Communities of Practice

Jacquie McDonald · Aileen Cater-Steel
Editors

Communities of Practice

Facilitating Social Learning in Higher
Education

 Springer

Editors
Jacquie McDonald
University of Southern Queensland
Toowoomba, QLD
Australia

Aileen Cater-Steel
University of Southern Queensland
Toowoomba, QLD
Australia

ISBN 978-981-10-2877-9   ISBN 978-981-10-2879-3   (eBook)
DOI 10.1007/978-981-10-2879-3

Library of Congress Control Number: 2016954699

Printed on acid-free paper

This Springer imprint is published by Springer Nature
The registered company is Springer Nature Singapore Pte Ltd.
The registered company address is: 152 Beach Road, #22-06/08 Gateway East, Singapore 189721, Singapore

The original version of the book was revised:
For detailed information please see erratum.
The erratum to this book is available at
10.1007/978-981-10-2879-3_29

Foreword

Communities of Practice Go to University

Going to university is usually a sign that you are growing up. You may still have some maturing to do, but higher education will help you do that. Therefore, as we reflect on the trajectory of the concept of community of practice, a pair of books written by and for people who use the concept in university contexts is a good sign: the concept is growing up.

The History of the Concept

The concept of community of practice took a circuitous route to the field of education. It was initially developed as part of a research program whose purpose was to rethink learning for an education audience. The aim was to inspect and reconsider the assumptions about learning that underlie current school design. The strategy was to study learning as a phenomenon in its own right: What does learning look like when it is not the result of teaching? Decoupling learning and teaching was meant to give rise to new ways of thinking about learning. This in turn was to enable new ways of approaching the design of schools and other institutions of learning. To our surprise the concept was first taken up by organizations outside of education, in business, government, healthcare, and international development.

The concept has had a long and notably diverse career, both as part of a social learning theory and as an approach to enabling learning. In retrospect we see the theory as having gone through three phases. Each transition builds on the prior phase, but involves a figure-ground switch.

In the first phase, the concept of community of practice was derived from studies of apprenticeship in various contexts. What was common across these contexts was that learning a practice entailed becoming a member of the community that "owned" that practice. You start at the periphery and gradually move toward full membership over time. In that phase of the theory, the existence of the community and its practice is taken as given and learning is theorized as an inbound trajectory into that community.

In the second phase, the community of practice is not taken as given. It is viewed as an emergent structure resulting from a learning partnership over time. This is a figure-ground shift from the first phase in the sense that, rather than the community defining learning, it is learning that defines the community. It was in this second phase that a question started to arise about whether you could be intentional about starting or cultivating a community of practice as a way to support learning. And indeed since then, this approach has been adopted in a large number of organizations across sectors. This applied use of the concept brought to the fore a number of new questions—about active cultivation, about leadership in convening and sustaining communities of practice, and about the relationship between communities of practice and organizational hierarchies.

In the third phase, there is again a figure-ground shift. While it was always clear that communities of practice exist in a broader landscape of different practices, the community remained the primary focus for analyzing and developing social learning capability. In the third phase, the primary focus is on a broader landscape of practice. In this landscape, learning capability depends as much on what happens at the boundaries between communities of practice as it does on the learning taking place inside them. In other words, boundaries between communities are learning assets just as communities are. From such a perspective, learning trajectories cut across a number of communities of practice in the landscape. It is not only a journey into the centre of one. Thus learning in a landscape involves two related but distinct processes. First it happens in communities of practice where learners define and develop specific forms of competence. Second it happens in relation to the broader landscape of practice: this includes many communities and practices in which we cannot claim membership or competence, but about which we can claim some level of knowledgeability that informs our participation.

In the complex world of the twenty-first century, the interplay of these two forms of participation—competence and knowledgeability—becomes central to what it means to know in practice. Applying this perspective to universities, we would pose the question: how can institutions of learning rise to this challenge? How can they enable forms of participation that encompass both competence and knowledgeability in complex landscapes of practice? A danger of ignoring participation is to simply view competence as a formal degree and knowledgeability as information. But social learning theory calls for approaches that go beyond degrees and information to a focus on robust identities that can successfully navigate a complex and changing landscape.

All three phases of the theory have pedagogical implications. These are relevant to universities as well as to education more generally.

Phase I highlights the importance of participation in practice for meaningful learning. Learning is viewed, not merely as the acquisition of information and skills, but primarily as a changing ability to participate in a human practice. Social participation shapes who we become. A substantial change in competence entails a corresponding change in identity.

Phase II suggests that a university needs to consider participation in learning partnerships as a way to increase its learning capacity as an organization with a special focus on learning. Where can the institution foster useful learning partnerships? Among staff for professional development? Among students for mutual support? Among faculty for better teaching? Among researchers for innovative approaches? And with partners in the broader community?

Phase III locates the university in the broader landscape of practice in which it operates: disciplinary practices, obviously, but also funding, regulation, policy, and business, as well as all the practices where research is relevant and where students move after graduation. Learning is not the exclusive prerogative of the university; it happens all the time, in every practice, and across boundaries. How the university contributes to the learning capability of this broader social landscape is a key question for higher education in the twenty-first century.

These questions about meaningful learning and social learning capability are central to our theorizing today. And they are well aligned with a number of trends in higher education. The scholarship of teaching and learning is an emerging field that needs to embrace and contribute to social learning theory. Universities need to rethink their approach to learning and their role in society, including alternatives to traditional university courses, MOOCs, work placements, and modular courses, among others. Inventiveness in a globalized world is now key for our students and those of us responsible for their preparation. People need to collaborate in order to explore and develop these new approaches in productive and imaginative ways. University administrators, faculty, and support staff need to accelerate their learning as new approaches to serving students and doing research require new practices. All these trends make the collection of scholarly works in these two volumes timely.

The two editors need to be commended for their work. We have known Jacquie McDonald for a number of years and have followed her work at the University of Southern Queensland, where she was a pioneer of the use of communities of practice for learning and teaching in higher education. In 2013, Jacquie joined our fellows program, in which each participant proposes a person project to work on during the year. When she suggested editing a volume of collected papers on the use of communities of practice in higher education, we thought it was an exciting idea. Higher education is a field where the use of social learning has not been well documented and the potential for application is endless. But we were not sure about the range of existing projects. We even wondered if she would be able to find enough people willing to contribute chapters for such a book. We had no idea that the response to her call for chapters would be so high that they would produce two volumes instead of the single book she originally planned.

For us this enthusiastic response is good news. In a field with as much potential for learning innovation as higher education, it is important to document cases both to understand what is happening in the field and to trigger people's imagination about what is possible. We are impressed by the variety of areas of application reflected in the chapters: professional development for faculty, pedagogical and curriculum innovations, collaborative research and writing, community–university partnerships, student communities, doctoral cohorts, and pedagogical approaches inspired by social learning principles. Projects are within and across institutions and disciplines, face-to-face and online, local and international. The response to the call for chapters is a clear indication of some fundamental shifts in the learning models underpinning higher education.

As communities of practice go to university, they bring social learning theory to bear on the practical and intellectual currents associated with these shifts. We believe that social learning theory stands to make a strong contribution and to mature in the process.

Grass Valley, CA, USA   Etienne and Beverly Wenger-Trayner
May 2016

Preface

Recognition of the positive impact of Communities of Practice and increased opportunities for social learning across discipline, national and international boundaries has seen growing interest in Communities of Practice in higher education. The authors in this book articulate the theoretical foundations of Communities of Practice (CoPs), the research into their application in higher education, CoP leadership roles and how CoPs sustain and support professional learning. The theoretical and leadership focus of this book provides the foundation for, and is complemented by, a companion book, *Implementing Communities of Practice in Higher Education: Dreamers and Schemers,* also edited by Jacquie McDonald and Aileen Cater-Steel, and published by Springer. The companion book has a more practical focus with examples and case studies of both student and academic CoPs, applications in sciences or humanities, curriculum development and virtual communities. The two books are the result of the marvellous response of 69 submissions to the initial call for proposals, demonstrating the impressive scope and interest in higher education CoPs. The wide geographic reach of the contents of this book is indicated by the fact that there are contributions from 71 authors from seven countries (Australia, Canada, Netherlands, New Zealand, Spain, UK, and USA). This is an indication of the extent and impact of higher education CoPs.

Etienne and Beverly Wenger-Trayner say that the term 'community of practice' is fairly recent, although the phenomenon it refers to is age-old (Wenger-Trayner and Wenger-Trayner 2015). As they articulate in the foreword of this book, community of practice theory is informed by, and informs, social learning theory (Bandura 1977). CoPs have gone through three phases, giving different perspectives on 'what is a community of practice' as the theory evolves through the different phases. CoP theory now seems well established (Tight 2015; Wenger-Trayner and Wenger-Trayner 2015) with a well-accepted definition used in this book. It is one which most of the authors explicitly or implicitly subscribe to, that Communities of Practice are "groups of people who share a concern or a passion about something they do and learn how to do it better as they interact regularly" (Wenger-Trayner and Wenger-Trayner 2015). Wenger-Trayner and Wenger-Trayner (2015) also say that the three characteristics, the domain, the community and the practice, are the three essential elements that constitute a CoP. These elements; building the domain of knowledge, creating a community of people, and sharing practice were initially presented in Etienne Wenger's 1998 seminal book, '*Communities of Practice: Learning, Meaning and Identity.*' These elements have been successfully adapted in the Australian Higher Education context as the organizing structure for a range of topic and cohort CoPs (McDonald and Star 2008, 2014; McDonald n.d.).

Defining what CoPs are, and are not, provides a perspective to explore how CoPs are useful as an approach to knowing and learning in higher education. Many CoPs operate outside and across formal institutional structures such as faculty, discipline teams, individual course offers, and, what is sometimes perceived as the academic and professional staff divide. The three different types of higher education CoPs identified in an Australian study (McDonald et al. 2012) were organic, nurtured or supported, and created or intentional. The research from that study found that members and/or facilitators may have intentionally set out to establish a CoP, or 'discovered' that they had created a CoP. Once they recognized that they were operating as a CoP, they were able to view the CoP activities through that particular lens, bringing an informed focus and understanding to past and future CoP activities. The CoP research and practice presented by the chapter authors will provide readers with such a lens to view how CoPs operate within different contexts. The chapters provide alternative perspectives to reflect on, and inform their own CoP activities.

Much has been written about the 'chilly climate' in higher education, which does not support collaborative activities; and about the changing role of academics, as government, institutional and student expectations are influenced by the corporatization of higher education. Palmer (2002, p. 179) noted that *academic culture is infamous for fragmentation, isolation, and competitive individualism, with no sense of being part of a community.* Changing educational and government expectations, and student demographics is also increasing pressure on staff as they are required to increase research output, teach diverse student cohorts, all with reduced administrative support, and increasing accountability and productivity requirements. There are also changes to the traditional autonomy of academic staff and the identity of higher education away from what is retrospectively viewed as a 'collegial' past, towards a more managerial and commercial entity, with efficiency and output measurements, and top down compliance audits (Probert 2014). The result is an intensification of academic work, a decline in collegiality and feelings of alienation and stress. Despite the changing context and 'chilly climate,' higher education staff and students have created ways to share and enhance learning through communities of practice. The authors in this book share their experiences as they articulate the theoretical foundations of Communities of Practice (CoPs) and its relevance in higher education; research their application in higher education; the CoP leadership roles and how CoPs can sustain and support professional learning in higher education.

The twenty-eight chapters of this book are collected in four themes, with an overview of each chapter is provided at the beginning of each part:

Part I—Theoretical Underpinnings Informing Communities of Practice
Part II—Research of Higher Education Communities of Practice
Part III—Leadership in Higher Education Communities of Practice
Part IV—Communities of Practice Sustaining Professional Learning and Development.

In conclusion, while we cannot be expert in all areas of CoP activities, through exploring the workings of other CoPs we can challenge our thinking and deepen our knowledge about CoPs. The authors' stories and research will inform our practice and how our own CoPs are positioned within national and international CoP activities. The authors raise, and, through their CoP initiatives, address opportunities and issues faced by all higher education leaders and educators. These include how CoP theory and practice aligns with, and can leverage on, evolving social learning theory, social media, changing community and learner expectations, and the fostering of personal learning journeys within, and outside, traditional higher education institutions. As well as these complex issues and opportunities, further research and practice will inform matters such as the impact of allegiance to own disciplines, boundary crossing.

We invite you to explore the different types of CoPs, their application in different contexts and foci, and share the challenges and triumphs presented by the contributing authors. It is our intention that the experiences detailed here may provide guidance to existing and future CoP facilitators and members in the Higher Education sector.

Book Development Process

A double-blind review process was used for all chapters submitted to the editors. Authors of selected chapters were invited to act on the reviewer's comments and resubmit their chapters to the editors. Chapters were checked and final revisions applied.

We have enjoyed the process of compiling these books and in particular working with the contributors who provided such wide-ranging contributions about Communities of Practice and Social Learning in Higher Education contexts. It is up to you, the reader, to decide whether the perspectives offered here are relevant to your research or practical application of CoPs in your context. We would be delighted to hear your feedback on the usefulness of these books in contributing to your Community of Practice activities

You are invited to contribute to the dedicated 'Books' page at the Communities of Practice Higher Education blog - https://jacquiemcdonald.com/books/.

Disclaimers

No product or service mentioned in this book is endorsed, nor are any claims made about the capabilities of such products or services. All trademarks are copyrighted to their respective owners.

Toowoomba, Australia   Jacquie McDonald
                                                                               Aileen Cater-Steel

References

Bandura, A. (1977). *Social learning theory*. Englewood Cliffs, NJ: Prentice Hall.

McDonald, J., Star, C., & Margetts, F. (2012). Identifying, building and sustaining leadership capacity for communities of practice in higher education. Final Report Office for Learning and Teaching. Australia. Accessed from www.olt.gov.au. 17 September 2014.

McDonald, J., & Star, C. (2008) The challenges of building an academic community of practice: An Australian case study, in Engaging Communities, Proceedings of the 31st HERDSA Annual Conference, Rotorua, 1–4 July 2008: pp. 230–240.

McDonald, J., & Star, C. (2014). Learning and teaching professional development: An Australian community of practice case study. *Learning Communities Journal*, 6.

McDonald, J. (n.d.). Facilitator Resources: ALTC Teaching Fellowship Community of Practice Facilitator Resources. http://www.usq.edu.au/cops/resources/altcfellowship/facilitator-resources. Accessed 10 February 2016.

Palmer, P. (2002). The quest for community in higher education. In W. M. McDonald (Ed.), *Creating campus community* (pp. 179–192). San Francisco, CA: Jossey-Bass.

Probert, B. (2014). Why scholarship matters in higher education (Discussion Paper No. 2). Sydney, NSW: Australian Government Office for Learning and Teaching.

Tight, M. (2015). Theory application in higher education research: the case of communities of practice. *European Journal of Higher Education, 5*(2). doi:10.1080/21568235.2014.997266.

Wenger-Trayner, E., & Wenger-Trayner, B. (2015). Communities of practice: A brief Introduction. http://wenger-trayner.com/introduction-to-communities-of-practice/. Accessed 10 February 2016.

Wenger-Trayner, E., Fenton-O'Creevy, M., Hutchinson, S., Kubiak, C., & Wenger-Trayner, B. (Eds.). (2015). *Learning in Landscapes of Practice: Boundaries, Identity, and Knowledgeability in Practice-Based Learning*. London: Routledge.

Wenger, E. (1998). *Communities of practice: learning, meaning and identity*. New York: Cambridge University.

Acknowledgements

The authors who contributed to this book deserve our heartfelt thanks for their contribution, patience, and cooperation throughout the long and complex process of compiling this book. All the contributors are listed with biographical details in the book.

The reviewers also played an essential role and we know the authors were very appreciative of the valuable comments provided by the reviewers. We sincerely thank the reviewers for taking the time to read and comment on the original submissions. These contributions were an essential ingredient necessary to improving the content and presentation of the chapters.

Thank you also to Etienne and Bev Wenger-Trayner for providing the thought-proving Foreword for the book. Their leadership and contribution to Communities of Practice and Social Learning is widely acclaimed.

A special note of thanks to Mohammad Mehdi Rajaeian (Mehdi) who provided prompt and valuable support to the Editors, especially in formatting manuscripts and assessing copyright requirements. Also thank you to the staff at Springer SBM Singapore, India and Australia who provided the necessary process, templates, reminders and project management of the entire process from our first proposal to this final publication. In particular we wish to express our thanks to Lay Peng Ang, Editorial Assistant and Nick Melchior, Senior Editor Education, Australia and New Zealand.

Finally, we dedicate this book to Aileen's grandchildren, Bea and Pippa, and to the inspirational leaders of Communities of Practice, Etienne and Bev Wenger-Trayner and Faculty Learning Communities, Milt Cox, CoP fellow travellers, and Jacquie's husband Bob Willis.

Jacquie McDonald
Aileen Cater-Steel

Contents

Editors and Contributors

About the Editors

Jacquie McDonald Associate Professor Jacquie McDonald is a Learning and Teaching Designer at the University of Southern Queensland (USQ) Australia. She has worked with higher education academics designing online and distance learning courses and programs for over 24 years. Her experience and research demonstrate the value of Communities of Practice (CoP) in building the learning and teaching capacity of educators, and contributing to scholarly practice and publications. Since 2006 she has led the successful implementation of communities of practice at USQ, which was recognized by a 2009 Australian Universities Quality Agency commendation and 2009 Australian Learning and Teaching Council (ALTC) Citation. She has led a number of institutional and national fellowships and grants to research and provide resources for leadership of communities of practice within the tertiary education sector. She has been invited by national universities to facilitate Community of Practice workshops and contribute to CoP initiatives. Jacquie is participating in a Social Learning Leadership Certificate program conducted by the international leaders of Communities of Practice—Etienne and Bev Wenger-Trayner.

Aileen Cater-Steel is a professor of information systems at the University of Southern Queensland (USQ). Her research interests include IT service management, IT governance, e-learning, and research supervision. At USQ she co-facilitates a community of practice for research supervisors. Aileen has led two Australian Research Council Linkage projects in the area of IT service management and is an active researcher in the Australian Centre for Sustainable Business Development. Aileen's work has been published in many top-tier international academic journals. She has published three edited collections of research articles. Aileen is a Fellow of the Australian Computer Society and received an award for Life-time Achievement from the IT Service Management Forum. Prior to her academic career, Aileen held senior IT positions in the public and private sector.

Contributors

Estibaliz Aberasturi-Apraiz's research and teaching career is primarily focused on teacher education, pedagogical innovation and visual arts in educational contexts. She is principal investigator of a community of practice where teachers reflect critically on learning from experiences in visual arts. Her professional development as a university professor at the University of the Basque Country (UPV/EHU) spans three distinct stages: her initiation into research and teaching in the Department of Didactics of Plastic Expression, the completion of her Ph.D. thesis, and her subsequent establishment as a university professor. She concentrates on visual arts as a field of study for teacher development and educational innovation. She has taken part in 20 studies (1 international, 5 national and 14 regional) and has participated in three thematic networks, involving teachers from more than five Spanish universities. In addition she has led three pedagogical innovation projects at the University of the Basque Country (UPV/EHU).

Lenore Adie is a Senior Research Fellow with the Assessment, Evaluation and Student Learning Research Program in the Learning Sciences Institute Australia, at the Australian Catholic University. Her research focuses on assessment and moderation processes as these contribute to supporting teachers' pedagogical practices and student learning. She has a further interest in the enactment of assessment policy and the validity of assessment processes. Sociocultural theories of learning are utilized within her work to interpret this dynamic context. Lenore has worked as a primary school teacher and in administration positions in state and private schools within Queensland, Australia.

Jennifer Alford is a Senior Lecturer in TESOL at Queensland University of Technology, Brisbane, Australia. She coordinates and teaches units in the Bachelor of Education related to English as a first and second (or additional) language learning. Her research interests are English teachers' knowledge, policy enactment and classroom pedagogy with a special interest in critical literacy in schools. Jennifer uses Ethnography and Critical Discourse Analysis methods to understand the relationship between texts and how power is played out in educational institutions. She is currently working on a book entitled *Critical Literacy with adolescent English language learners: policy and practice in global contexts* for Routledge Research in Language Education Series.

Peter J. Allen is a Lecturer in the School of Psychology and Speech Pathology at Curtin University, in Western Australia. Along with Peta Dzidic and Lynne Roberts, he was a convenor of the research group that developed into a community of practice as described in Chap. 10. Peter's teaching responsibilities are primarily in the areas of research methods and statistics. His areas of research interest include evidence-based learning and teaching, with a particular emphasis on the development of statistical decision-making skills.

Kay Aranda is a Lecturer at the University of Brighton. She has a long-standing involvement and interest in health and social inequalities. She has a working background in women's health and community development in the voluntary sector and in the NHS, primary care and community nursing. She has conducted research on resilience and strength or asset-based approaches to health and well-being, using communities of practice approaches. She has also worked as research advisor for qualitative research and was the public and patient involvement lead for the National Institute of Health Research, Research Design Service in the South East. She has led a number of qualitative research projects using participatory and creative methods for understanding inequalities, difference, disability and discrimination and is currently involved in a research exploring the value of practice theories for understanding inequalities in health.

Kim Aumann has worked as a community worker, parent support practitioner and manager of third sector organizations. She has successfully forged creative links with different university partners to tackle issues of disadvantage and inequalities together. In tandem with parents of disabled children, she led the development of a UK based support charity (www.amazebrighton.org.uk) applauded as an example of excellence and good practice. Her partnership work with the University and more recently with the UKs National Co-ordination Centre for Public Engagement led to the creation of a research and training programme at Amaze, a community interest company to pursue resilience research and practice (www.boingboing.org.uk) and the UK Community Partner Network. She has facilitated communities of practice comprised of academics, professionals and parent carers keen to develop resilience work with children and young people having tough times. Originally from Australia, Kim completed her studies in sociology, counselling, group work and research methods in the UK and is a Visiting Research Fellow at the University of Brighton.

Elizabeth A. Beckmann Australian National Teaching Fellow Dr. Beth Beckmann is an academic developer at the Australian National University. She has received multiple institutional and national teaching awards for her educational design and professional development work in university teaching, and is committed to advancing the professional recognition of university teachers. She is a Principal Fellow of the Higher Education Academy, and leads the Australian National University's Educational Fellowship Scheme.

Davina Boyd is a community and international development practitioner with 15 years' experience working in Australia and abroad. Davina works with diverse stakeholder groups, including private sector and non-government organizations, to design, manage and evaluate projects aimed at building individual and institutional capacity. Her practical experience is underpinned by research. Davina completed her Ph.D. in Capacity Development in 2009 and currently leads an Australian Development Research Award Scheme project that explores innovative ways to develop the capacity of smallholder farmers in Southern Africa to connect with markets. Davina also supervises students undertaking a research internship at Murdoch University.

Fiona Breen comes to student support from a Hospitality background and has a strong interest in supporting students from diverse and non-traditional backgrounds to succeed in vocational study programmes and graduate with work-ready skills. Fiona and Mervyn are colleagues and have been working together over a number of years to refine data collection approaches which provide evidence of the positive impact of learning advisers.

Natalie Brown is Head of the Tasmanian Institute of Learning and Teaching at the University of Tasmania. Her role encompasses policy, strategy and professional development in learning and teaching, and promotion of the Scholarship of Learning and Teaching. She continues to teach as well as supervising Ph.D. students. Natalie is a previous winner of an OLT Teaching Excellence Award.

Dr. Emily Castell is a Lecturer in the School of Psychology at Curtin University. In this role, Emily supervises final year research students, undertakes research in Scholarship of Teaching and Learning and is an educator in Community Psychology, Qualitative Research Methods, and Indigenous and Cross Cultural Psychology. Emily is a member of the of the research group that developed into a community of practice as described in this chapter, and is a recipient of two Teaching Academic Scholarship Seed grants to fund research exploring critical thinking and reflexivity among university students. Her research interests extend to; issues of social justice, community and applied psychology, Scholarship of Teaching and Learning, sexuality, and disability studies. Emily welcomes the opportunity to contribute to understandings and conceptualizations surrounding Communities of Practice.

Joseph W. Cates is Assistant Professor in the Department of Focused Inquiry at Virginia Commonwealth University, where he has taught since 2007. In addition to the first-year critical thinking seminars and writing workshops, he also teaches service learning courses that explore issues of food security in the local community. He earned an MFA in Poetry from VCU in 2002 and a BFA in Creative Writing from Bowling Green State University in 1997. He has recently presented work at the Teaching Professor Technology Conference, the International Association of Research in Service Learning and Community Engagement Conference and VCU's ALTfest. His latest projects include a screenplay, a new collection of poems, and academic writing related to his participation in the Learning Spaces Teaching Fellowship at VCU. He lives on a tree farm in Varina, Virginia with his wife and daughter.

Dr. Vinesh Chandra is a Senior Lecturer in Education at the Queensland University of Technology in Brisbane, Australia. His teaching areas are in Information and Communication Technology (ICT), Design Technology, Mathematics and Science. His research interests include the investigation of technology rich learning environments and teacher education. He has worked with teachers in Australia, Fiji, China and Zambia. Dr. Chandra leads the Share Engage Educate (SEE) Project (theseeproject.org) which has supported a number of schools in Fiji and other developing countries. One of the key objectives of the project is to enhance the quality of education in these countries through ICT. Collaboration, teamwork, and problem solving are some of the cornerstones of his initiatives.

José Miguel Correa-Gorospe has a Ph.D. in Pedagogy and works at the University of the Basque Country (UPV/EHU). He is faculty member of the Department of Teaching and School Organization (San Sebastian, Spain). In the last decade he has been teaching Information and Communications Technologies (ICT) to future Early Childhood Education teachers. His research interests include teacher education, educational innovation and ICT. He has numerous publications on teaching and teacher education, teacher identity, educational policies, and ICT practices at different educational levels. He has taken part in numerous research projects in Europe and Latin America, and he is the coordinator of the educational research group Elkarrikertuz. He is also a member of the network for research and educational innovation REUNI + D.

Milton D. Cox and colleagues designed and implemented faculty learning communities (FLCs) in 1979. Since that time he has been engaged in assessing their impacts on student learning and educational development in higher education. He has been project director of state and federal grants establishing FLC programs at other institutions, visiting over 100 institutions in the U.S. and abroad. He is author of several articles on communities of practice, the scholarship of teaching and learning, and is co-editor of the book, Building Faculty Learning Communities. Dr. Cox is founder and Director Emeritus of the Center for the Enhancement of Learning, Teaching, and University Assessment at Miami University where he initiated and continues to direct the annual Original Lilly Conference on College Teaching, just completing its 35th year. He is also founder and Editor-in-Chief of the Journal on Excellence in College Teaching and the Learning Communities Journal. He facilitates the Hesburgh Award-winning Teaching Scholars Faculty Learning Community, now in its 38th year. He is recipient of a certificate of special achievement from the Professional and Organizational Development Network in Higher Education in recognition and appreciation of notable contributions to the profession of faculty, instructional, and organizational development.

Elise G.C. Crawford is a Lecturer in the School of Human, Health and Social Sciences at CQUniversity, Australia. She lectures in the fields of Human factors, Safety Science, and Occupational Health and Safety. Elise has over 20 years' experience as an educator, initially in the performing arts, and more recently in the field of safety. Before working in higher education, Elise was a Work, Health and Safety (WHS) Advisor for the Queensland safety regulator where she was primarily responsible for supporting, educating and helping local businesses with their WHS related matters. Elise's primary research interest is in the field of human factors. She is currently exploring ways to optimize user adoption of new technology when introduced into complex working environments under safety critical conditions.

Special interests include: human factors engineering and innovation, transdisciplinary communication and teamwork, technology adoption in cognitively complex environments, safety science, professional communities of practice, and exploring ways to enhance learning opportunities in safety critical and higher education domains.

Ceri Davies is a Development Manager at the University of Brighton's award-winning Community-University Partnership Programme. She is responsible for leading a programme of community knowledge exchange which supports academic–community partnerships to explore contemporary social problems. Her research interest in Communities of Practice stems from this. Ceri draws on over 10 years' experience of working and volunteering in the community and voluntary sector in the UK and internationally, and currently chairs the board of a charity supporting people to have a voice that can influence policy and make change. Ceri is also completing her Ph.D., exploring how multiple forms of knowledge in community–university collaborations can address issues of social justice.

Maarten de Laat is Professor of Professional Development in Social Networks at the Welten Institute of the Open University of the Netherlands. His research concentrates on exploring social learning strategies and networked relationships that facilitate learning and professional development. He has published and presented his research extensively in international research journals, books and conferences. He is co-chair of the biannual International Networked Learning Conference.

Dr. Peta Dzidic is a Lecturer in the School of Psychology and Speech Pathology at Curtin University, Perth, Western Australia. With Peter Allen and Lynne Roberts, Peta was a convenor of the research group that developed into a community of practice as described in this chapter. Along with academia, Peta has worked in the public and private sectors contributing to over 20 community based research reports, and over 15 book chapters and journal publications in her 10 year professional career. In 2013 she was awarded the Curtin Student Guild award for Excellence in Teaching Award, Postgraduate Supervisor. Peta's primary teaching areas are in community psychology, and qualitative research methodology; her research focus is in community participation, dominant culture, and, social and environmental justice.

Michael A. Erskine is the Director of the Educational Technology Center at Metropolitan State University of Denver. He is a graduate of the Computer Science and Information Systems Ph.D. program at the University of Colorado Denver. His research interests include educational technology, disaster management, and spatial decision support systems. His research has been presented at the Americas Conference on Information Systems (AMCIS), the International Conference on Information Resources Management (ConfIRM), the IEEE Digital Ecosystems and Technologies Conference (DEST), and the International Conference on Project Management (ProjMAN). Additionally, his work has been published in the International Journal of Human-Computer Interaction and the Journal of Computer

Information Systems (forthcoming). He is a member of the Association for Information Systems and serves on the Board of Directors of the Association for Teaching and Learning Systems.

Suna Eryigit-Madzwamuse is a Research Fellow at the Centre for Health Research, University of Brighton, focussing on promoting well-being of children/young individuals and their families, taking into account biological and contextual risk and protective factors from a developmental perspective. She is currently involved in the Imagine Programme, emphasizing community–university partnership working and developing a resilient system of evidence-based community support for children and young individuals with life challenges.

Victor Fester is an experienced tertiary educator and has worked in a number of staff development roles in several New Zealand polytechnics. He has a strong interest in technology-enabled learning and is currently involved in a curriculum and teaching and learning renewal project.

Cath Fraser currently combines roles as a Research Leader at the Bay of Plenty Polytechnic with independent research and writing contracts for organizations across the higher education sector. Current research interests include mentoring, staff development and writing resources to support early-career teachers.

Vanessa Fredericks has been a sessional staff member at Macquarie University for over 6 years. During that time she has held various roles, including Program Research and Development officer for the Learning and Teaching and a casual tutor in Media and Cultural Studies. She first became involved with the BLASST project as events manager for the BLASST National Leadership Summit in 2013.

John Gilchrist is a Senior Research Fellow at the Australian Catholic University Academy of Law. He has a background of more than 20 years teaching in law at an undergraduate and postgraduate level. Over the last two years Dr. Gilchrist has been devoted to researching in law, to supervising and managing research in law and to continuing his TATAL involvement. He is a Fellow of the Higher Education Research and Development Society of Australasia.

Dr. Karen Guldberg is Senior Lecturer in Autism Studies, University of Birmingham, UK. She is also Director of the Autism Centre for Education and Research (ACER) and a Senior Fellow of the Higher Education Academy, UK. Karen conducts real-world research in the classroom, with a focus on pedagogy, social learning and the specific learning needs of children with autism. She has led a number of projects working in partnership with schools, practitioners and parents to research technology use and the learning arising from this. Karen has been involved in producing a number of online training resources, for educators as well as health practitioners. She led the development of the Autism Education Trust partnership school-based training and has recently led the adaptation of this to Early Years. She is now leading an Erasmus Plus strategic partnership (2014–2017) to research good autism educational practice in Greece and Italy in order to (i) better understand the cultural context for barriers to inclusion and (ii) identify and promote good outcomes for individuals on the autism spectrum.

Eleanor Hancock is Associate Professor of History at the University of New South Wales Canberra and has been a member of TATAL since 2009. She has just completed a three-and-a-half year term as one of the first learning and teaching coordinators at UNSW Canberra.

Angie Hart is Professor of Child, Family and Community Health at the University of Brighton where she loosely coordinates the efforts of a group of academics, students and community members who live and breathe collaborative research and practice development. She is also the Academic Director of the Community University Partnership Programme (Cupp) at the University of Brighton (http://www.brighton.ac.uk/cupp/). In collaboration with community practitioners and students, Angie has published widely on resilience-based approaches to supporting children and families. She has also written on community university engagement. Angie regularly consults on these issues to universities, charities and government agencies. Her academic background stems from the Universities of Sussex, Cambridge and Oxford, and she has a postgraduate diploma in Psychotherapeutic Counselling from the University of Sussex. Angie also directs a not-for-profit organization, Boingboing, in a voluntary capacity working with community members and academics (http://www.boingboing.org.uk/index.php/who-are-we). Together they have developed various practical resilience approaches to help children and families having challenging times including the Academic Resilience approach (http://www.youngminds.org.uk/training_services/academic_resilience). Angie's resilience profile is underpinned by professional and personal experience. She is a community psychotherapeutic practitioner in child and family mental health. And as the adoptive parent of three children from the care system, she is an experienced service user and advocate of health and social care services in both the voluntary and statutory sector.

Marina Harvey an OLT National Teaching Fellow and Principal Fellow of the Higher Education Academy, uses Participatory Action Research to investigate sessional staff issues. She has researched this topic for the past decade, including leading the Australian Government Office for Learning and Teaching (OLT) funded BLASST project, *Benchmarking Leadership and Advancement of Standards for Sessional Staff*. The BLASST project developed evidence-based national standards for enhancing quality learning and teaching with sessional staff. Marina continues to research and work towards national good practice and benchmarking with the BLASST framework across Australia and internationally. Her research is underpinned by, and also focuses on, the role of reflective practice and distributed leadership in higher education. This research passion for reflection has led to a series of projects focusing on the role of reflective practice for learning. Marina received a 2015 Australian Award for University Teaching. This Citation for Outstanding Contributions to Student Learning was in recognition of her co-creation of the goal orientated Spectrum Approach to Mentoring for learning and teaching in higher education.

Becky Heaver is a Research Officer in the Centre for Health Research in the Faculty of Health and Social Science. She recently completed a Ph.D. in Psychology, and now researches resilience in relation to children, young people and families, using methods including participatory research, literature reviews, and communities of practice. Her research interests also include psychophysiology, recognition memory, self-advocacy, and Asperger Syndrome. Becky is a volunteer for Boingboing, developing the online network via the website and social media.

Erika Hepple is a Senior Lecturer in Education at Queensland University of Technology. Erika coordinates and teaches undergraduate and postgraduate units in international teacher education, intercultural communication, and teaching/learning English as a Second Language. Her research focuses on internationalization in higher education, social constructions of identity and pedagogy in international teacher education, and teachers' professional development through community engagement both locally and globally. She has a long-standing professional interest in communities of practice in international teacher education.

Judith Honeyfield transitioned from nursing education and management to staff development 8 years ago, and has been a tertiary teacher for over 20 years. She is an active researcher and doctoral student and works closely with new teaching staff to promote a modern teaching and learning pedagogy.

Jesmin Islam has been Assistant Professor in the discipline of Accounting, Banking and Finance in the Faculty of Business and Government, University of Canberra, since 2009. Jesmin has extensive experience in teaching in accounting-related units across five major universities and other tertiary institutions in WA and ACT. She is currently working towards a HERDSA Fellowship.

Sandra Jones is Professor of Employment Relations and Director of the Centre for Business Education Research at RMIT University in Victoria, Australia and a Principal Fellow of the Higher Education Academy. Sandra has led a number of multi-university projects funded by the Australian Government Office for Learning and Teaching on the impact of distributed leadership in building leadership capacity for learning and teaching in universities. Professor Jones has published extensively on leadership in higher education with her most recent research being published as a Stimulus Paper on Developing and Sustaining Shared Leadership by the Leadership Foundation for Higher Education (UK) (Bolden, Jones, Davis & Gentle, 2015). Professor Jones is currently engaged in developing co-partnership research and learning opportunities as Living Learning Laboratories between university and external stakeholders.

Jeanne Keay began her professional life as a teacher of physical education in three secondary schools in England, before moving to Leeds Metropolitan University in 1992 to work within the School of Education. In 2002 she became Head of Initial

Teacher Education, and subsequently Dean of Education, at Roehampton University in London. In 2012 she became Assistant Director and Head of International Strategy at the UK Higher Education Academy and led the internationalization agenda for the HEA. In 2013 she moved to the University of the West of Scotland to become Pro Vice Chancellor (International) and in 2016 became Pro Vice Chancellor at Leeds Beckett University (UK). Throughout her academic career her research has been located within the area of professional development focusing on induction, quality assurance processes of CPD providers, CPD innovations and communities of practice. She is currently working on several projects examining issues around the impact of professional development on practice, including the professional development of primary teachers in the area of physical education.

Robert Kennelly is an Adjunct at the University of Canberra and has research interests in collaborative reflective practice and the development of academic skills in first-year management, second language students. He is a pioneer Fellow of the Higher Education Research and Development Society of Australasia (HERDSA) and a life member of HERDSA.

Barbara Kensington-Miller is a Senior Lecturer in the Centre for Research and Learning in Higher Education, at the University of Auckland, New Zealand. She teaches on the Postgraduate Certificate in Academic Practice, works with academic staff on aspects of their teaching and research, and supervises Masters and Ph.D. students. She holds a doctorate in mathematics education. Her research area fosters and promotes teaching and research of early-career academics. Within this area, her varied portfolio includes research on peer mentoring, academic identity, threshold concepts, teaching in large undergraduate classrooms, and flipped classrooms. She is currently leading a large government-funded project working with students, lecturers, and employers, investigating the learning outcomes that are invisible on transcripts and not formally assessed such as communication, persistence, affect.

Alice E. MacGillivray has a Ph.D. in Human and Organizational Systems. Her dissertation research participants were respected leaders, many of whom worked with communities of practice (CoP) and this research illuminated ways in which such leaders understand and work with boundaries. While directing an MA program for mid-career professionals at Royal Roads University, Alice developed and delivered the first full graduate course about communities of practice. It was designed to include an authentic CoP-like experience in partnership with Etienne Wenger, John D. Smith and the CPsquare.org community. That learning experience led to real-world differences in the organizations and communities of many students. Alice deeply values her learning as a participant and coordinator in communities of practice, and she continues to encourage and support them through her consulting. In higher education, Alice has worked with Royal Roads University, the University of Lethbridge, the University of Victoria, Capella University and is currently a Fellow with the Institute for Social Innovation at Fielding Graduate University.

Asunción Martínez-Arbelaiz holds a Ph.D. in Linguistics from Cornell University, New York. She is currently the Spanish Language Coordinator for the University Studies Abroad Consortium, where she also teaches a variety of courses of Spanish for speakers of other languages. Her research interests have evolved from theoretical linguistics to more applied aspects related to language, particularly second language acquisition, language pedagogy and sociolinguistics. She has published on a variety of topics such as technology for language learners and teachers, the design, implementation and evaluation of language tasks, and the development of language and culture acquisition in the study abroad context in various journals devoted to second language research. She is also part of the research group Elkarrikertuz, where she contributes ideas related to language and discourse to the challenge of how to prepare the teachers of the future. As a result of this collaboration, several presentations and publications have emerged that point to the need for a community of colleagues for teacher education.

Helen May began her career as a school teacher working in three schools across the UK, before specializing and moving into research, teaching and policy developments within HE. Helen joined the Higher Education Academy in January 2005—the leading body for learning and teaching based in the United Kingdom. She currently works as an academic lead. From 2012 until 2015, Helen was strategic lead for internationalization, where she led the development of a national framework for internationalizing higher education (2014, 2015), two research and practice networks on internationalization, and two one-year change programmes involving over 20 HE institutions to embed internationalization into learning and teaching. During her time at the HEA, Helen has also led a number of other thematic areas in academic practice, including inclusion, retention, assessment, disability, widening participation and strategic change. Throughout her career, Helen has researched and authored numerous publications. Her research interests include internationalizing higher education, inclusive learning and teaching; student engagement; equality and diversity; and preparing and implementing change. Helen holds a Doctor of Education and Masters of Education from the University of Leeds.

Trish McCluskey is Senior Lecturer and Manager of Course Enhancement in the Faculty of Health at Deakin University. She has worked in Tertiary Education in Australia and New Zealand for over 25 years, across a range of teaching, leadership, and governance roles including chair of Academic Board and member of University Council. Trish is a member of the Council of Australian Directors of Academic Development (CADAD) and in 2014, she led a joint project between CADAD and the Network of Australian Tertiary Associations (NATA) to research and develop a Social Media Toolkit for Academics. This toolkit has been widely adopted in both local and global networks. Her research/learning interests are around the value of Professional Learning Networks, Connected Leadership and Social Media in education.

Coralie McCormack is Adjunct Associate Professor at the University of Canberra specializing in capacity building for leadership in learning and teaching through institutional and national teaching awards and fellowships and teaching and learning communities of practice. Narrative approaches to teaching, evaluation and research are her passion. She is a life member of the Higher Education Research and Development Society of Australasia (HERDSA).

Alex McDaniel A former US Army Military Intelligence Non Commissioned Officer, Alex McDaniel earned his BS in Organizational Communication from Metropolitan State University of Denver and his MA in Instructional Design and Adult Learning from the University of Colorado Denver. Alex has presented on the benefits of virtual communities of practice to post-secondary education in a wide variety of academic venues and currently supports MSU Denver as the Senior Instructional Designer, Interactive Applications Developer, and Quality Matters Coordinator at the Educational Technology Center.

Bernadette Mercieca teaches at the Xavier College, Melbourne, and is the e-learning coordinator for the Senior Campus. She is also a sessional tutor/lecturer for pre-service teachers at Australian Catholic University. Bernadette is a Ph.D. candidate at the University of Southern Queensland who is researching the value that communities of practice might have for the professional learning of early-career secondary teachers.

Dr. Amanda Mergler is a Lecturer in the School of Cultural and Professional Learning in the Faculty of Education at Queensland University of Technology, Brisbane, Australia. Amanda is a registered psychologist with the Australian Psychological Society and an international affiliate with the American Psychological Association. Due to her interest in the healthy development of young people, Amanda's research focuses on personal responsibility in school students. She is particularly interested in how personal responsibility is operationalized and measured so that effective interventions can be harnessed. Amanda has also undertaken research examining the values held by pre-service teachers and young people, and examined well-being in university and school students. She has a keen interest in the area of positive psychology and has been involved in research exploring the notion of covitality; the effective combination of positive traits to enhance well-being in young and older Australians.

Kate Nash is a Lecturer in Media and Communication and Director of Student Education in the School of Media and Communication at the University of Leeds. Her research is focused on interactive factual media and its social and political impacts. She is also interested in media education and is currently leading a school research group on media education in the UK.

Thomas J. Nelson is Assistant Professor in the Department of Focused Inquiry at Virginia Commonwealth University. Dr. Nelson joined the department in 2007. He received his B.A. and M.A. from Western Washington University before moving on to earn his doctorate in English from the University of Texas in Austin. He has served as Faculty Development Coordinator for the department since 2011. He is interested in creating collaborative learning environments for faculty, for students, and between students and faculty.

Maria Northcote is an international leader in the area of Learning and Teaching, currently employed at the University of Southern Queensland (USQ) Australia. She has worked in the Education field nearly 20 years in a variety of capacities. Her experience with quality enhancement has focused on building institutional and individual capacity in the area of learning and teaching and scholarship. Dr. Newman has served as a consultant for institutions across the United States and is an international presenter on Faculty Learning Communities and other professional learning opportunities for faculty and staff in higher education.

Tara Newman is an international leader in the area of Learning and Teaching, currently employed at the University of Southern Queensland (USQ) Australia. She has worked in the Education field nearly 20 years in a variety of capacities. Her experience with quality enhancement has focused on building institutional and individual capacity in the area of learning and teaching and scholarship. Dr. Newman has served as a consultant for institutions across the United States and is an international presenter on Faculty Learning Communities and other professional learning opportunities for faculty and staff in higher education.

Edward R. Pember has an MA in Linguistics and has been providing academic and language learning support to international students for over 11 years. His research interests are primarily focused on the internationalization of education and its effect on students, staff and institutions. Over the last two years Edward has facilitated the community of practice on the Internationalization of the Learning Experience at Central Queensland University (CQU Australia) and has presided over the NSW/ACT Branch of the ISANA International Education Association (Australia).

Mervyn Protheroe's doctorate is in student support and statistical methods. His other research interests include mathematics education, physics education and models of learning advice.

Michelle Quail is a Clinical Coordinator within the Speech Pathology program in the School of Psychology and Speech Pathology at Curtin University in Perth, WA. Michelle is passionate about the clinical education of speech pathology students, and is interested in using innovative methods to overcome the financial and logistical challenges that universities currently face in supporting students' clinical learning.

Peter Reaburn is Associate Professor of Exercise and Sport Science at Central Queensland University (CQUniversity). He was Head of the Department of Health and Human Performance from 2000–2007. Peter was the winner of the CQUniversity Vice-Chancellor's Award for Excellence in Learning and Teaching in 2012 and won a National Office of Learning and Teaching Citation 'for sustained facilitation of inquiry-based learning and research project-based assessment practices in exercise physiology courses leading to outstanding student learning and career outcomes' in 2013. In that same year he was nominated by his cohort of nine postgraduate students as the 'Postgraduate Supervisor of the Year' which he won. Peter was instrumental in initiating the Community of Practice (CoP) 'movement' at CQUniversity in 2009 after hearing and reading of the impact CoPs can have on professional development of staff. CQUniversity currently has 13 CoPs with Peter facilitating both the Postgraduate Supervisors CoP and MetaCoP, a CoP for the facilitators of each CoP within the university. Peter has been happily married to Claire for 28 years and has two daughters. Peter enjoys overseas travel, surfing, cycling, open water swimming and sharing a love of sport and life with Claire and his daughters.

Lynne D. Roberts is Associate Professor in the School of Psychology and Speech Pathology and Director of Higher Education Research in the Faculty of Health Sciences at Curtin University in Perth, Western Australia. Lynne is an Office for Learning and Teaching (OLT) National Teaching Fellow and an executive member of Curtin Academy, and has received university and national awards for her teaching. Lynne is an active researcher and has published more than 70 peer-reviewed journal articles and book chapters. Lynne's interests in educational research range from teaching research methods, dissertation supervision, capstone units, learning analytics, and academic integrity through to interprofessional education. She has a particular interest in the changing shape of academia within Australia.

Millie Rooney is a Research Fellow in the Housing and Community Research Unit at the University of Tasmania. Millie is currently evaluating a program to improve thermal comfort and energy efficiency in low-income households in Tasmania. In 2014 Millie completed her Ph.D. in the School of Geography and Environmental Studies; an investigation into everyday sharing practices of suburban Australians. Millie has held a variety of roles in a number of departments across the University of Tasmania and has been a part of team-taught interdisciplinary units. Millie is an active member of an interdisciplinary campus book club on the practice of gratitude in the tertiary sector.

David Sadler is the Deputy Vice-Chancellor (Students & Education) at the University of Tasmania. In addition to establishing the Communities of Practice Initiative discussed in this chapter, David has also led many initiatives at UTAS in the areas of student engagement, education for sustainable development, open education resources, technology enhanced learning and increased social inclusion in higher education. David was formerly a Director of the Higher Education Academy in the United Kingdom with responsibility for the UK subject centre network. A former Dean of Social Sciences and Director of the UK Subject Centre for Sociology, Anthropology and Politics, David was recognized as a UK National Teaching Fellow for his work on innovative role-play teaching techniques in the social sciences. Davis also holds two Jean Monnet awards for his teaching.

Dr. Jacqueline B. Saldana is a college Professor at DeVry University (US based) with more than 25 years of managerial experience in program development and total quality management. She is an experienced leader, policy maker, and business practitioner; responsible for establishing goals, communication strategies, and monitoring systems for federal, non-profit, volunteer, and professional programs with outstanding and nationally awarded results. She collaborates as academic peer-reviewer and research practitioner with several journals and publishing initiatives, including higher education competence based developments. Saldana mentors doctoral candidates in several universities of the United States. She is also an active participant in organizations dedicated to empower female entrepreneurs and Hispanic populations. Saldana is often guest speaker for professional associations and colleges in topics related to leadership and management best practices. She was the first Puerto Rican member of the Society for Healthcare and Marketing Communications of the American Hospital Association (1996–2000), and distinguished Communications Professional by the PR House of Representatives in 1997, among other professional recognitions. Saldana has a BA in Communications from the University of the Sacred Heart, a MBA from the University of Phoenix, and a Doctoral Degree of Management in Organizational Leadership from the University of Phoenix, School of Advanced Studies.

Dr. Michelle Salmona is the Vice President of Research and Global Solutions at the Institute for Mixed Methods Research affiliated with UCLA. Michelle also works as an international consultant in program evaluation, research design and qualitative data analysis using software. Her research focus is to better understand how to support doctoral success and strengthen the research process. Recent research includes exploring the changing practices of qualitative research during the dissertation phase of doctoral studies, and investigates how we bring learning into the use of technology during the research process. Michelle is currently working on different projects with researchers from Education, Information Systems, Business Communication, Leadership, and Finance. Dr. Salmona is a Project Management Professional, a Senior Fellow of the Higher Education Academy, UK and full-time faculty at the Australian National University specializing in research methods. Before joining ANU, Michelle was an Assistant Professor in Information Systems at Central Michigan University. She graduated from the University of New South Wales with a Master of Business & Technology and received her doctorate from the University of Technology, Sydney. Michelle also holds graduate degrees in Project Management, and University Learning & Teaching and has completed a Master of Higher Education.

Sonia Saluja is a Senior Lecturer in the School of Medical and Applied Sciences at CQUniversity, Australia. She is a qualified physician with a keen interest in medical education and research. After graduating from medical school she further completed a postgraduate doctoral degree in medicine and was subsequently awarded a MD in Human Physiology. She has over 16 years of experience in teaching at a tertiary level in medical schools and universities in Australia and overseas. Currently she coordinates and teaches into Clinical Physiology courses in the Bachelor of Medical Sciences Program with a special interest in Neurophysiology. Her research interests are in the field of obesity, diabetes, chronic disease and health literacy. As chief investigator of health related research projects she has been awarded grants and published in peer-reviewed journals.

Karl Smart, Ph.D. is Professor and Chair of the Business Information Systems Department at Central Michigan University (CMU). He also serves as an Assistant Dean for Assessment and Assurance of Learning. In addition to teaching business communication, he teaches courses in visual communication and digital media and graduate courses in strategic communication and change management. His Department has recently created a degree in Applied Business Communication, focusing on communication, collaboration, and critical thinking skills. He also led an effort to establish a new Entrepreneurship Department at CMU, along with revising the entrepreneurship curriculum. Areas of research interest include information and document design, the impact of technology on communication and the workplace, collaborative learning and working in teams, and assurance of learning. He has published widely in professional and business communication journals, including International Journal of Business Communication, Business and Professional Communication Quarterly, IEEE Transactions on Professional Communication, Technical Communication, Journal of Business and Technical Communication, The Journal of Computer Documentation, as well as published articles in information systems and education/pedagogy journals. His most recent research focuses on the scholarship of learning, with a particular focus on active and experiential learning and technology-mediated instruction.

Sue Smith is the Director of the Centre for SME Development at the University of Central Lancashire in the United Kingdom. Sue is responsible for developing and delivering the SME business engagement strategy for the School of Management and delivering on the university-wide enterprise strategy. Prior to this, Sue led SME growth programmes at Lancaster University Management School and was the Director of LEAD. During her tenure at Lancaster University, Sue led the roll out of LEAD across the England and Wales to over 3000 SMEs. Sue has an extensive track record of university business engagement. She is passionate about how people learn to lead and manage and the real impact this can have on a business. Sue has designed and taught on many leadership development and entrepreneurship programmes for diverse learners in Higher Education from undergraduates and postgraduates to post experience adult learners who do not traditionally engage with universities. Her academic research focuses on two areas. The first is using social theories of learning to look at the impact of SME peer learning. The second is the relationship between universities, business and government and the impact this can have on the regional economy.

Laurie Smith is a Visiting Teaching Fellow at Lancaster University Management School in the United Kingdom. Laurie designs and delivers leadership programmes and action learning sets. Laurie has worked with small and medium sized enterprises to help them develop and grow, and realize their full leadership potential. Alongside the practical aspects of leadership development, Laurie has researched and evaluated the impact of leadership development on owner-managers and their businesses. Additionally, Laurie is an independent facilitator working with numerous Higher Education Institutions and private companies to develop their leaders and to embed reflective practice into their organizations. Developing people and enterprises along a sustainable path is something that really excites Laurie and he takes great pleasure in working with individuals and teams to create new learning opportunities that positively influence practice.

Claire Stubbs began her career as a youth worker in East Sussex as she felt passionate about supporting young people to overcome barriers in their lives and to offer them a different experience. Claire built on this passion through the management of health services targeting disadvantaged young people within East Sussex. With an interest in people and wanting to develop her skills and knowledge, Claire pursued training in Counselling Psychology and Psychotherapy. She now has ten years' experience working with young people in a psychotherapeutic capacity, supporting young people to work through a range of issues including addictions, self-harming, relationships, loss, bereavement, anxiety and depression She also delivers a psychotherapeutic programme targeted at women who experience disadvantage. Clinical and personal experience prompted the interest in the resilience research field in an attempt to understand what can be done in practice to nurture young people's resilience. Claire completed her doctoral research on the mechanisms that support young men's resilience to reoffending and is now part of the Boingboing team working with the University of Brighton. The focus of her work is on developing participatory research and practice in relation to resilience and disadvantaged young people.

Sarah Terkes is a science communication and public engagement professional at the University of New South Wales Australia. After wrapping up her role as network integrator for the project described in this chapter, Sarah moved from her research and communications position in the UNSW Institute of Environmental Studies into a communications and engagement role in the UNSW Faculty of Science. Sarah is an active and vocal advocate of STEM education and is currently the campaign manager of the Australian Research Council funded Science 50:50 initiative.

Dr. Kate Thomson is a Lecturer in the Faculty of Health Sciences at the University of Sydney. Her research interests include academic development and work integrated learning. Most recently, she has focused on facilitating student and staff learning through informal conversations, tailored online resources, and systems of peer support.

Antoine van den Beemt works as Assistant Professor at the teacher-training institute of Eindhoven University of Technology in the Netherlands, the Eindhoven School of Education. His teaching activities focus on diversity and differentiation in classrooms, social learning, and the use of ICT in education. Antoine's research focuses on teacher professional development, with special emphasis on (online) social learning and learning with ICT. In addition to practice-based publications and textbooks, he presented award-winning papers at (international) conferences and published in international peer-reviewed journals. He is staff member of the Dutch Interuniversity Center for Educational Research, and editorial board member and reviewer of several international journals on ICT and education. He currently works on digital pedagogies for online learning, social media in the classroom, and simulations in STEM education.

Emmy Vrieling is Assistant Professor of Teachers' Professional Development in Social Networks and Self-Regulation at the Open University of the Netherlands. Her work concentrates on exploring social learning dimensions as well as self-regulated learning processes that facilitate professional development in educational institutes. Her research addresses informal learning, social learning, social media, self-regulated learning, metacognition, reflection and motivation. She has published and presented her research in national and international research journals, books and conferences. Emmy is also Staff Member of the Dutch Interuniversity Center for Educational Research and Editorial Board Member of the Dutch Association for Teacher Educators.

Kristin Warr Pedersen is the Head of Student Leadership and Careers at the University of Tasmania. In her previous role as an Academic Developer in the Tasmanian Institute of Learning and Teaching she developed and co-coordinated the Communities of Practice Initiative described in this chapter. Kristin has held teaching and curriculum development positions in the School of Geography and Environmental Studies. She now leads a team of student leadership and career management professionals who work to enhance and recognize the co-curricular experiences of students across all fields of study at UTAS. Kristin is previous Office for Learning and Teaching (OLT) Citation Winner and was part of a team that won a national OLT Award for Programs that Enhance Learning in 2015.

Diane R. Watkins serves as the IT Services Communications Coordinator at Metropolitan State University of Denver. She holds a BS in Technical Communications and an AAS in Computer Information Systems. Highlights of Diane's professional experience include working as an instructional technologist and designer, developing computer-based training for the United States Air Force, exploring how military training can be enhanced and learner motivation increased by adding gaming aspects to computer-based training, and leading projects investigating the use of inquiry-based learning and the use of the Structured Content Development Model.

Melody West is an Academic Developer at the Tasmanian Institute of Learning and Teaching at the University of Tasmania. Her role is focussed on the reward and recognition of teaching excellence across institutional and national programs. She is co-coordinator of the Communities of Practice Initiative and has a broad engagement across a range of professional learning programs which support learning and teaching. Melody has a research background and avid interest in the area of social inclusion in the higher education sector.

Etienne and Beverly Wenger-Trayner are internationally renowned social learning theorists and consultants. Their pioneering work in the field of social learning has been influential in such diverse fields as business, government, international development, healthcare, and education. Their consulting practice specializes in contexts where there are large-scale social learning challenges. They bring people together across organizations, geography, sectors, and disciplines to address complex problems. Etienne is known for his seminal work on communities of practice, and is currently Visiting Professor at the University of Brighton. Beverly is known for her work with international organizations including cross-boundary processes and the use of new technologies. Together they are developing and publishing conceptual frameworks and practices to address the learning challenges facing public and private organizations today.

Part I
Theoretical Underpinnings Informing Communities of Practice

The six chapters in this part describe the theoretical underpinning of Community of Practice (CoP) and its relevance in higher education.

Chapter 1 "What is a Community of Practice?" by Mercieca develops a theoretical framework for the idea of a CoP and investigates the reasons why CoP is particularly relevant to the contemporary higher education.

Chapter 2 "Social Learning in Higher Education: A Clash of Cultures?" by MacGillivray explores cultural elements that may be inhibiting the emergence, nurturing and effectiveness of communities of practice in higher education.

Chapter 3 "Faculty Learning Communities & Community of Practice: Dreamers, Schemers, and Seamers" by Cox and McDonald who articulate the independent emergence of Faculty Learning Communities (FLCs) in the United States and Communities of Practice (CoPs) in an Australian higher education setting, and the defining features of FLCs and CoPs as separate and then as hybrid models within their institutional and national contexts.

Chapter 4 "Using Communities of Practice to Internationalise HEd: Practical and Strategic Considerations" by May and Keay investigates the usefulness of the concept of CoP in helping higher education institutions to meet their internationalisation aspirations.

Chapter 5 "Delivering Institutional Priorities in Learning and Teaching Through a Social Learning Model: Embedding a High Impact Community of Practice Initiative at The University of Tasmania" by Pedersen et al. describes the University of Tasmania's Communities of Practice Initiative (CoPI) that provides collaborative professional learning opportunities for staff.

Chapter 6 "Creating and Facilitating Communities of Practice in Higher Education: Theory to Practice in a Regional Australian University" by Reaburn and McDonald reflects the lessons learnt that are the keys to creating, sustaining and facilitating CoPs within an Australian regional university.

Taken together these chapters highlight the application of CoP in higher education, and provide the key concepts, theoretical underpinnings, and guidelines for creating, sustaining and facilitating CoPs within higher education institutions.

Chapter 1
What Is a Community of Practice?

Bernadette Mercieca

Abstract Communities of practice are voluntary groups of people who, sharing a common concern or a passion, come together to explore these concerns and ideas and share and grow their practice. This chapter develops a theoretical framework for the idea of a community of practice. It investigates the reasons why this form of social learning, as described by Bandura, is particularly relevant to the higher education sector in the light of contemporary change and upheaval in society and the university world and an increasing emphasis on a scholarship of learning and teaching. The history and defining features of a community of practice, as developed by Wenger is explained as well as the more recent thought on landscapes of practice by the Wenger-Trayner partnership. Three particular examples from varied situations, including a virtual community of practice, are discussed to illustrate some of the key features of communities of practice. The chapter concludes with encouragement for higher educational institutions to champion the establishment of these communities.

Keywords Community of practice · Higher education · Sociocultural theory · Landscapes of practice · Scholarship of teaching and learning · Identity · Online learning

1.1 Introduction

It is part of our human nature to gather and, when a group of people does so, with a common concern or problem to solve or ideas to share, a community of practice is formed (Wenger 2002). The idea of a Community of Practice (CoP) is essentially a

B. Mercieca (✉)
University of Southern Queensland, Darling Heights, Australia
e-mail: bernadette.mercieca@usq.edu.au

© Springer Nature Singapore Pte Ltd. 2017
J. McDonald and A. Cater-Steel (eds.), *Communities of Practice*,
DOI 10.1007/978-981-10-2879-3_1

very old and well-practiced concept, which has become increasingly well known, through the research and publications of Lave and Wenger (1991).[1] Wenger, in a recent interview, explains that he first became interested in a social theory of learning because of the difficulty of cognitive approaches to account for how adults make sense of their world (Omivar 2014). Through the use of anthropological data on apprenticeships in a number of different communities such as the Yucatec midwives in an American Indian community and the Vai and Gola tailors from West Africa, Lave and Wenger (1991) concluded that learning did not primarily occur with the transmission of facts in the master/apprentice relationship. Rather, learning was best facilitated within a community of apprentices and more experienced workers:

> We propose to consider learning not as a process of socially shared cognition that results, in the end, in the internalization of knowledge by individuals, but as a process of becoming a member of a sustained community (Lave and Wenger 1991, p. 65).

The concept of a community of practice has its theoretical roots in the psychology of socialization, which will be considered shortly. Its application covers a wide range of fields, including business, industry, health and education. The popularity of this idea has continued to grow and be developed with the Wenger-Trayner[2] partnership, both of whom are now globally recognized scholars and trainers.

Yet despite its momentum, the uptake of CoPs within higher education (HE) institutions has been surprisingly limited. Whilst a number of such institutions have trialled CoPs such as the University of Southern Queensland (USQ) and the University of South Australia (UniSA), the practice has not significantly spread in the twenty years since it was first promulgated. Bouchamma and Michaud (2011) suggest that although academics have generally been exposed to ideas about improving their methodology, many have lacked the support of a CoP to help them implement these ideas to improve their quality of teaching and learning.

A glimpse at HE will generally show that academics are often isolated in their practice and individualism, rather than collaboration, is the norm. McDonald (2012) suggests that for too long teaching has been a very private affair, conducted behind closed lecture room doors, whilst promotion continues to be traditionally based on research rather than teaching.

---

[1]These are representative of the key dates of Wenger and Wenger-Trayner's publications, but are not inclusive of all their textual and electronic output.

[2]Etienne Wenger has partnered with Bev Trayner, a learning consultant specializing in social learning systems.

However, the growing movement towards a Scholarship of Teaching and Learning (SoTL)[3] in HE, involving dedicated research into the practice of teaching in order to understand how students learn and to critically reflect on this, fits more comfortably with the concept of a CoP. As a seminal voice in this debate, Boyle (1990), concludes that if a vision of scholarship can be developed in HE institutions, "a true community of scholarship will emerge, one that is not only more collaborative, but more creative, too" (p. 80).

Exposing academics to new knowledge has traditionally been done through formal professional development activities, such as seminars and conferences, often with large numbers of attendees. Whilst there is still clearly value in these forms of learning, it tends to be a top/down approach, with internal or external 'experts' presenting to a relatively passive and unengaged audience. Research by the Australian Institute for Teaching and School Leadership (AITSL) (2011) indicated that there is growing dissatisfaction with this sort of professional development, conceived of as something that one 'does', or that is 'provided', or is 'done to' teachers. Current findings point to the need for professional development to be closely tied to the context of teaching and the capacities of teachers. Fullan (2007) goes so far as to suggest that traditional professional development, with its generalised ideas, has run its term and that "student learning depends on teachers learning all the time" (p. 35). Whilst he admits that institutions are not set up for teachers to engage in "continuous and sustained learning", the role of CoPs, is going at least part of the way to providing a regular, localised and supportive environment for engendering this sort of change in professional development, cannot be ignored.

This disparity between theory and practice and the urgent need for more relevant forms of professional learning in HE, provide the impetus for this book. The major part of this chapter will examine the theoretical basis behind the concept of a CoP from a socio-cultural perspective and its key principles to inform those who seek to establish them within their own institutions. The second part will present a brief survey of three very different CoPs that will assist in illustrating these principles in practical settings.

---

[3]The scholarship of teaching goes beyond scholarly teaching and is driven by a desire to understand how students learn effectively and how teaching influences this process. Thus, it is student-focused. The scholarship of teaching has two main components. The first is the use of creativity to develop original materials … that can be used beyond the boundaries of an individual instructor. The second component, a systematic evaluation of teaching and learning, can involve both informal and traditional research on teaching and learning, or curriculum related issues. Both research approaches require in-depth understanding of the literature, critical reflection, and sharing through publication.

1.2 The Socio-cultural Underpinning of Communities of Practice

Fundamental to an understanding of communities of practice is the importance of the social dimension of learning (Bandura 1977). Bandura argued that learning is a cognitive process that takes place in a social setting. Social learning theory expands on traditional behavioural theories, by placing emphasis on the important roles of various active, internal processes in the learning individual and social context of the learning situation. The work of 20th century Soviet psychologist, Vygotsky (1978),[4] is significant in this regard, his ideas having caused a paradigm shift in our understanding of human development and learning, from "ahistorical, cultural, individualistic unfoldings, to culturally historical, socially created processes" (Holzam 2009, p. 3). His unique ability to traverse the deeply rooted dualist concepts of his time that separated biology and culture, learning and development and the individual and society, allowed him to develop a form of social psychology that has inspired a quarter of a century of subsequent research.

Vygotsky saw social relations as preeminent, 'genetically' underlying all higher functions, and argued that the individual and their environment should not be viewed as distinct, separate factors that can, in some way, be added up to explain the individual's development and behaviour. Rather, each mutually shape each other in a "spiral process of growth" (Hall 1997, p. 22).

Wertsch (2009) provides a rich synthesis and critique of Vygotsky's ideas, using the terms inter and intra psychological processes to describe the way higher order thinking is developed. Inter psychological processes arise out of social interactions which, in turn, influence the intra psychological process of the person's higher order thinking. From the earliest months of a child's development, when they start to call on an adult's attention by pointing to objects, their intra psychological functioning begins to grow: "All higher mental functions are internalised social relationships" (Wertsch 2009, p. 66). Wertsch stresses that this process of internalization is not a case of external experiences being copied into an internal plane that already exists, but rather that it is the external reality that creates the internal consciousness.

This is a unique insight that goes to the heart of an understanding of the importance of community. It appears to parallel the thinking of another foundational figure in social psychology, Mead (1934), who, although coming from a quite different philosophical perspective to Vygotsky, had a remarkably similar understanding of the genesis of the mind in social processes, believing that the mind could never have come into being without a social environment to nurture it.

Vygotsky (1987) linked his ideas about the importance of social development with the notion of the Zone of Proximal Development (ZPD). The prevailing view

---

[4]Lev Semyonovich Vygotsky (1896–1934) was a Soviet psychologist, and the founder of a theory of human cultural and social development. He is best known for his theories on how higher order thinking is developed in children and for proposing the concept of the Zone of Proximal Development (ZPD).

of his time was that learning depends on, and follows, the developmental stage of the child. Vygotsky broke new ground in suggesting that instruction can move ahead of development, instead of following it, stretching the child's thinking and eliciting thinking structures.

He describes the ZPD as the distance between a child's 'actual developmental level' and the higher level of 'potential development' that they might be capable of achieving. It is a sensitive space, hovering between what a person already knows, and what is within their range to know, with the help of a more knowledgeable instructor. This has implications for adult learning in HE. Adult educators are becoming increasingly aware that traditional methods of presenting information and expecting students to memorize it are no longer satisfactory. Smith and Pourchot (2013), for example, point to the importance of scaffolding[5] instruction and fostering a more social environment for adult learners.

Further, the professional development of academics is not going to necessarily work with a 'one size fits all' approach, which tends to be the approach of traditional providers. Lander (2005), for example, suggests that a balance in terms of time, place and mode must be achieved in what is offered to academics, with online options being included. The advantage of a CoP is that an academic can check in at whatever level best fits their ZPD, picking up maybe just one idea at a time that might work in their particular situation, trialling it with students, then receiving feedback on how things went from a supportive group, before trying again.

Valsiner (1987) expanded Vygotsky's theory of the ZPD and related it to teacher learning, seeing it as "a set of possibilities for development that are in the process of becoming realised as individuals negotiate their relationship with the learning environment and the people in it" (Goos and Geiger 2010, p. 501). In so doing, he developed two additional zones, the zone of free movement (ZFM) and the zone of promoted action (ZPA). The ZFM relates to the environment in which a teacher works, including the students and the expectations of the institution and the community. In HE, this would include the professional context of the university, with its strategic plan and curriculum and assessment requirements, the socio-economic background of the students, the availability of ICT resources and community expectations. Goos and Geiger's (2010) research with mathematics teachers showed that there were different degrees of flexibility in this area between veteran and early career teachers. The latter were more constrained by what they perceived as 'required' by their school or institution, limiting their ability to significantly change their pedagogy. In contrast, the more senior teachers, whilst still aware of institutional requirements, felt a greater degree of autonomy and the confidence to make changes in their environment. The ZPA relates to the "activities, objects or areas in the environment in respect of which the person's actions are promoted" (Goos and Geiger 2010, p. 501). In reality, this means how much support a teacher receives to

---

[5]In education, scaffolding refers to the process of breaking learning into manageable steps with the teacher modelling and then stepping back and offering support. Bruner was first to use the term in the 1960s.

engender and sustain change in their pedagogy. If there is too little support, any attempts at pedagogical change may falter. This is where a CoP can play a vital role, providing necessary social resources to encourage and challenge the person.

In the complex environment of a school or university, the ZFM and ZPA intersect with each other in a variety of ways, but ultimately the ZPA is dependent on the ZFM. In practice, a teacher can only promote what they are allowed to do (Blanton 2005).

This brings us to a key question of this chapter: What is a 'community of practice'?

1.3   What Is a Community of Practice?

Lave and Wenger (1991) first coined the term, 'Community of Practice', in their seminal text, *Situated Learning: Legitimate peripheral participation*. This focused on what they termed 'situated learning' and arose out of the work of a number of social theorists, including (Vygotsky's 1978) theories of social learning. It challenged the conventional, cognitive understanding of the time that learning is internalised knowledge transmitted from teacher to pupil: "We suggest that learning occurs through centripetal participation in the learning community of the ambient community" (Lave and Wenger 1991, p. 100). This understanding of learning as a "trajectory into a community", rather than a handing down of facts, became their central theme, the 'flagship', for the institute Wenger-Trayner set up and all that was to follow in their theorizing (Omivar 2014, p. 169).

Lave's anthropological background was influential in their choice of a range of historical and cultural examples of a particular type of learning environment—an apprenticeship—to begin to develop their theory. This included the apprenticeship of Yucatec midwives in an American Indian community, Vai and Gola tailors from West Africa, US naval Quartermasters, modern meat cutters and non-drinking alcoholics in Alcoholics Anonymous. Their analysis of these examples showed that, in contrast to school situations, direct transfer of information in a formalised way was generally not as important as the involvement in a community that facilitated learning. In at least three of the examples, there was a noticeable absence of the conventional master-apprentice relationship. Rather, newcomers in these communities were able to experience what they define as 'legitimate peripheral participation':

> Legitimate peripheral participation provides a way to speak about the relations between new comers and old-timers, and about activities, identities, artifacts and communities of knowledge and practice. It concerns the process by which newcomers become part of a community of practice. (Lave and Wenger 1991, p. 29)

With the Yucatec midwifes, for example, Lave and Wenger (1991) drew on the anthropological research of Jordan (1989), to show how apprenticeships happen as a part of everyday life. Mayan girls are gradually introduced to the art of midwifery from an early age by observing their midwife mother or grandmother, hearing stories from their practice and gradually starting to take on increasingly significant roles in the practice as they get older. Similarly, the traditional Vai and Gola tailors, although experiencing a more formal introduction to their art than the new midwives, still moved from peripheral to full participation in their community, through a process of observation and increasingly significant and varied roles. There were no formal classes and, even though there was a distinct Master-apprentice relationship, where Master tailors sponsored new apprentices, the greater learning appears to occur between other old timers and their peers: "an apprentice's own master is too distant, an object of too much respect, to engage with awkward attempts at a new activity" (Lave and Wenger 1991, p. 29).

These traditional methods of learning are reflected in more contemporary examples such as the non-drinking alcoholic seeking membership in Alcoholics Anonymous, where the new members are not overtly lectured to or advised. Rather, older members act as sponsors and "with-hold advice and instruction appropriate to later stages; they hold back and wait until the newcomer becomes 'ready' to take the next step through increasing participation in the community" (Lave and Wenger 1991, p. 92). This is similar to many other contemporary organisations such as International Toastmasters or different sporting clubs that gradually induct members into their organisation through sponsorship, example and legitimate participation in increasingly complex roles.

Legitimate peripheral participation has particular importance in practice-based programs in HE institutions. Pre-service teachers and nurses, for example, need to move between distinct Communities of Practices of university and school or health service placement within the course of a year. Ensuring that they are supported to successfully negotiate the change in identity that this involves and the achievement of legitimate peripheral participation in each venue cannot be underestimated. This is developed in more detail in Wenger-Trayner's (2014) more recent writings on the landscape of practice that will be discussed later in this chapter.

1.4   Three Defining Features of Communities of Practice

Whilst Wenger and Lave's (1991) earlier work focused primarily on how a learner moves into a community, from legitimate peripheral participation to full membership, Wenger's later work in 1998, *Communities of Practice: Learning, Meaning and Identity*, gave significantly more prominence to the defining features of a CoP. Through a close study of a medical insurance claims processing office, Wenger outlined three key structural features of a community of practice: 'mutual engagement', 'joint enterprise' and 'shared repertoire'. However, his more recent writing and the Wenger-Trayner website now use the simpler terms of 'domain', 'community' and 'practice' which will be used here.

1.4.1 The Domain

The starting point of any CoP is its domain. It is what initially motivates people to gather, with a shared concern or interest—the knowledge base from which a group chooses to work. Within a HE setting, the domain might be an interest shared by teachers in facilitating learning in first year undergraduate courses or in integrating technology into lectures or tutorials across a faculty or range of faculties.

The domain is what keeps the CoP focused, and ensures its relevance over time. As a CoP develops, it may be refined and adjusted in response to the needs and interests of its members. This is essential for the sustainability of the CoP (Wenger 2012a, b). However, if interest in a domain starts to wane or it moves too far from its original conception that may well signal the end of the CoP.

A defining feature of a CoP is that membership is voluntary. This is what distinguishes a CoP from a faculty meeting or other forms of working party or group within an institution. Once mandatory requirements are introduced, the very heart of a CoP is challenged, although the exception to this is membership in online student CoPs, which have a necessary compulsory element to them.

A domain has the potential to draw together a great variety of participants who share their particular expertise. Although each group would have a facilitator, this is not necessarily the most senior member of the group—membership is essentially very egalitarian, from professors to sessional lecturers to tutors to librarians to administration staff. Over time, Wenger (1998) suggests, the members develop a level of competence through engaging with problems and trialling strategies. They become experts in their chosen domain.

1.4.2 The Community

If the domain is what establishes a CoP, it is undoubtedly the feature of community that sustains it, ensuring that members keep participating. Community is essentially about relationship and particular measures need to be set in place to ensure that this is fostered. As will be seen in the examples that follow, this might mean providing refreshments, allowing time for less formal interaction at the start or the end of proceedings, and affirming member successes on a regular basis. Wenger (1998) maintains, "Whatever it takes to make mutual engagement possible is an essential component of any practice" (p. 74).

Out of the passion that members feel for their shared domain comes their commitment to learn and share with each other. Their shared enterprise is the essence of what they are about, defined by members in the very act of doing what they do (Wenger 2006). Whilst a team or working party might work on a task, then disperse, a community continues over time, deepening its learning experience. Members grow in trust and mutual respect, with no one fearing ridicule for the questions they might ask or the experiences they might share.

Wenger (2002) stresses that, although participants need to connect on a regular basis, they don't necessarily have to meet every day or even every week for a CoP to flourish. Interaction between gatherings can be fostered by the use of available technologies and social media which allow for online discussions and reflection.

Virtual communities of practice (VCoPs) operate on the same principles of mutual trust and connection, although building these principles into a program is clearly more difficult in an online environment. A growing body of research has focused on 'social presence' as online learning has become ubiquitous. Bates (2014) refers to this as the degree to which individuals feel comfortable to engage with each socially. Whilst online participants obviously cannot be physically present to each other, research indicates that activities that stimulate a sense of community through the use of Web 2.0 technologies such as chat rooms and forums, and time taken at the start of the course to introduce participants is crucial for the success of programs (Bates 2014). These type of strategies will be illustrated in the third of the examples that appears later in this chapter.

Besides social presence issues, Bourhis et al. (2005) highlight problems such as low level IT skills of the academic or the students or the limited experiences of community of some participants. They see the solution lying in developing and supporting skilled leaders, who can build up trust and encourage participation in a variety of ways. As will be seen in one of the examples that follows, the leader of a VCoP needs to work as what (Wenger 2012a) calls a 'broker', bridging the gap between two very different communities, that of the university and the diverse world of online students.

1.4.3 Practice

As a CoP develops, sharing fellowship and histories of learning, the third defining feature, 'practice', begins to emerge. The investment of time in attending regular gatherings, and of self that comes from a genuine sharing of experiences and successes and failures inevitably leads to a CoP developing a particular, individual practice and collective identity. Participants develop "a shared repertoire of resources: experiences, stories, tools, ways of addressing recurring problems—in short a shared practice" (Wenger 2012a, p. 2). Whereas the domain has drawn participants together, and community has sustained their fellowship and learning, it is practice that crystallizes these experiences and shared knowledge.

A strong practice allows a CoP to deal with challenges as they arise and can lead to the development of what Wenger (1998) calls, 'reification'. In effect, reification is the observable output from the community, what it shares with the wider community. Reification could include the creation and distribution of stories of individual and community successes to capture best practices, opportunities for sponsored projects or encouraging the publication of articles about the community and its projects (Cambridge 2005). This is best illustrated in the first of the practical examples, where the success of one CoP led to the rise of many other similar CoPs and the extensive spread of the educational resources they created. Output from a community embodies its history and its perspectives on the world and begins to give it a profile in the wider academic community. Feedback from the wider community can also help a CoP to move forward and achieve great clarity about its purpose.

These three defining features of domain, community and practice are clearly linked and work together to create a dynamic learning community. A well-defined domain helps to generate the key issues and tasks that the community will steward. Within this shared context, as personal stories and experiences are shared, mutual trust and respect is generated. Further, through connecting people who might not otherwise interact with each other, new and stimulating learning can occur which may help participants to improve their classroom practice. More experienced participants have opportunities to mentor and coach younger members, whilst younger members can gain confidence in realising they are not the only ones grappling with particular problems.

Alternatively, if any one feature is out of balance, the overall functioning of the CoP can be threatened. If, for example, the domain is too broad or ill defined, the participants might not have enough in common to generate the engagement needed (community) or create meaningful practice. People may sign up but not contribute or honour their commitments. Further, if there is a clearly defined domain, but limited active involvement of participants or hierarchical leadership, the CoP could easily slip into being a traditional meeting. Wenger (2012a, b), although supporting the idea of leadership in a CoP, also points out the problem of too much dependence on a co-ordinator or central leader, which can make the group vulnerable if the person leaves, whilst also decreasing the diversity of perspectives in the group. Finally, there can problems if a group has a clearly defined domain and active community involvement but the practice is not in balance. Too much reification, where communities focus excessively on documentation, can damage the community's fellowship and genuine engagement with each other (Wenger 2012a, b). Alternatively, if there is not enough documentation and output, the community ultimately becoming stale and unappealing to participants.

Over time, a community creates its own history of learning and an experience of competence amongst its members. This competence includes:

1. Understanding what matters, what the enterprise of the community is and how it gives rise to a perspective on the world.
2. Being able (and allowed) to engage productively with others in the community.
3. Using appropriatedly the repertoire of resources that the community has accumulated through its history of learning (Wenger 2012a, b, p. 2).

1.5 Further Developments

Wenger's earlier writing and research essentially considered CoPs in terms of legitimate peripheral participation in a relatively unstructured social environment, where participants shared a field of practice. There was no explicit suggestion, at this stage, that there was either any formal leadership in the group, nor any talk of boundaries or how a CoP might relate to other CoPs in a participant's professional life. However, Wenger's later writings (1998, 2000, 2002, 2006, 2012a, b) and Wenger-Trayner's writings and website (2014),[6] move beyond this. In these later works, they suggested that there might be advantages to organisations where they find ways to harness this situated learning process in a semi-structured way, whilst still maintaining the essential features of domain, community and practice (McDonald 2012). Key terms such as identity, meaning, boundaries, brokers, and most recently, a landscape of practice, are introduced. These ideas have important implications for HE.

1.5.1 Identity and Competence

Although the idea of identity was implicit in Lave and Wenger's (1991) earliest seminal work, it was not until Wenger's publication of *Communities of Practice: Learning, Meaning and Identity* (1998) that he explicitly discussed the important role CoPs play in developing a person's identity. Wenger (1998) defines identity as a negotiated experience within a community, where "we define who who we are by the ways we experience ourselves through participation" (p. 145). Over time, this identity is strengthened and affirmed as a 'learning trajectory' taking us from where we have been to where we are now. As will be seen in some of the examples that follow, a person's professional identity is boosted through experiencing success in their own teaching and learning context as a result of their involvement in a CoP. This may lead participants to take on greater challenges, such as leadership roles, with increased confidence.

As participants further immerse themselves in a CoP, they build a level of competence through participating in shared decision-making and engaging creatively with problems as they arise (Wenger 1998). The construction of artifacts, such as resources for others to use, further testifies to this competence. The examples that follow show that as a CoP builds up the competence of its members, greater attention is received from higher authorities in the institution or in the public arena through publication and presentations.

There are different challenges to identity depending on the time a person has spent in a community. Newcomers are challenged to find a place in and forge a new identity within a new set of circumstances. There is a certain level of vulnerability

---

[6]This can be accessed at http://wenger-trayner.com/.

involved in this, as a person tries to find continuities between their past experiences elsewhere and their new experiences here. Old timers, on the other hand, may have a strong sense of identity within a particular CoP, but need to be challenged to be open to new possibilities that might arise: "they may want to invest themselves in the future, not so much to continue it, as to give it new wings" (Wenger 1998, p. 157).

1.5.2 Boundaries

An unavoidable but necessary consequence of a CoP as it develops over a period time, is that it develops a shared history and a particular way of doing things. A particular jargon or shared vocabulary can often develop and a focus on particular issues. This is what is known as a boundary of practice. It becomes very comfortable for those who belong to the CoP but not so easy for outsiders: "Participants form close relationships and develop idioscyncratic ways of engaging with one another, which outsiders cannot easily enter" (Wenger 1998, p. 113).

A boundary of practice is particularly necessary in VCoPs. Wenger et al. (2009) developed the concept of tech stewards in relation to online communities, whose role is to assist the VCoP to determine how broad its boundaries will be, how private and secure, and provide platforms to assist the community in determining their domain. The tech steward's choice of technology allows a community to sustain mutual engagement, confident that the technology will not fail them. It allows them to learn from each other, overcoming the isolation that members might feel. Over time, tech stewards assist the community in developing a practice, providing a digital space for the sharing of stories and other forms of reification. They become, in effect, brokers, as Wenger et al. (2009) goes on to describe.

1.5.3 Brokers

Brokers work at the boundaries of communities. They "are able to make new connections, enable co-ordination and—if they are good brokers—open up new possibilities for meaning" (Wenger 1998, p. 109). This is a complex process and requires the particular skills of chosen members, who must be prepared to forgo a certain degree of comfort in reaching out beyond their own community. There are two important processes associated with brokering. The first is being able to establish a climate of trust, which is important in all CoPs, but particularly so when participants come from quite different backgrounds. The second is being able to draw together different types of information and provide a shared focus to guide discussion and align and interpret experiences (Wenger-Trayner 2014).

The concept of brokering is evident in practice-based courses, where there is a particular role for facilitators to assist students in developing distinct, dynamic identities in the contrasting communities they are involved in. This might include helping them to reflect on the different competencies they need in each community. As will be seen below, as life becomes more complex and a person needs to be involved with a range of communities, the role of a broker becomes increasingly important.

1.5.4   Landscapes of Practice

Wenger-Trayner's more recent thinking focuses on the varied social landscape of communities that many of us belong to. A recent publication, *Learning in Landscapes of Practice* (2014), explores this issue from the perspective of what it means to live and work across the boundaries of a range of different practices that make up a professional landscape. In the HE landscape, this could include involvement in communities related to teaching, research and supervision as well as those related to professional associations and online communities. In terms of younger staff particularly, this could mean moving between different places of employment five or move times during their working career. From the perspective of students in practice-based courses, such as education or the health sciences, a landscape of practice could relate to simulaneous involvement in two separate, though related, communities. Because each of these practices have their own histories, moving between each of them mean negotiating one's identity and the boundaries of each community (Wenger-Trayner 2014).

A person entering a new community is faced with the difficult task of negotiating which aspects of their identity that they have brought with them from previous communities will be acceptable in this new community. This can be a complex and potentially emotionally fraught experience. Feelings of apprehension and confusion can arise as people find themselves moving from a situation where they felt secure and saw themselves as competent, to a situation where they might experience a sense of failure or incompetence. Shifts in the emotional investment of the new members occurs, as they experience acceptance and gradual confirmation of the provisional self they have projected (Wenger-Trayner 2014).

As mentioned earlier, a key outcome of belonging to a CoP is developing a sense of competence related to the knowledge defined and negotiated within the community. Wenger-Trayner (2014) suggests that the comparable dimension in a landscape of practice is knowledgeability: a person's ability to relate to a multiplicity of practices across a landscape of practices.

The metaphor of a landscape ensures that we pay attention to boundaries, to our multimembership in different communities and to the challenges we face as our personal trajectories take us through multiple communities (Wenger-Trayner 2014). It is a concept that they will undoubtedly continue to feature in their writings, reflecting a more nuanced understanding of contemporary society.

1.6   Practical Examples

In order understand how the theory of CoPs is enacted, three practical examples will be described. The first considers a longstanding community that, although not called a CoP at the time, certainly demonstrates a number of the key features of this. The Project for Enhancing Effective Learning (PEEL) began more than 30 years ago in a working class high school in Victoria (Australia) and highlights the value of academic/school teacher interaction. The second example examines a CoP that began operating at the University of Southern Queensland (USQ) in 2006. The final example comes from Umeå University in northern Sweden and looks at how a VCoP has been used to overcome the isolation of online students.

1.6.1   The Project for Enhancing Effective Learning (PEEL)

The learning community that is known as PEEL was begun by Ian and Julie Mitchell in 1985 as a joint venture between a Victorian State High School and Monash University. It arose out of a concern about the prevalence of passive, unreflective, dependent student learning in schools, even in apparently successful lessons. Mitchell's own research on conceptual change in the teaching of science, which strengthened his views on constructivism[7] as an important means of understanding learning, and his contact with John Baird from Monash University, whose doctoral thesis, *Improving learning through enhanced metacognition* (Baird 1986), addressed similar issues, formed the context for the formation of this community. The group initially consisted of a small number of teachers who agreed to work with John and conduct action research with their classes. Interestingly, in line with the formation of a CoP, the community arose at a 'grass roots' level rather than as an institutional initiative. In addition, although Baird's research formed the background for this community, it was "a collaborative action research project where ownership of all aspects, including research design, was shared by all participants" (Mitchell and Mitchell 2007, p. 22).

Thus, the desire to improve student learning through the use of metacognition strategies became the domain for this somewhat unusual group of high school teachers and academics. It led to the group formulating four key goals that guided their work:

1. To foster effective, independent learning through training for enhanced metacognition.
2. To change teacher attitudes and behaviours to ones that promote such learning.

---

[7]Constructivism is based on the belief that learning occurs as learners are actively involved in a process of meaning and knowledge construction as opposed to passively receiving information. Learners are the makers of meaning and knowledge. Constructivist teaching fosters critical thinking, and creates motivated and independent learners.

3. To investigate processes of teacher and student change as participants engage in action research.
4. To identify factors that influence successful implementation of a programme that aims to improve the quality of students' learning (Mitchell and Mitchell 2007, p. 20).

The small group of teachers, John Baird and several other academics from Monash University began meeting on a weekly basis during school hours, with the occasional addition of a full day's meeting. Their action research consisted of the teachers, with the support of the academics, trialling different meta-cognitive learning strategies in their classrooms and sharing their results within the community. Initially, the chosen classroom strategies proved to be more difficult to implement than anticipated. It is not easy to change teaching strategies that have been developed over many years. However, after 3 months of painful failure, the teachers began to experience success. They became "interdependent innovators, problematising and reflecting on their practice, sharing concerns, creating new teaching ideas, and sharing failures and successes" (Mitchell and Mitchell 2007, p. 22). This illustrates the importance of the community in a CoP. An individual might tend to give up after repeated failures in the classroom; however, with the support and suggestions of a community, the teachers gained the confidence to keep trying and eventually achieved success.

The academic staff were not directly involved in trialling teaching strategies, but took on the role of mentors in the community, providing advice and mirroring back to the teachers what they were doing. This is one of the key roles that (Wenger 2002) envisaged in a maturing community. As mentors, they were able to utilise their more developed skills of analysis and their greater familiarity with the research project, to help the teachers make sense of their experiences in the classroom and challenge them to look more deeply into them, whilst ensuring they stayed close to the research objectives.

It was also evident, in retrospect, that Mitchell took on the role of a broker in a landscape of practice, having the advantage of links to Monash University and John Baird, as well as being a teacher at the school. Teachers and academics, although sharing a common background in education, are seen as having different sort of skills and in 1986, teachers were sometimes suspicious and untrusting of academics. They were certainly unused to the process of active research and, indeed, of working in a sustained way with other teachers from different subject areas on broad learning issues. The CoP gave the teachers a new experience of their own professionalism and the possibilities that action research offers and they were pleasantly surprised by how valuable the group was for them. They appreciated how the academics listened to them, in ways that they had not previously experienced (Mitchell and Mitchell 2007).

Mitchell's research background also assisted him in helping the teachers align their teaching practice with the research objectives and understand the world from which the academics were coming. To a lesser extent, the teachers also needed to understand each others' worlds, as they each came from five different subject areas.

The ideas they developed, consequently, had to be generic, applicable to Science as well as Literature, to Physical Education as well Mathematics. Interestingly, Baird had conducted earlier research with a different school where the teachers involved had no opportunity to discuss their ideas or share their practice. There was significantly more progress made with this community where teachers met regularly and could "bounce ideas off each other" (Mitchell and Mitchell 2007, p. 22).

The regularity of these CoP meetings and the active role the teachers played in bringing back problems and challenges from their classroom created significant bonding in the group as well as developing their confidence and creativity:

> Collaborative action research helped the group develop synergy. They became innovators who fed off each other's ideas and built up creative practice. (Mitchell and Mitchell 2007, p. 25)

Such bonding is indicative of what can occur in a CoP after a sustained period of engagement with a particular domain. It was so strong in this PEEL group, that at the end of the 2 year research period, the teachers and their students did not want to stop. The competence and professional identity that had developed in the members of the group led to their ideas spreading, so that, as well continuing as a group themselves, they inspired many other communities to begin in other schools in Australia (both primary and secondary) and then overseas in countries such as Denmark, Sweden, Great Britain, Canada, New Zealand, and, most recently, China. Their reification included written reflections on their experience of the CoP, combined into a database of over 1400 articles, publication of the generic teaching strategies and graphic organisers they had developed, and books that are well accepted in schools. A widely dispersed newsletter (now a journal, know as PEEL SEEDS) still circulates some 30 years later. Conference presentations, meetings and consultation with other schools also followed. There is now a very large PEEL community connected by a domain of wanting to improve student learning. This high quantity of reification and public acclaim reflects the quality of the practice that was developed in that initial group.

PEEL was a very successful CoP, one that was, in many ways, ahead of its time. It was influential in encouraging teachers to reflect on their learning and support each other, in an otherwise, individualistic profession. Its impact, not only on the teachers themselves, but on the students, who began to consider themselves co-reseachers, cannot be underestimated. Reflecting the identity that can be fostered in a CoP, a number of the initial group of teachers have gone on to do higher degrees, produced classroom text books and taken on senior positions in other schools. Loughran (1999) believes the success of PEEL was due to its process and output being intelligible, plausible and fruitful. It was intelligible in that it came from the work of ordinary teachers, in ordinary classrooms, with a genuine passion for enhancing students' thinking skills. This is at the heart of what a CoP is about, bringing ordinary people together to create a shared history of learning. Secondly, it was plausible, in that the learning problems PEEL highlighted were ones shared by most other classrooms at that time, and, indeed, largely still today. Finally, it was fruitful "because, although it was demanding, examples of real gains in student learning were apparent" (Loughran 1999, p. 284). This model of professional development continues to inform professional development research. Thanks to the dream, passion and commitment of this small blended group of educators, a whole generation of teachers and students have experienced a better way to learn and seen how a CoP could effectively operate between a university and a school.

1.6.2 The Faculty of Arts Community of Practice

At USQ, the Faculty of Arts Teaching and Learning CoP began operating in 2006 and operated for almost 6 years. Its domain consisted of the teachers of first year courses offered by the Faculty of Arts. Clearly, a CoP that went for such a length of time, whilst beginning as a group of loosely connected academics, over time created significant personal and professional connections. These can ultimately become very tight nodes of inter-personal relationships (Wenger 1998). The vision of the Arts CoP was to improve the first year experiences for students in the Faculty of Arts and to empower academics to become more student-focused in their teaching practice, at a time when the student community was becoming increasingly diverse. Communal engagement for the group came through the discussion of issues related to assessment, the Faculty Learning and Teaching plan, student diversity and the student-learning journey. Their practice took various forms over the years, such as supporting academics with resources and strategies, instigating professional development for members of the Faculty and trialling new strategies in their own program.[8]

The Arts CoP met monthly for a 2 h session. The group consisted of a faculty-based facilitator, a facilitator from the Learning and Teaching Support Unit, and between six and nine regular attendees (Lawrence 2008). Features of their time together included typical community building activities of food and fellowship and celebrations of success, domain knowledge such as a member or an invited speaker giving input, and time to share practice related to the domain topic. The importance of sharing food and fellowship cannot be downplayed. This is where the bonds of community that Wenger (1998) refers to are developed and strengthened.

Important practical considerations for the group when it was first set up included membership—who would join and how many would be an ideal size for the group; workload—how much time and work commitment could be expected from busy members of the group; how often and at what time of day to meet and how to communicate between meetings; where to meet and how to manage budgeting, such as for food and drinks at meetings. More formal ongoing considerations for the group included their identified outcomes and how they aligned with USQ priorities.

---

[8]More details about this and other CoPs currently operating at the University of Southern Queensland can be found at http://www.usq.edu.au/cops/communities.

A quote from one of the members of this CoP gives an insight into how it was valued at the USQ:

> The good thing was to meet in an informal setting with staff. It's good to hear other people's ideas; yes, and I also think getting to know what is happening in other disciplines is useful because we're quite isolated in our discipline and quite often we don't know what is going on in other disciplines. (Lawrence 2008, p. 8, Interview 2)

The CoP was successful in instigating a change of practice in many participants. This included participants incorporating more academic skills and literacies in their units, making substantive changes to their assessment strategies and taking steps to create a more welcoming environment for their students. There was also clearly particular value for newer lecturers and tutors in being part of a welcoming and informative group of this nature, accelerating their sense of belonging in the university.

Although, as with any CoP, there were areas for improvement, such as a need for greater focus and structure in gatherings and better opportunities to more widely disseminate their practice, this was a very successful community, which would appear to have had a significant effect within the faculty and, arguably, the university generally, in terms of modelling to other faculties what can be achieved. There are now over 22 CoPs across the campuses at USQ, covering a variety of learning and supervisory areas. The Vice Chancellor of USQ, Professor William Lovegrove, in an interview with Dr Jacquie McDonald, the instigator of the project, reflects:

> The way I see them is, it's really staff with a real interest in given areas coming together to share experiences, I guess, and develop knowledge help to drive their particular initiatives in areas that they're quite passionate about. That's how I understand them ... and I think they're really useful because it's people who do the work, helping to drive the work rather than people who sit a level or two above trying to outline how it could be done. It's people really doing it. (McDonald 2011)

The fact that this CoP had a 'champion' in the senior echelons of the university is a significant plus for the group. A champion is identified as a senior manager who believes strongly that a CoP should be a primary mechanism for managing knowledge in an institution. Although they are not being personally involved in the group, they fully support development by providing guidance, funds, visibility and legitimacy in the wider community. There is a fine balance between maintaining the 'grassroots', non-hierarchical nature of a CoP, whilst at the same time harnessing the goodwill of the executive leadership of the institution. USQ appears to have achieved this balance.

1.6.3   Creating Online Community: A VCoP

The final example comes from Umeå University, a small, multi-campus university situated in a somewhat remote part of northern Sweden. This example differs from the previous two in that it involves students working with a leader, as opposed to teachers working with other teachers, and it took placed in a fully online environment. Although participation in this VCoP was clearly not voluntary, other salient features of a VCoP were evident making it useful to consider.

Umeå University, as a consequence of its location, has a long history of, and much experience with distance education with an estimated 45 % of students choosing to study in this mode (Deutschmann 2014). The challenge for this VCoP was to create a collaborative environment for online learning, a form of learning which, as was mentioned earlier, has inherent problems. The New York Times, for example, reported that the attrition rate for online courses is 90 %, even in smaller courses, and that while solely online courses are fine for highly skilled and motivated students, struggling students need much more personal contact to succeed (New York Times 2013). Deutschmann (2014) concurs, seeing a close correlation between the feelings of isolation that students can feel and unfinished courses, whilst (Gaytan's 2013) research found that the second highest rated factor affecting student retention in online courses was the quality of faculty and student interaction.

Deutschmann (2014) suggests that the reason for this unsatisfactory situation is that many lecturers have not been trained in how to run online courses. As a consequence, they tend to use the same strategies they would use in traditional courses, seeing their main role as content providers, "merely offering ready-made educational material to be downloaded, after which the individual is left to pursue his or her studies in relative isolation" (p. 1). The other reason, he adds, is that in a normal classroom, social interaction between students can be generally taken for granted—but this factor is lacking in online courses unless it is intentionally built in. The role of the leader of a VCoP becomes one of providing a framework for community building so that the academic and social worlds of the student can be integrated.

Another reason for creating community in online courses, Deutschmann (2014) suggests, goes back to the principles of social learning discussed earlier. Students learn more effectively when they can co-create knowledge through a learning community:

> Online learning is thus being transformed form 'silent solitary acts to lively, meaning-making events rich in discussion' where learning takes place with others in a social context. (Deutschmann 2014, p. 2)

Deutschmann (2014), who, in effect, was the leader of this VCoP, describes how, over a period of 6 years, the online courses in English language that he was involved with, experimented with social learning. One example from this period will help to demonstrate how the features of a VCoP were evident. This involved an English Grammar class that Deutschmann chose to structure using Johnson's

(1990) Key Element Model[9] as a starting point, elements of which include inter-dependence, interaction, accountability, social skills and self-evaluation.

The first activities that Deutschmann describes were 'warm up' tasks that primarily aimed at creating contact in an informal, fun way, but with links to the particular academic subject. For example, the Grammar students were asked to write humorous, short anecdotes from their schools days and different teachers they'd had. These were then posted to an online discussion board for others to read and comment on. This is similar, metaphorically, to fellowship activities, such as sharing food and drink, described earlier, that help to break down barriers and build community.

As the course progressed, Deutschmann set activities that included both an individual element and a group element, the latter of which involved students reading and discussing each other's work. He aimed to create opportunities for students to collaborate, whilst at the same time maintaining individual accountability. Students had the chance to give and receive feedback in a constructive manner (Deutschmann 2014).

The task for the Grammar students was to use the definite, indefinitive or zero articles in a number of sentences. The examples were made deliberately ambiguous to encourage discussion. Once each student had completed the task individually, they posted into a small group (of 4) discussion page. Each small group filled up as students submitted their work, adding an element of accountability to the task (Deutschmann 2014). The students then critiqued each other's work. Again we can see evidence of a VCoP, as with the shared domain of the subject they are studying and the developing bonds of community in place, students can then move into deeper social learning in defending their ideas and critiquing those of others.

Other types of group tasks that Deutschmann (2014) describes include PowerPoint presentations produced by several students, problem-based tasks and discussion seminars, where different issues were raised using real time audio and Skype.

Before leaving this example, it is worth pointing out several other VCoP features that are evident in Deutschmann's programs generally. He tried, for example, to ensure in particular programs, that mentors were involved to assist students who

---

[9]The Key Element Model aims produce the following elements in students:

- Positive interdependence: Students organize themselves by assuming roles which facilitate their collaboration.
- Promotive interaction: Students take responsibility for the group's learning by sharing knowledge as well as questioning and challenging each other.
- Individual accountability: Each student is held responsible for taking an active part in the group's activities, completing his/her own designated tasks, and helping other students in their learning.
- Social skills: Students use leadership skills, including making decisions, developing consensus, building trust, and managing conflicts.
- Self-evaluation: Students assess individual and collective participation to ensure productive collaboration.

were new to the university environment. Deutschmann also discussed in depth the role of the teacher as e-moderator, whose range of tasks included, not just providing information and evaluating assessment tasks but setting up communication channels, reassuring students and helping to build a community despite the challenge of distance and lack of physical presence. In many ways, the e-moderator is the one whose planning and approach will determine the success or failure of the online learning environment. This reflects (Wenger-Trayner's 2014) more recent thinking on landscapes of practice. In many ways, the teacher/e-moderator is a broker, working at the boundaries of the university community and the diverse communities from which the online students are drawn. Their role in establishing an atmosphere of trust and helping students engage with a new and unfamiliar environment is indispensable.

Although Deutschmann (2014) is hesitant to say that they have found all the answers to online learning, overall Umeå University would appear to offer a helpful perspective on ways of creating a VCoP. With the number of students in online courses continuing to grow, further research is needed into how this learning experience can be made even more engaging and effective for students.

1.7   Conclusion

In this chapter, CoPs have been presented as a way to provide an effective approach for dealing with the challenges facing higher education in the current environment of upheaval and change. They are recommended as a practical way of developing a scholarship of teaching and learning at a grassroots level, involving shared member concerns and interests from a wide range of participants. It is clearly very difficult as an individual to adapt to new circumstances and bring about change in an institution. But with the support of a CoP, in an environment where successes and failures are shared and new ideas workshopped, academics can develop their practice and be empowered to make lasting changes in their teaching. Over time, this involvement creates an "institutional memory regarding teaching and learning innovations" (McDonald and Star 2007, p. 117). In addition, CoPs can support younger academics and help them overcome the isolation that many other academics may feel in their professional lives. They are also, as we have seen, of particular value to online communities.

In other chapters, you will have the chance to read in more detail about a large range of other successful efforts to establish CoPs and VCops in a variety of HE settings. The challenge for those who wish to tap into this idea is to think broadly about the issues that confront your institution, seek out a champion who might support and encourage your initiative and recruit members who share an interest and concern in that domain. There are expanding avenues of support for those who decide to take up this challenge. No matter how small your beginning, know that you have begun on an exciting pathway to enhancing learning at your institution.

References

Baird, J. (1986). Improving learning through enhanced metacognition: A classroom study. *European Journal of Science Education, 8*(3), 263–282.

Bandura, A. (1977). *Social learning theory*. Englewood Cliffs, NJ: Prentice Hall.

Bates, T. (2014). *The role of communities of practice in a digital age*. Online learning and distance education resources. http://www.tonybates.ca/2014/10/01/the-role-of-communities-of-practice-in-a-digital-age/. Accessed 1 October 2015.

Blanton, M. W. (2005). Using Valsiner's zone theory to interpret teaching practices in mathematics and science classrooms. *Journal of Mathematics Teacher Education, 8*(1), 5–33.

Bouchamma, Y. (2011). Communities of practice with teaching supervisors: A discussion of community members' experience. *Journal of Educational Change, 12*(4), 403–420. doi:10.1007/s10833-010-9141-y.

Bouchamma, Y., & Michaud, C. (2011). Communities of practice with teaching supervisors: a discussion of community members' experience. *Journal of Educational Change, 12*(4), 403–420. doi:3.1007/s10833-010-9141-y.

Bourhis, A., Dubé, L., & Jacob, R. (2005). The success of virtual communities of practice: The leadership factor. *The Electronic Journal of Knowledge Management, 3*(1), 23–34.

Boyle, E. (1990). *Scholarship reconsidered priorities of the professoriate. The Carnegie Foundation for the Advancement of Teaching*. New york, NY: Jossey-Bass Books.

Cambridge, D. K. (2005). *Communities of practice design guide: A step-by-step guide for designing and cultivating communities of practice in higher education*. http://net.educause.edu/ir/library/pdf/nli0531.pdf. Accessed 14 October 2015.

Deutschmann, M. (2014). *Creating online community-challenges and solutions*. https://matsdeutschmann.files.wordpress.com/2013/01/creating-online-communitysecond-version.pdf. Accessed 30 July 2015.

Fullan, M. (2007). Change the terms for teacher learning. *Journal of Staff Development, 28*(3), 35–36.

Gaytan, J. (2013). Factors affecting student retention in online courses: Overcoming this critical problem. *Career and Technical Education Research, 38*(2), 145–155. doi:10.5328/cter38.2.147.

Goos, M., & Geiger, V. (2010). Theoretical perspectives on mathematics teacher change. *Journal of Mathematics Teacher Education, 13*(6), 499–507.

Hall, M. J. (1997). *The collected works of L.S. Vygotsky*. New York, NY: Plenum Press.

Holzam, L. (2009). *Vygotsky at work and play*. NY: Routledge.

Johnson, D. W., & Johnson, R. T. (1990). Using cooperative learning in math. In N. Davidson (Ed.), *Cooperative learning in mathematics* (pp. 103–125). Menlo Park, CA: Addison-Wesley Publishing.

Jordan, B. (1989). Cosmopolitan obstetrics; Some insights from the training of traditional midwives. *Social Science and Medicine, 28*(9), 925–944.

Lander, J. (2005). *Walk, don't run: Achieving balance in professional development for academics moving online*, School of Public Health, University of Sydney. www.ascilite.org.au/conferences/brisbane05/blogs/.../43_Lander.pdf. Accessed 15 July 2015.

Lave, J., & Wenger, E. (1991). *Situated learning: Legitimate peripheral participation*. Cambridge: Cambridge University Press.

Lawrence, J. (2008). Communities of practice: A sphere of influence enhancing teaching and learning in higher education. http://www.anzca.net/documents/2008-conf-papers/117-communities-of-practice-a-sphere-of-influence-enhancing-teaching-and-learning-in-higher-education-1/file.html. Accessed 12 October 2015.

Loughran, J. (1999). Professional development for teachers: A growing concern. *Journal of In-service Education, 25*(2), 261–273. doi:10.1080/13674589900200080.

McDonald, J. (2011). Interview with Professor Loveday. www.usq.edu.au/cops/resources/altcfellowship/vc-interview. Accessed 12 August 2015.

McDonald, J. (2012). Identifying and building the leadership capacity of community of practice facilitators. University of Southern Queenslandhttps://eprints.usq.edu.au/26120/8/McDonald_Nagy_Star_Burch_Cox_Margetts_LCJ_2012_AV.pdf. Accessed 4 October 2014.

McDonald, J., & Star, C. (2007) Making meaning of women's networks: A community of practice framework. In *2007 International Women's Conference: Education, Employment and Everything... the Triple Layers of a Woman's Life*, 26–29 Sep 2007, Toowoomba, Australia.

Mead, G. (1934). *Mind, self and society*. Chicago: The University of Chicago Press.

Mitchell, I. J. (2007). *Teaching for effective learning: The complete book of PEEL teaching procedures* (3rd ed.). Melbourne: PEEL Publishing.

Mitchell, I. J., & Mitchell, J. A. (1997). *Stories of reflective teaching: A book of PEEL cases*. Melbourne: PEEL Publishing.

Mitchell, I. J., & Mitchell, J. A. (2007). *PEEL in practice: 1400 ideas for quality teaching* (8th ed.). Melbourne: PEEL Publishing.

Omivar, O. (2014). The evolution of the communities of practice approach: Toward knowledge-ability in a landscape of practice—An interview with Etienne Wenger-Trayner. *Journal of Management Inquiry, 23*(3), 266–275.

Smith, C., & Pourchot, T. (2013). *Adult learning and development: Perspectives from national psychology*. NY: Routledge.

The Australian Institute for Teaching and School Leadership. (2011). *Professional learning: An introduction to the research literature*. http://www.aitsl.edu.au/. Accessed 14 October 2015.

Valsiner, J. (1987). *Culture and the development of children's actions: A cultural-historical theory of developmental psychology*. New York, NY: Wiley.

Vygotsky, L. (1978). *Mind in society: Development of higher psychological processes*. Cambridge, MA: Harvard University Press.

Vygotsky, L. S. (1987). Thinking and speech (N. Minick, Trans.). In R. W. Rieber & A. S. Carton (Eds.), *The collected works of L. S. Vygotsky: Vol. 1. Problems of general psychology* (pp. 39-285). New York: Plenum Press. (Original work published 1934).

Wenger, E. (1998). *Communities of practice: Learning, meaning, and identity*. Cambridge: Cambridge University Press.

Wenger, E. (2000). Communities of practice and social learning systems. *Sage Journals, 7*(2), 225–246.

Wenger, E. (2002). *Cultivating communities of practice: A guide to managing knowledge*. Boston, MA: Harvard University Press.

Wenger, E. (2006). *Communities of practice: A brief introduction*. https://www.academia.edu/6189864/Communities_of_Practice_A_Brief_Introduction. Accessed 14 October 2015.

Wenger, E. (2012a). *Communities of practice and social learning systems: The career of a concept.* http://wenger-trayner.com/resources/publications/cops-and-learning-systems/. Accessed 30 August 2015.

Wenger, E. (2012b). *Communities of Practice: A brief introduction,* http://wenger-trayner.com/wp-content/uploads/2012/01/06-Brief-introduction-to-communities-of-practice.pdf. Accessed 23 August 2015.

Wenger-Trayner, E. (2014). *Learning in landscapes of practice: Boundaries, identity, and knowledgeability in practice-based learning*. London: Routledge.

Wenger, E., White, N., & Smith. (2009). *Digital habitat: Stewarding technology for communities*. Portland, Oregon: CPSquare.

Wertsch, J. V. (2009). *Vygotsky and the social formation of mind*. Cambridge: Harvard University Press.

Chapter 2
Social Learning in Higher Education: A Clash of Cultures?

Alice E. MacGillivray

Abstract Social learning is a natural part of being human. Wenger's theory of social learning is also the theoretical underpinning for communities of practice. Learning is a key outcome of higher education. Yet, my experience suggests that communities of practice are not thriving in higher education compared to some other fields and sectors. This conceptual chapter explores cultural elements that may be inhibiting the emergence, nurturing and effectiveness of communities of practice in higher education. The chapter focuses primarily on faculty work. Social learning inhibitors may include higher priorities, boundaries that divide groups with potentially common interests, the disciplinary nature of leaning norms and the potentially overwhelming nature of diversity. The chapter lists benefits of enhanced community of practice work and includes ideas for future research.

Keywords Community of practice · Higher education · Social learning · Culture · Boundaries · Epistemologies

2.1 Introduction

This book includes successful examples of social learning through communities of practice (CoP) in higher education. Each example illustrates benefits to individuals and groups. The book fills an important niche; there is no book like it. And yet is that not surprising? Several researchers estimate that 80 % of our learning is informal (Cross n.d.). We learn as we practice. We learn through dialogue with each other. We learn when we reflect and share our successes and especially our failures. We learn socially: not just with a psychological perspective on interactions as described by

---

The original version of this chapter was revised: Punctuation has been updated. The erratum to this chapter is available at: 10.1007/978-981-10-2879-3_29

A.E. MacGillivray (✉)
Gabriola Island, BC, Canada
e-mail: Alice@4KM.net

© Springer Nature Singapore Pte Ltd. 2017
J. McDonald and A. Cater-Steel (eds.), *Communities of Practice*,
DOI 10.1007/978-981-10-2879-3_2

Bandura (Wenger 1998, p. 280) but through our practical and reflective experiences with each other, as described in subsequent theory development (Lave and Wenger 1991; Wenger 1999). And is education not the sector in which we care most about learning? In which we strive to deeply understand learning as a service to students, colleagues and communities? If we deeply value and understand learning, we can more effectively share important new findings from our research. And therefore, communities of practice should be thriving in all facets of higher education. This chapter explores this paradox: why aren't there more thriving communities of practice in higher education? Through this chapter, I hope to open a safe space for dialogue and learning about higher education cultures in relation to social learning.

Learning in higher education is associated with credentials. The validity and value of those credentials is determined within the higher education community through standardized tools such as credit hours, hierarchically organized degrees, criteria for quality within disciplines and methodologies, and double-blind peer-review processes. With regards to standards of excellence, higher education practitioners tend to be inward-focused.

Midgley's theory of boundary critique can help us explore this paradox and factors that may inhibit communities of practice in higher education. This theory is informed by the work of Churchman, Ulrich and others (Midgley 2000). A simplified version is presented in Fig. 2.1. It is "a normative theory (prescribing a course of action rather than simply describing an aspect of the world) about the need for reflection on boundaries during interventions" (Midgley 2000, p. 135). His work emphasizes that boundary judgments and values are interconnected, even if we are not consciously aware of that connection and related implications. The graphic uses boundaries to separates different groups; these are not necessarily barriers. Faculty are not staff, for example.

We can use this to consider formal education as having power and influence in the core (see Fig. 2.2). Non-formal and informal education, such as learning through communities of practice, is then situated in the margins. According to Midgley's theory, those in the core value or devalue groups and ideas in the

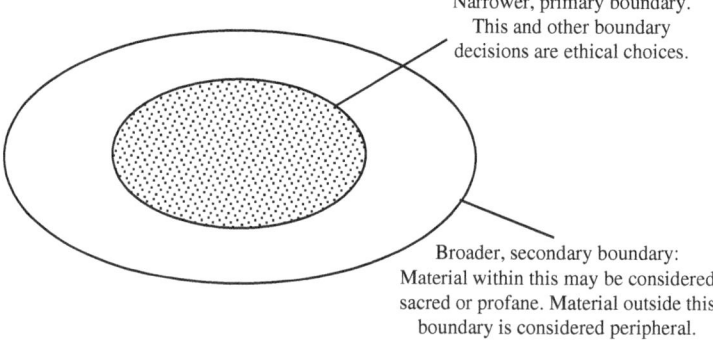

Fig. 2.1 Basic illustration of Midgley's theory of boundary critique. Adapted from Midgley (2005)

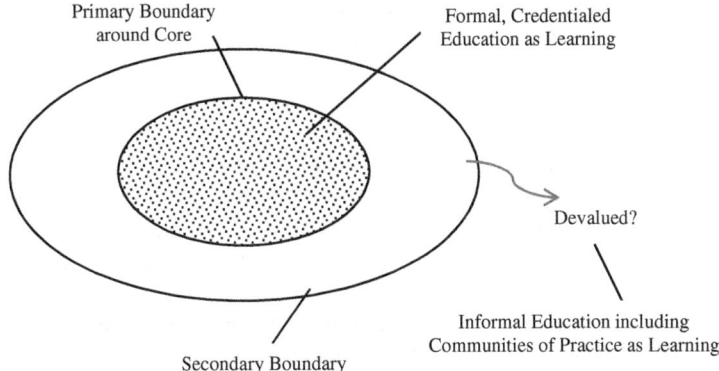

Primary Boundary
around Core

Formal, Credentialed
Education as Learning

Devalued?

Informal Education including
Communities of Practice as Learning

Secondary Boundary

Fig. 2.2 Theory of boundary critique to illustrate the primacy of the formal education construct in higher education, with communities of practice in the margin. Adapted from Midgley's (2005)

margins. The success stories in this book illustrate situations where CoP work has been valued and boundaries become more permeable.

Although I suggest ideas for future research, this is a conceptual chapter, which draws primarily on my professional experiences with communities of practice, work with several universities and the intersection of the two. My observations may resonate with some, and not apply in other contexts. I am a lifelong learner in the formal and informal sense. I enrolled in my doctoral program in my 50s (which was typical for the Human and Organizational Development PhD at Fielding Graduate University). By then, I knew my interests as a mature researcher and practitioner. I have taught or worked on thesis and dissertation committees with six universities. In 2002, I was fortunate to be able to design and teach the first full credit course about communities of practice (CoP), collaborating with Etienne Wenger, John D. Smith and others for a Master of Arts degree in Knowledge Management (see MacGillivray 2007, 2014a for more detail). I have been a member of many communities of practice and have studied others. To me, the intersection of higher education and communities of practice could be extremely fertile ground, but remains an under-populated landscape.

This chapter explores factors that may inhibit the growth and health of communities of practice in higher education, with a primary focus on faculty work. These culturally embedded factors relate to priorities, four types of boundaries, the nature of learning, the downside of expert cultures and the overwhelm factor. The chapter ends with an exploration of indicators of the desire to connect, implications of communities thriving—or not—in higher education, and ideas for future research.

To briefly clarify terms in this chapter, I use *community of practice* as described by Wenger et al. (2002): groups of people who self-select and regularly connect to create and share knowledge. In other words, getting together at an annual conference is not regular connection, and co-authoring a paper is more of a project than ongoing social learning and CoP membership.

The concept of CoP emerged through Xerox PARC's Institute for Research on Learning. It was embedded in an integrative social learning theory developed by Lave and Wenger and subsequently articulated by Wenger (1999, pp. 13–15) in Communities of Practice: Learning Meaning and Identity. Hoadley and Kilner (2005) have extended this thinking based on their work with CoP, outlying four key practices all related to the community's purpose: connection, conversation, exploration of context, and documentation of content. I have seen online spaces where documents are posted for faculty called communities of practice, but if they lack connections and ongoing contextual conversations for learning, they are merely repositories.

CoP members are more strongly interconnected than in communities of interest (where people participate in order to be informed) and are held together by a passion for their shared domain. In higher education, domains vary extensively. They could include an area of applied research (e.g. industrial symbiosis) a focus within a discipline (such as Jungian psychotherapy) skills (e.g. working effectively with International students or getting grants for community development work) or a career struggle (how to make time for research in a teaching university).

In communities of practice, it is difficult to know who is in and who is out, and they emerge and end organically, based on needs and energy. Scholar and humorist (Dr. Rumizen 2002) described the community of practice as a platypus, because it is such a strange beast in comparison with other workplace groups such as project teams or departments.

Because Wenger's theory of social learning and the CoP concept co-evolved, I sometimes use social learning almost interchangeably with community of practice. Although it is possible to have social learning in other contexts, social learning is a co-requisite for a community of practice. I use this term as Wenger (1999) does: a perspective that places learning "in the context of our lived experience of participation in the world...and a fundamentally social phenomenon" (p. 3). We are talking about learning that is deeply integrated with practice, community, meaning and identity. Without a *willingness* to engage in—and value—social learning, communities of practice cannot emerge and thrive.

2.2 Social Learning Inhibitors

2.2.1 Priorities

Tenure-track professors are under pressure to publish: particularly in peer-reviewed journals and perhaps only in the "A journals," and this can be all-consuming. At conferences, I have heard many mourn the work they had hoped to accomplish in fields important to them—such as environmental sustainability—where communities of practice could enable important social learning. But service and applied work were on the backburner, at least until their A-journal-reputations were established.

Many faculty also have significant administrative responsibilities, keeping them from the research they love.

Sessional instructors or adjunct faculty may have huge teaching loads or multiple jobs in order to survive. They may be expected to take on additional responsibilities (such as internal committee work) with no pay. This and a sense of disconnection from the large university community makes it difficult or impossible for the growing numbers of adjunct faculty to be leading or active in communities of practice (AcademicaGroup 2015, #3).

Communities of practice may fall into the "important but not urgent" category, even if they seem appealing.

2.2.2 Boundaries

Although cultural boundaries are gradually becoming more permeable in universities, they have strong roots. Boundaries can be vertical or horizontal; sometimes, they are fraught with ethical dilemmas. Some boundaries have created cultures referred to as: "Upstairs–Downstairs" (More Partnership and Richmond Associates 2014; PR Newswire 2014). The theory of boundary critique can again be used to illustrate four types of boundaries with potential to marginalize social learning and communities of practice.

2.2.2.1 Faculty/Student Boundaries

Faculty members—in the core—are expected to keep an aesthetic distance from students—in the margins—and maintain a higher status. For example, in one university, the term *learner* was used rather than *student*. This evolved because faculty members would comment that everyone in a course was a learner: the mid-career professional students collectively brought much more expertise into a class than a single faculty member could bring. For whatever reasons, the term *learner* is less common and is almost never used in public documentation now. At another university, a faculty member wanted a student—who did most of the research and analysis—to be the first author in a peer reviewed paper. A debate ensued because this did not fit with the long-term culture of faculty "deserving" first author status.

I have witnessed higher education environments where this boundary is permeable. I was fortunate to start undergraduate studies after a few years of work: at 20-something, I was technically a mature student. I had studied the natural history of the area and assumed that biology courses were essentially natural history courses. To my surprise, most professors knew little about natural history and I knew little about biology. I was regularly asked to contribute in the lecture hall and was invited into the faculty lounge. Not surprisingly, I eventually chose a doctoral program at Fielding Graduate University where the culture (influenced by Malcolm Knowles' work as a founding faculty member) was relatively egalitarian.

I remember the first faculty-student gathering I witnessed at Fielding. I was there in the role of a university administrator observing Fielding's model. It was at a summer session in Washington DC: much like a conference with optional attendance. Everyone present in the room was part of the first concentration offered in the doctoral program. The gathering was casual yet intense. People were sitting in a ragged, impromptu circle and leaning forward in their chairs. Much of the conversation that day revolved around how to research the phenomenon of multi-tasking with computers. Because of previous contact with the university, I happened to know which people in the room were faculty members. Otherwise, I would not have had a clue based on that gathering: faculty members and students were indistinguishable by age or by demeanor. It was during that session that I decided to sign up for the PhD that had not been in my life plan.

These atypical stories demonstrate the possibility of permeable boundaries between faculty and students in higher education. They also illustrate social learning—which binds faculty and students together through a common domain and sometimes a common practice. In the Fielding case, community of practice elements continued over time. For example, that particular conversation about multitasking led to research, publications and conference presentations by faculty and students, which were never pre-planned as anything resembling course assignments.

2.2.2.2 Faculty-Staff Boundaries

It is difficult to bridge the academic and administrative sides of universities, even though staff members have expertise that could help some faculty (group process skills as one example) and faculty have expertise that could help administration (leadership scholars might help with leadership challenges, for example). From a cultural perspective, faculty can be seen as in the core, and staff in the margins.

This artificial divide comes, in part, from our thinking of organizations in mechanical terms. We have *divisions* for example, and use terms such as *nuts and bolts* and *leveraging*. Accountability frameworks fragment groups. Collaborations across boundaries can be seen as optional and detracting from the core business of each fragment. Such fragmentation and specialization emulates efficient practices from the Industrial Era. Communities of practice across faculty-staff boundaries could be powerful. Consider an example from natural science. Where communities meet, there are often productive transition zones known as ecotones (Odum 1971). Their whole can be greater than the sum of their parts: one plus one plus one can equal more than three. Healthy estuaries are a magnificent example. Land, fresh water and salt water mix to create the most productive environments on the planet (NOAA). However, it is not easy to create these rich, estuary-like connections across the administration-academic divide.

One successful example of faculty/staff boundary blurring is the delivery of Instructional Skills Workshops (ISW). These workshops emerged in the late 1970s in British Columbia Canada to help faculty subject matter experts become more effective instructors (Day 2005). These workshops have spread across Canada and to more than 10 countries. Facilitators are often university staff members, but in some universities, faculty members have been very active. When I lead ISW workshops for faculty and for new ISW facilitators, it is common for staff and faculty to work closely together. Facilitators form communities of interest (with CoP elements) spanning multiple institutions. However, based on how ISW members identify themselves (ISW 2015) the online conversations are almost all amongst staff.

I asked Sylvia Currie, long time steward of the SCoPE community about the ratio of staff and faculty in her conversations. Despite being a very attentive facilitator, she had no idea (Pers. comm. 2015). This suggests a healthy blurring of lines, probably encouraged by the inclusive welcome, which introduces the platform:

> SCoPE brings together individuals who share an interest in educational research and practice, and offers opportunities for dialogue across disciplines, geographical borders, professions, levels of expertise, and education sectors. Our activities are facilitated by volunteers in the community, and membership is free and open to everyone (SCoPE 2014).

2.2.2.3   Faculty/University-Alumni Boundaries

In a typical, large, undergraduate lecture hall, the divide between faculty and students (before and after graduation) is typically huge. But what happens in graduate programs focused on lifelong learning for adults? Where terms such as andragogy and learning community are often used and where terms such as professor rarely are? Where the universities have egalitarian and inclusive cultures? Where students are accomplished professionals—often in their 40s–60s—and may be working on a second MA or PhD. What might social learning relationships look like amongst those alumni and faculty?

In this section, I share personal communication from two people who have worked—with uneven success—to enhance social learning in such contexts between alumni and universities. One is Victor Chears; whom I will cite as "1." He has been an active alumni member with various leadership roles in two universities. The other is Paul Corns; I will cite him as "2." One of his roles was as an Associate Vice-President of Community Relations and Advancement in a university. In both cases I have permission to share personal communication (2015). Both Chears and Corns spoke about how collaborative learning relationships are often severed once people graduate:

> Alumni are often the outliers in the discussion of constituencies within higher education. Once they reach the status of no longer being students there can be a disconnect with regard to their ongoing role as a member of the academic community. This is especially true for graduates who choose not to formally join the Academy. Presumably, if one has gone through the rigor of classes, researching, reading, completing coursework, being critiqued, rising to new levels of critical thinking, drafting and defending a serious academic treatise (aka dissertation), and a myriad other occasions of discourse, one would have earned a

recognizable and laudable place in the realm of consideration as a critical component of the organization's culture. This is not necessarily so. Rather the graduate, now alumnus, while having achieved the goal that they entered the institution to obtain, is relegated to a functional role that often severs the intellectual alliance to which they had become accustomed (1).

Several systems issues contribute to this disconnect: standard university software platforms are not designed for inclusion of alumni; expenses associated with library access are not in the budget, and so on. There are structural considerations as well. Most universities shift the relationship with those who have graduated to the administrative side of the house, where emphasis may be on financial contributions, so "little attention is paid to whether the former student now alumnus has other ideas and desires for ongoing connection and contribution" (1). Those ideas and desires may relate to the recent academic accomplishments and identities of the alumnae. They may crave scholarly conversations and collaborative research and publishing opportunities, for example. Promoting the university may be woven into those activities, but promotion and fundraising will rarely be primary motivators for alumni. Some administrative leaders have taken other approaches:

> Typically universities ask the question "How best to reconnect with alumni?" Our plan flipped that question, asking "How best to not disconnect from our learners?" The [inclusive and blended] learning model already created this seamless flow between face-to-face and online experience, generating a kind of technical fluency and positive dependency for the learning community. The university could not make this transition. Some of the reasons, both operational and cultural, are referenced in this chapter particularly with regard to faculty-staff boundaries and the time limited contracts imposed on professors…The establishment of strong communities of practice requires a commitment to releasing control and the adoption of a less formulaic approach to relationship and information management (2).

Over the years, I have heard promoters of social learning in higher education use terms such as "strategic partners," and "practitioners of progressive change." Is loss of control a key inhibitor? Rumizen's metaphor of the community of practice as a platypus is mentioned elsewhere: an oddity requiring a very different kind of management. Wenger et al. (2002) write:

> The spread of communities of practice throughout an organization is usually not a conventional pilot-rollout process by which a successful template is applied programmatically. Rather, it is an organic diffusion that expands as people get the idea, see its potential, and develop new aspirations. The process gains momentum through various combinations of top-down directives and encouragement and bottom-up initiative and responsiveness (p. 201).

This separation and disconnection can be magnified for alumni who choose not to enter the formal academy. At this time in our history, "the scholar/practitioner is not held in the same level of regard as the scholar/educator similar to how lawyers not admitted to a bar are viewed against those who are" (1).

How might university-alumni boundaries be blurred, at least for graduate programs where mid-career alumni bring advanced academic credentials and considerable applied academic experience?

2 Social Learning in Higher Education: A Clash of Cultures?

1. Recognition of the issues. Along the path to becoming an alumnus there must be a means for level setting expectations about what lies ahead in the ongoing relationship with the institution (1).
2. Willingness to consider all forms of diversity. What are the benefits for all parties as the roles shift? The scholar/practitioner brings a diversity of thought, undergirded by the academic experience, which the scholar/educator may not have, but is useful to the overall fabric building of the institution (1).
3. Openness to non-traditional Communities of Practice (CoP). Alumni bring unique and worthy perspectives that are more outward-focused yet critical to how higher education is perceived and framed (1).
4. Recognition of the strengths of hierarchies as different than the strengths of more organic communities of practice, where there are new opportunities to connect teaching, research and service to the increasingly complex problems so evident in our world (2).

2.2.2.4   Faculty Rank Boundaries

Other boundaries in most universities separate faculty by rank. There are many layers in a typical university and terms vary from nation to nation. I will limit reference here to tenured faculty, tenure track faculty and contracted faculty.

Tenure gives a large degree of freedom and job security. It often comes with the privilege of doing more research and less teaching. Tenured professors have published in the A journals: the most prestigious journals in their field. Tenure track faculty members must prove their expertise over long periods of time before they might gain tenure status.

Contracted faculty members are typically part-time instructors. *Adjunct faculty* and *sessional instructor* are among terms used for these positions. Although these individuals may have PhDs and experience applying knowledge from their discipline to the "real world," they often have low status and pay. Contracted instructors are increasingly common and can carry two thirds of a university's teaching load (CBCRadio 2015; The Adjunct Project 2015) and the percentage may be higher in some institutions.

These differences in status can impact the potential for social learning across ranks. Again, we can use the theory of boundary critique to examine this relationship. Although there are exceptions—research is typically considered high-status work in the core and teaching is devalued in the margins. This dynamic has developed in part because research can be a major source of revenue and can boost a university's reputation.

Tenured faculty members generally have very strong records publishing in journals with high impact factors and may teach very few courses. Tenure track faculty members strive for this depth of publishing experience. Contracted faculty may or may not make the effort to publish in peer-reviewed journals. Some tenured professors treat more junior faculty and staff as assistants. They may not even consider working with contracted faculty. As a matter of fact, they may have no exposure to contracted faculty, even in their field. If full time professors wanted to collaborate, the funding system might not allow contracted faculty to be paid. When contracted faculty members publish independently in journals, it is often without any financial support (time, research grants, travel expenses and so on) from their institutions.

Although some contracted faculty members are well paid, respected and given significant responsibilities, others feel stressed by workload and low pay. Data from the Adjunct Project (2015) show that fees for a three-credit course can be as low as $450 USD. Even with higher fees, income may be equivalent minimum wage, depending on the university's learning and teaching models. Contracted faculty members are typically responsible for their own expenses (information technology, Internet access, office equipment and so on). In the Adjunct Project, one PhD describes her work with universities as a community service; she needs to rely on other sources of income, adding: "If for any reason I miss a class meeting—whether it's sickness, delivering a baby, a dead battery, or a volcanic eruption—my pay is docked for that day" (The Adjunct Project 2014 post). Contracted faculty may be hesitant to add social learning activities and voluntary membership in communities of practice to their schedules.

Ironically, such pressures have pushed adjuncts towards what might be called short-term communities of practice. For several months, #adjunctchat on twitter brought contracted faculty together to brainstorm topics such as "Innovative ways to include the collective adjunct voice in the national higher education conversation" (AdjunctChat 2014, #4). Recently in Canada, instructors connected across the country (University of Toronto, the University of Northern BC and York University) to go on strike (Pathe 2015). And National Adjunct walk out day (NAWD 2015) was promoted through Facebook. Given the increasing reliance on contracted instructors, these indicators may signal significant challenges in the future.

Why do boundaries of rank and status matter? As one example, consider research as an important university function: a source of presumably accurate, insightful and unbiased knowledge about things that matter in the world. What if that knowledge were systemically diversified, deepened and enriched by more collaboration across boundaries of rank and status? When I worked as a program director in higher education I found it interesting to reflect on these concepts. Some of the contracted faculty I hired charged more for a day's consulting in the business world than some full time faculty made in a month. But status shifts with context. I was not successful in developing opportunities for contracted faculty to bring their deep, real-world experience to collaborations with core faculty with deep scholarly expertise.

In another setting, a colleague started a grant program at a major funding institution. He proposed a structure in which proponents must outline plans for collaborations between communities and universities. Initially, academics were not supportive because the science would be tainted or diluted by non-experts. So my colleague and others proposed a formal experiment in which the proposal would be tested and evaluated. Everyone, including deep experts, was surprised and impressed by the quality of the results. The program ran for several years, and the research groups did have community of practice elements as they worked through challenges, and learned from each other's contexts.

2.2.2.5 Disciplinary Boundaries

These are prominent in most institutions of higher education. A tenured professor who works within a discipline (microbiology, clinical psychology, art history, and so on) may be one of few in his or her institution. It is unlikely that they will be encouraged to collaborate with peers in other schools or programs within the university. That is an understandable stance for researchers working at the leading edges of their disciplines, yet their deep expertise is probably relevant in other fields. Faculty work is sometimes described as lonely. Experts undoubtedly relate to others in their field, but those experts may be in other parts of the world.

Some faculty members take initiative. Decades ago, I attended a fascinating panel session on climate change organized by Dr. Eric Higgs at the University of Victoria. The surprising thing was that all panelists came from different humanities disciplines rather than from the sciences.

When I present at conferences (with a range of disciplines) I ask participants about how they connect and learn from each other. Not surprisingly, they all say conferences. And they almost always mention the conversations between sessions as where the real learning takes place. Conferences can become micro, time-bound communities of practice, largely through social learning in the corridors. But they lack the element of regular connection mentioned earlier. When I ask people if they are involved with online forums or communities to connect and learn between conferences, the answer is almost always no (information technology and e-learning conferences being notable exceptions). At these conferences, a few of us with positive online community experiences find each other between sessions, and talk about unrealized potential. But it rarely goes farther.

Universities are being pressured to provide relevant education. Sometimes this means involving the public in dialogue or decisions. Peter Levesque describes a transition he has watched: Scientists have acknowledged they are in a special, privileged group where they sometimes make or influence important decisions. He has heard scientists hesitate to work with lay people who "don't know what we are doing." But then he goes on to muse: "What if we could teach them? What if we let people teach people? That's what the Danish have done. They said, Yes: we need a level of democratic involvement in science policy. So we're going to hold consensus conferences" (MacGillivray 2009, p. 135).

We are seeing many examples of citizen science projects, which are essentially disciplinary boundary-blurring activities. These projects can be catalysts for communities of practice where citizens and scientists from universities learn together. One Canadian example is the volunteer program helping to conserve the Greater Kejimkujik Ecosystem in Nova Scotia. Over 10,000 volunteer hours per year have been logged. Scientists orient and train citizens to actively participate in scientific research and conservation efforts. Citizens bring expertise from their disciplines. Citizens and scientists get to know each other. Many come to Kejimkujik National Park year after year to reconnect with fellow citizen scientists, share ideas, make a difference to species such as the endangered Blanding's turtles. People are pulled together by a passion for specific conservation efforts, they develop a community in which they improve their practice, and the scientific body of knowledge grows through social learning as well as the scientific method.

2.2.3 Nature of Learning

The concept of discipline is important in higher education and professors tend to work within the communities and cultural norms of their discipline. These norms include specific ideas about what constitutes high quality research and learning. Once in a while, scholars break through disciplinary barriers. For example, complexity theory draws from ecology, chemistry and other disciplines, and communities of practice have grown up around such trans-disciplinary concepts. Similarly, there are tools and practices that span boundaries (social and organizational network analysis, for example). Scholars passionate about these topics may regularly connect with each other to share ideas and publish, even—or perhaps especially—if their backgrounds are diverse.

As one example, Cross et al. have published as a trio (e.g. 2001) and in other configurations. Cross holds degrees from the University of Virginia and Boston University School of Management in business administration, organizational behavior and information technology. Parker has degrees from Northeastern University, the London School of Economics and from Stanford in sociology. Borgatti's degrees are from Cornell in anthropology and University of California in mathematical social science. Collectively, this covers a lot of territory both geographically and conceptually, but they connected through different ways of approaching social networks. However, many faculty members do not realize they are working with similar interests and problems at different scales or in different contexts.

Disciplines have had embedded ontologies, epistemologies and cultures, which may be almost invisible to members. Anthropologist Matt Hamabata has come to believe that ethnography is the most empirical of the research methodologies because you are immersed in the actual experience of a culture (pers. comm.). Yet a biologist might say that such experience is not valid knowledge because it cannot be tested and measured. In that biologist's eyes, ethnography is not empirical. Concepts such as social learning and constructivism do not drop equally well into different disciplines. Furthermore, some disciplines and fields—such as high-energy physics—are intrinsically more collaborative than others—such as microbiology (Knorr-Cetina 1999).

2.2.4   The Downside of Expert Culture

Academics spend their careers developing deep expertise. Confidence around expertise may be central to their identities. In some cases, this could inhibit their willingness to open up to new forms of learning or admit how little they know about some things that might be valuable. In today's academic world, there may be a digital divide: not in terms of bandwidth but in terms of comfort. For example, a senior professor may have published books and dozens of peer-reviewed papers, but may be misinformed about the value and potential of social media, CoP platforms, the potential for meaningful relationships through online interactions, and online leadership. If scholars in a field are spread around the globe, there will be gaps in conversations and collaborations without the use of technologies. The individuals may not even be aware of potentially valuable colleagues until they discover and search on platforms such as academia.edu.

It is rare to see someone shift from no knowledge or interest to intense interest in information technologies, but I have witnessed this transformation a few times. One memorable event many years ago was from the K-12 education field. There had been a large bulk purchase of computers for classrooms with little uptake in use. People noticed and female teachers were less likely than males to experiment with the computers. I was working for an education ministry in Canada at the time, and co-facilitated a process to design workshops for female classroom teachers. We had a diverse design team of women from many backgrounds, with varying degrees of computer expertise. Some without this expertise joined hesitantly, nor sure whether they were interested or what they might contribute. At one point, my colleague Susan opened a website from a well-known university listing *Great Canadian Scientists*. A woman with a trades and technology background asked: "Why don't they have any women?" Susan replied: "Why don't you ask?" The woman's body literally slumped as she said—more quietly—"yes, I should get around to sending them a note." Susan countered: "No—you can do it right here. Let me show you." Instantly re-energized, she crafted a query to the university. At our next planning meeting, we opened the reply, which essentially said: 'because there aren't any.' At that meeting we happened to have a guest who had recently researched 100 female Canadian scientists and we fed highlights of her research into our reply to the university. By the time we had our next meeting, there were women included on the website. This simple experience infused the group with even more energy for the workshop design. Yes, this was a project, but it would not surprise me at all if some of the contacts made through that project led to expanded networks, social learning and perhaps communities of practice related to women in science, technology, engineering and mathematics.

2.2.5   The Overwhelming Nature of Diversity

Faculty members are busy people, balancing tasks such as applying for grants, research, course design, teaching, thesis supervision, committee work, administrative duties, crafting of recommendations for alumni in the workforce, and community service. Compounding this, we live in an era of increased boundary blurring. Some universities are adopting business models similar to those in the private sector. Some are offering more applied courses. Disciplines themselves are losing their hard edges. Innovators experiment with new topics such as organizational ethnography and scholars adopt methodologies from other fields. For example, historians may be using anthropological methods and "a psychologist may be studying emotions in on-line environments using e-mail as data" with such shifts echoing larger questions about the nature of knowledge and Harding's *epistemological crisis of the West* (Bentz and Jeremy 1998, p. 2). Closed and elite are becoming open and egalitarian. This boundary blurring can be unsettling to some.

Social learning through communities of practice can initially amplify this diversity of perspectives. For some, exposure to diversity (different epistemologies, for example) could add to the overwhelm factor. Without a foundation of positive community of practice experiences, the concept may have little appeal.

2.3   Indicators, Implications and Future Research

2.3.1   Indicators

Are there indicators that faculty want to connect more or in new ways? Other chapters in this book provide examples. And social media platforms give us others.

Consider the microblogging tool *twitter* as just one option for sharing online. There are many higher education-related hashtags (i.e. keywords) in use for filtering. These include #HigherEd, #elearn, #edtech, #PhDchat, #research and #MOOC. Hoadley and Kilner (2005) suggest that connecting is a key initial step in the development of communities of practice. Hashtags enable people with similar interests to find each other amidst all the noise in social media platforms. The hashtag #ScholarSunday is intended precisely for that purpose: to introduce your twitter followers to scholars you recommend following.

People also host chats on twitter. These are regularly scheduled online conversations with a name that reflections the general domain (e.g. #HigherEdchat #AdmissionsLive) and with predetermined topics for each chat. However, many of these chats are staff-centered rather than faculty-centered.

Two recent stories illustrate the social—rather than the technical—side of scholars wanting to connect more. The first was a sad story for many of us who followed scientist @BoraZ on twitter and frequently shared his posts. Here is context from James (2013), Staff Scientist at Mount Desert Island Biological Laboratory:

> Over the course of a few days in mid-October, it emerged that Bora Zivkovic (@BoraZ on Twitter), a trusted and beloved leader of the ScienceOnline community and the blog editor at Scientific American, had sexually harassed at least three women. The science blogosphere and Twitterverse erupted. Expressions of shock, anger, and sadness flowed forth onto the Internet at a rate that left even the most seasoned Twitterers—myself included—feeling overwhelmed.

James created a #ripplesofdoubt hashtag, and thousands of tweets flowed in from people concerned about sexual harassment and its implications. Many interchanges were community of practice-like, sharing resources, experiences and tips. The domain was not a discipline, but it was one that resonated for many people building careers in the sciences and as scholars.

At the time of this publication, there is another interesting hashtag phenomenon that suggests scholars would like to be better connected. Glen Wright conducts research at the Institute for Sustainable Development and International Relations. A year ago he had not used twitter much. Despite that, he bet a friend that: "he could get 10,000 people to follow a twitter account dedicated to the amusing side of academe" (Kolowich 2015). His friend claimed no one would ever read his posts, but he launched the idea and now has over 16,000 followers. They play with hashtags such as #BadAdviceForYoungAcademics, suggesting tongue-in-cheek that young academics write their theses in comic sans, take lots of adjunct jobs, and tie all research to cancer because that's where the money is. This may seem like nothing but cathartic silliness, but some of Wright's strange hashtags quickly became powerful attractors. They show a desire to connect and interact, even if it is not [yet] focused on expected community of practice domains.

2.3.2 Implications

If the higher education landscape is under-populated with communities of practice, there are significant implications. There are many reasons why more high quality, nurtured communities of practice could be valuable for faculty, staff, students and society as a whole. They include the potential to:

1. Catalyze innovation and progress within disciplines across geographic and cultural boundaries;
2. Engage and empower students as quickly as possible by spanning faculty-student boundaries, so they can work to address the important challenges facing the world today;
3. Enrich learning by sweeping in new perspectives as encouraged by systems scholar C. West Churchman (Midgley 2000). There may be rich intersections across the faculty/staff boundary, such as better use of social media for conversations about research and dissemination of findings;

4. Help promising new faculty feel part of a community with emergent mentorship rather than climbing a ladder towards recognition;
5. Better connect scholar-practitioners (often adjuncts) with career academics to enrich research and move it into more applied settings;
6. Make space for faculty to enjoy time together outside of the pressures of work in institutions. Members tell us that experiences in communities of practice can be "energizing, healing, or comforting environments in which they could feel appreciated, at home and where they could speak their own specialist language" (MacGillivray 2009, p. 146).
7. Address complex problems in higher education. Some community members in other fields see CoP work as "ways of solving problems considered intractable in vertical structures, or as ways of being more effective with service to customers, clients, and citizens" (MacGillivray 2009, p. 146).

2.3.3 Further Research

This book may—in itself—encourage scholars to think more about social learning and further research presented here. Areas for further research include:

1. [How] do disciplines influence the perceptions of value of communities of practice? Karen Knorr Cetina's work is a promising foundation. Are there certain disciplines in higher education—such as her example of microbiology— where collaboration is relatively rare and social learning or constructivism might not be particularly valued?
2. Why might more social learning be attractive to faculty? Do faculty feel isolated from [potential] colleagues? Do they have learning needs unrelated to their disciplines? Are they interested in branching into more inter- or trans-disciplinary work?
3. If safe research spaces were set up for dialogue about interesting higher education topics—with names and roles (student, staff, adjunct, dean…) withheld— would participants accurately guess roles? Might they be surprised by the depth and value of contributions by people in "unlikely" roles?
4. What are the current social networks at play? These could be mapped over time with action research interventions.
5. Where are there innovations in higher education encouraging sustained action research and social learning across boundaries described in this chapter? What could we learn from these experiences?
6. Where are the innovations in higher education where students are supported in the formation of networks and communities integral to their research? What can we learn from them?
7. Who has tried hard to encourage communities of practice in higher education and has failed? What could we learn from these experiences?

2.4   A Cultural Shift?

When I saw the call for chapters and thought about what I might contribute to this book, an old publication kept coming to mind. Its title was Education for Judgment. It, too, was an edited book, with each chapter written by a faculty member. At the time Harvard Business School was strongly encouraging discussion (social learning of a sort) in its lecture halls. They were pioneering a shift from teacher-centered to active-learning approaches. In the book, the editors emphasize that in all levels of formal education, as much as 80 % of class periods are spent in teacher-centered mode with interactions limited largely to question and answers between individual students and instructors. "And why not?" they write. "If the goals are information transfer and the accumulation of knowledge, the process is practical, efficient, and well-understood" (Christensen et al. 1991, p. 3).

Education for Judgment drew me in for two reasons. It felt like a privilege to witness the struggles of faculty members as they made sense of this new, dynamic and inclusive habitat. I was also intrigued by how different their stories and their voices were. As I read it, I sensed that the authors had tapped deeply into their own values and dreams as well as into the more intellectual aspects of the shift.

This book came to mind because it, too, was exploring a paradox. Here were professors in a world renowned business school, who would not be there if they did not have subject matter expertise and some skills with lecturing. And yet hidden under the surface of that excellence, many were craving something different. Harvard administrators handed them the opportunity to explore new learning approaches and new ways of thinking about what they could bring to a classroom.

Is that so very different than the intersection of communities of practice and higher education? In my experience, most faculty members are working long hours, feel the pressure to do more, and wish they had more time to follow their passions. Communities of practice could become more common and accessible venues in which those passions could thrive and fuel academic reform.

References

AcademicaGroup. (2015). *Part-time faculty: What we know, and what we don't*. http://academica.ca/blog/part-time-faculty-what-we-know-and-what-we-dont. Accessed 2 June 2015.

AdjunctChat. (2014). Innovative ways to include the collective adjunct voice in the national higher education conversation. Accessed September 2014.

Bentz, V. M., & Jeremy, J. S. (1998). *Mindful inquiry in social research*. Thousand Oaks: SAGE Publications.

CBCRadio. (2015). *Contract university lecturers strike, demand quality education*. http://www.cbc.ca/radio/thecurrent/the-current-for-march-6-2015-1.2984153/contract-university-lecturers-strike-demand-quality-education-1.2984260. Accessed 7 March 2015.

Christensen, C. R., Garvin, D. A., & Sweet, A. (1991). *Education for judgment: The artistry of discussion leadership*. Boston: Harvard Business School Press.

Cross, J. (n.d.). *Informal learning blog: Where did the 80 % come from?* http://www.informl.com/where-did-the-80-come-from/. Accessed June 2013.

Cross, R., Parker, A., Prusak, L., & Borgatti, S. P. (2001). Knowing what we know: Supporting knowledge creation and sharing in social networks. *Organizational Dynamics, 30*(2), 100–120.

Day, R. (2005). The instructional skills workshop: The heart of an educator learning community in British Columbia and beyond. Paper presented at the ISSoTL Conference, Vancouver, B.C., http://iswnetwork.ca/wp-content/uploads/2012/07/Hand_ISW_ISSoTL1.pdf. Accessed June 2006.

Hoadley, C. M., & Kilner, P. G. (2005). Using technology to transform communities of practice into knowledge-building communities. *ACM SIGGROUP Bulletin, 25*(1), 31–40. doi:10.1145/1067699.1067705.

ISW. (2015). Instructional skills workshop network: ISW community. http://iswandfdw.ning.com/profiles/members/. Accessed February 2015.

James, K. (2013). What I learned from #ripplesofdoubt https://chroniclevitae.com/news/143-what-i-learned-from-ripplesofdoubt. Accessed 15 December 2013.

Knorr-Cetina, K. (1999). *Epistemic cultures: How the sciences make knowledge.* Cambridge: Harvard University Press.

Kolowich, S. (2015). Meet the 26-year-old behind academic twitter's most popular hashtags. The Chronicle of Higher Education. http://chronicle.com/blogs/wiredcampus/meet-the-26-year-old-behind-academic-twitters-most-popular-hashtags/55857. Accessed 25 February 2015.

Lave, J., & Wenger, E. (1991). *Situated learning: Legitimate peripheral participation.* Cambridge: Cambridge University Press.

MacGillivray, A. (2007). Learning at the edge-Part 2: Scholar-practitioner reflections on boundaries. *Emergence: Complexity and Organization, 9*(4), 44–55.

MacGillivray, A. (2009). Perceptions and uses of boundaries by respected leaders: A trans-disciplinary inquiry. Retrieved from ProQuest Dissertations & Theses Global (UMI 3399314).

MacGillivray, A. (2014a). *Intellectual estuaries in higher education I.* https://www.youtube.com/watch?v=xzUaRJ73crA. Accessed March 2015.

Midgley, G. (2000). *Systemic intervention: Philosophy, methodology, and practice.* New York: Kluwer Academic.

Midgley, G. (2005). An introduction to systems thinking for tackling the 'Wicked Problem' of antimicrobial resistance. Presented at International Workshop on Complexity and Policy Analysis, June 22–24, Cork, Ireland.

More Partnership and Richmond Associates. (2014). An emerging profession: The higher education philanthropy workforce. A report to the Higher Education Funding Council for England. Dundee: More Partnership. http://www.givingnorthernireland.org/sites/default/files/research/An%20emerging%20profession-The%20higher%20education%20philanthropy%20workforce.pdf

NAWD. (2015). National Adjunct Walkout-Day https://www.facebook.com/pages/National-Adjunct-Walkout-Day/340019999501000. Accessed 20 February 2015.

Odum, E. P. (1971). *Fundamentals of ecology.* Philadelphia: Saunders Philadelphia.

Pathe, S. (2015). How a hashtag turned into an international adjunct movement. http://www.pbs.org/newshour/making-sense/hashtag-turned-international-adjunct-movement/. Accessed 27 February 2015.

PR Newswire. (2014). Review of pay and finance will not end the "upstairs–downstairs" culture in higher education, Says Unite. http://www.prnewswire.co.uk/news-releases/review-of-pay-and-finance-will-not-end-the-upstairs-downstairs-culture-in-higher-education-says-unite-152955365.html. Accessed 5 January 2015.

Rumizen, M. C. (2002). *The complete idiot's guide to knowledge management.* Madison: CWL Publishing.

SCoPE. (2014). *An open, online community for people like you.* http://scope.bccampus.ca/. Accessed February 2014.

The Adjunct Project. (2014). http://adjunct.chronicle.com/on-working-for-free/. Accessed 9 March 2015.

The Adjunct Project. (2015). http://adjunct.chronicle.com/. Accessed 9 March 2015.

Wenger, E. (1998). Communities of practice: Learning, meaning, and identity. Cambridge: Cambridge University Press.

Wenger, E. (1999). *Communities of practice: Learning, meaning, and identity*. Cambridge: Cambridge University Press.

Wenger, E., McDermott, A., & Snyder, W. (2002). *Cultivating communities of practice: A guide to managing knowledge*. Boston, MA: Harvard Business Press.

Chapter 3
Faculty Learning Communities and Communities of Practice Dreamers, Schemers, and Seamers

Milton D. Cox and Jacquie McDonald

> *These FLC's have totally reinvigorated me after 21 years of teaching!!!! Member quote* (Beach et al. 2006, p. 87).
> *I love Communities of Practice—I know I'm not alone. Member quote* (McDonald et al. 2008).

Abstract The authors articulate the independent emergence of Faculty Learning Communities (FLCs) in the United States and Communities of Practice (CoPs) in an Australian higher education setting. Based on 35 years of experience beginning with Miami University FLCs (Cox) and 10 years of experience starting with University of Southern Queensland CoPs (McDonald), the authors report what they see as the defining features of FLCs and CoPs as separate and then as hybrid models within their institutional, national and international contexts. Similarities and differences are outlined, with a discussion around why each approach evolved within the particular local and then national context. The chapter concludes with ideas about collaborative activities and practical adaptions of each approach to suit different higher education contexts and needs.

Keywords Faculty learning communities · Communities of practice · Higher education · Landscapes of practice · Professional learning

3.1 Introduction

The authors of this chapter are intrigued by the similarities and differences they observe between two models of situated learning in higher education, namely faculty learning communities (FLCs) in the U.S. and communities of practice

M.D. Cox (✉)
Center for Teaching Excellence, Miami University, Oxford, OH, USA
e-mail: coxmd@miamioh.edu

J. McDonald
University of Southern Queensland, Toowoomba, QLD, Australia
e-mail: mcdonalj@usq.edu.au

© Springer Nature Singapore Pte Ltd. 2017
J. McDonald and A. Cater-Steel (eds.), *Communities of Practice*,
DOI 10.1007/978-981-10-2879-3_3

(CoPs) in Australia. When the authors began collaborating in 2009, there was no evidence of awareness, interaction, or cross-fertilization of ideas or practice between the two models. The focus of this chapter is to draw on the experiences of the authors' involvement in the visioning (dreaming), implementing (scheming), and integrating (seaming) of FLCs and CoPs within both their higher education contexts. This new weave has produced a fabric that has promising versatility and strength in enhancing community, interdisciplinarity, organizational development, and the scholarship of teaching and learning (SoTL). Now colleagues and institutions across the academy will have the opportunity to tailor academic fashions that incorporate diverse patterns and designs to find, achieve, and celebrate new styles in higher education. And the authors claim that these will be more than just fashionable—they will be sustainable.

Based on 35 years of experience beginning with Miami University (Miami) FLCs (Cox) and 10 years of experience starting with University of Southern Queensland (USQ) CoPs (McDonald), the authors articulate what they see as the defining features of FLCs and CoPs as separate and then as hybrid models within their institutional and national contexts. Similarities and differences are outlined, with a discussion around why each approach evolved within the particular local and then national context. The chapter concludes with ideas about collaborative activities and practical adaptions of each approach to suit different higher education contexts and needs.

3.2 Faculty Learning Communities

3.2.1 History of Faculty Learning Communities

From 1974–1988 universities in the U.S. focused their educational development and rewards on establishing early-career academics as producers of disciplinary discovery scholarship while providing little support for their pedagogical development. Recognizing this, the Lilly Endowment, a private foundation, invited selected research universities to apply for three-year grants that would support the design and implementation of pedagogical development programs for early-career academics (Austin 1992). In 1979, Miami University received such a grant and built a program using a small-group learning community approach to engage junior colleagues in a yearlong effort to enhance teaching and learning.

Also, this program at Miami was designed to address some long-term problems in U.S. higher education. Dewey (1933) pointed out the lack of active, student-centred learning, and Meiklejohn (1932), concerned about increasing disciplinary specialization, called for a coherence and unity of curricula across disciplines. These two educators independently proposed a new approach to eliminate these impediments to student learning. This approach involved small cohorts of 20 or so students all taking two or three topic-linked courses planned by instructors teaching those courses. The instructors pointed out the connections and contrasts between the different disciplinary approaches to the cohort in the linked courses. Programs adopting this new curriculum are now called student learning communities (SLCs), but this model was not successfully implemented until the 1980s (Gabelnick et al. 1990).

Research on student learning in SLCs in the 1980s and 1990s reported that there were higher rates of retention, cognitive intellectual development, and civic engagement for students in SLCs when compared with students not in SLCs (MacGregor et al. 2001). Research on early career academics in the Miami program over the same period revealed rates of higher tenure (retention) (Cox 1995), cognitive development (Cox 2003), and civic engagement (Cox 2003) when compared with early-career academics not in the program. With these similarities with SLCs in hand, the small groups of Miami's early-career academics program were then named faculty learning communities (FLCs). However, FLCs were developed independently of SLCs.

The evolution of FLCs has occurred in four phases: one-dimensional, cohort development for early-career academics, 1979–1988, at Miami (Cox 1994, 1995); local multidimensionality—the broadening of the model to other cohorts and to topic-based FLCs at Miami, 1989–1998 (Cox 2001); state and federal grant-supported extension of the model to the state of Ohio and U.S. with assessment of the model in multiple venues, 1999–2008 (Beach and Cox 2009; Cox 2006; Cox and Richlin 2004); and international extension of the model, 2009–present, for example (Wong et al. 2016).

In 2008–2009, peak FLC programming occurred at Miami University. Its teaching and learning centre managed 18 FLCs involving 17 % of the full-time faculty, and looking back, 52 % of the full-time faculty and 54 % of department chairs had participated in an FLC. Since 1990 there have been 169 FLCs at Miami University, with 46 of them cohort-based and 123 topic-based. This managed density offered Miami the opportunity of becoming a learning organization, one that connects its units and members to the mission, goals, and challenges of the institution, thus enabling it to meet the demands of change (Cox 2001; Haynes et al. 2010; Senge 1990).

3.2.2 Definition and Properties of FLCs

A Faculty Learning Community is defined as "a voluntary, structured, yearlong, multi-disciplinary community of practice of around 6–12 participants (8–10 is ideal) that includes building community and the development of scholarly teaching and the scholarship of teaching and learning" (Cox et al. 2014, pp. 1–5). Sixteen recommendations for designing, implementing, facilitating, assessing, and sustaining FLCs are listed in "Appendix 1". These recommendations for FLC infrastructure are based on 35 years of experience with and research about the effectiveness of FLCs.

There are two types of FLCs: cohort-based and topic-based. A topic-based FLC has a curriculum with a focus on a particular topic that addresses a campus teaching, learning, or institutional challenge or opportunity. Examples of such topics include using mobile technology in courses, developing e-portfolios, introducing team-based learning, enhancing the experience of first-year students, or remaking student-advising systems. Topic-based FLCs offer membership to and provide opportunities for learning and SoTL open to all academic ranks and cohorts. Cohort-based FLCs offer the FLC experience to a group of academics in the same category of career development or interest group, for example, early-career academics (the original FLC model now in its 37th year at Miami University) (Cox 2013), senior academics, lecturers and clinical academics, sessionals, department chairs, and STEM educators. These cohort-based FLC participants shape their curriculum to include a variety of teaching and learning topics of interest to them.

The literature is generous on the topic of facilitating FLCs, for example Ortquist-Ahrens and Torosyan (2009) and Petrone and Ortquist-Ahrens (2004). In a leadership role, the facilitator selects the FLC topic or cohort, determines its goals, plans its components, applies to have the FLC offered, and helps recruit members. Afterwards, in the yearlong FLC meeting phase, the facilitator sheds the leader role and as a member of the group functions in a non-linear way as coordinator and energizer, modelling the behaviour he or she wants FLC colleagues to assume. One concern has been that FLC facilitators might behave as directive leaders in working with their FLC members; hence, academic developers have downplayed the use of the term 'leadership' and 'leader' in favour of 'facilitator'.

However, there are different leadership roles in the broader institutional structure involving FLCs (Cox 2016). These leadership roles are (1) the investigator, who is interested in learning about FLCs and leads the efforts to attend FLC workshops and then brings related information to the institution; (2) the implementer, who leads efforts on campus to establish FLCs as effective and sustainable academic development approaches; (3) the FLC program director, who, once FLCs have been established at an institution, each year organizes, advises, assesses, champions, and supports the FLCs that are in place. Each of these three leadership positions can be held by one or more persons, and the same person may fill two or more of the three roles. Often the three leadership roles are per-formed by members of the institution's teaching and learning centre.

To conclude this overview of FLC infrastructure, observe that an FLC is not a committee, task force, course, book club, or action learning set. These structures may lack community or SoTL development. An FLC is a yearlong, structured, small group learning community with a process that enables its participants to investigate and provide solutions to about any problem or opportunity in higher education.

3.2.3 Assessment and FLCs

Assessment has played a key role in the development of the FLC movement. In 1979 when the first FLC was established at Miami, a well-planned assessment process was engaged, and the outcomes and evidence generated were influential in convincing the central administration and the university senate to continue and support FLC efforts. The three original FLC assessment questions are still used today, asking about member development, student learning as a result of the FLC, and effectiveness of the components used in the FLC operation. Over the years the questions have been expanded to include additional outcomes due to the increasing objectives of FLCs. Two of the original three questions and resulting outcomes are discussed in Sect. 3.5.1.3 and are located in Tables 3.3 and 3.4.

Here are additional FLC assessment outcomes: (1) FLCs provide an effective platform for working with academics to develop SoTL (Beach and Cox 2009; Cox 2003); (2) According to implementation science, FLCs provide the most effective educational development programming model for implementing evidence-based interventions (Fixsen et al. 2005; Cox 2014a, b); and (3) Academics in FLCs report that the top ten impacts on their students' learning as a result of their FLC participation are all high on the Bloom taxonomy (Beach and Cox 2009).

In conclusion, now that the development of FLCs has moved to the international phase, the major FLC assessment survey developed in the U.S. and reported in Beach and Cox (2009) should be adapted internationally for use by educational developers. This will enable comparison of outcomes from FLC initiated in different countries, with similar structures such as CoPs. For example, in Sect. 3.5.1 see a straightforward adaptation and comparison for FLC–structured CoPs in Hong Kong (Kwong et al. 2016). The adaptation and comparison for FLC–structured CoPs offers a potential area of research that covers important components of educational development.

3.3 Communities of Practice

3.3.1 Australian Context of University of Southern Queensland CoP Approach

How did a member move from—"When I was first invited as a fairly cynical, jaded and tired cores course leader, the idea of another two hour meeting was not one that I was enamoured with" (McDonald et al. 2008)—to bouncing into the CoP a year later saying "I love Communities of Practice—I know I'm not alone" (personal communication 2008). This section provides a brief overview of the journey from the first University of Southern Queensland (USQ) Community of Practice (CoP) pilot, started in 2006 for Faculty of Business First Year Core Course Leaders, to date. The pilot initiative was informed by the CoP doctoral research of

McDonald (2007); her Learning and Teaching designer role in a central support unit, and co-facilitator (McDonald and Star 2008) experience as core course leader in a Business Faculty. USQ is an Australian regional university with a strong focus on distance and online learning, a mix of local and international students in transition from secondary school, and mature age students. Academic staff operate in a challenging educational context, with many first in family students, teaching courses over three semesters to on-campus, distance or online students; shrinking administrative support and tension between teaching and research focus. Further discussion of the Australian Higher Education context follows in Sect. 3.3.3.

After collaborating on the redesign of a first-year undergraduate course, Star and McDonald (2007) agreed that a CoP would be an effective way to support and enhance professional learning and also share learning and teaching innovations with other members of the Faculty, particularly other first-year course leaders. As articulated in the CoP literature, specifically that which placed the learning component as central and situated in practice (Lave and Wenger 1991; Wenger 1998; Wenger et al. 2002), McDonald and Star believed the CoP would create a space where teachers could share positive experiences (domain knowledge and practice), successes and "war stories" about their practice, and build learning resources and professional expertise.

3.3.2 Theory of Communities of Practice

USQ CoPs are informed by social learning and CoP theory. Early work by Bandura (1977) saw the focus of learning moving from the individual to a cognitive process that takes place, or is situated, in a social context. Vygotsky (1978) made a major contribution to social learning theory, arguing that social relations and supporting learners to relate what they already know with what they could know, influencing educational approaches and the importance of learning in a social environment. Mercieca (2016) provides an extended discussion on the social–cultural underpinning of CoPs. Mercieca notes that (Vygotsky 1978) saw social relations as an important component of developing higher level thinking, and suggested that there should not be an artificial separation between intellectual and social activities. The combination of the essential CoP elements–building domain knowledge, growing community and sharing practice (Wenger 1998; Wenger-Trayner and Wenger-Trayner 2015)—weave together intellectual and social activities.

The term 'Communities of Practice' emerged from research into learning at the Xerox Palo Alto Research Centre in California in the 1980s (Tight 2015). The work of Lave and Wenger (1991) that investigated the apprenticeship model of learning showed that, rather than the novice apprentice learning from the master craftsman, learning took place through a complex set of social relationships. A whole social network, including other apprentices, supported the learning journey within the particular practice field, and eventually, recognition as a fully-fledged member of the Community, hence the term 'Community of Practice' that indicates a whole community supports the development of a new practitioner.

Wenger et al. (2002) describe communities of practice as:

> Groups of people who share a concern ... and who deepen their knowledge and expertise in this area by interacting on an ongoing basis ... [As they] accumulate knowledge; they become informally bound by the value that they find in learning together. Over time ... [t]hey become a community of practice (pp. 4–5).

Increasingly CoPs are seen as dynamic places where members engage in sharing knowledge and learning together, in business, community and education. The acceleration of the growth of information has created an environment where individuals, communities, and institutions seek to manage and harvest information to generate knowledge. The Community members have valuable local knowledge and strategies to share with their colleagues. Within the CoP literature, this is highlighted by the emphasis on the practice of the participants, the sharing of tacit knowledge, and the role of apprentices, who learn the craft of their masters through observation, imitation and practice (Wenger 1998). The explosion of knowledge and use of technology in higher education is equally reflected in its impact on business, government and all aspects of society. While increasing knowledge is valued, how to manage and share knowledge is a challenge to Higher Education institutions, educators and learners. As noted by Wenger et al. (2002) early attempts at knowledge management originated from information technology departments that tended to confuse knowledge and information. Huge resources have been devoted to building (often unused digital graveyards) information systems and databases. These can capture explicit information as knowledge 'objects', however, tacit knowledge is "an accumulation of experience" (p. 9) that continues to grow with everyday experience, and people are the living repositories of the knowledge. People are not often aware that they possess tacit knowledge, or of how it can be valuable to others. Wenger et al. (2002) argued that tacit aspects of knowledge are often the most valuable, and sharing requires extensive personal contact and trust, and the interaction and informal learning as experienced in CoPs. This reflects Vygotsky's (1978) research on the importance of social relations.

As CoPs are more widely implemented, shared experiences, publication of evidence-based practice and research means CoP theory and practice is continuing to evolve. It has moved from describing organic communities, emerging in a single practice field (Wenger 1998); to approaches on how to create intentional and strategic communities; to viewing an individual's membership in, not only a single practice field community, but as membership across a number of different communities of practice. This research is led by Etienne and Bev Wenger-Trayner, who have moved their social learning and Community of Practice research and theory from CoPs in a specific practice field to social learning and knowledgeability across a whole landscape of practice (Wenger-Trayner et al. 2015).

3.3.3 Higher Education Context

Faculty teaching is a demanding role and tends to be isolated and private, with Faculty working as 'lone rangers,' despite working with the same students in the same programs. Reflecting on this isolated practice, Palmer (2002, p. 179) noted that "academic culture is infamous for fragmentation, isolation, and competitive individualism". Changihg educational and government expectations, and student demographics are also increasing pressure on staff as they are required to increase research output, teach diverse student cohorts, with reduced administrative support, and increasing accountability and productivity requirements. There are also changes to the traditional autonomy of academic staff and the identity of higher education away from what is retrospectively viewed as a 'collegial' past, towards a more managerial and commercial entity (Probert 2014). This has changed academic 'ways of working', viewing students as customers, cost effective, efficiency and output measurements, with top down compliance audits. The result is an intensification of academic work, a decline in collegiality and feelings of alienation and stress. Chalmers (2011) noted the dominance of the research agenda in Australia, which has privileged research over learning and teaching activities, creating a climate where learning and teaching academics feel their role is undervalued and teaching focus not a positive career path. The corporatization of the Australian higher education sector, internationalisation and globalisation of higher education, and information and communication technology developments (Kemp and Norton 2014; Universities Australia 2013) is discussed further in Reaburn and McDonald (2016).

McDonald and Star (2008) believed that a CoP could address staff, student and institutional needs, with the three elements providing the context for isolated first year course leaders to collaborate to share and grow their learning and teaching practice. This credibility of this belief and the impact of USQ CoPs was recognised by the Australian University Quality Agent (AUQA) who awarded USQ with a highly prized commendation in 2009 and invitation to contribute to the AUQA Good Practice Database, stating that "AUQA commends USQ for the creative space it provides for academic staff through the Communities of Practice to share good practices and continue professional conversations across faculties".

3.3.4 The USQ Community of Practice Approach

The USQ Community of Practice approach was designed to suit the educational context and acknowledgement that first-year teachers are time-poor. To retain the integrity of Wenger's (1998) three fundamental CoP elements; community, domain of knowledge and shared practice; while ensuring members had value for time and not attending 'just another meeting', these three elements were used by McDonald and Star (2008, 2014) as an organising agenda framework for CoP gatherings. An example of the agenda structure is outlined below. The order of agenda items is flexible, depending on the planned activities.

Example of University of Southern Queensland Community of Practice Agenda
Welcome and Community time
Introductory activities: (Title) (5–15 min)
Building our domain knowledge: (Title and presenter) (30–40 min)
Food and fellowship (30 min)
Sharing our practice: (Title and presenter) (30–40 min)
Next meeting: _____ (Date and time) _____ (Venue)

Resources:
McDonald, J. (n.d.). Facilitator Resources: ALTC Teaching Fellowship Community of Practice Facilitator Resources. http://www.usq.edu.au/cops/resources/altcfellowship/facilitator-resources.

This structure has provided a consistent framework for monthly meetings and for addressing member priorities and sharing practice. This structure has proved robust in a range of different CoPs and university contexts. Most CoP meetings are 1–2 h, usually monthly, as decided by the members. As noted in Reaburn and McDonald (2016), this CoP structure is effective in building a domain of knowledge, through invited speakers, members sharing practice by open and frank discussions, and developing the sense of community of people by having time at the start and/or end of the meeting to interact informally to foster the social fabric of learning.

USQ CoPs have positively impacted on students, staff and the institution. The CoPs facilitate academic professional conversations on learning and teaching, with positive impacts on the student experience by inspiring members about teaching; promoting reflection on teaching practice and, encouraging innovation. They provide collegial support for new teachers. The cohort CoPs also facilitate a consistent approach to teaching issues across programs. For example a coordinated assessment timetable for first year Faculty of Business courses was implemented following CoP assessment discussions. Sharing of practice means proven and effective teaching practices are made explicit. For example an online toolkit for first year teachers was generated from the yearlong CoP sessions. It incorporated practical responses to common issues facing course leader, disseminating practical solutions to common teaching issues and, spreading awareness of good practice.

Data collected in the Faculty of Business CoP indicates positive impact on the first year student experience:

- Average fail rates in first year courses declined between 2004 and 2007 from 19.5 to 9.5 % of students.
- An increase in student performance—the average number of grades awarded above a B increased from 12.8 % in 2004 to 14.6 % of students in 2007.

- Retention in the courses of CoP members improved between 2005 and 2007. For on-campus students it increased from 88.4 to 95.4 % and for external students from 62.5 to 90.25 %.
- Faculty retention of students in first year increased between 2004 and 2008 from 68.3 to 81.8 % of students.

While other initiatives have influenced these results, the work of the Faculty of Business CoP in all areas of the student experience, including policy change, helped achieve these significant improvements.

3.3.5   Leadership Roles and Facilitation of Higher Education CoPs

As CoPs evolved at USQ the significance and impact of the facilitation or leadership role became apparent. An analysis of the academic literature identified confusion around the understanding of CoPs, a dearth of literature specifically on higher education CoPs, and a gap regarding the leadership role within CoPs (McDonald et al. 2012a, 2012c; McDonald 2014).

Experience showed that the facilitation/leadership role within CoPs can be challenging as the CoP may have an uneasy fit within the context of higher education institutions. Most USQ CoPs are member driven, rather than a top-down initiative, so they are not aligned with formal institutional structures. The CoP facilitation role differs significantly from those of the familiar institutional roles of committee chair, department head or unit/course leader. Often CoP members will be from different disciplines and may include both professional and academic staff. The dynamics of collaboration within such diversity will require significant leadership skill to manage personalities and power dynamics, cultivate a supportive receptive context and provide outcomes useful for both members and institutions. At USQ and, as noted in the Australian Office of Learning and Teaching report, *Identifying, building and sustaining leadership capacity for communities of practice in higher education*', the 'leadership' role in the CoP is designated the 'facilitator' (McDonald et al. 2012c).

The research (McDonald et al. 2012c) identified different types of CoPs— organic, nurtured/support and created/intentional and recognised that CoP facilitators would be facing different challenges depending on their experience, context and type of CoP. The different types of higher education CoPs are presented in Table 3.1.

Similar research and experience is noted in the Faculty Learning Communities literature, and the exchange of research and experience led to collaboration and cross fertilisation of CoP and FLC ideas between the authors, Milton Cox and Jacquie McDonald. The reports and resources from these collaborations to build CoP facilitator capacity are described in detail by McDonald et al. (2012c) and McDonald (2014). Resources relating to this unique leadership role in an Australian

Table 3.1 Types of CoPs and contextual issues (*Source* McDonald et al. 2012c, p. 22)

Type of CoP	Organic	Nurtured/supported	Created/intentional
Structure	Bottom-up	Modified bottom-up	Top-down
Support level	Minimal	Subsidised	Provided
Membership	Voluntary	Voluntary/suggested	Encouraged
Themes	Discipline-related	Discipline or issue related	Guided issues and cross discipline
Agenda	Self-determined	Self-determined/steered	Guided theme
Timing for outcomes	Self-determined	Self-determined and funding-related	Short-term rather than long-term

context have been developed through two Australian Office of Learning and Teaching grants and can be accessed via McDonald (n.d.) and McDonald et al. (2012b).

3.4 Faculty Learning Communities and Community of Practice Similarities and Differences

In Table 3.2 the authors indicate what they see as the defining features of FLCs and CoPs.

3.5 Dreaming, Scheming, and Seaming the Two Models

The authors continue their observations about FLC and CoP structures and activities, collaborating and consulting with colleagues around the practical adaptions of each approach to suit different national and international higher education contexts and needs.

3.5.1 Integrating FLCs and CoPs at Hong Kong Baptist University

An example illustrating the collaborative activities and practical adaptations of a combination of both FLC and CoP approaches is the case at Hong Kong Baptist University (Wong et al. 2016).

Table 3.2 Comparison of the defining features of FLCs and CoPs

Defining features	FLC—Miami University—now U.S. model	CoP—USQ Australia
Initiation by	Academic and/or professional who usually facilitates the FLC	Academic and/or professional who usually facilitates the CoP, occasionally management
Institutional support	Usually teaching and learning centre or other professional unit; sometimes provost, deans	Usually learning and teaching centre or other professional unit; sometimes management, research office, deans
Centralised management	Teaching centre; provost and/or deans; units such as Library	N/A
Champion/s and sponsor/s	Teaching Centre; FLC Program director; proposer; facilitator	Learning and teaching centre, management, research office, deans
Cohort or topic based	Both	Both
Time frame membership	One academic year voluntary	No time limit voluntary
Membership process	By application	By invitation
Member status	Academic and/or professional	Academic and/or professional
Meeting scheduling	Every 3 weeks for 2 h recommended, but members can adjust	Members decide, usually monthly, 1–2 h
Meeting structure/agenda	Determined by members; coordinated by facilitator	Three CoP elements, community, sharing practice, building domain knowledge
Goals and objectives determined by	Goals by facilitator; objectives by members	Visioned by facilitator, negotiated by members
Agenda decisions	Determined by members	Determined by members
Meeting leadership	Facilitator or co-facilitator as full participant in FLC; models behaviour	Facilitator, not leader; with co-facilitators, distributed leadership approach
Program leadership	Three roles: investigator, implementer, program director	Informal coaching and facilitation role
Impact assessment	3 areas: member development, FLC components engaged, and related student learning	Funded CoPs evaluated
SoTL component	Learning, teaching, or institutional project, assessment, and refereed presentation on campus and beyond	Informal, some research, presentations and publications, on campus and beyond
Community building and social aspect	Food at meetings; inclusion of family at some events	Dedicated community time for refreshments and conversation

(continued)

Table 3.2 (continued)

Defining features	FLC—Miami University—now U.S. model	CoP—USQ Australia
Rewards/thank you for members	Varies from nothing to $1000 USD; Usually available as professional expenses, not stipend	Informal, sharing and profiling member activities
Budget for entire year	Varies $0–$10,000 USD funded by Centre via Central Administration	Not centrally funded
Student involvement	Associate member; provides student perspective on projects	Research CoPs only

3.5.1.1 Background and Overview

The Hong Kong Special Administrative Region (HKSAR) consists of connected cities in the People's Republic of China. Hong Kong's higher education institutions experience opportunities and challenges due to their global situation. The University Grants Committee (UGC) of Hong Kong is a non-statutory advisory committee responsible for advising the HKSAR government on the development and funding needs of higher education institutions in Hong Kong. By 2010, major curriculum changes and increasing numbers of students entering universities in Hong Kong created challenges such as retention, curriculum review, outcomes assessment, and the establishment of engaged and active learning. After a review of post-secondary education in Hong Kong, the UGC provided recommendations to the HKSAR government that could help meet the challenges. Among the recommendations for the continuing enhancement of teaching and learning, the UGC suggested to "collectively consider the establishment of communities of practice (CoPs) to promote sector-wide collaboration on teaching and learning issues" (University Grants Committee 2010, p. 84). To fund this recommendation, UGC provided seed funding (HK $16 million in total, around US $2 million) to its eight institutions during the 2012–2015 triennium. The experience of Hong Kong Baptist University (HKBU) sets forth both the opportunities and the challenges of this venture. Details about HBKU's eight faculties, academic organization, students, undergraduate graduate attributes, and whole-person education are provided in Wong et al. (2016).

3.5.1.2 The Dreaming, Scheming, and Seaming Phases

The HBKU teaching and learning centre, named the Centre for Holistic Teaching and Learning (CHTL), designed (dreaming), implemented (scheming), and managed (seaming) the CoP approach at HKBU. In the dreaming stage, the CoP approach sought to address five themes selected by the Centre:

1. Assist the development of the new (previously 3-year) 4-year undergraduate student cohort curriculum by enhancing the existing mentoring system to become an academic advising system.
2. Assess learning outcomes to ascertain that students are achieving the intended learning outcomes of their programs and attaining the University's Graduate Attributes.
3. Enhance teaching and learning with online resources and e-Tools; for example social networking, e-communities and mobile learning.
4. Enable students to achieve excellence—showcasing/publishing high quality student works, particularly their capstone experience like Honours Projects.
5. Establish a community of scholars to further the cause for interdisciplinarity.

Investigating the goals, properties and outcomes of CoPs in general in the dreaming phase, the Centre sought a structured academic CoP model with the goals of building community and the scholarship of teaching and learning. As they studied the literature, they discovered FLCs (Cox 2004) and decided, in the scheming phase, that they wanted their CoPs to have the following FLC components: multidisciplinarity; action learning; social gatherings organized to ensure participants' enjoyment and commitment; community to ensure safety and trust, openness, respect, responsiveness, collaboration, relevance, challenge, enjoyment, a feeling of loyalty and pride, and empowerment; connection of the subject matter of the CoP to the members' own teaching and interests, and the sharing of related outcomes with the university and beyond. Many of these FLC properties are listed in "Appendix 1" (Cox 2016).

In the seaming phase, CHTL selected the following process to seam FLC and CoP approaches:

> In order to enable a common understanding of CoPs among the University community, the definition of Faculty Learning Community (Cox 2004)—a cross-disciplinary group of faculty and staff members engaging in collaborative activities for enhancing teaching and learning—was adopted for CoPs at HKBU. In consequence, to facilitate successful establishment of CoPs, Dr. Milton Cox, who has had extensive experience in helping institutions set up CoPs in various countries, was engaged as HKBU's CoP consultant. A number of consultation sessions and workshops (both online and in person) ensued in 2013 to engage faculty members in this new endeavor of staff development to enhance teaching and learning (Wong et al. 2016).

CHTL invited CoP applications from staff, and these were blind reviewed by five reviewers in a formal selection process including criteria such as adherence to the FLC model, use of budget, and alignment with the CHTL five themes. Seven CoPs were selected and are currently in various phases of operation:

1. Whole Person Education in Medical Services.
2. Development of a Teaching Portfolio Framework.
3. Enhancing Students' Graduate Attributes Through Problem-Based Learning and Service Learning in Formal Academic Courses.
4. Creation of a Model for Student e-Portfolios as a Tool for Life-long Learning and Assessment.

5. Environmental Science Education.
6. Enhancing Student Learning Through a Holistic Mentoring Programme and a Comprehensive Proficiency Test in Analytical Science.
7. The Data and News Society.

Each CoP had at least one CHTL colleague within its membership for logistics and consultation assistance. Details about membership, months in existence, and presentations at international conferences are provided in Wong et al. (2016).

3.5.1.3 Assessment

Assessment of CoP outcomes at HKBU was an extremely important part of their CoP initiative. Kwong et al. (2016) describe a master assessment plan that gauged the effectiveness of CoPs established at HKBU. An overall survey questionnaire (Kwong et al. 2016) was adapted at HKBU based on and very similar to the one developed by Beach and Cox (2009) used in the evaluation of FLCs established in the U.S. The survey asked CoP participants at HKBU and FLC participants at six universities in the U.S. (Beach and Cox 2009) for responses to questions that included the following: (1) in 13 offered areas, indicate the degree to which your professional life has been impacted by your participation in a CoP (Table 3.3); (2) in 31 offered areas, indicate the degree of change in student learning outcomes that the you detected as a result of CoP participation or activities (Table 3.4); (3) in 8 offered areas, indicate the degree to which changes in your personal attitude affected student learning as a result of your CoP participation; (4) in 19 offered teaching and learning activities or approaches, indicate the extent to which these activities or approaches in your CoP focus courses resulted in changes in student learning; (5) in 21 offered assessments, indicate the degree that those were used as evidence for judging changes in student learning in your CoP focus courses, selected from 31 outcomes that were offered, that were detected as a result of CoP participation or activities.

Tables 3.3 and 3.4 (Kwong et al. 2016) provide the results and HBKU-U.S. comparisons from survey questions (1) and (2). For all survey questions and tables, Kwong et al. (2016) discuss the results of the survey and comparisons of the HKBU CoPs and U.S. FLC results. While administration of the Beach and Cox survey for FLCs across institutions in the U.S. yields consistent rankings of the same items at and near the top selections, the HKBU CoP selections at and near the top are sometimes different than in the U.S. A detailed study of reasons for these similarities and differences provide opportunities for future research.

Kwong et al. (2016) reported "Results from both the survey and interviews showed that participants benefited from participating in this CoP project—that, for instance, they changed attitudes towards teaching, and adopted various teaching and learning approaches and assessment methods, which led to improved and enhanced student learning".

Table 3.3 Individual participant changes as a result of CoP participation (*Source* Kwong et al. 2016)

	HKBU (CoPs 1, 3, 4, 5 and 6)			Beach and Cox (2009) 6 universities in US			
	Mean	SD	N	Mean	SD	N	p value
01. Awareness of how diversity influences/enhances teaching and learning	4.11	0.88	36	3.25	1.30	351	0.0000*
02. Interest in teaching process	3.94	0.87	35	3.86	1.08	361	0.6121
03. Comfort level as a member of the university community	3.91	0.96	37	3.55	1.18	374	0.0340*
04. Awareness of how to serve student learning needs	3.84	0.98	38	3.33	1.19	354	0.0031*
05. View of teaching as an intellectual pursuit	3.82	0.83	35	3.74	1.16	364	0.6011
06. Awareness of ways to integrate teaching/research experience	3.76	1.04	35	3.41	1.27	365	0.0633
07. Understanding and interest in scholarship of teaching	3.74	1.14	33	3.80	1.14	368	0.7722
08. Perspective on teaching and learning/other aspects of higher education beyond discipline	3.71	0.84	35	3.93	1.11	369	0.1520
09. Confidence in addressing student needs in/out of class	3.69	1.01	38	3.29	1.20	352	0.0235*
10. Total effectiveness as a teacher	3.68	0.92	36	3.55	1.14	354	0.4309
11. Understanding of your role at the university	3.59	0.99	38	3.26	1.23	358	0.0575
12. Technical skill as a teacher	3.50	1.00	33	3.38	1.46	341	0.5306
13. Research and scholarly interest with respect to discipline.	3.48	0.96	34	3.18	1.27	366	0.0918

Measurement scale (degree of impact): 5 = a very substantial impact; 1 = no impact
To follow the presentation pattern of Beach and Cox (2009), survey items have been ordered by decreasing means of HKBU responses for this table
* $p < 0.05$

One assessment factor for an FLC is dissemination of the outcomes of the FLC projects, usually refereed presentations or publications of the results of each member's project and/or outcomes of the entire FLC. The CoPs at HKBU confirmed the achievement of that FLC component by presenting eleven such papers in 2015 at the International Lilly Conference on College and University Teaching in

Table 3.4 Changes in student learning outcomes as a result of CoP activities (*Source*: Kwong et al. 2016)

	HKBU (CoPs 1, 3, 4, 5 and 6)			Beach and Cox (2009) 6 universities in US			
	Mean	SD	N	Mean	SD	N	p value
01. Ability to think holistically—to see the whole as well as the parts	3.87	1.19	32	3.39	1.23	241	**0.0336***
02. Understanding of perspectives and values of course or discipline	3.83	1.14	31	3.39	1.21	228	**0.0464***
03. Development of an openness to new ideas	3.80	1.16	32	3.46	1.20	235	0.1226
04. Ability to think creatively	3.79	1.15	31	3.38	1.22	242	0.0646
05. Development of the capacity to think for oneself	3.77	1.23	32	3.44	1.21	237	0.1547
06. Skill in using materials and tools central to course or discipline	3.77	1.09	28	3.30	1.23	234	**0.0345***
07. Development of an informed concern about contemporary social issues	3.77	1.34	25	3.10	1.31	210	**0.0187***
08. Development of a multidisciplinary perspective	3.74	1.21	29	3.15	1.28	211	**0.0152***
09. Ability to synthesize and integrate information and ideas	3.73	1.18	32	3.37	1.19	244	0.1061
10. Improved learning of concepts and theories	3.73	1.17	28	3.36	1.17	241	0.1144
11. Analytical skills	3.73	1.13	32	3.32	1.13	234	0.0553
12. Skill in use of techniques and methods used to gain new knowledge	3.69	1.16	29	3.31	1.13	231	0.0966
13. Ability to draw reasonable inferences from observations	3.69	1.11	28	3.22	1.18	233	**0.0365***
14. Ability to evaluate methods and materials in a course or discipline	3.68	1.21	28	3.24	1.20	221	0.0708
15. Ability to apply principles and generalizations already learned to new problems and situations	3.65	1.22	28	3.35	1.15	236	0.2170
16. Problem-solving skills	3.62	1.18	31	3.35	1.17	240	0.2312
17. Development of an ability to work productively with others	3.57	1.39	32	3.50	1.17	233	0.7859
18. Ability to ask good questions	3.57	1.20	30	3.28	1.18	242	0.2121

(continued)

Table 3.4 (continued)

	HKBU (CoPs 1, 3, 4, 5 and 6)			Beach and Cox (2009) 6 universities in US			
	Mean	SD	N	Mean	SD	N	p value
19. Ability to develop appropriate study skills, strategies, habits	3.54	1.32	29	2.96	1.21	211	**0.0260***
20. Improved learning of terms and facts	3.54	1.24	28	2.91	1.24	217	**0.0120***
21. Development of respect for others	3.50	1.45	32	3.26	1.26	220	0.3750
22. Development of a capacity to make informed ethical choices	3.48	1.46	27	2.97	1.40	205	0.0878
23. Development of a commitment to exercise the rights and responsibilities of citizenship	3.48	1.43	28	2.72	1.36	194	**0.0088***
24. Development of a lifelong love of learning	3.46	1.24	31	3.14	1.23	219	0.1795
25. Development of an informed appreciation of other cultures	3.45	1.42	25	2.98	1.35	210	0.1172
26. Skill in using technology	3.41	1.15	31	3.14	1.32	214	0.2321
27. An increased rate of intellectual development	3.39	1.20	31	3.12	1.26	198	0.2485
28. Development of an informed historical perspective	3.39	1.45	27	2.82	1.32	197	0.0542
29. Development of an aesthetic appreciation in a course or discipline	3.36	1.45	28	2.98	1.33	202	0.1907
30. Utilization of internship experience	3.23	1.74	20	2.41	1.39	118	**0.0473***
31. Improved writing skills	3.19	1.31	28	3.00	1.27	220	0.4689

Measurement scale (degree of changes): 5 = a very substantial amount; 1 = not at all
To follow the presentation pattern of Beach and Cox (2009), survey items have been ordered by decreasing means of HKBU responses for this table
* $p < 0.05$

Washington DC, the Higher Education Research and Development Society of Australasia, and the International Conference: Assessment for Learning in Higher Education. Titles and presenters are listed in Wong et al. (2016). In addition, ten articles generated by the CoPs have been accepted for publication in the *Learning Communities Journal*, volume 8, issues 1 and 2.

3.5.1.4 FLC–CoP Differences and Integration Challenges

The CHTL encountered start-up challenges during the FLC–CoP initiation process at HKBU. One concern was finding space for the CoPs to meet, a persistent, general problem in Hong Kong due to dense population and the premium put on real estate. A second problem was finding and obtaining approval for funding of refreshments at CoP meetings. As a publicly funded institution, this required that rules and regulations be changed to enable special budget arrangements. Another challenge was obtaining cooperation from academic departments and support units where members were invited to engage and contribute time to an unknown and unusual teaching and learning development structure. Obtaining time commitment from CoP members who were meeting three times per week and doing action research required special efforts to make programming and proposed outcomes of value to departments, participants, and their students. To ensure the success and sustainability of CoPs, the CHTL placed one of its members in each CoP. This, along with the ambitious assessment efforts, placed a strain on CHTL personnel. This sometimes created a tension between CoPs and CHTL, with CoP members fearing that reviews were not formative but would cause them to lose their funding. Finally, because disciplinary research received the highest prestige and rewards at HKBU, as at most research universities, the strong encouragement for members of CoPs to produce SoTL presented challenges that are still being addressed. Wong et al. (2016) noted that, "From various perspectives, the CoP initiative at HKBU can be considered as pioneering" (p. 11).

There were some differences between the FLC–CoP model at HKBU and the FLC model in the U.S. The structural differences consisted of CoPs meeting for more than 1 year in order to complete the SoTL publication plan. Also, each CoP had a member of CHTL as participant of the CoP in order to make sure the CoPs were faithful to the FLC–CoP model. In addition, the generous UGC grant provided each CoP with a budget that far exceeded that of most FLCs in the U.S.

There were a few terminology differences, for example the use of the term 'coordinator' for CoPs instead of 'facilitator' used for FLCs. And of course the CoP term was selected instead of FLC because of the different meanings of 'faculty' which are used for an individual instructor in the U.S. versus a disciplinary collective of colleagues in most Commonwealth countries.

The FLC–CoP model at HKBU had only these few differences with the U.S. FLC model, a result of the CHTL's conviction and dedication to achieve the goals and objectives of its major grant-supported CoP initiative while preserving the values and integrity of the university culture.

3.5.2   Integrating CoPs and FLCs at the University of Southern Queensland

In 2015 USQ adapted the FLC model to implement a limited number of funded Learning and Teaching Communities to promote and support learning and teaching initiatives within USQ. The aim is to generate projects that provide institutional impact as well as enhance the capacity to investigate and resolve specific issues that were identified by senior management as of key importance to USQ. Participants nominated to work in a Community on one of the pre-identified priority areas which were: experiential learning; academic start-up skills for higher degree research and multimodal education. Key aims of the initiative included the formation of academic communities focused on enhanced scholarship of teaching and learning, improved educational practice; and the identification and support of emerging researchers at USQ.

Academic and professional staff were invited to come together (via a competitive process) to work in one area, and each Community had access to $10,000 and $20,000 (AUD) to support its scholarly activities. Information sessions, then application and a selection panel process identified potential members. Details of the 2015 USQ Learning and Teaching Community grants are available online.

The initiative was championed by the Pro Vice-Chancellor (Scholarly Information and Learning Services) and facilitated by academics from the central Learning and Teaching Services unit. An external evaluator and researcher worked with participants to investigate the impact of participation in this initiative to explore best practices for using a community model as a professional development strategy; and cultural change evidenced throughout and following the implementation process. The research focus was on the lived experience of participants, with data collected using observations, interviews and focus group methodology.

The Learning and Teaching Community approach differed from the existing USQ bottom-up CoP approach, given it was a top-down funded initiative. It was also a modification of the usual FLC process (Cox et al. 2014). Community members applied to join one of the three topic communities, but there was no nominated facilitator as in the Miami FLC process. At start up in April 2015, Communities came together to establish guiding principles, drawing on community qualities articulated in the literature, discuss commitment and contribution to the community, and work on ways to collaborate, and how to share on-going conversations and document activates on Moodle (the USQ Learning Management System). The Communities participated in whole project meetings, planning their community approach and activities. After July 2015 each community worked independently, then came together for a public presentation of results in December 2015 and presented a final report in January 2016.

3.5.2.1 Learning and Teaching Community Outcomes and Research Findings

Members initially found it challenging to work with staff from different disciplines and roles, i.e. academic and professional staff. Working collaboratively in cross-discipline groups to establish what knowledge each member brought to the group, how they would address their nominated topic and how individual members could work together as a community proved to be quite difficult and time consuming. Eventually each community was reduced to a core of willing workers either by people voluntarily dropping out, or by moving into smaller groups. In the interviews with the external evaluator members said that identifying a common goal was a key to success; however, most members found they had to establish good working relationships before they could agree on a common goal. Participants reflected that successful outcomes were influenced by the degree to which members were open to each other's ideas and through sustained discussion, were able to work together on ways to implement those ideas. As previously noted by Palmer (2002, p. 179) "academic culture is infamous for fragmentation, isolation, and competitive individualism". Despite time being dedicated for informal interaction with refreshments at each initial meeting, more scaffolding and extended time is required to establish 'community,' trust and collaborative approaches. Interviewed members articulated that working through initial difficulties was the only way to develop better practice, saying that "we started off talking a lot, now we are listening a lot". One member reflected on the process and how it positively changed their practice saying that:

> I have learnt that collaborative research requires strategic and planned effort in practice—it doesn't always just happen—and it is built on a clear understanding of roles and the workload of others. Most significantly, a well-connected group is the platform—and these concepts are now guiding my research collaboration practice (participant interview 2015).

As this initiative was a FLC adaption, within an academic year time framework, the timeframe was tight and members felt more time was required to explore their topic in depth. However, all of the interviewees had plans for continuing work in their focus areas, and suggested that their findings and activities could be further developed within the University. Impacts on personal learning and teaching approaches, and what members learnt about ways to collaborate with across discipline colleagues were positive outcomes of the initiative. Some members noted that they were better supported in their roles than they had thought previously, and mentioned increased confidence in their academic role, with one adding 'I have grown in myself and learned to be more strategic with my time' (participant interview 2015).

An issue to be addressed in future USQ Learning and Teaching Community initiatives is clarification of the collaborative community approach. Several potential members, who had not attended the information sessions, thought they were applying for funding to complete a nominate project, which is a standard academic and research process. Articulation of Community building process is clearly stated articulated in the 2016 offer and an informal interview to clarify expectations will be part of the selection process. The USQ Learning and Teaching Communities approach whereby participants explore a broad subject area together, decide what is of interest to that group at that time and then pursue more focused investigations, was felt to be a useful one for fostering scholarship of teaching and learning, as well as potentially alerting participants to some pedagogic issues which could improve their practice.

3.6 Conclusion and Way Ahead

The results of these two examples that describe the integration of the FLC and CoP approaches in Hong Kong and Australia provide encouraging prospects for development and use by educational developers in higher education. An FLC is a CoP, but the structure and operation of FLCs that are integrated within CoPs enable CoPs to achieve their FLC-type goals and objectives in higher education.

The educational development value of FLCs and CoPs for the academic cultures of other countries needs to be investigated. Such efforts are also underway in Colombia and Lebanon, and the use of the Beach and Cox (2009) assessment instruments as employed at HBKU (Kwong et al. 2016) are recommended.

FLCs and CoPs can be successfully seamed provided scholarly visioning (dreaming) and well-informed implementation (scheming) are engaged prior to the implementation of these approaches across institutional, national and international landscapes of practice.

Acknowledgments The authors wish to acknowledge the previous and current FLC and CoP members, facilitators, sponsors and champions as the FLC and CoP models continue to evolve in international settings.

Appendix 1

Sixteen Recommendations for Creating and Sustaining Effective FLCs

1. Limit your FLC to a workable size: 8–10 (6–12 maybe) faculty, professionals, and administrators.
2. Make membership voluntary and by an application process with department chair sign off.
3. Consider having affiliate partners: mentors, student associates, consultants.
4. Select a multidisciplinary FLC, cohort, topic, goals, and membership: three reasons: participant curiosity, rich innovations, dysfunctional unit relief.

5. Meet every 3 weeks for 2 h for one academic year, and determine meeting time at the point of member applications.
6. Provide social moments, community, and food at meetings; an FLC is not just a committee or task force.
7. Make the facilitator a key participating member who models desired behavior and initially determines goals.
8. Have members determine FLC objectives, meeting topics, budget.
9. Focus on obtaining and maintaining FLC member commitment.
10. Assess 3 areas of FLC impact: member development, student learning/effectiveness of innovation, and FLC components engaged.
11. Employ an evidenced-based, scholarly approach leading to SoTL.
12. Present the FLC outcomes to the campus and conferences.
13. Blend online/distance FLCs with an initial and 2 or 3 face-to-face meetings when possible.
14. Include enablers such as rewards, recognition, and a celebratory ending.
15. Imbed an FLC Program of two or more FLCs in a Teaching and Learning Center and have an FLC Program Director there.
16. Adapt the FLC model for your readiness and institutional culture.

Note These items are applicable for a CoP if its structure is the FLC–CoP model.

References

Bandura, A. (1977). *Social learning theory*. Englewood Cliffs, NJ: Prentice Hall.

Beach, A. L., & Cox, M. D. (2009). The impact of faculty learning communities on teaching and learning. *Learning Communities Journal, 1*(1), 7–27.

Beach, A. L., Ndebe-Ngovo, M., & Dirks, D. (2006). *Developing faculty learning communities to transform culture for learning*. Final FIPSE Grant Evaluation Report. Kalamazoo, MI: Western Michigan University.

Chalmers, D. (2011). Progress and challenges to the recognition and reward of the Scholarship of Teaching in higher education. *Higher Education Research & Development, 30*(1), 25–38.

Cox, M. D. (1994). Reclaiming teaching excellence: Miami University's Teaching Scholars Program. *To Improve the Academy, 13*, 79–96.

Cox, M. D. (1995). The development of new and junior faculty. In W. A. Wright & Associates (Eds.), *Teaching improvement practices: Successful strategies for higher education* (pp. 283–310). Bolton, MA: Anker.

Cox, M. D. (2001). Faculty learning communities: Change agents for transforming institutions into learning organizations. *To Improve the Academy, 19*, 69–93.

Cox, M. D. (2003). Fostering the scholarship of teaching through faculty learning communities. *Journal on Excellence in College Teaching, 14*(2/3), 161–198.

Cox, M. D. (2004). Introduction to faculty learning communities. In M. D. Cox & L. Richlin (Eds.), *Building faculty learning communities. New Directions for Teaching and Learning, No. 97* (pp. 5–23). San Francisco: Jossey-Bass.

Cox, M. D. (2006). Phases in the development of a change model: Communities of practice as change agents in higher education. In A. Bromage, L. Hunt, & C. B. Tomkinson (Eds.), *The realities of educational change: Interventions to promote learning and teaching in higher education* (pp. 91–100). Oxford UK: Rutledge.

Cox, M. D. (2013). The impact of communities of practice in support of early-career academics. *International Journal for Academic Development, 18*(1), 18–30.

Cox, M. D. (2014a). Foreword. In P. Blessinger & J. M. Carfora (Eds.), *Inquiry-based learning for faculty and institutional development* (Vol. 1, pp. xiii–xvi). Innovations in Higher Education Teaching and Learning. Bingley: Emerald.

Cox, M. D. (2014b, November). *Leveraging sustainable change using FLCs, faculty development, and implementation science.* Paper presented at the 39th annual conference of the Professional and Organizational Development Network in Higher Education, Dallas, TX.

Cox, M. D. (2016). Four positions of leadership in planning, implementing, and sustaining faculty learning community programs. In B. Flinders & J. Bernstein (Eds.), *Enhancing teaching and learning through collaborative structures. New Directions for Teaching and Learning*, (Vol. 148). San Francisco: Jossey-Bass.

Cox, M. D. & Richlin, L. (Eds.). (2004). *Building faculty learning communities. New directions for teaching and learning* (Vol. 97). San Francisco: Jossey-Bass.

Cox, M. D., Richlin, L., & Essington, A. (2014). *Faculty learning community planning guide.* Los Angeles, CA: International Alliance of Teacher Scholars.

Dewey, J. (1933). *How we think.* Lexington, MA: Heath.

Fixsen, D. L., Naoom, S. F., Blase, K. A., Friedman, R. M., & Wallace, F. (2005). *Implementation research: A synthesis of the literature.* Tampa, FL: University of South Florida, Louis de la Parte Florida Mental Health Institute, National Implementation Research Network (FMHI Publication #231).

Gabelnick, F., MacGregor, J., Matthews, R. S., & Smith, B. L. (1990). *Learning communities: Creating connections among students, faculty, and disciplines. New Directions for Teaching and Learning, No. 41.* San Francisco: Jossey-Bass.

Haynes, C., Cummins, R. H., Detloff, M., Dixon, L., Ernsting, K., & Fuehrer, A. (2010). Learning communities and institutional transformation. *Learning Communities Journal, 2*(2), 149–167.

Kemp, D., & Norton, A. (2014). *Review of the demand driven funding system report.* Canberra: Australian Government.

Kwong, T., Cox, M. D., Chong, K., Wong, W. L., & Nie, S. (2016). Assessing the effect of communities of practice in higher education: The case at Hong Kong Baptist University. *Learning Communities Journal, 8*(2), 171–198.

Lave, J., & Wenger, E. (1991). *Situated learning: Legitimate peripheral participation.* USA: Cambridge University Press.

MacGregor, J., Tinto, V., & Lindbald, J. H. (2001). Assessment of innovative efforts: Lessons from the learning community movement. In L. Suskie (Ed.), *Assessment to promote deep learning: Insight from AAHE's 2000 and 1999 assessment conferences.* Washington, DC: AAHE.

McDonald, J. (2007). *The role of online discussion forums in supporting learning in higher education* (Unpublished doctoral thesis). University of Southern Queensland, Toowoomba, Queensland. http://eprints.usq.edu.au/3588/

McDonald, J., Collins, P., Hingst, R., Kimmins, L., Lynch, B., & Star, C. (2008). Community learning: Members' stories about their academic community of practice, in Engaging Communities. In *Proceedings of the 31st HERDSA annual conference, Rotorua* (pp. 221–229). 1–4 July 2008.

McDonald, J., Nagy, J., Star, C., Burch, T., Cox, M. D., & Margetts, F. (2012a). Identifying and building the leadership capacity of community of practice facilitators. *Learning Communities Journal, 4*, 63–84.

McDonald, J., & Star, C. (2008) The challenges of building an academic community of practice: An Australian case study, in Engaging Communities. In *Proceedings of the 31st HERDSA annual conference, Rotorua* (pp. 230–240). 1–4 July 2008.

McDonald, J., Star, C., Burch, T., Cox, M., Nagy, J., & Margetts, F. (2012b). Project resources: Identifying, building and sustaining leadership capacity for communities of practice in higher education Office of Learning and Teaching, Australia. http://www.cops.org.au/resources/

McDonald, J., Star, C., & Margetts, F. (2012c). *Identifying, building and sustaining leadership capacity for communities of practice in higher education*. Final Report, Office for Learning and Teaching. http://www.olt.gov.au. Accessed 17 September 2014.

McDonald, J. (2014). *Community, domain, practice: Facilitator catch cry for revitalising learning and teaching through communities of practice*. Final Report. Office for Learning and Teaching. Accessed http://www.olt.gov.au. 17 September 2014.

McDonald, J., & Star, C. (2014). Learning and teaching professional development: An Australian community of practice case study. *Learning Communities Journal, 6*, 109–126.

McDonald, J. (n.d.). Facilitator Resources: ALTC Teaching Fellowship Community of Practice Facilitator Resources. http://www.usq.edu.au/cops/resources/altcfellowship/facilitator-resources. Accessed 10 February 2016.

Meiklejohn, A. (1932). *The experimental college*. New York: HarperCollins.

Mercieca, B. (2016). What is a community of practice? In J. McDonald & A. Cater-Steel (Eds.), *Communities of practice—Facilitating social learning in higher education*. Singapore: Springer.

Ortquist-Ahrens, L., & Torosyan, R. (2009). The role of facilitator in faculty learning communities: Paving the way for growth, productivity, and collegiality. *Learning Communities Journal, 1*(1), 29–62.

Palmer, P. (2002). The quest for community in higher education. In W. M. McDonald (Ed.), *Creating campus community* (pp. 179–192). San Francisco, CA: Jossey-Bass.

Petrone, M. C., & Ortquist-Ahrens, L. (2004). Facilitating faculty learning communities: A compact guide to creating change and inspiring community. In M. D. Cox & L. Richlin (Eds.), *Building faculty learning communities. New Directions for Teaching and Learning, No. 97* (pp. 137–148). San Francisco: Jossey-Bass.

Probert, B. (2014). Why scholarship matters in higher education (discussion paper no. 2). Sydney, NSW: Australian Government Office for Learning and Teaching.

Reaburn, P., & McDonald, J. (2016). Creating and facilitating communities of practice in higher education: Theory to practice in a Regional Australian University. In J. McDonald & A. Cater-Steel (Eds.), *Communities of practice—Facilitating social learning in higher education*. Singapore: Springer.

Senge, P. (1990). *The fifth discipline*. New York, NY: Doubleday.

Star, C., & McDonald, J. (2007). Embedding successful pedagogical practices: Assessment strategies for a large, diverse, first year student cohort. *International Journal of Pedagogies and Learning, 3*(2), 18–30.

Tight, M. (2015). Theory application in higher education research: the case of communities of practice. *European Journal of Higher Education*. doi:10.1080/21568235.2014.997266.

University Grants Committee. (2010). *Aspirations for the higher education system in Hong Kong: Report of the University Grants Committee*. http://www.ugc.edu.hk/eng/doc/ugc/publication/report/her2010/her2010-rpt.pdf

Universities Australia. (2013). *An agenda for higher education 2013–2016: A smarter Australia*. Canberra, Australian Capital Territory: Universities Australia.

Vygotsky, L. (1978). *Mind in Society: development of higher psychological processes*. Cambridge, MA: Harvard University Press.

Wenger, E. (1998). *Communities of practice: Learning, meaning, and identity*. Cambridge: Cambridge University Press.

Wenger-Trayner, E., & Wenger-Trayner, B. (2015). *Communities of practice: A brief Introduction*. http://wenger-trayner.com/introduction-to-communities-of-practice/, Accessed 10 Feb 2016.

Wenger, E., McDermott, R., & Snyder, W. (2002). *Cultivating communities of practice*. Massachusetts: Harvard Business School Press.

Wenger-Trayner, E., Fenton-O'Creevy, M., Hutchinson, S., Kubiak, C., & Wenger-Trayner, B. (Eds.). (2015). *Learning in landscapes of practice: Boundaries, identity, and knowledgeability in practice-based learning*. London: Routledge.

Wong, E., Cox, M. D., Kwong, T., Fung, R., Lau, P., Sivan, A., et al. (2016). Establishing communities of practice to enhance teaching and learning: The case at Hong Kong Baptist University. *Learning Communities Journal, 8*(2), 9–26.

Chapter 4
Using Communities of Practice to Internationalise Higher Education: Practical and Strategic Considerations

Helen May and Jeanne Keay

Abstract Most Higher Education Institutions (HEIs) include a commitment to internationalisation within their corporate strategies covering a range of activities focusing on students, staff, finance and culture, which inevitably has led to questions about how HEIs can meet these varied and sometimes competing demands. This chapter asks questions about the usefulness of the concept of a community of practice in helping HEIs to meet their internationalisation aspirations. We acknowledge different purposes, functions, structures and participants in communities of practice and provide a critical analysis of the concept and its usefulness in promoting collegiality and collaboration to achieve an HEI's internationalisation aims. We draw on particular UK examples to illustrate this point. We address practical and strategic considerations and conclude by highlighting issues, proposing opportunities and identifying key messages for institutions seeking to use communities of practice to internationalise higher education.

Keywords Communities of practice · Internationalisation · Collaboration

4.1 Introduction

Most Higher Education Institutions (HEIs) include a commitment to internationalisation within their corporate strategies and they identify the breadth of the work involved in meeting the targets they have agreed. These targets cover a range of

The original version of this chapter was revised: Author affiliation has been updated. The erratum to this chapter is available at 10.1007/978-981-10-2879-3_29

H. May (✉)
Higher Education Academy, York, UK
e-mail: Helen.May@HEAcademy.ac.uk

J. Keay
Leeds Beckett University, Leeds, UK
e-mail: j.k.keay@leedsbeckett.ac.uk

© Springer Nature Singapore Pte Ltd. 2017
J. McDonald and A. Cater-Steel (eds.), *Communities of Practice*,
DOI 10.1007/978-981-10-2879-3_4

activities focusing on students, staff, finance and culture, which inevitably has led to questions about how HEIs can meet these varied and sometimes competing demands. This chapter asks questions about the usefulness of the concept of a community of practice in helping HEIs to meet their internationalisation aspirations. Wenger (1998) states that a community of practice is defined as a group that coheres through sustained mutual engagement on an indigenous enterprise, creating a common repertoire, a definition that assumes all involved in the community are there voluntarily and for the same purpose. In this chapter we acknowledge that this is not necessarily the norm and provide a critical analysis of the concept of a community of practice and its usefulness in promoting collegiality and collabora- tion to achieve an HEI's internationalisation aims.

In 2014, the Higher Education Academy (HEA), the leading body for learning and teaching in the UK undertook research (O'Mahony 2014) to explore the ways in which UK HEIs ensure a high quality learning experience for students under- taking degrees through transnational education (TNE) partnerships. In a subsequent article, we examined the potential for using (Wenger's 1998, 2006) characteristics of communities of practice to highlight potential and suggest practical ways to create more effective TNE partnerships (Keay et al. 2014). Through this work we argue that the development of communities of practice, promoting a focus on the quality of the relationship between partners for the enhancement of practice, could be used to raise the quality of learning experiences for students. We suggest that partners can use *joint enterprise* in order to co-develop the TNE 'product'; that *mutual engagement* will promote shared responsibility for developing the part- nership; and that focus on a *shared repertoire* can highlight the importance of working collaboratively to create contextually appropriate practices.

In this chapter we develop these ideas to consider the broader internationalisa- tion agenda in higher education and explore how communities of practice can be used to encourage collegiality and collaboration in this field of work. We focus on internationalisation activities in higher education and consider the circumstances, strategy and structures, which may hinder or support the development of such learning communities.

While our previous work promoted communities of practice as a vehicle for ensuring that TNE provided an excellent student learning experience, we also recognise that the broad range of internationalisation activities undertaken in a HEI may not always encourage collaborative working. Many international activities are competitive in nature, both within a HEI and between groups of HEIs. For example, recruiting international students; promoting brand awareness; striving for and being recognised as providing an excellent student experience through national and international surveys; and offering language support, outward mobility opportuni- ties and a truly internationalised curriculum are all examples of how HEIs compete against one another in relation to internationalising their offer. The task of striving for international recognition may prevent cross sector collaboration and sharing of resources; for example, one of the HEI mission groups in the UK tried and failed to form an international interest group because of the competitive nature of interna- tional activity. One example of a cross sector group successfully sustaining what they call communities of practice is the Universities UK International Unit (http://www.international.ac.uk/about-us/what-we-do.aspx), which has country wide focused communities. However, they possibly continue to exist because the purpose, of each community for HEI members, is on gaining information rather than sharing it. It is not only between institutions that competitiveness disrupts collaboration and its benefits, within institutions budgets are often devolved and success and organisational investment often relies on meeting targets. This sometimes prevents the sharing of good practice within an institution, which would result in increased improvements in all areas of internationalisation.

Drawing on our own research and professional practice, derived from working for the national body, the HEA (http://www.heacademy.ac.uk/home) facilitating research and practice communities, as well as working with and within HE institutions and using contributions from the higher education sector in the UK, we propose that partnership, collegiality and collaboration are 'good things' and that communities of practice in higher education can be useful ways to situate learning and promote these elements. We ask how communities of practice can be used to encourage collegiality and collaboration and even help achieve and lead organisational change in the field of the internationalisation of higher education.

In order to situate the discussion the chapter will firstly examine definitions of internationalisation; then it will explore the characteristics of communities of practice, what they are, what they do, how and where they operate, who participates and what are the benefits. The chapter will then focus on strategic considerations, using research evidence and our own practice in higher education and working within institutions and for a national agency to illustrate the points made, concluding with a summary of opportunities, issues and key points.

4.2 Internationalisation

Knight (2003) defines internationalisation as an integration process, which brings an international, intercultural or global dimension to education and in its broadest and most aspirational sense this is what internationalisation should achieve. More recently, the (British Council 2015) refers not only to students' experiences but also to university staff, stating that 'internationalisation must be engrained in the culture of the university, that it must be part of an institutional ethos catalysed by each individual's experiences' (p. 4). However, an analysis of the internationalisation strategies of a range of HEIs based in Australia, the UK and Europe reveals a slightly different definition. Most strategies and plans provide a broad definition of the term internationalisation, which reflect Knight's views, but a closer examination of such strategies and intended outcomes also reveals a somewhat different intention. The focus of such strategies appears to be on laudable claims about internationalising the institutional curriculum, programmes, research, student and staffing base, developing international collaborations, providing students with a preparation to become global citizens and achieving an international community. However, the following areas also appear on a regular basis in such strategies: reputation enhancement, being the best, the institution of choice, recruitment growth, global presence, developing strategic partnerships and quality positioning in the market. Focus on these areas is of course expected and if an institution is to internationalise itself all of these outcomes are important, but in the context of suggesting that communities of practice, which are by nature collaborative, can enhance internationalisation activities, this is an important element of the definition.

In 2013, the HEA held a learning and teaching summit focusing on internationalisation, involving 30 national and international experts in order to identify the core principles for the agenda in UK HE. What emerged over the course of the summit was the central importance of collegial and collaborative ways of working to all aspects of internationalisation including internationalising the student experience, recruiting and retaining international students and staff and all forms of TNE. Whilst there may be a range of reasons for wanting to internationalise an organisation, if collaboration is centrally important to achieving these, it can follow that communities of practice could be key. The International Association of Universities (IAU), in their 2012 Call for Action identified unintended consequences of universities' internationalisation agendas. They suggested that 'competition is in danger of displacing collaboration as the foundation for internationalization (p. 3). It is about the use of communities of practice in internationalisation we will further consider through the discussion below.

4.3   Communities of Practice

In making the case for communities of practice to be useful in encouraging collegiality and collaboration in the field of internationalisation we want to ask a series of questions in order to explore the nature, development and sustainability of such groups:

1. What are communities of practice?
2. What can communities of practice do?
3. How are communities of practice formed, developed and sustained?
4. Where do communities of practice operate?
5. Who are the participants in communities of practice?
6. Who benefits from communities of practice?

In answering and discussing these key practical questions, we use a range of examples to illustrate different forms of communities of practice and show how their purposes differ. These examples are drawn in particular from the UK higher education system, but draw on our experience of working internationally.

4.3.1 What are Communities of Practice?

Early use of the term communities of practice focused on learning in the workplace; Lave and Wenger (1991) promoted a model of situated learning, examining how workers learned in communities and how they learned to become members of those communities through legitimate peripheral participation. Over time the concept has been redefined to describe communities of practice as: 'groups of people who share a concern, a set of problems, or a passion about a topic, and who deepen their knowledge and expertise in this area by interacting on an on-going basis Wenger et al. (2002, p. 4). So, if we take this revised concept and apply it to the focus of this chapter, using a community of practice to develop an HEI's internationalisation agenda, we need to ask whether everyone has a passion, or a concern for internationalisation. Or, as will be discussed below, is that what a community of practice is designed to develop?

Naturally there are different kinds of communities of practice and inevitably not all those groups that are called, or call themselves, communities of practice actually behave as might be expected of a community of practice (Wenger 2006). The issue, he claims, is the criteria. Lave and Wenger's (1991) and Wenger's (1998) work is cited in most writing that considers communities of practice and the characteristics that we used in our previous work, joint enterprise, mutual engagement and shared repertoire, are useful in setting the criteria for such groups. Despite using a set of agreed criteria, Lave and Wenger (1991, p. 42) suggest that a community of practice is never defined precisely, however, what appears to be consistent in defining communities of practice is the focus on learning. 'A surface reading would see a community of practice as a unified, neatly bounded group, whereas what is intended is a more subtle concept .... those involved have different interests and viewpoints' Cox (2005, p. 3).

Communities of practice are not homogenous, and these differences have an impact on the way criteria are applied. They are different sizes, they operate in different contexts, both within and across organisations and while some are recognised, others are hidden; communities contain core and peripheral members and membership is not necessarily limited to one community of practice. One person may belong to several communities of practice and play different roles in each community. Therefore, applying different definitions to the concept and ways of working of a community of practice may provide different answers to questions about the usefulness of communities of practice in achieving the aims of internationalisation in HEIs. For example, if a community of practice is comprised of academics who have the internationalisation of student learning as their main focus the fact that they operate from different parts of the organisation will not necessarily hinder the work of the community. In fact, they are more likely to share practice and learn from one another.

4.3.2   What can Communities of Practice Do?

If the common denominator for the outcomes of communities of practice is learning, then how that learning takes place and whether, as Wenger (Smith 2003) suggests, learning is the reason the community comes together or the outcome of the community coming together are important questions to consider. In this chapter we are proposing that communities of practice can provide the context for developing and achieving HEIs' internationalisation agendas. Drawing on the characteristics of communities of practice (Wenger 1998), we suggest they can provide the context for drawing participants together to work towards the common goal of internationalising the HEI; they can promote the notion of shared responsibility of all participants to work towards achieving the agreed outcomes; and through sharing knowledge, understanding and resources they can ensure that learning is a corporate and common outcome.

Cultivating communities of practice is not only in the interests of the participants of the community but also, as discussed below, in the interests of the HEI leaders. In the context of an HEI, the beneficiaries of a community of practice are not limited to the participants, who are likely to be employees of that organisation, but also include the students; for example, in a community formed to share practice and understanding of internationalising the student experience or the wider society, as discussed below. However, as we promoted in our previous publication (Keay et al. 2014), communities of practice are important because of the process and not just the product. The benefits of a community of practice that is focusing on internationalising the institution will ensure that a range of outcomes are the focus of the work of the group rather than simply considering one element, for example, recruitment of international students to generate income.

> When it is given a name and brought into focus, it becomes a perspective that can help us to understand our world better. In particular it allows us to see past the more obvious formal structures such as organisations, classrooms, or nations, and perceive the structures defined by engagement in practice and the formal learning that comes with it. (Wenger 1998, p. 247)

The question this raises is whether learning of any community of practice could be further enriched if what was shared and developed was across institutional or national contexts? Would an insight into such contexts brought about through the community help facilitate a more objective view of localised structures or approaches or indeed endorse and bolster local activity? Furthermore, could the outcome(s) of joint activity be enhanced? Working within a cross-discipline/organisational/national community of practice could not only help to counter competition, get beyond structures and understand other viewpoints but the process has the potential to enhance the learning of participants and the organisation as well as the outcome.

To reflect further on the impact of diverse perspectives and contexts on what communities do, we can look to an example community of practice in the context of internationalisation. In 2013, the HEA invited those with internationalisation expertise from across the world to form a community of practice to help shape a UK strategy (HEA 2014). The group first met through a two-day summit, which acted as a means of surfacing points of divergence and convergence. What was co-created through the summit was a set of agreed principles for internationalisation. Community representatives, who formed a small working group, developed these principles over a period of seven months and this led to the development of a sample framework. During this time, a reference group from the community of practice critiqued various drafts. The members of the community were reconvened to debate and discuss before it went out for sector wide consultation. Those responding to the consultation included those from different national contexts.

Whilst some might debate whether the methodology for creating this UK strategy, the Internationalising HE framework HEA (2014) articulated here does represent a community of practice, what was created was a strong sense of community amongst those involved. The intention had been to facilitate the development of a co-created product and to promote a sense of collective ownership and responsibility for what was created, so to maximise its quality and impact. What distinguishes them as community was their common sense of purpose and through working together new ways of thinking were achieved. The fact that the outcome had been informed by evidence derived from different contexts helped to significantly enhance it. Those involved in the development of the outcome reported a sense of ownership and responsibility for what was created. The diversity of perspectives brought together through the process not only served to enhance the experience of those involved but also what was created. Furthermore its potential impact is also increased by virtue of more knowing about it and it having resonance with a range of contexts.

4.3.3 How are Communities of Practice Formed, Developed and Sustained?

If we accept that although communities of practice do not have a set form and that their participants will play different roles both inside and outside the community and that the process of group learning and development is the focus, then it is important to ask how they are formed, developed and sustained and become of value. This is particularly important in the field of internationalisation where the outcomes are not only qualitative and collaborative but are also the result of competition and are commercial in nature.

4.3.3.1 Forming Communities of Practice

Wenger's (1998) early work suggests that communities of practice are formed naturally, that they are formed through social interaction and a focus on participants coming together with authentic learning being the result rather than a planned process of learning (Cox 2005). If we subscribe to this definition of communities of practice we must ask whether what we are proposing is appropriate. Are we proposing a form of community of practice that is not organic in its growth but formed externally and if so, will this be effective?

We are proposing in this chapter that communities of practice are useful in enabling collaborative processes to support the internationalisation agenda in HEIs but what if the forming of these communities is contrived? Hargreaves (1994) noted a culture of contrived collegiality in examining school cultures where groups are formed externally to achieve specific outcomes and Williams et al. (2001) compare this with 'structural collaboration' claiming that this is a better form of culture for learning. Is a community of practice that has been contrived in formation any less valuable than one that has been formed naturally? More recently, Wenger et al. (2002) suggest a shift in thinking and a focus on a commodification of the notion of communities of practice (Cox 2005). If a community of practice becomes a management tool does this detract from its value? Will communities of practice to support the development of internationalisation in HEIs form naturally or will it be necessary to help the agenda to be achieved through forcing communities to form? Viewing communities of practice as a management tool may not be detrimental to learning but it does have an impact on the definition of the concept.

In examining an example of a community of practice that has been externally generated and formed by the senior management of a HEI to address a specific strategic purpose it is possible to see both perspectives. The example relates to a HEI in the UK that applied to engage in one of the HEA's services—a year-long programme to enable and facilitate whole organisational change (https://www.heacademy.ac.uk/consultancy-services/change) an HEA Change Programme (described in more detail in the next section) focusing on internationalisation. The institution had a clear mission to extend the good practice in some areas of the organisation to enable all schools and programmes to ensure that the learning experiences offered to students had a global outlook. However, engagement in the HEA's Programme was driven by the PVCs responsible for Learning and Teaching and Internationalisation and while this has ensured a cross-institution focus it has also resulted in a process that, rather than being driven by the community, it is driven by participation in a group that has been externally formed. A community of practice is growing and the group is sharing learning but it is not clear from their participation in this programme whether the contrived nature of this group has hindered progress or alternatively whether it has actually hastened its formation.

4.3.3.2 Cultivating Communities of Practice

Communities of practice emerge in different forms, for example, they may be comprised of local, national or international members; they may be within an organisation or across organisations; and the establishment of such groups begs questions about how best to cultivate or develop a sense of community amongst those individuals who are part of the community. In order to collaborate, as Wenger (1998, 2006) argued, participants need to be committed to working together. One could further surmise that they would need to value other participants' contributions and to interact in a purposeful way. A review of relevant literature, Keay (2006) relating to collaboration generated the following four criteria; when collaborating:

- Relationships between participants are supportive and not supervisory and members hold each other in mutual respect;
- Individuals are motivated and committed to learning and collaboration;
- Activity takes place in a culture in which professional dialogue is possible and where participants seek feedback and constructive criticism;
- Participants engage in reflective practice.

These characteristics of collaborative engagement are useful when exploring how communities of practice operate and what types of behaviour will support the cultivation of such groups.

Participants in communities of practice also have to learn to be members of the community and this links to Lave and Wenger's early work using the notion of legitimate peripheral participation to describe how new members learn the rules of the community and are gradually able to, and allowed to, contribute. Given the questions raised in the previous section about contrived collegiality and communities of practice that are brought together rather than emerging in an organic way, we must ask whether legitimate peripheral participation is a way for those forming the communities to ensure that all participants are focused on the same outcomes. It also raises questions about the participants, the stakeholders and the beneficiaries of such communities.

As we consider the cultivation of communities of practice we must ask questions about how individuals are empowered to learn in such contrived communities and indeed who, if anyone, 'owns' the community and its outcomes. For example, as a result of some of its more longitudinal work with HEIs, the HEA has in the past set up a number of social networking ('SharePoint') site for interested participants. The sites provided the facility to upload and comment on documents as well as hold asynchronous discussions and helping connect people across institutions with one another outside of the face-to-face contact. Over the last 7 years of doing so, it has become evident that in the instances where the HEA instigated or facilitated the site, it was little used. However where the site was instigated, owned and facilitated by members of the group, it was regularly used, as evidenced through email notifications, and became an integral part of the programme. Feelings about the site being imposed on the group appear to have affected their willingness to engage with it and benefit from the facility. Whilst the programme did not attempt to create a community of practice, the site facilitated one when it served the interests of those using it rather than of the programme. Indeed, Kimble and Hildreth (2005) argue that being self-directed or self-motivated and a self-serving interest is what distinguishes a community of practice from working or task groups, which may serve the interests of the wider organisation.

4.3.3.3 Sustaining Communities of Practice

Wenger et al. (2002) defined communities of practice as groups of people who share a concern or a passion for something they do and learn how to do it better; however, we should ask, what if the passion is not theirs but one forced on them by others? Would such a circumstance have an impact on the sustainability of the community?

We should also ask questions about the leadership of communities of practice; who are the leaders, what are their goals and motivations for leading the group; and is power and control through such leadership detrimental to the outcomes? Some cultures and organisation may limit the development and positive effects of communities of practice and many of these typify higher education communities. For example, Cox (2005) developed (Eraut's 2002) work, which describes cultures and practices that are not conducive to the development of effective communities of practice, many of which are recognisable in HE:

- Frequent reorganisation, so that engagement between individuals is not sustained.
- Employment of temporary or part time staff, no relationships build up.
- Tight management, where the organisation wishes itself to "own" the task.
- Individualised work, so there is no collective engagement.
- Very competitive environments, inhibiting collaboration.
- Time pressurised environments, so there is a lack of time to develop collective understanding.
- Spatially fragmented work, so that there may be no available common, unsupervised space.
- Heavily mediated activities, e.g. by computers, so that interaction is (arguably) less immediate and intense.

Sustaining communities of practice may depend on members having an on-going sense of purpose or value in continuation, which can last beyond the original purpose. In a previous article (Keay et al. 2014), we argued for the significance of the process rather than the products of communities of practice. If the process of interacting or collaboration has an inherent value, members may continue to meet even after the completion of products. The network created by the community may serve new purposes and outcomes over time.

One example of this happening in the UK is through change programmes led and facilitated by the HEA. As indicated previously, these help HEIs to lead cultural change on particular strategic themes or areas, including internationalisation. The opportunity provided through the programme enables the group to form and to start acting like a community of practice. The HEA provides a set number of meeting points for all participating providers typically over the course of a year. Senior leaders from an HEI usually elect to apply to participate in the programme and those participating are mandated to form a core 'team' who work together to plan, implement and evaluate a change initiative during the course of the programme.

The existence of the programme often enables groups of staff (or staff/students) within and across institutions to meet who would not have done otherwise, despite having a common and vested interest in the theme. Through a HEA evaluation survey to participants of previous change programmes over the last 10 years, several individuals reported continuing to meet and work with others from the programme after it closed. Examples included collaborating with others to submit research proposals, writing chapters or articles, institutional visits and exchanges, and generating group email lists to exchange ideas and request support. Whilst it is not known from the survey for how long these activities lasted, and was certainly not the case for every individual or programme, it does illustrate that the programme instigated communities to form. This does recognise that the themes and work involved in leading change is on-going. Internationalisation is a process of continual enhancement that cannot be achieved in a defined period of time. As such communities of practice on topics of this nature may help sustain them into the future.

4.3.4   Where Do Communities of Practice Meet?

The question of where communities of practice meet is significant when considering the practicalities of what can be achieved or considering who can be involved. Whilst traditionally communities of practice may have met in real time and/or face to face, one might question whether this is still necessary to enable a community of practice to run effectively. Do communities of practice, especially those involving membership from around the world, need to physically meet to be able to achieve their outcomes or goals? Indeed, one could argue that where a community of practice meets could affect its future sustainability. Individuals may be more willing to participate if they do not have to invest resource and time in travel to partake in such communities? It may be simply not practical or financially viable for them to do so. In this section, we address some of these practical considerations and the impact on the effectiveness of a community of practice.

The issue of virtual, rather than face to face, communities of practice, has been scrutinised within the literature c.f. Kimble and Hildreth (2004, 2005), Daniel et al. (2003) and McDermott and O'Dell (2001). What is common to these works is the importance of virtual communities staying true to the characteristic features of a 'community of practice'—of building trusting relationships, having a joint endeavour, making social connections and developing a shared 'repertoire'. Undoubtedly technology can facilitate virtual communities to achieve these, especially given the significant advancements in recent times, with mobile technology and social media evolving and changing the mode and frequency of interactions between people across the world. Whilst technology may open up new possibilities and opportunities for who, how, when and where we interact with one another, Kimble and Hildreth (2005) argue that a shared interest, desire and motivation remains critical. They argue that regular interaction and task focus can support motivation, operating as a virtuous circle. Hence, whilst members can evidently benefit from a virtual world, operating synchronously or asynchronously, and whilst communities of practice may have formed or continued to meet through technology where they may not have done otherwise, virtual members will need to commit as much, if not more, time and energy in the community to enable it to succeed as a community of practice.

It does need to be recognised however, that whilst technology can facilitate it can also be a barrier to participation in certain parts of the world (or indeed country) where connections are poor or technology is less advanced. Not everyone has equal access to technology, the hardware or software, or the capabilities. Who is informing the community of practice is an important question, which we will come onto in the next section. Who contributes to the co-created outcomes of the community or whose voices are heard within the community should not be down to who has access to resources to do so. Such issues are not exclusive to technology of course; given that access may be restricted by other factors including time, financial means, language(s)/dialect used or rights to freedom of speech. Resources (such as technology and funding) can act as key enablers to communities of practice in some contexts, helping them grow and maximise their effectiveness, impact and reach. However, attention should be paid to how barriers to participate can be overcome and those without resources can be enabled to participate.

4.3.5   Who Are the Participants in Communities of Practice?

The question of who participates in any one community of practice and, in the context of internationalisation, who might participate are important questions to ask. Would it be those who are interested in internationalisation through their practice or research? Would it be those who have a remit or role in the agenda? Would it be those with the resource (time, money, technology) available? If we take a broad definition of internationalisation, as we stated earlier, to encompass the recruitment and retention of those coming from overseas to study in the UK, those studying for a UK degree overseas (TNE) as well as enabling a more internationalised education for all students, then internationalisation can be addressed as a collective responsibility. Therefore, would it translate that a wide range of stakeholder voices need to be involved in such communities to be effective or have impact?

In our experience, the make-up of communities of practice can vary enormously from one to another, involving a range of those employed by a HEI (such as academic, professional service, student union staff); those affiliated to a provider (such as service users, employers, community) or those benefiting from higher education (prospective students, students and/or alumni).

Furthermore, within any one HEI there may be several communities of practice in operation. These may exist within one programme, department, service, faculty or campus or across several. Work in the UK such as Gibbs (2010, 2012) has done much to promote collaboration and community at the programme level. If we argue that communities are best formed by those within the community rather than imposed then questioning who they actually involve or invite to join are crucial questions. A key issue therefore is one of how communities of practice seek to widen the membership of the group to ensure they have input from a range of stakeholder groups and enable equity of access and opportunity.

In 2012, the HEA formed two communities of practice on internationalisation, one focusing on internationalising the curriculum and the other on transnational education; with a specific remit to consider how they could widen engagement in that particular theme. Originally set up as special interest groups and later named research and practice networks, they were convened by one or more individual(s) from the sector selected through a competitive tendering process. The two incorporated a collective membership of over 300 staff of those working in the UK and transnationally. The convenors and members determined their terms of reference, the location and frequency of meetings and define their goal or purpose. The HEA offered support, in the form of funding, resources, administration, and so on, to enable the community to interact. Typically the community met face to face 3 times per year, as well as virtually through a group email list. Both communities identified a number of sub-themes or areas, and tasked particular members to lead the work on behalf of the community. Not all members could attend each meeting, nor get involved in generating the joint product, but membership continued to grow during period of funding and individuals talked of their commitment to enabling the wider engagement of others. Their name change was significant in recognising this remit and goal.

Over the course of 2 years, both communities worked on joint products. The transnational community created a digest of practice, structured around 6 key areas of operation. It provides advice and examples pooled from different sources. The curriculum community applied an enquiry methodology to reflect on and examine their practice and created a series of posters, which were the focus of a conference for the wider community. The outputs were also aligned to the HEA's development of a national framework (discussed in detail later) centralising notions of community, globalisation, inclusivity and collaboration. Whilst these communities did not directly address issues of inequity of access, they did go beyond being a community with a common interest. It was their goal or outcome towards which the community's efforts were directed that was significant to addressing the issue of widening those engaged in the community.

4.3.6 Who Benefits from Communities of Practice?

As discussed earlier in this chapter, communities of practice vary considerably in their membership and the outcomes and beneficiaries of the group can extend beyond those who are members of the group. For the purposes of this chapter, the key beneficiaries have been categorised as follows:

- Students
- Staff
- Institution
- Wider community/society.

4.3.6.1 Students

Most communities of practice in HE would acknowledge that their work benefits students in so far as the work of the community is directed towards the enhancement of the student learning experience. Indeed many would recognize this as the core purpose of the group. There is strong evidence also that a student's engagement in a community of practice has inherent value both to them as an individual but also to the student learning experience more broadly. It is advised that enabling students to engage in global academic communities provides the opportunity for them to make and contribute to international connections and networks, ultimately enriching the learning process (HEA 2014). Recognising the benefit to learning is not a new one; Lave and Wenger (1991) argued that social interaction and participation in communities of practice facilitates learning. In other work, it has been shown that being 'part of' a community can have positive repercussions on student success. One of the key findings of the *'What Works? Student Retention and Success Programme'* was that student engagement and a sense of belonging are critical factors in enabling students' progression, retention and attainment on a programme (Thomas 2012). What this serves to illustrate is that a student's engagement in an internationalisation focused community of practice could have wider repercussions beyond the theme itself. If communities of practice help to foster learning, engagement and sense of belonging, might their involvement also impact upon their progression, retention and attainment in HE?

Considering the issue of the wider benefit to the student learning experience, there has been a move globally to ensure the students' voice is represented and heard across the institution. Engaging students as part of the communities in which decisions are made or quality is assured or enhanced is now highly regarded, and increasingly common, practice. Students can help ensure decisions are authentic and valid as well as play a significant role as change agents, benefiting the wider student population now and in the future.

In summary, students can gain from both the process and the products of communities of practice. This is of benefit to the individuals directly involved in those communities, facilitating their own learning and development associated with internationalisation but also potentially impacting upon their retention and success. There may be associated benefits to the student community at large, as the products and learning may help impact upon their life in and beyond HE.

4.3.6.2   Staff

Whilst there are student led communities emerging in the UK, facilitated nationally or locally, communities of practice are more commonly instigated by staff and comprised of staff members. By way of illustration, the two HEA internationalization communities of practice, discussed above, with a collective membership of 300 members, were led by staff, convened by staff and included around 10 student members. When considering the benefits, it is our experience from working with communities of practice locally and nationally, that unless staff regard the community to have inherent value, to them as an individual or to a common good (where, for example, internationalisation is part of their role), they will not commit on an ongoing basis. Staff report having to juggle busy schedules and workloads and manage conflicting priorities and commitments. They also report different motivations for participating. There is value for some in the process of interaction, reflection, sharing and celebrating with others, whilst others are more motivated by the co-created product, towards which the community's efforts are directed.

In the Internationalising HE Framework (2014), the HEA argues that being part of global communities helps to 'enhance the occurrence, relevance and impact of the process and products of international alliances, providing potential sources of evidence to support achievement and progression in teaching and research'. This recognises both the value of being part of global communities and the personal benefit to staff in terms of their research, development, reward, recognition and/or promotion. Increasingly research tenders require and value global alliances and connections, which membership of communities of practice can provide.

4.3.6.3   Institution

An institution can benefit from communities of practice in multiple ways. In the Internationalising HE Framework, the HEA (2014) states that global communities benefit organizations by providing the opportunity for them to 'learn from and contribute to global expertise to maintain credibility and currency in learning, teaching and research, assisting academic advancement and sustainability'. With the current state of flux and rate of change in HE, it is more important than ever that institutions remain current and credible, helping them remain in good standing to secure their future. It could be advantageous in a competitive market place to be able to use engagement in communities of practice as evidence of an institution's willingness to listen and learn from other contexts. Dissemination of the existence and work of the community can help contribute to their reputation, where members are (or seek to be) involved from across the world.

4.3.6.4 Wider Communities or Societies

Many UK HE institutions reach out into their local communities and go to great lengths to make an effective contribution to society at large. They have a strong sense of corporate social responsibility, which is exercised not just to their students and their employees, but also to education, the economy, the environment and society. This is evident in numerous services and aspects of institutional operation, including within the formal and co-curricula, their strategies for knowledge exchange, sustainability and widening participation, as well as their partnerships with industry and service users. When the internationalizing HE Framework HEA (2014) was first conceived, it was driven by strong values and sense of collective responsibility. It also aspired to address inequality and injustice experienced by many people worldwide, hence the inclusion of embedding social responsibility as key strand. Furthermore, its overarching purpose was defined as 'preparing 21st century graduates to live in and contribute responsibly to a globally interconnected society'; thus recognizing that significant role that internationalization and HE can play in benefiting society in the UK and across the world.

4.4 Strategic Considerations

Thus far, we have argued that the most effective communities of practice are owned and developed from grass roots level, where the benefits are integral to all community members and associated with its defined purpose. In this section we highlight the central role of strategy (both locally and nationally) in ensuring that communities of practice, relating to internationalisation, are as effective as possible and are sustained over time. We argue that strategy can play a vital role in legitimising, resourcing and recognising the work of a community of practice, elements which are essential to its impact and survival. Importantly though, we are not arguing for strategy to play a role in mandating or imposing communities of practice on staff and/or students.

4.4.1 Local Strategy

Most institutions within the UK have a number of strategies or plans in operation, which typically relate to the overall corporate strategy. Many have a specific international or internationalisation strategy that may work in conjunction with other strategies such as the learning, teaching, assessment, employability or recruitment. This was identified in a survey of UK Pro-Vice Chancellors (2013) led by the HEA on the theme of internationalisation. They were asked whether their institution had a distinct strategy for internationalisation and, if so, what they prioritised within them. Of the 43 institutional responses (26 % of UK institutions),

64 % (27) had an internationalisation strategy and a further 11 % (5) addressed internationalisation as a specific subsection within other strategies. Amongst those with a distinct internationalisation strategy, institutional need was clearly prioritised (raising reputation and international recruitment); with aspects of the student learning experience prioritised within the strategy less so. A number of PVCs also referred to the priority of global partnerships and networking, and the role it played in enhancing research, transnational education and/or the student experience. In the following quote, identifying the strategy's key priorities, the respondent highlights the multiple levels of partnership and the benefit of doing so:

> To enhance our ability to engage with individuals, organisations and societies around the world in meeting the challenges of the 21st century through education.

The link between internationalisation and strategy is not a new one. Krause et al. (2005) developed a framework of internationalisation indicators, which included five dimensions: strategic, teaching and learning, student, faculty and research. In a blog, entitled 'Internationalisation strategy: supporting all aspects of HE strategy?' following the **European Association for International Education** conference in 2011, van Gaalen and Becker (2011) argue that 'international linkages at the policy level are necessary to solve higher education problems'. In 2009, Maringe conducted a study into the strategies and challenges of internationalisation in HE, involving a range of UK providers, and concluded that there was a need for better integration of internationalisation into policy at all levels of the institution.

The need for better integration into policy is not unique to internationalisation. Indeed a number of areas of academic practice, including education for sustainable development, employability, retention and success and inclusion require such consideration. Each of these areas have implications for the operations within and across the whole institution, affecting the collective aspects of operation such as policy, systems and processes as well as the individual aspects such as beliefs, behaviours, approaches or attitudes. Thus, they need to be embedded into all constituent parts of the organisation. This was highlighted in a research study (May and Bridger 2010), investigating how ten UK providers went about developing and embedding inclusion across the institution. All of them found it necessary to prompt change at the level of the institution (policy) as well as the individual (practice) in order to maximise the impact and sustainability of their work. Policy and practice was argued to operate as 'two sides of the same coin' (p. 36) since 'attention to one requires attention to the other and changing one has implications for the other.' (p. 98). Encouraging staff to operate differently or engage in new initiatives without the substantiation or validation of a strategy can lead to resistance, and equally having a strategy without the buy in or engagement of staff can be ineffectual. One participant in the May and Bridger research stated:

> It is very difficult to make change if all the attitudes, behaviours and systems are against you, so I think it is very difficult to do one without the other. (p. 36)

Such barriers to change were exemplified in comments raised by delegates in a national conference organised by two communities of practice in the UK on internationalisation of the curriculum and transnational education on behalf of the HEA in 2014. Institutional systems and rules of engagement were reported to act as barriers to staff working internationally. There were reports that staff had trouble getting their institutions to value and reward their work transnationally. Barriers such as these can impede internationalisation, where institutional processes and systems are out of sync with what is happening 'on the ground'; even in cases where the institutional strategy may endorse such practice. A holistic consideration of the whole institution's operation is thus important and encouraging and facilitating communities of practice, whether across the organisation as a whole, within faculties and departments or as we have previously promoted (Keay et al. 2014) in relation to developing international partnerships.

In order to operate smoothly and efficiently and have impact and sustainability, communities of practice require resourcing. The investment of time is part of this resource issue, as alluded to earlier, but there is also a financial investment, for example, in terms of travel, technology and subsistence, to enable the community to meet physically or virtually. Where communities of practice operate across departments, services, institutions or even national boundaries, there may be further resource implications. Interestingly, when the HEA was no longer able to resource two national communities of practice in internationalisation, they ceased to exist. The resource investment provided a nominal sum as an honorarium to recognise the work of those who convened the communities and a further grant mandating an output to engage the wider HE population in the theme. Each community met physically and virtually at regular intervals throughout the duration of the funding. Individual members invested time and money in the community; needing to justify their involvement to their own institution. HEA funding was certainly not sufficient to pay for members' travel or time, but nevertheless the existence of such resource was clearly significant. The endorsement of communities of practice within strategy can certainly help warrant the investment of resource by individual institutions.

4.4.2 National Strategy

In an earlier section, the development of the HEA's framework (2014) was noted as an example of a community of practice. Now in this section, we consider the role it has played in promoting a national approach to internationalisation and in promoting the principles and practice of communities of practice. Following its publication, the framework has been distributed to all HEIs in the UK and the HEA has since commenced a year-long enhancement programme involving 13 providers to help them apply the framework across the whole institution or department.

Integral to the HEA's framework is the promotion of collegial and collaborative approaches to education, research and partnership that transcend local, national and international boundaries. It recognises and promotes interaction between people for the benefit of education. As an underpinning principle, collaboration is evident in the aspirations and objectives of the framework, in the key strands, knowledge and values being promoted as well as in the roles and responsibilities for their implementation. The framework aspires to enhanced connection between the three principal audiences: people, organisations and curriculum.

The experts who produced the framework, selected for their contribution to knowledge in this area, raised the strategic importance of collegial and collaborative approaches and community in internationalisation throughout. Before the group met for a two-day summit, the HEA asked individuals to define the purpose of internationalisation in HE. A strong theme emerged around the importance of global interconnections, relationships and partnerships but also one about enabling effective working between cultures and nations. During the summit, the group were tasked to devise a set of mutually exclusive categories, which define and characterise the practice of internationalisation; these later became the areas of focus at the core of the framework. The two of significance in the context of this chapter are global academic community and intercultural engagement (HEA 2014). Coupled with other stands covering the embedding of an inclusive ethos and social responsibility, it can be recognised that notions of community and collaboration are centrally addressed within the framework. Arguably, therefore, it can play a key role in helping establish communities of practice on a national agenda for internationalisation.

It is too early to determine the impact of such a strategy on the development of communities of practice or on UK higher education more broadly. However, what is known is that there was significant support for collegial and collaborative ways of working and the strand of facilitating global academic communities amongst those who responded to the consultation on the framework. Furthermore, 91 % of responses considered a framework of this nature was needed for the UK. Institutions will apply it in different ways; indeed this was recognised in how it was conceived in its design. It was developed to be used as a tool for self-reflection, communication, professional development, curriculum review and/or planning.

It is also known, through reports to the HEA and through those working on the enhancement programme, that some HEIs have reported an intention to integrate the framework within institutional strategy and adopt it in full, whereas others report using it to help shape particular aspects of their work. It would certainly be interesting to establish whether it helps endorse and promote the impact of local activity.

4.4.3   Global Communities of Practice

Global communities involving staff and/or students across different national boundaries are beginning to be recognised to be of inherent value. For example, the European Union's funding opportunities require a collaborative approach between organisations and many of the research funding opportunities, for example the Horizon 2020 and the Seventh Framework Programme (http://www.welcomeurope.com/horizon2020.html) and curriculum development programmes such as Erasmus

Plus   (http://ec.europa.eu/programmes/erasmus-plus/documents/erasmus-plus-programme-guide_en.pdf), begin as functional operating groups and become communities of practice. Other examples demonstrate where interest groups form communities of practice, two such examples have been formed between institutions in the UK and Australia. The first one was a group that emerged from bench-marking work undertaken in relation to promoting teaching by academics in four institutions in the UK and Australia (Wills et al. 2013). The HEA sponsored the work, but did not drive the outcomes and development of the group who, if we apply the characteristics to their work certainly emerged as a community of prac-tice.The learning outcomes were relevant to both countries and products have been used in change programmes within both the UK and Australia. However, one of the unanticipated outcomes of this community of practice was the extension of the relationships between one of the institutions and a different HEI to use the benchmarking process used in the first project to explore internationalisation in both institutions and this has also enabled development between specific areas in both contexts Booth et al. (2014).

   In summary, in this section, we have argued that strategic endorsement of communities of practice or their underpinning principles such as collaboration, inclusion and partnership can play a crucial role in maximising their impact and sustainability. It can help others to see that the potential (or actual) work/time invested is worthwhile or secure the investment required to ensure they are effec-tive. It can help ensure that the work of the community goes beyond being ad hoc and localised to being embedded within institution as part of the norm. Explicit promotion of communities within institutional strategies alone is not enough however. Internationalisation more broadly and specifically communities of prac-tice have ramifications for institutional systems and processes. Effort needs to be made to embed internationalisation into all aspects of institutional operations, as the HEA Framework (2014) and others (such as Maringe 2009) promote. A holistic approach is needed, looking at the culture of the organisation. As we discussed earlier working collegially and collaboratively within communities of practice can have multiple strategic benefits for different audiences. The existence of national agendas or endorsement can play a big role in framing, promoting or communi-cating communities of practice.

4.5   Issues and Opportunities

In the final sections of this chapter we summarise and discuss the issues we have raised concerning the relationship between communities of practice and interna-tionalisation agendas and propose opportunities that can be found through such a relationship. We have adopted a broad definition of internationalisation, recognis-ing the relationship between the qualitative aspects of culture and experience and the quantitative aspects of brand, recruitment and finance. For example, recruitment contributes to the culture of an organisation through the influences of having students from a number of different countries on home campuses and working overseas within TNE partnerships offers development opportunities for both those students and staff involved in the programmes. Inevitably, the sections below overlap as issues can also offer opportunities.

4.5.1 Issues

For those within an existing community of practice or planning to develop one, one issue worthy of consideration is how its work aligns with the strategy of the institution, its policy, mission, values or plans, as well as with national strategy. This can be important to demonstrate when seeking to convince others of the value or impact of the community. Another related issue is whether there are any policies, procedures or systems that adversely impact upon the work of any planned or existing community of practice. Making a case for changing these to enable and facilitate the work of the community and drawing out any misalignments between strategy and practice is vital. To support the development of communities of practice and overcome organisational barriers relating to internationalisation requires focus on three aspects of the context by those holding senior management positions:

- *Culture*: encourage the development of relevant communities of practice and ensure that there is an expectation that such groups are a strategically important part of the organisation;
- *Strategy*: ensure that there is clarity about the direction of travel and institutional expectations about internationalisation outcomes;
- *Structure*: ensure that there is sufficient investment in the policies, processes and practices to enable communities of practice to function efficiently and enable representation from a range of stakeholder groups.

The formation of communities of practice requires careful consideration of the purpose and the specific context and stage of development of internationalisation within the organisation. Who forms a community of practice and for what purpose are issues that require consideration? If the formation is organic, does the community have a focus that will meet the HEI's needs? But if its formation and development is contrived by the organisation will this detract from the potentially positive outcomes noted in communities that are organically formed? Communities of practice can used to develop a passion or can bring people together because participants share a passion; the issue here is whether both can lead to improved practice as an outcome or will the first one just lead to increased interest and concern but no impact?

If the process of learning is the main purpose of a community of practice can this form of group really be useful in addressing internationalisation agendas? As suggested at the beginning of this section, issues can also be opportunities; given the nature of internationalisation agendas and associated activities there could be different outcomes from a community of practice that focuses on internationalisation. The development of collaborative working and partnerships could combat the negative elements of competition while still delivering against for example, the recruitment elements of a strategy.

Legitimate peripheral participation Lave and Wenger (1991) can have both positive and negative outcomes for a community of practice. Participants joining a community of practice are often expected to learn the behaviours and 'rules' of the group before contributing to the outcomes and developments. This process can be useful in supporting new members to learn about internationalisation in the HEI context but it can also be restricting if the leadership of the group restricts the contributions of new members and controls the outcomes. New members offer an opportunity to extend the impact of the community but if tightly controlled will restrict impact. However, new members may be required if, as we argue above, attention is given to whose voices are or need to be represented as well of providing equity of access and opportunity to all potential members. The growth in a community's size and/or scope may have an impact on its original purpose, affecting how people interact within it or how its value is perceived. If internationalisation is an issue for all, staff and students alike, then can communities of practice be one of the key activities to enable this wider engagement?

4.5.2   Opportunities

Communities of practice have the opportunity to develop, as Knight (2003) suggests, intercultural, international and inter-global dimensions through a context where learning is situated. Developing a culture that will enable this to happen will not only support internationalisation agendas but will also contribute to organisational development. Reversing Eraut's (2002) list of contextual cultures and practices, which mitigate against the development of communities of practice provides the opportunity to address some of the issues highlighted in the previous section. For example, avoiding cultures that only promote competition; ensuring that participants have time to develop; and promoting and enabling interaction between participants are not only positive ways of working within a community of practice but will also contribute to organisational development by valuing and empowering staff and students.

Using the community of practice characteristics proposed by Wenger (1998) to examine how such groups can be effective in organisational cultures that have an internationalisation agenda is an opportunity to encourage collaboration and collegiality. For example, *joint enterprise,* will ensure clarity of direction; *mutual engagement* will encourage working towards the same outcomes and has the potential to overcome the challenges of competition; and a *shared repertoire* will develop contextually appropriate practices. There is also the opportunity for a community of practice to offer the opportunity for participants to understand other perspectives, to gain information and to address the quality of the student experience. In a community of practice focusing on internationalisation other opportunities include developing links outside through members' links, for example research collaborations can develop into outward mobility and curriculum development opportunities.

4.6 Key Messages

In summary, communities of practice are of benefit to those involved. The process of mutual engagement and invention of practice, particularly between those sharing similar aspirations, approaches, and concerns, is seen as inherently beneficial; warranting members to continue to commit time and energy on an on-going basis to the group. The work of communities of practice extends far beyond the community, with the potential to have a mutually influencing effect upon the wider student and staff population as well as policy and practice at multiple levels of the institution and beyond. It is important to consider ways to extend the reach, promote equity of access and maximise the impact of any one community. Drawing from the discussion in the sections above we conclude with some key messages relating to the usefulness of communities of practice in meeting internationalisation agendas in higher education.

- Partnership, collegiality, collaboration are good things, which can be beneficial to different partners but the process of developing a community of practice requires facilitation;
- Commitment to the concept of the community of practice is essential if the opportunities are to be realised;
- Communities of practice are not homogenous and therefore can accommodate different purposes in different contexts with varied intended outcomes, they do not have to be in real time and can be virtual communities. Communities of practice, especially those developed across institutional, nations and national boundaries are not always formed locally;
- The success of a community of practice requires a clear strategy on internationalisation leading to policies, which inform processes, systems and investment. Having an external impetus, such as funding or a piece of work, can bring a new community together who may not otherwise have met;
- Despite the complexities of the HE sector and this specific focus, staff and students can benefit from interacting within communities;
- The process of co-creation is inherently useful to those within the community as well as the wider academic community.

References

Booth, S., Keay, J., Sadler, D., Duffy, T., & Klekociuk, S. (2014). Benchmarking international student experience. In I. Dobson, M. Conway & R. Sharma (Eds.), *TEMC—Refereed papers 2014 ATEM Inc. and TEFMA Inc.* ISBN 978-0-9808563-5-4.

British Council. (2015). Broadening Horizons: The value of the overseas experience. British Council, siem.britishcouncil.org. Accessed 26 June 2015.

Cox, A. M. (2005). What are communities of practice? A comparative review of four seminal works. *Journal of Information Science, 31*(6), 527–540. doi:10.1177/0165551505057016.

Daniel, B., Schwier, R., & McCalla, G. (2003). Social capital in virtual learning communities and distributed communities of practice. *Canadian Journal of Learning and Technology, 29*(3), 113–139.

Eraut, M. (2002). *Conceptual analysis and research questions: Do the concepts of 'learning community' and 'community of practice' provide added value?* New Orleans: Annual Meeting of the American Educational Research Association.

Gibbs, G. (2010). *Dimensions of quality.* York: Higher Education Academy.

Gibbs, G. (2012). *Implications of dimensions of quality in a market environment.* York: Higher Education Academy.

Hargreaves, A. (1994). *Changing teachers changing times.* London: Cassell.

Higher Education Academy. (2013). *Pro-vice chancellor survey of UK internationalisation strategies.* Unpublished.

Higher Education Academy. (2014). *Internationalising higher education framework.* York: Higher Education Academy.

International Association of Universities. (2012). *Affirming academic values in internationalization of higher education: A call for action.* Oslo: IAU.

Keay, J. (2006). 'Collaborative learning in physical education teachers' Early Career Professional Development. *Physical Education and Sport Pedagogy, 11*(3), 285–305.

Keay, J., May, H., & O'Mahony, J. (2014). Improving learning and teaching in transnational education: Can communities of practice help? *Journal of Education for Teaching: International Research and Pedagogy, 40*(3), 251–266. doi:10.1080/02607476.2014.903025.

Kimble, C., & Hildreth, P. (2004). Communities of practice: Going one step too far? *Social Science Research Network.*

Kimble, C., & Hildreth, P. (2005). Dualities, distributed communities of practice and knowledge management. *Journal of Knowledge Management, 9*(4), 102–113.

Knight, J. (2003). Updated internationalization definition. *International Higher Education, 33,* 2–3.

Krause, K., Coates, H., & James, R. (2005). Monitoring the internationalisation of higher education: Are there useful quantitative performance indicators? In M. Tight (Ed.), *International relations.* London: Emerald.

Lave, J., & Wenger, E. (1991). *Situated learning: Legitimate peripheral participation.* Cambridge: Cambridge University Press.

Maringe, F. (2009). Strategies and challenges of internationalisation in HE: An exploratory study of UK universities. *International Journal of Educational Management, 23*(7), 553–563.

May, H., & Bridger, K. (2010). *Developing and embedding inclusive policy and practice in higher education.* York: Higher Education Academy.

McDermott, R., & O'Dell, C. (2001). Overcoming cultural barriers to sharing knowledge. *Journal of Knowledge Management, 5*(1), 76–85.

O'Mahony, J. (2014). *Enhancing student learning and teacher development in transnational education.* (pp. 1–38) York: Higher Education Academy. pp. 1–38. http://www.heacademy.ac.uk/resources/detail/internationalisation/enhancingTNE

Smith, M. K. (2003, 2009) 'Jean Lave, Etienne Wenger and communities of practice. *The Encyclopaedia of Informal Education.* www.infed.org/biblio/communities_of_practice.htm

Thomas, L. (2012). *Building student engagement and belonging in higher education at a time of change: Final report from the what works? Student retention and success programme* (HEA, HEFCE, Action on Access). London: Paul Hamlyn Foundation.

Van Gaalen, A., & Becker, R (2011). Internationalisation strategy: Supporting all aspects of HE strategy?   https://www.nuffic.nl/en/news/blogs/internationalisation-strategy-supporting-all-aspects-of-he-strategy. Accessed 3 March 2015.

Wenger, E. (1998). *Communities of practice: Learning, meaning and identity.* Cambridge: Cambridge University Press.

Wenger, E. (2006). Communities of practice—A brief introduction. Accessed 23 October 2011. http://www.ewenger.com/theory/index.htm

Wenger, E., McDermott, R., & Snyder, W. M. (2002). *Cultivating communities of practice.* Boston, MA: Harvard Business School Press.

Williams, A., Prestage, S., & Bedward, J. (2001). Individualism to collaboration: The significance of teacher culture to the induction of newly qualified teachers. *Journal of Education for Teaching, 27*(3), 253–267.

Wills, S., Brown, C., Cashmore, A., Cane, C., Sadler, D., Booth, S., et al. (2013). *Promoting teaching: Making evidence count.* York: Higher Education Academy.

Chapter 5
Delivering Institutional Priorities in Learning and Teaching Through a Social Learning Model: Embedding a High Impact Community of Practice Initiative at the University of Tasmania

Kristin Warr Pedersen, Melody West, Natalie Brown, David Sadler and Kate Nash

Abstract This chapter describes the University of Tasmania's Communities of Practice Initiative (CoPI), established in 2011 by the Deputy Vice Chancellor (Students and Education). The purpose of the CoPI is to provide collaborative professional learning opportunities for staff around priority and special interest areas in learning and teaching. Importantly, the CoPI is supported with strategic funding, allocated to promote the development of emergent, evolving and broad-reaching Communities of Practice (CoP). Coordinated by the central learning and teaching unit of the University of Tasmania, the CoPI provides on-going professional development for participants to support them to establish, facilitate, disseminate and sustain their work. Since 2011, the CoPI has funded over 30 CoPs in three distinct programs. The initiative has raised the profile of learning and teaching across the institution and increased the number of staff actively participating in learning and teaching scholarship. The CoPI is recognised by staff to provide collegial learning opportunities and space to engage with colleagues from other parts of the University with similar interests. This chapter outlines the background, establishment, and on-going development of the CoPI, including the professional learning opportunities afforded to participants through the initiative. In doing so, this chapter showcases a whole-of-institution program that has delivered professional learning opportunities for individuals and groups leading to institutional change and the enhancement of the learning and teaching culture across the University of Tasmania.

Keywords Communities of practice · Institutional priorities · Peer learning · Professional learning · Recognition · Teaching fellowship · Collaboration

K.W. Pedersen (✉) · M. West · N. Brown · D. Sadler
University of Tasmania, Hobart, Australia
e-mail: Kristin.Warr@utas.edu.au

K. Nash
University of Leeds, Leeds, UK

© Springer Nature Singapore Pte Ltd. 2017
J. McDonald and A. Cater-Steel (eds.), *Communities of Practice*,
DOI 10.1007/978-981-10-2879-3_5

5.1 Introduction

Communities of practice (CoP) are increasingly being recognised in international literature as providing opportunities for organisations to promote social learning, leadership development and organisational change (Anderson and McCune 2013; Blackmore 2010; Hildreth and Kimble 2004; Wenger et al. 2002). Lave and Wenger coined the term 'community of practice' when they recognised the power and potential for informal learning experiences to enhance individual job performance, learning and job satisfaction, as well as collaboration and the sharing of good practice across an organisation (Lave and Wenger 1991). Since that time, the collaborative CoP model has been attributed to a variety of informal learning experiences that often go unrecognised by an organisation (Boud and Middleton 2003; Wenger et al. 2002). However, increased attention on the value of CoPs in enabling the sharing of practice amongst often disparate individuals have led many organisations to now support and even attempt to cultivate this method of collaborative social learning (Blessinger and Carfora 2014; Cox 2004; MacKenzie et al. 2010).

Through active collaboration and sharing experiences with colleagues from across an organisation, CoPs enable individuals to learn from, and contribute to, enhancing the practice of an organisation (Anthony et al. 2009). CoPs can harness a variety of perspectives and knowledge in ways that help organisations to identify, share and ultimately instigate a shift in organisational norms and patterns of behaviour (Wenger et al. 2002). Unlike more hierarchical forms of mentoring historically supported in workplace professional development a CoP model supports collaborative and distributed forms of peer learning and leadership. These include building peer support structures for review and improvement of individual practice; providing opportunities for the development of peer mentoring relationships; and identifying gateways to use shared understanding about key organisational issues to influence, contribute to, and lead organisational learning and change (Cox 2004; Kramer and Benson 2013; Shapiro and Levine 1999). The capacity to promote the progression of learning from individual motivation and interest through to organisational change is one of the most celebrated aspects of the CoP model but often one of the most difficult to formally cultivate (Blessinger and Carfora 2014; Crossan et al. 1999; Wenger et al. 2002). Nevertheless, the potential to foster such a learning shift from individual to group to whole-of-organisation learning is a key motivating factor for large organisations to support the social learning model intended by a CoP.

Like other large organisations recognising the potential for social learning to instigate change, higher education institutions are increasingly drawing on the CoP model to enhance collaborative engagement and learning amongst often disparate staff (Cox 2004; Hill and Haigh 2012; Ng and Pemberton 2013). Through sharing, integrating and co-developing aims, outcomes and processes, higher education institutions are leveraging the CoP model to bridge divides, create efficiencies and enhance innovation across the sector (Hildreth and Kimble 2004; Lea 2005; Shapiro and Levine 1999). Research has shown that traditionally siloed academic disciplines as well as academic and administrative functions of the university can become better connected through CoP participation (Hildreth and Kimble 2008; Pharo et al. 2014). These models have operated under a variety of names and through the support of a diversity of structures; see for instance examples of *faculty learning communities* supported across the United States (Cox and Richlin 2004) and the increase of virtual communities of practice in HE (Dubé et al. 2005). However, at the heart of all of these approaches lies the motivation to unite people for the enhancement of both individual and collective learning and practice.

While many CoPs in the higher education domain commence as organic, grass-roots initiatives, the significant impact of this approach on promoting institutional change in key learning and teaching areas has given rise to many formal CoP initiatives that are supported by strategic funding with formal recognition and support for those involved (McDonald and Palani 2011; McDonald et al. 2012; Shapiro and Levine 1999). This chapter will outline the background and evolution of one such whole-of-institution program, the University of Tasmania's Communities of Practice Initiative (CoPI). The initiative is delivered through three centrally funded programs that cater to the development and continued cultivation of small to large CoPs. We will describe the categories under which CoPs are identified through the initiative, the funding allocated to each stage of CoP development and the opportunities for on-going professional learning provided for CoP members. We will outline the establishment and continued evolution of this initiative, followed by a discussion of the outcomes and impact of four years of implementation. We will also outline ways in which participation in this whole-of-institution initiative has been embedded in formal recognition processes at the University of Tasmania to ensure staff understand, and are rewarded for, the positive contributions CoP participation makes to the institution as well as their own individual career goals.

5.2 Institutional Context

The University of Tasmania is a medium sized, multi-campus higher education provider with five national and two international campuses. Like most other Australian institutions, an institution-wide *Strategic Plan for Learning and Teaching* (University of Tasmania 2012a) outlines the vision and priority areas the University of Tasmania intends to deliver on. While the plan is centrally proposed and endorsed by the representative University Learning and Teaching Committee, the implementation of that plan through learning and teaching initiatives and programs must occur across the full range of academic disciplines, programs, courses, administrative units and individual classrooms.

With over 5900 staff (including academic, professional, permanent and casual staff) and 33,000 students, the delivery of the University of Tasmania's learning and teaching goals faces many of the challenges widely documented in the literature including: siloed disciplines; providing equity in multi-campus delivery; provision of quality student experience for both on-shore and off-shore student cohorts; and casualisation of the work force (Gaither 1999; Pharo et al. 2014; O'Mahony 2014; Brown et al. 2010). The CoPI was proposed as an attempt to invigorate collaboration across the institution around shared priority areas in learning and teaching. Recognising that a CoP model can provide enhanced collaborative learning opportunities, offering benefits for the collective as well as for the individuals involved (MacKenzie et al. 2010; Wenger et al. 2002; Wenger 2006), the CoPI aims to employ this model in ways that identify and empower collaborative engagement with shared institutional priorities. In doing so, the CoPI is designed to bring together individuals and initiatives that are often working in isolation across the institution to address shared challenges. The overarching objective of the program is to empower individuals to contribute to the delivery of strategic initiatives through collaboration, integration and recognition.

5.3 Theoretical Underpinnings of Design

The design of the CoPI is largely inspired by the work of (Etienne Wenger 1998, 2002, 2006). The CoPI uses (Wenger et al. 2002) description of a CoP as a 'group of people who share a concern, a set of problems, or a passion about a topic, and who deepen their knowledge and expertise in this area by interacting' (p.4). Recognising the importance of informal learning communities in the creation and sharing of knowledge in an organisation (Lave and Wenger 1991), the CoPI is designed to foster informal learning in ways that can drive strategic change in an institution. Using the foundational characteristics of a CoP as identified by Wenger (2006), all funded CoPs in the program are required to identify their (1) shared *domain*; (2) accepted method of interaction to identify the ways in which they work as a *community*; and (3) shared *practice* and how it contributes to the learning and performance of the group as a whole and of each of the individuals involved. Taken together, these three foundational characteristics are the building blocks for establishing engagement between often dispersed staff at the institution. By bringing together individuals to work on shared areas of interest in an agreed upon way, with a clear set of advantages for the individuals involved, the CoPI outlines a method through which the institution can communicate with a broad range of staff on key learning and teaching priorities. Building on Wenger's foundational characteristics of a CoP, the Swiss Agency for Development and Cooperation (2009) outlined an additional three characteristics (*motivation, structure* and *mandate*) that have also been utilised in the design of the CoPI, particularly relating to the two upper streams (Fig. 5.1). The additional attention given to motivation, structure and mandate for CoP participation has helped to recognise how small learning communities can best participate in, and often lead broader institutional initiatives.

Motivation to participate in a CoP is often driven by individual interest, which is outlined in Wenger's attention to a shared domain area that builds bridges between the practices of individuals in a community. However, as a centrally driven

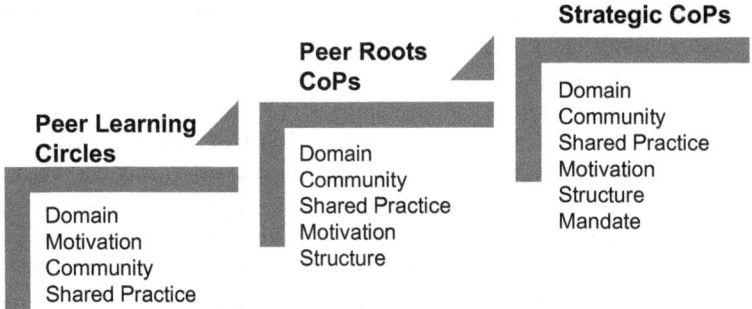

Fig. 5.1 The three funding streams of the CoPI and the theoretical design elements of each as they relate to Wenger (2006) and the Swiss Agency for Development and Cooperation (2009)

initiative, the CoPI also links to job performance measures of the individual, school, faculty, discipline and/or institution. As such, the CoPI provides a dual motivation for staff to participate in a CoP. The structure of the CoPI provides space for individual CoPs to utilise both formal and informal structures to manage their collaboration. However the central organisation, reporting requirements and professional development opportunities provided to CoPI participants offer a shared framework for CoPs to benchmark their work across the institution. This mix of freedom to operate with an expectation to report and engage with others allows both formal and informal structures to emerge from each of the CoPs. In particular, the initiative provides opportunities for staff enthusiasm around key interest areas (often informal) to contribute to, and even drive, strategic initiatives (formal). With three tiers of the CoPI, there is scope for individuals and groups to develop through a more informal, interest driven structure towards a broader, whole-of-institution formal structure once their work is embedded in institutional practice or culture. While participation in the CoPI is not mandated, institutional support of the CoPI is validated by the recent inclusion of CoPI participation as a creditable part of the Teaching Performance Expectations that staff are assessed against in annual performance management (University of Tasmania 2014a). Such recognition of the potential for collegial engagement to positively contribute to career performance highlights the extent to which the CoPI is seen to enhance strategic visions for the enhancement of learning and teaching. Through formal recognition that CoP participation can make valuable contributions to individual job performance and strategic visions in learning and teaching, the institution helps to guarantee engagement and sustainability of the initiative, despite its non-mandated status.

CoPI participants are encouraged to engage with the University of Tasmania Peer Learning Framework (Skalicky and Brown 2009), which provides a planning tool to assist CoP participants to plan the establishment, support and evaluation of their shared practice. This tool is built around Wenger's three foundational characteristics of a CoP, and emphasises the collaborative and horizontal peer learning opportunities of the CoP model. The tool also aims to assist CoPs to become self-sustaining and grow their impact through broader engagement with the university community. While Boud and Middleton (2003) have noted the CoP model in a large organisation often provides more benefit and opportunities to staff in senior positions, the CoPI is designed to be developmental for both individuals and groups and it supports the progression of individual and group learning and leadership across all levels of the institution. The CoPI recognises that passion drives practice for staff from early career through to senior levels, and passion can motivate horizontal and vertical collaboration. In a higher education environment that increasingly relies on a casual workforce and blended professionals who blur the line between academic and professional roles (Whitechurch 2008) it is increasingly important to provide opportunities for early career staff to develop productive and collegial working relationships across traditional boundaries (Szekeres 2011). This has been recognised as critical to guaranteeing job satisfaction, sharing and transferring institutional knowledge and providing support for career progression (Ponjuan et al. 2011). The CoPI employs a peer learning approach to attempt to distribute leadership and mentoring roles across a group of learners by bringing together staff (and in some cases students) from a variety of positions in the institutional hierarchy. There is no preference for senior positions and there are no identified leadership roles in a CoP. CoP 'leaders' are designated as contact points for funding agreements and central communication with each CoP; however, a non-hierarchical structure is required to define the community itself. Even the TILT Teaching Fellowship (described below) is targeted to academic staff from early career to senior positions. In many ways the CoPI preferences opportunities for early career and professional staff to engage, recognising the important ways CoP participation can orientate staff to the learning and teaching culture of the institution, particularly through fostering cross-departmental connections that may be otherwise difficult for individuals to initiate on their own (Whitechurch 2008; Pifer and Baker 2013).

Wenger et al.'s (2002) definition of a CoP also notes that 'over time, [CoPs] develop a unique perspective on their topic as well as a body of common knowledge, practices, and approaches. They also develop personal relationships and established ways of interacting' (p. 5). It is this aspect of a CoP that has inspired both the design and the strategic institutional support for the initiative. An overarching aim of the CoPI is to promote the progression of learning from individual passion to peer interpretation and integration of practice, eventually to organisational learning and change (Crossan et al. 1999). In line with Lave and Wenger's (1991) early work identifying CoPs as a recognition of informal learning in the workplace, the more organic format of two of the streams of the CoPI recognises and attempts to support the informal learning initiatives that crop up and inspire individuals to collaborate, sometimes in unlikely or unrecognised places. A third stream is more formally aligned with a teaching fellow and identified strategic priority of the institution, but still allows for organic development and individual inspirations to guide the work of each CoP. Through the CoPI, the University of Tasmania recognises and supports cultural change and the enhancement of learning and teaching as identified in the innovations, passions and good practice of its staff and students from across the institution. The CoPI is our attempt to ensure that passion and motivation are both recognised and encouraged through the promotion of peer learning opportunities.

5.4   Establishment and Leadership

The University of Tasmania's CoPI was established in 2011 by the incoming Deputy Vice Chancellor (Students and Education) (author Sadler). The purpose of the CoPI was to provide collaborative professional learning opportunities for staff around priority and special interest areas in learning and teaching, in order to empower institutional change and organisational learning. Specifically, a CoP model was sought to guide the initiative in a way that would ensure staff were supported to collaborate across traditionally disparate areas of the University (both academic and administrative) and to promote cross-institutional progress in strategic learning and teaching challenges. Those challenges included enhancing the overall student experience for an increasingly diverse student cohort; ensuring quality curriculum design and delivery that responded to industry and community needs; promoting quality teaching and professional learning in a fast changing academic environment and providing a space for staff across distributed campuses to work collaboratively and distribute leadership of specific CoPs across geographical and disciplinary boundaries.

Strategic funding totalling $102,000 from the DVC (S&E) was provided to the CoPI in its inaugural year (2012). To ensure opportunities for the development of emergent, evolving and broad-reaching CoPs, the funding was divided between strategic, commissioned initiatives that would be determined annually by the DVC (S&E), and a small scale grant program that would provide opportunities for staff to propose focus areas for CoP development (Table 5.1). CoPI funding is tiered in a way that enables small, start-up CoPs to develop over time and apply for funding in other CoP categories or other teaching development grant funding to further progress their work. The CoPI funding scheme also included designated money to provide professional development opportunities for CoP participants, dissemination activities and programs for the future development of the initiative. The latter allocation of funding was intended to ensure the impact of the CoPI would be sustainable and extend to the broader UTAS community to create institutional learning and change.

The design and leadership of the CoPI has been coordinated by the central learning and teaching unit of the institution, the Tasmanian Institute of Learning and Teaching (TILT). TILT provides professional learning support to staff in all areas of learning and teaching with a particular focus on the delivery of peer learning programs. Using a peer learning model that includes a variety of approaches to peer-led professional development, TILT staff support peer mentoring, review and observation activities for programs across the learning and

Table 5.1 CoPI funding streams and number of CoPs funded under each stream between 2012 and 2015

	2012		2013		2014		2015	
	Number funded	Total funds allocated	Number funded	Total funds allocated	Number funded	Total funds allocated	Number funded	Total funds allocated
Peer learning circles	Program initiated in 2014				9	$4500	5	$2500
Grass roots CoPs	4	$11,061	4	$11,342	2	$5127	4	$11,722
Strategic CoPs	2	$70,000	1	$35,000	4	$41,000	1	$8000

teaching domain. TILT staff from the 'Recognition and Professional Learning' area established the design of the CoPI and continue to support the initiative today. This section of TILT is responsible for the design and delivery of a number of successful peer-led professional learning programs that focus on the enhancement of learning and teaching practice and recognition through grants, CoPs and formal awards. The staff focused on delivering the CoPI have included two part-time academic staff members (authors Warr Pedersen and West) and one full-time administrative staff member. The location of the CoPI within this team portfolio enables the considered support of CoP development across a number of professional learning and recognition schemes. Warr Pedersen and West are also responsible for supporting staff in the development of teaching awards and projects, including internal and national grants, allowing them to assist CoP participants in development, recognition and funding of their work. The section below titled 'Professional Learning and Support for the CoPI' outlines the variety of ways the CoPI is integrated into other TILT professional learning activities.

5.5 Design of the CoPI: A Tiered Structure

5.5.1 Strategic Priority Community of Practice Program

The largest pool of funding for the CoPI is allocated to the Strategic Priority Fellowship/CoP Program (up to $70,000). As the strategic CoPs are based on key areas of the institution's Learning and Teaching plan, getting buy-in from most areas of the institution has not been difficult, because the outcomes of the fellowship and supporting CoP help to support individuals, schools and programs achieve their own goals. To date eight Strategic CoPs have been funded and have focused on Education for Sustainability (2011); Internationalisation (2012); Peer Mentoring (2013); Student Engagement and the Student Experience (two CoPs funded in 2014); Breadth Units (2014); Quality Assurance (2014) and Peer Review for Quality Assurance (2015).

There are up to two Strategic CoPs funded annually (except in 2014 where funding was split between four CoPs), which are attached to a TILT Teaching Fellowship. The DVC (S&E) annually determines two strategic priority areas under which TILT Teaching Fellowships are offered on a competitive basis. A key criterion for the assessment of applications is the extent to which the applicant can justify their capacity to initiate, recruit and support the establishment of a large, cross-institutional CoP in their strategic focus area. This model of CoP activation and initial facilitation through a dedicated TILT fellow is based on the successful work of one of author Warr Pedersen's previous national Australian Learning and Teaching Council projects on building interdisciplinary teaching teams at four Australian institutions through a supported CoP model (Davison et al. 2012; See Chap. 16). In this model a dedicated person with knowledge and experience in the scholarship of the domain area identifies, recruits and supports the inclusion of CoP membership. This person is then supported by others in TILT to facilitate inter- actions of the CoP and to build collaborative will between members. With a ded- icated fellow to embed a scholarly approach in the work of the CoP, the role continues to enrich CoP interactions and practice. Fellows identify, develop and disseminate resources for the group to consider and use, and inspire collaborative engagement with scholarly literature in the domain area of the CoP. The relation- ship between the fellow and the CoP then becomes mutually beneficial as the fellow contributes to the facilitation and enrichment of the CoP and the CoP contributes to the peer review, engagement and dissemination of the fellow's scholarly work.

The rationale for linking large CoP establishment to the work of a teaching fellow comes from over a decade of lessons in the dissemination of fellowship work at the University of Tasmania. Following an assessment of the impact of previous University of Tasmania teaching fellowships, it was determined that the most broad-reaching impact occurred when the work was widely disseminated through active engagement with a CoP throughout the time of the fellowship. Similar observations have been made in research conducted in the UK (Jones 2010), and have led to enhancing the work of fellows through the collaborative CoP model. The UK focus has been on promoting excellence in teaching by ensuring teachers awarded for good practice through formal recognition pathways are supported to disseminate their work through a combined fellowship/CoP approach. While the CoPI does not exclude previously recognised teachers from the fellowship program, the TILT Teaching Fellowship is intended to support the professional development of staff regardless of whether they have been previously recognised for their good practice in a given area. The Strategic CoP Fellowship is thus driven by individual motivation and passion for a subject, and as a result previously recognised teachers are neither excluded nor preferenced in the initiative.

Prior to the establishment of the CoPI, this CoP/Fellowship model had been most successfully used in the University of Tasmania Assessment Fellowships (2006) and the institution-wide, Criterion Based Assessment project (2006–2009). The appointment of Assessment Fellows from each faculty in 2006 was in response to the need for a review, and subsequent transformation, of assessment practice at the university. The six fellows, many of them early career academics at the time, worked together to pave the way for approval of a criterion-referenced assessment (CRA) system across the institution. Through sharing their collective experiences the fellows came to understand the power of a CoP to enable professional learning, professional support and the ability to shape change. This was highly influential in the design of the CRA implementation plan and subsequent projects for institution-wide rollout of this plan. A centrepiece of the plan was the establishment of a network of 34 School Champions who connected the central implementation team with individual school contexts. The champions themselves were supported through a CoP, which facilitated their induction into learning and teaching leadership. The initiative adopted an approach to change management that com- bined a corporate (top down, policy driven) imperative with a shared values approach developed through the CoP. The resulting impact went beyond assessment change, building leadership capacity of staff and increasing scholarly publications of academics through supported opportunities for action research (Cordiner and Brown 2009).

In evaluating the assessment initiative it was recognised that the work of the fellows was greatly enhanced in terms of outcomes in comparison to what had been achieved previously by individual fellows working on specific projects, even when those projects had institution-wide relevance. Moreover, utilising a broader CoP in fellowship work consisting of both appointed representatives and those staff who became involved voluntarily had particular value in embedding and sustaining the change.

Like the highly successful assessment initiative, the Strategic CoP Fellowship scheme is dedicated to providing peer leadership development opportunities for staff who are passionate about areas of strategic interest to the University. An important aspect of the Strategic CoP Fellowship scheme is found in the secondment of the incumbent fellow into TILT during the life of the fellowship. This relocation better supports the fellow to initiate an institution-wide CoP through a more centralised position than would be allowed by their substantive disciplinary role. Because the Strategic CoPs are based around institutional priority areas, the work is supported by TILT with the fellowship and the CoP both being integrated into, and supported by, the work of the entire TILT team. This centralised support enables the work of the CoP to become better embedded in the work of TILT, sustaining the work of the CoP and the fellowship well beyond the funding year.

5.5.2 Grass Roots Communities of Practice Program

A small CoP grant program is delivered through the allocation of Grass Roots Communities of Practice grants (GRCoP) that are funded under a broader Teaching Development Scheme offered annually by the DVC (S&E). These small grants award up to 4 CoPs per year to the amount of up to $3000 each. The aim of this program is to provide staff from across the institution the opportunity to propose the establishment of a new CoP, or to support the on-going development of an existent CoP in an area of special interest to the participants. Because these grants are funded under a broader teaching development grant scheme, CoPs seeking funding through this outlet have number of requirements to fulfil, which as a result, guide the structure of activities of the CoP in the funding year. All GRCoPs must:

- devise and undertake a significant practice-based or scholarship activity that will advance learning and teaching at the University of Tasmania and/or nationally;
- produce a deliverable or output with broad applicability and/or enhancing scholarship in the field of learning and teaching;
- disseminate their outcomes widely; and
- benefit the University's Strategic Plan, Learning and Teaching Plan and/or other strategic institutional/national priorities (University of Tasmania 2014b).

When applying for funding for a GRCoP, applicants must outline how they will achieve these program objectives in addition to identifying the domain area that their CoP will focus on and an initial method of interaction that will be used to mobilise the group. GRCoP grant applicants must also identify a set of enhanced practices that are likely to result from their collaboration, with final identification and reflection on the interaction and impact of CoP practices discussed in final reporting and dissemination events at the conclusion of the funding year.

While the GRCoP grant scheme is designed to allow for organic development of a CoP, the reporting requirements of the funding program provide a semi-structured framework to guide that development. The structure is intended to assist CoPs in growing their shared practice, and to ensure that practice continues to provide professional learning opportunities that benefit the individuals involved as well as the context of their specific domain area (Stuckey and Smith 2004; Wenger et al. 2002). This structure moves GRCoPs away from being identified as informal learning experiences and instead recognises the work of CoPs as strong contributors to institutional change.

Importantly, GRCoP grants are open to any staff member, academic or professional. The scheme also accepts a broad definition of 'learning and teaching' to ensure the inclusion of a myriad of initiatives and ideas. While GRCoP grants are required to benefit institutional priorities, the interpretation of that benefit can translate across the spectrum from whole-of-institution down to a very specific issue identified in a classroom. The number of participants in a GRCoP is not mandated, however it is a requirement that a full community be identified at the application stage. This membership is not intended to be stagnant and a funded GRCoP is supported to grow in size both during and after the funding year.

Some examples of previously funded GRCoPs include those addressing: cross-faculty priority areas (such as clinical practice); scholarship development (in learning and teaching); innovations (mobile technology in learning); and small-scale projects or resource development that can contribute to larger institutional priorities (such as the first year transition CoP). Like other Teaching Development Grants provided under this funding scheme, GRCoP grants are designed to be seed funding, with successful applicants being encouraged and supported to build their work into larger institutional projects or to apply for national funding. This support is provided by the TILT Professional Learning and Recognition team as well as the individual Schools and Faculties of participating members.

5.5.3 Peer Learning Circles

Peer Learning Circles (PLC) officially became a third stream of the CoPI in 2014, following their introduction to TILT peer learning initiatives via the 2013 TILT Teaching Fellow (author Nash) in the year of her fellowship. Initially funded as part of the fellowship, the immediate success of the program led to an allocation of $6000 to fund up to 12 PLCs on an annual basis. The PLC concept was largely influenced by the Faculty Learning Circle concept advocated for by Cox (2004). The aim of PLC is to provide a flexible framework within which individual staff can increase their engagement in learning and teaching by working on a short-term project with a group of colleagues. PLCs were trialed in 2013 with 12 groups formed and 7 successfully completing projects.

PLCs can be divided into three broad groups: (1) project oriented groups that form around a shared issue in learning and teaching (one such group included staff from the Schools of Business and Computing interested in collaboratively exploring blended learning); (2) skills oriented groups that provide an opportunity to complete learning and teaching tasks such as creating a teaching portfolio or building evidence for a teaching award (such as one group of interdisciplinary, early career academics using a peer learning model to review and develop their portfolios for the performance management of their teaching); and (3) cohort based groups that work together to achieve a specified outcome (such as early career staff or staff working within a specific school to deliver a course review).

PLCs are made up of small numbers of staff, usually between 4 and 10 participants. Importantly, PLCs are encouraged, and in some cases required, to have enrolment of staff from different faculties and schools. It is a requirement that a broad range of staff are engaged in any centrally funded initiative such as the PLCs. While interdiscplinarity is preferenced, there are instances where a single discipline or school PLC will be funded if they can show how their practice will be disseminated more broadly through the project.

An annual call is made at the start of the academic year for potential PLC participants to propose a project through an Expression of Interest (EoI). Interested staff must submit a proposed domain area and project they would like to pursue that would contribute to that domain area. While not a requirement of an EoI, staff can also identify other PLC participants they know, or think, may be interested in participating. TILT will assist PLCs to find additional members if a project is granted funding and still requires this support. Funding of up to $500 is provided to support each PLC. Groups meet with a TILT representative once to refine their project and develop a timeline. The TILT representative is designated to a group by the PLC coordinators (authors Warr Pedersen and West), based on portfolio areas and/or areas of interest and expertise from across TILT. Following an initial meeting with a TILT staff member, it is up to each PLC to determine if the TILT member will continue to work with the group. If this on-going support is not required, the PLC works independently according to their established plan, meeting several times over the course of a year.

Unlike other grant schemes provided under the CoPI, such as the GRCoP grants, there is not a formal reporting requirement for PLCs. Instead, individual PLC participants have the option of providing TILT coordinators with a short report at the end of the year, detailing their participation, their own learning outcomes and their plans for developing their work further. Following receipt of this report, individual participants receive a formal letter of recognition from the Head of TILT and the program coordinators. As part of this letter, the TILT coordinators also provide advice on how PLC participants might take their work forward in other professional learning opportunities or activities offered by TILT.

5.6 Professional Learning and Support for the CoPI

Due to its coordination by TILT, a key element of the CoPI is the provision of on-going professional learning opportunities for CoP participants. These opportunities have been designed to support CoPs to establish, facilitate, disseminate and sustain their work. From the inception of the CoPI, it was decided that the various supports would need to assist CoPs develop and to "…catalyse [their] evolution" (Wenger et al. 2002, p. 54), rather than impose formal design or structure. The various levels of support were introduced to be responsive to the evolution of the CoPI over time, starting with generalised tool-kit based resources and plenty of space for broad community conversations through to more targeted support aimed at synthesising outcomes and aligning the activities of CoPs with evolving strategic learning and teaching priorities. Underpinning the design and delivery of professional learning for the CoPI is a budget of $10,000 per year, in addition to a further $10,000 used to support the CoP dissemination event at the annual *Teaching Matters* conference. This event includes a plenary Pecha Kucha presentation given by CoPs funded in that year. A CoP networking and roundtable discussion session is also available as part of the day. In addition to the formal conference day, CoP dissemination workshop sessions accompany the conference in a second half-day session.

The key starting point to assist staff to conceptualise and form CoPs is the *Communities of Practice: Readings and Resources* publication (Skalicky and West 2012). This compilation of seminal readings and resources was designed to stimulate conversations and to guide the potential ways in which staff might consider or develop a CoP at the University of Tasmania. It contains two key parts: The Blue Section—*Toolkit Readings* which includes a variety of documents pertaining to what a CoP is and some common ways in which one might work, and The Green Section—*Case Study Readings*, to illuminate readers as to how CoPs have been applied in particular contexts within the Australian higher education landscape. When the CoPI was launched at the University of Tasmania, over 50 physical copies of the reader were disseminated, with an electronic copy made available on the CoPI website. New CoP participants are directed to the site upon application and approval of their funding, although the site is live and available throughout the year as an open resource to all. TILT staff have been contacted on a number of occasions by groups outside of the University of Tasmania who have utilised this resource in the establishment of their CoPs.

TILT staff facilitate on-going face-to-face support for CoPI participants via a number of mechanisms: information workshops directed towards staff wishing to apply for funding under both the GRCoP grant and the PLC streams (facilitated in person on the major campuses, and by video-link to satellite campuses); one-to-one support to fellows leading the strategic CoPs, including informal presentations to members of their communities; and, one-to-one support for staff who attend weekly grants consultation hours to discuss issues, ask questions, describe activities, and sometimes simply to unpack the excitement and emerging knowledge and practice occurring in so many of the CoPs over time. In addition to the provision of static resources and on-going support services for the development of CoPs in the initiative, TILT staff introduced an additional in situ professional learning program in the first year of the program. Despite the oft-reported advantages and benefits of being a CoP member it was also reported by members in the first year that they felt in somewhat unfamiliar terrain in terms of knowing if their CoP was *working*. Conversations common to this theme often involved staff wanting to know how many members constituted a successful CoP; whether or not the various types of participation in the communities was appropriate; and how to ensure community sustainability. In response, TILT staff invited the then current Australian Learning and Teaching Council Teaching Fellow for Communities of Practice, Associate Professor Jacquie McDonald, to facilitate a customised and discursive workshop about 'How to do communities of practice'. The workshop was open to all University of Tasmania staff with special invitation to our CoP participants to attend.

This workshop provided two-fold benefits for participants. This was the first opportunity since the launch of the CoPI for participants to come together and share practice, providing the valuable opportunity to learn from the experience of other CoPs. McDonald also invited participants to nominate key questions, interests, themes, limitations and/or areas of concern as the basis for the workshop. In this way, it was the experiences of the CoP participants that drove the discussions for the day, increasing the relevance and applicability for the participants and enabling in situ learning. Specific messages from the day were recorded and McDonald and staff from TILT co-developed a response document that was circulated to participants. In addition to providing specific strategies and reflection points for participating CoPs, this document also sought to position the CoPI more broadly as (among other things):

- A site for **culture change**;
- Operating within a **supportive institutional framework** and a vehicle for **innovation and change** which is **influencing learning and teaching practices**;
- A space for **intellectually stimulating** and **invigorating conversations**;
- A forum for **developing** and **testing innovative communication strategies**; and
- Successful in terms of **engagement and influence** because the **CoPI aligns with the overall strategic priorities of the university**.

Taken from: McDonald and West (2012), Response to: *Generating Excitement, Relevance and Value: How to make the most out of your Community of Practice*

Prof McDonald's workshop and the subsequent response document were well received by participants. The resources from the workshop and the response document are available on the CoPI website and continue to be used by subsequent

CoPs. The response document has also helped TILT staff to provide a descriptive framework and justification for the CoPI when communicating about the initiative to new audiences and senior managers.

Recognising the value of these high impact, in situ professional learning opportunities, TILT co-supported a visit by Etienne Wenger to the University of Tasmania in 2013 to present of a series of staff based and public workshops. The first of these, *Cultivating Communities of Practice in UTAS*, looked at the relevance of the concepts of CoPs in terms of the pedagogical implications, organisational implications and as a foundational concept and theory of learning. The second, *Learning and Leading in Organisations*, explored organisational design and leadership in the context of learning efficiently, and the third workshop, *Learning in and across Landscapes of Practice: Recent Developments in Social Learning Theory*, presented a perspective on learning as an inherent dimension of everyday life and a fundamental social process. These workshops were pivotal in helping staff to ground the CoPI and its evolution in its value for learning—for staff who were community members, and for the students of many of those staff.

TILT continues to support professional learning of the CoPI by connecting communities with institutional and national fora with the purposes of disseminating and extending knowledge, outcomes and outputs. This support has included funding attendance at internal and national conferences and symposiums; providing dissemination and professional learning opportunities for CoP participants to attend state-based Promoting Excellence Network workshops, Office for Learning and Teaching events and symposium run by branches of the Higher Education Research and Development Society of Australasia. Significantly, staff working in TILT are also invited to participate in specific communities of interest to them, particularly at the PLC level. This is an integrative strategy where the skills and expertise of TILT staff are readily shared with the broader university community. All professional learning opportunities offered by the CoPI are designed to further enhance a dynamic group of learning and teaching champions who continue to realise strategic learning and teaching priorities, within and beyond the University.

5.7   Outcomes

Since 2011, the CoPI has supported the establishment of 8 Strategic CoPs, 14 GRCoPs and 22 PLCs. These CoPs have collectively delivered outcomes against all four of the University of Tasmania's Strategic Goals in the *Strategic Plan for Learning and Teaching* (2012–2014). This has included specific delivery of 14 of the 16 identified key objectives of that plan. The DVC (S&E) has publically recognised the CoPI as one of the most important programs of change and innovation at the University of Tasmania (Sadler 2013). As a consequence of this initiative the University of Tasmania has made enormous strides in various areas and won both internal and national awards for both teaching and community engagement activities. In the specific area of Sustainability, the University of

Tasmania now has an enviable record of national and international recognition, in part drawn from the stimulus of the CoPI and drawing from a close partnership between professional and academic staff. This has led in turn, to members of the CoPI inspiring a heightened institutional awareness of sustainability and a new University strategy.

The CoPI has been recognised as having significant impact on raising the profile of learning and teaching across the institution, and increasing the number of staff actively participating in learning and teaching initiatives and scholarship (Warr Pedersen and Brown 2013). More than 400 staff members have participated in the initiative, with many CoPs also including students and members external to the University. Importantly, due to the interdisciplinary and inter-organisational structure of the CoPI, staff from all of the seven academic Faculties have been involved in this initiative, as well as staff from the central Division for Students and Education and administrative and service units including Commercial Services and Development. The impact of the CoPI can also be measured in the integration of staff and disciplines from the distributed campuses, with leadership being provided in some cases from the smaller and more remote locations. This ensures greater institutional coherence in relation to strategies as well as easing possible tensions. Good practices present in one location or discipline have easily transferred to other locations and disciplines. In addition, the CoPI has brought professional learning opportunities to historically excluded staff, such as community clinical teaching associates and satellite tutors. The initiative has also bridged a number of historical divides at the institution including those between academic and professional staff; 'teachers' and 'researchers'; and seemingly diverse academic disciplines.

The CoPI is perceived by staff as an 'in-road' to the learning and teaching space, and most specifically, a collegial space to learn both from and with colleagues from other parts of the University with similar interests. A survey of participants indicated three common motivations for engagement: collaboration with colleagues (96 % nominated peers as their primary source of information on learning and teaching); skills development; and increased professional demands to participate in learning and teaching activities. The CoPI has responded to the increasing number of staff wanting to engage in professional development in learning and teaching, in particular staff who are new to this area has likely driven the high demand for flexible 'entry level' activities such as PLCs.

In testimony to the value placed on the CoPI by the institution, recognition of participation in a CoP has been formalised through the previously mentioned Teaching Performance Expectations (TPEs) outlined for academic staff at the University of Tasmania. The TPEs are a formal measure through the annual performance management cycle, and are used to guide promotion applications. Involvement in CoPs is specifically recognised in both Domain 2 (Excellence in contemporary curriculum design) and Domain 3 (Excellence in Scholarly Teaching). In the latter category CoP membership can evidence the adoption of a scholarly approach to learning and teaching, engagement in on-going professional development and a contribution to peer learning.

There are success stories from across the initiative that include examples of staff using the CoPI to write their first scholarship of learning and teaching publications; to run institution-wide expos to engage staff with educational technologies; to write winning teaching award applications; and to successfully apply for teaching grants based on the ideas and practices developed from their CoP. Other CoP participants have attributed their participation in the initiative as a key factor in increasing their job satisfaction levels, or providing an identity in their work as a teacher that they have not had before. A number of outcomes have developed from individual CoPs across all three streams of the CoPI and examples of each follow.

5.7.1 Examples of CoPs in Practice

Noting the potential for a CoP to grow through the initiative, one of the inaugural PLCs in 2013 formed an interfaculty CoP interested in pooling and peer reviewing resources for reviewing curriculum across a range of disciplines. This group went onto to form a larger inter-institutional CoP through Strategic CoP funding in 2014. They are now trialling a curriculum review tool at the University of Tasmania that is being peer reviewed by national partners as part of a pilot for a larger multi-institutional project currently under development.

Evidencing the 'seeding' potential of the GRCoP scheme, a CoP funded in this category in 2012 has used online technologies including Twitter and blogging to grow their membership to more than 200 online members from across the globe. This CoP has developed and shared a number of resources from a multitude of health disciplines to enhance professional learning experiences for clinical nursing facilitators. Joining the ranks of other virtual CoPs, this GRCoP is making scholarly contributions (including 13 publications to date) that are enhancing the developing landscape of how virtual collaboration can lead learning and teaching initiatives that bridge geographic divides.

In 2014, the University of Tasmania launched an innovative curriculum renewal project that involved the development of a set of 'breadth units' by interdisciplinary teaching teams. The trial of this project was supported by the Strategic CoP Program with the designation of a TILT Teaching Fellow, a TILT Educational Developer and funding to support the establishment of an institution-wide CoP. The purpose of the CoP was to bring together the individuals and teams developing the first round of breadth units to establish a methodology of peer learning and collaboration as the model by which this initiative would progress. The Breadth Unit project is ambitious as it attempts to provide the first formal integration of curricula drawn from all undergraduate courses at the institution. Ultimately, the CoP model has enabled lessons learned from the inaugural year of this project to be widely shared amongst participants, recorded for future reference for new participants and promoted institutional learning through on-going documentation and dissemination of the work to date.

Another example of a highly successful Strategic CoP was the pilot for the program funded in 2011 under the strategic priority area 'Education for Sustainability'. Before this formal recognition, an informal network of sustainability educators and researchers existed at the University, but a lack of recognition often stagnated progress and limited the impact of this disparate group. Through the CoPI, the Education for Sustainability Community of Practice (EfS CoP) grew in 12 months to a more than 60 members that included representatives from every Faculty, including students, academic and professional staff, and staff in voluntary positions. The EfS CoP has contributed the University of Tasmania's *Open To Talent: Strategic Plan 2012-Onwards* (University of Tasmania 2012b), holds representation on the University's Sustainability Committee, developed one of the first ever breadth units under the 2014 curriculum renewal project, successfully applied for national funding with national collaborations; and most recently extended their CoP to a state-wide Sustainability CoP through an internal Community Engagement grant. Due to individual motivation and a passion for the domain area of this CoP, the 2011 TILT Teaching Fellows that supported the uptake of this work have continued to cultivate and motivate this large CoP, along with assistance from around 20 other highly motivated core members. The remaining members engage with CoP activities based on interest and time and this participation rate ebbs and flows. The informal and formal structure, combined with a strong sense of motivation and identity in the group has helped to sustain this CoP well beyond the funding year provided through the CoPI, making this CoP one of the most celebrated examples of this UTAS initiative.

5.8 Conclusion

This chapter has provided a description of an institution wide program that showcases the potential for the CoP approach to deliver on strategic learning and teaching priorities through a supported social learning model. Through a tiered approach to funding, the CoPI promotes the engagement of staff at a variety of levels and ensures the sustainability and progress of established CoPs as they are given the option to develop through the initiative. Significantly, the CoPI has evolved the ways in which staff at the University of Tasmania have been able to access, actively engage with, and enhance the learning and teaching culture within the institution.

Characteristics of effective CoPs in the program have included: a clearly defined domain area and initiatives that have relevant and achievable outcomes; institutional recognition of participation in CoPs as enhancing teaching performance; institutional support (from TILT) to enable groups to tap into relevant expertise and opportunities; and commitment from participants to the shared goals of the CoP. A key value of the CoPI has been in harnessing and sharing these success stories with CoPs across the institution. As a centrally coordinated initiative, the CoPI provides a vehicle through which lessons can be gathered, shared and built upon. This point of contact for CoPI information has enabled the evolution of the program as it responds to an ever-changing higher education environment.

While the CoPI has been catalysed by and adheres to a structure that is driven from a top-down mandate, a commitment to supporting organic development and learning through a CoP model has allowed individual passions and motivations to drive participation and identify success. Inspired by the shared interests of its participants, the CoPI allows staff from across the institution to use peer learning as a vehicle to extend their knowledge, practices and passion across disciplines and professional boundaries. In doing so, individuals have been supported to identify the need for, and lead progress towards, positive change across a variety of institutional priorities to enhance learning and teaching for all.

Key to the success of the CoPI and the sustainability of the CoPs funded under this initiative has been attention to the links that can be made between streams of the program as CoPs grow and develop their work. The potential for CoPs to move through funding categories and access a variety of levels of support and professional learning throughout their participation in the initiative has helped to create a culture of collaboration and professional growth. Aligning these various forms of participation with the formal recognition frameworks that staff performance is assessed against has further enabled the CoPI to redefine engagement and success in learning and teaching scholarship and cultural enhancement. With attention to the scholarly foundations of the CoP model as a social learning approach, the University of Tasmania CoPI has provided a framework through which institutions can align their strategic priorities with the provision of professional learning opportunities, rewards and recognition of all staff. In doing so, the outcomes for the institution and the full range of individuals involved can be positive and many.

Acknowledgments The authors would like to acknowledge the dedicated contributions of all of the Communities of Practice participants in the Communities of Practice Initiative at UTAS, without whom the success of the initiative would not be possible.

References

Anderson, C., & McCune, V. (2013). Fostering meaning: Fostering community. *Higher Education, 66*(3), 283–296.

Anthony, J. A. J., Rosman, S. N., Eze, U. C., & Gan, G. G. G. (2009). Communities of practice the source of competitive advantage in organizations. *Journal of Knowledge Management Practice, 10*(1). www.tlainc.com/articl181.htm. Accessed February 25, 2015.

Blackmore, C. (Ed.). (2010). *Social learning systems and communities of practice*. Doredrecht: Springer.

Blessinger, P., & Carfora, J. M. (Eds.). (2014). *Inquiry-based learning for faculty and institutional development: A conceptual and practical resource for educators*. Bingley: Emerald Group Publishing Limited.

Boud, D., & Middleton, H. (2003). Learning from others at work: Communities of practice and informal learning. *Journal of Workplace Learning, 15*(5), 194–202.

Brown, T., Goodman, J., & Yasukawa, K. (2010). Academic casualisation in Australia. *The Journal of Industrial Relations, 52*(2), 169–182.

Cordiner, M. C., & Brown, N. (2009). Using a distributed leadership strategy to improve the quality of assessment across a university: Initial results of the project. ATN Assessment Conference. (2009). *Assessment in different dimensions conference proceedings* (pp. 104–110). Melbourne: Australian Technology Network.

Cox, M. D. (2004). Introduction to faculty learning communities. In M. D. Cox & L. Richlin (Eds.), *Building faculty learning communities* (pp. 5–23). San Francisco: Jossey-Bass.

Cox, M. D., & Richlin, L. (Eds.). (2004). *Building faculty learning communities*. San Francisco: Jossey-Bass.

Crossan, M. M., Lane, H. W., & White, R. E. (1999). An organisational learning framework: From intuition to institution. *Academy of Management Review, 24*(3), 522–537.

Davison, A. G., Pharo, E. J., & Warr, K. (2012). *Demonstrating distributed leadership through cross-disciplinary peer networks: Responding to climate change complexity*. Sydney: Australian Learning and Teaching Council.

Dubé, L., Bourhis, A., & Jacob, R. (2005). The impact of structuring characteristics on the launching of virtual communities of practice. *Journal of Organizational Change Management, 18*(2), 145–166.

Gaither, G. (Ed.). (1999). *The multi-campus system: Perspectives on practice and prospects*. Sterling: Stylus Publishing.

Hildreth, P., & Kimble, C. (2004). *Knowledge networks: Innovation through communities of practice*. London: Idea Group Inc.

Hildreth, P., & Kimble, C. (2008). Introduction and overview. In C. Kimble, P. M. Hildreth, & I. Bourdon (Eds.), *Communities of practice: Creating learning environments for educators* (Vol. 1, pp. ix–xix). Charlotte: Information Age.

Hill, M., & Haigh, M. (2012). Creating a culture of research in teacher education: Learning research within communities of practice. *Studies in Higher Education, 37*(8), 971–988.

Jones, J. (2010). Building pedagogic excellence: Learning and teaching fellowships within communities of practice at the University of Brighton. *Innovations in Education and Teaching International, 47*(3), 271–282.

Kramer, S., & Benson, S. (2013). Changing faculty use of technology—One cohort at a time. *Journal of Applied Research in Higher Education, 5*(2), 202–221.

Lave, J., & Wenger, E. (1991). *Situated learning: Legitimate peripheral participation*. Cambridge: Cambridge University Press.

Lea, M. R. (2005). Communities of practice in higher education. In B. Bartin & K. Tusting (Eds.), *Beyond communities of practice: Language, power and social context* (pp. 180–197). New York: Cambridge University Press.

MacKenzie, J., Bell, S., Bohan, J., Brown, A., Burke, J., Cogdell, B., et al. (2010). From anxiety to empowerment: A learning community of university teachers. *Teaching in Higher Education, 15*(3), 273–284.

McDonald, J., & Palani, A. (2011). Building leadership capacity for community of practice facilitators: Edgy professional development. In *Research and development in higher education: Reshaping higher education* (pp. 198–206). Gold Coast: The Higher Education Research and Development Society of Australasia.

McDonald, J., Star, C., & Margetts, F. (2012). *Identifying, building and sustaining leadership capacity for communities of practice in higher education*. Canberra: Australian Government Office for Learning and Teaching.

McDonald, J., & West, M. (2012). *Response to: Generating excitement, relevance and value: How to make the most out of your community of practice*. Hobart: Tasmanian Institute of Learning and Teaching.

Ng, L., & Pemberton, J. (2013). Research-based communities of practice in UK higher education. *Studies in Higher Education, 38*(10), 1522–1539.

O'Mahony, J. (2014). *Enhancing student learning and teacher development in transnational education*. New York: The Higher Education Academy.

Pharo, E., Davison, A., McGregor, H., Warr, K., & Brown, P. (2014). Using communities of practice to enhance interdisciplinary teaching: Lessons from four Australian institutions. *Higher Education Research and Development, 33*(2), 341–354.

Pifer, M. J., & Baker, V. L. (2013). Managing the process: The intradepartmental network of early-career academics. *Innovative Higher Education, 38*(4), 323–337.

Ponjuan, L., Conley, V. M., & Trower, C. (2011). Career stage differences in pre-tenure track faculty perceptions of professional and personal relationships with colleagues. *The Journal of Higher Education, 82*(3), 319–346.

Sadler, D. (2013, November). Closing plenary. In *Presented at the tasmanian institute of learning and teaching 12th annual teaching matters conference*, Sandy Bay, Australia.

Shapiro, N. S., & Levine, J. H. (1999). *Creating learning communities: A practical guide to winning support, organizing for change, and implementing programs*. San Francisco: Jossey-Bass.

Skalicky, J., & Brown, N. (2009). *Peer learning framework: A community of practice model*. Report to the University of Tasmania Student Transition and Retention Taskforce. Hobart: Centre for the Advancement of Learning and Teaching, University of Tasmania.

Skalicky, J., & West, M. (2012). *UTAS community of practice initiative: Readings and resources*. Hobart: Tasmanian Institute of Learning and Teaching.

Stuckey, B., & Smith, J. D. (2004). Building sustainable communities of practice. In P. M. Hildreth & C. Kimble (Eds.), *Knowledge networks: Innovation through communities of practice* (pp. 150–164). London: Idea Group.

Swiss Agency for Development and Cooperation. (2009). *Communities of practice—From own to shared knowledge*. www.sdc-learningandnetworking.ch/en/Home/Library?applState=detail&itemID=7287. Accessed October 10, 2014.

Szekeres, J. (2011). Professional staff carve out a new space. *Journal of Higher Education Policy and Management, 33*(6), 679–691.

University of Tasmania. (2012a). *University of Tasmania strategic plan for learning and teaching 2012–2014*. www.utas.edu.au/__data/assets/pdf_file/0005/268160/Learning-and-Teaching-Strategic-Plan.pdf. Accessed February 25, 2015.

University of Tasmania. (2012b). *Open to talent: Strategic plan 2012—Onwards*. www.utas.edu.au/__data/assets/pdf_file/0006/327498/UTMC8112_Strategic-Plan_Large-V4.pdf. Accessed February 25, 2015.

University of Tasmania. (2014a). *The UTAS academic*. www.utas.edu.au/provost/the-utas-academic-performance-expectations-for-academic-staff. Accessed February 25, 2015.

University of Tasmania. (2014b). *Teaching development grant guidelines*. www.teaching-learning.utas.edu.au/awards-and-grants/national-and-other-awards/utas-teaching-development-grants. Accessed February 25, 2015.

Warr Pedersen, K., & Brown, N. (2013, July). *Collaborative promotion of learning and teaching: The UTAS communities of practice initiative and the Tasmanian Institute of Learning and Teaching*. Poster presented at the meeting of the Higher Education Research and Development Society of Australasia, Auckland, New Zealand.

Wenger, E. (1998). *Communities of practice: Learning, meaning and identity*. Cambridge: Cambridge University Press.

Wenger, E. (2006). *Introduction to communities of practice: A brief overview of the concept and its uses*. http://wenger-trayner.com/theory/. Accessed February 25, 2015.

Wenger, E., McDermott, R., & Snyder, W. M. (2002). *Cultivating communities of practice*. Boston: Harvard Business School Press.

Whitechurch, C. (2008). Shifting identities and blurring boundaries: The emergence of third space professionals in UK Higher Education. *Higher Education Quarterly, 62*(4), 377–396.

Chapter 6
Creating and Facilitating Communities of Practice in Higher Education: Theory to Practice in a Regional Australian University

Peter Reaburn and Jacquie McDonald

Abstract Communities of Practice (CoPs) have been operating successfully at Central Queensland University Australia (CQU) since 2009. The major purpose of this chapter is to use a scholarly reflection approach to share what we have learnt are the keys to creating, sustaining and facilitating CoPs within an Australian regional university. A second purpose of the chapter is to bridge the gap between the theory and practice of creating, sustaining and facilitating CoPs within a higher education setting. We highlight the importance of meeting the CoP members' needs, of keeping the focus on the domain of the CoP, of engendering trust within the CoP, and when in the role of facilitator, sharing your passion for the domain through regular engagement with CoP members between CoP meetings. Critically within the higher education sector, we also highlight the importance of 'managing up' and engaging the senior leadership/management of the university to ensure the sustainability of CoPs. Finally, and based on our extensive experience as drivers of CoPs within regional universities, we share our *Top 10 Tips* to creating and facilitating CoPs within a higher education setting.

Keywords Communities of practice · Higher education · Facilitating · Creating · Regional university

P. Reaburn (✉)
CQUniversity, Rockhampton, QLD, Australia
e-mail: p.reaburn@cqu.edu.au

J. McDonald
University of Southern Queensland, Toowoomba, QLD, Australia
e-mail: mcdonalj@usq.edu.au

© Springer Nature Singapore Pte Ltd. 2017
J. McDonald and A. Cater-Steel (eds.), *Communities of Practice*,
DOI 10.1007/978-981-10-2879-3_6

6.1 Introduction

Communities of Practice (CoPs) were initiated at Central Queensland University, Australia (CQU) in 2009. The lead author (PR) was the instigator of the CoP 'movement' at CQU and remains the key driver of CoPs at CQU. The second author (JM) has acted as a mentor, advisor and critical friend to the lead author. She is widely regarded as the lead academic researcher of CoPs within Australian higher education.

While they vary in focus, membership and activities, the common denominator of CoPs at CQUniversity is that they are meeting the needs of their members and are facilitated well by experienced 'champions' (leaders of their respective CoP). Importantly, we have also learnt that the CoPs that have aligned their activities with the strategic and organisational plans of the university have been sustained since their inception.

The major purpose of this chapter is to bridge the gap between the theory and limited empirical research related to the role of CoPs within the higher education sector and relating this theory to the practice of creating, sustaining and facilitating CoPs at CQU. The chapter is not based on empirical research examining the outcomes of CoPs at CQU. The chapter is framed upon the scholarly reflections and 7 years' experience as the driver and leader of CoPs at CQU under the mentorship of a critical friend, the second author of this chapter.

6.2 The Context of CoPs Within CQU

CQU is a relatively 'young' Australian University. It achieved full University status in 1992 after being an Institute of Advanced Education from 1967. Now more than 20 years on, and following a merger with the Central Queensland Institute of Technical and Further Education (CQITAFE) on 1 July 2014 to become Queensland's first dual sector university. CQU is responsible for providing a diverse range of training and education programs (degrees) and courses to more than 30,000 students studying qualifications from certificate to post-doctorate level. Compared to other Australian universities, CQU has the highest ratio of students from mature age, Aboriginal and Torres Strait Islander, first-in-family, and low socio-economic backgrounds.

CQU is a complex organisation with multiple campuses and study locations, a large and diverse student population, internal and external modes of delivering learning and teaching, a complex and ever-changing corporate structure, and increasing demands for academic staff to become more research productive. Along with 12 locations in regional Queensland, CQU has expanded its presence throughout Australia with campuses in Adelaide, Brisbane, Melbourne, Noosa and Sydney; Study Centres in Biloela and Yeppoon within Central Queensland; a

Cairns Distance Education Study Centre; a delivery site in Edithvale, Victoria; and Partner Study Hubs in Cannonvale, Queensland and Geraldton, Western Australia.

Adding to the complexity of the organization, CQU has nine corporate directorates including the Higher Education Directorate that has six academic schools and two schools related to the TAFE Directorate. Further complexity is added by the fact that, apart from the Vice-Chancellor and a Provost, there are five Deputy Vice-Chancellors and four Pro-Vice Chancellors with various corporate responsibilities, and 10 Associate Vice-Chancellors managing the large number of campuses and study locations. The university has approximately 1500 academic staff across a wide range of disciplines and schools and 800 professional staff across the many schools and directorates.

At CQU we began to initiate the creation of CoPs in 2009 for reasons that will be examined in Sect. 6.4 later in this chapter. Using the experience, guidance and advice of the second author (JM), the first author (PR) used the CQU general e-mail list to call an open meeting of potential CoP 'champions' (at CQU we call CoP facilitators/convenors 'champions'). These 'champions' were identified as well-respected leaders in their field who also had a demonstrated commitment within a domain of knowledge and a passion to share that knowledge.

6.3   Operational Definitions of CoPs at CQU

At CQU, we define CoPs as groups of people who share a passion for something that they know how to do and who interact regularly to learn how to do it better (Wenger et al. 2002). With effective leadership and facilitation, CoPs encourage active participation and collaborative decision-making, problem solving or simply sharing of practice by all individual CoP members. They are thus different to the more traditional organisational structures within universities such as committees, project teams and working groups. At CQU we strongly support the position taken by McDonald et al. (2012), in their project report on identifying, building and sustaining leadership capacity for CoPs in (Australian) higher education when they suggest CoPs provide one mechanism through which academics can engage in sustained learning and teaching inquiry within supportive communities situated in their learning and teaching practice. At CQU we not only encourage and assist individuals with a 'passion for something' to share their knowledge of learning and teaching, we also encourage and assist 'champions' to initiate their own CoPs that can be focused on any aspect of University practice. The major criteria we use for the creation of CoPs at CQU is that the 'champion' is passionate about their topic/domain and has the capacity and energy to bring other people together to share practice and learn from each other.

6.4 Why CoPs in Higher Education and CQU?

We began encouraging the creation of CoPs at CQU for four reasons. Firstly, in the years leading up to 2009, CQU was an unhappy place to work. Staff morale was very low and staff were working behind closed doors and not engaging with each other in a collegial or collaborative way. Interestingly, evidence of the low staff morale at CQU was being observed across the sector at the time (Churchman 2005; Winefield et al. 2008). Thus the major driver to initiate CoPs at CQU was to bring like-minded individuals together during a period of rapid change as our University became increasingly bureaucratized and individual staff more isolated as the sense of collegiality and consensual decision-making was becoming lost with the increase in bureaucracy. We saw CoPs as a way to have staff open doors and engage in collegial and collaborative dialogue. Indeed, once we looked at the research literature related to CoPs, it became obvious that CoPs were *the* way to engage staff in collegial dialogue.

Through a professional colleague at CQU, the lead author became aware of the work of the widely-acknowledged 'founder' of the term and concept of CoPs, Wenger (1998). The work of Wenger highlighted that a CoP is a combination of three elements:

1. A *domain of knowledge* that creates a common ground and sense of common identity,
2. A *shared practice* that that community of people develops to be more effective in that domain, and
3. A *community of people* who care about that domain and want to learn more about it.

Two of these core elements of CoPs, 'community of people' and 'shared practice' struck a chord with the lead author of this chapter. In contrast to formal higher education groups such as committees, project teams, schools or faculties, a CoP allows for both personal and professional development of the participants that is grounded in their current practice and driven by their individual needs, rather than the organisations' needs. Furthermore, and as identified in a review of CoPs in academe in Australia (Nagy and Burch 2009), CoPs are different from traditionally formal university meetings in a number of ways including:

- Non-hierarchical
- Informal
- No formal leader
- Membership is voluntary
- Agendas are not imposed or intentionally prescribed
- Tacit knowledge becomes articulated
- Participants may just listen/observe and choose not to contribute
- Involves social time to build sense of community and trust.

Taken together, CoPs started at CQU as a means of (re)connecting academic staff in collegial and collaborative activities that were different to the increasingly corporatized and bureaucratic activities of their normal university work life.

The second reason for establishing CoPs at CQU was that through a review of the research literature, the lead author became aware that the lack of collegiality observed at CQU also existed across the Australian higher education sector. This lack of collegiality appeared due to the erosion of the traditional self-management practices of academics as a result of changes in government policy forcing universities to corporatize which in turn lead to new managerial-style leadership (Marginson 2006; Sharrock 2012). This corporatization of the Australian higher education sector arose as a result of greater need for government compliance and accountability, greater need for efficiency and value for money, internationalisation and globalisation of higher education, and information and communication technology developments (Huisman and Currie 2004; Kemp and Norton 2014; Universities Australia 2013). Indeed, when describing the present climate of the Australian higher education sector, Sharrock (2012) suggested "it is often claimed that scholarly communities are subject to 'command and control' leadership styles and institutional processes, geared increasingly to 'corporate and commercial profit-seeking purpose' (p. 324). Similar to large corporate organizations, it now appears that universities and their leadership must now develop their strategic goals, visions and mission and ensure all individual and organizational efforts are aligned with those strategic educational and economic goals (Sharrock 2012). A number of higher education CoP researchers have suggested that this increased corporatization has led to decreased staff autonomy and increased accountability, both of which decrease the amount of time available and willingness to engage in collegial and collaborative work such as CoPs (Buckley and Du Toit 2010; Houghton et al. 2015; Nagy and Burch 2009). This decrease in collegiality in decision making works against the desire of 78 % of Australian academics previous research has shown to value collegiality as 'very important' in academic life (Anderson et al. 2002). At CQU it became obvious that compliance and corporatization influences at a national level were driving academic and professional staff away from collegial decision making and into an increasingly bureaucratic workplace. Thus, because of their collegial nature in bringing people together who have a similar interest or passion, CoPs were seen as a way of (re)connecting people in an informal way.

Thirdly, through having worked in academia for over 20 years, the lead author was aware that academic life can be a very individualistic activity, particularly in a regional university such as CQU where a critical mass of staff in each discipline was and still remains difficult to achieve. We were motivated by Palmer (2002) who reflected our belief that

> Academic culture is a curious and conflicted thing. On the one hand, it holds out the allure and occasionally the reality of being a 'community of scholars'...On the other hand, it is a culture infamous for fragmentation, isolation, and competitive individualism – a culture in which community sometimes feels harder to come by than in any institution on the face of the earth. (p. 179)

Again CoPs appeared a way to bring people together as a community of scholars with a common interest to learn from each other in a non-threatening way.

Finally, in 2009 when CoPs were initiated at CQU, the university was preparing for an external audit of its activities including learning and teaching. In 2009 the lead author was seconded into a project team for the 5-yearly audit of the university. It was through this process that he became aware of the CoP work in higher education of co-author Associate Professor Jacquie McDonald and others at the University of Southern Queensland. Specifically, this group had established a number CoPs around learning and teaching for a number of purposes including both professional development and leadership development (McDonald and Star 2006, 2007, 2008). With the support of the other members of the CQU audit project team, it was decided to initiate the formation of CoPs at CQU under the mentorship of the second author.

Taken together, the above reasons provide the rationale for the creation and facilitation of CoPs in Australian higher education in general (Churchman 2005; Churchman and Stehlik 2007; Nagy and Burch 2009; McDonald et al. 2012) and CQU specifically. Through reading and ongoing communication with the co-author of this chapter, the lead author became aware that CoPs, as the definition suggests, is a way of bringing together both academic and professional staff across disciplines, schools, faculties and divisions to share practice and learn from each other in a collegial and collaborative way. Thus, we believe that in the modern corporate university where there is increasing alienation of staff from collaborative pursuits and collegial participation in decision making, that CoPs are a means by which universities can reconnect individuals within their own terms of reference.

6.5 Types of CoPs at CQU

Over a number of years of working with CoPs within their own university and then a number of other Australian universities in Australia, including The University of Queensland; University of Tasmania; University of Adelaide; and Griffith and Flinders Universities, McDonald et al. (2012) have identified three types of CoPs operating within Australian higher education:

1. *Intentional* CoPs that are created to satisfy a particular organisational need or strategy;
2. *Nurtured* CoPs that are created and facilitated from grass roots university staff. They maintain a participant-driven agenda and focus, but have university awareness and support from senior leadership; and,
3. *Organic* CoPs that evolve or emerge at universities through participants sharing issues or concerns but not engaging formally with the university or its leadership for support.

Table 6.1 summarises the key characteristics of these three types of CoPs in higher education. The table also gives examples of both past and currently operating *intentional* and *nurtured* CoPs within CQU.

Lead commentators and researchers on CoPs in universities have strongly suggested that *nurtured* CoPs are preferred within higher education (Buckley and Du Toit 2010; McDonald et al. 2012; Nagy and Burch 2009; Pemberton et al. 2007). They recommend that CoPs be *nurtured* rather than 'imposed' (*intentional*)

Table 6.1 Characteristics of three models of communities of practice in higher education.

Characteristic	Organic	Nurtured	Intentional
Initiation	Individual or member initiated	Individual or group initiated	University initiated
Group structure	Informal	Formal but grass roots	Formal and university endorsed
Membership	Participant defined	Optional and cohort or topic focused	Mandatory membership institutionally defined
Leadership	Distributed, informal and shifting	Distributed and lead by a convenor(s)/ champion(s)	Formal and hierarchical based on institutionally defined and endorsed
Priorities	Simply evolve or emerges from shared practice, shared concerns or issues	Established to address shared practice, shared concerns or issues	Established to address institutional concerns or priorities
Relationship to University	No formal university awareness, acknowledgement or support	Negotiated university awareness, acknowledgement and support	Formally part of university structure, officially endorsed, funded and supported
Lifecycle	Limited linear lifecycle	Cyclical with potential to recreate lifecycle	Linear but potentially an open lifecycle
CQU example(s)		1. Postgraduate supervisors 2. Work-related learning 3. Education for sustainability 4. Teamwork 5. New staff 6. Internationalisation of the learning experience 7. Technology in learning and teaching 8. First year experience 9. Interprofessional simulation learning 10. Open online courses (OOCs)	Heads of Program MetacoP (meeting of all CoP champions to share their practice)

Adapted from McDonald et al. (2012)

otherwise the CoPs may be viewed sceptically by academics as a pretence for a predetermined agenda that may simply be another university committee hierarchical in nature and not driven by the needs of the individual CoP members. However, both the present authors and the commentators above strongly suggest that CoPs in higher education can and do provide the scaffolding for establishing collegial relations in a safe place that is free of hierarchical power and politics typically observed in schools and faculties. Moreover, CoPs offer a collegial environment free of organisational constraints that might negatively influence behaviour and discussion within the CoP.

CoPs usually exist within a wider context or larger organisation such as a university. The organisation's attitude towards CoPs can impact on both the development and success of both the individual CoP and the organisation itself (Buckley and Du Toit 2010; McDermott 2002, 2004). As shown in Table 6.1, most of the CoPs at CQU are CoPs that have been created from the bottom-up by passionate individuals who create and facilitate a CoP focused on a domain of interest (e.g. work-related learning) or a cohort of individuals who share a practice (e.g. postgraduate supervisors). Through supporting these 'bottom-up' CoPs, the learning organisation such as a university is allowing staff to take the initiative for activities and projects that will enhance the CoP members learning and personal growth.

6.6   Theory of CoPs to Practice of CoPs

The theory of CoPs is based on social learning theory. In the early 1970s, the work of Bandura (1972) signalled the move of ideas about learning from an individual, objectivist approach to considerations about the context of learning, by theorising that learning was a cognitive process that takes place in a social context. The 'Communities of Practice' concept is informed by further study of the social nature of human learning inspired by anthropology and social theory (Lave 1988; Lave and Wenger 1991; Vygotsky 1978; Wenger 2010).

Indeed, the term 'Communities of Practice' emerged from Lave and Wenger's (1991) study that investigated the apprenticeship model of learning which showed that, rather than the one-on-one master/apprentice model, it was a complex set of social relationships within the whole practicing community that supported both learning and membership. The idea of 'learning situated in practice' is an essential element of CoPs. Indeed, this early work by Lave and Wenger highlighting the importance of social learning within CoPs has recently been reinforced through Jane Hart's writings and blog that focuses on learning in the social workplace. She notes that social collaboration, as demonstrated in CoPs and social teams, is where we learn implicitly from one another as a consequence of working together (Hart 2015).

Thinking about CoPs as social learning systems enables us to reflect on both individual and group learning, and the relationships, interactions, and learnings that we forge or experience within these CoP social systems. Wenger (2010, p. 179) suggests CoPs "exhibit many characteristics of systems more generally: emergent structure, complex relationships, self-organization, dynamic boundaries, ongoing negotiation of identity and cultural meaning, to mention a few." This systems approach is also articulated by Senge (2006) whose work the lead author strongly believes in and supports.

In his book *The Fifth Discipline: The Art and Practice of the Learning Organization*, Senge (2006) conceived of learning in any form as a combination of five disciplines:

1. *Personal mastery* implies that personal growth and learning takes place when individuals are in a safe place where inquiry is normal and those same individuals have the capacity and desire to take responsibility for their own professional development. At CQU we have learnt that a CoP that is well facilitated by the 'champion' can create this safe place where CoP members can openly share practice, solve problems, and address issues that are of personal or professional interest and focused on a domain of mutual interest.

2. *Mental models* include the testing and improving of our own interpretation of how the world around us works. For example, within the Postgraduate Supervisor CoP at CQU that the lead author 'champions' an award-winning supervisor of international research higher degree students presented on why his practice is so successful. CoP members who are younger or more inexperienced supervisors of international postgraduate students can then test their methods and practices through interacting with the 'expert' and other members of the CoP.

3. *Shared vision* around which a group can rally and focus. In a CoP this shared vision may be their shared passion or practice (e.g. Education for Sustainability CoP at CQU), the topic on which the CoP focuses (e.g. Work-Related Learning CoP at CQU), or the CoP cohort (e.g. New Staff CoP at CQU).

4. *Discussion and dialogue* is Senge's fourth discipline. This implies that the group develops the capacity to carry out their vision through discussion and dialogue. At CQU we base our CoPs on open discussion of topics, issues and problems directly related to the domain of the CoP and the interests of the CoP members. For example, our Education for Sustainability CoP identified that the university did not have a policy related to sustainability. Through open dialogue and discussion, the CoP worked with their strategically chosen senior CQU leader, in this case the PVC (Learning and Teaching) to develop a policy. At CQU we encourage every CoP to choose a 'mentor' who is directly approached by the 'champion' to engage with the CoP based on their position and sphere of influence related the domain of the CoP. Working with their 'mentor', the Education for Sustainability CoP members collaborated together to develop a CQU policy on education for sustainability that has since been approved by CQU's Academic Board as a university policy.

5. *Systems thinking* is the way the CoP members integrate, develop and engage in the other four disciplines. Senge (2006) suggests that systems thinking affects the degree to which any organization becomes a learning organization as well as the degree of success an individual CoP can have.

While theories about learning organizations such as universities suggest systems thinking and change need to be synergistic, this change often takes place at the group level. This suggests that CoPs might become an ideal component of any learning organization involved in change. Indeed, Hackman and Edmondson (2007) noted that group learning is far more successful than individual learning whenever issues or topics involve more than one person. Thus, groups such as CoPs that are groups of individuals passionate about a topic or issue should thus become an 'indispensible part of a learning organization' (Henrich and Attebury 2010). The individual CoP members as a collective bring a diverse range of experiences and skills that they can share and learn from to implement and change practice that may be more sustainable at the grass-roots level than change imposed from the top-down.

Importantly, the late Professor of Social and Organizational Psychology at Harvard University, Richard Hackman has identified a number of characteristics of successful groups within learning organizations (Hackman and Edmondson 2007). These characteristics include: accomplishing their tasks, continually learning and adapting, be a real team and not just a group with a name, have a clear direction and purpose, have competent coaching to facilitate work, not be over-or under-bounded, have adequate autonomy, and have a balance between performing and learning. As suggested by Henrich and Attebury (2010), the success of a number of these above characteristics rests within the group and specifically with the individual CoP 'champion' to create the climate within the CoP group. However, other characteristics involve the leadership and management of the larger organization, suggesting the need to engage with senior leadership if leading CoPs within a university setting. At CQU we have learnt over the years to strategically engage a senior leader ('mentor') of the university. The 'champion' of each CQU CoP has handpicked their own 'mentor' who is invited to every CoP meeting, invited to speak at the CoP at least once per year, and kept informed of CoP activities through notes of meetings being sent to them and being a part of a CoP e-mail list for interaction between CoP meetings. Both of the current authors have learnt the need to 'educate' the senior leadership of our respective organisations as to the benefits of supporting CoPs within the university.

6.7 Benefits of CoPs in Higher Education

Over the last few decades there has been a significant increase in the number of journal articles, books, book chapters, conference papers and online documents mentioning CoPs or using the term 'communities of practice' in the title of the documents (Tight 2015). Moreover, the same paper highlights that there is increasing application of the theory of CoPs within empirical higher education research, suggesting that the higher education sector sees benefits in the application of CoP theory to many aspects of practice within a university setting.

CoP theory has been used to empirically examine the positive impact of CoPs in a number of areas of university practice. These include the professional development of academic staff (Blanton and Stylianou 2009; Buckley and Du Toit 2010; Drouin et al. 2014; Nixon and Brown 2013), development of new academic staff (Cox 2013; Gourlay 2011; Morgan 2014), mentorship and development of university library staff (Henrich and Attebury 2010; Sanchez-Cardona et al. 2012; Van Wyk 2005), development of research higher degree student learning (Kriner et al. 2015; Sense 2015; Wisker et al. 2007), learning and teaching (Baker-Eveleth et al. 2011; Lawrence and Sankey 2008; McDonald and Star 2014; Morton 2012; Pharo et al. 2014; Richards 2012), online learning and teaching using virtual communities (Bourhis et al. 2005; Johnson 2001; Palloff and Pratt 2007), development of the scholarship of learning and teaching (Bishop-Clark et al. 2014; Buysse et al. 2003), improving the quality and effectiveness of medical education Mazel and Ewen (2015), research development (Kozlowski et al. 2014; Ng and Pemberton 2013), and university leadership development (Debowski and Blake 2007; Flavell et al. 2008; Higgins 2009; McDonald et al. 2013).

Furthermore, empirical research has shown that encouragement of university staff engagement in CoPs within higher education leads to many individual and organisational benefits. These benefits include:

- Overcoming institutional isolation and increasing collaboration (Churchman and Stehlik 2007; McDonald 2014; Nagy and Burch 2009; Ng and Pemberton 2013; Pharo et al. 2014; Reaburn et al. 2012; Sanchez-Cardona et al. 2012; Van Wyk 2005)
- The exchange, acquisition and evaluation of knowledge through social learning (Ng and Pemberton 2013; Pharo et al. 2014; Sanchez-Cardona et al. 2012; Van Wyk 2005)
- Improved learning and teaching (Beach and Cox 2009; McDonald and Star 2008; Morton 2012)
- Increased research outcomes (Ng and Pemberton 2013)
- Improved work performance through sharing of experiences and best practices (Buckley and Du Toit 2010; McDonald and Star 2008; Ng and Pemberton 2013; Sanchez-Cardona et al. 2012)
- Encouraging interdisciplinary practice (Henrich and Attebury 2010; McDonald and Star 2008)
- Establishment of professional networks and alliances (Buckley and Du Toit 2010; Sanchez-Cardona et al. 2012)
- Innovation and promotion of new practices (Henrich and Attebury 2010; Sanchez-Cardona et al. 2012; Van Wyk 2005)
- Leadership development (Debowski and Blake 2007; Flavell et al. 2008; Higgins 2009; McDonald 2014; McDonald et al. 2012).

Taken together, the above benefits and increasing use of CoP theory for maximising both organisational and individual staff outcomes within higher education strongly suggest that application of CoP theory and creation of CoPs is needed and warranted within the higher education sector. At CQU, we used both the above theory and experience of the second author to create a CoP 'movement' at CQU that was driven from the bottom-up.

6.8 Creating CoPs: Theory to Practice

From a theoretical perspective, the creation and development of a CoP is similar to the Tuckman (1965) stages of group development (forming, storming, norming, performing). Similarly, Wenger (1998) identified that CoPs go through stages of creation and development beginning with an initial *potential stage* where individuals who face similar situations but don't share practice find each other and discover commonalities. Wenger suggests CoPs then go through a *coalescing stage* where these same individuals come together, recognise their potential and explore their connectedness to then enter an *active stage* through engaging in joint activities. Finally, CoPs go through a *dispersed stage* where CoP participants no longer engage intensely but stay in touch before entering the *memorable stage* where the participants remember their CoP as a significant part of their identity and tell stories of their involvement.

Based on the original work of Wenger (1998) within actual communities and industry, Star and McDonald (2015) have identified both *nurtured* and *intentional* CoPs are the most commonly observed CoPs within higher education in Australia. Moreover, these same CoP researchers have identified five phases in the evolution of a nurtured CoP within higher education in Australia. Together with key issues for each phase, these five phases are presented in Table 6.2.

These resources are specifically designed for CoP facilitators ('champions') in higher education. They focus on leadership as an enabling influence to achieve desired CoP outcomes. The websites provide resources that are intended as professional development tools for individual facilitators. Critically, each of the resources is designed as a concise commentary of no more than two pages that distil the knowledge and experience gained from a large international team of higher education CoP researchers.

From a practical point of view, higher education CoPs such as those at CQU usually start up around a particular issue or topic (e.g. Work-related learning CoP; Education for sustainability CoP; Internationalisation of the learning experience CoP) or practice (e.g. Heads of Program CoP; Postgraduate supervisors CoP) or are cohort-focused (e.g. New staff CoP, Heads of Program CoP, Postgraduate supervisors CoP). The issue or practice then becomes the domain of the CoP and is the trigger to create the CoP. The person or small group of individuals who identify the *domain* usually takes the role of facilitating the CoP because of their knowledge of the issue or practice (*nurtured* CoP) or hierarchical position in the university (*intentional* CoP).

The authors of the present chapter have been both the leaders of the CoP movement and facilitators or co-facilitators of a number of CoPs at their respective

Table 6.2 Phases and key issues associated with a nurtured CoP within higher education.

Phase	Key issues	Examples from CQU
1. Initiation	• Topic or cohort focus • Identify the 'spark' or reason to connect practitioners or the cohort • Scope landscape for CoP alignment with university goals • Identify senior leaders to sponsor/champion the CoP • Identify resources such as administrative support • Identify potential members	Identify key individuals who exhibit 'best practice' or cohorts of staff identified as benefiting from 'connecting' Familiarise key individuals with university planning documents Identify senior leaders with an interest in the CoP domain Brainstorm potential CoP members
2. Creation	• Get buy-in from potential members and senior leader(s) • Sell the CoP • Get the critical mass • Leverage local knowledge and contacts • Nurture the spark • Seven design principles (see Table 6.3)	• Make potential CoP members (e-mail or face-to-face) and senior leaders (face-to-face) aware of benefits of membership (see benefits section) • Using the seven design principles, call an initial face-to-face (with video-conferencing if available) meeting • Ensure a credible core group of 'leaders in practice' are engaged
3. Infancy	• Nurture and develop membership • Ensure value from membership and attendance at meetings • Build trust • Build CoP profile • Ensure credibility of core members and champions/convenors • Back-channelling (CoP convenor/facilitator(s) regularly check with CoP members that the CoP is meeting their needs and to identify any group dynamic issues or other problems aren't arising)	• Create an e-mail list of CoP members • Keep them informed of activities/speakers well in advance • Communicate between meetings • Create a sense of trust, transparency and openness within meetings • Invite senior leaders or experts in practice within or outside the university to share practice at meetings • Ensure a credible core group of 'leaders in practice' are engaged and foster development of CoP newcomers • Share and celebrate success stories through media such as newsletters and reports
4. Maturing/sustaining	• Avoid university leveraging or taking over • Membership changes • New member induction • Protect the 'space' • Keep the role of CoP focused	• Educate senior leaders on need for CoPs to remain autonomous to bureaucratic imperatives • Ensure CoP activities are member driven • Welcome new members and encourage their interaction and involvement at every meeting • Ensure the domain of the CoP is the focus

(continued)

Table 6.2 (continued)

Phase	Key issues	Examples from CQU
5. Recreating	• Re-assess the critical issues or new trigger • Evolve the membership • Rebuild the critical mass • Renegotiate the relationship with university	• Keep all stakeholders informed and engaged in all aspects of decision making • Involve CoP members in reflective practice and evaluation of CoP activities and outcomes • Keep senior leadership involved and informed of CoP activities

Readers are strongly advised to refer to the CoP facilitator resources described in detail by McDonald et al. (2012). Moreover, the key issues relating to each phase of a nurtured higher education CoP are examined in detail at two excellent websites created and updated by the second author of this chapter: (1) http://www.usq.edu.au/cops/resources/altcfellowship/facilitator-resources; (2) http://www.cops.org. au/resources/. Adapted from McDonald Fellowship resources (2012)

universities. From both the authors' experience, the 'champion' needs a high level of passion, commitment and determination to create and then sustain the CoP. Furthermore, for *nurtured* CoPs at CQU we have learnt the importance of both aligning CoP activities with university strategic goals and objectives articulated in strategic and/or operational plans as well as the importance of identifying and forming ongoing relationships and regular quarterly meetings with senior leadership who can act as 'mentors' of the CoPs.

Identifying the CoP 'champion' of each CoP is a critical step in the creation phase of any *nurtured* or *intentional* CoP. Typically this person is self-selected through either of two mechanisms. First, by directly approaching the CoP driver at CQU (PR) with a topic/cohort and reason to connect fellow practitioners or a cohort. Second, and more importantly for the creation of *intentional* CoPs, the 'champion' may be seen by senior leadership or the wider university community as the recognised leader in the proposed CoP practice or cohort. With the mentoring support of the lead author, the 'champion' then starts recruiting potential participants by e-mail and/or verbal invitation to other academic or professional staff they know who may be interested in the issue, topic, cohort or practice. At CQU, we also identify and approach a mentor from senior leadership to work with the 'champion' to promote the initial meeting and ideally speak at that first meeting. We then send out an invitation by e-mail to all university staff or specific e-mail lists (e.g. postgraduate supervisors) inviting them to an initial CoP meeting. The e-mail details the date, time, venue and purpose of the initial CoP meeting.

This *creation* phase is also the appropriate time to address the seven CoP design principles articulated by Wenger et al. (2002). In Table 6.3 we list both these theoretical design principles and examples of how we have applied them at CQU.

Table 6.3 Theoretical design principles of CoPs (Wenger et al. 2002) and examples of how we have applied the principles at CQU

Design principle	Examples in practice at CQU
Design for evolution	CoP convenor/facilitator(s) work with participants to identify a and promote a schedule of activities, sharing experiences for the upcoming year
Open dialogue between inside and outside perspectives	CoP champions work with participants to identify other stakeholders from within the university (senior leaders, postgraduate/undergraduate students, academic or professional staff), other universities, or outside the university (education department, business or public service professionals) and invite their involvement in the CoP
Invite different levels of participation	CoP champions work with participants to brainstorm who else should be encouraged to participate in the CoP Senior leaders identified as having an interest or responsibility for the CoP *domain* are invited to actively participate or speak at the CoP
Develop both public and private community spaces	CoP champions work with administration support to arrange regular meeting dates/times/venues Individual members share practice and resources via e-mail, video-conference, blogs or informal meetings CoP champions work with administration support to arrange an annual CoP Showcase of individual CoP activities
Focus on value	CoP champions work with participants to identify and prioritise issues or topics and individuals to share practice Create a 'bottom-up' agenda ensuring CoP members own the CoP and its activities Invite relevant senior leadership and community/industry leaders to speak at the CoP meetings
Combine familiarity and excitement	CoP champions work with participants to arrange activities (e.g. guest presenters to share practice, research projects) At the first meeting, CoP champions work with participants to establish operating principles (e.g. trust and confidentiality, equality of standing, openness)
Create a rhythm for the community	CoP champions work with participants to arrange convenient dates and times for CoP meetings that are then locked into diaries for the upcoming year

Once created, the combined experience of the current authors suggests the success or failure of a CoP revolves strongly around the commitment and practice of the CoP 'champion'(s).

6.9 Facilitating CoPs: Theory to Practice

Effective facilitation is critical to both creating and sustaining an environment in which CoPs can thrive (Ortquist-Ahrens and Torosyan 2009). Just as CoPs differ from groups such as committees and other work groups in universities, the role of CoP 'champion' also differs from that of a chairperson or hierarchical leader.

From a practical point of view, both Table 6.3 and the resources identified at the website http://www.cops.org.au/resources/ identify a number of key roles and responsibilities for the 'champion' creating and facilitating CoPs in a higher education setting. Apart from initiating and creating a CoP through engaging and encouraging potential CoP members and then 'selling' the benefits of participating in a CoP, the facilitation of the CoP during and between meetings is equally important.

Ensuring value for members is critical for maintaining the relevance of the CoP. The experience of both authors is to encourage 'buy-in' and ownership of the CoP activities by the members. One way of achieving this is by providing time for members to identify their priorities at the first meeting of the CoP and then at the first meeting of the CoP held at the beginning of each academic year. This might be done by online survey prior to the initial meeting, or by brainstorming and small group discussion at the first CoP meeting of the year. Ideas are then prioritised by consensus and the activities or topics and associated speakers for future meetings circulated. This initial meeting is also the time and place for the 'champion' to establish the CoP operating principles such as the confidentiality of discussions, the equality of each member's standing in the CoP, and the importance of every member being encouraged to be open and frank in discussion.

The first meeting of the CoP is also the place for members to decide meeting times and lengths and lock them in for the year. At CQU we have found lunchtimes (12–2 pm) to be convenient for CoP meetings that usually are 1.0–1.5 h in length. At CQU we have even sought and received university funding for light lunches to be provided to members as an incentive to participate. The structure of each meeting is suggested to be divided into the three equal elements as recommended by Wenger (1998) and used by McDonald and Star (2008) as an organising agenda framework for University of Southern Queensland CoPs:

1. Addressing the *domain of knowledge* where an invited speaker from within or outside of the CoP present for 20–30 min on the agreed-to topic related to the domain,
2. Members *sharing practice* by open and frank discussion with the invited speaker while also sharing their own experience or practice,
3. Developing the sense of *community of people* by having time at the start and/or end of the meeting to interact informally to create the social fabric of learning.

Within each meeting, the role of the 'champion' is to engender and develop the building of trust within the members. New members are encouraged to introduce themselves and share their own practice and experiences and core members seen as practice experts are encouraged to share practice in a non-threatening way. Readers are strongly encouraged to read the paper by Ortquist-Ahrens and Torosyan (2009) that explores the nature of facilitation; outlines key facilitative attitudes, skills and tasks; and considers a number of key concepts about adult collaborative learning and group development and dynamics that are important to successful and effective facilitation during CoP meetings. Moreover, readers wanting to become effective facilitators of CoPs within the higher education sector are strongly advised to consult the concise resources for CoP 'champion'(s) at: http://www.cops.org.au/ resources/.

The role of the 'champion' is equally important between meetings. At CQU, we have a 0.4 professional staff appointment to assist the CoP 'champion'(s). This person keeps brief notes (not minutes) from each meeting. These notes simply list attendees and major discussion items and any actions or recommendations that arise during the CoP meeting. These notes are then circulated by the 'champion' via e-mail with warm and friendly dot-pointed list of resources (e.g. websites, papers, links for further reading, shared learnings) relevant to the domain or recent or future meeting. Finally, the e-mail identifies the next CoP meeting date, time, venue, focus item and speaker profile as well as any relevant pre-reading for that meeting. We have learnt this between-meeting interaction greatly encourages the development and sense of community sharing within the CoP.

Critically, during the early *infancy phase* of CoP development where trust is being developed among CoP members, and as identified in Table 6.2, back-channelling (Wenger 1998) by the 'champion' is encouraged on an ongoing basis. This process involves the 'champion' 'checking-in' on the CoP group dynamic as well as the perceptions and concerns of any individual CoP member outside of the regular CoP meeting. This might be done by the 'champion' encouraging feedback from CoP members by e-mail or by spontaneous social interaction in corridors or around campus. During the *infancy phase* the 'champion' needs to also keep senior leadership and in particular their CoP 'mentor' informed of CoP activities and outcomes, especially as they relate to aligned university goals and objectives.

During the *maturing and sustaining phase* of CoP development when the CoP has established its identity and is demonstrating benefits to both individual CoP members and the university, there may be a danger that senior university leadership may see the CoP as a means of implementing university processes or innovations. The role of 'champion' becomes critical in achieving the balance between maintaining the distinction between the institutionalisation of CoPs and the institutional awareness of the CoP's existence (Langelier 2005). This dilemma is a fine line for a 'champion' who must 'protect' the independence of the CoP by educating university leadership about the value and role of CoPs in universities and how CoPs are different to committees, project teams or working groups that are used to implement university policies and projects related to organisational aims and objectives.

Other roles of the 'champion' during the *maturing/sustaining phase* are to be aware that members will leave but that new members will join and need to be introduced and encouraged to actively participate in CoP activities and discussions. Finally, the authors' experience also suggests that the 'champion' must keep focused on the CoP domain and member-agreed topics while also addressing topical issues relevant to CoP members. This currency and focus ensures the CoP remains dynamic and provides value to the members.

Sustaining CoPs has been suggested by lead commentators on industry-based CoPs as a more difficult task than the 'champion' may have expected. Issues that inhibit the CoPs growth and development include loss of momentum, loss of relevance, and a sense the CoP may have become too localised (McDermott 2004). While to our knowledge no empirical research has explored the keys to sustaining CoPs in higher education, an Australian Office of Learning and Teaching project by McDonald et al. (2012) and the project resources at http://www.cops.org.au/resources provide ideas for sustaining CoPs within higher education settings. These include the importance of the 'champion' role in creating a shared sense of context for all CoP members and ensuring equal participation in discussions so that imbalances in experience and power are minimised.

In order to assist facilitators sustain their CoP, McDermott (2004) has identified six characteristics of mature and successful CoPs within both business and community organisations. Both the current chapter authors have seen these characteristics contribute to the longevity and sustaining of CoPs within our respective universities. These success factors are:

1. *Clear purpose.* The CoP sets and evaluates short-term and long-term goals. The CoP might establish annual goal setting and assessment processes or ensure the CoP purpose is clearly articulated. For example, the Postgraduate Supervisor CoP at CQU set out to run a workshop on *Key success factors in postgraduate supervision* and ran a workshop on the topic facilitated by a Dean of Graduate Studies from an internationally-recognised university.
2. *Active leadership.* CoP leadership needs to be passionate and actively promoting the CoP within the university, particularly amongst senior leaders.
3. *Critical mass of engaged members.* CoPs thrive on the work of a committed, stable, and active core group of members who see their CoP membership as part of their job/career. The 'champion' needs to be working with this group at and between meetings.
4. *Sense of accomplishment.* CoP members gain a sense of accomplishment in knowing they are addressing issues relevant to the organisation. By having the CoP members decide the issues, topics and CoP speakers develops this sense of ownership and accomplishment.
5. *High management expectations.* While this factor may be more relevant to business-based CoPs, our experience within higher education strongly suggests the need to 'manage-up' and keep senior university leadership aware of CoP outcomes and achievements, especially those that align with university goals and plans.
6. *Real time.* CoP members see their involvement as core to their role within the university, not secondary to their role.

Finally, the role of the 'champion' may also change during the *recreating phase* of the CoPs development. Annual revisiting of the previously-agreed to priorities and activities needs to be undertaken by the 'champion' to keep the CoP member-focused. Succession planning for leadership of the CoP is also essential and provides members with opportunities to develop their leadership and facilitation skills within and between meetings in a non-threatening environment. Furthermore, *intentional* CoPs may be decommissioned during this phase if the purpose of the CoP has been met. Alternatively, an *intentional* CoP may morph into a *nurtured* CoP if the membership of the original *intentional* CoP desires to keep meeting to share practice, address issues or solve problems. During the *recreating phase*, *nurtured* CoPs may also decommission or recreate themselves if the members feel it will benefit them. For example, at CQU, one of our more successful CoPs focuses on postgraduate supervisors as a cohort. However, over time the size of the CoP has become too large and interests of the members too diverse. Thus, the 'champion' (PR) is encouraging the creation of a new CoP focused on postgraduate supervision of international students.

A number of previous studies have identified characteristics of 'champion'(s) of successful CoPs in industry, public organisations and higher education. One of the earliest studies was conducted by Bourhis et al. (2005) who identified the key leadership factors within eight virtual and *intentional* CoPs within public and private organisations. They observed that CoPs whose success exceeded expectations had very involved leaders who possessed the ability to build political alliances, to foster trust, and to find innovative ways to encourage CoP participation. Importantly, the researchers identified that the organisations who created the successful *intentional* CoPs allocated time within the CoP leader's workload to facilitate their CoP. More recently, and within the higher education sector, McDonald et al. (2012) reported on an Australian project that conducted a sector-wide needs analysis and quantitative interviews to identify CoP leadership roles, challenges and development needs. Similar to the finding of Bourhis et al. (2005), these researchers identified CoP leaders need to be passionate about their domain, ensure their CoPs become 'of interest' to their institutional managers through aligning their CoP outcomes or activities with institutional objectives, facilitate the establishment of interpersonal relationships through informal interaction, and encourage their CoP members to interact in a trusting and non-hierarchical way that is collaborative.

In summary, the facilitator/'champion' of CoPs within a higher education setting has a critical role in both creating and facilitating the CoP during and between meetings (McDonald et al. 2012). Moreover, the role also demands soft skills to ensure the theoretical underpinnings and suggested activities at every stage of the CoP creation and development are met. Finally, the CoP creator and facilitator/'champion' needs to be aware of what the research suggests are the key CoP success factors in creating and sustaining CoPs.

6.10 Success Factors in Creating and Sustaining CoPs

Over the last 5–10 years, the authors of the present chapter have observed CoPs both succeed and fail within their respective universities. While empirical research on CoPs in higher education has yet to determine these factors, research and experience from industry suggests 10 factors contribute to the success of CoPs (McDermott 2000; Probst and Borzillo 2008) and five factors contribute to the failure of CoPs (Probst and Borzillo 2008).

While presenting the 10 success factors explaining CoP creation and sustainability, there also appear four key challenges in starting and supporting CoPs that have been able to share knowledge and think together (McDermott 2000). Firstly, the *management challenge* is to communicate that the organisation values sharing knowledge and practices. Secondly, the *community challenge* is to create real value for CoP members and ensure the members share cutting edge thinking rather than copying what is already there. Thirdly, the *technical challenge* is to design both human and information systems that not only make information available but help members think together. Fourthly and finally, the *personal challenge* is for members to be open to the ideas of others and maintain a thirst for developing the CoPs practice. Table 6.4 highlights the ten success factors related to each of these four challenges.

Table 6.4 Critical success factors in building community and how CQU has used these factors to sustain and build CoPs

Success factor	CQU implications
Management challenge	
1. Focus on topics important to the members	Create and facilitate CoPs that are nurtured from the bottom up CoP members choose focus items to discuss and speakers to address the item
2. Find a well-respected CoP member to coordinate the CoP	Encourage 'best practice' leaders to create CoPs or encourage the initiator to work with the 'best practice' leader as co-'champion'
3. Ensure people have time and encouragement to participate	Timetable meetings around both non-teaching weeks and lunchtime or low teaching days (e.g. Fridays) Provide light lunch at meetings 'Champion' well-trained in soft skills and facilitation skills
4. Build on the core values of the organisation	Ensure the 'champion' is aware of the university strategic and operational plans as well as the university mission and values Educate the CoP on the need to try and align activities with these plans

(continued)

Table 6.4 (continued)

Success factor	CQU implications
Community challenge	
5. Get key thought leaders involved	Invite a senior leader to be the CoP 'mentor' and act as the CoP voice/advocate at senior leadership meetings Invite senior leaders and 'best practice' leaders from both within and outside the university to share practice at CoP meetings Ensure meeting notes and e-mail updates are circulated to 'mentors' and senior leaders
6. Build personal relationships among members	Timetable social interaction time before and after CoP meetings Welcome new members and ask them to introduce themselves Encourage different activities and projects (e.g. topic preparation, research projects) within and between meetings and encourage all members to get involved Communicate between meetings via creating and using a group e-mail list
7. Develop an active and passionate core group	Deliberately plan for group projects and activities Engage with key 'best practice' leaders or enthusiastic new staff between meetings
8. Create forums for thinking together and systems for sharing information	Create a CoP group e-mail list, blog, Wiki or website Facilitate meetings well to encourage all CoP members to input and share knowledge and practice
Technical challenge	
9. Make it easy to contribute and access the CoPs knowledge and practices	Create a CoP group e-mail list, blog, Wiki or website Create a friendly and non-threatening atmosphere of trust and openness at meetings to encourage all CoP members to input and share knowledge and practice
Personal challenge	
10. Create real dialogue about cutting edge issues	Encourage CoP members to own the focus of each CoP meeting Be flexible in the topic of each planned meeting

The chapter authors hope their shared experiences and practices outlined in Table 6.4 might assist current CoP facilitators to improve their practice. Moreover, it is hoped that future CoP facilitators may benefit from our collective experience. Just as there are factors relating to the success of CoPs, researchers and lead CoP commentators have also examined both challenges that CoPs face, as well as factors leading to the failure of CoPs.

6.11 Challenges and Failure Factors in Creating and Sustaining CoPs

In contrast to the research examining CoP success factors, empirical research consisting of both survey and semi-structured interviews with 12 leaders of unsuccessful corporate CoPs in European and US companies has identified five major reasons for failure common to the 12 CoPs (Probst and Borzillo 2008). These were:

1. *Lack of a core group.* The lack of a core group (regular attendees at meetings, bringing in fresh ideas, supporting other members on problem solving) actively engaged in the CoP activities lead to failure of the CoP. The lesson learnt is that the CoP 'champion' needs to nurture and encourage this core group early in the initiation and creation stages of CoP development.
2. *Low level of one-to-one interaction between members.* The lack of one-to-one interaction between CoP members (face-to-face, telephone, e-mail etc.) in discussing practices or helping one another solve common problems was observed as a major contributor to failure of the CoP. The implication for the 'champion' is to facilitate personal interaction at CoP meetings and encourage member interaction between meetings.
3. *Rigidity in competences.* Reluctance to learn from others was observed to impede CoP member's capacity to absorb and use new practices. Thus, the 'champion' needs to encourage the trialling and use of new ways of doing things to personally and professionally develop CoP members.
4. *Lack of identification with the CoP.* The research focused on corporate CoPs showed that members of failed CoPs did not view participation in the CoP as meaningful to their daily work. Moreover, they did not perceive other CoP members as peers who could assist them with useful knowledge and practices. The 'champion' thus needs to ensure the members needs and priorities are being met when planning CoP meetings and activities. Furthermore, they need to ensure guest speakers are seen as 'experts' in the domain area and/or topic being discussed or activity being undertaken.
5. *Practice intangibility.* This occurs when CoP members fail to engage with one another in a way that allows them illustrate their practice to make it concrete enough to understand and visualise what they do. The 'champion' thus needs to ensure that the speaker and both written and visual resources illustrate the practice being discussed in a way that members can understand and incorporate into their practice.

While Probst and Borzillo's (2008) research examining reasons why CoPs succeed or fail might help inform our higher education practice, to our knowledge there are limited empirical studies that has examined barriers to academics not forming and engaging with CoPs within higher education (Buckley and Du Toit 2010; Houghton et al. 2015). Buckley and Du Toit (2010) surveyed academics from a range of academic levels from the Faculty of Management within the University of Johannesburg in South Africa. The survey identified four the reasons preventing academics from engaging with a CoP at the university. The most important factor preventing engagement was lack of time with 75 % of respondents agreeing they did not have enough time to participate in CoPs. Their heavy workloads and administration commitments (e.g. meetings, workshops) were identified as the major factors affecting the lack of engagement. The second major barrier was that the academics expected the university leadership/management to should have an incentive to forming and engaging in CoPs. Thirdly, mistrust (e.g. stealing ideas) also played an important role with 41 % of respondents agreeing that mistrust as the reason for not engaging with CoPs. Finally, a sense of uncertainty as to whether other CoP members would contribute equally to the CoP was seen as a barrier with 47 % of respondents saying this factor prevented their involvement in CoPs. In a more recent Australian study, Houghton et al. (2015) used a case study approach to explore reasons why academics did not engage with an online teaching CoP developed by academics within a large multi-campus, multi-disciplinary business school within an Australian metropolitan university. The researchers identified difficulties in finding technologies to fit the CoP purpose, concerns about confidentiality and lack of time as the major reasons for non-engagement of staff.

Despite these barriers to CoP creation and engagement (lack of time, lack of incentive from management, mistrust, concern about confidentiality, and fear of inequity of contribution) in CoPs in a university setting, the Buckley and Du Toit (2010) also identified a number of success factors in CoPs at the University of Johannesburg. These factors included management participation, personal development of CoP members, provision of infrastructure (hardware and software) to share knowledge and practice, desire for knowledge sharing, and relationship building.

Based on 7 years of experience with CoPs at CQU and 10 years of experience at USQ, a number of the CoP success and failure factors identified within the South African higher education sector research above could be used to explain the success and failure of CoPs at CQU and USQ. In particular, our CQU and USQ experience strongly suggests that engagement of university leadership/management in each CoP is a critical success factor. Moreover, the energy, passion and commitment of the CoP 'champion', meeting CoP members' professional development needs, and informal relationship building are important success factors. Indeed, the very reason the co-author of this chapter undertook her fellowship was to develop resources to enable CoP facilitators to be more effective in leading and driving CoPs in the Australian higher education sector.

6.12   Top 10 (11) Tips for Creating and Facilitating CoPs in Higher Education

At CQU, our Office of Learning and Teaching has developed a series of *Top 10 Tips* on many aspects of learning and teaching. In 2011, our Metacop (a CoP made up of the 'champion' from each of CQUniversity's individual CoPs) developed a *Top 10 Tips for Creating and Facilitating a Community of Practice* as a Metacop group activity. Each of our individual CoP facilitator/'champion'(s) was asked independently to develop their own list which we then workshopped together in a collaborative way to arrive at the final list. Below are what we at CQU, based on 7 years of experience in CoPs, believe are the Top 10 Tips for creating and facilitating a CoP. The lead author, as the 'champion' of Metacop and creator of the CoPs 'movement' at CQU, has taken the liberty of adding one more to the list based on his experience in initiating and supporting CoPs from their inception at CQU.

1. *Select a domain name (title) for your CoP*
   The focus of the CoP must be something people are genuinely interested in and want to focus upon. This will generally be started by one person (the 'champion') who takes the initiative to initiate the formation of a CoP. The 'champion' role is a chance to develop leadership skills and influence practice across the university.
2. *Make contact with the existing CoP network*
   The Office of Learning and Teaching at CQU has provided funding for a professional staff member (cops@cqu.edu.au) to provide administrative support for CoPs. Speak with them about the support they can provide including calling the first meeting, organizing venues, Jabber (video-link from desktops), phone and ISL (video-link from teaching rooms), links, and taking notes. Also speak directly to other existing CoP facilitators ('champions') about how they function. Maybe sit in on another CoP meeting to see how they operate.
3. *Make personal approaches to potential CoP participants*
   Personal invitations either face-to-face, e-mail or videoconference are more effective than a generic e-mail. Invite new people along to the next CoP meeting. At every meeting welcome newcomers and encourage them to share their practice.
4. *Call your first meeting and create a relaxed atmosphere*
   Work with the CoP support staff to arrange the venue, teleconference or videoconference links for you. Make everyone feel welcome and invite them to introduce themselves and have input into every meeting. The CoP belongs to all members.
5. *Lock in the calendar of meeting dates early*
   To help participants with time management, schedule meetings at the beginning of the year for the rest of the year using *Outlook* invitations. Our professional staff support person can do this for you. We are all busy, so planning well ahead makes life easier for all. We've found before-term, mid-term and end of term

breaks are best for meetings with 12–2 pm (lunchtimes) the best time of the day to host meetings.

6. *Have a speaker for every meeting*

The purpose of CoPs is to share practice. Consult CoP members to determine guest speakers for future meetings. Guest speakers can be from within or outside the CoP. They can be bought in for face-to-face, ISL or *Jabber* (video-conferencing software) meetings. A standard agenda has been developed for CoPs and usually takes the following format—welcome and social time (10 min), guest speaker (20–30 min), sharing of practice (20–30 min), social time (5–10 min).

7. *Engage every participant in every meeting*

Everyone in a CoP has a contribution to make. Ideally, the chair of the group engages everyone by encouraging the quieter/newer members and inviting those attending virtually to have input first.

8. *Be patient and flexible and consider working with a fellow co-champion*

CoPs are built on trust and relationships that take time to develop. Use face-to-face, ISL, Jabber, teleconference, email, Facebook or LinkedIn—all these channels are good ways to communicate but each has a different purpose. Use the collective wisdom of the CoP to decide the direction and activities in which to engage. If you can find an equally-committed person to work with you as a 'champion', it not only shares the load but keeps each of you 'honest' in planning and achieving outcomes.

9. *Have outcomes and share success*

Choose smaller projects to work on as a group. It may be a research project, a symposium, a research grant, a problem, developing or reviewing a policy, developing a resource or simply discussing practice. Spread the word on what you are doing both within and outside your CoP. Showcase CoP achievements; be they individual or group achievements. Celebrate these and get CQU Communications staff to promote the success or initiative through internal university communications such e-mail updates or newsletters.

10. *Maintain regular contact*

To keep the momentum going ensure regular contact is maintained with CoP participants. Participants are busy managing their own priorities so keep them in the loop with brief dot-pointed e-mails and regular interaction, face-to-face or online via a *Moodle* site, *LinkedIn* 'members only', *Facebook* page, or other media. Again, let the CoP participants decide what the best way to stay in touch is.

11. *Manage up*

Previous research on business CoPs highlights the need to engage with senior leadership/managers as a critical success factor in sustaining CoPs (McDermott 2004; Probst and Borzillo 2008). Moreover, research from business also suggest that aligning CoP needs and values with those of the organisation the CoP sits in is a critical success factor (Van Winkelen 2003). Aware of these needs within a higher education setting, at CQU we communicate with senior leadership about our CoP activities, our alignment with university goals and priorities, and our outcomes related to those goals and priorities. Since we began doing this at CQU we have maintained the funding of a 0.4 professional staff member as a support person for CoPs for the last 5 years. Based on both the initial suggestion by Wenger (1998) and our own practical experience, we 'manage up' in four ways:

a. quarterly face-to-face meetings with both the Deputy Vice-Chancellor and Pro-Vice-Chancellor (Learning and Teaching) whose office funds the 0.4 professional staff appointment,

b. six-monthly written reports of activities and outcomes to the Vice-Chancellor's Advisory Committee that consists of all senior leaders within the University,

c. strategically inviting senior leaders to be 'mentors' for individual CoPs and this get invitations to the respective CoP meeting and also receive the meeting notes, and

d. invitations to senior leaders/managers to speak and present to at least one CoP meeting per year.

6.13   Conclusions

CoPs are increasingly being recognised as a means of building sustained communities of practitioners to share practice, address issues, solve problems and professionally develop staff in Australian higher education (McDonald et al. 2012). Our extensive experience as the 'drivers' and facilitators of CoPs within our respective universities has taught us that the longevity and success of CoPs within higher education revolves around four critical factors:

1. CoP champions being well read in the theory of CoPs.
2. Regular and open communication with the CoP members at and between meetings and the leadership/decision-makers within the university.
3. Group facilitation skill development for each of the CoP facilitators/ 'champions'.
4. The drive, energy and commitment of the CoP facilitator/'champion' as possibly the most critical factor in CoP success. Without that commitment to meet the needs of the CoP membership and to effectively communicate with all stakeholders, the theoretical positive outcomes of CoPs may not be met.

We sincerely hope that through our experience in leading CoPs within higher education settings, this chapter brings the theory and practice of CoP facilitation together to enable the reader to effectively lead the development and sustainability of CoPs within their own organisation. We know CoPs are THE way to share practice, learn from each other, and feel a part of a community of adult learners.

Resources

Resources for leaders of Communities of Practice: http://www.cops.org.au/resources/.

These resources have been designed specifically for those who facilitate CoPs. They focus on leadership as an enabling influence to achieve desired CoP outcomes, and are not intended to address activities around how to form a CoP.

Australian Teaching Fellowship Community of Practice Facilitator Resources: http://www.usq.edu.au/cops/resources/altcfellowship/facilitator-resources.

These resources are prepared as an outcome of the Australian Learning and Teaching Council (ALTC) Teaching Fellowship, 'Community, Domain, Practice: Facilitator catch cry for revitalising learning and teaching through communities of practice' to provide CoP facilitators/'champions' with ideas and practical resources at different phases of a CoPs evolution.

References

Anderson, D., Johnson, R., & Ssaha, L. (2002). *Changes in academic work, implications for universities of the changing age distribution and work roles of academics.* Canberra: Department of Education Science and Training. http://pandora.nla.gov.au/pan/33861/20030326-0000/www.dest.gov.au/highered/otherpub/academic_work.pdf

Baker-Eveleth, L., Chung, Y., Eveleth, D., & O'Neill, M. (2011). Developing a community of practice through learning climate, leader support, and leader interaction. *American Journal of Business Education, 4*(2), 33–40.

Bandura, A. (1972). Modeling theory: Some traditions, trends, and disputes. In R. Parke (Ed.), *Recent trends in social learning theory* (pp. 35–61). New York, NY: Academic Press Inc.

Beach, A. L., & Cox, M. (2009). The impact of faculty learning communities on teaching and learning. *Learning Communities Journal, 1*(1), 7–27.

Bishop-Clark, C., Dietz, B., & Cox, M. (2014). Developing the scholarship of teaching and learning using faculty and professional learning communities. *Learning Communities Journal, 6*, 31–53.

Blanton, M., & Stylianou, D. (2009). Interpreting a community of practice perspective in discipline-specific professional development in higher education. *Innovative Higher Education, 34*(2), 79–92.

Bourhis, A., Dube, L., & Jacob, R. (2005). The success of virtual communities of practice: The leadership factor. *The Electronic Journal of Knowledge Management, 3*(1), 23–26.

Buckley, S., & Du Toit, A. (2010). Academics leave your ivory tower: Form communities of practice. *Educational Studies, 36*(5), 493–503.

Buysse, V., Sparkman, K., & Wesley, P. (2003). Communities of practice: Connecting what we know with what we do. *Exceptional Children, 69*(3), 263–277.

Churchman, D. (2005). Safeguarding academic communities: Retaining texture and passion in the academy. In T. Stehlik & P. Carden (Eds.), *Beyond communities of practice: Theory as experience* (pp. 11–30). Adelaide: University of South Australia.

Churchman, D., & Stehlik, T. (2007). Transforming academic work: Communities of practice in Australian universities. *Journal of Organisational Transformation & Social Change, 4*(3), 263–278.

Cox, M. (2013). The impact of communities of practice in support of early-career academics. *International Journal for Academic Development, 18*(1), 18–30.

Debowski, S., & Blake, V. (2007). Collective capacity building of academic leaders: A university model of leadership and learning in context. *International Journal of Learning and Change, 2*(3), 307–324.

Drouin, M., Vartanian, L., & Birk, S. (2014). A community of practice model for introducing mobile tablets to university faculty. *Innovative Higher Education, 39*(3), 231–245.

Flavell, H., Jones, A., & Ladyshewsky, R. (2008). Academic leadership development for course coordinators and the influences of higher educational change. In *Paper presented at the Proceedings of AUQF 2008: Quality and standards in higher education: Making a difference*, Canberra, Australia, 9–11 July 2008.

Gourlay, L. (2011). New lecturers and the myth of "Communities of Practice". *Studies in Continuing Education, 33*(1), 67–77.

Hackman, J., & Edmondson, A. (2007). Groups as agents of change. In T. Cummings (Ed.), *Handbook of organizational development*. Thousand Oaks, CA: Sage.

Hart, J. (2015). *Difference between social learning and social collaboration*. http://www.c4lpt.co.uk/blog/2015/03/18/the-difference-between-social-learning-and-social-collaboration/ Accessed October 28, 2015.

Henrich, K., & Attebury, R. (2010). Communities of practice at an academic library: A new approach to mentoring at the University of Idaho. *Journal of Academic Librarianship, 36*(2), 158–165.

Higgins, D. (2009). *Promoting learning and teaching communities*. http://www.olt.gov.au/resource-promoting-learning-teaching-communities-anu-2009. Accessed October 28, 2015.

Houghton, L., Ruutz, A., Green, W., & Hibbins, R. (2015). I just do not have time for new ideas: Resistance, resonance and micro-mobilisation in a teaching community of practice. *Higher Education Research & Development, 34*(3), 527–540.

Huisman, J., & Currie, J. (2004). Accountability in higher education: Bridge over troubled water? *Higher Education: The International Journal of Higher Education and Educational Planning, 48*(4), 529–551.

Johnson, C. (2001). A survey of current research on online communities of practice. *The Internet and Higher Education, 4*(1), 45–60.

Kemp, D., & Norton, A. (2014). *Review of the demand driven funding system report*. http://www.education.gov.au/report-review-demand-driven-funding-system. Accessed October 28, 2015.

Kozlowski, K., Holmes, C., & Hampton, D. (2014). The effectiveness of a college-wide research learning community in increasing the research self-efficacy of new faculty. *Learning Communities Journal, 6.*

Kriner, B., Coffman, K., Adkisson, A., Putman, P., & Monaghan, C. (2015). From students to scholars: The transformative power of communities of practice. *Adult Learning, 26*(2), 73–80.

Langelier, L. (2005). *Work, learning and networked: Guide to the implementation and leadership of intentional communities of practice*. http://www.cefrio.qc.ca/media/uploader/GuideFinal_ANGLAIS.pdf

Lave, J. (1988). *Cognition in practice: Mind, mathematics and culture in everyday life*. New York, NY: Cambridge University Press.

Lave, J., & Wenger, E. (1991). *Situated learning: Legitimate peripheral participation*. New York, NY: Cambridge University Press.

Lawrence, J., & Sankey, M. (2008). Communities of practice: A sphere of influence enhancing teaching and learning in higher education. In *Paper presented at the power and place: Refereed proceedings of the Australian and New Zealand communication association conference*, Wellington. http://eprints.usq.edu.au/4268/1/Lawrence_Sankey_ANZCA2008.pdf

Marginson, S. (2006). Dynamics of national and global competition in higher education. *Higher Education: The International Journal of Higher Education and Educational Planning, 52*(1), 1–39.

Mazel, O., & Ewen, S. (2015). Innovation in indigenous health and medical education: The leaders in Indigenous Medical Education (LIME) Network as a community of practice. *Teaching and Learning in Medicine, 27*(3), 314–328.

McDermott, R. (2000). Knowing in the community: 10 critical success factors in building communities of practice. *IHRIM Journal* (March). http://archive2.nmc.org/projects/dkc/sfccp_1.shtml

McDermott, R. (2002). Measuring the impact of communities. *KM Review, 5*(2), 26.

McDermott, R. (2004). How to avoid a mid-life crisis in your CoPs. *KM Review, 7*(2), 10–13.

McDonald, J. (2014). *Community, domain, practice: Facilitator catch cry for revitalising learning and teaching through communities of practice.* Final report 2012 (published 2014).

McDonald, J., Nagy, J., Star, C., Burch, T., Cox, M., & Margetts, F. (2013). Identifying and building the leadership capacity of community of practice facilitators. *Learning Communities Journal, 4.*

McDonald, J., & Star, C. (2006). Designing the future of learning through a community of practice of teachers of first-year courses at an Australian University. In *Paper presented at the designing the future of learning: Proceedings of the first international LAMS conference*, Sydney, Australia.

McDonald, J., & Star, C. (2007). Making meaning of women's networks: A community of practice framework. In *Paper presented at the education, employment, and everything: The triple layers of a woman's life: Refereed Proceedings of the international women's conference*, Toowoomba, Queensland, Australia.

McDonald, J., & Star, C. (2008). The challenges of building an academic community of practice: An Australian case study. In *Paper presented at the engaging communities, Proceedings of the 31st HERDSA annual conference*, Rotorua.

McDonald, J., & Star, C. (2014). Learning and teaching professional development: An Australian community of practice case study. *Learning Communities Journal, 6*, 109–126.

McDonald, J., Star, C., Burch, T., Cox, M., Nagy, J., & Margetts, F. (2012). *Final report: Identifying, building and sustaining leadership capacity for communities of practice in higher education.* http://www.olt.gov.au/project-identifying-building-and-sustaining-leadership-capacity-communities-practice-higher-educatio. Accessed October 28, 2015.

Morgan, S. (2014). Mentoring and support for new faculty: Enhancing social capital using communities of practice. *Learning Communities Journal, 6.*

Morton, J. (2012). Communities of practice in higher education: A challenge from the discipline of architecture. *Linguistics and Education: An International Research Journal, 23*(1), 100–111.

Nagy, J., & Burch, T. (2009). Communities of Practice in Academe (CoP-iA): Understanding academic work practices to enable knowledge building capacities in corporate universities. *Oxford Review of Education, 35*(2), 227–247.

Ng, L., & Pemberton, J. (2013). Research-based communities of practice in UK higher education. *Studies in Higher Education, 38*(10), 1522–1539.

Nixon, S., & Brown, S. (2013). A community of practice in action: SEDA as a learning community for educational developers in higher education. *Innovations in Education & Teaching International, 50*(4), 357–365.

Ortquist-Ahrens, L., & Torosyan, R. (2009). The role of facilitator in faculty learning communities: Paving the way for growth, productivity, and collegiality. *Learning Communities Journal, 1*(1), 29–62.

Palloff, R., & Pratt, K. (2007). *Building online communities: Effective strategies for the virtual classroom* (2nd ed.). San Francisco, CA: Josey-Bass.

Palmer, P. (2002). The quest for community in higher education. In W. M. McDonald (Ed.), *Creating campus community* (pp. 179–192). San Francisco, CA: Jossey-Bass.

Pemberton, J., Mavin, S., & Stalker, B. (2007). Scratching beneath the surface of communities of (mal)practice. *The Learning Organization, 14*(1), 62–73.

Pharo, E., Davison, A., McGregor, H., Warr, K., & Brown, P. (2014). Using communities of practice to enhance interdisciplinary teaching: Lessons from four Australian institutions. *Higher Education Research and Development, 33*(2), 341–354.

Probst, G., & Borzillo, S. (2008). Why communities of practice succeed and why they fail. *European Management Journal, 26*(5), 335–347.

Reaburn, P., Donovan, R., & McDonald, J. (2012). Evaluation of the effectiveness of communities of practice in enhancing learning and teaching: A pilot study at an Australian regional university. In *Paper presented at the HERDSA 2012*, Hobart.

Richards, D. (2012). Leadership for learning in higher education: The student perspective. *Educational Management Administration & Leadership, 40*(1), 84–108.

Sanchez-Cardona, I., Sanchez-Lugo, J., & Velez-Gonzalez, J. (2012). Exploring the potential of communities of practice for learning and collaboration in a higher education context. *Procedia: Social and Behavioral Sciences, 46*, 1820–1825.

Senge, P. (2006). *The fifth discipline*. New York City: Doubleday.

Sense, A. (2015). Work-based researchers and communities of practice: Conceptual and gestational dilemmas. *Australian Journal of Adult Learning, 55*(2), 283–308.

Sharrock, Geoff. (2012). Four management agendas for Australian universities. *Journal of Higher Education Policy & Management, 34*(3), 323–337. doi:10.1080/1360080X.2012.678728.

Tight, M. (2015). Theory application in higher education research: The case of communities of practice. *European Journal of Higher Education, 5*(2), 111–126.

Tuckman, B. (1965). Developmental sequence in small groups. *Psychological Bulletin, 63*(6), 384–399.

Universities Australia. (2013). *An agenda for higher education 2013–2016: A smarter Australia*. https://www.universitiesaustralia.edu.au/news/policy-papers/Universities-Australia-Policy-Statement-2013-2016#.VS7t3WR–70. Accessed October 28, 2015.

Van Winkelen, C. (2003). Why aligning value is key to designing communities: CoPs thrive when both employees and organization see benefits. *Knowledge Management Review, 5*(6), 12–15.

Van Wyk, B. (2005). *Communities of practice: An essential element in the knowledge management practices of an academic library as learning organisation*. Unpublished Masters thesis, University of Pretoria, Johannesburg, South Africa.

Vygotsky, L. (1978). *Mind in society: The development of higher psychological processes*. Cambridge, MA: Harvard University Press.

Wenger, E. (1998). *Communities of practice: Learning, meaning, and identity*. New York, NY: Cambridge University Press.

Wenger, E. (2010). Communities of practice and social learning systems: The career of a concept. In C. Blackmore (Ed.), *Social learning systems and communities of practice* (pp. 179–198). London: Springer.

Wenger, E., McDermott, R., & Snyder, W. (2002). *Cultivating communities of practice: A guide to managing knowledge*. Cambridge, USA: Harvard Business School Press.

Winefield, T., Boyd, C., Saebel, J., & Pignato, S. (2008). Update on National University Stress Study. *Australian Universities' Review, 50*(1), 20–29.

Wisker, G., Robinson, G., & Shacham, M. (2007). Postgraduate research success: Communities of practice involving cohorts, guardian supervisors and online communities. *Innovations in Education & Teaching International, 44*(3), 301–320.

Part II
Research of Higher Education Communities of Practice

Several instances of application of CoP within the higher education are presented in this part that illustrate the lessons learned from research and practice of CoP.

Chapter 7 "Facilitation of Social Learning in Teacher Education: The 'Dimensions of Social Learning Framework'" by de Laat et al. presents a framework regarding dimensions of social learning that enables teachers to assess the alignment of the learning goal a group of teachers with the group's configuration.

Chapter 8 "Communities of Practice in Community-University Engagement: Supporting Co-productive Resilience Research & Practice" by Davies et al. de-scribes application of CoP in community-university engagement, focused on resilience with children, young people and families.

Chapter 9 "Promoting a Community of Practice Through Collaborative Curriculum Reform in a University Business School" by Salmona and Smart presents an innovative model for collaborative curriculum reform developed using CoP.

Chapter 10 "Reflections on the Emergence and Evolution of a Scholarship of Teaching and Learning Community of Practice within a Research-Intensive Higher Education Context" by Dzidic et al. explains a critical case study analysing the emergence and evolution of a higher education CoP centred on the Scholarship of Teaching and Learning (SoTL).

Chapter 11 "Building a Faculty-Centric Virtual Community of Practice (vCoP) within the Post-Secondary Education Environment: A Systems Approach Frame-work" by Watkins et al. describes the process used to design, develop and assess a faculty-centric, system approach based, virtual CoP within the environment of globally distributed faculty post-secondary educational.

Chapter 12 "Enhancing the Impact of Research and Knowledge Co-production in Higher Education Through Communities of Practice" by Guldberg describes the application of CoP in dissemination of research to practice by portraying a professional development programme for school staff who work with pupils with autism.

Chapter 7
Facilitation of Social Learning in Teacher Education: The 'Dimensions of Social Learning Framework'

Maarten de Laat, Emmy Vrieling and Antoine van den Beemt

Abstract To understand the organization of social learning by groups in practice, this chapter elaborates on the use of a framework of dimensions and indicators to explore social learning within (prospective) teacher groups. The applied framework that we call the 'Dimensions of Social Learning (DSL) Framework' is built upon four dimensions including 11 indicators corresponding to these dimensions. The DSL Framework was prompted by a literature review that applied notions of social networks, communities of practice and learning teams as the main underlying perspectives and has been tested empirically in higher education. In this chapter, to validate the framework, we present the findings of a case study that applied the DSL Framework to explore the social dimensions of particular teacher learning groups and to reflect on the usefulness of the indicators in terms of compiling an image of the learning group's social configuration. The case study suggests that the framework appears fruitful for assessing the social configuration of teacher learning groups. Moreover, the resulting image allows teachers to analyse whether their group's configuration fits its learning goals, or whether adjustments are required. It is therefore possible to improve learning processes within teacher learning groups.

Keywords Social learning · Collaborative learning · Teacher groups · Professional development

M. de Laat (✉) · E. Vrieling
Welten Institute, Open University, PO Box 2960,
6401 DL Heerlen, The Netherlands
e-mail: maarten.delaat@ou.nl

A. van den Beemt
Eindhoven School of Education, Eindhoven University of Technology,
Eindhoven, The Netherlands

© Springer Nature Singapore Pte Ltd. 2017
J. McDonald and A. Cater-Steel (eds.), *Communities of Practice*,
DOI 10.1007/978-981-10-2879-3_7

153

7.1 Introduction

Social learning in teacher groups receives growing attention as a stimulus for the professional development of teachers. The literature on professional development increasingly calls for more bottom–up oriented perspectives for sustained professional development connected to everyday organizational life and work (Boud and Hager 2012; Hargreaves and Fullan 2012; Marsick and Volpe 1999; Pahor et al. 2008). While the controlled organizational approach tends to focus on individual skills and knowledge acquisition through the provision of training, the bottom–up approach tends to focus more on spontaneous processes and perceives learning as a way of participation and a process of becoming through engagement in professional practices (De Laat 2012).

The top–down approach, driven by knowledge acquisition, has been criticized for several years (refer to Hargreaves 2000 in the case of teacher professional learning, for example), and researchers have been calling for a broader appreciation of what professional development entails. This implies that we are in need of an improved theory of professional development (Knight 2002) by changing its metaphors (Büchel and Raub 2002; Hargreaves and Fullan 2012; Hodkinson and Hodkinson 2005; Lave and Wenger 1991; Wenger 1998). Boud and Hager (2012) argue that professional development is an ongoing process. They emphasise terms such as organic growth, evolution, and gradual unfolding and perceive professional development as a process of becoming. In this process professionals continuously develop their own identity and abilities in response to events in their professional environment. In their view, 'learning is a normal part of working, and indeed, of most other social activities. It occurs through practice in work settings from addressing the challenges and problems that arise. The majority of learning takes place not through formalised activities but through the exigencies of practice with peers and others, drawing on expertise that is accessed in response to needs. Problem-solving in which participants tackle challenges that progressively extend their existing capabilities and where they learn with and from each other appears to be a common and frequent form of naturalistic development' (Boud and Hager 2012, p. 22). In this view, the main metaphors that we should be using in the context of professional development are participation, construction and becoming (Wenger 1998; Boud and Hager 2012; Hargreaves and Fullan 2012). From a developmental perspective, participation in a professional practice is needed in order to learn and improve. Being a member of a teacher group provides access to a social group where their ways of doing and being are shared, discussed and improved. Participation in such a group provides a platform where issues or problems can be introduced and where the group can construct new solutions and reflect on them together. As a social group they develop their practice and shared knowledge of their profession together. Boud and Hager's statement reads in this context as a strong plea for recognizing professional development as a social learning process where professionals work and learn together, changing and innovating both their professional practice as well as who they are. Participation in this social context contributes to a sense of collective membership and together they build a shared identity related to their profession. In other words, participating in teacher groups facilitates the process of becoming a professional teacher. Enabling this perspective of learning involves being in touch with one's professional colleagues, building the networked connections needed to participate in constructive professional dialogues about what it means to become a professional, and being able to continue to perform in the workplace (De Laat 2012).

Professionals in demanding jobs, in particular, are often faced with complex issues and Lohman (2006) found that they rely on others to a great extent to solve work-related problems. Although professionals may be informed about new approaches individually during training workshops, it is through their informal social networks with colleagues and peers that they learn how to interpret, embrace, share, compile, contextualize and sustain this new knowledge (Baker-Doyle and Yoon 2010; Lane and Lubatkin 1998). The three metaphors discussed earlier form key elements of a social theory of learning and this theory has helped to increase our understanding of the importance of informal learning in the workplace (Clarke and Hollingsworth 2002; Eraut 2000; Marsick and Watkins 2001; Richardson and Placier 2001). This type of learning is relational rather than isolated (Lave 2012). People develop interconnected relationships that provide support, shared risks, trust, access to information and knowledge. These relationships result in an open and engaging social 'web' that facilitates learning, development of professional capital, and the process of how things get done (Cross et al. 2003; Cross and Parker 2004; Hargreaves and Fullan 2012; Thomas and Brown 2011; Villegas-Reimers 2003).

Teachers are expected to take more active control and participate in change processes together with their peers (Hargreaves 2000). With it comes the prevalence of organizational models of self-organization and governance that feed this process —such as communities, networks and teams. Self-regulated groups that operate in a culture where increased professional autonomy and distributed leaderships thrives, give rise to questions about the nature of social learning and how teachers benefit from it. By sharing problems and insights in a constructive way, teachers are able to collaboratively construct new knowledge and skills (Wenger et al. 2011). This knowledge construction is important for a continuous learning and development mode among teaching professionals.

However, the preparation of prospective teachers for their social role as colleagues in schools is weakly conceptualized in teacher education curricula in many countries (Dobber 2011). It is therefore relevant to consider the ways in which teacher educators can prepare prospective teachers for participation in teacher groups. In this chapter we will focus on a specific case in the Netherlands.

Collaborating in teacher groups as an integral part of teacher education curricula can provide models for prospective teachers through which they can learn the practices of working in teacher groups by means of experiencing social practices themselves and understanding the challenges, stimulating the process of participation, co-construction and becoming. The development of social competence can be stimulated with the creation of learning groups of (prospective) teachers and their educators around a central theme with explicit attention for the role of prospective teachers within the group. Prospective teachers can thus benefit from social learning opportunities in teacher groups under the condition of sufficient guidance from more experienced teachers (Vrieling 2012).

Facilitation of social learning in teacher groups is considered a prerequisite for innovative learning (Wenger 1998). According to Büchel and Raub (2002), the facilitation of group learning is a condition for establishing professional development. In general, ongoing negotiation and searching for legitimization and realization are experienced in teacher groups. This continuous negotiation and searching for meaningfulness provides a certain contingency within social learning groups. Although social learning in teacher groups is not a fixed condition, it can be enhanced. Hanraets et al. (2011) distinguish five recommendations to facilitate social learning that largely resemble the design principles for self-regulated learning as formulated by Vrieling et al. (2010): (1) Facilitators must demonstrate a facilitating role instead of a directing role; (2) Participants must feel responsible for their network activity (i.e. shared ownership); (3) Participants must possess sufficient networking skills; (4) Face-to-face and online interactions need to be combined; (5) Support from management and direct supervisors is necessary. These recommendations illustrate the importance of facilitating learning processes within teacher groups.

7.2   The 'DSL Framework' as a Facilitation Instrument

To facilitate teacher groups in assessing their potential social value as a guideline for professional development, Vrieling et al. (2015) have described a 'Dimensions of Social Learning (DSL) Framework' (refer to Table 7.1). With this framework, the behaviour of the group in relation to their learning goals can be explored. The framework characterizes social learning processes in teacher groups on all-embracing commonalities ('dimensions') and associated characteristics ('indicators'). The dimensions serve as a lens through which to observe the current social configuration of teacher groups. It helps to view the group's activities from a learning perspective, containing aspects of teams, communities and networks. Moreover, based on this analysis, the group can reflect on how their social configuration fits with their purpose and learning goals.

The framework is based on four superordinate dimensions: (1) practice; (2) domain and value creation; (3) collective identity and (4) organization, with their corresponding indicators. These indicators are based on the extent to which the group shows specific attitudes and behaviour. They can therefore serve as the foundation for understanding their social learning in practice.

The first dimension, *Practice*, indicates the necessity for a relationship between the knowledge created and shared in the group and teachers' day-to-day activities. This dimension encompasses two indicators: (1) 'Integrated or non-integrated activities', representing the extent to which group knowledge and activities are

Table 7.1 Social learning dimensions and their indicators

1. Practice
1a. To what extent does the group exhibit integrated or non-integrated group activities in daily work?
1b. To what extent does the group exhibit temporary or permanent social activities?
2. Domain and value creation
2a. To what extent does the group focus on sharing or broadening/deepening knowledge and skills?
2b. To what extent does the group experience value creation, individually or collectively?
3. Collective identity
3a. To what extent do participants exhibit a shared or unshared identity?
3b. To what extent does the group exhibit weak or strong ties?
3c. To what extent do the participants view one another as task executors or knowledge workers?
4. Organization
4a. To what extent does the group operate externally directed or self-organized?
4b. To what extent does the group exhibit 'local' or 'global' activities?
4c. To what extent does the group exhibit hierarchic or equal relationships?
4d. To what extent does the group exhibit shared or non-shared interactional norms?

integrated in their practice and (2) 'Temporary or permanent activities', which describes the social learning attitude as reflected in the duration or sustainability of learning activities.

Domain and value creation, the second dimension, is referred to as the sharing of experience and expertise among group members. Key indicators are: (1) 'Sharing or broadening/deepening knowledge and skills', reflecting the extent to which the group develops collective knowledge and skills through dialogue and (2) 'Individual or collective value creation', which describes the level to which the group develops shared value such as group ownership, mutual inspiration or positive interdependence.

When group members work interdependently with a shared purpose and responsibility for collective success, the group can demonstrate a *Collective Identity* (third dimension). This dimension can be characterized by: (1) 'Shared or unshared identity', which is related to group history and social and cultural background; (2) 'Strong or weak ties', which reflects the sense and intensity of general contact among group members and (3) The extent to which group members perceive each other as 'task executors or knowledge workers'.

The final dimension, *Organization,* exhibits how the group is organized. Teacher group organization can be indicated by: (1) The extent to which the group shows 'externally directed or self-organized learning'; (2) The focus on 'local or global activities'; (3) The presence of 'hierarchic or equal relationships' and (4) The extent to which the group shows a shared interactional repertoire, reflected in 'shared or non-shared interactional norms'.

7.3 The Case Study

In line with the importance of facilitation, this chapter further elaborates on the findings of a case study within Dutch pre-service teacher education (Vrieling et al. 2014) which demonstrates the validity of the Dimensions of Social Learning (DSL) Framework. In this study, the social configuration of a group of primary (prospective) teachers and their educators is successfully explored and facilitated with the DSL Framework. We use the framework to help bring the current situation of group organization into focus. The importance of this approach is to acknowledge the unique social setting, dynamics and desires of each group as it is situated in practice. From this view, we take a practice-driven approach rather than an ideal typical approach that favours a particular perspective on learning. To us it is not a question of choosing a community structure above teams or networks but rather the opposite in which aspects of group work and organization benefit from a community, network and/or team approach.

We start by describing the social fabric of a particular group with the DSL Framework as it is experienced in practice. This description or snapshot is applied to explore the current situation to understand how various aspects of social learning can help stimulate an informal professional development culture. It provides a snapshot of the group's learning at a certain point in time and this insight can be applied to reflect on how this current situation fits with the participants' learning goals or ambitions. In other words: Are the group's learning aspirations in line with the way in which they organize their learning? Based on this assessment of group learning the chapter ends with a reflection on how the framework can be used to facilitate teacher group learning in practice. It concentrates on how assessment can inform group facilitation and it provides practical guidelines and operationalization activities to support teacher groups that work with the DSL Framework.

7.3.1 Participants and Analyses

To gain insight into social learning activities within teacher education, the explorative study is conducted in a college of primary teacher education, which predominantly serves schools in a rural area in the eastern part of the Netherlands. This is an independent, relatively small institution with approximately 500 prospective teachers per academic year. Most prospective teachers enter its program after graduating from the middle level of general secondary education and the highest level of secondary vocational education.

In the group we followed, primary teachers (N = 12) from ten different schools interacted with prospective teachers in their third and fourth year (N = 12) and teacher educators (N = 2), as they tackled real-life professional challenges such as counselling of children with special needs. The group's objective was to improve the language teaching and learning within primary schools. All primary teachers and teacher educators participated on a voluntary basis. Network participation was compulsory for the prospective teachers who chose to work on their assignments in the involved schools. The primary teachers in their workplace schools as well as the teacher educators within the institute guided the prospective teachers in the form of feedback opportunities, knowledge provision, practice of research skills, etc. The idea was to narrow the gap between the educational institute and the primary schools by designing and experimenting with new teaching practices.

The group meetings (N = 7) were videotaped. In addition, six in-depth retrospective semi-structured interviews (two prospective teachers, two teacher educators and two primary teachers) were conducted after the final group meeting to ensure in-depth insight into the object of the study. Group meetings and interviews were held in Dutch. on how the participants experienced the group activities from the perspective of the social learning dimensions (refer to Sect. 2.1 and Table 7.1). For this matter, the interview topics corresponded to the dimensions of the DSL Framework. The indicators of the framework were used to formulate more specific questions. For the interview guideline, a biographical approach (Bornat 2008) was used to activate participants into rethinking the social processes from the start towards the present situation of the group.

Analyses consisted of summarizing the raw data, consisting of video recordings of group meetings and audio recordings of interviews, into a content analytic summary matrix (Miles et al. 2014). This matrix was checked reciprocally by two of the authors, which did not result in any major inconsistencies of interpretation. This process resulted in a second matrix containing the final data for analysis as well as codes and themes related directly to the DSL Framework. This second matrix was also used for a member debriefing, which involved presentation of the results to respondents.

7.4 Exploring Social Learning in Teacher Groups

In the following sections, a description of the group is presented for each dimension, as well as lessons learnt, to consider for professional development of (prospective) teacher groups.

The DSL Framework provided an impression (i.e. current status) of the group, based on the analysis of the data of the case study's group meetings. This impression of the group on dimensions and indicators was discussed in the group asking the following questions: Does the group share this impression as a result of the dimensions and indicators? What are the different views between the group participants in response to this impression? In addition, future directions and ideas for professional development were discussed within the group by way of the following question: 'Keeping the group goals in mind, on what dimensions and indicators would the group like to make some changes to improve their learning?'

7.4.1 Practice: Non-integrated or Integrated Group Activities

In line with earlier research findings (Agterberg et al. 2009; Hanraets et al. 2011), all group members emphasized the importance of actual integration of group knowledge and activities into everyday practice. Therefore, the group transformed their experiences into concrete artefacts (tools) to be applied in actual classroom practice.

> Primary teacher: 'For me it is important that the meetings are practical. For example, during the last meeting we made a movie and I really enjoyed that. In response, I did the same with my students and I learned a lot from them.'

Although the meetings provided useful tools, there were no agreements about the actual integration of the group products into classroom practice. Also, the experiences in classroom practice were only occasionally communicated during the meetings.

> Primary teacher: 'Within school I notice that other activities are more urgent and are considered more important by colleagues, which means that the network activities are pushed into the background.'

For some prospective teachers and their corresponding schools, the group activities actually matched their assignments. In these cases the group products were integrated into classroom practice. Other prospective teachers experienced a mismatch between their assignments and the group activities: their work could not be associated directly with the group's goals and activities. Prospective teachers were invited to present their work in an attempt to enhance the integration between the network activities and prospective teachers' assignments. Opportunities for feedback were also provided.

> Prospective teacher: 'All participants performed their own activities and occasionally we worked together. I am not aware of any group products.'

For teachers as well as prospective teachers, it is of importance that the group activities make sense immediately for their own practice of teaching. To formalize agreements on experimenting with group products, the group agenda can list two items: (1) Experiences with the group products in classroom practice and (2) Necessary changes of the group products, based on the group experiences. In addition, making sure that prospective teachers have finished their working plan at the start of the network meetings can enhance the connection between the network activities and prospective teachers' assignments. Even then, it is necessary to closely observe prospective teachers' progression and stimulate them to actively participate in the network for maximum output.

7.4.2   Practice: Temporary or Permanent Activities

The learning network intended to discuss work-related topics to broaden or deepen their knowledge and skills in cooperation with people who shared the same questions or challenges. The teacher educators described long-term (3 years) and short-term (1 year) goals that were discussed with the group members. In the case of the teacher educators and two primary teachers that participated from the start, a more permanent social learning attitude was demonstrated. In terms of the main metaphors that were mentioned earlier, these participants developed professionally through participation, via construction towards becoming. The primary teachers and more prominently the prospective teachers who started to collaborate this year were more focussed on temporary learning activities, i.e. finishing their assignments. They had a more product-centred (short-term) attitude instead of a process-centred (long-term) attitude aimed at getting something out of networked learning immediately. Although prospective teachers valued incoming feedback, it was aimed at improvement of their work and not at the value of learning as a process.

> Prospective teacher: 'For me it is important that I can communicate my ideas and that I receive useful feedback on my ideas.'

Through the creation of awareness, among prospective teachers, of the importance of networked learning for the development of their social competences as a teacher, the product-oriented learning style of many prospective teachers might gradually switch towards a more process-oriented learning style, necessary for long-term learning.

7.4.3   Domain and Value Creation: Sharing or Broadening/Deepening of Knowledge and Skills

Besides prospective teachers' short central presentations of their working progress, it was common to develop collective knowledge and skills through dialogue in small working groups where feedback was provided and accepted. The level of knowledge sharing was therefore demonstrated by way of the sharing of experience and expertise among group members (Agterberg et al. 2009).

> Primary teacher: 'It is pleasant to collaborate with prospective teachers: they have time and opportunities to enhance their knowledge concerning our network theme and their output becomes input for our school. This leads to innovation.'

However, due to the diverse starting situations of the group members, group learning resulting from these activities, by way of sharing a particular interest or (knowledge) domain that brings people together (Wenger 1998), did not occur. The shared interest or domain did not develop into a basis for 'deep level similarity' among group members (Van Emmerik et al. 2011). The teacher educators finalized the group products based on the critical thinking processes of the group meetings. The output from all sessions was collected and shared with the group members in the final meeting.

Group facilitators, i.e. teacher educators, are advised to create opportunities for listening to the perspectives of others in dialogues. This allows for new views to be examined so that old views can be altered. These dialogues, often enforced by questions from novices (Barak et al. 2010; Leh et al. 2005), can lead to reframing: a process of transforming existing perceptions into a new understanding or frame, possibly resulting in the broadening or deepening of knowledge and practice. The group therefore integrates these views into a new mental construct that is collectively held. To rise above the level of knowledge sharing and reach for knowledge creation, it is important that prospective teachers gradually learn how to ask for and provide feedback on their assignments (Vrieling et al. 2010). The feedback process can be practised by modelling, using the following four Schunk and Zimmerman (2007) steps: (1) observation: learners can induce the major features of the skill by watching a model learn or perform; (2) emulation: the learner imitates performances of a model's skill with social assistance; (3) self-control: the learner independently shows a model's skill under structured conditions; and (4) self-regulation: the learner shows an adaptive use of skills across changing personal and environmental conditions. The emulation phase in particular is often underestimated in teacher education curricula (Vrieling 2012) and can therefore be integrated within teacher groups.

7.4.4 Domain and Value Creation: Individual or Collective Value Creation

Individual or collective value creation refers to the level to which the group develops shared value such as group ownership, mutual inspiration or positive interdependence. The group selected and agreed upon a central theme at the start of the learning network. However, in the course of the year it appeared difficult to hold on to the central goals and participating group members strived for individual instead of common goals. The main reason for this individual instead of collective value creation was the focus of the primary and prospective teachers on temporary learning activities (see Sect. 3.2.2).

> Prospective teacher: 'With a common goal as a group, we can develop towards a higher level; however, at this moment the group members strive for their own individual goals.'

As a consequence, the group facilitator again arranged a meeting aimed at more alignment for the second semester meetings. However, because of the diversity in the specific working conditions, no shared goals developed and the collective goals were not reflected upon. To summarize, no capacity was developed within the group to create shared value.

Prospective teacher: 'It seems like the learning materials that we are developing are not connected to students' activities.'

A shared vision is necessary to inspire all group members to actively participate in the group activities. Only members who share mutual values with peers create real learning opportunities and professional growth. One possible way to achieve a shared agenda is for group members to perform collaborative research and consequently generate shared knowledge (Barak et al. 2010). In this process, attention is necessary for achieving a balance between individual accountability and positive interdependence linked to group goals (Hornby 2009). Individual accountability refers to the extent to which the performance of each individual group member is assessed as well as the results given back to the group and the individual. In the case of positive interdependence, group members perceive that they can only reach their learning goals if the other group members also reach their goals.

7.4.5 Collective Identity: Shared or Unshared Identity

Only the teacher educators and two prospective teachers who participated from the start shared the same history and purpose. The prospective teachers and most of their guiding primary teachers had the goal to finish prospective teachers' assignments resulting in new products or ideas for their schools. Although the group facilitator stimulated the group to discuss what was meaningful by engaging them in conversations about needs and objectives, no shared identity evolved. Collective reflection and open dialogue were enhanced resulting in learning within schools. However, group learning in between schools did not occur. The group members did not feel like they belonged to the group, did not feel responsible for the group process and did not plan any meetings other than the group meetings.

Prospective teacher: 'I did not have the feeling that we were one group. I don't even know the names of the primary teachers involved other than the ones in my school.'

When we apply the fourfold taxonomy of Katz and Earl (2010) as a guideline, the first phase, which is 'Storytelling and Scanning for Ideas', was illustrated in our group while the participants gained information by exchanging stories in small groups in search for specific ideas. Phase two, 'Aids and Assistance', also occurred in the form of mutual assistance and feedback when people asked for help. However, because there was no open exchange of ideas and opinions or a feeling of shared responsibility, the final two phases, 'sharing' and 'joint work', were not achieved in the observed group.

Prospective teacher: 'I would like to receive some help from group members for the implementation of the group products in classroom practice, because only then will real innovation occur.'

Groups that aim to stimulate a shared identity are advised to discuss the questions of who they are and how they can be important for each other. For instance,

storytelling and scanning (Meirink et al. 2010) can create a sense of belonging to
the group (De Laat 2012). For teacher groups to function and exist, it is important
that the participants feel responsible for their group activity, by integrating their
perspectives and by ensuring an interwovenness of individual tasks (Doppenberg
et al. 2012) through 'aid and assistance', allowing colleagues to observe the
teaching practices of one another, 'sharing' or exchanging of instructional materials, methods, ideas and opinions, and 'joint work' in which teachers sense a collective responsibility for their teaching (Meirink et al. 2010).

7.4.6 Collective Identity: Strong or Weak Ties

The 'Strong or weak ties' indicator reflects the sense and intensity of general
contact among group members. All group members sensed a strong connection with
the group facilitators (teacher educators) who, in turn, sensed close relationships
with prospective teachers and primary teachers who showed real engagement by
attending all meetings and actively participating in conversations and discussions.

> Teacher educator: 'I feel strongly connected to prospective teachers and primary teachers
> who work pro-actively on their working assignments and actively participate in the
> meetings of the group: the critical thinkers.'

The relationships between the group members of the same school (prospective
teachers and primary teachers) were strong. These strong ties can be characterized
as proximal, frequent and reciprocal, which made participants experience a strong
inward focus that enhanced deeper knowledge within schools. Between schools, the
relationships reflected as weak and were analysed as distant, infrequent and non-
reciprocal. Interaction was kept to a minimum outside of the group meetings. No
real knowledge sharing occurred, because of the lack of cohesive, interpersonal
relationships or ties within the group as a whole.

> Primary teacher: 'The relationships are strong within schools, but weak between different
> schools.'

The teacher educator in his role as group facilitator demonstrated an innovative
and outward focus (Hanraets et al. 2011). Such an external view of the group
requires weak ties outside of the group and is valued for professional development
(Carmichael et al. 2006).

If group members aim for long-lasting social relationships related to their
practice and domain, it can help to analyse the structure of connections among
people. In such learning groups, questions concerning the content, direction, and
strength of these interactions can be elaborated by using 'Social Network Analysis'
(Schreurs et al. 2014). The study of relationships between individuals, referred to as
'Social Network Analysis', operationalizes a social structure in nodes (i.e. the
individual actors within a network) and ties (i.e. the relationships between the
actors).

7.4.7 Collective Identity: Task Executors or Knowledge Workers

In line with the 'Temporary or permanent activities' indicator (Sect. 2.2.2), the primary teachers who participated from the start, and the teacher educators, to a greater extent, demonstrated a long-term attitude towards learning. They not only worked on their tasks, but also shared knowledge within their group in the form of new rules, routines, strategies, best practices, implementation, etc. This attitude enabled the group to develop a more long-term perspective with a focus on continuous learning. Although the opportunities for such a long-term driven perspective were present, a knowledge-driven perspective did not evolve. A first cause for the lack of a knowledge-driven focus in the group was found in the fact that the prospective teachers and starting primary teachers aimed at individual instead of collective value creation (Sect. 2.2.4), i.e. finishing the learning assignments resulting in improvement within their individual schools.

Primary teacher: 'The learning attitude differs between "old" and "new" group members.'

Secondly, it was observed that most group members with a short-term focus sensed their participation in the group as obligatory and members with a long-term perspective considered participation to be voluntary.

Primary teacher: 'Although we were not supported in terms of extra hours, for example, participating in this learning network felt voluntary. I attended all meetings, even on my day off, because the group products are useful. I really want to remain part of this group in the coming years to further extend my expertise.'

To establish a learning situation where the participants can flourish in a self-regulated manner from a continuous learning mode, it is of importance to fulfil various positions within groups (Haythornthwaite and De Laat 2012). Besides more familiar positions such as the 'network star' (people who give information or other resources to several individuals), 'gatekeepers' (people who bring outside information into the network) and the 'technological guru' (people who are everyone's resource for questions on the use of technologies), recent work is beginning to reveal new learning positions in online learning environments (Haythornthwaite and De Laat 2012), such as 'e-facilitators' (people who help in online learning environments to shape the argument, provide summaries and influence the direction of the discussion), 'braiders' (people who take the online community discussions and reinterpret these into different styles and for different audiences), and 'accomplished fellows' (people who set up working parties to explore a subject more in-depth). These new learning positions are examples of how group members can collaborate as knowledge workers, which stands in contrast to groups where members are focused on execution of the given tasks.

7.4.8 Organization: Directed or Self-organized Learning Activities

The teacher educators directed the group externally during the meetings. They made the agenda and the notes, directed the group, and collected and spread information. One of them was also the content expert of the group. In general, the participants were satisfied with these working conditions and identified the important role of the network facilitator in providing good leadership and facilitation. In line with Hanraets et al. (2011), different roles of the facilitator were discerned by the group members, which roles are especially important during the start-up phase of the group: information source, inspirer, guide, public relations manager and investigator.

> Primary teacher: 'We need a chairman who sticks to the appointments that have been made; this way we don't lose any precious time for communication.'

Although the group did not aim to develop regulation of the organizational process, it appeared crucial for the facilitator to make some changes in order to achieve a meaningful, shared context within the group.

> Primary teacher: 'Sometimes we felt like the group facilitator was the only one who had a good idea of the aims of the group and we were the executors of the assignments.'

Therefore, the group elaborated on two fundamental questions, representing the domain (meaningful activity) and the identity (shared activity) of the group: (1) 'How are we relevant to each other?' and (2) 'Who are we and where are we going?' (Akkerman et al. 2008). After the intervention, prospective teachers were more involved in the preparation of the sessions. However, the leadership activities were not taken up by a group of people to arrive at a division of responsibilities.

The leadership activities can be distributed across multiple people to enhance a shared agenda for the group. It is of importance for all members to be actively involved to enhance feelings of responsibility for a proper outcome of the group. In such settings, distributed leadership appears as an attractive concept to enhance professional development of teacher groups. Based on the expertise of the participants, learning environments can be created in which all members can contribute to problems and challenges concerning school improvement. Tasks and roles can be divided to formalise this process. However, the regulation of group activities among group members, and more eminent, the prospective teachers, should be a gradual process (Vrieling 2012). In an optimal learning situation, group facilitators who can be seen as experts, gradually decrease assistance when the (prospective) teachers are able to perform more independently. To reach for this aim, the necessary regulation skills can be modelled to novices upon four regulatory skill levels (Schunk and Zimmerman 2007).

7.4.9 Organization: Local or Global Activities

Overall, the group displayed an inward focus towards local activities within their own schools. No general themes were discussed. The group facilitator was the only party who was more generally-oriented and proactively sought for collaborative partners and publication opportunities.

Primary teacher: 'Our group products are applied within and between the involved schools.'

Although teachers often act locally, it is fruitful for teacher groups to share their knowledge and expertise. This allows for small and local teacher groups to be cultivated towards more globally-oriented groups. Successful groups with a global orientation draw people together from disparate contexts around shared challenges, yet also sustain the ability to stay close to the local needs of their members.

7.4.10 Organization: Hierarchic or Equal Relationships

A different level of expertise occurred because of the diversity of group members. This resulted in a learning climate where some group members were observed as dominant in their behaviour. As a result, the discussing climate within the group meetings did not feel safe for all members, especially the prospective teachers. No group activities were executed to enhance equality between the group members.

In the second semester meetings, when the group composition had been altered (the two primary teachers that participated from the start decided to leave the group), the group participants generally perceived each other as equals and appreciated the input of others. In the group meetings, prospective teachers and primary teachers often interacted in small groups where no hierarchical structures were observed.

Primary teacher: 'Primary teachers may be experienced, but they are not per se the experts.'

However, some prospective teachers only felt confident in conversations with the group members of their own schools.

Prospective teacher: 'Because I am more familiar with the primary teachers from my own school, I feel more confident to discuss matters with them.'

In addition, prospective teachers remarked that their assignments were judged by one of the teacher educators, a possible complicating factor when equal relationships are strived for.

The hierarchical structures within groups can hinder spontaneous learning. For prospective teachers in particular it is of importance to learn how to discuss different topics in groups where various levels of expertise are present. Instead of viewing such a situation as not quite as safe, through the use of modelling (see Sect. 2.2.3), prospective teachers can learn how to profit from these circumstances by way of dividing roles for example.

7.4.11 Organization: Shared or Non-shared Interactional Norms

Although opportunities were provided to discuss relevant themes within the group as a whole, prospective teachers in particular did not always possess sufficient confidence to freely add to group discussions, ask questions or ask for feedback. This was caused by the size of the group, which consisted of 25 members, as well as the lack of collective identity. The communication procedure was not discussed within the group. However, to meet the expectations of the participants, the group facilitator did organize many opportunities for discussion and interaction in small groups during the second semester meetings. In these meetings, different perceptions within the group were openly discussed.

> Prospective teacher: 'For me the most valuable output of the meetings is the opportunities to interact with colleagues in small groups.'

By using a range of activities that can be found in the 'Toolkit Networked Learning' (Wenger et al. 2011), interactions can be facilitated between group members, establishing and maintaining positive interdependence. Group members can therefore be supported to find a balance between individual goals and accountability, and group goals.

7.5 Creating an Impression of the Group's Social Learning

The features of social learning as discussed in Sect. 7.4 are a guide to explore and reflect upon the configuration of a group, rather than to make a value judgment to assess the effectiveness of the teacher groups. Teacher groups differ on the 4 dimensions of social learning, because they address different goals. The DSL Framework helps to obtain a clearer picture of how groups organize and focus their activity and this knowledge can be used to reflect upon and discuss future actions. Based on our observations of the group as described in Sect. 7.4, the case study provides an impression of the group that is visualized in Fig. 7.1. Here the dimensions of the framework are used as sliders, where the star roughly marks the impression based on our explorations:

This impression was reviewed with the group facilitator, resulting in an image that was subsequently discussed with the group and altered where appropriate. For example, the 4c indicator ('To what extent does the group exhibit hierarchic or equal relationships?') was viewed as rather hierarchical. However, according to the group, the members felt equal, at least in the second semester of the research period. The dimensions therefore served as a lens or framework through which to observe the current social configuration of the group in relation to their learning goals, and provided feedback to the group.

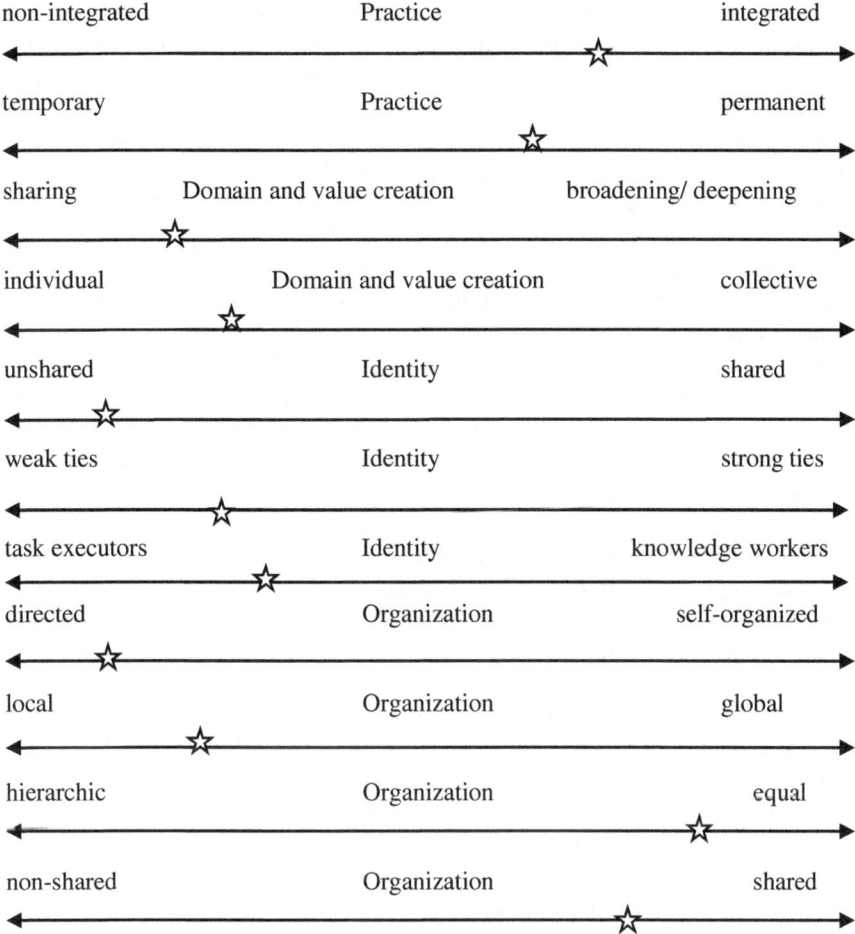

non-integrated   Practice   integrated

temporary   Practice   permanent

sharing   Domain and value creation   broadening/ deepening

individual   Domain and value creation   collective

unshared   Identity   shared

weak ties   Identity   strong ties

task executors   Identity   knowledge workers

directed   Organization   self-organized

local   Organization   global

hierarchic   Organization   equal

non-shared   Organization   shared

Fig. 7.1 Visualization of the group's social configuration from a dimension perspective

7.6 Making the DSL Framework Practice-Ready

The development of learning groups, over time, is emphasized by Büchel and Raub (2002), for instance, who describe four stages of development. During the first stage the learning group should gain focus, for instance, by defining learning goals and ensuring management support. The second stage is used to create the network context, while subsequently in stage three the network activities are routinized. The fourth stage is used to leverage network results. Although useful, these four stages appear to be ideal, but typical and network development in everyday practice may not follow this smooth pathway. Boud and Hager (2012), as discussed in the introduction to this chapter, perceive network development as a movement of both the learning group and its participants through the metaphors of participation, construction and becoming.

The DSL Framework, as may have become clear from the case study results, provides a snapshot image of the learning group. The results also showed that the learning group without support could hardly construct this image. However, when a learning group defines long-term learning goals, for instance, participants want to know whether the group's development is heading towards those goals. The DSL Framework describes this as the extent to which the learning group displays permanent activities.

The case study displays two important issues related to the original DSL Framework. Firstly, the participating teachers were looking beyond the snapshot image of the group's social configuration. They were looking for an instrument with which to follow the group process and development over a longer period of time with several measurements. Secondly, the teachers wished for more practice-related phrasing within the framework. The dimensions and indicators of the DSL Framework originally served as a research instrument to assess learning groups. However, applying the framework in everyday practice, as we did in our case study, taught us that, although the original framework indicators were visible and recognizable, they were formulated in a manner that is too abstract for independent use by learning groups.

Having formulated these issues, the question that arises is 'What is needed in order to enable learning groups to assess development on their own?' How can we make the DSL Framework practice-ready? We first approached this question by means of biographical interviews with learning group members (Van den Beemt et al. 2015). Biographical interviews (Bornat 2008; Van den Beemt and Diepstraten 2016) are interviews during which we ask respondents to look back over a period of time and narrate experiences related to a certain topic, in this case, the learning group. Our biographical interviews discussed dynamics and development of the learning group by focusing on the first participation of respondents in the learning group, the subsequent pathways of participation and the experienced relations with other group members. Interview questions were guided by topics such as learning goals, activities, participants and network development. The interviews and simultaneous observations of learning group meetings taught us how to rephrase the DSL Framework indicators into 29 so-called viewpoints (Van den Beemt et al. 2015).

Table 7.2 presents an example of how the dimensions 'Collective identity' as well as 'Organization' were translated into viewpoints. The feedback from learning groups during the process confirmed the usefulness of the viewpoints to chart both the development and quality of the learning process. These viewpoints can therefore facilitate (support) learning networks to assess their development on these characteristics.

Table 7.2 Translation of dimensions 'collective identity' and 'organization' into viewpoints

Dimension: collective identity
Indicator: 3a. To what extent do participants exhibit a shared or unshared identity?
Viewpoints: • Informal network activities during the meetings to strengthen relatedness • Sense of belonging to the group • Contact between group members outside the meetings
Dimension: Organization
Indicator: 4a. To what extent does the group operate externally directed or self-organized?
Viewpoints: • Reflective quality of the learning group for self-guidance during preparation, performance and evaluation of activities • Division of roles based on expertise among members

7.7 Discussion

There is growing attention for social learning in teacher groups as a stimulus for the professional development of teachers. In this chapter the social configuration of a learning group of (prospective) teachers and their educators is observed and facilitated based on the 'Dimensions of Social Learning (DSL) Framework' which includes 4 dimensions and 11 indicators of social learning. The DSL Framework helps to put the metaphors, used to reflect upon professional development, into perspective. This is done by reflecting on the extent to which there is group participation, collaboration (i.e. co-construction) to change practice and a sense of belonging and shared identity within the group.

The case study demonstrates that social learning in teacher groups can be associated with the DSL Framework. The social configuration of the group is visualized by using the DSL Framework. The framework can therefore support the awareness of the group's members towards the dimensions of social learning. The participants recognized the dimensions and their indicators and were able to reflect on the social configuration of their group by using the framework. Moreover, it showed that the framework could support the participants in observing and facilitating group development. The dimensions serve as a lens or framework through which to observe the current social configuration of a teacher group. The behaviour of the group in relation to its learning goals is therefore assessed. Based on this analysis, the group can reflect on how its social configuration fits the purpose and learning goals. As a result, teacher groups become more aware of the potential value of their group for future development.

As for the facilitation of the prospective teachers' roles in learning groups, a shared domain and identity for all participants is difficult to achieve, although it is conditional for learning. Unless goals are clearly stated and agreed upon, teacher groups can easily lose energy and underperform. Even if group facilitators develop and communicate goals, this is not a guarantee that the goals will animate members. To achieve a shared agenda, teacher group facilitators can influence group members' behaviour trough group design and facilitation. The facilitator is advised to investigate the needs and expectations of the group members at an early stage and use this information for co-developing the group. Through dividing the responsibilities between group members, the role of the facilitator will evolve into a coach instead of a director of the group, and that can mean the difference between enthusiasm and cynicism, illustrating the important role of the facilitator. Without facilitation, it is difficult for teacher groups to self-regulate their learning process. In line with self-regulated learning theories, it is essential for group facilitators to gradually diminish their support (scaffolding) during the process. Successful knowledge building of the group's participants is therefore ensured, which is a prerequisite for self-regulation of learning.

By way of identifying and modelling the expected behaviours, prospective teachers can be thoroughly guided in developing sufficient networking skills. Areas of interest in this matter are: (1) create a link between the group activities and prospective teachers' assignments (practice); (2) ask prospective teachers what they want to get out of the community (domain and value creation); (3) set up short social activities before moving on to 'working' activities (identity) and (4) assign social and facilitative roles until roles emerge naturally (organization).

The operationalization of the DSL Framework is an example of the iterative process between literature and (educational) practice. We started our exploration with a review of current literature on teacher social learning (Vrieling et al. 2015. The dimensions and indicators support the assessment of the social configuration of teacher groups. However, practice required a framework that is formulated in a less abstract manner. The resulting viewpoints facilitate teacher-learning groups in assessing their learning processes and social configuration. The question is whether these viewpoints serve as a means to assess the complete lifetime of learning groups. To answer this question, in current research, the framework is operationalized into qualitative (interview guideline) and quantitative (online questionnaire) instruments with supportive guidelines for teacher groups to observe and facilitate their professional development. The purpose of the operationalization is to extend the group's assessment (one moment snapshot) into support (development over time).

Social scientific research based on perceptions and hindsight is always coloured by memory and narration. However, perspectives such as the DSL Framework enable us to discuss these perceptions and sharpen their consequences. The translation of the DSL Framework dimensions into practice-related viewpoints facilitates participants in learning teams to discuss their perceptions and to initiate new developments based on the resulting diagnosis.

References

Agterberg, M., Van den Hooff, B., Huysman, M., & Soekijad, M. (2009). Keeping the wheels turning: The dynamics of managing networks of practice. *Journal of Management Studies, 47* (1), 85–108.

Akkerman, S., Petter, C., & De Laat, M. (2008). Organizing communities-of-practice: Facilitating emergence. *Journal of Workplace Learning, 20*(6), 383–399.

Baker-Doyle, K., & Yoon, S. A. (2010). Urban teacher support networks. *Social Network Theory and Educational Change*, 115–126.

Barak, J., Gidron, A., & Turniansky, B. (2010). 'Without stones there is no arch': A study of professional development of teacher educators as a team. *Professional Development in Education, 36*(1–2), 275–287.

Bornat, J. (2008). Biographical methods. In P. Alasuutari, P. L. Bickman, & J. Brannen (Eds.), *The Sage handbook of social research methods* (pp. 344–356). London: Sage.

Boud, D., & Hager, P. (2012). Re-thinking continuing professional development through changing metaphors and location in professional practices. *Studies in Continuing Education, 34*(1), 17–30.

Büchel, B., & Raub, S. (2002). Building knowledge-creating value networks. *European Management Journal, 20*(6), 587–596.

Carmichael, P., Fox, A., McCormick, R., Procter, R., & Honour, L. (2006). Teachers' networks in and out of school. *Research Papers in Education, 21*(2), 217–227.

Clarke, D., & Hollingsworth, H. (2002). Elaborating a model of teacher professional growth. *Teaching and Teacher Education, 18*(8), 947–967.

Cross, R. L., & Parker, A. (2004). *The hidden power of social networks: Understanding how work really gets done in organizations.* Harvard: Harvard Business Press.

Cross, R., Parker, A., & Sasson, L. (Eds.). (2003). *Networks in the knowledge economy.* Oxford: Oxford University Press.

De Laat, M. (2012). *Enabling professional development networks: How connected are you?* Heerlen: LOOK, Open University of the Netherlands.

Dobber (2011). *Collaboration in groups during teacher education.* Doctoral dissertation, Leiden University, The Netherlands.

Doppenberg, J., Bakx, A., & Den Brok, P. (2012). Collaborative teacher learning in different primary school settings. *Teachers and Teaching: Theory and Practice, 18*(5), 547–566.

Dron, J., & Anderson, T. (2014). The Distant Crowd. *International Journal of Learning and Media, 4*, 3.

Eraut, M. (2000). Non-formal learning and tacit knowledge in professional work. *British Journal of Educational Psychology, 70*(1), 113–117.

Hanraets, I., Hulsebosch, J., & De Laat, M. (2011). Experiences of pioneers facilitating teacher networks for professional development. *Educational Media International, 48*(2), 85–99.

Hargreaves, A. (2000). Four ages of professionalism and professional learning. *Teachers and Teaching: Theory and Practice, 6*(2), 151–182.

Hargreaves, A., & Fullan, M. (2012). *Professional capital: Transforming teaching in every school.* New York: Teachers College Press.

Haythornthwaite, C., & De Laat, M. (2012). Social network informed design for learning with educational technology. In A. D. Olofsson & J. O. Lindberg (Eds.), *Informed design of educational technologies in higher education: Enhanced learning and teaching* (pp. 352–394). New York: Amazon.

Hodkinson, H., & Hodkinson, P. (2005). Improving schoolteachers' workplace learning. *Research Papers in Education, 20*(2), 109–131.

Hornby, G. (2009). The effectiveness of cooperative learning with trainee teachers. *Journal of Education for Teaching: International Research and Pedagogy, 32*(5), 161–168.

Katz, S., & Earl, L. (2010). Learning about networked learning communities. *School Effectiveness and School Improvement, 21*(1), 27–53.

Knight, P. (2002). A systemic approach to professional development: Learning as practice. *Teaching and Teacher Education, 18*(3), 229–241.

Lane, P. J., & Lubatkin, M. (1998). Relative absorptive capacity and interorganizational learning. *Strategic Management Journal, 19*(5), 461–477.

Lave, J. (2012). Changing practice. *Mind, Culture, and Activity, 19*(2), 156–171.

Leh, A., Kouba, B., & Davis, D. (2005). Twenty-first century learning: Communities, interaction and ubiquitous computing. *Educational Media International, 42*(3), 237–250.

Lohman, M. C. (2006). Factors influencing teachers' engagement in informal learning activities. *Journal of Workplace Learning, 18*(3), 141–156.

Marsick, V. J., & Volpe, M. (1999). The nature and need for informal learning. *Advances in Developing Human Resources, 1*(3), 1–9.

Marsick, V. J., & Watkins, K. E. (2001). Informal and incidental learning. *New Directions for Adult and Continuing Education, 2001*(89), 25–34.

Meirink, J., Imants, J., Meijer, P. C., & Verloop, N. (2010). Teacher learning and collaboration in innovative teams. *Cambridge Journal of Education, 40*(2), 161–181.

Miles, M. B., Huberman, A. M., & Saldaña, J. (2014). *Qualitative data analysis: A methods sourcebook*. London, UK: Sage Publications Ltd.

Pahor, M., Škerlavaj, M., & Dimovski, V. (2008). Evidence for the network perspective on organizational learning. *Journal of the American Society for Information Science and Technology, 59*(12), 1985–1994.

Richardson, V., & Placier, P. (2001). Teacher change. In *Handbook of research on teaching* (pp. 905–947).

Schreurs, B., Van den Beemt, A., Prinsen, F., Witthaus, G., Conole, G., & De Laat, M. (2014). An investigation into social learning activities by practitioners in open educational practices. *The International Review of Research in Open and Distance Learning, 15*(4), 1–20.

Schunk, D. H., & Zimmerman, B. (2007). Influencing children's self-efficacy and self-regulation of reading and writing through modelling. *Reading and Writing Quarterly, 23*(1), 7–25.

Van den Beemt, A., & Diepstraten, I. (2016). Teacher perspectives on ICT: A learning ecology approach. *Computers & Education, 92–93*, 161–170.

Van den Beemt, A., Vrieling, E., & De Laat, M. (2015). *Toepassing en validering van het 'Dimensies van Sociaal Leren'-raamwerk. [Application and validation of the 'Dimensions of Social Learning' Framework]*. Paper presented at the 2015 Dutch Educational Research Conference, Leiden, Netherlands

Van Emmerik, I. J. H., Jawahar, I. M., Schreurs, B., & De Cuyper, N. (2011). Social capital, team efficacy and team potency. The mediating role of team learning behaviors. *Career Development International, 16*(1), 82–99.

Villegas-Reimers, E. (2003). *Teacher professional development: An international review of the literature*. Paris: International Institute for Educational Planning.

Vrieling, E. M. (2012). *Promoting self-regulated learning in primary teacher education*. Doctoral dissertation, Open University, The Netherlands.

Vrieling, E. M., Bastiaens, Th. J., & Stijnen, P. J. J. (2010). Process-oriented design principles for promoting self-regulated learning in primary teacher education. *International Journal of Educational Research, 49*(4–5), 141–150.

Vrieling, E., van den Beemt, A., & de Laat, M. (2015). What's in a name dimensions of social learning in teacher groups. *Teachers and Teaching: Theory and Practice*. doi:10.1080/13540602.2015.1058588.

Vrieling, E., van den Beemt, A., de Laat, M. (2014). *Dimensies en indicatoren van sociaal leren in een pabo leernetwerk [Dimensions and indicators of social learning within a pre-service teacher education network]*. Paper presented at the 2014 Dutch Educational Research Conference, Groningen, Netherlands.

Wenger, E. (1998). *Communities of practice: Learning, meaning and identity*. Cambridge: University Press.

Wenger, E., Trayner, B., & De Laat, M. (2011). *Telling stories about the value of communities and networks: A toolkit*. Heerlen: Open University of the Netherlands.

Chapter 8
Communities of Practice in Community-University Engagement: Supporting Co-productive Resilience Research and Practice

Ceri Davies, Angie Hart, Suna Eryigit-Madzwamuse, Claire Stubbs, Kim Aumann, Kay Aranda and Becky Heaver

Abstract For the last 10 years, we have been exploring Communities of Practice (CoPs) as both a conceptual and practical approach to community-university engagement, most notably in our work on resilience with children, young people and families. We have found elements of CoP theory and practice to be a powerful

C. Davies (✉)
Community University Partnership Programme, University of Brighton,
Falmer, Brighton BN1 9PH, UK
e-mail: c.davies@brighton.ac.uk

A. Hart
Centre for Health Research and Community University Partnership Programme,
University of Brighton, Falmer, Brighton BN1 9PH, UK
e-mail: a.hart@brighton.ac.uk
URL: http://www.boingboing.org.uk

A. Hart · C. Stubbs · K. Aumann
BoingBoing Community Interest Company, Brighton, UK
e-mail: info@boingboing.org.uk
URL: http://www.boingboing.org.uk

K. Aumann
e-mail: info@boingboing.org.uk
URL: http://www.boingboing.org.uk

S. Eryigit-Madzwamuse · B. Heaver
Centre for Health Research, University of Brighton, Falmer, Brighton BN1 9PH, UK
e-mail: s.eryigit-madzwamuse@brighton.ac.uk

B. Heaver
e-mail: b.heaver@brighton.ac.uk

K. Aranda
School of Health Sciences, University of Brighton, Falmer, Brighton BN1 9PH, UK
e-mail: k.f.aranda@brighton.ac.uk

© Springer Nature Singapore Pte Ltd. 2017
J. McDonald and A. Cater-Steel (eds.), *Communities of Practice*,
DOI 10.1007/978-981-10-2879-3_8

and pragmatic way to approach many of the tensions, considerations and nuances of this work. This chapter focuses on our experiences (academics and community partners) of running a CoP with a diverse membership that meets monthly to discuss, disagree and debate about resilience research and practice. We outline those theoretical areas we have found invaluable in getting us started with CoPs, but we also discuss where we have found ourselves needing to develop our own approaches to help us with the complex circumstances and systems, rather than within one single domain. We identify a series of paradoxes that we have to navigate in making our CoP work—particularly the tensions between being social but intentional in our practice, and how we can disentangle the blend of participation and learning that occurs in our CoP space. We conclude by turning to the future, to consider the conceptual development that might be helpful in this area and to reflect on the potential of supporting co-productive research and practice in pursuing social goals through communities of practice.

Keywords Communities of practice · Community university engagement · Resilience

8.1 Introduction

At the University of Brighton, together with community partners, we have been exploring the Community of Practice (CoP) approach in our work on community-university engagement for the last 10 years. Taking a lead from Lave and Wenger's (1991) work on situated learning, we have been inspired by the guiding principle that learning takes place in the context in which it is applied, and that knowledge is a co-constructed social process in cultivating social learning spaces. Both these ideas have great resonance for our community-university engagement activities; happening as they do across different cultural, social, political and knowledge domains.

We understand CoPs to be "groups of people informally bound together by shared experience and a passion for a joint enterprise" (Wenger and Snyder 2000, pp. 139–140). This chapter focuses on our interpretation and use of CoP theory; those underpinning concepts that we find most valuable to our work; and how we put those ideas into practice. To illustrate how we apply CoP theory, we draw on the work of a specific research cluster whose members work across university and community spheres co-developing research and practice in the area of resilience among young people and families.

We conceptualize resilience as overcoming adversity, whilst also potentially subtly changing, or even dramatically transforming (aspects of) that adversity (Hart et al. 2013b). Within this perspective, the academics writing this paper work and/or live with children and young people with mental health issues, with disabilities, who are adopted or in foster care, who over/misuse drugs or alcohol, whose parents over/misuse drugs or alcohol, as well as "mainstream" children and young people and their families, service providers and policy-makers. The key principles that we include in our approach to resilience research and practice are knowledge co-production and using an inequalities imagination. For us this includes co-leading research and practice development; transformative practice, including the promotion of psycho-political literacy; inclusion and supporting researchers to be aware of groups of people who are systematically excluded from research because they are perceived as too difficult to include; and having a whole-system orientation rather than working solely with individuals.

In this chapter, we focus on our experiences of running our Resilience Forums—CoPs which meet monthly and are communicated as being "open to anybody (with a pulse!) involved with or interested in resilience research and practice". Starting in 2010 in Brighton, and run jointly between the University of Brighton and boingboing, a local community interest company (http://www.boingboing.org.uk/index.php/resilience-forum), in 2014 the Forum expanded to Hastings. In 2015, through collaboration with YoungMinds, a national charity, we have also set up a joint Forum in London. These CoPs are a space that we organise, welcoming and encouraging discussion, disagreement and debate about resilience research and practice. They are free to attend and topics for discussion to date have included child protection, sociological critiques of resilience, hope, inequalities, reoffending, collective resilience and building resilience in practice. We draw on experiences from these CoPs to form the empirical basis of this chapter and from this point refer to them collectively as "the Forum" for the purposes of discussion. Since 2007, we have also convened time-limited, closed CoPs funded by external income sources from local councils and health authorities which we have discussed elsewhere (for example Aranda and Hart 2014). More recently, and with other collaborators as part of Imagine (http://www.imaginecommunity.org.uk/), a funded research project, we have set up a series of time-limited/closed, and open/Forum-style CoPs in the UK and beyond. In this chapter, we mostly draw on our experiences of convening the open/Forum-style CoP in our local community. Because of this, we have deliberately anonymized examples in order to protect the identities of Forum participants.

In this chapter we want to move beyond making the case for situated learning and the core conceptual underpinnings of CoPs; plenty before us have done this (Brown and Duguid 1991; Edwards 2005; Graber 2013; Roberts 2006; Wenger 1998; Wenger et al. 2011). Instead, we set out why we think CoPs are worth exploring in the unique landscape of community-university engagement and in the field of resilience. Guided by the Resilience Framework that we co-created with other practitioners, parents and young people (Boingboing 2010; Hart et al. 2007a), a communities of practice approach also helps us explore this domain at the interface between research and practice.

We also discuss how our practice experiences align with, as well as challenge, existing wisdom on CoPs and what they do. One key issue is that there is no clear consensus over what a CoP is and the variation in application of CoPs has resulted in a body of theoretical work that largely has its origins in professional, and indeed, mono-professional, contexts. We have previously argued that the resulting presentation of some of this work therefore is overly neutral and does not align closely with disparities in power, resource, knowledge capital and subject position that is the reality of working with different people across varied contexts rather than within a largely homogenous context (see Hart et al. 2013a).

Our chapter begins by offering a brief history of community-university engagement at the University of Brighton. We also share a short history of our resilience research and how we came to develop our current Forums. We then turn to an exploration of which CoP concepts we have mobilized within the Forums, including boundary spanning, social artistry and legitimate peripheral participation. In reviewing our experiences we share what we have learned so far about cultivating social learning spaces and address the tension of making CoPs useful across, rather than within, domains. This includes highlighting three particular challenges of our work—leadership, learning and participation, and the issue of situation. We address existing theory and how we (re-)interpret and extend this thinking into our practice contexts. From this mix we try to identify what we think is good enough in getting started with and purposefully using CoP ideas. The final parts of this chapter turn to the future, to consider the conceptual development that might be helpful in this area and to reflect on the potential of supporting co-productive research and practice in pursuing social justice goals through communities of practice.

8.2 Community-University Engagement

Contemporary debates on the role and purpose of universities in society are wide ranging—encompassing aspects of access, student fees, the knowledge economy and increasingly the role of research and the impact it can have in the public sphere. For the Community University Partnership Programme (Cupp) at the University of Brighton we have been concerned with how partnerships between communities and the university can unlock solutions, address contemporary social issues and develop partnerships for mutual benefit. As outlined by Hart and Wolff (2006), our framework is rooted in a sense of place and a commitment to engage with issues of locality. We approach this in a number of ways including: providing a first point of contact for all enquiries through our community helpdesk (Hart et al. 2009), delivering a programme of seed funding that helps catalyze early partnership working between academics and community partners (Cupp 2011), and linking community engagement to the curriculum (Millican and Bourner 2014).

These pathways have allowed us to support a broad variety of partnership work from using campus green space for allotments open to the community, to working with Lesbian, Gay, Bisexual, Transgender and Queer (LGBTQ) activists as co-researchers on influencing local authority service delivery. Multiple stakeholders from academic, community and public sector backgrounds have been working together for mutual benefit. Of course this agenda is also situated in broader policy, strategic and civic contexts and the interpretation of engagement, to what purpose and for whom, are all variably understood depending on the complex interaction of these factors (for an overview see Benneworth et al. 2009; Brennan 2008; Hart et al. 2007b; Watson et al. 2011). Most recently in the UK, for example, with the rise in student fees and changes to the measures by which research funding is allocated, local connectivity can distinguish an institution and acting on the imperative of engagement can result in increased standing and financial success for the university.

Regardless of this changing context, the art of working across different domains of practice, cultures, languages and norms is a constant consideration for those involved in community engagement research and practice. The UK Community Partner Network, which was co-founded by one of the authors, in one of their practical guides (UKCPN, n.d.) pulls together an overview of the importance of the following in partnership working:

- Negotiating different cultures
- Agreeing and managing expectations
- The balance of power and equity
- Funding and capacity
- General communications

What we know is that a range of underpinning skills and process need to be in place to achieve collaborative work—these include building trust, finding a shared language, paying attention to relationships and aiming for co-production.

8.2.1 So Why CoPs?

CoPs initially fit into this picture by providing us with a theoretical debate from which to draw when thinking about the venture of community-university engagement. Such efforts have implications from strategic through to project levels but all require a re-definition of what is possible in process, practice and outcome of university relationships with their communities. We thought this might offer us a new "landscape of practice" (Wenger 1998, p. 118), and a language through which to conceptualize some of the complexity inherent in working with community and university actors. CoPs, perhaps more pragmatically, give us some ideas and language to "get on" with trying things out. Taking this lead, we have looked for opportunities to coalesce groups of academic and other stakeholders to regularly meet to share learning, information and practice. Hart and Wolff (2006) offer an overview of our early use of this concept in some of our Cupp projects to date, and discuss the origins of how this more organic and anthropological approach to collaboration could be best conceptualized and cultivated.

In 2010, in collaboration with another local university, we went further, securing national higher education council funding to develop four CoPs. These focused on older people, young people and families, LGBT communities and the Deaf community. These projects brought together academics, community practitioners, students, service users and community members to address areas of local and national concern in relation to enhancing health and wellbeing. They were also an important demonstration of how the intellectual and other resources of universities can be put to good use by communities. The CoP model was used to offer a conceptual home for these cross-boundary groupings of people, which were specifically supported to develop key outcomes through this way of working, including evaluating how effectively these had been achieved (see http://www.coastalcommunities.org.uk/sussex.html).

More recently (see Hart et al. 2013a), we have turned our attention to how CoP ideas in Community-University Partnerships (CUPs) can support us to cultivate social learning spaces in which knowledge is mobilized, as Wenger (2009) would put it, through genuine encounters where people can engage with their experiences of practice. We have interpreted this through the Forums by providing a regular open space—anybody can attend, which we have continually made explicit. We use a range of presenters that have included parents, young people, academics and practitioners. Our focus is on how people access, share and use the "practices" that are being mobilized through discussion and debate. With this approach we have so far been seeking to generate democratic social spaces, although there has also been a sometimes explicit expectation from those attending the Forum that we create spaces that involve at least some degree of pedagogical intent.

The Forums have all been prompted with a degree of "getting on" and trying things out, particularly as we had not found much in the literature that could guide us about getting started with CoPs in a community-university partnership context. We have used CoPs in a number of different ways and the CoP theory has offered us some key insights and guidance by helping us to mobilize new languages, explore new forms of co-working and bring new understandings to our context. We expand below on those conceptual elements of CoPs that have had the greatest resonance for our Forum work so far.

8.2.2   Situated Learning

First proposed by Lave and Wenger (1991) as a model of learning in CoPs, situated learning is built on an acceptance that learning cannot be separated from the context in which it is generated. In community-university working, this focuses us on the social process of co-constructing knowledge and is therefore a foundational starting point for how we consider what CoPs offer us. We are concerned with not just who is in the conversation on resilience research and practice, but also what their experience is like.

For us, this means we have had to consider both the physical environment within which we gather but also how attention to participative dynamics in this space might enable or constrain people's learning experiences. Wenger and Trayner (personal communication November 11, 2013) emphasize that modes of learning should take place in a meaningful context and it is this that drives the learning.

As Hart and Wolff (2006) identify, an analytic focus on practice helps us to put an emphasis on such practical considerations. We think this can offer us something of a "preserved" social space through which to negotiate our partnership work, one that supports the questioning of assumptions about who participates and what legitimate contributions they make and take from the CoP they are involved in. For example,

Roberts (2006) argues that knowledge that is aligned with the predispositions of a community, which supports the identity and practices of its members, is more likely to be adopted than knowledge that challenges identity and practice. (No surprises there!)

8.2.3   Boundary Working

The mixed constituencies of people that are coming together in our CoPs require us to consider what is happening both at the intersection of people's practices but also in moving across them. Lave and Wenger (1991) identify this feature of CoPs as where a great deal of learning can take place and innovation in practices often happens at these boundaries. In reality we think this requires some support. Particularly as in the context of the Forums, we can have a room that includes say, for example, 11 academics, 2 teachers, 3 parent carers of children with complex needs, 2 educational psychologists, 7 students, 5 family workers, 2 policy makers, 2 young adult service users, 2 charity chief executives, 3 mentors and 4 youth workers. Visitors often remark on the mix of people present and we are continually struck by the fact that we always have large numbers of attendees, usually between 20 and 30, and sometimes as many as 200 people will attend.

For the academic and practitioner convenors of the Forums in particular, facilitating these intersections is best achieved with some knowledge of the practices that are represented. The individuals who can span different "worlds" are known as boundary spanners (see Wenger 2000). They are those people who can broker and translate across different practice settings. We have previously identified the important role that these boundary spanners have in CoP work (Hart and Wolff 2006; Hart et al. 2013a).

Whilst the idea of bringing different perspectives together makes a lot of sense, we acknowledge some limitations from practice that stem from the assumption that everyone who attends does so with a full understanding of what the CoP is, and what conceptually it hopes to achieve. For example, some of the medical professionals who have attended the Forums through their interest in resilience have felt their role and professional identity challenged in the space. This has in fact inhibited them from sharing their practice as they work out both whether the Forum is for them, and whether they can operate at the intersection of theirs and others' practices in order to learn. This requires both their own competencies to be realized, but also to recognize others—in something of a "learning partnership". In some of these cases, this stems from their only experiences of being professionals, and "listened to" without challenge in that capacity. The Forum provides a different kind of space where what is considered expert might not map onto their other experiences—and in our case, parent carers and young people themselves may also hold expert views on what it means to work with the resilience concept, which they may or may not realize they hold. This disruption of conventional power relationships of course has the potential to act across the many constituencies of the Forum, and this simple example is one way to show what are otherwise complex flows and processes. Importantly, however, Wenger (2010) identifies that a learning partner isn't someone who agrees with you or even shares your background necessarily; he sees it as someone with whom focusing on practice together creates a high learning potential.

8.2.4 Legitimate Peripheral Participation

Connected to both how people might learn in a CoP, and ideas of movement across boundaries, Legitimate Peripheral Participation (LPP) describes how someone might enter a community of practice, or as Lave and Wenger (1991) put it—how newcomers become experienced members and eventually old timers of a community of practice or collaborative project. Within our Forum there are numerous examples of variations on this theme. We have seen fairly typical, expected paths of newcomers participating in the life of the CoP regularly growing their involvement, e.g., a parent carer and a researcher who, whilst coming from different starting points, shared an interest in resilience ideas and began developing their practice in this space.

This idea is also discussed by Borzillo et al. (2011) as legitimate peripherality, which members gain before they become fully participating members of a CoP. An important consideration here is the interplay of who is being legitimated and who is doing the legitimating. This is also closely related to the trajectory of identity that Wenger (2009) picks up in his exploration of this theme. Let's take the parent carer or the researcher, as they regularly attend the CoP, their own practice develops and with it their view of the CoP and how others view them. At what point these individuals are deemed to be moving through the pathway of LPP, and by whom, rests in part on their recognition as "expert" enough to be at the center—a core CoP member. Not only does this raise questions of power relations, it is also slightly problematic if your starting point, as ours is, is that there is no one expert.

Another way to think about this perhaps is related to the question of belonging, which can take various forms at various levels (Wenger 2000). As opposed to "lurking" on the edges of a CoP (Handley et al. 2006), individuals can be understood to be at different levels of participation in the CoP. Wenger identifies three modes—engagement, imagination and alignment—that each have implications for a person's contribution to the formation of a social learning system and their personal identity. They each also require a different kind of work, from joint activities to having a degree of distance.

We ourselves have questioned those who may adopt a position of "illegitimate peripheral participation"—the lurkers, who only ever stay on the periphery. We often find ourselves mulling over strategies that might support peripheral people to become more involved, even venting occasional frustration at what we perceive as extreme passivity on the part of some CoP members. This is particularly the case in our more formal, time-limited communities of practice where members make an explicit commitment to share and develop practice when they sign up. However, even in relation to the Forum-style CoP, we have to admit to hoping that members might take more responsibility for convening the space and developing shared practice. Of course, we also have to challenge our thinking on this, reminding ourselves that the beauty of the Forum space is that it is open to anybody to participate in any way.

8.2.5 Social Artistry

Wenger (2009) tells us that enabling social learning spaces is an art and in reflecting on how this happens in our CoP work, who is doing the enabling is a key question. We are faced with the tension of how our CoP is convened, led and facilitated, and in trying out a number of different versions have settled on a mixture of all three that is mostly done by those of us in the university. This leaves us with tricky questions of how this intersects with issues of participation and power that we indicate above, and explore further below. The concept of social artistry is relevant here then as our focus is on who can provide authenticity in this leadership to deal with the paradoxes it presents. And so we are translating this into a type of stewardship that may be performed by a person, or people, who can understand and perform different roles to keep the CoP on course. Without this, we don't think our Resilience Forums would continue to operate very successfully. Gathering as it does a diverse membership, and relying as it does on an impetus and direction that cannot assume that everyone wants to know the language of CoPs or would prioritize time to organize these social learning spaces.

What we experience in practice are overlaps between these concepts, and they share many cross cutting issues—of participation, power, and hierarchies of knowledge. Our CoP work to this point only takes us so far, and it doesn't fully help us with the complex circumstances in which we practice. As a result, we have also found ourselves needing to develop our own approaches, which we explore further as part of the discussion about how we put our own CoP into practice.

8.3 Resilience Research and Practice

One of the reasons for setting up the Forum was to provide a space for people involved in previous projects or formal time-limited resilience CoPs to continue to meet and connect to develop their resilience based work We were also keen to hold a space in which we could attend to the many enquiries and requests for meetings and research collaborations that we receive, and for researchers to present their ideas or findings, so we have much invested in offering the space. In that way it has certainly served as a holding space, and one which sees different partnerships flourish. All of these are located in the domain of resilience research and practice.

With a growing popularity over the last 40 years the concept of resilience has captured the attention of researchers, practitioners, policy-makers and other community stakeholders alike. The origin of this concept goes back to the longitudinal studies of understanding developmental outcomes in relation to various risk factors and identifying the heterogeneity in children's responses to risk situations (Garmezy et al. 1984; Werner and Smith 1982). Although it has been conceptualized in various ways, the core features of resilience are experience or potential for experiencing adversity and being able to deal with that adversity (Luthar 2006). The enthusiastic uptake of resilience-based approaches lies in these core aspects, as the concept of resilience is capable of capturing a positive imagination of the future under conditions of adversity and a hope for change. The shift of focus from risk to resilience has the potential to give a sense of purpose and future direction to various fields of studies on the wellbeing of individuals and communities.

As Aranda and Hart (2014) discuss more recently, resilience has "acquired something of a galvanizing force… as it seems to resonate with the immediate concerns of everyday practice and lived experiences or struggles with disability, disadvantage or exclusion" (p. 2). According to Yates and Masten (2004), in order for a resilience-based program to be successful and have sustainable impact on later developmental and life outcomes, interventions should have three aims: to deal with the adversity condition, to build capacity, and to activate a social support system. However, unless resilience interventions also target the adversity factors and/or conditions of adversity (i.e., inequalities structure, lack of services) the programs, even if they are successful, would not go beyond a sticking plaster impact and result in temporary improvements until the adversity re-appears in a different format or as a different risk factor. Therefore, a comprehensive resilience research and practice agenda should incorporate capacity building, challenging risk situations, creating resilient social networks and service re-design or improvement. We suggest that bringing resilience research and practice together with activism by explicitly uniting resilience with a social justice approach could have the potential to respond to the current limitations of resilience research and practice development.

It is within this framework that we hold monthly Resilience Forums to create a regular, open space where we share and discuss resilience research and practice and exchange academic, professional and experiential knowledge. The Forums bring together a diverse mixture of people who share a passion for resilience ideas and practice. We have always been keen to learn how members experience the Forum. However, in the spirit of joint ownership and responsibility, we did not seek formal evaluation feedback in the early days of the Forum CoP, although we do have data sets for the time-limited, closed CoPs which were part of formal research projects mentioned at the beginning of this chapter. Some of us remain troubled about how we capture feedback data, not wanting to perpetuate the notion that we were providing a service to members that they might "evaluate". In the early days there was another practical reason for not seeking formal evaluation data; we simply did not have the capacity to collate and analyze it, and aspired to running the Forum CoP as near to cost neutral as we could. Rather, we occasionally sought feedback via email, and received many unsolicited verbal or email communications regarding members' experiences. However, in the past year, despite the concerns described above, we have formalized feedback for the open monthly Forum CoP, The main way in which we receive this data is via reflection forms compiled by members at the end of each Forum. Our aim has been to make this "reflection" rather than "evaluation", which also makes clear that everyone has the opportunity to get involved in the convening and delivering of CoP sessions. We also have an observation sheet that anyone who attends is free to fill in. Feedback from those who attend often relates to how valuable a space it is to them.

> To be able to reflect on how I am integrating resilience into practice was so valuable. I really do appreciate the forums which are consistently excellent, inspiring and challenging.

Each Forum starts with a brief talk on a specific aspect of resilience and then opens to everyone in order to create an interactive session. The emphasis is on creating an environment that supports sharing and mutuality, and also dissolves the fixed boundaries between expert and non-expert knowledge. The perspectives of resilience researchers, practitioners, policy-makers, service users including young people (there are some Forums that young people attend which we try to gear more explicitly towards them) and their families, have equal standing in these sessions and in the networks created. While not wanting to privilege one knowledge set over another, it can be challenging to get the balance right when such a diverse community of individuals attend.

> I enjoyed the points of discussion and the difference of opinion. Good to hear other people's perspectives.

Within resilience research Rutter (1999) highlights the significance of turning points as a key mechanism in nurturing resilience. Through the creation of a holding space that invites a range of identities to attend, we have observed how the Forum has been a mechanism for the facilitation of turning points that can create positive outcomes for the individual and wider systemic change.

For example, at one Forum, a practitioner wanted to introduce a service user to the concept of resilience. She brought the young man along to the Forum and his presence had a significant impact on professionals who were present, as he eloquently articulated his adverse experiences, bringing a "realness" into the room. Spotting his potential, the coordinator of the Forum wanted to offer him further development opportunities. He has since gone on to co-deliver sessions within the Forum and external training. He advised that this opportunity had changed his life, since nobody had ever created a job for him before and he could now tell people that he was a lecturer.

Furthermore, as a result of the work he is doing with the university, the organization he was working with are now looking at setting up a mentor scheme so that he can mentor other young people who have offended. The decision made by the worker to bring him along to the Forum was a crucial turning point that interrupted the flow of chain effects; influencing the resilient outcomes for the young man and practices within the organization which will also impact on other young people.

Hence the Forum aims to create opportunities for its members to work across organizational, identity and disciplinary boundaries, allowing participation by anyone with an interest. Part of this is based on the idea that we challenge current hierarchies and structures of knowledge generation, but we are not always successful. We sometimes get feedback that lets us know we missed the mark:

> I didn't think the speaker really focused enough on making what they are doing under-standable to non-academics.

And we are always conscious that the quality of the space is in part reliant on good facilitation:

> ... this time it was great because the facilitator knew how to get people talking and get different people involved. Sometimes they don't.

In response to these criticisms we have developed a briefing sheet for Forum conveners, however it remains a significant challenge for many of us to facilitate the space in a way that supports everybody to have a positive learning experience. As a significant contribution to the field of resilience, the Forums are expected to create networks that will develop a unique perspective on the resilience issues, a common body of knowledge, practice and approaches that can be mobilized by members in, across and between the other social learning spaces they inhabit.

Maintaining the domain in the Forum itself though can be hard, but we have various strategies to support this. For example, we ask speakers to fill in a form saying how they relate to the domain, we can brief them before they attend and we often look up their profiles to see how they are using resilience ideas in their work and lives in an effort to keep the focus on resilience research and practice. However, people don't always stick to the domain, they often have other reasons for wanting to present at the Forum. That can include wanting to capitalize on our profile in this field, or they may want access to the unique range of participants who attend, or they may be touting for work or contact or want a platform for their own work. In one of the worst cases, we experienced presenters working with definitions of resilience from a cursory web search in an attempt to locate their interests in the domain with no other genuine connections. This left us needing to intervene in the CoP space to re-assert the domain of the CoP as we wanted to do our best to ensure that the Forum was a relevant and useful space for those attending. We are well aware that many attendees have had to go out of their way to get time out of work or arrange childcare to come.

8.4 Making CoPs Work for CUPs—Navigating Theory and Practice

We began this chapter by offering the definition of a CoP we use: "groups of people informally bound together by shared experience and a passion for a joint enterprise" (Wenger and Snyder 2000, pp. 139–140). As Wenger (2010) has also noted, many practitioners find the CoP concept good in theory but hard to apply in practice, and for us applying guiding principles in our Forums and our community-university engagement work more generally brings inherent complexity and a number of paradoxes. We have identified three that we expand upon here, all of which have been reflected to us through the formation and on-going practice of the Forums.

They are: being social but intentional; disentangling participation and learning, and the issue of situation in situated learning. We then conclude this section with an overview of the best tips we can think of for cultivating a CoP within a community-university engagement activity.

8.4.1 Being Social but Intentional

In starting off our CoPs, the issue we were immediately faced with was one of offering a vision that could attract people to participate, but not making the offer so fixed that people are then effectively co-opted into what it is doing. We found ourselves wanting to create a space that others could discover—perhaps rather naively hoping that within it would emerge an organic set of relationships that would produce an on-going learning community. Whilst we no doubt began cultivating a set of relationships that are developing into a learning enterprise, in reality it turned out that someone also needed to do the practical stuff like booking venues and coordinating presenters. We have also realized that because of the diverse group of people we wanted to attract to the CoP, we had to be able to talk about it in a particular way, link in with our existing networks, and offer something of a starting point for people to get what it was all about. For example, our advertising for the CoP included a promise to make people feel welcome, an acknowledgement that some of them might not have been to an event at the university before, and that we wanted to keep numbers reasonable so everyone could join in if they want to. We continue to have a large number of attendees, and to make this happen takes at least a day or two a month of administrative work—advertising the Forums, coordinating content, updating the website and dealing with individual queries. The Forum is popular, but it is certainly not cost-neutral.

This effort and energy goes beyond the administration required to make them happen, and the idea of social artistry is important here for understanding how we both help people come together and hold a conceptual vision of the CoP and of resilience research and practice work; one that may require us to practice some intentionality—offering direction for the CoP and using forms of stewardship to make sure that it actually happens.

Despite it not being our explicit focus in the beginning, Wenger (2009) emphasizes CoPs as the learning space of a community built through a history of learning over time; he argues that the continuity this develops contributes to relationships and trust that enable joint enquiry into practice. We mentioned the medical professionals earlier as an example of some newcomers who weren't convinced of the learning enterprise, even though they shared the passion for resilience research and practice. Everyone has a practice, and there is knowledge in each, yet engaging with knowledge as lived practice requires a lot of trust (Wenger 2010). To make this more difficult, learning in social spaces cannot be imagined separately to learning across social spaces that members will inhabit, with all the rules, rituals, assumptions and dynamics they may contain. And so it is likely to raise questions of identity, competence and trust for individuals, dynamics we think are heightened in such a diverse mix of members and that we need to pay attention to.

Another take on this is to understand that as we participate in various social learning spaces, our actions affect the nature of these spaces and those we interact with. How we manage our participation here is what Wenger (2009) calls "learning citizenship" (p. 15). Whilst this has clear implications for those members of our CoP—it also has implications for those of us who wanted to develop this social learning space in the first place as our actions affect the spaces we enter, create, connect or leave. For Wenger (ibid), convening is one of the most significant acts we can perform. Some of our experiences have involved going so far as to approach a participant in a break to encourage them to ask a question that would open discussion in an instance where participants were overawed by a respected international speaker. From our perspective, this "intervention" began to unlock the dialogue and enabled discussion and debate to flow.

The intersection of the social and intentional, as well as the social and the learning enterprise we aspire to, then leaves us with a tricky set of issues to navigate. Notions of convening seem to fit quite well to explain the origins of our Forums, but we feel something else is needed for the on-going pragmatics of making it work. And so we want to make use of the idea of "learning governance". Conceptually this orients us to both an overview of decisions that the stewards/convenors might take that matter to what the CoP is doing, and at the same time have responsibility for an awareness of how the CoP and its members are linked into broader systems and other social learning spaces and practices. Box 8.1 lists some of the different agendas that we can think of that form part of this governance. They reflect both a vertical (associated with traditional hierarchy and decisional authority) and horizontal (engagement in joint activities and a commitment to collective learning) accountability that strengthens our ability to manage governance of this type.

Box 8.1 Agendas at play in the CoP

- Widening participation of CoP membership
- Conventional academic imperatives (e.g. research and publishing)
- International research/practice links
- CoP as the container to help the convenors deal with individual email and telephone requests to meet or connect
- Intellectual integrity of the domain
- Therapeutic or pastoral
- Practice development in relation to our resilience approach
- Basic networking
- Academic and social capital development
- Sustainability
- Socialising

- Individual skills development and capacity building
- Positively managing those who tout for work
- Keeping the members to the domain
- Facilitating discussion and sharing

Importantly, we think this takes us beyond boundary spanning. Such an approach appears to center a lot of power in the convenor, yet this reflects and honors the skills and capacities of that person to manage a complexity higher than Wenger might imagine in his conception of these spaces. It is this meeting of skills and knowledge that enables the social learning space the Forum provides. For example, the social space the Forum provided that meant a practitioner attended but was too unsure or uncomfortable to speak, needed to be balanced with basic ethical issues about engagement that requires taking responsibility for sometimes supporting an individual's needs. Powerful feelings can also get generated. We have experienced situations where a speaker or participant comes across to others as blaming a particular group in the room for an issue or problem being discussed. This can require intervention to bring people back to context and re-direct conversations that maintain the aim and purpose of the space. This requires some basic group work skills and knowing the purpose and priorities for the session. In a further instance, a service user who had complex experiences as a client of mental health services took offence at the view of an academic and was visibly shaken by their experience, needing support after the CoP. In another, a commissioner was annoyed at spending time out of the office to hear an inexperienced presenter not complete her presentation, leaving little time for focused discussion.

And so within this context, we are also seeking to understand CoPs in a way that clearly identifies responsibility and remit for the space being created, animated and held, but one in which participants can be enabled to develop joint ideas and practices, often across these tensions. We aspire to those leading to the development of a shared language; one that can be continually built and developed, rather than reflect a series of separate identities that come together at certain intervals in sometimes contested and uncomfortable ways.

But it's a tricky job. We would like more distributed responsibility for this with Forum members. It can become burdensome and an emotional tax for the convenor. Some people who have convened a Forum admit themselves afterwards that they haven't got the skill set required to navigate and sustain the CoP space, even with support. This is in part because the span of agendas identified in Box 8.1 being balanced in the convening role requires being on your toes most of the time. This is also overlaid with the desire we have of wanting the CoP to be a positive space for people who can be having a bad time in life, and a responsibility we feel for taking some basic care of people emotionally. However, we don't always achieve this.

We have done some previous thinking about leadership in the area of community-university engagement, identifying it as at the heart of arrangements where diverse groups must come together with different goals and motives to take part in a collective process (see Hart and Church 2011). Whilst traditional notions of top–down leadership, where the idea of the individual leader persists (see Bolden 2011), notions of flexible or more distributed leadership may further assist our thinking in the paradox of being social but intentional. Such collective approaches invite a more systemic perspective to the functions that can or should be carried out by a group and puts a focus on how this happens through the relationships between CoP members, rather than concentrated in one individual.

As we grapple with some of these ideas, we think it is important not to lose sight of the fact that for the social and learning spaces we currently convene, there is more than just learning on the agenda. This is in part because the stakes are high for some people to be participating in our CoP, often investing as they are in the legitimacy of the academic work in this area to also deliver on meeting some of their needs. We have at times been concerned for the welfare of some CoP members, because of the intensity of the experience or closeness of discussions to their lived experience. After all, the domain of interest is resilience and "navigating adversity" is in the room. So we extend a further characteristic to the paradox of being social but intentional. In our CoP experience, this must also contain consideration of responsibility.

8.4.2 Participation and Learning

It is difficult to disentangle the blend of participation and learning we encounter in working CoPs through CUPs. For sure, these are considerations for any CoP, but our experience of the Forums—across a diverse membership, and trying to pay attention to the quality of participation and people's learning experience, is subject to multiple complexities. Participation occurs during various shared learning activities within CoP boundaries (Borzillo et al. 2011; Lave and Wenger 1991) locate learning not in the acquisition of structure but in the increased access of the learner to participatory roles in expert performances.

The Forum arrangement of our CoP means that our diverse membership is not necessarily a consistent one. People are signed up to a mailing list that alerts them to an upcoming Forum, and depending on the topic, and their availability to attend, they may or may not come. The Forum has now expanded to operate in three geographic locations, so it's also the case that, again topic dependent, someone might attend in different places at different times. This fluidity is in part why we know the Forums work. Evaluations and feedback suggest that CoP members find the space useful and the growth in the number of Forums is testament to it being a style that people are keen to access.

Yet to further problematize this, the notion of experts takes on a dual meaning in our Forum. Wenger tells us that everyone has a practice and that no practice is privileged or subsumes another, but the reality of a context that includes academic, practitioner, young people, student, parent and professional input reflects existing hierarchies of knowledge that we cannot ignore. Although of course, Lave and Wenger (1991) discuss "expert" performances as those which form the core of a CoP that others may engage in as practice is developed, the word expert here also links into the dynamics and assumptions of who attends the CoP. This is at risk of being further re-enforced by the use of speakers at most Forums, however, we try hard to ensure that this reflects the constituency of the broader group. It has been more difficult to secure practitioner and service user presentations, as this is not a usual or straightforward activity for those groups. The reality is that one of the main reasons that CoP members come along is that they are keen to hear from those they deem to have a particular type of knowledge about an issue. It is worth noting that the most well attended Forums have been those where the speakers are professors with international reputations for their resilience research and practice development. However, some people come along to hear them because they know that it is likely that the speaker will present in an inclusive and lively way. Hence, many Forum members seem to welcome the ethos we are trying to create, yet privilege the expertise of formal "experts".

We are also challenged to think about how legitimate peripheral participation in particular works in something as fluid as the Forum. We experience people coming from the "outside in", but they may also choose to remain lurking on the boundaries, or indeed drift off from the center to the edge, or out of the CoP altogether. And further, as Handley et al. (2006, p. 649) ask, "can an individual be 'going through the motions'— appearing as a full participant—yet not participating in the sense of experiencing a feeling of belonging and perhaps, of mutual commitment and responsibility?" There is no requirement for members to follow relatively linear trajectories of participation in the Forum, and to some degree this may be an attraction. This also somewhat decenters a further tension of who deems a peripheral member to have become expert enough to be considered a core participant. Of course, the risk here is that the learning partnership that CoPs rely on—of people acting on their learning citizenship—impedes the development of practices within the group and is reinforced by members' ongoing participation. This will have consequences for the nature and experience of other members of the CoP and the sense of identity that Borzillo et al. (2011) suggest builds through increased participation in developing practices in their group. Handley et al. (2006) go on to suggest that in fact only those individuals who successfully navigate a path from peripheral to full participation can be categorized as "participating" in the sense implied by Lave and Wenger's early work. It is difficult to pinpoint the shared practice that evolves from the CoPs sometimes, as it is not something we have the resources to track.

This classical view of participation does not match neatly on to our CoP experience. Yet the juxtaposition of pedagogy and participation is also subject to influences that are not necessarily accounted for in LPP. Although we have mentioned some participants that have gradually developed their practice to now be considered more "core" CoP members through an LPP-type process, we also have examples where, when people attend, they have found it very hard to get out of their work commitments. In trying to come out of their daily practice they have had to go through maybe two managers to release their time. We have had circumstances where they then arrive in the CoP space and don't really learn anything. So the pedagogical element of the CoP is critical for us and underscored by our intention of being respectful of the people who come, and so we need to be prepared to flex to ensure this is fulfilled for people.

Edwards' (2005) critique of the perspective of situated learning implied in these processes is that it does not adequately deal with how new knowledge is produced and does not elucidate how or what people are learning. Wenger (2000) would argue that we need a balance of core and boundary processes, so that the practice is at the same time an enabler of deep learning and linked with other parts of a system as a way of developing a learning capability, but he hasn't really expanded on the pedagogical beyond this. Rather than find an absolute definition of participation and learning here—as Wenger and Trayner (personal communication November 11, 2013) suggest we should refrain from doing—and instead trying to generate a definition not in the absolute but in relation to the landscape, we suggest there are two further ways to think about these ideas in our context. One is Wenger's (2000) concept of "alignment"—making sure that activities "local" to the CoP are sufficiently aligned with other processes so they can be mobilized beyond engagement with the CoP, which builds on his point above. The other is Practice Theory, which broadly refers to an epistemological position that is concerned with action or how things get done in everyday life, in which "the social is located in practical knowledge or routinized dispositions, or networks and assemblages of activities and things or in processes of embodied performativity" (Aranda and Hart 2014, p. 4). By adopting this position, Gheradi (2009) argues our practices can be opened up to inspection, allowing us to understand them as a knowledgeable collective action.

Both of these ideas begin to alert us to the portability of skills and knowledge, gained through co-participation in entangled actions and practices (Reckwitz 2002) in something like our CoP, which can be used in other settings. In other words, we can think about how practice travels as a way of understanding what people might be learning in the CoP. This could be, for example, listening to a story everyone knows in the CoP about, say, a family mediation meeting, and from which they then develop a narrative of that story that can be applied in their own situation. Aranda and Hart (2014) discuss in more detail how practice theory can generate new ways of thinking about resilience in the context of some formally constituted CoPs, but in our Forum we can suggest that the whole notion of practice has also travelled with the Forum itself—to new geographic locations. Each time, the practice has had to be changed to be contextually relevant, and in some places the work is harder to maintain and sustain than others. This further underscores our need to get the space of our CoP right; to foster learning and pay attention to the alignment of the learning enterprise the CoP provides across the other social spaces its members are within and between.

8.4.3   The Issue of Situation

Situated learning tells us much about the importance and the argument for learning taking place within the context it is applied. There is a growing body of literature that promotes a view of socially constructed knowledge and the pedagogical implications and possibilities of viewing learning in this way. On the topic of "situation", the Forum has prompted us to think about precisely where our CoPs are situated, in a physical as well as conceptual way. As Smith (2003) identifies, the nature of the situation impacts significantly on the process and Wenger (2009) recognizes learning citizenship as very sensitive to context.

We mostly hold our Resilience Forum in a university space, although our recent expansion of the Forum through a collaborative venture with YoungMinds in London sees us holding it jointly with them at their London offices. Also, since there are often far more members external to the university who come, ironically we might lose academic participation if the Forums are not held in the university. This hasn't yet happened in our London Forum, but that may be because YoungMinds is seen as an important national organization with which academics would want to collaborate. Furthermore, the speakers at that Forum have so far been academic professors with international reputations, so our earlier point about them attracting large audiences may apply here too.

An abstract reading of the situation of our university-based Forum would raise questions of power—on the face of it, there are clear imbalances between the university and its resources, and many of the people we have participating in our CoP. Yet we have found that some community members in fact privilege the university as a physical location, and some have commented on the fact that they like to come to the university as it takes them out of their practice worlds. Others have said that they found it difficult at first to come and to participate because they felt that they wouldn't know as much about the issues as the academics, but that over time the friendly format and atmosphere helped them relax and participate.

We have found that CoPs can challenge assumptions and place actors in non-traditional positions; this also helps to relocate the "experts" that people observe in the CoP as coming from a number and range of different places. Some writers still maintain that core members' power status is a potential barrier that could initially prevent peripheral members from participating (Borzillo et al. 2011) and others have critiqued Wenger for not dealing adequately with issues of power (see Fox 2000, for example).

But more recently, Wenger and Trayner discuss that claims to competency are negotiated in the politics of community formation (personal communication November 11, 2013), which once again reinforces that how the CoP emerges, and the precise configuration of skills legitimacy and leadership (see Cashman et al. 2007) within it, has implications for the precise configuration of participation, pedagogy and "situation" it sits within. Returning to ideas of practice theory, we could understand this process of configuration and re-configuration as a strength, as it reflects the entangled nature of "doing" learning as embedded in the social world.

For us, the three paradoxes we have discussed above enable rather than constrain us to do good CoP work that helps us meet our goals in our domain. Many of the tensions we have identified between classic CoP theory and the pragmatic and specific elements of our practice are located in a frame we use for much of our community-university partnership work—that of "learning by doing". And we have put together the sorts of guiding ideas, planning and approaches that we would consider to do this again in Box 8.2, which builds from our own experiences of establishing and sustaining a cross-discipline but also cross-practice heterogeneous CoP. We now find ourselves developing our own approaches alongside the existing theory that can work for us, as we and our participants do, across and within the Forum and our other social learning spaces—perhaps the ultimate in alignment that Wenger suggests.

Box 8.2 Getting started with CoPs in CUPs.

- Accept that there will be contradictions in what you are trying to achieve
- Ensure that the convenor has good facilitation skills and can explicitly hold the group dynamics
- Brief speakers about the Forum and what it is trying to achieve
- Brief speakers about the domain and ensure that they explicitly connect their talk to it
- If more vulnerable participants come, make sure that someone has the responsibility to offer a debrief with them afterwards—it's a good idea to buddy up
- Produce a jargon-busting sheet that is given to all participants at every Forum
- Create a social space afterwards—we have a cup of tea together, but in the spirit of trying to make the Forum as sustainable as possible, people buy their own
- Ensure the space is not eaten up by presentation alone

For further ideas, see Hart and Wolff (n.d.)

8.5 Imagining Our CoPs in the Future

We find ourselves in complex landscapes of practice, which together can begin to constitute a body of knowledge on resilience research and practice. And in looking to the future of these Forums, and others that might grow within the resilience domain, we concur with Wenger on the risks of determinism for which others have critiqued CoPs (see Wenger 2009). We believe CoPs should be used as a perspective rather than a technique and one that honors underlying principles. Yet as we have discussed above, the pragmatism that we think should accompany this work means those principles may be stretched, re-interpreted and extended to meet our real time needs and balance our real time agendas.

We want to argue for context as central to making choices about your CoP—as we have illustrated above, this is indeed the only way we have been able to navigate this terrain with a broad membership of academics, practitioners, parents, students and young people. Within this we have been confronted with the paradoxes that we discussed above and a number of further nuances which we have not been able to expand on in this chapter. These include wanting to see a review of CoPs that are not based on assumptions of mainstream learning styles. This is also an area underexplored by us empirically and one that we think needs further attention in order to achieve the conceptual CoP ambition of maximizing learning capabilities. We are also curious to extend our thinking to how our own knowledge of inclusive and democratic practices to support participation more generally in community-university engagement intersects with Wenger's firm belief that CoPs are a learning, not a democratic, enterprise. Although we would tend to agree in the sense that our current Forum is hugely reliant on a few to maintain it, we are also acutely aware that without specific attention to the inclusion and engagement of our diverse CoP membership, who participates and attends, would be radically altered. We have questions about whether this blurring of boundaries between participation through shared learning activities, and actually getting people to a CoP in the first place, would make the CoP more or less effective and/or valuable for participants.

And on the idea of value we also want to further explore how we gather and use empirical information on the value of the learning enabled by our CoP approaches. Wenger et al. (2011) have begun development of a conceptual framework that might help us with this. They position "value creation stories" developed through social learning as a format for proposing questions and suggesting indicators that orient us to what to look for to make an assessment of the value of this learning. They suggest cycles of value creation in CoPs that can accommodate retrospective and future opportunities. In tandem with our identification of "alignment" in the preceding section as an important component for supporting the pedagogic aspects of a CoP member's participation in the Forum, we think this could be a key way to uncover not just the potential acquisition of knowledge from Forum spaces, but how what individuals may be learning in the space can be represented and realised elsewhere in their daily practices. This is an area of future conceptual and empirical development that we think would add to our ability to understand the power of CoPs as learning enterprises.

Our final thoughts turn to what all of this means for connecting people together in learning communities. Coming as we do from diverse starting points and residing as we do in diverse organizational locations—and in some instances, no organization at all—we each face slightly different considerations in coming together to share our practice in the domain of resilience. For some this means, as we have seen, negotiating the time with managers in our work places to attend, for others it means translating the value and potential of this space to fit with the imperatives of an academic context. And for some others, finding ways to navigate their marginalized positions to engage with what they deem to be a critical contribution to sometimes very vulnerable lives.

But for all of us, it means building links within and across our daily places and practices in ways we simply don't do through other means. CoPs have given us a language and a vision to begin this work, expand our networks and provide new viewpoints on questions and issues that we often jointly share. The Forum has also been a good example of establishing a space that has continued to operate regularly for over 4 years, expand into new locations and include an increasing number of people and perspectives. If we accept Wenger's (2009) thoughts on learning as the production of social structure—an aspirational extension of this work is to think about how we are re-making possibilities for not just learning, but how CoP members live and learn across a multiplicity of practices. We think this can have implications for structural relationships between those in the CoP and outside of it. And in viewing our joint enterprise in these terms, it leads us to imagine how such change cannot just identify, but also alter important asymmetries in how this domain is understood, and how practice is developed that reflects the inclusion and learning capability of the diverse range of people that co-produce it.

Acknowledgments Many thanks to the participants in all the communities of practice to which we belong for stimulating our thoughts and for helping us develop and refine our own CoP practices. The discussion in this chapter is informed by our ongoing research programme on CoPs for resilience practice, most notably as part of the ESRC-funded Imagine Project which is part of the Connected Communities Programme (http://www.imaginecommunity.org.uk/).

References

Aranda, K., & Hart, A. (2014). Resilient moves: Tinkering with practice theory to generate new ways of thinking about using resilience. *Health*. doi:10.1177/1363459314554318.

Benneworth, P., Conway, C., Charles, D., Humphrey, L., & Younger, P. (2009). *Characterising modes of university engagement with wider society: A literature review and survey of best practice*. http://www.tufts.edu/talloiresnetwork/downloads/Characterisingmodesofuniversityen gagementwithwidersociety.pdf. Accessed 1 February 2015.

Boingboing. (2010). *Boingboing: resilience research and practice*. http://www.boingboing.org.uk/ . Accessed 30 June 2015.

Bolden, R. (2011). Distributed leadership in organizations: A review of theory and research. *International Journal of Management Reviews, 13*(3), 251–269. doi:10.1111/j.1468-2370. 2011.00306.x.

Borzillo, S., Aznar, S., & Schmitt, A. (2011). A journey through communities of practice: How and why members move from the periphery to the core. *European Management Journal, 29*(1), 25–42. doi:10.1016/j.emj.2010.08.004.

Brennan, J. (2008). Higher education and social change. *Higher Education, 56*(3), 381–393. doi:10.1007/s10734-008-9126-4.

Brown, J. S., & Duguid, P. (1991). Organizational learning and communities-of-practice: Toward a unified view of working, learning, and innovation. *Organization Science, 2*(1), 40–57.

Cashman, J., Linehan, P., & Rosser, M. (2007). *Communities of Practice: A new approach to solving complex educational problems*. Alexandria, VA: National Association of State Directors of Special Education.

Cupp. (2011). *Community knowledge exchange briefing paper.* University of Brighton. http://about.brighton.ac.uk/cupp/images/stories/Static/materials_and_resources/cupp_briefing_CKE_web.pdf. Accessed 3 November 2015.

Edwards, A. (2005). Let's get beyond community and practice: the many meanings of learning by participating. *Curriculum Journal, 16*(1), 49–65. doi:10.1080/0958517042000336809.

Fox, S. (2000). Communities of practice, Foucault and actor network theory. *Journal of Management Studies, 37*(6), 853–868. doi:10.1111/1467-6486.00207.

Garmezy, N., Masten, A. S., & Tellegen, A. (1984). The study of stress and competence in children: A building block for developmental psychopathology. *Child Development, 55*(1), 97–111. doi:10.2307/1129837.

Gherardi, S. (2009). Introduction: The critical power of the 'practice lens'. *Management Learning, 40*(2), 115–128. doi:10.1177/1350507608101225.

Graber, R. (2013). *Evaluation of a targeted youth support resilient therapy community of practice.* Unpublished Paper: University of Brighton.

Handley, K., Sturdy, A., Fincham, R., & Clark, T. (2006). Within and beyond communities of practice: Making sense of learning through participation, identity and practice. *Journal of Management Studies, 43*(3), 641–653. doi:10.1111/j.1467-6486.2006.00605.x.

Hart, A., Blincow, D., & Thomas, H. (2007a). *Resilient therapy: Working with children and families.* Hove: Routledge.

Hart, A., & Church, A. (2011). Research leadership for the community-engaged university: Key challenges. *Metropolitan Universities, 22*(2), 45–64.

Hart, A., & Wolff, D. (n.d). *Communities of practice.* http://www.publicengagement.ac.uk/do-it/techniquesapproaches/communities-practice. Accessed 1 February 2015.

Hart, A., & Wolff, D. (2006). Developing local 'communities of practice' through local community–university partnerships. *Planning, Practice & Research, 21*(1), 121–138.

Hart, A., Davies, C., Aumann, K., Wenger, E., Aranda, K., Heaver, B., et al. (2013a). Mobilising knowledge in community–university partnerships: What does a community of practice approach contribute? *Contemporary Social Science, 8*(3), 278–291. doi:10.1080/21582041.2013.767470.

Hart, A., Gagnon, E., Aumann, K., & Heaver, B. (2013b). *What is resilience?* http://www.boingboing.org.uk/index.php/what-is-resilience?id=50:defining-resilience&catid=1. Accessed 1 February 2015.

Hart, A., Maddison, E., & Wolff, D. (2007b). *Community-university partnership in practice.* London: Niace.

Hart, A., Northmore, S., Gerhardt, C., & Rodriguez, P. (2009). Developing access between universities and local community groups: A university helpdesk in action. *Journal of Higher Education Outreach and Engagement, 13*(3), 45–59.

Lave, J., & Wenger, E. (1991). *Situated learning: Legitimate peripheral participation.* Cambridge: Cambridge University Press.

Luthar, S. S. (2006). Resilience in development: A synthesis of research across five decades. In D. Cicchetti & D. J. Cohen (Eds.), *Developmental psychopathology: Risk, disorder, and adaptation* (pp. 740–795). New York: Wiley.

Millican, J., & Bourner, T. (2014). *Learning to make a difference: Student community engagement and the Higher Education curriculum.* London: Niace.

Reckwitz, A. (2002). Toward a theory of social practices: A development in culturalist theorizing. *European Journal of Social Theory, 5*(2), 243–263. doi:10.1177/13684310222225432.

Roberts, J. (2006). Limits to communities of practice. *Journal of Management Studies, 43*(3), 623–639. doi:10.1111/j.1467-6486.2006.00618.x.

Rutter, M. (1999). Resilience concepts and findings: Implications for family therapy. *Journal of Family Therapy, 21*(2), 119–144. doi:10.1111/1467-6427.00108.

Smith, M. K. (2003). *Michael Polanyi and tacit knowledge. The encyclopedia of informal education.* http://www.infed.org/thinkers/polanyi.htm. Accessed 1 February 2015.

UKCPN (n.d.). *UKCPN guides and resources*. http://www.publicengagement.ac.uk/work-with-us/community-partner-network-test/find-helpful-stuff/ukcpn-how-guides. Accessed 1 February 2015.

Watson, D., Hollister, R., Stroud, S. E., & Babcock, E. (2011). *The engaged university: International perspectives on civic engagement*. New York: Routledge.

Wenger, E. (1998). Communities of practice: Learning as a social system. *Systems Thinker, 9*(5), 2–3.

Wenger, E. (2000). Communities of practice and social learning systems. *Organization, 7*(2), 225–246. doi:10.1177/135050840072002.

Wenger, E. (2009). Social learning capability. Four essays on innovation and learning in social systems. *Social Innovation, Sociedade e Trabalho Booklets, 12*, 5–35.

Wenger, E. (2010). Communities of practice and social learning systems: The career of a concept. In C. Blackmore (Ed.), *Social learning systems and communities of practice* (pp. 179–198). London: Springer.

Wenger, E. C., & Snyder, W. M. (2000). Communities of practice: The organizational frontier. *Harvard Business Review, 78*(1), 139–146.

Wenger, E., Trayner, B., & de Laat, M. (2011). *Promoting and assessing value creation in communities and networks: A conceptual framework*. The Netherlands: Ruud de Moor Centrum.

Werner, E. E., & Smith, R. S. (1982). *Vulnerable but invincible: A study of resilient children and youth*. New York: McGraw-Hill.

Yates, T. M., & Masten, A.S. (2004). Fostering the future: resilience theory and the practice of positive psychology. In P. A. Linley, & S. Joseph (Eds.), *Positive psychology in practice* (pp. 521–539). Hoboken, NJ: John Wiley & Sons. doi:10.1002/9780470939338.

Chapter 9
Promoting a Community of Practice Through Collaborative Curriculum Reform in a University Business School

Michelle Salmona and Karl Smart

Abstract The purpose of this research is to describe and investigate an innovative model for collaborative curriculum reform developed using Communities of Practice (CoP) theory which can work in any discipline. It is an engaging story for readers in higher education about an academic CoP from the coalface; academics who are dealing with real problems and issues. The narrative includes practical examples and critical reflection by educators directly engaged in curricular reform. This research addresses a need to ensure quality in university teaching and learning by supporting the development of an integrated curriculum. It investigates how faculty engage in this process and illuminates the complex ways in which they work. There are four main findings: faculty improve their practice through the implementation of the new framework using a CoP; the promotion of students' innovation skills is an essential component of a successful program; communication and collaboration mitigates resistance to change; and a shared vision promotes faculty involvement. We reveal complexities in relationships between faculty and administration, and show successful collaboration and organizational change can be achieved through a community of practice under challenging conditions.

Keywords Communities of practice · Curriculum reform · Organizational change · Faculty engagement

M. Salmona (✉)
College of Business and Economics, Australian National University,
Canberra, Australia
e-mail: michelle.salmona@anu.edu.au

K. Smart
Department of Business Information Systems, Central Michigan University,
Michigan, USA

© Springer Nature Singapore Pte Ltd. 2017
J. McDonald and A. Cater-Steel (eds.), *Communities of Practice*,
DOI 10.1007/978-981-10-2879-3_9

199

9.1 Introduction

In this chapter we describe and investigate an innovative model for collaborative curriculum reform designed using Communities of Practice (CoP) theory. This curriculum development framework (CDF model) can work in any discipline and allows us to consider how faculty change the way they view developing and strengthening curriculum through learning community connections developed through this implementation. Using communities of practice theory we investigate how faculty learn and develop professionally as they engage in this process. It is an engaging story for readers in higher education about an academic CoP from the coalface; academics who are dealing with real problems and issues. The narrative includes practical examples and critical reflection by educators directly engaged in curricular reform.

Our story considers a case study where this CDF model was used to meet a university need. It is an account of a university initiative in the USA to develop and improve applied learning outcomes for an entrepreneurship program, building on interdisciplinary approaches in a business college. It presents and outlines a CDF model drawing on communities of practice theory to engage faculty in interdisciplinary curriculum reform.

The transformation of universities towards a stronger emphasis on the market and fees, through the privatization and marketization of higher education, has led to changes in academic staffing and their employment conditions. A general worldwide trend towards increasing fixed-term, or adjunct, appointments has increased, not just in higher education, and it is seen as a key feature of a flexible labour market (Vandenheuval and Wooden 1999; Pocock et al. 2004; Brown et al. 2008). Internationally these types of employment conditions are known as either adjunct, sessional, casual, contingent, part-time, non-tenure track, fixed-term, or temporary. Although such workers have few rights and limited benefits (May et al. 2005; Pocock et al. 2004), fixed-term employees are generally on a contract and do accrue some benefits.

We report the outcomes of our research into this process where we demonstrate the effective engagement of mostly fixed-term faculty in strengthening the program using this curriculum development framework developed through a community of practice. The issue here is how collaborative curriculum processes have productive and transformational outcomes which improve student experiences and outcomes. We look at how a community of practice develops inside a more traditional curriculum design process.

The framework addresses a need to ensure quality in university teaching and learning by supporting the development of an integrated curriculum. Our research contributes to the literature by investigating how faculty engage in this process and illuminates the complex ways in which they work.

9.2 Framing Our Approach

What follows is a review of relevant research framing the development of the CDF model. Then the forming of the community of practice is described, followed by the model implementation process. It is an account of the research process employing an interdisciplinary approach to curriculum reform and the specific outcomes of this curriculum realignment effort.

9.2.1 Developing the Model

The CDF model we use is an application of this development, and uses graduate attributes as a way of collaboratively engaging faculty in fostering a shared vision of the program. In this research we investigate this model for collaborative curriculum reform. In business education it is not enough just to build students skills, we must develop initiatives throughout the program that develop and foster creativity, and provide a framework that helps students to creatively respond to challenges in innovative ways (Florin et al. 2007). We draw upon the literature of higher education, curriculum and learning, workplace collaboration, together with communities of practice and organizational change. During the study, we continued to use the literature to inform our analysis to assist in making sense of the data.

An understanding of curriculum was one of the central ideas in developing this new CDF model. Generally, work in higher education has been dominated by research on individual student learning, and the term *curriculum* has not been engaged in the literature until recently (Hicks 2007). One significant way that student learning has impacted curricula reform is through the development of graduate attributes (Barnett and Coate 2005; Lee 2005; Barrie 2007). The CDF model we use is an application of this development, and uses graduate attributes as a way of collaboratively engaging faculty in fostering a shared vision of the program. The framework also draws on another key component of curriculum using Biggs' (1996, 2003) constructive alignment as a foundational concept to improve teaching through improving student learning.

Constructive alignment is the blending of theoretical underpinnings of constructivist theories of learning with those of instructional design's emphasis on the purposeful agreement among learning goals, instruction, and assessment so that all components of a course or program work together to achieve the same ends (Frielick 2004). It posits that course objectives, teaching context, teaching activities, and assessment processes should be consistent in encouraging students to use the same learning processes. In constructive alignment, constructive refers to what the student does, which is to construct meaning through relevant learning activities. Alignment refers to what the teacher does, which is to set up a learning environment that supports the learning activities appropriate to achieving the desired learning outcomes (Biggs 1999, 2003). Constructive alignment provides a device and framework to use for the CDF model.

In proposing the use of this new framework, we advocate the advantage of linking educational development with the strategic priorities of the institution (Boud and Walker 1998; Boud 1999). Development activity related to research and scholarship makes little difference overall if isolated from "normal" academic practice or from the particular setting in which people operate. Lee and Boud (2003) propose that educational development should be conceptualized not only as a university-wide process, but also as a local practice and as a process of peer learning in the workplace, as articulated by us in this study (Boud 1999; Lee and Boud 2003).

Research has shown that fixed-term and casually employed academics strongly desire a voice, respect, and inclusion (Junor 2004; Wallin 2007). This study goes some way to addressing how fixed-term faculty gained a voice and became a contributing part of the curriculum redesign effort.

9.2.2 *Forming the Community of Practice*

Important to this study is collaboration and how people work together, where constructive alignment focuses on changing teaching practice in a collaborative and supportive way. A dynamic link exists between the concept of change and communities of practice theory, where such communities are an effective strategy for curriculum reform (Defise 2013). Communities of practice focus on the learning process and improving knowledge and practice of all CoP members at both the individual and community level (Monaghan 2011).

Communities of Practice (CoP) theory (Boud and Middleton 2003; Chua 2006; Hodkinson and Hodkinson 2004; Kosky 2005; Lave and Wenger 1991; Wenger et al. 2002) informed the development of the framework, primarily with the group coming together with the aim of improving practice. CoP theory is based on theoretical understandings with shared meanings in a discipline, where community members come together to inform and improve their practice. It is a way to promote change in professional practice in a formal way (Wenger 1998b).

Using this perspective, the group is a community of individual members, who engage in meaningful discussion through interaction and participation to convert ideas into practical actions with a common goal. By engaging faculty in the process of curriculum development, through the development of a community of practice, meaningful long-term changes can be put in place. Success for faculty developers can be contingent on their ability to clearly see relevant issues, understand their organizational roles and work context, and learn how to develop whole communities of practice (Stein et al. 1999; Land 2004; Connelly et al. 1997). CoP theory is also put forward as a useful lens to consider the data and is a thread throughout this article.

The context for this curriculum reform is described later in the Sect. 9.3. To achieve our goals an interdisciplinary group was formed by the Dean to review the current program. We will refer to this group as the Curriculum Realignment (CR) group. The goal was to identify deficiencies and develop a more integrated program focusing on strengthening entrepreneurship outcomes in a real-world setting.

Although the composition of the CR group included a diverse mix of tenured faculty, fixed-term or adjunct faculty, program administrators, and practicing entrepreneurs; the majority of the group were adjunct faculty who teach in the program. The increased use of fixed-term or adjunct faculty and faculty credentials is recognized as a significant issue in higher education (Feldman and Turnley 2001; Greisler 2002; Kabongo and McCaskey 2011). With the charge to review, evaluate and improve the curriculum, the CR group began to meet regularly to review the program. Through a series of facilitated work sessions during the summer, described in Fig. 2.1, the CR group followed an interdisciplinary curriculum development framework (CDF model). Through the work sessions, the group identified weaknesses in the current program; sought subject matter expert reviews in respective disciplines; gathered input from students who were in the program and from alumni who had graduated; benchmarked top-ranked entrepreneurship programs in the United States; and solicited feedback from practicing entrepreneurs in all aspects of the review. These efforts, which we investigate, resulted in a more focused, integrated major in the ENT degree, with increased buy-in from faculty from multiple disciplines within business, greater involvement with entrepreneurs, and clearer objective and goals for the program itself. A discussion about the forming of the CoP can be found in the Findings section—Finding 4: Improving Practice.

9.2.3 The Model Implementation

Fundamental to this curriculum reform effort was using the CDF model. The CDF model draws on resources from the curriculum literature, in particular Biggs' notion of constructive alignment (1996), to provide a frame and to scaffold the curriculum work. Constructive alignment is defined as a system in which components including context and learning activities work together and support each other. It is based upon the constructivist view that knowledge is constructed through experiences combined with outcome-based instruction with clear outcomes delineated. Through this process instructional material is aligned to the desired outcomes, with critical assessments verifying the outcomes have been reached.

The implementation of the framework consisted of a series of facilitated work sessions. The first work session focused on the different abilities of the students at different levels of their study program, and discussed what skills and abilities a student would need to be successful in their studies; these became the key graduate outcomes for the program. In following work sessions the students' progress through the program was discussed beginning with the outcomes the students

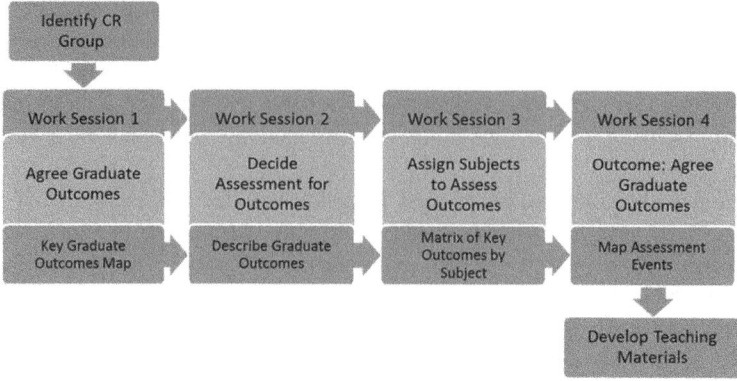

Fig. 9.1 Mapping the approach to curriculum reform [adapted from Salmona (2009)]

would be expected to achieve after each semester of study. Following Biggs' (1996) constructive alignment, the focus then shifted to considering how these outcomes would be assessed, which then led to discussions about how the different assessments were linked, and how they built on each other during the semester. A key element to this conversation was to think about which subject objectives and which key outcomes were being assessed in each assessment event. A possible outcome to this approach is to give faculty space to 'rethink' how they engage students in learning tasks and preparation (Salter et al. 2009). The approach used in this study is outlined in the following Fig. 9.1 and the site for the curriculum reform is described in the Sect. 9.3.

9.3 Case Study Context

Historically, entrepreneurs have played an important role in the economic development and stability of countries, often spurring growth and innovation (Landes 2010; Samila and Sorenson 2011). Through the economic downturn in the late twentieth and early twentyfirst centuries, renewed emphasis has focused on the significance of entrepreneurs in stimulating economic growth (Manev and Manolova 2010; Song et al. 2010). As the importance of entrepreneurship continues to grow, colleges and universities have sought to find ways to train and prepare individuals to become entrepreneurs. Courses and programs in entrepreneurship have been added to the curriculum of many colleges and universities through the past 20 years, both in the United States and in other countries throughout the world. Programs in entrepreneurship have now become an integral part of many business schools globally (Damodharan et al. 2010; Finkle et al. 2006; Kuratko 2005; Sonfield 2000).

Historically, entrepreneurs have played an important role in the economic development and stability of countries, often spurring growth and innovation (Landes 2010; Samila and Sorenson 2011). Through the economic downturn in the late 20th and early 21st centuries, renewed emphasis has focused on the significance of entrepreneurs in stimulating economic growth (Manev and Manolova 2010; Song et al. 2010). As the importance of entrepreneurship continues to grow, colleges and universities have sought to find ways to train and prepare individuals to become entrepreneurs. Courses and programs in entrepreneurship have been added to the curriculum of many colleges and universities through the past 20 years, both in the United States and in other countries throughout the world. Programs in entrepreneurship have now become an integral part of many business schools globally (Damodharan et al. 2010; Finkle et al. 2006; Kuratko 2005; Sonfield 2000).

In 1997, the College of Business at a Mid-Western University (MWU) [a pseudonym] in the United States launched a new degree program in entrepreneurship (ENT). The program proved unusual in a couple of ways: (1) the degree required significant hands-on experience with both an internship and a real-life consulting project, and (2) the required content courses had a specific entrepreneurship focus, such as marketing or accounting for entrepreneurs. The program was among the first in the United States to offer an undergraduate degree in ENT and grew steadily so that after 13 years, the ENT major had become the second largest major in the College of Business and the eighth largest at MWU, with over 350 students enrolled with an ENT major, as seen in Fig. 9.2.

With an increasingly positive reputation, the ENT curriculum remained relatively unchanged through 2007. However, with growth, staffing issues arose. Although the ENT program had a program director, administrative oversight was

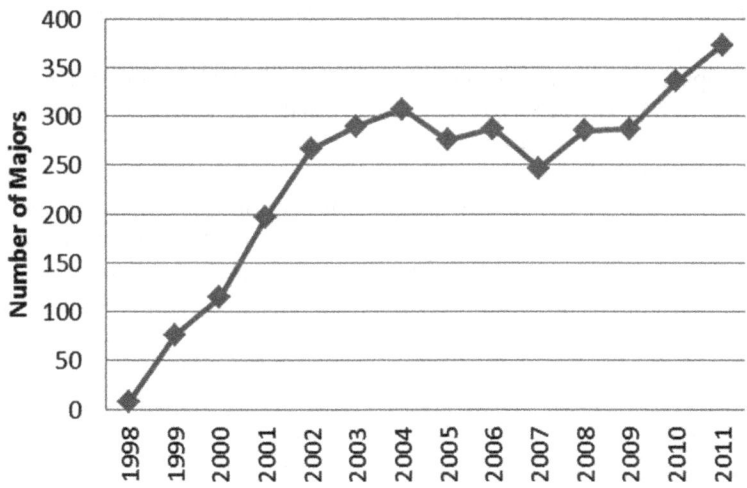

Fig. 9.2 Growth of entrepreneurship major at MWU

not provided by a specific department within the college. The interdisciplinary design of the program resulted in a lack of organizational structure. For example, ENT courses were not a priority for most department chairs, and increasingly, chairs relied on fixed-term or adjunct instructors to teach courses. With the lack of a cohesive faculty, courses were taught in isolation of other courses, and the resulting degree represented more of a collection of courses strung together with ENT course titles than an integrated program.

These factors, along with a new college dean and a new ENT program director, drove a decision to conduct an internal formative review of the program. All stakeholders agreed that a more integrated program was needed to better prepare students to become successful entrepreneurs. As McCormick and Gray (2010) argue the idea that business is a learnable skill is foundational to business education. Our approach supports a plan to build an integrated degree, which sequentially developed toward a capstone experience, with a focus on practical applications of real-world concepts. This emphasis on experiential learning focuses on learning being a process built on integrating experience and interactions between individuals and their environment (Kolb 1984; Kayes 2002; Viswanathan 2012).

9.4   Research Design

In this study we explore how faculty change the way they view developing and strengthening curriculum through the implementation of a curriculum development framework. Using communities of practice theory we investigate how faculty learn and develop professionally as they engage in the process using the CDF model in their curriculum reform effort. A main outcome is the construction of an integrated curriculum with buy-in from faculty across disciplines. Secondary outcomes include the sharing of teaching and learning materials produced in all courses across the program.

Participants in the study include administrators along with regular and fixed-term faculty at MWU who attended work sessions and were involved in the design and development of the structure of the program. They came together on a number of separate occasions during the development period and took time to reflect on their practice with each other. Faculty engagement developed and grew with the group wanting to revitalize the curriculum while gaining a better understanding of the complexity of the context and the interaction of the participants with the change.

A grounded theory approach frames the theoretical orientation of this qualitative research which is a flexible form of research that seeks to understand social interactions of individuals within different contexts. It does not have to be technical, but it can be used as an adaptable and open-ended approach to developing understandings about human situations (Denzin 2010). The key features of grounded theory are an iterative and flexible process to create a model grounded in empirical data of the voices; to construct meanings from the participants (Corbin and Strauss 2008; Charmaz 2006).

In our research we address the following research questions:

1. What can we learn from examining an innovative model for collaborative curriculum reform developed using Communities of Practice (CoP) theory?
2. How can curriculum quality be strengthened in interdisciplinary higher education contexts through collaborative inquiry?

Exploring these questions helps us to understand the complex realities from the perspectives of the participants. The design process aims at theory generation and is influenced by us and the context of the study (Lincoln and Guba 1985). Over a period of 3 months, we systematically gathered data about the activities and characteristics of the participants to illuminate understandings about the research questions. Participants' experiences in the research were collected through interviews along with other data, including site documents and field observations of curriculum review meetings.

One of the most challenging aspects in conducting any qualitative research is the analysis and interpretation of the process and the data, which can be informed by quality studies published previously (Anfara et al. 2002; Miles and Huberman 1994; Strauss and Corbin 1998). In this endeavour, the focus of the research guided the qualitative enquiry and helps us develop the relationship between the research questions and the data sources. Credibility and dependability are the key criteria for judging the adequacy of research (Anfara et al. 2002).

Early data collection and analyses help us to identify subsequent sampling and inductive analysis. This grounded theory approach to theory building and our reflections, as recorded in the data collection, is integral to an understanding of the impact of any changes in practice. Such understanding provides opportunities for strengthening our understanding about how we develop and build curriculum.

We used a qualitative data analysis software program, NVivo, as a tool to assist in the management and analysis of the data. Patton (2002) cautions that although analysis programs can assist in categorizing, grouping, and comparing data, the researcher not the program must decide how to frame a study, how much and what to include, and how to tell the story. So we used NVivo to help us with data management and supporting transparency (Gibbs 2002; Richards 2005; Bazeley and Jackson 2013).

9.5 Findings

In this research we examine some of the difficult situations that arise when implementing change initiatives. Using constructive alignment as a theoretical base for the CDF model, provides us with a common epistemological space in the work sessions. We found that reaching a shared understanding of terms and concepts was both rewarding and frustrating to participants. The frustration came through the extraordinary amount of time it takes for some participants to come to the same understandings as the rest of the group. The reward comes when a paradigm shift occurs and shared understanding emerges.

There are four main findings in this study which relate to the way faculty improve their practice through the implementation of this new framework; students' skills; communication and collaboration, and sharing the vision. We use the three dimensions of a community of practice proposed by Wenger (1998b)—mutual engagement, negotiated joint enterprise, and shared resources—as a framework for exploring the challenges of engaging the faculty. The four findings are a result of the CR group's work revising the ENT program. We reveal complexities in relationships between faculty and administration, and show successful collaboration and organizational change can be achieved under challenging conditions.

9.5.1 Finding 1: Improving Practice

A community of practice exists where a group of like-minded professionals come together with the aim of improving practice. Such a community can, not only help individuals improve their own practice, but can also foster increased commitment and facilitate change—which is what happened at MWU. Using the work session format and approach outlined in this chapter, we present practical processes and tools that contribute to CoP success.

The faculty demonstrated an engagement and commitment to the CDF project, beginning at the first work session as they saw a possibility of personal benefit through the process. "It opens I think communication among people involved in a program in a way that seldom happens" (Participant 012). The CR group shared ways of working together in a community of practice as described by Wenger (1998b) and Wenger et al. (2002). Significantly, we found that faculty began to link the work session process to improvements in their own practice.

This analysis suggests that the curriculum development innovation provided the opportunity for educational development that otherwise would not have happened. The faculty particularly liked the common aims of the CR group and the shared ways of engaging in doing things together along with the framework's structure and the process which followed. "The thing that I saw evolve and develop was this sense of shared excitement and then just sharing, really developing more the community of practice" (Participant 021). Such observations are among the key indicators Wenger identifies that show a community of practice is developing. We found the faculty were working together at another level, and by going through the process, they were given an opportunity to reflect on and work to improve their practice.

Some implementation problems did arise, including the different skill levels of the participants, the lack of clarity in some CR group goals, and a noticeable lack of time. A common feeling also existed that the CR group would benefit from a more focused review and reflection on the process. This accords with Brew's (2004) argument that a rigorous framework of evaluation, review and research reflects a growing trend of searching for new ways to understand and present the nature of educational development.

Keeping the faculty engaged through the process was complicated, but as faculty grasped the process of aligning the new curriculum in the first work session, the expectation of doing more work during subsequent sessions increased. Maintaining open and clear communication became key to optimizing the chance of successful change (Fiss and Zajac 2006). As Participant 013 pointed out "Yeah, I mean I always like collaborating with other teachers but I guess I don't really know what the payoff is going to be. I don't know if it's going to work out. I don't know if it's going to be a lot of extra work but working through the process, I kind of understand what my colleagues are doing and they understand what I'm doing and so I think it's easier to collaborate on things like that."

9.5.2 Finding 2: Promotion of Students' Innovation Skills Is Essential

Promotion of students' innovation skills is an essential component of a successful program. A breakthrough in the process came with the insight that students lacked skills in innovation and idea analysis. This conceptual change came from the realization that the students were not really being given the opportunity to innovate, nurture, and analyse ideas in the existing program—skills essential for a successful entrepreneur. The CR group discussed this and proposed to add a new course in this area to focus on developing this opportunity for the students. Drawing on the concepts of constructive alignment, discussed earlier, the CR group agreed that it was essential to strengthen the program by reinforcing these concepts in other courses throughout the program.

Using CDF process, and having the space to collaborate and communicate, allowed the CR group to discover this missing area, and showed other faculty at MWU that the CR group was not just rearranging existing courses. It also shows the value of faculty achieving a shared understanding. Additionally, the process reflected that the CR group was genuinely looking at, and being driven by, outcomes as we described earlier in the paper.

9.5.3 Finding 3: Communication and Collaboration Mitigates Resistance to Change

Critically examining this CDF process through the growing awareness of the faculty is achieved through successfully navigating issues of defensiveness, lack of preparation, lack of cohesion, and lack of trust. Our second finding suggests that clear communication, working together and building trust in the process and each other, are all factors in overcoming the faculty's initial resistance to this change. "Nobody likes to change, even if—I mean, very few people like to change, I should say—and you either have to change them so much so that they can never go back or you have to change them little bits at a time so that they can adapt and accept it. But, you know, if you don't include them in the process they tend to resist a lot more." (Participant 011).

9.5.4 Finding 4: A Shared Vision Promotes Commitment and Involvement

Previously, development of new teaching materials at MWU had been done by individual faculty in isolation, and the participants saw this new framework as a chance to collaborate with their peers and to be part of a change in an inclusive way. All of the faculty were interested in trying something different and were keen to be involved. They also felt that MWU's support of the process demonstrated interest in what they, as faculty, had to say. Hanrahan et al. (2001) propose that an educational development activity makes little difference in the long term if isolated from usual and relevant practice. So we thought that the CDF model approach was more likely to work and engage the faculty, if participants saw its relevance and meaning to their usual practice.

In the past the faculty at MWU had only communicated intermittently about developing new curriculum. This new CDF model now gave the faculty space to work with each other at MWU and share their work with colleagues. It supports the view that the CDF model created a neutral platform for share voice where organizational status was neutral. The CDF model was designed to promote professional engagement in developing new curriculum at MWU. The goal in using the model was to be responsive to the needs of the faculty, cost–effective and scalable, and take into account the fixed-term status of some of the faculty. As the curriculum development process progressed, the faculty begin to see benefits in engaging in the process; this engagement grew as levels of trust increased both their own community and MWU.

The faculty found it valuable to have the time and space to reflect collaboratively on the content, delivery, and assessment in courses. "In this particular series of meetings and discussions, it's good to see the passion that individuals brought to the table and the willingness to work outside of what their requested teaching load … I just hope there's more out there that I've not met, if they're like the ones that we've got together here on this team" (Participant 019). This was the first time that any of the participants had taken part in this type of development work, and they strongly supported the implementation of the new approach and found it useful to work with. "The groundswell is always very effective if you can get a ground to swell, so that's usually more effective than from the top down, but if you can create kind of a process so that the goals are linked from above and below, then that's great" (Participant 021).

In summary, we found the faculty were committed to their work and to their students, and they commented that they noticed a greater commitment from MWU in assisting staff. Throughout the sessions all participants entered into the process in an open and enthusiastic way. Although there were strong indicators that a community of practice had formed, elements of tensions also emerged that could not be accounted for within the framework. These tensions included the casually employed status of the faculty and the challenge of engaging them in the process.

9.6 Lessons Learned

Reflecting on the tensions that emerged in the data analysis demonstrates that the complexities in the relationships are important to this study. This section describes how a successful collaboration can lead to improving practice and successful change in the workplace. It also describes the tensions that exist when change takes place and how a community of practice can help with this process.

To fully understand how a community of practice works, the process of working together or collaborating needs further investigation. Working *jointly on an activity or project*, as proposed by Elliott and Woloshyn (1997), can be understood as a common definition of collaboration. A successful collaboration can lead to learning and improving practice and change in the workplace. Collaboration is both an individual and social pattern of interaction, with the potential to stimulate ways of thinking that are normally inaccessible to individuals working on their own. In this work collaboration is considered as a process or series of actions, changes, or functions bringing about a result or achieving a goal. This idea supports a community of practice where a group of practitioners come together to share with the aim of improvements to practice, a negotiated joint enterprise (Wenger et al. 2002; Wenger 1998a).

On the surface, the CR group was excited and eager to be involved, yet early on in the project, the idea of collaboration or joint enterprise was missing: "working together is really a new perspective for me" (Participant 014). This curriculum development project proposed a new framework to develop teaching materials where faculty could work together or collaborate with each other and the institution. As defined by Elliott and Woloshyn (1997), collaboration exists where participants can be seen to be working jointly towards a common goal—the essence of a community of practice. However, as time passed the participant faculty started to learn about each other and working together at a more complex level: "Yeah, I realized that I wasn't alone. I think it was good getting the different perspectives and, again, I think that whole how your course sits in with everyone else's, and then being able to fill gaps in" (Participant 016).

We found the faculty began to realize that they could learn from each other: "One of the things just getting together and talking about with other faculty. What are you teaching and how does it fit together?" (Participant 014). "It helps us articulate what it is that we're doing which is helpful to—I mean, I think we know what we're doing. Each of us individually thinks we know, but amongst ourselves, [this process prepares and helps us] so that we're all kind of on the same page when we're making decisions and then when we try to articulate what we're doing to students and administrators, I think it helps in that way." (Participant 013).

The faculty enjoyed working together and saw the benefits from the process: "I have seldom seen, particularly with curricula issues, that sort of excitement amongst colleagues, and I think there was a—I don't want to use the term synergy but a way in which we each came with our own experiences and then as we shared ideas things just kind of built in such a way that the end product was certainly more than what individually any of us could have done, and what we would have expected" (Participant 012).

The tensions found in this study are similar to those found in critiques of communities of practice, where CoPs theory is found to downplay the role of off-the-job learning and overlooks tensions that might emerge along with issues of social power and inequality (e.g. Hodkinson and Hodkinson 2004). We propose that the ideas of social power and inequality are particularly important in this study, as the fixed-term employment status of some of the participant faculty required their voluntary engagement in the process if the framework was to work.

The changes that took place during this curriculum development project led to many tensions surfacing: relationship tensions as well as competing, sometimes conflicting interests of work and time commitments. Faculty reported tensions in where to direct their focus: should they be aligned with the institution's goals, should they focus on their own professional practice, or should they be focused on promoting strong outcomes for their students? The institution goals are primarily focused on promoting strong financial gains for MWU, with quality in teaching as a secondary goal. The faculty, on the other hand, are clear that their main focus is the students. Even so, the faculty are open to aligning their focus with the institution goals when these goals were similar to their own.

An additional layer of complexity also becomes evident as the faculty are balancing their teaching at MWU with their own external work commitments and professional practice. These tensions are framed under three headings in the following diagram, Fig. 9.3. First, the employment status of the teachers is discussed above. Second, the relationship between the teachers and the institution is closely related to this idea and we expand it to include the relationship between the teachers and students, and other faculty. The final tension is about lost opportunities which we capture through the constraints of the process and identify ways the process could be improved. These tensions are represented in Fig. 9.3. Tensions and Alignment in the Data. This diagram attempts to captures the key elements of the tension and alignment we reveal in this study, where alignment of goals, as discussed following Fig. 9.3, promotes a stronger outcome to the process.

This diagram shows that successfully working together, in this case in a community of practice to engage the fixed-term and full-time faculty, can promote the alignment of goals and balancing of different needs to achieve a successful outcome. For example, within the tensions manifesting through the relationship between the faculty and MWU are the elements of the faculty's focus on the students, MWU's focus on achieving a quality experience for the greatest profit,

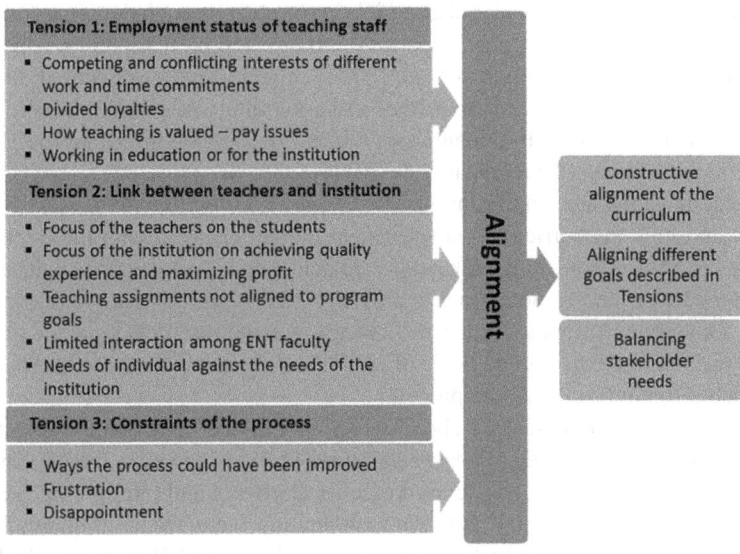

Fig. 9.3 Tensions and alignment in the data [adapted from Salmona (2009)]

and institution versus individual needs. Alignment in this study is shown through three elements: constructive alignment in the curriculum development work; alignment of goals; and balancing the different needs of interested parties.

Although curriculum work is complicated and apt to trigger strong feelings and tensions, the diagram is put forward as a way of interrogating, or asking questions about, the curriculum development process more deeply. The research process gave the faculty an opportunity to engage in their own professional development that would not have been available to them if this project had not taken place. When asked to consider the process, the participants affirmed that the series of work sessions was successful in its aim of identifying outcomes for courses, and presented an opportunity to engage in developing their own teaching materials and learn from colleagues. They found the work sessions productive, although they had to work very hard together as a CR group when learning a new practice. Even though tensions emerged, the participants reported that it was interesting to see how other faculty went about their teaching and it was productive to have time to reflect with their colleagues on their work.

9.7 Conclusion and Practical Implications

This research brings this issue of working together to produce integrated and relevant curriculum to the forefront in an effort to engage the reader, college administrators and educators. A secondary outcome of this study was the development of the new teaching and learning materials, and it became clear through the process that the faculty were also being given an opportunity to develop professionally, which was an unanticipated result. Hanrahan et al. (2001) suggest "that professional development that is discipline-specific and located in a community-of-practice is more likely to be relevant and productive than a centralized, decontextualized approach". For change to work it must be relevant and meaningful to the participants. We consider how these tensions are manifestations of the particular employment conditions of faculty, and how the curriculum development project engaged with these tensions. We also discuss how the different tensions are managed and suggest how educational development can be promoted in a setting like MWU. In this paper we present a critical examination about the tensions in the educational development process, where we look at the needs and goals of MWU and the more complex interpersonal relationship dynamics inside the process.

The work sessions described above were not the end of the story. During the following year the individual departments worked, with this new shared vision of the program to get the new and revised courses approved and through the curricula process. Further adjustments and accommodations were made as more faculty became part of the realignment/redesign process. The core CR group worked with both additional regular and fixed-term faculty, and further adjustments were made to accommodate feedback from department, college, and university curriculum committees. The core CR group continued to work on the process; and a sense of community has continued with sharing of information, articles, ideas, and making adjustments as the curriculum approval process progressed.

In this paper we express some of the particular challenges of working with a fixed-term workforce in a higher education institution, an area where there is no significant literature. In this changing higher education environment, with its unstated underlying assumption of full-time employment, any curriculum or educational development has to be mindful of fixed-term teaching staff. A real contribution of this work is to highlight how the participants to engage in curriculum reform, and we illuminate the different ways in which people are working. Through our data analysis, we add a new dimension to communities of practice, further illuminating our understanding of its application in an environment with a high percentage of fixed-term faculty. We argue, through our discussion that both full-time and fixed-term employed faculty can be successfully engaged in their own professional development through a collaborative framework such as a community of practice. The end result of the CR group's work using the CDF process was an updated, current, relevant and integrated curriculum for the ENT program in a Business College, with clear graduate outcomes and meaningful assessment to ensure outcomes are met.

The process also serves as a model for initiating institutional change in higher organization and for engaging faculty. By providing this space for the faculty to come together, they are able to share ideas and goals, and feel valued by the institution. MWU's need to improve the quality of teaching, to meet the growing quality focus in higher education is addressed by developing the institutional capacity for alignment of goals between the faculty and MWU. Future work on this topic could investigate how this model could be used in other settings.

References

Anfara, V. A., Jr., Brown, K. M., & Mangione, T. L. (2002). Qualitative analysis on stage: Making the research process more public. *Educational Researcher, 31*(7), 28–38.

Barnett, R., & Coate, K. (2005). *Engaging the curriculum in higher education.* New York: Society for Research into Higher Education and Open University Press.

Barrie, S. C. (2007). A conceptual framework for the teaching and learning of generic graduate attributes. *Studies in Higher Education, 32*(4), 439–458.

Bazeley, P., & Jackson, K. (2013). *Qualitative data analysis with NVivo* (2nd ed.). London: Sage.

Biggs, J. B. (1996). Enhancing teaching through constructive alignment. *Higher Education, 32*(3), 347–364.

Biggs, J. B. (1999). What the student does: Teaching for enhanced learning. *Higher Education Research and Development, 18*(1), 57–75.

Biggs, J. B. (2003). *Aligning teaching and assessing to course objectives.* Paper presented at the teaching and learning in higher education conference: New trends and innovations, University of Aveiro, April 13–17.

Boud, D. (1999). Situating academic development in professional work: Using peer learning. *International Journal for Academic Development, 4*(1), 5–10.

Boud, D., & Middleton, H. (2003). Learning from other at work: Communities of practice and informal learning. *Journal of Workplace Learning, 15*(5), 194–209.

Boud, D., & Walker, D. (1998). Promoting reflection in professional courses: The challenge of context. *Studies in Higher Education, 23*(2), 191–206.

Brew, A. (2004). Editorial: The scope of academic development. *International Journal for Academic Development, 9*(1), 5–7.

Brown, A. J., Goodman, J., & Yasukawa, K. (2008). Casualisation of academic work: Industrial justice and quality education. *Dialogue, 27*, 17–29.

Charmaz, K. (2006). *Constructing grounded theory: A practical guide through qualitative analysis.* London: Sage.

Chua, A. Y. K. (2006). The rise and fall of a community of practice: A descriptive case study. *Knowledge and Process Management, 13*(2), 120–128.

Connelly, F. M., Clandinin, D. J., & He, M. F. (1997). Teachers' personal practical knowledge on the professional knowledge landscape. *Teaching and Teacher Education, 13*(7), 665–674.

Corbin, J., & Strauss, A. (2008). *Basics of qualitative research: Techniques and procedures for developing grounded theory.* London: Sage.

Damodharan, V. S., Majumdar, S., & Gallant, M. (2010). Relevance of education for potential entrepreneurs: An international investigation. *Journal of Small Business and Enterprise Development, 17*(4), 626–640.

Defise, R. (2013). Supporting the implementation of curriculum reform through learning communities and communities of practice. *Prospects, 43*, 473–479.

Denzin, N. K. (2010). Grounded and indigenous theories and the politics of pragmatism. *Sociological Inquiry, 80*(2), 286–319.

Elliott, A. E., & Woloshyn, V. E. (1997). Some female professors' experiences of collaboration: Mapping the collaborative process through rough terrain. *Alberta Journal of Educational Research, 43*, 23–36.

Feldman, D. C., & Turnley, W. H. (2001). A field study of adjunct faculty: The impact of career stage on reactions to non-tenure-jobs. *Journal of Career Development, 28*(1), 1–16.

Finkle, T. A., Kuratko, D. F., & Goldsby, M. G. (2006). An examination of entrepreneurship centers in the United States: A national survey. *Journal of Small Business Management, 44*(2), 184–206.

Fiss, P. C., & Zajac, E. J. (2006). The symbolic management of strategic change: Sensegiving via framing and decoupling. *Academy of Management Journal, 49*(6), 1173–1193.

Florin, J., Karri, R., & Rossiter, N. (2007). Fostering entrepreneurial drive in business education: An attitudinal approach. *Journal of Management Education, 31*(1), 17–49.

Frielick, S. (2004). *The zone of academic development: An ecological approach to learning and teaching in higher education*. Johannesburg: University of the Witwatersrand.

Gibbs, G. (2002). *Qualitative data analysis: Explorations with NVivo (understanding social research)*. Buckingham: Open University Press.

Greisler, D. (2002). Adjunct to what? A non-traditional perspective on teaching and social sciences. *International Journal of Public Administration, 25*(9), 1125–1141.

Hanrahan, M., Ryan, M., & Duncan, M. (2001). The professional engagement model of academic induction into on-line teaching. *International Journal for Academic Development, 6*(2), 130–149.

Hicks, O. (2007). *Curriculum in higher education in Australia–Hello?* Paper presented at the enhancing higher education, theory and scholarship, proceedings of the 30th HERDSA annual conference, Adelaide, Australia, July 8–11.

Hodkinson, P., & Hodkinson, H. (2004). A constructive critique of communities of practice: Moving beyond Lave and Wenger. In *Integrating work 7 learning, contemporary issues seminar series, OVAL research working paper 0402*, May 11, 2004.

Junor, A. (2004). Casual university work: Choice, risk, inequity and the case for regulation. *Economic and Labour Relations Review, 14*(2), 276–304.

Kabongo, J. D., & McCaskey, P. H. (2011). An examination of entrepreneurship educator profiles in business programs in the United States. *Journal of Small Business and Enterprise Development, 18*(1), 27–49.

Kayes, D. C. (2002). Experiential learning and its critics: Preserving the role of experience in management learning and education. *Academy of Management Learning and Education, 1*(2), 137–149.

Kolb, D. A. (1984). *Experiential learning: Experience as the source of learning and development*. Englewood Cliffs, NJ: Prentice-Hall.

Kosky, L. (2005). *The university and its engagement with the community*. Paper presented at the Town and Gown Dinner, University of Melbourne, May 25, 2005.

Kuratko, D. F. (2005). The emergence of entrepreneurship education: Development, trends, and challenges. *Entrepreneurship Theory and Practice, 29*(5), 577–598.

Land, R. (2004). *Educational development: Discourse, identity and practice*. Maidenhead: Open University/Society for Research into Higher Education.

Landes, D. S. (2010). Global enterprise and industrial performance: An overview. In D. S. Landes, J. Mokyr, & W. J. Baumol (Eds.), *The invention of enterprise: Entrepreneurship from ancient Mesopotamia to modern times* (pp. 1–7). Princeton, NJ: Princeton University Press.

Lave, J., & Wenger, E. (1991). *Situated learning. legitimate peripheral participation*. Cambridge: University of Cambridge Press.

Lee, A. (2005). *Discussion paper—Knowing our business: The role of education in the university*. Callagan, NSW: Australian Council of Deans of Education.

Lee, A., & Boud, D. (2003). Writing groups, change and academic identity: Research development as local practice. *Studies in Higher Education, 28*(2), 187–200.

Lincoln, Y. S., & Guba, E. G. (1985). *Naturalistic inquiry*. Beverly Hills, CA: Sage.

Manev, I. M., & Manolova, T. S. (2010). Entrepreneurship in transitional economies: Review and integration of two decades of research. *Journal of Developmental Entrepreneurship, 15*(1), 69–99.

May, R., Campbell, I., & Burgess, J. (2005). *The rise and rise of casual work in Australia: Who benefits, who loses?* Paper presented at the IR changes report card, University of Sydney, June 20.

McCormick, B., & Gray, V. (2010). Message in a Bottle: Basic business lessons for entrepreneurs using only a soft drink. *Journal of Management Education, 35*(2), 282–310.

Miles, M. B., & Huberman, A. M. (1994). *Qualitative data analysis* (2nd ed.). Thousand Oaks, CA: Sage.

Monaghan, C. H. (2011). Communities of practice: A learning strategy for management education. *Journal of Management Education, 35*(3), 428–453.

Patton, M. (2002). *Qualitative research and evaluation methods* (3rd ed.). Thousand Oaks, CA: Sage.

Pocock, B., Buchanan, J., & Campbell, I. (2004). Meeting the challenge of casual work in Australia: Evidence, past treatment and future policy. *Australian Bulletin of Labour, 30*(1), 16–39.

Richards, L. (2005). *Handling qualitative data: A practical guide*. London: Sage.

Salmona, M. (2009). *Engaging casually employed teachers in collaborative curriculum and professional development: Change through an action research enquiry in a higher education pathways institution*. Sydney: University of Technology.

Salter, D., Pang, M. Y. C., & Sharma, P. (2009). Active tasks to change the use of class time within an outcomes based approach to curriculum design. *Journal of University Teaching and Learning Practice, 6*(1).

Samila, S., & Sorenson, O. (2011). Venture capital, entrepreneurship, and economic growth. *The Review of Economics and Statistics, 93*(1), 338–349.

Sonfield, M. C. (2000). Establishing and developing entrepreneurship and small business growth in a post-communist economy: The case of Hungary. *Academy of Entrepreneurship Journal, 6*(2), 16–26.

Song, L. Z., Song, M., & Parry, M. E. (2010). Perspective: Economic conditions, entrepreneurship, first product development, and new venture success. *The Journal of Product Innovation Management, 27*(1), 130–135.

Stein, M. K., Smith, M. S., & Silver, E. A. (1999). The Development of professional developers: Learning to assist teachers in new settings in new ways. *Harvard Educational Review, 69*(3), 237–269.

Strauss, A., & Corbin, J. (1998). *Basics of qualitative research: Techniques and procedures for developing grounded theory* (2nd ed.). Thousand Oaks, CA: Sage.

Vandenheuval, A., & Wooden, M. (1999). *Casualisation and outsourcing: Trends and implications for work-related training*. Adelaide: National Centre for Vocational Education Research (NCVER).

Viswanathan, M. (2012). Curricular innovations on sustainability and subsistence marketplaces: Philosophical, substantive, and methodological orientations. *Journal of Management Education, 36*(3), 389–427.

Wallin, D. L. (2007). Part-time faculty and professional development: Notes from the field. *New Directions for Community Colleges, 140*, 67–73.

Wenger, E. (1998a). Communities of practice. Learning as a social system. *Systems Thinker, 9*(5), 5.

Wenger, E. (1998b). *Communities of practice: Learning, meaning and identity*. New York: Cambridge University Press.

Wenger, E., McDermott, R., & Snyder, W. M. (2002). *Cultivating communities of practice*. Boston, MA: Harvard Business School Press.

Chapter 10
Reflections on the Emergence and Evolution of a Scholarship of Teaching and Learning Community of Practice Within a Research-Intensive Higher Education Context

Peta Dzidic, Emily Castell, Lynne D. Roberts, Peter J. Allen and Michelle Quail

Abstract In this chapter we present a critical case study analysing the emergence and evolution of a higher education Community of Practice (CoP) centred on the Scholarship of Teaching and Learning (SoTL). This CoP exists in the context of an institution attempting to re-position itself as 'research intensive', where there are ongoing tensions between research and teaching, with prevailing perceptions that research is more valued than teaching, and disciplinary research is more valued than teaching and learning research. The chapter draws on the findings from a workshop with the CoP members, conducted within a Futures Studies anticipatory action-learning framework, and analysed using Causal Layered Analysis. Findings highlighted the importance of social context. Three themes emerging from the workshop were members' perceived systemic exclusion from the wider research community, exploration and contestation of dominant university culture and values, and perceptions that teaching and SoTL are undervalued within the university setting. Individual and collective experiences of exclusion and othering prompted a movement of defiance, fostering the development of a CoP which, over the first 3 years of operation, has achieved institutional recognition, access to resources, competitive research funding success, significant publication outputs, and, growth and stability in research group membership. Multidisciplinary engagement and focus, the research group's interpersonal style which is based on mutual respect and support, and flexibility through empathy have fostered successes. Ultimately the success of a CoP is not determined by tangible outputs alone. Rather, it is characterised by equity, collaboration, genuine participation and empowerment.

P. Dzidic (✉) · E. Castell · L.D. Roberts · P.J. Allen · M. Quail
School of Psychology and Speech Pathology, Curtin University, GPO Box U1987,
Perth, WA 6845, USA
e-mail: peta.dzidic@curtin.edu.au

© Springer Nature Singapore Pte Ltd. 2017
J. McDonald and A. Cater-Steel (eds.), *Communities of Practice*,
DOI 10.1007/978-981-10-2879-3_10

Keywords SoTL · Scholarship of teaching and learning · Futures studies · Causal layered analysis

10.1 Introduction

In August 2012, as part of a faculty-wide exercise to promote collaborative research, all academic staff members in our school (situated in a mid-sized, mid-ranked Australian university) were assigned to a 'program of research' by the head of school, based on their research history and interests. All but one of these programs represented an area of research strength for the school. The remaining program of research, seemingly pulled together to 'capture' staff not involved in areas of research strength for the school, was labelled 'teaching approaches/internet use'. This was the only program of research to have a Scholarship of Teaching and Learning (SoTL) focus. Two co-leaders and four other members were initially assigned to this group, representing a mix of predominantly teaching/research and teaching academics. Within this original small group there were varying degrees of engagement and association with the domain of research. Indeed, some members had not conducted any research in the areas of teaching or online behaviour previously. The group had no representation on the school's research committee.

The dynamic of the research group is perhaps best described as atypical of other research groups that developed from this process. SoTL emerged as the common theme amidst a group of individuals whose research interests were deemed to not fit anywhere else. During the group's establishment, there was seemingly limited institutional investment by the school or faculty, and the resultant dynamic was, in effect, due to members being left to their own devices. Members created and negotiated their own roles, rules, and focus. While this may have been the objective and process that emerged in other discipline specific research groups, this emerged with seemingly little scrutiny or interest by those in positions of power. In effect, a sense of being 'the forgotten', 'the disregarded', and the 'the undervalued' led to a scenario where the research group began to manifest as a CoP. Its members with diverse disciplinary backgrounds, years of expertise, and levels of authority within the university structure found solace as institutional misfits, and common ground in their shared interest in SoTL.

Conceptually, it appears that while the group was formed alongside other research groups, the discipline non-specific focus of SoTL perhaps in part accounts for the way in which the group has, at times, been institutionally forgotten or disregarded as a research group. This dynamic may have contributed to the necessity of the group members to operate like a CoP. The dynamics of a CoP has been conducive to the development of an inclusive culture, seemingly in part a response to the exclusion from other groups felt by members.

From this inauspicious beginning just over 3 years ago, a thriving community of practice (CoP) has emerged. Our CoP is consistent with Wenger's (2010) model of Community of Practice, with CoP as a social learning system situated within broader social learning systems (Wenger 2000, 2010). This CoP has a 'bootlegged' relationship (Wenger et al. 2002) with the school within which it is embedded, with a history of fighting for recognition, resources and legitimacy. Over time, the success of this CoP has resulted in increased visibility and recognition within the broader faculty teaching and learning community, providing a form of legitimization. In this chapter, we (five members of the CoP) present a critical case study analysing the emergence, evolution and future directions of this higher education CoP, which has become increasingly (although not exclusively) centred on SoTL. We trace the organic growth of the CoP, from a small group of 'Odd Bods'[1] pushed together as part of a bureaucratic re-shaping exercise to a thriving CoP with 17 members today. In doing so, we capture a shared history of the CoP through providing the perspectives of the leaders, original members, and newer members. We then articulate the challenges and tensions of conducting research in an area marginalised within higher education, and highlight the advocacy by members to legitimise the CoP as a research group in order to access resources and esteem.

10.2 Background

At the time of the initial assignments to programs of research, the university's vision was to be among the top 20 universities in Asia by 2020, with a particular focus on increasing the quantity and quality of research outputs. With its origins as an 'institute of technology', only transitioning to university status in the late 1980s, the university was now competing directly in a market with sandstone universities with established research credentials. As an institution attempting to re-position itself as 'research intensive', there were (and continue to be) ongoing tensions between research and teaching, with prevailing perceptions that research is more valued than teaching, and that disciplinary research is more valued than teaching and learning research. These attitudes are not specific to our institution, but are widespread throughout Australian (Freudenberg 2012; Probert 2013) and overseas (Schroeder 2007) universities.

Across the Australian higher education sector, there is also increasing division between research and teaching staff, with increasing numbers of staff employed as 'teaching only' academics over the last 5 years (Probert 2013, 2014). Consistent with this, a major restructuring within our own institution over the last 2 years has seen the emergence of new categories of academic staff: Teaching-Focussed, Teaching-Focussed Clinical-Professional, and Scholarly Teaching Fellow. With no formal time allocation for research, academics in these positions need to establish a record of engagement in SoTL in order to meet criteria for promotion. Engagement in SoTL is now "an imperative, not a choice" (Huber and Hutchings 2005; cited in Mathison 2015, p. 98). It is also becoming increasingly imperative for staff with traditional teaching/research roles, with SoTL now a common criterion for

---

[1]Our original colloquial name for the group.

performance management (Mathison 2015; Vardi 2011; Vardi and Quin 2011). Despite this, academic staff have not traditionally been trained in the area of SoTL. Although PhDs provide disciplinary training, the methodologies used within disciplines are not always transferable to SoTL research (Mathison 2015; see, for example, Borrego 2007, on difficulties engineering academics experience in transitioning to SoTL). This places academic staff occupying teaching roles in a difficult transition, where they must focus their career progression on SoTL, despite this being a new and unique domain to many, and quite often distinct from their path to, and progression through, academia to date.

This context causes further tension for staff members wishing to continue pursuing research specific to their discipline and area of interest/specialty when this lies outside of SoTL. Without being recognised within workloads or career progression frameworks, it is easy to assume that this discipline specific research is not deemed valuable to the university, and should instead be left to the 'research' academics. Thus teaching focussed and teaching/research academics are forced to find a balance between their research interests and research requirements, while maintaining both job satisfaction and career progression opportunities. As a result of these challenges, it is essential that staff focusing on SoTL band together within this context and form a sub-discipline that nurtures progression in the area of SoTL. Williams et al. (2013) argue that to effectively integrate SoTL into higher education requires networks of scholars, rather than isolated individuals. The CoP approach, with a focus on social learning (Wenger 2000), provides one means of engaging and up-skilling staff in SoTL.

In situating our CoP within the literature on SoTL communities of practice, it is important to distinguish between SoTL and scholarly teaching. The terms 'SoTL' and 'scholarly teaching' are sometimes used interchangeably, but represent qualitatively different concepts. Building from Boyer's (1990) original conceptualisation of the scholarship of teaching, SoTL has recently been defined as "the systematic study of teaching and learning, using established or validated criteria of scholarship, to understand how teaching (beliefs, behaviours, attitudes, and values) can maximize learning, and/or develop a more accurate understanding of learning, resulting in products that are publicly shared for critique and use by an appropriate community" (Potter and Kustra 2011, p. 2). Further, the public sharing should be through peer-reviewed publications (Wilson-Doenges and Gurung 2013). It is this focus on producing research outputs that are scrutinised by others (peer-review) that sets SoTL apart from scholarly teaching, where the focus is on "teaching grounded in critical reflection using systematically and strategically gathered evidence, related and explained by well-reasoned theory and philosophical understanding, with the goal of maximizing learning through effective teaching" (Potter and Kustra 2011, p. 3). Further, divisions in relation to the quality of SoTL have been proposed. For example, Wilson-Doenges and Gurung (2013) identify three levels of SoTL research: entry-level SoTL with weaker designs, mid-level SOTL with some methodological shortcomings and high-level SOTL with rigorous methodology.

The majority of CoPs around SoTL featured in previous publications (e.g., Cox 2013; Duffy 2006) actually focus on scholarly approaches to teaching. Further, a survey across 86 learning communities (a type of structured higher education CoP that is typically focused on SoTL; Cox 2013) indicated that while the majority were engaged in some form of scholarly teaching, only a minority reported publishing activity (Richlin and Cox 2004). Previous research has identified multiple barriers in moving beyond scholarly teaching to engaging in SoTL research that results in peer-reviewed publications. These include competing time demands and priorities; unfamiliarity with higher education literature, research methods and suitable journals for publishing; ethical challenges; and differences between disciplinary and SoTL practices (Hubball et al. 2010). Where SoTL CoPs have moved beyond scholarly teaching to engaging in teaching and learning research, mentorship of new CoP members by experienced SoTL researchers appears key. SoTL mentors are able to model SoTL practice, facilitate SoTL research and provide networking opportunities (Hubball et al. 2010). While mentorship provides one avenue for increasing SoTL research, there is a paucity of case studies available that examine how CoPs can work within the contested academic space to effectively engage members in SoTL in ways that result in recognised academic outputs. In this chapter, we present the evolution of our SoTL focussed CoP, which has developed capacity to achieve such outputs.

10.3 Research Approach

This research uses a case study design, based on the analysis of a Futures Workshop with CoP members. Futures Studies is a field within the social sciences that advocates the necessity and value of in-depth deconstruction of social issues. The argument is that the difficulty that can emerge in addressing social issues can come from failing to get to the root of an issue, and instead focussing on superficial and uncontested understandings of it. Within this field it is felt that by examining deeper cultural mythologies, worldviews, and value systems, the drivers of social issues can be identified. Knowing and addressing these drivers (as opposed to the resultant impact of these issues) gives opportunity for genuine long-term change to occur. A Futures Workshop is based on Causal Layered Analysis (CLA) methodology (Bishop and Dzidic 2014; Inayatullah 2006). The methodology is contextualist in its epistemology and presents as a useful analytical framework for the analysis of complex issues. The complex issue that we wished to examine related to identifying and deconstructing the apparent resilience of a group, that by institutional definition, was not valued, and did not warrant support. A Futures Workshop aims to deconstruct a complex issue by prompting participants to explore it according to increasing levels of scrutiny. For example, questions posed at the beginning of a Futures Workshop can prompt participants to provide accounts of the uncontested history or qualities of the issue. In this instance, participants were asked to describe their history of participation in the group. The complexity of the questions then escalates, such that towards the end of the workshop, epistemological and onto-logical questions relating to the issue under investigation can be posed. For example, questions that call on participants to reflect on how others may socially construct the group, and what the underpinning of such constructions may be.

Conducting a Futures Workshop to deconstruct our CoP enabled an in-depth discussion of the dynamics of a group by its members. Tensions can emerge in instances that researchers are also embedded within the community they are investigating. The complexity arises whereby immersion in that community can inhibit the propensity for discoveries to be made and for thorough deconstruction to occur. The questioning style fostered in a Futures Workshop is one that forces participants to question underlying assumptions pertaining to the nature of the topic under investigation. The approach also recognises and values that researchers can perform dual roles, as traditional researchers engaging in a process of inquiry, but also as participants who have a contribution to make to the study.

10.4 Participants

In total, 11 members of the CoP participated in the Futures Workshop. Participants were from the same school, but represented two overarching disciplines and at least six sub-disciplines. Participants represented a range of academic levels, from early career to 40 years within academia. All participants taught at either an undergraduate or postgraduate level within their discipline, however their allocation of teaching and research differed as per their appointment. Some participants had no research allocation but were permitted to engage in SoTL, others had upwards of 20 % research allocation and were permitted/expected to engage in discipline specific research. All but two participants identified as female, reflecting the composition of gender in the school.

10.5 Procedure

After this project was reviewed and approved by our local human research ethics committee, members of the CoP were invited to participate in a Futures Workshop facilitated by two of the authors (Dzidic and Castell). In the workshop, members were encouraged to discuss the history of the group (including external and internal factors that shaped its development), and reflect on its purpose, leadership and possible futures. The workshop was audio recorded and, after transcription and de-identification, the recording was securely erased. Following analysis, a feedback letter summarising key findings was presented to participants for comment. In reply, participants indicated that the summary captured their experiences of engaging in the CoP. In their feedback, some participants emphasised particular qualities of the CoP, or particular factors in the development of the CoP. This feedback has been integrated with, and has contributed to the depth and richness of, the analysis and interpretation of findings.

10.6   Analysis

The de-identified transcripts were analysed using CLA (Inayatullah 1998, 2004), an emerging Futures methodology for examining data at four levels: the litany, social causative, discourse/worldview and myth/metaphor. The aim of this approach is to deconstruct deeper, more complex underpinnings of social issues or processes. While akin to a thematic analysis in that the interpretation leads to the identification of themes, the process of analysis is informed by identifying data content pertaining to the conceptual layers. The layers assist in the identification of surface level themes (litany layer), as well as more complex systemic (social causes), discursive and ideological, and cultural and historical (myth/metaphor) themes. The inter-pretations and findings reflected in this chapter constitute the final phase of a CLA, where issues are synthesised and reconstructed to form meta-themes and messages. Our analysis draws on the community psychology concepts of barometers of change (Sarason 2000), a critique of genuine participation (Arnstein 1969; Taylor and Bogdan 1980), and concepts of liberalism and neoliberalism (Newbrough 1995) to understand the growth of membership, engagement, and resultant schol-arly activity by CoP members over the first 3 years of operation.

10.7   Findings

Analysis of the Futures Workshop transcripts resulted in the identification of themes. For meaningful interpretation and ease of reading, these findings have been synthesised into three meta, or overarching themes of *systemic exclusion, contested institutional and group values*, and *changing constructions and undervaluing of academia* (see Table 10.1 for a summary). Despite the research group's institutional recognition, milestones, and success in challenging the systemic barriers that had prevented genuine participation and opportunity for the group, participants reported that the dominant cultural value and message that teaching research is not valued, prevailed. In this section, each theme is examined in depth with quotes used for illustration and justification.

10.7.1   Systemic Exclusion

Participants were invited to reflect on their personal history of engagement as a member of the research group. Given the gradual growth in membership, accounts of the history were diverse. Some participants were founding members and reflected on the beginnings of the group out of an institution-wide push to create formalised research groups. Others had joined more recently, as new staff members, and/or due to mutual research interests and opportunities for collaboration. Despite diversity in

Table 10.1 Summary of themes emerging from causal layered analysis of futures workshop

Theme	Description
Systemic exclusion	• Individual and collective histories of engagement in CoP • Constructed as 'different' • Looking for a 'home' • Deprivation of resources • Collegiality through adversity
Contested institutional and group values	• Hierarchy in perceived value of roles and activities • 'Core business' • Operating within dominant university culture • Accessing esteem without compromising group values
Changing constructions and under-valuing of academia	• Notions of an 'academic' • Contrasting a 'bygone' era with contemporary notions of academia • Garnering opportunities to engage meaningfully in one's role as an 'academic'

stories, a collective chronological account emerged and was met with consensus. Notably, irrespective of the duration of engagement in the group, some participants lamented that they did not qualify for membership in other research gruops, felt 'different', as 'other', and as 'under valued'. Specifically, participants described their experience of being excluded from the wider research community but had "found a home" as a member of the research group. Founding members reflected on the emergence of the research groups more broadly within the university, and what this meant for them. A participant stated:

> I can remember that scramble when the faculty decided that it was gonna have these research groups and people had to be aligned with them and there were all sorts of rules about who could and couldn't join each group and everything else. …it was imposed now in the school and as we said, there was a kind of this group of elite – the faculty was realigning itself, I think, as wanting to focus almost exclusively on health-related research. And there were people like myself who were thinking 'well, I don't really give a toss about health'.

Here, the participant reflected on top-down decision making processes and suggested that a particular domain of research (health) was valued more than others. With restructuring came the expectation that academics' research interests and expertise should align with the faculty's current interest. Participants further deconstructed and critiqued the imposed processes and character of the group membership, stating:

> Participant A: but if you were a level two [a grading system that identified group members on their level of experience and power afforded to them as members], there were things you weren't allowed to do, and it was just like this whole hierarchical thing.
> Participant B: it's very much like a class system, almost instantly.
> Participant A: You're right. That validated [you] as a researcher or not.

For participants who were afforded the opportunity to join health related research groups, the hierarchical class structure was off-putting, acting as a deterrent for future engagement. Other participants found themselves allocated to a group that appeared to fall out of the valued research domain, a participant reflected:

...the faculty had programs of research and they decided to sort of replicate it within the school to get collaboration going within the school. So they were able to map out all the other areas and they then they had a few people left over.

Being constructed as 'left overs' was a sentiment echoed by other participants, for example, "so it did seem very much that it was the odd bods, that was people who didn't fit into the existing programs of research". In response to these systemic pressures, the group initially self-identified and labeled itself as the 'Odd Bods'. The name represented a collective experience of exclusion, being constructed as different, and a sense that the value of their disciplinary expertise and contribution was undermined and not appreciated by the school or faculty.

Participants also discussed the transformation of the research group from the 'Odd Bods' to a collectively determined nomenclature and formally identified research group. Participants noted that over time the group identified systemic barriers that prevented a presence and voice in decision-making and opportunities experienced by other research groups and individual researchers. As discrepancies were identified, the research group systemically challenged dominant cultural values pertaining to the value, role and contribution of teaching and learning research. A major issue that the research group contended with was systemic oppression, a participant noted:

...I remember one of the things that we kept pushing for was to be recognised as researcher, as a research group, because every time research was mentioned in staff meetings, we were always left off... It was more about accessing resources because if you're not recognised as a research group, then you can't apply for the school research grants. You can't – you gotta get recognised in your workload.

Another participant stated:

...I think when we realised that this was the only group that didn't have representation on the R&D committee, it was – I mean it was described at the time as being 'an oversight'...

Deliberate or otherwise, the exclusion described in the two previous accounts illuminated a perceived difference between the CoP and other research groups and researchers within the school. This introduced unique procedural challenges that other research groups (aligned with faculty programs of research) had not endured.

10.7.2   Institutional and Group Values in Contest

Participants explored and contested dominant university culture and values, arguing that the culture resulted in a class system that privileged some academics and excluded others. A competitive academic climate was identified that valued particular research (that aligned with faculty programs of research) over teaching related research. Further, participants criticised the more general institutional culture that valued research over teaching. For example, a participant stated, "...I still think that anything to do with teaching is considered to have no value", and another, "It's an interesting idea that if you're doing teaching, it must be because you couldn't get a research position... but that's not the case".

This hierarchy in perceived value of roles and activities resonated with participants who tended to either empathise with or identify as performing a role outside those valued and celebrated within the university. The potential impact this current value system has on future academics was lamented during the workshop,

> A big legacy of the group would be that young people starting out don't see teaching as – or a teaching focussed role as a consolation prize. ...that it's just considered a career path the same way as any other role.

Following this, a participant responded, "and maybe a booby prize for some people. I mean, that sounds weird, not even a consolation prize, but a booby prize".

Having emerged as a research group in part out of adversity and being constructed as 'outsiders', the culture of the research group aligned itself with values of inclusion and agency. For example, one participant reflected on the group's response to the broader dominant university culture, stating, "...the humour, the irreverence of it all; the acknowledgement of the teaching as core business of the university". Here, the roles of group members are valued as being "core business", as opposed to being undervalued and positioned on the periphery. The imposition of hierarchical and value laden processes and structures was also critiqued by participants, for example,

> I think that seems to be a pattern over the years is that anything that's imposed will fail at some point. Anything where people are allowed to let their creativity and their individual thing grow will mean it will work.

Membership within the research group created a 'safe' place for exploration, learning, development, advocacy, capacity building, collaboration and mentorship. One participant reflected on the group's collective endeavors to garner agency and autonomy, perceiving these efforts as illustrative of "self-empowerment",

> [This group is a] really classic example of empowerment or self-empowerment. I mean really, it's the nature of the group has been in fact, it's been supportive, non-competitive, but still effective, and I think the group support was provided for people to actually do their own thing and feel protected... So they're not gonna be penalised for being who they are and I think that's allowed the growth of the group.

It was also evident that the research group was empathic to the lived experience of its members, for example,

> I think just that common understanding of what it's actually like to be teaching on the ground, because I think it's very easy when you have teaching in your workload to become very insular because you've just got to put your head down and write this lecture or mark these six billion assignments or whatever. And I find that I feel very disconnected from

everybody at my peak times of the year. But this gives a sense of, you know, at least I know I'm gonna see people once every couple of weeks.

The emergence of the research group as a CoP is perhaps a product of members contesting the broader exclusionary and hierarchical culture of the institution in which they are embedded. Participants recognised their values and practices fell outside of those recognised and legitimised by the university. For example, it was evident that to be aligned with the qualities praised by the university would require participants adopting the university's values at the expense of their own. Absolving values presents as inherently unjust and, irrespective of the injustice, the adoption of alternative roles (including those roles valued by the university) presents to participants as an impossibility. Some participants were structurally bound by their appointment and contractually inhibited from engaging in research outside of SoTL.

10.7.3 The Changing Value of 'Academia'

Participants reflected on the perceived value of academia, reflecting on changes in common understandings around what being an 'academic' means, and how conceptualisations of academia have changed over time. One participant stated:

I can remember a time when [the University] had the reputation of being an applied university and that we had a distinct marketable brand... about actually developing theory in application and that seemed to me to be – yeah – something that attracted students... good students who came here because they really wanted to do things...

Here the participant lamented on the changing nature of both the institution and of academic pursuit, making an explicit connection between teaching style and student expectations and perceptions. The notion of a 'bygone' era where students "really wanted to do things" was paralleled in CoP members' reflections on the value of the group for promoting opportunities to conduct research, hold conversations and collaboratively engage in ways which were perceived as personally and professionally meaningful or "actually important".

Notions of what could be valued as "actually important" among CoP members were contrasted with broader commentary on the nature of academia and perceptions regarding the "core business" of the university. For example, one participant reflected that, "...teaching and learning research is always disregarded. And I suspect that people still don't necessarily think of us as being a research group". Participants' reflections on a changing academic climate, that teaches differently and fails to recognise SoTL as research, suggested that participants located themselves as individuals and a collective within a dominant socio-cultural context.

Participants recognised that there were sections within the university who questioned the legitimacy of the group, a sentiment that group members contested with conviction. For example, one participant commented on how the research group was able to succeed despite structural impositions, stating, "we had these research groups imposed on us and we made it work... it's possible to kind of do your own thing a bit underneath the radar". The metaphor of 'flying under the radar' was pervasive, and reflected other 'war' metaphors adopted by participants during the workshop. Words such as "battle", "fight", "underdog", "challenge" and "win", were symbolic of the ostracism and threat participants experienced in the broader competitive cultural context of the university. For example,

> It's like you have to fight and it seems like this has been safety in numbers. So there's like, I suppose, awareness of the systemic things that we have to fight for. And that this is an avenue [through] which we can, I suppose, work within the system to kind of break the system down and get what we want from it.

Participants reflected on engaging in the "fight", to challenging existing policies so to be afforded the same access and opportunities as other research groups. A discursive shift within the school and faculty recognising the group's work as 'research' (a valued construct), as opposed to teaching 'scholarship' (a trivialised construct) afforded the research group new rights, previously only experienced by other research groups. The research group drew links between achieving recognition as 'researchers' with significant milestones in their development, namely; membership in decision-making circles (e.g., the school research and development committee), access to resources (e.g., conference support), competitive research funding success, significant publication outputs, and growth and stability in research group membership (see Table 10.2). For CoP members, attainment of these resources and access to esteem within the university context were symbolic of a shifting perception of the group, from 'Odd Bods' to a legitimate research group. Legitimation of the group has been an ongoing process. It is apparent that using the metrics of success adopted by already legitimate research groups has meant that the CoP has indisputable evidence of its success. In doing so, the CoP has in effect 'played the game'; they have conformed to what is valued by the broader institution, but have done so in a way that they have been able to garner control of their subject matter.

Participants reflected on the advantages that came with being recognised as a *legitimate* research group. Participants derived a sense of legitimacy from the

Table 10.2 Group size and key objective performance indicators from 2012 to 2014

	2012	2013	2014
Members	6	15	17
Peer reviewed publications	2	10	10
Conference presentations	5	4	18
Research funding (AU$)	12,000	259,000	140,500

Note The 2013 funding figure includes two nationally competitive grants. In the first 2 months of 2015 (to February 28), there have been three papers published (and another five accepted), six conference presentations (and another five accepted) and AU$50,000 in funding earned research group being identified as an exemplar, and as leaders in teaching research at a faculty and university level. For example, one participant reflected,

> I think we're recognised in the faculty as leading the teaching research in the faculty. And the faculty is seen as leading teaching research in the university. So that puts us right at the forefront of it.

Another stated,

> It [the research group] also maybe raised the profile of the school in a way ... from the faculty's perspective; I think we've kind of done the whole school a favour in the sense of them [the faculty] kind of giving us a tick for what we're doing.

10.8 Reflections on the CoP

The aim of this chapter was to present the evolution and current status of the CoP, in part to serve as an exemplar of how CoPs in a research-intensive higher education setting can develop. On reflection, it could be argued that this CoP is perhaps 'non-replicable' in that the group emerged out of adversity; individuals found themselves in an exclusionary social context that valued a particular type of academic over another. These 'Odd Bods' found each other and autonomy through endeavouring to work outside of a system that labelled them as different and valued them less. To propose a template, or set of parameters to replicate the success of the research group as a CoP is perhaps antithetical given that it was the imposition of pre-determined rules, structures, and processes that lead to group members finding themselves excluded. To offer rules and structures potentially replicates the system and processes criticised by the group in the first place.

Despite this paradox, we argue that much can be learnt from the emergence of the group. Rather than solely 'looking in' at the specific dynamics and processes of the group, there is necessity to 'look out' and examine the social and historical context that the group emerged from and is now embedded within. This claim is well supported given themes from the workshop analysis reflect issues surrounding autonomy and exclusion, and is consistent with the contextualist and systemic focus promoted by the use of CLA. We suggest that for 'successful' CoPs in research-intensive higher education settings to emerge, there is a need for a supportive, safe and inclusive context. Indeed, these characteristics are commonly cited as instrumental to the development of successful CoPs (e.g., McDonald and Star 2008; Nagy and Burch 2009; Ng and Pemberton 2013). In this chapter, we offer a deconstruction of the context that gave rise to this successful CoP.

In the following sections, we reflect and build on the themes and messages that emerged from the Futures Workshop. We present these reflections according to qualities or parameters that may 'typically' be considered when establishing a CoP. In doing so, we offer alternative 'parameters' for consideration of a successful CoP. When considering *Leadership* and *Lifecycle* we offer *History, Context and*

Structural Considerations, when considering *Planning* we offer *Engagement*, and, when considering *Processes, Protocols and Tools for Success*, we offer *Foundations*. In our offerings, we endeavour to deconstruct and question the presumptions of what makes for a successful CoP. We do this by not only 'looking in' at the qualities of the group but also by 'looking out'; examining the context and history that lead to the group's emergence. What appears to make the CoP somewhat unique is its struggle for legitimacy within the institution. It thus makes sense to explore institutional ideology.

10.8.1 History, Context and Structural Considerations

The research group's structure as a CoP emerged somewhat organically, in the sense that the dynamics emerged out of necessity. It was obvious to the group members that the way in which they would receive the necessary support as academics was through supporting each other. As such, the CoP was not a deliberate attempt to give name or structure to the research group. Rather, it presented as an unsaid operationalisation of a research groups' response to a challenging academic context.

Participants' personal and collective struggles within the dominant university culture appeared to have prompted members to construct a social setting that protects its members; allowing for personal and collective needs to be met. In contest with participants' experiences within the broader university context, where participants' experiences reflected being afforded little agency or control, the structure of the research group is negotiated and responsive to the needs of its members. While there are leadership roles in the group, the leadership is constructed as more of a 'facilitator' role, convened by two members (as opposed to a single member) of the group. Conveners have tended to change annually, with regular changes motivated by a desire to enable up-skilling and experiential learning for other members of the group. Regular fortnightly meetings are scheduled, however attendance is encouraged rather than enforced. This is in recognition of the practical constraints experienced by teaching staff, and an understanding that there will be periods during the year which are particularly time demanding. Standing items on the agenda are negotiated so as to be responsive to the needs and direction of the group.

As such, a quality of the research group that appears to have strengthened its effectiveness is its collective fight for agency and creative control, within the broader institutional context. By fighting for power, the group has been able to co-construct its format, focus, and overall, its identity. Arnstein (1969) presents a 'ladder' of participation as a typological framework for understanding how different forms of participation grant access to power, resources and opportunities for change. At the higher rungs of the ladder, Arnstein suggests that citizens engage in renegotiation of power, and actively shape the nature of their participation. This process of renegotiation sees those who are not in a position of power afforded power, and, those in a position of power, resign some of theirs. At the lower rungs of the ladder, citizen participation is tokenistic, reflecting coercive processes and disempowerment. We speculate that the dynamics evident within the CoP might reflect participation as it pertains to the higher rungs of the ladder. Participation is characterised by empowerment. The kind of power held within/by the group has not been gifted. or afforded to them. Rather has come as a consequence of the group actively rejecting the rules, structures and processes imposed on them.

10.8.2   CoP Engagement

The formation of the research group was iterative, organic and in response to systemic barriers preventing its members from engaging meaningfully in other research groups. In response, one of the foundational values of the group is *inclusivity*. This value marks a rejection of intellectual elitism and celebrates engagement between group members, irrespective of their status, experience within academia, or disciplinary background. The specific nature of engagement is multifaceted and reflected in the research group's interpersonal style, flexibility (through empathy), and multidisciplinary focus.

The *interpersonal style* between members is one based on mutual respect and support, and is responsive to group members' diverse needs (e.g., appointment, academic experience etc.). There is a desire in the group for meetings to be a space where participants can engage in meaningful research or teaching related discussions, and a forum to ask questions or seek advice. Importantly, all questions are taken seriously and are valued equally. This mindset appears to have fostered a safe, value-free setting that encourages inquiry and the exchange of information and knowledge.

The group dynamic is characterised by its *flexibility (through empathy)*. There is an appreciation within the group that the demands of teaching place legitimate pressures on group members, and that there are times in the academic calendar where research may present as a competing demand to teaching. Given this, levels of engagement in the research group can fluctuate. Importantly, this fluctuation is *accepted without penalty* and, arguably, has contributed to the longevity and robust nature of the research group.

The group has adopted a *multidisciplinary focus*, and while not all research projects are necessarily multidisciplinary in nature, diverse disciplinary perspectives shape group discussions. Multidisciplinary collaboration within the group has fostered not only creativity, but also methodologically and statistically robust research projects that have substantive applicability. Adopting a multidisciplinary orientation has therefore helped to build capacity.

Collectively, these qualities in the engagement style help to create, as termed by participants, a "home" for group members; presenting as qualities enabling both personal and collective self-determination and autonomy.

10.8.3 CoP Foundations

It is perhaps tempting to identify processes, protocols and tools that promote and support the development and sustainability of a CoP. However, it would seem that these qualities are rendered meaningless unless a 'level playing field' exists. A level playing field within the context of this chapter refers to assurances that systemic and ideological factors do not result in favouritism or privileges being afforded to one research group and not another. When the playing field is not level, process, protocols and the adoption of tools that are common practice for one group can be an impossibility for another. It may be impossible because a group is not aware of opportunities. If they are aware, they may be precluded from engaging through mechanisms such as policy, value-laden rhetoric or labeling, or, are disempowered to the extent that efforts at resistance are perceived as too great, or deemed to be too risky or damaging. A level playing field did not exist when the research group was conceived, and it can be argued that it was these inequities, seen through systemic exclusion and deprivation of resources and opportunities, that prompted the subsequent development of the group. It is important to note, however, that while the playing field external to the group could not be considered 'level', internally, within the research group, the playing field was characterised by equity and inclusion.

Determining if the playing field is level requires examining the broader social and cultural context for evidence that a CoP has access to the resources and opportunities that *should* be afforded it. This serves as a necessary *foundation* for a CoP. Across various stages of the research group's development, members became aware of inequities, and were active in contesting and challenging these barriers to their success. Participants reflected upon indicators of changing perceptions toward the research group, noting "…I think we're winning if, when we open our mouths at a meeting, people roll their eyes." Here, the participant reflected that disrupting the status quo is indicative of their success as a research group, and is evidence that perceptions of the research group as a legitimate presence have taken hold. This is evidence that the group now has a voice, because they are being heard.

Achieving legitimacy in this group did not come from achieving 'esteem' as a research group in ways that are applied to other research groups within the university. Rather, indicators of having achieved legitimacy as a group were reflected in instances where the group achieved notoriety in their capacity to effect change at school and faculty levels, for example, via having a presence at meetings, exercising a voice and influence, and forging opportunities to command resources. Sarason's (2000) barometers of change theory refers to the identification of nuances in hindsight that are indicative of change. For the CoP, achieving legitimacy over time is seen through these aforementioned barometers. These barometers appear illustrative of the fact that the group is still an outsider within the dominant university culture and value system. The appraisal of success is not through conventional measures, but instead reflected in indicators that the group does not conform. That is, they remain the perpetual 'Odd Bods'.

It can be argued that it was the members' determination and fighting spirit that lead to changes in policy and resource access. However, it was also the group's collective agency. Unlike individual efforts at resistance that may result in heightened vulnerability, collective resistance has greater propensity to offer protection through numbers and also capacity building through sharing of knowledge.

10.9   Conclusions, Final Reflections, Implications and Future Plans

In contrast to many SoTL CoPs with 'imposed' membership and institutional support, such as faculty learning communities (e.g., Cox 2013; Richlin and Cox 2004), our group experienced organic growth. It is apparent that our individual and collective experiences of exclusion and othering prompted a movement of defiance; collective endeavours have not only made a home for a group of 'Odd Bods' but have resulted in significant personal, institutional and social contributions.

Our SoTL CoP is successfully overcoming the previously identified barriers in moving beyond scholarly teaching to engaging in SoTL research that results in peer-reviewed publications (Hubball et al. 2010). Our CoP operated as a social learning system (Wenger 2000, 2010) with group members sharing practice and expertise, resulting in a demonstrable increase in SoTL related grants, peer-reviewed publications and conference papers over the preceding 3 years. With a focus on outputs, our SoTL CoP on the surface mirrors some of the previously identified values specific to higher education research based CoPs: responding to research pressure and intellectual isolation through moving towards collaborative research with a focus on tangible returns (Ng and Pemberton 2013). However, while these outputs might be considered indicators of a successful CoP using traditional measures of success, it is valuable to deconstruct those indicators of change that gave rise to the contexts, and opportunities, in which our group as a successful CoP could flourish (Sarason 2000).

The experiences of the research group as a CoP reflect a tension between the values of its members and that of its institutional setting. However, the root causes of these value tensions extend far beyond the physical university setting and rather, are a reflection of broader changes in dominant socio-economic ideology and governmentality within Australia. Under neoliberalism, it is not surprising that the traditional notions and values of education have undergone transformation, whereby notions of learning, enquiry, and the pursuit of knowledge have been challenged. It is similarly unsurprising that under neoliberalism, top-down decision making processes valuing hierarchy and control are deemed appropriate strategies for re-structuring. (Indeed, the perceived value and utility in re-structuring is, in itself, reflective of neoliberalism.)

Table 10.3 Qualities of liberal and neoliberal governmentality in higher education

Qualities	Liberal (traditional)	Neoliberal (emergent)
Governance	Collegial, flat, negotiated	Competitive, hierarchical, dominated
Restructuring	Professional autonomy	Determination of 'which' professional autonomy
Power and agency	The right and freedom for academics to define their role	Rights and freedom of academics are dependent on markets

Specific qualities that distinguish liberal (the former ideology) and neo-liberal orientations (a contemporary ideology) with higher education settings are posited in Table 10.3.

On reflection, neoliberal conceptualisation of governance, constructs of power and agency, and the emphasis on restructuring, offer socio-political terms to explain the challenges experienced by members of the CoP during its development. However, such threats to autonomy through the "commodification of teaching and research" (Olssen and Peters 2007, p. 316) resonate with the experiences we, the CoP members *continue* to experience in our day-to-day lives as academics. Neoliberalist regulation within higher education manifests to create settings whereby "targets and performance criteria are increasingly applied from *outside* the academic role that diminish the sense in which the academic—their teaching and research—are autonomous" (Olssen and Peters 2007, p. 326). Through academic restructuring, our roles (through the distribution of either teaching or research dominant roles), and research practices (through the formation of programs of research) have been determined *for* us. Outside determination of roles (title) and performance of that role (duties, tasks) have deprived us of professional autonomy (Olssen and Peters 2007).

Neoliberalism within the higher education system is expected to result in greater productivity, the same outcome expected of the more traditional market economy. However, from a neoliberalist perspective, productivity is fostered through competition. Marginson (1997; cited in Olssen and Peters 2005) gives commentary on the cultural shifts within Australian universities observed to accompany higher education reform. Of particular note,

> The removal from collegial view of key decisions regarding governance.... The creation of limited life areas of research or research centres, sponsored from above for research funding purposes.... Research management is subject to homogenizing systems for assessing performance.... A diminishment of the role of peer input into decisions about research. (p. 327).

While it could be argued that these qualities identified by Marginson (1997) are conducive to competition, these qualities also depict the rhetorical, reactionary and individualistic demands placed on academics under this system of governance.

Within a broader social and cultural context that celebrates competition over more collegial academic pursuits, and favours organisational control over autonomy, CoPs perhaps serve as a 'safe haven' for those within higher education settings who find themselves excluded, othered and deprived of personal agency and autonomy. Put simply, a neoliberal context does little to create a supportive and inclusive context. Rather, as was experienced by the 'Odd-Bods', this position has the propensity to ostracise and stifle productivity. That was until the 'Odd-Bods' found sufficient collective agency to challenge the system. Rittel and Webber (1973) reflect:

> ...planning for large social systems has proved to be impossible without loss of liberty and equity. Hence, for them the ultimate goal of planning should be anarchy, because it should aim at the elimination of government over others..." (p. 158). It is speculated that the success of CoP has come as a result of overt engagement in a metaphorical perpetual 'battle' to disrupt and challenge the dominant neoliberal context.

Taylor and Bogdan's (1980) work on 'defending the illusion of the institution' provides a commentary on the governing capacity of broad systemic structures. The authors note that scope for action, participation and engagement among citizens is perpetually governed by broad systems and structures. The 'illusion' to which Taylor and Bogdan refer is the capacity for institutions to shape-shift at a surface level, while still operating under the same legitimating myths which established conditions for non-participation, exclusion and disempowerment in the first place. Institutions will make use of devices that are cloaked in the rhetoric of supporting citizen engagement, empowerment and action. However, these devices merely serve to sustain prevailing power distances and structures. The processes therefore are deceptive and manipulative as changes give a false impression of institutional improvement. In the case of this CoP, we may speculate that it emerged in response to similar rhetorical devices (e.g., new categories of employment for academic staff and the formation of programs of research). It is apparent that the group members have actively contested the apparent systemic changes to achieve individual and collective gains, which are considered meaningful for those who form the CoP.

Newbrough (1995) similarly theorises the tensions between liberty (the self) and equality (justice), but does so with the added dimension of fraternity (the collective). It is perhaps through Newbrough's theorising that we can garner the greatest insights regarding COP. That is, a COP is indeed a *community*, and the sole pursuit of liberty over fraternity has the unintended propensity to stifle creativity, agency, a connection with others, and quite possibly productivity. Ultimately, we speculate that it is not possible to set about to 'create' a successful CoP. Rather, perhaps it is the case that a CoP appears to develop its strength and success through a solid foundation. In this particular instance, the foundation was a shared experience of adversity, and the desire to make an, at times, adverse social setting amenable to the interests of group members. Specifically, the CoP used the metrics and processes imposed on them as a means of legitimising the SoTL research they felt was undervalued within the broader university context. It is undisputable that the outputs generated by the groups have been successful, and this seemingly provides leeway for the group to continue to engage in research not considered 'in vogue'. In summary, we argue that this CoP has been successful because it has been able to work within the constraints of a neoliberal tertiary education sector. However, the success of a CoP is not determined by tangible outputs alone. Rather, it is characterised by equity, collaboration, genuine participation and empowerment among all members to meet the individual and collective aims of the group.

Acknowledgments Thank you to the members of the CoP without whom this research would not have been possible. Fight the power!

References

Arnstein, S. R. (1969). A ladder of citizen participation. *Journal of the American Institute of Planners, 35*, 216–224. doi:10.1080/01944366908977225.

Bishop, B. J., & Dzidic, P. L. (2014). Dealing with wicked problems: Conducting a causal layered analysis of complex social psychological issues. *American Journal of Community Psychology, 53*, 13–24. doi:10.1007/s10464-013-9611-5.

Borrego, M. (2007). Conceptual difficulties experienced by trained engineers learning educational research methods. *Journal of Engineering Education, 96*(2), 91–102. doi:10.1002/j.2168-9830. 2007.tb00920.x.

Boyer, E. (1990). *Scholarship reconsidered: Priorities of the professoriate.* San Francisco, CA: Jossey-Bass.

Cox, M. D. (2013). The impact of communities of practice in support of early-career academics. *The International Journal for Academic Development, 18*, 18–30. doi:10.1080/1360144X. 2011.599600.

Duffy, D. K. (2006). COPPER: Communities of practice: Pooling educational resources to foster the scholarship of teaching and learning. *Community College Journal of Research and Practice, 30*(2), 151–152. doi:10.1080/10668920500433306.

Freudenberg, B. (2012). Show me the evidence: How the scholarship of learning and teaching is critical for modern academics. *Journal of the Australasian Tax Teachers Association, 7*, 171–190. https://www.business.unsw.edu.au/About-Site/Schools-Site/Taxation-Business-Law-Site/Journal%20of%20The%20Australasian%20Tax%20Teachers%20Associati/JATTA2012Vol7No1-Freudenberg.pdf

Hubball, H., Clarke, A., & Poole, G. (2010). Ten-year reflections on mentoring SoTL research in a research-intensive university. *International Journal for Academic Development, 15*(2), 117–129. doi:10.1080/13601441003737758.

Inayatullah, S. (1998). Causal layered analysis: Poststructuralism as method. *Futures, 30*, 815–829. doi:10.1016/S0016-3287(98)00086-X.

Inayatullah, S. (2004). Causal layered analysis: Theory, historical context, and case studies. In S. Inayatullah (Ed.), *The causal layered analysis (CLA) reader* (pp. 1–54). Taiwan: Tamkang University.

Inayatullah, S. (2006). Anticipatory action learning: Theory and practice. *Futures, 38*, 656–666. doi:10.1016/j.futures.2005.10.003.

Mathison, K. (2015). Effects of the performance management context on Australian academics' engagement with the scholarship of teaching and learning: A pilot study. *The Australian Educational Researcher, 42*, 97–116. doi:10.1007/s13384-014-0154-z.

McDonald, J., & Star, C. (2008). The challenges of building an academic community of practice: An Australian case study. In *Engaging communities: Proceedings of the 31st HERDSA annual conference, Rotorua, New Zealand* (pp. 230–240). NSW, Australia: HERDSA.

Nagy, J., & Burch, T. (2009). Communities of practice in academe (CoP-iA): Understanding academic work practices to enable knowledge building capacities in corporate universities. *Oxford Review of Education, 35*, 227–247. doi:10.1080/03054980902792888.

Newbrough, J. R. (1995). Toward community: A third position. *American Journal of Community Psychology, 23*, 9–37. doi:10.1007/BF02506921.

Ng, L. L., & Pemberton, J. (2013). Research-based communities of practice in UK higher education. *Studies in Higher Education, 38*, 1522–1539. doi:10.1080/03075079.2011.642348.

Olssen, M., & Peters, M. A. (2005). Neoliberalism, higher education and the knowledge economy: From the free market to knowledge capitalism. *Journal of Education Policy, 20*(3), 313–345. doi:10.1080/02680930500108718.

Potter, M. K., & Kustra, E. D. H. (2011). The relationship between scholarly teaching and SoTL: Models, distinctions, and clarifications. *International Journal for the Scholarship of Teaching and Learning, 5*(1), Article 23. http://digitalcommons.georgiasouthern.edu/ij-sotl/vol5/iss1/23

Probert, B. (2013). Teaching-focused academic appointments in Australian universities: Recognition, specialisation, or stratification? *OLT report*. http://www.olt.gov.au/secondment-probert

Probert, B. (2014). Why scholarship matters in higher education. *OLT Report*. http://www.olt.gov.au/secondment-probert

Richlin, L., & Cox, M. (2004). Developing scholarly teaching and the scholarship of teaching and learning through faculty learning communities. In M. Cox & L. Ricklin (Eds.), *Building faculty learning communities* (pp. 127–136). San Francisco, CA: Jossey-Bass.

Rittel, H. W. J., & Webber, M. M. (1973). Dilemmas in a general theory of planning. *Policy Sciences, 4*, 155–169. doi:10.1007/BF01405730.

Sarason, S. B. (2000). Barometers of community change: Personal reflections. In J. Rappaport & E. Seidman (Eds.), *Handbook of community psychology* (pp. 919–929). New York, NY: Springer.

Schroeder, C. (2007). Countering SoTL marginalization: A model for integrating SoTL with institutional initiatives. *International Journal for the Scholarship of Teaching and Learning, 1*(1), Article 15. http://digitalcommons.georgiasouthern.edu/ij-sotl/vol1/iss1/15

Taylor, S. J., & Bogdan, R. (1980). Defending illusions: The institution's struggle for survival. *Human Organization, 39*, 209–218.

Vardi, I. (2011). The changing relationship between the scholarship of teaching (and learning) and universities. *Higher Education Research and Development, 30*, 1–7. doi:10.1080/07294360.2011.536968.

Vardi, I., & Quin, R. (2011). Promotion and the scholarship of teaching and learning. *Higher Education Research and Development, 30*, 39–49. doi:10.1080/07294360.2011.536971.

Wenger, E. (2000). Communities of practice and social learning systems. *Organization, 7*, 225–246. doi:10.1177/135050840072002.

Wenger, E. (2010). Communities of practice and social learning systems: The career of a concept. In C. Blackmore (Ed.), *Social learning systems and communities of practice* (pp. 179–198). London: Springer.

Wenger, E., McDermott, R. A., & Snyder, W. (2002). *Cultivating communities of practice: A guide to managing knowledge*. Cambridge, MA: Harvard Business Press.

Williams, A. L., Verwoord, R., Beery, T. A., Dalton, H., Mckinnon, J., Strickland, K., et al. (2013). The power of social networks: A model for weaving the scholarship of teaching and learning into institutional culture. *Teaching and Learning Inquiry: The ISSOTL Journal, 1*(2), 49–62. http://muse.jhu.edu/journals/teaching_and_learning_inquiry__the_issotl_journal/v001/1.2.williams.html

Wilson-Doenges, G., & Gurung, R. A. R. (2013). Benchmarks for scholarly investigations of teaching and learning. *Australian Journal of Psychology, 65*, 63–70. doi:10.1111/ajpy.12011.

Chapter 11
Building a Faculty-Centric Virtual Community of Practice (vCoP) Within the Post-secondary Education Environment: A Systems Approach Framework

Diane R. Watkins, Alex McDaniel and Michael A. Erskine

Abstract This chapter describes the process used to design, develop and assess a faculty-centric virtual Community of Practice (vCoP) within the environment of post-secondary educational. The primary goals for developing a faculty-centric vCoP were to provide: on-demand, multi-modal learning opportunities for globally-distributed faculty with diverse abilities, a forum for faculty members to share their ideas and best practices, and a self-supported, sustainable and scalable learning community, while increasing social capital. To guide the development of the resulting community artifact, the systems approach model was applied (Dick in The systematic design of instruction. Pearson/Allyn and Bacon, Boston, 2005). Further guided by the empirical work of Chiu (Decis Support Syst 42(3):1872–1888, 2006) regarding knowledge sharing and the development of social capital in vCoPs, as well as the 21 typology elements outlined by Dubé (Interdiscip J Inf Knowl Manag 1(1):69–93, 2006), this study extends the understanding of effective vCoP implementations. In an ever-expanding realm of instruction and the digitization of instruction within post-secondary education, a supportive Community of Practice is deemed critical to the effective dissemination of skills, techniques and information. Thus, to address this gap, a faculty-centric vCoP development framework is proposed and examined in detail. This chapter provides a comprehensive literature review, presents a theoretical framework, discusses challenges and goals of a faculty-centric vCoP, explains the framework development methodology used, highlights key findings and discusses benefits and limitations of the findings. This chapter examines a suggested development framework and processes to develop a vCoP in the post-secondary educational setting with the goal of fostering knowledge creation and knowledge sharing among participants.

D.R. Watkins · A. McDaniel · M.A. Erskine (✉)
Metropolitan State University of Denver, Denver, CO, USA
e-mail: erskinem@msudenver.edu

© Springer Nature Singapore Pte Ltd. 2017
J. McDonald and A. Cater-Steel (eds.), *Communities of Practice*,
DOI 10.1007/978-981-10-2879-3_11

Keywords Virtual community of practice · Development framework · Systems approach · Content seeding · Social capital · Communities of practice

11.1 Introduction and Literature Review

Regardless of the nature of an organization, be it corporate, higher education, or non-profit, the necessities of today's work environments dictate that employees are frequently located remotely from one another. In addition to geographically distributed individuals, functional teams, groups, and even physical workspaces are often scattered, and may be combined with temporal considerations that discourage or make physical contact impractical. Bridging organizational knowledge gaps through common databases and technology infrastructure are only partial solutions to creating unity of knowledge for such a dispersed organization.

Therefore, focus needs to be brought to how knowledge is shared, managed, and distributed from within a dispersed organization. Spontaneous and voluntary Communities of Practice (CoPs) are discussed by Wenger (1998b), while Lave and Wenger (1991) describe how members united to form a community of learning to overcome challenges. However, these early descriptions of such communities do not emphasize the potential limitations caused by significant temporal or geographic differences between knowledge sharing participants. The need to overcome such differences has inspired many organizations to look for digital alternatives to facilitate virtual teams (vTeams) and virtual Communities of Practice (vCoPs). Such virtualized knowledge sharing communities allow organizations to realize many of the benefits that traditional teams and CoPs share, including knowledge transfer, community building, and creating social capital (Lesser and Storck 2001), while simultaneously mitigating challenges of physical and temporal gaps.

While vCoP members may occasionally interact face-to-face, the primary means of communication are most often asynchronous and separated by distance. vCoPs are typically online social environments (Chiu et al. 2006) that allow members to communicate and share knowledge about common interests, goals and practices (Dubé et al. 2006). As a primarily virtual community (Koh et al. 2007), the central topic helps to define the purpose of the vCoP and provide it with a separate feeling of identity.

While contemporary vCoP implementations reply on electronic information systems, it is important to recognize that a vCoP might also employ more conventional communication technologies such as fax, telephone, email, newsgroups, or even physical mail. Furthermore, this chapter suggests that the ability to generate interpersonal bonds and a sense of community, recognized as important for conventional face-to-face meetings (Bourhis and Dubé 2010; Ardichvili 2008), can also be achieved within a vCoP when implemented using a strategic development framework. Therefore, face-to-face interaction is not a focal point for the vCoP strategies discussed within this chapter, rather the focus will be on a proposed development framework that can be used to span the time and geographic distance that may necessitate the use of a vCoP.

The similarities between vCoPs and physical CoPs include the composition of members communicating thematic knowledge and experiences with one another. Members share the common goal of advancing specific objectives, ideas or practices that can span significant periods of time (Wenger 1998a). vCoPs and CoPs help members assimilate into organizational cultures (Chang et al. 2009), form workplace identities, gain skills and knowledge, establish and enhance motivations (Barab and Duffy 2000; Bradsher and Hagan 1995), and may serve as a motivating force for improving overall performance and effectiveness (Allen 2005).

The overall relationship between the effect on the individual member and the organization, however, is not as well established. The evidence presented by Wenger and Snyder (2000) indicate that the benefits realized from involvement in such communities positively influence performance, communication, and goal accomplishment. The aforementioned benefits of vCoPs and CoPs align well with knowledge sharing requirements that commonly occur in the post-secondary education environment.

11.2 Knowledge Sharing in Post-secondary Education Environments

With an ever-expanding depth and breadth of instruction, and the continual digitization of instruction within post-secondary education, a supportive community is often deemed critical to the effective dissemination of skills, techniques and information. While such organizational knowledge sharing can exist in physical communities, this chapter emphasizes the benefits of a virtual community. Specifically, a faculty-centric vCoP development and implementation approach is suggested. A vCoP can facilitate the following benefits to members: situate learning to their work environment, provide just-in-time solutions, and increase employee interaction. Furthermore, post-secondary education organizations can utilize vCoPs to provide the following advantages to faculty: self-help resources, motivation to consider embracing innovative tools and methods, and to a forum for sharing best practices.

Furthermore, from an organizational perspective, a vCoP also delivers several advantages including increased interaction among experts, increased communications between faculty and administrators, communications outside of face-to-face interactions, codification of practices and solutions to problems, and facilitations of formal and informal training which often foster innovation and cost reductions (Allen 2005). Such benefits are helpful to post-secondary educational organizations as they strive to overcome several possible constraints, including decreasing budgets, increasing performance expectations and demands on faculty time, and decreasing faculty development opportunities. Furthermore, a well-designed vCoP could provide the motivation to integrate innovative technologies and instructional methodologies to support the various aspects of teaching and learning.

These benefits to individuals and organizations within the post-secondary educational environment emphasize the need to consider the use of vCoPs. As the implementation of a successful vCoP has not been exhaustively explored in research, this gap provided the motivation to define a detailed vCoP development framework. This framework is designed to allow organizations with limited resources to align their vCoP development efforts with best practices to better ensure successful implementations.

11.3 Methodology

In response to Bond and Lockee (2014), who suggest a more cyclical approach to vCoP development, we suggest a modified development framework considering the natively iterative nature of the systems approach model (Dick et al. 2005). Thus, this chapter extends the recommendations and steps outlined by Bond and Lockee (2014), in addition to applying the systems approach model to an organizational knowledge-sharing network. This model was considered ideal because many post-secondary education institutions are already familiar with its foundational principles. The preceding literature review was used to formulate the development framework, with an ongoing emphasis on building community and enhancing social capital.

In alignment with the systems approach model (Dick et al. 2005), the proposed vCoP development framework suggests iterative steps that can, and should, be revisited as the implementation progresses. The primary phases of the model consist of planning, development, operation and evaluation. The planning phase includes goal development, analysis of organizational characteristics, analysis of member characteristics and defining objectives. The development phase consists of establishing benchmarks and measurements, developing content and collaboration strategies and developing and seeding content. The operations phase refers to the continued and self-sustained community and its iterations. The ongoing assessment phase includes both formative and summative assessments necessary for continued improvement. While the operation phase informs the formative and summative assessments, it is not exhaustively described or examined as it is not within the scope of the development framework. These phases are visualized in the following model (see Fig. 11.1).

Within the four distinct phases, the vCoP development framework consists of nine distinct stages. It should be noted that although the framework includes nine stages, individual organizations may choose to implement only specific stages based on their needs and constraints. The development framework stages are described in the following sections.

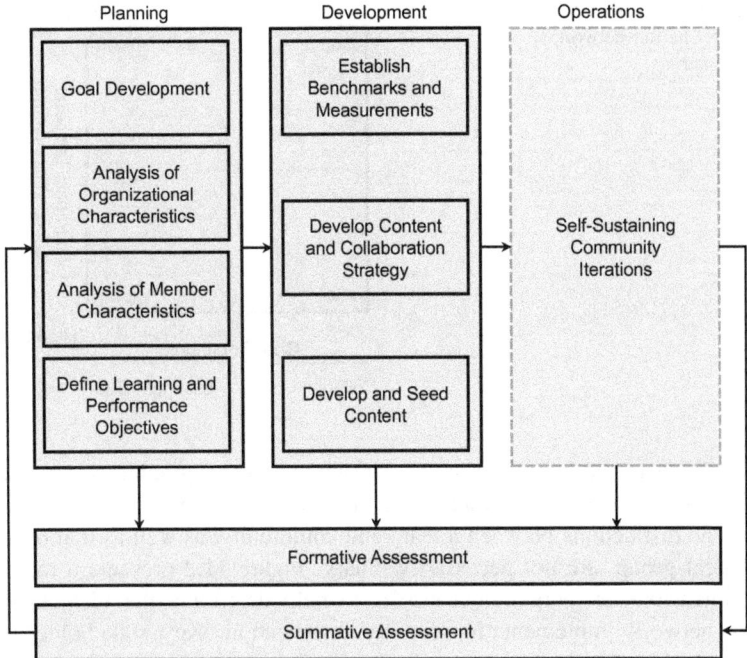

Fig. 11.1 vCoP development framework

11.3.1 Stage 1: Goal Development

The first stage of the vCoP development framework includes three distinct steps. The first step is to determine if a vCoP is the most appropriate method to foster and share knowledge within a particular organization. The second step is to define the purpose and establish executive support. The third step is to clearly define and develop goals for the planned vCoP creation or improvement initiative. In regards to a vCoP improvement project, the third step evaluates the performance gaps of any existing knowledge sharing networks to ascertain new goals. This is in alignment with the first stage of the systems approach model (Dick et al. 2005), which compares actual and perceived participant needs to establish goals.

While a team generally has a superordinate goal, a CoP is driven by parallel or common goals (Allen 2005). This distinction also applies with virtual participants, as one important distinction between a vTeam and a vCoP is that vTeams have interdependent performance goals, while vCoPs are based on a shared goal (Ardichvili 2008). These subtle distinctions are essential, and will ultimately determine the most appropriate implementation approach. Furthermore, in a team, cooperation is often mandatory and essential for success, while in a community, participation generally is voluntary and collegial. By determining where a suggested vCoP goal plots on a goal continuum, ranging from collegial to essential, the determination to implement a team or a community can be made.

Fig. 11.2 Organizational knowledge sharing network decision matrix

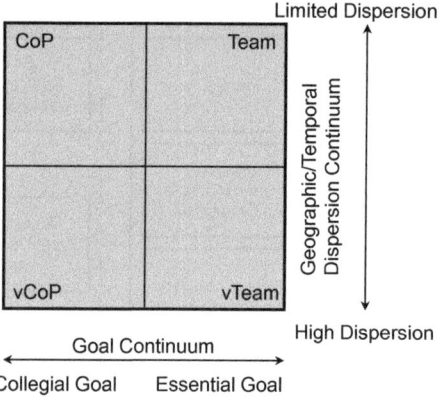

In addition to the goal continuum, the amount of geographic or temporal distribution of members will impact the decision to form a virtual or physical group. The distinctions between a team and community, as well as that of a virtual or physical group, are not necessarily binary. Figure 11.2 presents a matrix with both dimensions on perpendicular axes to help determine the ideal knowledge sharing network implementation for an organization. Key stakeholders should collectively plot their expectations for each of these attributes for a new group, while current members of an established group should evaluate where their team or community is positioned. The proposed or existing placement within one of the four quadrants will determine the best approach for developing or expanding an organizational knowledge sharing network. If the results of this step indicate that a vCoP is not the optimal solution, stakeholders should pursue information regarding implementation strategies for their relevant quadrant. This chapter continues with the assumption that a vCoP implementation is the warranted approach.

Upon making the determination of the appropriate knowledge sharing network strategy for an organization, the second step of the first stage is to define the purpose of the vCoP, as well as to identify the appropriate sponsors and champions. This critical step is essential to any technology implementation (Baccarini 1999).

The purpose of an organizational vCoP spans from being operational to strategic (Denning 1998). However, vCoPs tend to have greater success if implemented in alignment with an existing organizational mission as this may reduce challenges related to uncertainty (Dubé et al. 2006). When defining the purpose of the vCoP, attention should be given to the elements that shifted the decision to form a vCoP in the preceding step. This is particularly essential for groups that plot on or near a quadrant boundary in step one of the goal development stage. Furthermore, this process should clearly state the needs for an organizational knowledge sharing network and why the vCoP approach is superior to other knowledge sharing efforts.

Upon defining the clear purpose of the vCoP initiative, it is essential to gather executive support. As with other formal projects and technology implementations, the success of a vCoP development effort can be positively influenced through the support of a champion and sponsor. Such a support can come from either an administrator or an executive committee who are empowered to ensure that sufficient resources are available for the vCoP development effort. While sponsors and champions advocate for the vCoP (Crawford and Brett 2001), if the virtual community is being created external to a formal organization framework, the initial members may themselves serve as sponsors and champions, thus the establishment of clear purpose may be sufficient.

Upon defining the vCoP purpose and identifying executive support, the final step of the first stage involves establishing and defining the fundamental goals that shape the subsequent vCoP development stages. Thus, identifying the knowledge gaps and setting appropriate goals to address these gaps is essential to the first stage of the vCoP development model. These goals should identify skills, knowledge and attitudes that are to be achieved by the community. Brainstorming sessions, stakeholder discussions, or personal interviews can be utilized to generate goals for a new vCoP. Alternately, for an existing vCoP, Ríos et al. (2009) suggest that interview and surveys of experts and administrators can be used to define vCoP goals. These interviews and discussions with prospective participants can be facilitated using various synchronous and asynchronous tools. These community goals will help establish the scope of the subsequent analysis stages.

11.3.2 Stage 2: Analysis of Organizational Characteristics

The second stage of the vCoP development framework involves performing an in-depth analysis that will ultimately inform the subsequent stages and phases. More specifically, this stage should examine constraints and opportunities within the organizational context, as well as define requirements and specifications. Such an analysis has been shown to directly impact success (Dvir et al. 2003).

This stage requires an analysis of the organizational and technological context of the institution hosting the vCoP. The organizational context can determine how the vCoP aligns with an existing organization, specifically through the identification of the creation process, boundaries, environment, organizational slack, degree of institutionalized formalism and leadership. The technological context addresses the technological requirements of the as well as the degree of reliance on technology (Dubé et al. 2006).

One of the essential structuring characteristics of a vCoP is the identification of the vCoP leadership (Bourhis et al. 2005). Specifically, the creation of a vCoP can occur organically or be intentionally fostered through organizational leadership (Fontaine 2001). Specifically, Fontaine (2001) identifies two types of community leadership roles: community leaders and sponsors. While an organically developed vCoP may be successful, the proposed vCoP development framework assumes an intentionally structured and formal development process.

As organizations and communities often encompass internal and external boundaries, these should be identified and examined. For instance, a vCoP may be developed to foster knowledge sharing among faculty members in different departments, therefore spanning an internal boundary, or cross multiple institutions, consequently spanning external boundaries. While vCoP implementations can inherently cultivate knowledge sharing across internal and external boundaries, the ability to establish community trust may become more difficult as boundaries are crossed (Wenger et al. 2002).

In addition to understanding the extent of the existing boundaries, the organizational environment and culture should be examined. Cothrel and Williams (1999) suggest that the organizational environment may have a facilitating, neutral or hostile attitude toward the establishment of a vCoP. Understanding the environment of an organization allows subsequent design steps to address associated risk. While Dubé et al. (2006) consider this as a single vCoP typology item; Hara et al. (2009) expand this single typology item to independently examine the organizational knowledge sharing culture and organizational sponsorship. A comparison of the strengths of the project sponsor and project champion, as identified in the first stage of the framework, with the risks of the organizational environment and culture is essential when planning the vCoP implementation.

The available resources will also impact the scope of the vCoP development. If an organization has limited resources to devote toward a vCoP implementation, it may be beneficial to limit the scope or plan to leverage external resources to ensure success. However, such constraints may impact the potential success as the purpose or goals may no longer be met. The availability of resources could also be impacted by the perceived legitimacy of the vCoP implementation. Dubé et al. (2006) state that the degree of institutionalized formalism has been shown to be an essential component of the success of a vCoP. Thus, the sponsor and champion role becomes essential toward impacting the legitimacy of the vCoP development.

Finally, consideration should be given to the leadership role of the vCoP. Specifically, a vCoP may utilize an organic and continuously negotiated leadership structure or opt for a clearly assigned leadership and governance model. Institutional legitimacy, culture and boundaries will influence these important leadership considerations.

In addition to the context of organizational structure, the technology capacity and readiness of the organization must also be considered. Specifically, the degree of reliance on technology as well as the technological requirements should be clearly defined.

Whereas some vCoP implementations may provide most interactions through a virtual environment, other vCoP implementations may utilize some non-virtual interaction. This is not unusual as some non-virtual interaction has been shown to strengthen the effectiveness of virtual communities (Hildreth et al. 2000; Dubé et al. 2006). Understanding the degree of reliance on technology and physical distances will influence the design considerations. Thus, this step confirms the necessity of a vCoP versus other knowledge sharing network options.

Additionally, the availability and access to various technologies can influence the capabilities of a vCoP. For instance, a high degree of technological variety could allow synchronous and asynchronous interaction, document storage, and collaborative document sharing. Such flexibility could empower community members to develop and share knowledge through a variety of techniques. However, a high degree of technological capability may also overwhelm and frustrate community participants who prefer simplicity.

In addition to understanding the organizational context, the individual membership characteristics must also be considered. Thus, the next stage of the development framework extends the analysis to individual members.

11.3.3 Stage 3: Member Characteristics

In addition to performing an analysis of the organizational context, the individual vCoP membership context also impacts important design considerations. Such context includes the membership quantity, geographic dispersion, selection processes, enrollment processes, experience, stability, technology literacy, cultural diversity and relevance. As this development framework is an iterative process, the results of this stage may warrant changes to the findings of the previous stages.

One of the primary member characteristics is the projected quantity of vCoP members. Membership levels can be similar to small groups, departments, organizations, or encompass global communities of practitioners. The projected size will further impact the vCoP organization and required technology resources. As participation metrics will likely need to be estimated, it is essential to determine possible maximum number of participants in order to facilitate planning concerning the organizational and technological scalability.

Once the membership sizes has been estimated, the geographic and temporal dispersion of members should be examined as these can impact the complexity and success of a vCoP. Specifically, temporal dispersion complicates the ability to provide a synchronous community. Furthermore, large geographic dispersion creates psychological distance between members and makes in-person collaboration difficult (Dubé et al. 2006). This metric, and its analysis, will facilitate the determination of the technology specifications and leadership decisions. Once more, the iterative nature of the development model may necessitate revisiting prior stages as such metrics are established.

Another consideration concerning membership is the selection, or inclusivity, threshold. The potential vCoP inclusivity can range on a spectrum between open and closed. Specially, an open vCoP may encourage participation with anyone that can access the community, while closed membership selection may require participants to be part of an existing team, department or organization (Dubé et al. 2006).

Additionally, the membership enrollment process will impact goals related to the vCoP size, as well as that of active participation. Member enrollment may consist of voluntary, encouraged, compulsory, or mixed participation. Motivation to participate is generally greatest for voluntary participants and weakest for mandatory participants (Mitchell 2002).

The members of a newly formed vCoP tend to fall into one of three groups, (1) those that may already have existing relationships, (2) those that may already have virtual relationships, or (3) those that may have no existing relationships. As some vCoPs extend existing relationships from other virtual or physical communities, such groups can apply existing norms, roles and legitimacy to a new community. In addition to the existing communities, individuals may have existing experience with other virtual communities, allowing them to quickly feel comfortable in such environments.

The permanence of the community will be a further influence to the success of a vCoP. Organizations that experience high employee turnover may need to devote a significant amount of resources to adapting and integrating new community members, instead of furthering social capital. Furthermore, open vCoP models tend to provide more stability as the membership is tied to an individual not an individual's relationship with an organization (Dubé et al. 2006).

Technological literacy, or technology self-efficacy, of the participants may impact the willingness to adopt a new technology such as those often found in a vCoP. Thus, a clear understanding of the technological literacy of the community will be essential to designing a successful vCoP that does not overwhelm novice members or frustrate more experienced members who may feel limited by the technology.

Cultural diversity is another important consideration that should be addressed during the design process (Dubé et al. 2006). Diverse cultural perspectives based on national, organizational and professional backgrounds provide great benefits to any community, such as incorporating different contexts and unique existing knowledge. However, there are significant challenges that would need to be addressed, such as potential language barriers and unfamiliar communication norms.

Community goal selection can also influence the success of a vCoP. For instance, community members may find immediate benefits when the goal topics align closely with existing organizational themes. The selected topics should provide value to both the hosting organization as well as the participating individual (McDermott 2000; Dubé et al. 2006). An early understanding of topic preferences will greatly inform subsequent stages concerning vCoP content strategy and development.

To address all of the aforementioned factors, it is suggested that twenty-three common vCoP typology elements, comprised of the twenty-one Dubé et al. (2006) elements, in addition to two elements established by Hara et al. (2009), be examined to understand the impact of organizational and member characteristics on the vCoP development effort.

11.3.4 Stage 4: Define Objectives

This stage of the vCoP development process requires that the community goals be expanded to specific knowledge sharing, community building and performance objectives. Specific and measurable objectives should be developed for each community goal. The starting point of this stage involves distilling the results of the brainstorming sessions, stakeholder discussions or personal interviews conducted in the first stage of the vCoP development framework. Specifically, the results of these sessions and interviews should be converted into objectives that are specific, measurable, assignable, and realistic and have a defined implementation time frame (Doran 1981). Through the establishment of clear and measurable objectives, the subsequent development of evaluation metrics is simplified (Baccarini 1999).

Development of clear and measurable objectives is accomplished by systematically deconstructing each community goal into smaller, more easily measured objectives. It may be important to distinguish between each of the objectives developed through this process as each might require a different implementation and support strategy. Objectives typically consist of information or acquired knowledge that is relevant to the overarching goal, and can be further clarified into additional objectives that focus specifically on acquired skills or tasks to be accomplished.

Regardless of the disposition of each objective (learning or performance), all objectives should be written to adhere to the SMART philosophy of objective construction. This is to say that each objective should be Specific, Measurable, Achievable, Realistic and Time bound (Doran 1981). A review of each objective should be conducted, and each objective that does not meet the SMART criteria should be rewritten until all stakeholders agree that each objective aligns with its respective vCoP goal.

The ABCD process, an alternative to SMART, also helps break down the construction of objectives by determining the Audience, Behavior, Condition and Degree necessary for creating clear learning and performance objectives (Reiser and Dick (1996). Using ABCD, the audience should be evaluated as either the entire, or a specific subset, of the vCoP. Next, the behavior should intelligibly define the exact action or knowledge required for the completion of the objective. A condition should be established to narrow the focus of each objective, making it both realistic and time bound. Finally, the degree should establish the measurement for an objective. As with the SMART criteria, objectives should be rewritten until all of the ABCD criteria are met for each vCoP goal. An organization should select and utilize the most familiar systematic objective development process (e.g., SMART, ABCD).

Through the development of well-defined learning and performance objectives, stakeholder expectations can be managed through documentation and communication, and the vCoP can be better evaluated for success during the subsequent evaluation phase. As with prior steps, the creation of objectives may reveal that some of the initial definitions, sponsors, champions, goals, community characteristics, and member characteristics may need to be refined.

11.3.5 Stage 5: Establish Benchmarks and Measurements

The purpose of this stage of the development framework is to ensure that an organization can accurately assess incoming skills and knowledge, as well as, inform the continued development of vCoP members and leaders. This process continues throughout the duration of the vCoP to allow for continuously improved alignment with the ongoing needs of the members. The establishment of benchmarks and measurement strategies may indicate the need to revisit the learning and performance objectives defined in stage four.

To establish knowledge benchmarks, which will then inform the content development and subsequent measurements of success, it is suggested that a focus group of potential vCoP members from a variety of contexts be established and assessed. This sample will allow potential objectives to be identified to see if any have already been met and thus will not need to be focused upon. Any unmet objectives will need to be further assessed to determine the members' degree of previous mastery. The results of these assessments help direct the development of content for the vCoP and inform the definition of the ongoing measurements to evaluate the success of the vCoP.

Embracing the iterative nature of the systematic model, such ongoing, periodic assessments should be used to identify areas of vCoP performance that are deficient and need to be revisited. It is often the case that when one learning objective is not being met, there may be problems with the degree of mastery of preceding learning objectives.

Methods for conducting the initial assessments may include, but are not limited to: (1) focus groups representing cross sections of potential vCoP members and leaders, (2) surveys, (3) questionnaires, (4) use cases, (5) anecdotal evidence, (6) facilitated leader and stakeholder discussions, and (7) recommendations from previous projects or studies.

Samples of ongoing, periodic formative evaluations may include, but are not limited to: (1) member satisfaction surveys, (2) measuring engagement and activity levels, (3) informal member-based rating systems, (4) guided practice sessions, (5) evaluated practice sessions, (6) use case scenarios, and (7) solicited or unsolicited reports of application of concepts and skills in their relevant fields.

It is important to note that the objectives are not meant to be restrictive or overly rigid, and changes may be necessary to keep the vCoP on track with the ultimate goals. This iterative formative evaluation process serves to ensure that the vCoP remains relevant, engaging and beneficial to the members.

11.3.6 Stage 6: Develop a Content and Collaboration Strategy

The second stage within the vCoP development phase is the sixth stage of the vCoP development framework. The focus of this stage is on developing an appropriate and relevant content strategy based on the collegial goals and objectives, the newly established benchmarks and evaluation tools, and the dynamic needs of vCoP leaders and members.

One of the greatest challenges within a community of practice is encouraging members to contribute to the shared knowledge of the community (Chiu et al. 2006). The social exchanges and shared knowledge help to sustain a virtual community, so encouraging these interactions is vital to the success of a community (Chiu et al. 2006). Engagement building research reveals that higher levels of social capital increase the engagement and contribution levels of the organization members, which in turn increases the overall creation of value within the organization as well as the potential for innovation (Nahapiet and Ghoshal 1998; Tsai and Ghoshal 1998). A reciprocal effect is that involvement in a community of practice also increases social capital (Kline and Alex-Brown 2013; Lesser and Prusak 1999). The following section defines social capital, describes the dimensions of social capital and how the facets of social capital influence community members' motivation to share knowledge, and explores the effect that being part of a community of practice has on social capital.

Halpern (2005) provides the following eloquent description of the concept of social capital:

> Societies are not composed of atomized individuals. People are connected with one another through intermediate social structures – webs of association and shared understandings of how to behave. This social fabric greatly affects with whom, and how, we interact and cooperate. It is this everyday fabric of connection and tacit cooperation that the concept of social capital in intended to capture. (p. 3)

Nahapiet and Ghoshal (1998) extend the definition of social capital to also include "the sum of the actual and potential resources embedded within, available through, and derived from the network of relationships possess by an individual or social unit" (p. 243). At the most basic level, social capital theory states that members within a network of relationships, as well as the network as a whole, gain benefits from being part of the network that otherwise would not be possible (Kline and Alex-Brown 2013). Thus, benefits of a vCoP include access to the wealth of shared knowledge, open communication between like-minded individuals, and the opportunity for innovation within the community.

To explore how social capital might influence the sharing of knowledge within a professional virtual community, Chiu et al. (2006) examined three closely interrelated dimensions of social capital: structural, relational and cognitive. These dimensions were originally defined by Nahapiet and Ghoshal (1998). Chiu et al. (2006) describe the manifestations of each dimension as, "the structural dimension of social capital is manifested as social interaction ties, the relational dimension is manifested as trust, norms of reciprocity, and identification, and the cognitive dimension is manifested as shared vision and shared language" (p. 1873). They focused on the how each of these facets of social capital influence the amount of knowledge shared within a virtual community as well as the quality of that knowledge. Their research revealed that these facets did have an impact on the quantity or the quality of the knowledge that was shared.

Kline and Alex-Brown (2013) suggest that being an active member of a community of practice can increase social capital through participant engagement within the community. They share that the key to increasing engagement in the community is through the development and implementation of engaging activities. Furthermore, they suggest that the CANFA model (Kline and Barker 2012) may be used to create engaging activities through, "*collaboration, application, negotiation, facilitation and active-practice*" (Kline and Alex-Brown 2013, p. 286). Specifically, "CANFA prescribes that activities need to be *collaborative* between participants; *apply* to the work they are performing; *negotiate* the outcomes and products of the community; structure *facilitation* into the community, and focus on *active-role participation* at the workplace" (p. 289). Having members of a CoP participate in engaging activities enhances their social connections, which in turn increases their social capital.

A content and collaboration strategy should also be developed to leverage the reciprocal relationship between social capital and participation in a vCoP, by using the vCoP as a facilitated platform for members to share knowledge and participate in collaborative activities. This will help to expand and strengthen the members' social connections and increase their social capital, which in turn leads to greater knowledge sharing.

11.3.7 Stage 7: Develop and Seed Content

A critical and particularly valuable period for a vCoP is immediately after its launch. Without a critical mass of community engagement or knowledge sharing, the new vCoP may not offer members enough of a participation incentive or perceived value to engage. Thus, a new vCoP could benefit from the seeding of information and resources. It has been shown that seeding encourages members to generate associated content to what is already available (Solomon and Wash 2012). By providing a reason for participants to begin discussions around specific topics, seeded content can be a catalyst for engagement.

Effective content seeding requires a content strategy to be developed and catalyst content elements to be developed and implemented prior to the vCoP launch. This strategy serves to pre-populate the vCoP, thus making it a valuable resource at launch without requiring substantial member contributions to be relevant. Xu et al. (2006, p. 31) describe the need for seeding in their vCoP for educators example, "Most of new teachers came to the forums for solving their problems and looking to help. Before any new teachers started to contribute, they had to be convinced that this was the right place to do so. So the further [*sic*] system should not start from an empty skeleton." In addition to selecting and developing catalyst content, it is essential to determine when and how to most effectively expose or release content to the vCoP members.

The social nature and community-generated direction of a vCoP requires additional considerations to those of more formally produced projects. Therefore the design context of a vCoP demands that the roles of design and leadership be evolved in order to encourage active participation and create a hospitable environment (Hagen and MacFarlane 2008). This production evolution should include limiting the development and deployment to strategic content and avoiding the tendency to differentiate between the ideas generated by developers and those of community members. Consequently, it is important to seek out and identify specific areas and opportunities for seeding that spark the greater levels of knowledge reciprocity. While the seeding process is most critical during the early stages of vCoP development, it can also be applied to foster continued relevance and usefulness for community members (Hagen and MacFarlane 2008).

Seeding content can be implemented in a variety of methods including producing content, reusing existing content, integrating third party content, or any other means of injecting relevant information where additional discussion or content creation on the part of vCoP members is desired. This last point is crucial when considering seeding any content into a vCoP. The strategic use of seeding should be included into the development phase of the overall vCoP design, and agreed upon by all appropriate stakeholders, as there can be potential negative side effects to this strategy. One of the significant concerns associated with seeding is that this technique has been shown to decrease the overall contributions of unstructured content when compared to new community members being presented with a blank canvas (Solomon and Wash 2012). Therefore, it is important to purposefully employ this tactic with content that is not necessarily dependent on the creation of original thought or member solutions, but is designed to trigger initial engagement and encourage knowledge sharing on specific topics or objectives.

11.3.8 Stage 8: Conduct Formative Evaluations

Throughout the development process and following an initial launch formative evaluations are encouraged as the results from such evaluations will allow appropriate and necessary modifications prior to active community participation. There are four types of formative evaluation that should be performed during the vCoP development and immediately after the initial launch. These types are proactive, clarificative, interactive and monitoring. The proactive evaluation is conducted at the onset of the project and formalizes the steps completed earlier in stages. However, a second *ex ante* formative evaluation is clarificative. The clarificative evaluation occurs during the development phase of the project and will explicitly define the theory of change that applies to the project (Owen and Rogers 1999). Examples of this approach include, but are not limited to, the development of a logframe matrix

(Crawford and Bryce 2003) or the establishment of program logic (Cooksy et al. 2001). During the operations phase of the vCoP both interactive and monitoring evaluations should be conducted (Boulmetis and Dutwin 2005). Interactive formative evaluations can consist of additional focus groups or semi-structured interviews with stakeholders. Formative evaluations conducted through monitoring can consist of surveys, observations and other system generated metrics.

As with previous stages of the vCoP development framework, the results of this stage should not only inform the subsequent, but also the preceding stages.

11.3.9   Stage 9: Summative Evaluation

This final stage evaluates the overall success of the community and informs incremental improvements and redesigns. Unlike the *ex ante* formative evaluation, the *post ante* summative evaluations occur after each community iteration.

There are multiple approaches toward conducting a summative evaluation including positivist, interpretist and critical methodologies. The positivist approach allows for the quantitative evaluation of the system based on performance benchmarks set by the objectives established earlier. An example of a positivist evaluation is to determine if the vCoP is meeting the estimated participation metrics as defined in a previously developed objective. The evaluation of such quantitative measures allows the vCoP leadership to determine if the goals have been met, and respond accordingly if not. However, as quantitative measures alone may not be the only indicators of success, additional approaches are also suggested. The interpretist approach suggests that the evaluator assess the perspectives, experiences and expectations of each of the system stakeholders through qualitative evaluation, such as interviews and focus groups (Potter 2006). An example of this may reveal that the vCoP is not meeting participant expectations, while the qualitative goals are met. Finally, the critical approach suggests that the social, political and historical context of the vCoP development and implementation be considered for their impact and constraints on the system (Klecun and Cornford 2005). An example of this may reveal that the interpretist findings were largely based on assumptions or that hidden objectives exist and have not been met. While one of these approaches may be sufficient to evaluate the success of the vCoP, a combination of all three approaches will provide the greatest insight into whether the vCoP is meeting the prescribed goals, providing unforeseen benefits, or is in need of continuous improvement.

11.4   Limitations and Future Research

While the proposed vCoP development framework can inform a successful vCoP launch, the development framework has not yet been fully validated through a comprehensive evaluation process consisting of all nine stages. Thus, a significant limitation of the vCoP development framework is a lack of summative evaluation results for an actual implementation. Future research examining the validity of the development framework is suggested. Another limitation of the proposed vCoP development framework is that it was examined only in the context of a post-secondary education environment. Future research will need to assess how the vCoP development framework assists with the implementations in the context of varying cultures, environments and goals. Doing so will help determine limitations of the vCoP development framework and ultimately lead to modifications to ensure generalizability.

Another limitation is that an understanding of the value of each step toward overall success has yet to be established. Understanding which steps are critical success factors would allow resource-constrained institutions to maximize their investment. While a post-secondary educational institution with prior community-building experience and management resources could absorb the steps of the development framework, institutions with limited resources may need to consider partnering with other institutions, limiting the scope, or finding external resources to ensure a successful implementation. Thus, a final limitation is the significant resource investment required to complete the nine-stage development framework. As some institutions of post-secondary education may lack the resources necessary to fully implement the recommended framework, additional suggestions for future research include an identification of the essential development stages for vCoP success, an identification of stages that can be distilled or even eliminated to meet institutional constraints, and an empirical evaluation of the proposed framework.

11.5   Conclusion

This chapter provides a comprehensive literature review, presents a theoretical development framework, discusses challenges and goals of a faculty-centric vCoP, suggests benefits to post-secondary educational institutions, presents key findings and discusses benefits and limitations of these findings. Specifically, this chapter suggests a nine-stage iterative implementation framework to facilitate the successful development of vCoPs. The proposed framework emphasizes the importance of completing a detailed planning phase prior to beginning the development phase. Finally, evaluation strategies are suggested for continuous improvement.

This chapter provides a comprehensive literature review, a decision matrix to aid in identifying the optimal type of knowledge sharing network and theoretically-based vCoP development framework. Specifically, this chapter suggests a nine-stage iterative implementation framework to facilitate the successful development of vCoPs. The proposed framework emphasizes the importance of completing a detailed planning phase prior to beginning the development phase. The possible challenges, goals, benefits and ongoing evaluation strategies of a faculty-centric vCoP are also discussed. This chapter concludes by emphasizing the need for an examination of the proposed framework in practice.

The use of the proposed vCoP development framework could provide immediate and practical benefits to contemporary organizations, because employees are often separated by physical and temporal distance. Thus, bridging organizational knowledge gaps and building a sense of community has become an ongoing challenge. The implementation of a vCoP helps to overcome this challenge, while enhancing communication, building social capital, increasing shared knowledge, and fostering innovation. Furthermore, a vCoP in the post-secondary education environment provides the opportunity for faculty to have an open forum for sharing ideas and best practices, while building a self-supported and sustainable learning community.

References

Allen, S. (2005). Communities of practice as organizational knowledge networks. *Proceedings of The National Convention of the Association for Educational Communications and Technology, Orlando, FL, 2*(25), 25–31.

Ardichvili, A. (2008). Learning and knowledge sharing in virtual communities of practice: Motivators, barriers, and enablers. *Advances in Developing Human Resources, 10*, 541–554.

Baccarini, D. (1999). The logical framework method for defining project success. *Project Management Journal, 30*(4), 25–32.

Barab, S. A., & Duffy, T. (2000). From practice fields to communities of practice. In D. Jonassen & S. M. Land (Eds.), *Theoretical foundations of learning environments* (pp. 25–56). Mahwah, NJ: Lawrence Erlbaum Associates.

Bond, M. A., & Lockee, B. B. (2014). *Building virtual communities of practice for distance educators* (Vol. 1). Berlin: Springer.

Boulmetis, J., & Dutwin, P. (2005). *The ABCs of evaluation: Timeless techniques for program and project managers*. Hoboken: Wiley.

Bradsher, M., & Hagan, L. (1995). The kids network: Student-scientists pool resources. *Educational Leadership, 53*(2), 38–43.

Bourhis, A., & Dubé, L. (2010). 'Structuring spontaneity': Investigating the impact of management practices on the success of virtual communities of practice. *Journal of Information Science, 36*(2), 175–193.

Bourhis, A., Dubé, L., & Jacob, R. (2005). The success of virtual communities of practice: The leadership factor. *The Electronic Journal of Knowledge Management, 3*(1), 23–34.

Chang, J., Chang, W., & Jacobs, R. (2009). Relationship between participation in communities of practice and organizational socialization in the early careers of South Korean IT employees. *Human Resource Development International, 12*(4), 407–427.

Chiu, C. M., Hsu, M. H., & Wang, E. T. (2006). Understanding knowledge sharing in virtual communities: An integration of social capital and social cognitive theories. *Decision Support Systems, 42*(3), 1872–1888.

Cooksy, L. J., Gill, P., & Kelly, P. A. (2001). The program logic model as an integrative framework for a multimethod evaluation. *Evaluation and Program Planning, 24*(2), 119–128.

Cothrel, J., & Williams, R. L. (1999). On-line communities: Helping them form and grow. *Journal of Knowledge Management, 3*(1), 54–60.

Crawford, L., & Brett, C. (2001). Exploring the role of the project sponsor. In *Proceedings of the PMI New Zealand annual conference, PMINZ Wellington, New Zealand*.

Crawford, P., & Bryce, P. (2003). Project monitoring and evaluation: A method for enhancing the efficiency and effectiveness of aid project implementation. *International Journal of Project Management, 21*(5), 363–373.

Denning, S. (1998). Building communities of practice. In S. Elliott, C. Henderson, & V. Powers (Eds.), *Knowledge management: Lessons from the leading edge* (pp. 48–50). Houston, TX: American Productivity and Quality Center.

Doran, G. T. (1981). There's a SMART way to write management's goals and objectives. *Management Review, 70*(11), 35–36.

Dick, W., Carey, L., & Carey, J. O. (2005). *The systematic design of instruction* (6th ed.). Boston: Pearson/Allyn and Bacon.

Dubé, L., Bourhis, A., & Jacob, R. (2006). Towards a typology of virtual communities of practice. *Interdisciplinary Journal of Information, Knowledge, and Management, 1*(1), 69–93.

Dvir, D., Raz, T., & Shenhar, A. J. (2003). An empirical analysis of the relationship between project planning and project success. *International Journal of Project Management, 21*(2), 89–95.

Fontaine, M. (2001). Keeping communities of practice afloat. *Knowledge Management Review, 4* (4), 16–21.

Hagen, P., & MacFarlane, J. (2008). Reflections on the role of seeding in social design. In *Proceedings of the 20th Australasian conference on computer–human interaction: designing for habitus and habitat* (pp. 279–282).

Halpern, D. (2005). *Social capital*. Cambridge: Polity Press.

Hara, N., Shachaf, P., & Stoerger, S. (2009). Online communities of practice typology revisited. *Journal of Information Science, 35*(6), 740–757.

Hildreth, P., Kimble, C., & Wright, P. (2000). Communities of practice in the distributed international environment. *Journal of Knowledge Management, 4*(1), 27–38.

Klecun, E., & Cornford, T. (2005). A critical approach to evaluation. *European Journal of Information Systems, 14*(3), 229–243.

Kline, J., & Alex-Brown, K. (2013). The social body of knowledge: Nurturing organizational social capital via social media based communities of practice. *Technical Communication, 60* (4), 279–292.

Kline, J., & Barker, T. (2012). Negotiating professional consciousness in technical communication: A community of practice approach. *Technical Communication, 59*(1), 32–48.

Koh, J., Kim, Y. G., Butler, B., & Bock, G. W. (2007). Encouraging participation in virtual communities. *Communications of the ACM, 50*(2), 68–73.

Lave, J., & Wenger, E. (1991). *Situated learning: Legitimate peripheral participation*. Cambridge: Cambridge University Press.

Lesser, E., & Prusak, L. (1999). Communities of practice, social capital and organizational knowledge. *Information Systems Review, 1*(1), 3–10.

Lesser, E. L., & Storck, J. (2001). Communities of practice and organizational performance. *IBM systems journal, 40*(4), 831–841.

McDermott, R. (2000). Why information technology inspired but cannot deliver knowledge management. *Knowledge and Communities, 41*(4), 21–35.

Mitchell, J. (2002). *The potential for communities of practice to underpin the national training framework: Findings from an evaluation of pilot projects of communities of practice that were managed by reframing the future and funded through the Australian National Training Authority, 2001*. Adelaide, South Australia: Reframing the Future/Australian National Training Authority (ANTA). Retrieved from NCVER website: http://hdl.voced.edu.au/10707/108459

Nahapiet, J., & Ghoshal, S. (1998). Social capital, intellectual capital, and the organizational advantage. *Academy of Management Review, 23*(2), 242–266.

Owen, J. M., & Rogers, P. J. (1999). *Program evaluation: Forms and approaches* (2nd ed.). St. Leonards, NSW: Allen & Unwin.

Potter, C. (2006). Program evaluation. In M. T. Blanche, K. Durrheim, & D. Painter (Eds.), *Research in practice: Applied methods for the social sciences* (2nd ed., pp. 410–428). Cape Town: UCT Press.

Reiser, R. A., & Dick, W. (1996). *Instructional planning: A guide for teachers.* Allyn and Bacon.

Ríos, S. A., Aguilera, F., & Guerrero, L. A. (2009). Virtual communities of practice's purpose evolution analysis using a concept-based mining approach. In J. Velasquez, S. Rios, R. Howlett & L. Jain (Eds.), *Knowledge-based and intelligent information and engineering systems: Lecture notes in computer science* (Vol. 5712, pp. 480–489). Berlin: Springer. Retrieved from Springer website: http://link.springer.com/chapter/10.1007%2F978-3-642-04592-9_60

Solomon, J., & Wash, R. (2012). Bootstrapping wikis: Developing critical mass in a fledgling community by seeding content. In *Proceedings of the ACM 2012 conference on computer supported cooperative work* (pp. 261–264).

Tsai, W., & Ghoshal, S. (1998). Social capital and value creation: The role of intrafirm networks. *Academy of Management Journal, 41*(4), 464–476.

Wenger, E. (1998a). *Communities of practice.* Cambridge: Cambridge University Press.

Wenger, E. (1998b). *Communities of practice: Learning, meaning, and identity.* Cambridge: Cambridge University Press.

Wenger, E., McDermott, R. A., & Snyder, W. (2002). *Cultivating communities of practice: A guide to managing knowledge.* Brighton: Harvard Business Press.

Wenger, E., & Snyder, W. M. (2000). Communities of practice: The organizational frontier. *Harvard Business Review, 78*(1), 139–145.

Xu, W., Kreijns, K., & Hu, J. (2006). Designing social navigation for a virtual community of practice. In Z. Pan, R. Aylett, H. Diener, X. Jin, S. Gobel, & L. Li (Eds.), *Technologies for E-learning and digital entertainment* (pp. 27–38). Berlin: Springer.

Chapter 12
Enhancing the Impact of Research and Knowledge Co-production in Higher Education Through Communities of Practice

Karen Guldberg

Abstract Communities of Practice (CoP) are increasingly being nurtured in higher education but there is little literature on how CoP can be used to enable the dissemination and impact of research, to support the academic community to engage with its stakeholders or to encourage knowledge transfer, knowledge exchange or knowledge co-production with the end users of research. This chapter focuses on how a group of researchers worked with school practitioners and other stakeholders to develop a professional development program for school staff who work with pupils with autism. The chapter outlines how this community became a thriving community of practice that helped bridge the gap between theory and practice and also generated new knowledge. Themes such as the 'landscape of practice', 'structural and organizational issues', 'knowledgeability', 'competence', and 'engagement' are explored as a way of discussing the key considerations that need to be taken into account when examining how CoP can support the process of ensuring that research is of relevance to the communities it seeks to serve.

Keywords Communities of practice · Knowledge co-production · Impact

12.1 Introduction

Higher education in the UK is undergoing fundamental changes, moving from being public institutions to becoming private enterprises and increasingly needing to justify the value of the research endeavor by showing evidence of impact in terms of the wider social, economic, cultural and environmental benefits. Academics are strongly encouraged to consider how to ensure that gaps between research and

K. Guldberg (✉)
University of Birmingham, Birmingham, UK
e-mail: K.K.Guldberg@bham.ac.uk

© Springer Nature Singapore Pte Ltd. 2017
J. McDonald and A. Cater-Steel (eds.), *Communities of Practice*,
DOI 10.1007/978-981-10-2879-3_12

practice are bridged and that they engage in 'knowledge transfer' and 'knowledge exchange'. Whilst knowledge transfer suggests a one-way application of research from researchers to practitioners, knowledge exchange suggests a more reciprocal relationship between researchers and practitioners. Here the focus is on sharing learning, ideas and experiences, creating a dialogue between communities, and with it the notion that collaborative activity can lead to a better understanding of the ways in which academic research can add value and offer insights to key issues of concern for policy and practice (ESRC, not dated).

It has also long been recognized that educational enquiry should be about researchers and teachers nourishing each other through a common purpose of generating knowledge of value to those engaged in a common mission (Stenhouse 1983), thus focusing on co-production of knowledge. This entails consideration of new ways of working, recognizing that educational research is an area of enquiry with its own unique features, which needs to develop its own methods and approaches (Gee 2001). Research ownership and participation are key factors in the quality of educational research (Rose 2015), and Communities of Practice (CoP) can facilitate the knowledge transfer and exchange process. Yet whilst there is increasing interest in communities of practice theory in higher education, particularly related to teaching, research, faculty transfer and knowledge management (Kimble and Hildreth 2008), there is little research examining how communities of practice can enhance knowledge transfer, knowledge exchange and knowledge production, and through this make an impact on those that matter.

This chapter focuses on how a collaborative partnership enabled educational researchers to engage in genuine knowledge production with school practitioners, thus ensuring that educational research and enquiry had value for policy makers, teachers, parents and children. The chapter takes readers through a journey that examines the experiences of a unique partnership in which the outcomes of the work featured as a Research Excellence Framework Case Study for University of Birmingham, UK in 2014. I discuss this particular project in the context of some of Wenger et al. (2014) themes and conceptualizations around knowledge creation and landscapes of practice. The chapter focuses the lens on the concepts of 'landscapes of practice', 'structural and organizational issues', 'knowledgeability', 'competence', and 'engagement'. The organizational and structural issues that enabled the community of practice to develop are explored (Wenger 2004) before focusing on the interrelationship between the different stakeholders and how this enabled new forms of knowledge, evidence and practices to emerge. This then opens up discussion on the nature of knowledge generated through this work. The concepts of 'knowledge transfer', 'knowledge exchange' and 'knowledge co-creation' are explored in relation to Wenger et al. (2014) concept of 'knowledgeability' and by referring to discussions around 'evidence based practice' in education.

12.2 The Autism Education Trust Partnership

The Autism Education Trust (AET) is a national partnership that operates across all of England and was launched in the Houses of Parliament in November 2007 with support and funding from the Department of Education and from Ambitious about Autism, The Council for Disabled Children and The National Autistic Society in the UK. The Autism Education Trust (AET) was awarded £1.2 million in 2011 to create a 2-year national professional development program from the Department for Education, England. The aim of this professional development program was to build skills in the school work force to meet the needs of children and young people with autism between the ages of five and sixteen. The work originally consisted of a set of national standards that describe the key factors common to current good practice in settings; three levels of training materials in autism education and a competency framework for practitioners. The National Autism Standards allow schools to self-review against a framework of good practice; and the competency framework guides professional development. The school-based program also consists of autism training for school staff at level 1 (general awareness), level 2 (for staff working with young people with autism on a daily basis) and level 3 (for specialists such as special educational needs coordinators). Readers can access some of these resources on the Autism Education Trust website (www. autismeducationtrust.org.uk).

When the AET received funding from the Department for Education in England in 2011, their model was one whereby the national standards, competencies and training materials would all be interlinked. Tenders were announced for the development of the content of the materials, with separate tenders going out for the delivery of training. The AET was therefore at the center of appointing and identifying the members of the partnership that would develop and deliver the training. Criteria for the appointment of the hubs were that the individual hubs would cover a certain area of the country, and they should be organizations that had large networks of people to deliver the training to. They should also consist of a range of organizations, including local authorities, the voluntary sector and a school. It was crucial that the AET chose organizations that already had high levels of competence and expertise in order to ensure that they could work well together and have respect for one another. They appointed content developers and the training deliverers at the same time in order to ensure that those people delivering the training would be involved in commenting on and engaging in the development of the materials throughout.

The Autism Centre for Education and Research (ACER) at University of Birmingham, UK, were commissioned by the Autism Education Trust partnership to create the content for this professional development program and therefore to address how to enhance the understanding, knowledge and skills of staff working with autistic pupils in schools. Whilst ACER developed the training materials and the Standards and Competency frameworks, regional hubs were appointed to deliver the training across England. The hubs included local authorities, voluntary sector organizations and a large special school. The partnership therefore has multiple stakeholders and represents a partnership between higher education institutions, voluntary, statutory and private sector organizations, including a design consultancy. This collaborative inter-professional team of policy makers, practitioners and individuals on the autism spectrum were tasked with developing a shared ethos and a vision for autism education, which linked the public, private and voluntary sector together. The structure of the collaboration therefore brought together a number of organizations that shared the domain of autism education, albeit with different vantage points for approaching that domain, with different experiences and practices, but nevertheless with a shared ethos and values. The partnership represented different communities of practice interacting, driving forward new understandings, and through this process impacting significantly on the field of autism education in England.

As a result of this partnership, the AET now offers the largest national training program in England for education-based staff with around 50,000 staff having been trained in over 100 local authorities by the end of 2014. It has led to new conceptualizations of how to effectively teach pupils with autism, thereby redefining the domain, with a trainer stating that it has "changed the way we conduct training for staff. We now focus on the differences and strengths of pupils with autism rather than their deficits" (Jason Hakin, trainer). Changes in day-to-day practice in autism education have led to a 'statistically highly significant rise' in the knowledge and understanding of participants after the training and is also stimulating positive and lasting changes in practice (Cullen et al. 2013). The work has been described as transforming autism education, with Steve Huggett, Director of AET stating: "This program is transforming autism education and is making a real impact because all elements of the program have been developed collaboratively, involving a number of different stakeholders and sectors, and including people with autism. This also means that there is strong commitment and support for it."

12.3 Autism Education as a Landscape of Practice

The partners brought together by the AET involve a number of communities of practice consisting of individuals who share a craft or profession within a particular domain whilst having very unique knowledge bases and competences based on their positions within that domain. For example, the Autism Centre for Education and Research (ACER) specializes in educational intervention and provision for individuals on the autism spectrum, across the lifespan. This center is based at University of Birmingham, UK and delivers a range of courses, with several modes of delivery (campus, distance and web-based) and levels of study (from University Certificate through to PhD level study). In addition to a large network of students and regional tutors, ACER engages in substantial interdisciplinary research projects with colleagues from a number of different Universities. ACER has an ethos of using collaborative and participatory research methodologies to explore evidence based practice in the education of individuals on the autism spectrum, working closely with individuals on the autism spectrum and including them in research whilst striving to have close synergies between research, teaching and knowledge exchange.

Other partners on this project include the training deliverers, or hubs as they are termed. For example, the Birmingham Local Authority Communication Autism Team (CAT) are a team of professionals who work for the local authority in a support role with nearly 3000 pupils on their caseload and supporting over 400 schools. Most of the trainers in the team are qualified teachers who previously worked in different stages of education. They are now specialist teachers who support other school-based staff to meet the needs of children with communication difficulties and pupils on the autism spectrum. Their roles are wide-ranging and include visiting schools, supporting the schools with overall development plans as well as meeting the needs of individual children; offering training to schools, running a service for children out of school and also running services such as social skills groups. Another hub/training deliverer is a special school for children with autism. The Bridge School has teachers who are experienced in teaching children with autism and complex needs and their community of practice is focused around the school and the activities generated around that, with the school having a particular expertise in understanding practices and competencies around meeting the needs of children with complex needs and autism. The National Autistic Society is a hub representing the non-profit sector and is an organization offering services and advice to people who want to know more about autism. It was initially a parent led organization and the organization itself has its own culture around the development of a service. These organizations only represent a section of the partnership, but illustrate the different type of stakeholders that were involved.

This partnership is therefore a complex system of communities of practice in which individuals are more or less engaged with multiple communities of practice (Omidvar and Kislov 2013). Crucially, Wenger et al. (2014) highlight that no practice can claim to contain or represent the whole in such a complex interrelated system of communities of practice. Kimble and Hildreth (2008), also stress this focus on CoPs not being one large community, but that we are usually describing

a constellation of interrelated CoPs that can even spread beyond the borders of the 'host' organization.

12.4 'Knowledgeability' and Knowledge Co-creation

Through the development of the professional development programme for schools, this community was focused on the creation of new knowledge and understandings that emerged from the joint work of the different communities across the landscape of practice, and it went further than having shared repertoires, mutual engagement and joint enterprise. In order to also be a genuine learning community, there was commitment towards co-construction of knowledge (Garrison and Anderson 2003). The community needed to focus on being both a collaborative learning environment and a collaborative working environment. The former emphasizes productivity in terms of evidence of change in participants whilst the latter emphasizes change in terms of outputs. In relation to the work being discussed here, there is no doubt that this community consisted of a 'learning partnership among people who find it useful to learn from and with each other about a particular domain' (Wenger et al. 2011, p. 2).

The community had mutual engagement around the domain, with the focus being on identifying, developing and communicating what is considered 'best autism practice' in the education of pupils with autism. This mutual engagement meant that all parts of the community had something to contribute and a reason to engage. Mutual engagement was clearly focused on the task of improving the skills, knowledge and competencies of the workforce, in the form of developing and delivering the professional development program outlined above. The community was therefore involved in a joint enterprise around the creation of three tiers of training materials, a set of competencies for practitioners and a set of standards for settings to self-evaluate their practice. All members of the community engaged with one another in this development, albeit at different levels, with various levels of participation. The ACER team and Genium (the design consultancy) represented the core team responsible for the overall development of the content. The AET ensured that this core team met regularly with the people who would be delivering the training throughout the creation of the materials. Different levels of participation and engagement were encouraged in the form of regular partnership meetings; setting up a team of consultants from different hubs who regularly commented in detail on different drafts and through engaging trainers in 'train the trainer' events once the materials were completed. The different roles and responsibilities coupled with organizational structures that encouraged engagement, led to participation happening at a number of different levels, ranging from active to occasional and peripheral.

The involvement of the training deliverers from the outset meant that they had input into the development throughout and were therefore engaged and had a sense of ownership. Their input was invaluable and they had major influences on a number of levels. This ranged from influencing how long each level of training should be, to identifying the resources that should accompany the training materials and ensuring that concepts and materials were explained in a way that would make sense to practitioners. The researchers were drawing on the research evidence in the creation of the materials but did not always have a current experiential understanding of key issues facing practitioners. Equally, training deliverers were in touch with the day-to-day implementation of government policies and had better understandings of how the practitioner community was responding to these on a practical level. The perspective of the training deliverers was therefore invaluable in ensuring that the materials would connect with practitioners. Similarly, the engagement and involvement of adults with autism was crucial in ensuring that the materials truly reflected the perspective of people with autism.

Through this process, participants clearly developed a shared repertoire expressed in resources or tools used to negotiate meaning. Examples of these include teaching resources, training presentations, documentations and resources for use in training materials, concepts and words used, as well as ethos and values. These words, symbols, concepts and images were shared amongst the community, and were often contested and discussed in the creation of the materials, with the final product leading to written resources that represented a truly shared repertoire.

Although all the different communities of practice within this landscape of practice share their overall landscape, or domain (autism education), there were very different competences, experiences and practices in place in the different 'sub domains' or 'constellations' of these multiple communities of practice. Partners brought their own unique experiences and expertise, and they would often view the development of materials through using the lens of their own positioning and expertise. For example, the ACER researchers' expertise were rooted in not only understanding the research evidence, but also being able to translate that research evidence, and ethos and values into easily accessible materials that had a clear rationale and content. However, these were not developed in isolation, as the researchers would then circulate the materials to training deliverers and individuals with autism. Practitioners would raise issues about the extent to which the materials would make sense to school staff, and whether they were grounded enough in practice. Our consultant with autism would challenge wording and ways of putting things, making absolutely sure that the materials were consistent in taking a 'capacity approach' to working with people with autism, rather than a focus on deficits. The different stakeholders would therefore bring different competencies, experiences and knowledge to the project. The Birmingham Local Authority CAT team, for example, would bring recent and relevant grounding in working directly with mainstream schools and would offer perspectives on what the key issues are that practitioners are dealing with in those settings. The Bridge school would bring perspectives on the needs with children with autism and additional learning difficulties, whilst the National Autistic Society would often look at the materials through the lens of parents of children with autism, and their needs. Our consultant with autism would critique and give feedback on the materials from the perspective of a person with autism. Bringing all these different lenses to bear on the development of the materials ultimately not only enriched the materials themselves but also the knowledge base of all those involved in creating them.

In terms of the pedagogy of the program, it was clear from the start that the people writing the materials were not going to be the people delivering the program. In fact, the same materials were going to be delivered by a wide range of different hubs and trainers. These people would deliver materials in different areas of the country and to different audiences. The danger arising from this was that although the knowledge co-creation process was dynamic during the creative process of developing the materials, the training could be in danger of quickly becoming stagnant, out of date and 'technical' in delivery if everyone was delivering training to a 'script'. It was therefore important to get the balance right between ensuring that certain key points were covered in the training, particularly key information about understanding autism and how it might impact on the individual pupil. Simultaneously, the materials needed to be flexible enough to engage and involve the trainers and keep them motivated when they were delivering the training, as well as enabling trainers to adapt the materials according to their audiences and according to their own personal styles. The materials were therefore developed as interactive presentations with video clips, activities, case studies and links to resources embedded within them and a distinction was made between core slides and resource slides. The core slides represented content that was crucial for all trainers to get across, regardless of who delivered it, where and to whom.

Equally important were the resource slides, which were slides in which there were links to video clips, activities and additional resources that trainers could draw upon depending on their preferences, the nature of their particular audience and their own teaching style. The creation of the materials thus offered a balance between key content that everyone had to deliver, whilst enabling every trainer to deliver the content in their own style, and building on their own strengths by choosing which resource slides, activities, video clips and case studies to draw upon. This process resulted in trainers being able to bring their own resources to the training and to continuously keep the materials fresh and engaging, and strongly rooted in practice, as they moved forward with training, thus enabling 'knowledgeability' to be sustained beyond the completion of the materials.

12.5 Knowledge Co-creation Using Different Evidence Bases

The work clearly represented knowledge co-creation drawing upon the perspectives of a number of individuals and organizations. Wenger argues that "knowledge is not a separate object from the people who produced it or even the process that produced it". It is part of the mutual engagement through which participants refine and expand their 'experiences of practice' (Wenger 1998, p. 4). This knowledge needs to consist of both tacit knowledge, referring to those valuable context-based experiences that cannot easily be captured, codified or stored (Davenport and Prusak 1997; Kimble and Hildreth 2005) as well as the knowledge creation that leads to direct outcomes and products.

Whilst it is crucial to acknowledge the way in which knowledge is shaped by mutual engagement with people, resources and objects, in a project like this, and in fact in any educational research, we need to examine how different knowledge bases interact with one another and what the status of those knowledge bases might be. This is particularly important in relation to this work, as the autism research community on interventions and teaching approaches tends to privilege scientific evidence over the evidence base of practitioners. This is clearly illustrated in the way in which the concept of evidence based practice (EBP) is understood, with EBP being defined as scientific research that informs practice. In the autism field, it is generally accepted that valuable scientific research paradigms are experimental designs and instrumental research (Mesibov and Shea 2009). EBP in education clearly privileges scientific evidence over evidence from practice (Thomas 2012). Yet in addressing how knowledge develops, we need to understand that the way that knowledge develops dynamically in relation to people, experiences and objects, and that it is also influenced by outside factors and contextual ways in which different knowledge bases are perceived in the wider context (Biesta 2011). This is particularly pertinent when certain forms of knowledge are privileged over other forms of knowledge. In this project, we did not accept the notion of one form of evidence or knowledge being superior to the other. The starting point for co-production of knowledge was that both research findings and professional expertise are equally important. Practice had an important contribution to make to the knowledge base, and there was strong recognition that good research should be respectful of those for whom we search for an evidence base for. This means that researchers must make efforts to engage our activity with wider audiences and to make our work accessible to all who may have an interest in what we do. In that respect, we questioned the value of educational research without teachers, learners or schools, as these are simply the subject of our investigations, but should be partners in the research process at every stage.

In the field of research into educational interventions and teaching approaches for pupils with autism, Wenger et al. (2014) concept of 'knowledgeability' becomes particularly important in considering how to bridge a 'persistent disconnect between research and practice' (Parsons and Kasari 2013). The term 'knowledgeability' is defined as the complex relationships people establish with respect to a landscape of practice, which make them recognizable as reliable sources of information. Wenger et al. (2014) argue that the ability to be recognized as such depends on the depth of one's competence in one or more core practice(s), and it also depends on one's 'knowledgeability' about other practices and significant boundaries in the landscape. The gap between research and practice in educational research cannot be bridged without researchers becoming more able to understand practice and practitioners becoming more able to understand research through developing new methodologies that enable co-construction of knowledge with practitioners. This knowledge co-creation (Parsons et al. 2015) needs to entail a shift away from traditional conceptions of knowledge transfer and knowledge exchange towards a much more shared endeavor (Leibowitz et al. 2013) in which collaboration and dialogue are key features. This leads to a focus on the culturally specific and situated nature of knowledge, and how evidence is an outcome of knowledge co-creation (Houston et al. 2010).

In the context of the partnership described in this paper, 'knowledgeability' captures how the different partners in the project were able to travel across the landscape of practice, and through this process both the research based perspectives and the practice-based perspectives were enhanced. This 'knowledgeability' could be seen in the way the training materials and their delivery through the hubs were created through an interactive synergy with the hub delivery teams bringing to life and supplementing the core materials developed by the researchers. Of importance here, is the fact that all members (core development team, regional hubs and the AET) saw their roles as important to the creation of the materials, leading to open communication, the existence of autonomy, engagement with the program, and ownership of resources. In practical and concrete terms, 'knowledgeability' developed as different members of the community worked with individuals on the autism spectrum, accessed their views and ensured autistic voices were authentically and strongly represented in the development and in the materials. The 'knowledgeability' also informed the creation of new knowledge that in turn connected with teachers, and persuaded them of the value of learning about autism, because in understanding autism, they would develop better expertise about educating all children in the classroom.

12.6   Competencies

A concept that is discussed by Wenger et al. (2014) in this context is the notion of 'competences'. Members of this community need to be competent in their own practice, but as Wenger et al. (2014) point out, they were also expected to be knowledgeable with respect to practices in the landscape relevant to the specialization of others in the community. Trainers needed to have specific competences in their core practices of delivering training, and researchers needed a different set of core competences. Yet these different perspectives, experiences and outlooks regarding the world of autism educational practice needed to understand each others practices across boundaries because understanding these different perspectives contributed to the task of increasing the knowledge and understanding of practitioners.

There are a number of processes that are particularly important for ensuring good flow of 'knowledgeability' and 'competences'. An important factor in this is to carefully consider the issue of engagement by doing things, working on issues, talking, using and producing artifacts, debating, and reflecting together. This project had regular but focused engagement on a number of different levels and this increased the competence and 'knowledgeability' of the community. Firstly, there was differentiation in the engagement of different members of the community, where different levels of participation were welcomed. For example, the project team had a core team that was responsible for the writing of the content. Within the core team, writers had clear and specific responsibilities for different aspects of content creation, whether that was the core slides, the additional resources, the case studies or the video clips. The core team worked intensively and also took on the leadership of the project, working regularly and consistently on those aspects. Then there was another level of engagement, which constituted the 'consultative group.' This group participated regularly as a result of activities initiated by the core group, but not as regularly as the core group. There was also a larger, more passive group of project partners, the expert reference group and other stakeholders, who were more passive but were still involved in the learning process. This included many of the trainers who were not involved in the creation of materials, but who were involved in delivery, for example. Engagement and participation was also designed to happen in a 'ripple effect'. Once the materials were completed, for example, the core team organized a 'train the trainer event' including a written trainers guide. This training provided the first group of trainers with the necessary training for them to move out and deliver training to other trainers in their own services.

The design of activities and tasks were focused on enabling productive cross-boundary encounters to help reconfigure the partnerships in the landscape (Wenger 2010). This involved designing learning activities that engaged people in doing something concrete relevant to their practice. Organizing practical 'train the trainers' sessions which modeled how to run the training and which were run by people who would also be engaged in the delivery of the training, were of importance in this respect. Other activities included setting up a wiki where draft materials and completed documents were made available to everyone involved in the project. Crucially, this became an excellent way of involving the wider group of consultants and hubs, and also became a space were the community could discuss contentious issues. This space was used productively to challenge the content team on some of our terminology, with our autistic consultant being particularly vocal in this respect. We had regular face to face as well as skype meetings and these focused on practical issues of close relevance to the project, giving opportunities for shared reflection and learning and addressing concrete challenges.

12.7 Shared Ownership

The way in which different stakeholders were engaged in it, was at times both challenging and time consuming, but it did mean that there was a shared sense of ownership and values, and that progress mattered to all stakeholders. It also meant that people could engage their own practice in 'boundary activities' (Wenger et al. 2014). Thus researchers were involved in brokering information across different stakeholder groups in a way that enabled growing understanding of the different sectors. Creating film clips of good practice in classroom settings was an example of such an activity, as was the writing of practical case studies, which involved collaboration between different sectors of the community (researchers, individuals with autism and school practitioners).

The learning spaces were therefore diverse and they supported different kinds of interaction. We also used multiple ways of connecting people through using technologies such as skype, the wiki, and email, as well as connecting people regularly through physical face to face meetings and visits to different settings (such as schools, for filming). The work can therefore be perceived as a learning journey, where engagement gives us 'direct experience of regimes of competence' (Wenger et al. 2014). Previous research has also found that productive outcomes depend on a number of factors including the nature of the task (Fung 2004), affective and social relationships (Guldberg and Pilkington 2006) and the notion that meaningful learning is constructed out of experience, including the notion that the sharing of experience through discussion is a stimulus for reflection that can impact on practice (Garrison and Anderson 2003). We tried to find time for focused and deep reflection time and to emphasize the importance of exploratory talk (Mercer 1995) in meetings and communication. This included creating an enabling environment where we encouraged all participants to offer reasons for their own propositions, to welcome alternative suggestions; and ask others for justifications.

Boundaries were often the places where diverse viewpoints co-existed, leading at times to heated discussions at partner meetings, training events and the expert reference group. Some of these discussions related to the role of different organizations and members, some to the financial model behind the partnership or with disagreements relating to the technological tools chosen to deliver the training materials. Wenger argues that reflection across boundaries can also be a fruitful source of inspiration and new thinking (Wenger et al. 2014). Although boundaries can be places where innovation happens, they can also be sources of possible conflict and a possible reason for the minimization of learning (Wenger et al. 2014). The professional identity of participants was at times challenged by engaging in boundary communities, with tensions emerging from the different practices, values, outlooks and agendas in those boundary communities, yet social engagement around this shared work supported various forms of learning by taking into account craft and personal knowledge as well as consideration of how evidence can be systematically 'marshalled' and used (Pring and Thomas 2004).

12.8   Changing Cultures

The collaborative model and practices that emerged within the community turned out to be significant in shaping the flexibility of the materials to be used by the hubs in a range of educational settings (mainstream, special and specialist) and with a wide range of school-based professionals across England. It enabled change in the culture and attitudes of school staff in their areas and initiated a willingness to update, renew and revise existing approaches, strategies and provision for pupils with autism, and therefore deepened the 'knowledgeability' of the landscape of practice. As understandings developed through a dynamic and dialectic process of negotiation with context, the knowledge creation process in this community existed in a dynamic duality of practice and reification.

Regimes of competence were further developed through the creation of strong relationships in which partners created a common language, which moved all parts of the community away from language which presented autism as a deficit towards language in which autism was presented as a different way of being; from a lens which overly focused on the difficulties and 'problems' presented by pupils with autism to a lens which looked at the strengths of people with autism; from a world were research dominated thinking about what was considered 'good autism practice' to a world where the voice of practitioners was heard and firmly put on the agenda; and finally but certainly not least, moving towards a world where the perspective and voice of people with autism was embedded in all aspects of the project and the resulting materials. This ranged from people with autism being involved in commenting at all levels on the materials during their production, to the materials themselves being embedded with quotes from people with autism and video clips taking on board both their perspectives and the perspectives of their families. Reconfiguring the landscape of practice in autism education through new forms of engagement has therefore given more of a voice to individuals with autism and although differences were overtly expressed during the creation of the materials, this also led to ways of discovering true mutual interest.

12.9 Structural and Organizational Issues: Horizontal and Vertical Accountability

This work indicates that, when trying to understand what is involved in creating a productive community, it is necessary to examine infrastructure, resources and processes required for successful implementation; the roles of community members and the sharing of goals, activities and tasks; as well as the kinds of learning taking place through ethics, trust and social capital (Rasmussen 2005; Pilkington and Guldberg 2009). We also need to locate studies in the social conditions, cultures and contexts in which they take place. This contextual level needs to take into account the wider field of policy-making and institutional change (Jones and Cooke 2006), or even the culture of the country (Alexander 2000). Culture and context are clearly complex concepts with both historical and dynamic aspects (Mercer and Littleton 2007) and covers both the wider context of legislative changes and policy foci in the field of special educational needs and also the changes that are taking place in higher education. For this chapter, the most important issue for the moment is the piecemeal and ad hoc nature of training that was available for staff before the creation of this professional development program, with training in mainstream schools being the least adequate. Policies in the field of autism have recognized the importance of training and there is recognition that school staff, particularly in mainstream schools, need further training, given that 70 % of children with autism are being educated in mainstream schools in the UK (Mackay and Dunlop 2004). This highlighted the need for a national, coherent training program that could be focused on the needs of pupils in mainstream schools, with the Autism Education Trust setting up a partnership model for developing and delivering this training.

Although Wenger's original conceptualization of communities of practice was that they are often informal in nature and complement formal organizations, communities of practice have increasingly also been defined in the literature as those that are structured, or where CoPs are used as an organizational tool to harness the learning and knowledge of its members (Polin 2008). In the partnership work described here, the AET partnership was set up as an organizational model to create a collaborative professional development program to be rolled out across England, and I will argue that the organizational mechanisms that were set up were crucial to the success, but so were the more informal ways in which participants in the community shared knowledge. This informal sharing of knowledge often emerged from the passion and commitment of the members. As argued elsewhere (Guldberg et al. 2013), Wenger's social learning theory enables examination of both the formal organizational mechanisms put in place to support the 'knowledge management' process and the informal ways in which knowledge is shared. Social learning spaces can therefore sit within the context of institutional accountability structures (Wenger 2004). In Wenger (2004) work, he talks about vertical accountability representing hierarchy, evidence based prescription; codification and regulation. He contrasts this to horizontal, which covers communities and networks, peer-to-peer learning, personal meaning, engagement and creativity.

Wenger et al. (2002) have argued that if the strategic goals of a parent organization are aligned with the passion and commitment of its members, then a community is much more likely to thrive. The clear organizational structure that informed the governance of the AET partnership involved multiple organizations and stakeholders, and it also ensured that each organization and stakeholder had clear roles and structures within that. This could at times lead to tensions, but crucially it enabled all partners to be focused about their own roles, and it was clear to all stakeholders what their contribution could be. There was also a critical mass, so if some hub members did not engage, there were others who would, thereby allowing engagement at different levels. In addition to the clear structure, the success of the community was also rooted in the choice of organizations and individuals who were part of this community. In the selection of researchers who created the first set of materials, ACER was commissioned to undertake the work because the researchers had credibility within the autism educational community of practice, for example, and had the respect of the training deliverers. It was also important that key individuals were people who were passionate and clear about their own expertise, but who were also clear about what their own limitations were and how they could learn from what other people could provide. Although the AET partnership represented a project team with clear deliverables and shared goals, milestones and results; with designated members who had consistent roles, it has not dissipated once the first project was completed. Instead it has organically evolved, become defined by the knowledge of its members; with the community itself organically identifying what it needs to do next in order to continue existing.

The relationship between the organizations outlined above and the AET has been critical to the successful delivery of the AET program as it has allowed an ongoing dialogue between the AET and the people it supports. This ongoing dialogue helps inform and develop its programs, especially since the model combines national reach and consistency with a local training network that ensures close contact with local early years settings, schools, colleges and Local Authorities. The interactive relationship between the AET and its stakeholders drives the organic growth of the AET's products and outputs, which is another key feature of the AET model. For example, the AET Director highlighted that it was AET users and partners who first asked for the 2013/15 expansion into the early years and the post 16 sectors. Recently published AET guidance for parents on schools was both instigated and developed by parents themselves. In addition, feedback from users of the AET offer drives revision and improvement of the training and materials and the schools training materials have already benefited from an interim revision whilst major revisions and updates of the whole schools program including the AET Autism Standards and competency framework will be delivered in the 2015/16 government funded program. The partnership has also led to further natural and organic development, with almost all hubs now being financially self-sustaining. It has been extended to other sectors, with a parent guide, an early years and a post 16 program currently being developed. It has grown from seven hubs to nineteen thus extending its reach to the whole country. With evaluation built into the training from the start, it has robust quality assurance procedures and a systemic process-driven management. All of this contributes to the success, reach and sustainability of the program.

The work has been important in encouraging relationships to develop, and enabling different partners in the community to build on their relationships, and this has continued through the development of the program over time. Thus the partners came together in 2011 to create the school-based program and once this was completed, the AET won funding to adapt this to early years and post 16. Although the configuration of different partners changed according to who was commissioned to take on these adaptations, it created further opportunities for the foundation for learning together and collaborating. The work of reconfiguring the landscape of practice is clearly long-term, and further funding has enabled this long-term configuration to continue, especially as there has been some continuity in the people and institutions that have been involved at different stages of the project.

One of the reasons for this is that participating in the endeavor brings high value for time. Training hubs benefit from having clear structures and parameters round their work with schools and teachers; they do not have to generate new training materials from scratch and they are able to deliver training that has credibility with teachers. There is therefore buy-in for them. An example of how it gives high value for time, can be found in the way that the Birmingham Local Authority Communication Autism Team (CAT) work with schools now as a result of the training, the set of national standards and the competency framework. The CAT team use the Standards as a framework for working with schools, helping schools to create school development plans based on the standards in order to improve their practice as a setting. They use the competencies to help individual practitioners to identify their own training needs.

Having said this, there are also tensions related to whether this activity represents high value for time. Although impact, 'knowledge transfer' and 'knowledge exchange' are valued in higher education in the UK, the relative value of researchers undertaking this kind of consultancy work is quite low compared to spending time engaging in writing publications for peer reviewed journals, for example. The researchers' orientation to the project has been firmly rooted in their commitment to wanting to make a difference in the field, and has not necessarily generated additional value for them in terms of the hierarchies of the institution and their promotion as academics. It has, however, provided high value in relation to professional and personal development, building new understandings and engaging closely with the field of practice.

For the academics, it has also meant that they have been able to become particularly creative in continuing the aspirational narrative of wanting to make a difference to the world of educational practice in autism. As such, it has provided a passion and impetus for continuing to build on the processes and ways of working through extending the work of the community and building on the experiences that have been outlined in this chapter. This has resulted in new opportunities and challenges related to gathering a community of researchers, policy makers and practitioners in the UK, Italy and Greece to research current educational practices in autism in those respective contexts and to create collaborative professional development programs in Greece and Italy. This has been possible through receiving funding of nearly half a million Euros from the European Union Erasmus Plus Strategic Partnership Program, Key Action 2. A new challenge has therefore now emerged in re-configuring the landscape of practice to build 'knowledgeability' in international practices in autism education, combining different multiple voices and perspectives to understand an even bigger and more complex landscape.

This project, with new partners rooted in their own communities of practice, is aptly named 'Transform Autism Education'. Although we are at an early stage in this project, the aim is for transformation by all partners learning from each other through engaging across boundaries in each others' communities, with the engagement taking the form of transnational project meetings involving visits to schools and settings, discussions of each others education systems, identifying similarities and differences and co-creating resources.

12.10 Concluding Comments

Wenger argues that the tacit, dynamic and socially distributed nature of knowledge means that it cannot be managed and measured like a physical asset (Wenger et al. 2002, p. 166). The direct and active encounters with other practices that have been described in this chapter are conducive to learning and reflection because they 'offer a chance to see oneself through other eyes' (Wenger et al. 2014). They have the potential to yield both better knowledge of other practices and better understanding of one's own practice in its relation to the landscape. As such, it is important to understand how Communities of Practice can be important ways of not only enabling the transfer of scientific knowledge to practice, but also in enabling educational researchers to focus on methodologies that allow the development of co-creation of knowledge. This co-creation of knowledge is of fundamental importance if we are to find evidence bases for teaching approaches and interventions that will work in real classrooms and that will be meaningful for pupils with autism, their families and their teachers.

Acknowledgments The author would like to thank everyone involved in the AET partnership, with a special thanks to Ryan Bradley, Dr. Glenys Jones, Dr. Kerstin Wittemeyer and Martin Kerem for their collaboration in producing the materials; to Dr. Steve Huggett and Sarah-Jane Critchley from the Autism Education Trust for their continued passion and commitment and to Damian Milton for his tireless and patient input. My deepest thanks are extended to all the schools, families and pupils who generously gave their time.

References

Alexander, R. (2000). *Culture and pedagogy: International comparisons in primary education.* Hoboken: Blackwell.

Biesta, G. (2011). Disciplines and theory in the academic study of education: A comparative analysis of the Anglo-American and Continental construction of the field. *Pedagogy, Culture and Society, 19*(2), 175–192.

Cullen, M.-A., Cullen, S., Lindsay, G., & Arweck, E. (2013). *Evaluation of Autism Education Trust Training Hubs programme 2011–2013. Final report.* London: Autism Education Trust.

Davenport, T. H., & Prusak, L. (1997). *Working knowledge: How organizations manage what they know.* Boston: Harvard Business School Press.

ESRC. (not dated). Knowledge exchange. http://www.esrc.ac.uk/collaboration/knowledge-exchange/. Accessed August 5, 2014.

Fung, Y. Y. H. (2004). Collaborative online learning: Interaction patterns and limiting factors. *Open Learning, 19*(2), 135–147.

Garrison, D. R., & Anderson, T. (2003). *E-learning in the 21st century.* London: Routledge Palmer.

Gee, J. P. (2001). Identity as an analytic lens for research in education. *Review of Research in Education, 25,* 99–125.

Guldberg, K., Mackness, J., Mariyannis, E., & Tait, C. (2013). Knowledge management and value creation in a third sector organisation. *Journal of Knowledge and Process Management, 20*(3), 113–184.

Guldberg, K., & Pilkington, R. (2006). A community of practice approach to the development of nontraditional learners through networked learning. *Journal of Computer Assisted Learning, 22* (3), 159–172.

Houston, N., Ross, H., Robinson, J., & Malcolm, H. (2010). Inside research, inside ourselves: Teacher educators take stock of their research practice. *Educational Action Research, 18*(4), 555–569.

Jones, E. J., & Cooke, L. (2006). A window into learning: Case studies of online group communication and collaboration. *ALT-J, Research in Learning Technology, 14*(3), 261–274.

Kimble, C., & Hildreth, P. (2005). Dualities, distributed communities of practice and knowledge management. *Journal of Knowledge Management, 9*(4), 102.

Kimble, C., & Hildreth, P. M. (2008). Communities of practice: Going one step too far? http://ssrn.com/abstract=634642. Accessed February 04, 2014.

Lave, J., & Wenger, E. (1991). *Situated learning: Legitimate peripheral participation.* New York: Cambridge University Press.

Leibowitz, B., Ndebele, C., & Winberg, C. (2013). 'It's an amazing learning curve to be part of the project': Exploring academic identity in collaborative research. *Studies in Higher Education.* doi:10.1080/03075079.2013.801424.

Mackay, T., & Dunlop, A. (2004). *The development of a national training framework for autistic spectrum disorders.* London: The National Autistic Society.

Mercer, N. (1995). *The guided construction of knowledge.* Clevedon: Multilingual Matters.

Mercer, N., & Littleton, K. (2007). *Dialogue and the development of children's thinking.* London: Routledge.

Mesibov, G., & Shea, V. (2009). Evidence-based practices and autism. *Autism, 15*(1), 114–133.

Omidvar, O., & Kislov, R. (2013). The evolution of the communities of practice approach: Toward knowledgeability in a landscape of practice—An interview with etienne Wenger-Trayner. *Journal of Management Inquiry.*

Parsons, S., & Kasari, C. (2013). Editorial: Schools at the center of educational research in autism: Possibilities, practices and promises. *Autism, 17*(3), 251–253.

Parsons, S., Guldberg, K., Porayska-Pomsta, K., & Lee, R. (2015). Digital stories as a method for evidence-based practice and knowledge co-creation in technology-enhanced learning for children with autism. *International Journal of Research Methods in Education, Special Issue: E-research in Educational Contexts. 38,* 247.

Pilkington, R., & Guldberg, K. (2009). Conditions for productive networked learning among professionals and carers: The WebAutism case study. In L. Dirckinck-Holmfeld, C. Jones, & B. Lindstrom (Eds.), *Analysing networked learning practices in higher education and continuing professional development* (pp. 43–63). Netherlands: Sense Publishers.

Polin, L. G. (2008). Graduate professional education from a community of practice perspective. In C. Kimble, P. Hildreth, & I. Bourdon (Eds.), *Communities of practice. Creating learning environments for educators* (2nd ed.). North Carolina: Information Age Publishing.

Pring, R., & Thomas, G. (Eds.). (2004). *Evidence-based practice in education.* Berkshire: Open University Press.

Rasmussen, A. (2005). Case: Productive learning processes and standardisation. In L. Dirckinck-Holmfeld & B. M. Svendsen (Eds.), *Report on theoretical framework on selected core issues on conditions for productive learning in network learning environments, Kaleidoscope Deliverable 24.3.1.* Denmark: Aalborg University.

Rose, R. (2015). Learning from each other: Respecting cultural differences in an international research agenda. Paper presented in Becoming Visible seminar in Brazil, March 12th–15th 2015.

Stenhouse, L. (1983). Research is systematic inquiry made public. *British Educational Research Journal, 9*(1), 11–20.

Thomas, G. (2012) Changing our landscape of inquiry for a new science of education. *Harvard Educational Review, 82*(1), 26–51. http://her.hepg.org/content/6t2r0891715x3377/

Wenger, E. (1998). *Communities of practice: Learning, meaning, and identity.* Cambridge: Cambridge University Press.

Wenger, E., McDermott, R., & Snyder, W. (2002). *Cultivating communities of practice.* Boston, MA: Harvard Business School Press.

Wenger, E. (2004). Knowledge management as a doughnut: Shaping your knowledge strategy through communities of practice. *Ivey Business Journal.*

Wenger, E. (2010). Communities of practice and social learning systems: The career of a concept. In C. Blackmore (Ed.), *Communities of practice and social learning systems.* New York: Springer.

Wenger, E., Trayner, B., & De Laat, M. (2011). Promoting and assessing value creation in communities and networks: A conceptual framework. Rapport 18, Ruud de Moor Centrum, Open University of the Netherlands.

Wenger, E., Fenton-O'creevy, M., Hutchinson, S., Kubiak, C., & Wenger-Trayner, B. (Eds.). (2014). *Learning in landscapes of practice: Boundaries, identity, and knowledgeability in practice-based learning.* New York: Routledge.

Part III
Leadership in Higher Education Communities of Practice

The seven chapters in this part focus on the adoption of CoP for Leadership education, practice and also the role of leadership within the CoP.

Chapter 13 "Mediating Role of Leadership in the Development of Communities of Practice" by Saldana demonstrate the mediating role that leadership exerts over CoP knowledge creation.

Chapter 14 "Revealing the Nexus between Distributed Leadership and Communities of Practice" by Jones and Harvey discusses the relation between Distributed Leadership and CoP in higher education context.

Chapter 15 "The Leadership Link: A hybrid Professional Learning Network for Learning and Teaching Leaders" by McCluskey describes a Professional Learning Network (PLN) that utilises a range of collaborative spaces and digital technologies to engage Learning and Teaching Leaders in collaborating and sharing their experiences and wisdom about leadership in a contemporary university.

Chapter 16 "The Road Less Travelled: A Conversation Between Four Communities of Practice Facilitators About Their Experiences, Learning and Professional Outcomes From the Role" by Pedersen et al. presents the experiences of four previous CoP facilitators from three different Universities.

Chapter 17 "Facilitating a Community of Practice in Higher Education: A Case Study" by Pember presents a chronological case study of development of a CoP, and discusses the challenges experienced and success achieved during the development.

Chapter 18 "The Role of Higher Education in Regional Economic Development Through Small Business CoPs" by Smith and Smith describes the learning experiences of a group of small business owner-managers on a leadership programme called LEAD.

Chapter 19 "Teacher Educators' Critical Reflection on Becoming and Belonging to a Community of Practice" by Adie et al. reports reflections of a diverse group of teacher on their experience of being brought together to form a CoP in the scholarship of teaching, and how the group members learned how to work collaboratively across the boundaries of their disciplines.

Chapter 13
Mediating Role of Leadership in the Development of Communities of Practice

Jacqueline B. Saldana

Abstract This chapter aims to demonstrate that leadership is a Community of Practice (CoP) mediating influence for problem solving and innovation that should be incorporated in the contemporary CoP model. Jean Lave and Etienne Wenger (1991) coined the term "Community of Practice" to describe how groups of professionals network to identify common solutions to everyday problems. Wenger et al. (Cultivating communities of practice: a guide to managing knowledge. Harvard Business School Press, Boston, 2002) elaborated a CoP theory explaining how field practitioners develop and share working skills through the dimensions of domain, practice, and community, each related to diverse activities and life cycle stages of knowledge creation. Today, numerous organizations have adopted CoPs to promote innovation among their professional constituencies. CoPs have been characterized as spontaneous networks of people that operate without hierarchies or leadership structure. However, the current CoP literature suggests the mediating role of leadership over the capacity of members to produce problem-solving and innovation. A revised CoP structure in which leadership appears a mediating influence for CoP development is necessary to validate the existence of considerable research reporting leadership expressions as influence over CoP socialization and knowledge creation. By acknowledging the mediating role that leadership exerts over CoP knowledge creation, organizations sponsoring communities of practitioners may be able to overcome the challenges in leveraging the spontaneous nature of the community with the legitimization of knowledge creation structures.

Keywords Communities of Practice · Leadership · CoP life cycle · CoP developmental stages

---

Dedication: To my father's memory (Heriberto Baez-Vargas, RIP).

J.B. Saldana (✉)
College of Business of Management, DeVry University, Highland Landmark V,
3005 Highland Parkway, Downers Grove, IL 60515-5683, USA
e-mail: jsaldana@devry.edu

© Springer Nature Singapore Pte Ltd. 2017
J. McDonald and A. Cater-Steel (eds.), *Communities of Practice*,
DOI 10.1007/978-981-10-2879-3_13

13.1   Introduction

The proliferation of Web 2.0 technologies has removed barriers for communication, allowing practitioners to exploit cross-cultural opportunities for collaboration and innovation. Culturally diverse groups within interconnected networks increase opportunities for collaborative participation and high-performing capabilities (West 2009). Documented peer-collaboration case studies, such as the scientific work on the dangers of chlorofluoro-carbons (CFCs) that lead to the Basel Convention of 1989, and the creation of the Linux software (Lee and Cole 2003) demonstrated that the collaborative participation of diverse experts in a field can promote progressive learning, creative solutions, and radical change. Tapscott and Williams (2010) named Wikinomics to the accelerated production of innovation that can emerge when industries practice global peer production through the contemporary "weapons of mass collaboration" (p. 50) as result of contemporary Internet capabilities.

Capitalizing on the promises of these collaborative networks, professional associations, multinational enterprises, pharmaceutical companies, educational, and information technology organizations around the world have adopted Communities of Practice (CoPs) to promote innovation among professional constituencies (Stuart 1993). As result of this interest for peer-collaboration among organizations, a theory of CoPs has proliferated during the last 25 years, with Wenger et al. (Wenger 2004; Wenger et al. 2002; Wenger and Snyder 2000) as main proponents. CoPs have been described as "...groups of people who share a concern, a set of problems, or a passion about a topic, and who deepen their knowledge and expertise in this area by interacting on an ongoing basis" (Wenger et al. 2002, p. 4).

In the contemporary theory of CoP, the nature of collaboration has been described as one of spontaneous evolution in which any member of a CoP can aspire to champion knowledge initiatives and leadership does not belong to specific members (Cargill 2006). However, a number of recent CoP studies (Cheng and Lee 2014; Lee et al. 2014; Mabery et al. 2013) have increasingly identified leadership expressions as mediating influence in the success of peer collaboration. Transformational leadership paradigms, for example, facilitate the dispersion of ideas and peer collaboration among multiple constituencies with the assistance of technological platforms (e.g. Wikipedia, YouTube) (Bass and Riggio 2010). Behaviors such as idealized influence, intellectual stimulation, individualized consideration, and inspirational motivation manifest and influence the way CoP members produce, steward, and disseminate knowledge. Emergent theory of CoPs has documented how diverse business sectors, such as the European traveling industry, have implemented planned leadership efforts to assist practitioners in achieving high performance (Akkerman et al. 2008). Cargill (2006) emphasized that leadership is a mediating factor in the performance of CoPs through negotiation, informal agreements, and followership.

Leadership expressions will influence how groups of practitioners develop common values, commitment, and loyalty, all of which improve group performance (Hulpia et al. 2009). Shared practice, for example, can be inspired by the intensity of leadership expressions (Schroeder 2010). Managers who understand these leadership expressions could facilitate working environments for creative thinking. Leadership is a mediating influence that affects the manifestation of CoP dimensions (e.g. community, practice, and domain) at the diverse stages of the community lifecycles. Theoretically, studies have demonstrated that expert and referent leadership are salient characteristics of practitioners as they translate themselves from the periphery to the core championship of a CoP (Maistry 2008). Moreover, leadership influence over knowledge creation has been evidenced since the seventeenth century through the work of scientific communities.

13.2 Literature and Theory

13.2.1 Predecessors of the CoP

Inspired by the origins of the Royal Society of London in the seventeenth century, Price and Beaver (1966) named invisible colleges to the concept of networks of peers interchanging knowledge to solve scientific dilemmas. In his book, Little Science, Big Science, Price published the results of his work with scientists collaborating in projects while located in different geographies, demonstrating that practitioners with similar interests can increment their expert and cognitive abilities through collaboration, promoting simultaneously industry advancement. Later, Crane (1969, 1971) expanded Price's theory, with the publication of the book *Invisible Colleges: Diffusion of Knowledge in Scientific Communities*. According to Crane, invisible college members are often expert volunteers who join efforts to solve industry problems, create new production paradigms, and identify operational anomalies. Similarly to Wenger's et al. (2002) CoP concept, invisible colleges exhibit central and peripheral structures, social groups, and shared leadership networks.

Adler and Haas (1992) theorized during the 1980s on the concept of *epistemic communities* that were seen as groups of subject matter experts who share practices, working methods, and knowledge to solve common industry problems. Members of epistemic communities try to validate knowledge through the empiric application of science within diverse fields and industries, motivated by the goal of finding reliable practices to replicate, standardize, and disseminate knowledge to a bigger community of practitioners. As they participate in activities for collective creation of working methods, not only do they expand their levels of expertise, but they also can provoke disruptive technologies and radical change. The work of epistemic communities has been documented as fundamental in influencing worldwide efforts to protect the ozone layer and enact global regulation toward cleaner air (Adler and Haas 1992). Both epistemic communities and CoPs validate knowledge by transferring its applicability to diverse working circumstances, establishing the boundaries of legitimate knowledge, and defining rules for best practice (Kinsella and Whiteford 2009).

As the theory of epistemic communities proliferated, Senge (1993) used the term *learning communities* to describe the interaction of groups of scholars at the Massachusetts Institute of Technology (MIT) during the explosion of the total quality management movement in the 1990s. During this time, Japanese philosophies on how to convert occupational expertise into explicit knowledge through collaborative learning were already known globally (Nonaka et al. 2001). Simultaneously, organizations in the United States launched diverse initiatives to transform the work of traditional teams into cohesive and innovative communities of practitioners Senge (1993). Senge suggested that learning communities would be a contemporary platform from which to create new professional paradigms, provoke changes, and promote creative inquiry. Theory of learning communities does not differentiate highly educated experts from occupational groups, placing both scientists and rural midwives into the same category of knowledge creators. In both learning communities and CoPs, the origination of knowledge emerges from interconnected associations, social networks, and relationships between like-minded individuals (Wenger et al. 2002). Contemporary leadership scholars (Scharmer 2007) associated these collaborative behaviors to leadership forces capable to promote change.

13.2.2 Contemporary CoP Theory

The term "Community of Practice" was introduced by Lave and Wenger (1991) as part of a study of how social collaboration produced situated learning within labor settings. *Situatedness* was the term used by Lave and Wenger to describe these collaborative interactions; a term that acquired industrial relevance during the late 1990s and early 2000s, and which referred to a process of collective interpretation of knowledge, meaning, and practice through the incorporation of cultural backgrounds, worker's characteristics, and circumstances (Rohlfing et al. 2003). Most often, situatedness emerges when practitioners share pre-existing knowledge of industry jargon and working methods (Goel et al. 2011). As a result of the dynamics of situatedness, workers develop professional identity, apprenticeship networks, and a common discourse.

Although Orr (1996) and Brown and Duguid (1998) also published seminal work explaining the dynamics of CoPs, it was (Wenger et al. 2002) who globally popularized the CoP concept. Wenger used Orr's work during the 1980s with Xerox technicians to explain how practitioners in an occupational community (i.e. gremial community) develop cohesiveness and sense of common purpose when trying to solve common problems. Moreover, occupational groups will establish their own rules and rebel toward organizational authority when they see the integrity of their practice compromised. Orr (1996) coined the term "non-canonical" to define the unofficial leaning that emerges from informal practices that lead to spontaneous problem-solving, and which are not always incorporated to the formal organizational body of knowledge. While official (e.g. canonical) knowledge is the practice related to prescriptive guidance that serves as roadmap for practice execution, Orr (1996) suggested that most of the important practices in organizations happen at an unofficial level of knowledge.

Organizational behaviorists (Lee et al. 2014) suggested that leadership strategies, such as rewards can promote spontaneous collaboration within teams, committees, and ad hoc groups, However, Wenger et al. (2002) differentiated CoPs from other organizational cohorts because the spirit of the community is committed primarily to institute reliable and effective practice regardless organizational objectives. The CoP structure is not delimited by organizational procedures or mechanistic working methods. Members of the CoP will evolve their occupational practice progressively as they engage in occupational inquiry and dialogue, trial-error activities, and dissemination of knowledge. Although organizations try to legitimize the role of CoPs through mechanisms for resource allocation, this legitimization endangers the community's identity. As practitioners experience these changes in policies and jurisdiction, they become more mechanistic and lose the ability to experiment with new practices.

Through the observation of groups of practitioners from different geographies and cultures, such Alcoholic Anonymous, Mexican midwifes from Yucatan, and the United States Navy.

Wenger et al. (2002) defined a contemporary CoP social structure based on the dimensions of community, domain, and practice. Taken together, these three factors represent a series of dynamic interpretations, behaviors, and manifestations that serve as foundation for knowledge creation among groups of practitioners seeking for deepening subject matter content. The need for sharing information to solve common problems among groups of individuals create a social fabric in which they self-organize to use this information. As groups mature, they can constructively develop information-sharing networks and ways to steward and disseminate knowledge (Contu and Willmott 2003).

CoP members have also demonstrated to abide by the Pareto laws (Hardy 2010) that seem to govern numerous organizational systems. Approximately 20 % of its membership seems to drive the activity of the community by sustaining continual epistemic dialogue whereas 80 % remain at the "periphery" (Wenger et al. 2002). Contemporary CoP theory named "champions" to members *driving* community, and placed them at the center of the CoP traditional structure (see Fig. 13.1). A direct relationship seems to exist between level of expertise and positioning from the periphery to the center of the CoP. This means, as the level of expertise of the practitioner increases, so does the motivation and initiative to contribute to the community. Wenger et al. (2002) identified as *legitimate peripheral participation* the relationships between experts, a phenomenon that happens through the sharing professional identify, stories, and artifacts of production.

Champions (e.g. sponsors, facilitators) are passionate volunteers who originate CoPs by facilitating knowledge, guidance, legitimacy, and visibility (Wenger 2004). Champions exercise leadership behaviors with direct influence on social activity (Venters and Wood 2007), group performance (Wright 2007), quality outcomes (Akkerman et al. 2008), and successful learning (Bishop et al. 2008).

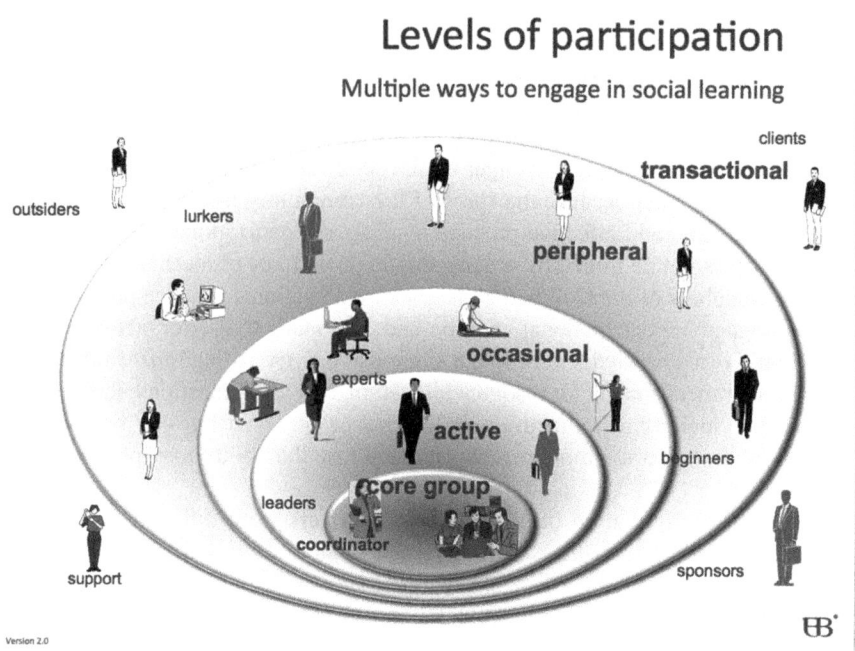

Fig. 13.1 Degrees of community participation *Source* Wenger-Trayner and Wenger-Trayner (2015) Used with permission

Within a CoP, champions promote activities of socialization and knowledge sharing that result in professional identity and common practice. The second layer of CoP participants are those known as core or active participants (Wenger et al. 2002). Core participants demonstrate fluctuations in the intensity of their participation and engage in CoP activities that respond to their individual interests. At the periphery, the rest of the members engage in limited activity in what seems to be common social ranks among CoPs (Corso et al. 2009; Guldberg and Mackness 2009). Wenger et al. (2002) identified this CoP social phenomenon as the 10-15 % rule (e.g. 80/20). CoPs social structures demonstrate a small number of champions or facilitators initiating reflective collaboration and knowledge projects in comparison with a larger group of members who remain as passive participants or recipients of a body of knowledge in a specific subject matter field.

CoPs' structures vary, ranging from voluntary informal networks to globally dispersed learning communities (Li et al. 2009). Professional CoPs usually do not develop mechanisms and protocols. CoPs are not formal departments, operational teams, or business units. Members enlist to participate in CoPs based on their passion for a topic or mutual expertise despite the fact that these structures share common characteristics. CoP membership evolves spontaneously (e.g. organically) as long as members find value in their common interest. Some organizations take intentional steps to legitimize and support CoPs, which results in the *institutionalization* of communities forced to defend their jurisdictions and group identity (Ferlie et al. 2005).

Institutionalization (Wenger et al. 2002) happens because organizations try to align their objectives to the goals of groups of practitioners. The process of institutionalization is a delicate process, structurally and culturally, because it forces the introduction of formal guidelines trying to legitimize CoPs as custodians of knowledge within informal socialization dynamics. Wenger et al. (2002) explained that professional organizations should promote only guidelines that elicit genuine passion for knowledge-sharing activities, enabling CoPs to safeguard knowledge for both individual and organizational benefits. The organic, informal, and spontaneous characteristics of CoPs challenge organizations that want to nurture knowledge communities because these are resistant to supervision and managerial intervention.

However, Wenger et al. (2002) emphasized that CoPs in specific contexts could benefit from institutionalization, especially if they receive support in the areas of administration (Siebert et al. 2009) and information systems (Moreno 2001). The use of information systems to facilitate virtual communication among dispersed professional groups is a common practice in the world of CoPs. CoPs benefit from the advantages of Internet, social network, and virtual forums to develop technical jargon, exchange roles, and communicate. Technologies facilitate that participants in CoPs develop a mutual vocabulary and shared meaning (Hawk et al. 2009). Not only do technologies promote knowledge sharing, they also facilitate knowledge stewardship and knowledge dissemination (Abdullah et al. 2005).

Finally, degrees of formalization (e.g. lifecycle stage) and leadership dynamics are research constructs to consider as the theory of CoP evolves. Professional CoPs today manifest different degrees of formalization and leadership expressions related to their role and purpose within professional organizations. In this context, CoPs develop different degrees of formalization that influence social structures and leadership roles among participants. Appropriateness of social systems and leadership dynamics shape the conditions for individuals' creativity with direct influence on collective innovation (Sahin et al. 2009) and knowledge diffusion.

13.2.3 Community, Practice, and Domain

Wenger et al. (2002) theorized that all activities inside a CoP happen under the frames of community (social activities), practice (send of common purpose), and domain (expertise and knowledge). Community (social activities) is the CoP dimension that defines the activities practitioners execute on a regular basis. Wenger and Snyder (2000) suggested that community activities provides members with quality of *closeness centrality* or the stretching of links and relationships to evolve from a simple network of field experts to a mature CoP with common purpose. According to Wenger et al. (2002), as the social fabric in which experts collaborate expands, the dimension of community assists in intensifying cohesion.

The community dimension reflects a type of *legitimization* of the CoP through knowledge outputs inside the community or co-creations with members from other communities of practitioners.

The expansion of knowledge also relates to the social activity (community) that Wenger et al. (2002) defined as *peripheral participation*. This means that each CoP possesses at its center a group of champions or core participants who voluntarily take responsibility for the work of the community, with peripheral groups that participate sporadically in the creation of knowledge and become often "consumers" of knowledge. However, at the center of the CoP, leadership roles are shared as the community practitioners consider all members as "peers." Members of a CoP can move from the center of the CoP to the periphery at any time.

Simultaneously, Wenger et al. (2002) described practice as the articulation of a common purpose among practitioners to produce and disseminate knowledge through time. The dimension of practice allows CoP members sustaining cohesion while members are continually engaged in adding value to the field by creating methods to share both explicit and implicit knowledge (Nonaka et al. 2001). Within the practice dimension, communities of practitioners create joint enterprise, working methods, artifacts, stories, and practices that contribute to the growth and maturity of the CoP. As the CoP matures, members are able to articulate a body of knowledge distinctive of a working culture. This body of knowledge can increase in sophistication as the members of a CoP steward knowledge through time. Wenger et al. (2002) described that CoPs possess developmental stages that are similar to the classic theory of organizational life cycle (Smith et al. 1985).

Finally, Wenger et al. (2002) defined domain (knowledge) as the representation of the expertise among the community of practitioners. Examples of domain include industries, fields of expertise, or work specializations. Furthermore, the domain dimension explains how members of communities with similar expert interests combine their epistemic realities through context, knowledge, language, cognition, and experience to produce creative solutions and innovations, capable of promoting socio-technical advantage despite of geographic dispersion (Noriko 2007). In the tradition of occupational or gremial groups, domain represents a shared passion that evolves through mutual accountability for the advancement of a field of expertise (Wenger et al. 2002). In Wenger's vision of the gremial structure, domain is the dimension that corresponds to structural capacities to steward and disseminate knowledge. Dane (2010) argued that domain is also fundamental in developing new knowledge systems, augmenting as well the capabilities of field experts in adopting change. As practitioners develop a body of knowledge, the community evolve throughout life cycle dynamics.

13.2.4 CoP Life Cycle

Like most organizational systems, CoPs demonstrate signs of traditional life-cycle dynamics rooted in the diverse stages of knowledge creation among groups of

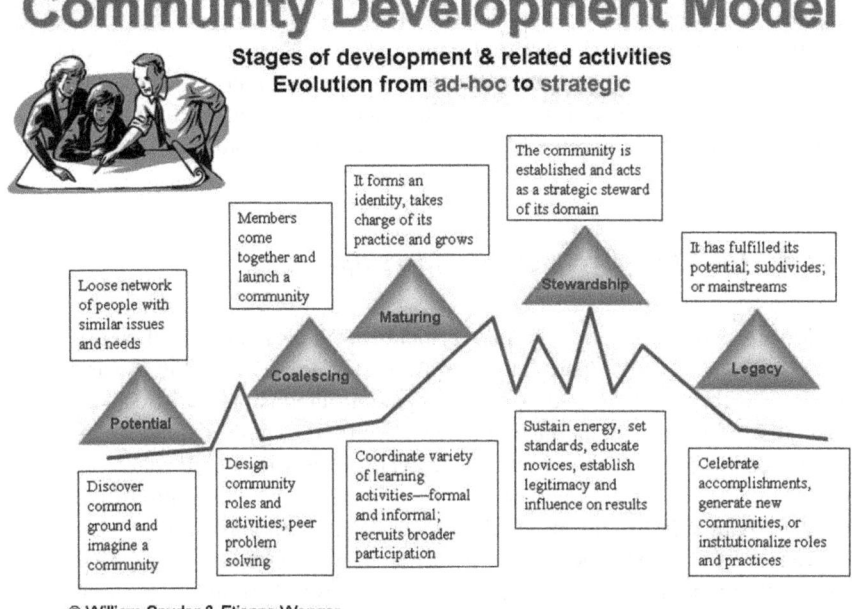

© William Snyder & Etienne Wenger

Fig. 13.2 CoP developmental stages *Source* used with permission from Snyder and Wenger. Accessed from http://knowledgecommunities.org/cops.htm

practitioners. Based on McDermott's studies with geoscientist teams at Shell Oil in the 1990s, Wenger et al. (2002) suggested that CoP members can evolve from loose networks to cohesive gremial cohorts as they go through the phases of potential, coalescing, maturing, stewardship, and transformation (see Fig. 13.2). Members of CoPs show different behaviors in the way they collaborate and communicate in each of the life cycle stages. Wenger et al. (2002) named *developmental stages* to the phases of the CoP life cycle.

Wenger et al. (2002) reported that members of CoPs experience different behaviors in the diverse lifecycle phases in each of the dimensions of community, domain, and practice. Seminal literature systems' life cycles (Smith et al. 1985) identified how networks of professionals can evolve from a lack of formal structure to centralized activities, from informal to formal communication, from personalized to impersonal rewards, and from entrepreneurship to collective bargaining. It is presumed that mature CoPs will show core members dedicating more time to community projects; however, the CoP lifecycle exists regardless of maturity of some of the participants. As CoP have groups of experts continually integrating and emigrating from the community, it is difficult to predict the status of peripheral groups in cases of dissolution. Nevertheless, it is expected that practitioners in CoPs decrease their industry "learning curve" as they stay longer as part of the community of practitioners (Lesser and Storck 2001). Members of CoPs can adopt formal and informal roles during the life of the community. Furthermore, CoP studies have shown these formal and informal roles manifest through leadership expressions during the diverse life cycle stages of the community of practitioners.

13.2.5 CoP Life Cycle and Leadership

Leadership expressions are not only evident, but they manifest differently during the diverse stages of the CoP life cycle. As part of their leadership dynamics, CoP members with peripheral and core participation demonstrated distinctive identity, behaviors, and power relationships (Lawless 2008). These distinctive behavioral and leadership paths at the different life cycles stages of a CoP make possible to predict quality, frequency, and cohesion of interactions and relationships of CoP members (Katja 2009), all of which influence collaboration within the CoP.

Wenger et al. (2002) described the different manifestations that CoP members exhibit throughout the life cycle continuum. Several authors agreed that CoP members experience changes in the focus of their practice, relationships, and cohesion through the evolution of a community or practitioners. From starting to the sustaining of the community, CoP members experience different relationships and dynamics. These include finding like-minded people to form the community and creating stewardship methods to disseminate intellectual interests. In the same way, leadership expressions manifest differently through the evolution of the CoP. Community members can go from loose networks of volunteers to develop an increased dialogue that can lead to new ideas (see Table 13.1).

Leadership scholars such as Bandura et al. (as in Bowen 2010) emphasized how leadership can influence social, adaptive, and generative learning as members of a group develop cohesiveness. A shared passion for knowledge through time can provoke entrepreneurial spirit, which consequently influences the adoption of projects and creation of new industry practices. Although all of these outcomes are supposed to happen within spontaneous collaborative networks, Shin (2011) reported that sometimes 'light-touch' leadership approaches are necessary to aid the CoP in the allocation of support, resources, and training. Moreover, while (Vavasseur and MacGregor 2008) reported that positive leadership increased efficacy among CoP members. On the contrary, CoP members who cannot develop positive leadership networks see their capacity to create knowledge diminished (Venters and Wood 2007). Shared leadership frames are beneficial in redefining the direction and intensity in which knowledge is disseminated among industry practitioners (Schroeder 2010).

Table 13.1 CoP life cycle and membership manifestations (Saldana 2014, p. 47)

Structural element	1 Potential	2 Coalescing	3 Maturing	4 Stewardship
Community	Finding like-minded people	Developing ability for collaborative reflection	Transforming from loose networks to tight networking relationships	Keeping intellectual tone according to community interests
Domain	Eliciting the interests and passion of participants	Establishing the value of knowledge sharing	Defining community roles within organizational contexts	Maintaining relevance and voicing concerns
Practice	Identifying common knowledge among members	Identifying what knowledge to share	Defining systematically content and identifying knowledge gaps	Practicing innovation and producing knowledge
Leadership	Building of loose networks in which core members volunteer to lead	Developing trust and increased dialogue among members	Initiating projects, sharing vision and community focus	Developing openness toward new ideas and new members

Cargill (2006) emphasized that leadership indeed exists among CoP members, and it is visible through the informal agreements and negotiations that are part of the knowledge creation process. However, it is also true that CoPs operate more effectively with participative leadership, flexibility, and decentralization. The egalitarian nature of the CoP requires that peers perceive themselves under similar conditions of value and domain. Any followership emerges from the interest of the community members to advance industry practice and the mutual admiration of expertise. However, the continual engagement in common practice among cooperative social structures develops loyalty, sense of common purpose, and commitment (Hulpia et al. 2009).

One interesting aspect of in the development of CoP champions is that leadership expressions do not progress sequentially (Wenger et al. 2002). This suggests that any CoP member can move from the periphery to leading activities at the center of the community at any moment, or regress when the interest for a topic decreases or a specific practice is no longer needed. CoP members will accept and regress from leadership roles based on interest, similarity, or level of experience. Other leadership traits, such as initiative and motivation, are also factors that influence the presence of leadership expressions. These leadership fluctuations have demonstrated to be a mediating influence in the ability of CoPs to produce innovative solutions (Cargill 2006).

13.3 Mediating Role of Leadership

Recent CoP research studies have acknowledged the mediating role of leadership as a critical factor in the success of subject matter development among groups of practitioners from different disciplines. Table 13.2 illustrates a list of research studies by area of expertise.

Research studies such as Retna and Ng (2011) reported that members from technology CoPs in Singapore developed individualized motivation under the influence of industry domain leadership and community culture in which guided facilitation and distributed leadership contributed to successful knowledge outcomes. Furthermore, longitudinal case studies in multinational companies (Borzillo et al. 2012) found that strong collaboration networks between leaders of the CoP exist as a factor for success across diverse industry fields. Earlier, Weaver et al. (2009) researched power influence behaviors exhibited by CoP members, reporting supportive profiles of power, leadership influence, and reference and expert power.

Table 13.2 Research addressing the mediating role of leadership over CoPs (2001–2011)

Discipline	Studies
Agriculture	O'Kane et al. (2008)
Banking	Moreno (2001)
Construction	Bishop et al. (2008)
Consulting firms	Anand et al. (2007), Hayes and Fitzgerald (2009), Kasper et al. (2008), Shin (2011), Tomcsik (2010)
Creative industries/arts/culture	Dabback (2010)
Disaster management	Goldstein and Butler (2010)
Education	Ash et al. (2009), Blanton and Stylianou (2009), Buckley and Du Toit (2009), Carey et al. (2009), Clark (2010), Creech et al. (2009), De Palma and Teague (2008), Guldberg and Mackness (2009), Hew and Hara (2007), Hodgkinson et al. (2008), Kisiel (2010), Linehan (2010), Luebke et al. (2008), Price (2005), Rivern and Stacey (2007), Steele (2011), Vavasseur and MacGregor (2008), Vega and Quijano (2010), Velez (2011), Weaver et al. (2009), Wright (2007)
Healthcare	Bowen (2010)
Hospitality	Akkerman et al. (2008)
Insurance	Hemmasi and Csanda (2009)
Management	Borzillo (2009), Li (2010)
Military	Adkins et al. (2010)
Politics	Venters and Wood (2007)
Real state	McElyea (2011)
Technology	Bach and Carroll (2010), Bechky (2003), Chang et al. (2009), Hansten et al. (2005), Lee and Cole (2003), Teng (2011), Thompson (2005), Yang and Wei (2010)
Volunteer organizations	Iverson and McPhee (2008)

Power relationships observed among CoP members influenced epistemic values, collective sense making, and communication frequency.

Weaver et al. (2009) studied how informal leadership positions within CoPs influenced communication among academic peer groups in understanding core issues and achieving group goals through the frame of Janusian leadership. Leaders with Janusian capabilities are able to reflect on situations from contrasting viewpoints, place themselves on diverse mindsets, learn from leadership lessons, and apply those lessons in the future. Leadership scholars (Kouzes and Posner 2000) identified Janusian qualities as necessary to engage leadership as continual process for growth and development, and not as a destination, position, or role. Leaders who continually develop their abilities, and subsequently help develop others around them are characteristic of high-performance organizations. Janusian leaders are motivated by collective goals, do not need to be appointed officially to take responsibility over projects, and are able to see the perspective of macro-scenarios. As result, they are able to establish epistemic dialogue across different organizational networks and do not mind engaging in tasks that could be considered menial by others if this ensures achieving the overall goals of the organization.

In contrast, Wartburg and Teihert (2006) identified the transformational leadership model as the most suitable paradigm for the work that the CoP performs because practitioners who volunteer to advance industry practice are inspired by the attributes of transformational leaders. Although political scientist James Downtown used the term 'transformational leader' for the first time in 1973, James MacGregor developed a transformational leadership theory (Burns and Avolio 2004) that changed organizational landscape during the 1980s and 1990s. MacGregor presented the transformational paradigm as a more effective approach than the classic transactional leadership approach in which the leader "transacts" with followers to accomplish goals. On the contrary, transformational leaders inspire subordinates to accomplish the goals because they (the leaders) exhibit highest moral standards, character, and integrity.

13.3.1 Leadership Theories Related to CoPs

From the existing leadership theories, the transformational paradigm seems to be most appropriate relevant to the dynamics of a community of practitioners. During the 1980s, Bass contributed to the transformational leadership paradigm by solidifying a taxonomy of behaviors and behavioral dimensions related to transformational leadership. Transformational leaders demonstrate characteristics such as idealized influence, inspirational motivation, intellectual stimulation, and individualized consideration (Bass and Riggio 2010). Peers who exhibit these characteristics are often more successful in motivating individuals to perform at higher levels of productivity and innovation. Transformational expressions are recognized for instilling enthusiasm, promoting constructive criticism, and producing new solutions.

Dionne et al. (2004) reviewed the transformational leadership paradigm and its effects among groups of practitioners from the four perspectives of idealized influence, inspirational motivation, intellectual stimulation, and individualized consideration. The authors found that each of the four dimensions influenced performance executions among groups of practitioners. For example, idealized influence and inspirational motivation were both associated to the development of cohesion, as observed among collaborators in financial institutions and information technology firms. Cohesion also emerged from sharing a common vision. Transformational leaders are often now for the articulation of collective through power vision, or the ability that groups and individuals have to envision and work in plans to make possible a collective future (Kopeikina 2005). By engaging in visionary conversations about how this future should look for the community of practitioners, CoP members can establish a solid ground for the improvement of industry practices.

Intellectual stimulation influenced the creative capacities of CoP members through the exhibition of rationality, problem-solving engagement, and questioning of current protocols and working methods. Dionne et al. (2004) associated intellectual stimulation to the forces of functional conflict in which oppositional viewpoints (especially task-oriented conflicts) are confronted, discussed, and negotiated through renovated industry practice. The confrontation of different perspectives encourages non-traditional thinking and suggests new ways of performing tasks. Moreover, CoP members experienced individualized consideration through mentoring, coaching, and supporting apprenticeship within the group of practitioners. Not only did individualized consideration assist CoP members in developing industry skills, it also assisted in moving members from the periphery to the championship core of the CoP. CoP members who exercise individualized consideration often listen attentively to others while helping them to develop their professional abilities.

Transformational leadership, in all its dimensions and expressions, can be mapped to the work and practice creation of CoP memberships. Although CoPs are self-organized networks of individuals in which leadership positions are not formally appointed, many studies have demonstrated that leadership expressions, especially those associated to transformational paradigms, are able to influence CoP outcomes (Saldana 2014). Moreover, the deliberate introduction of leadership stimuli has been shown to promote effective performance among CoPs from multiple industries (Akkerman et al. 2008). In general, CoP members with positive leadership environments are able to develop better communication and cohesiveness, and long-term relationships that exist even after a CoP has been dissolved (Zboralski et al. 2006). Leadership is a mediating influence that should be embedded to the contemporary CoP model (see Fig. 13.3).

Adkins et al. (2010) reported that the success for knowledge sharing in CoPs depends on the role of informal leaders acting as champions, mentors, and facilitators, who sustain pace and frequency of interactions because they consider themselves the *owners* of the body of knowledge. Although formal mechanisms do not exist among CoPs to regulate leadership, emerging literature demonstrates that

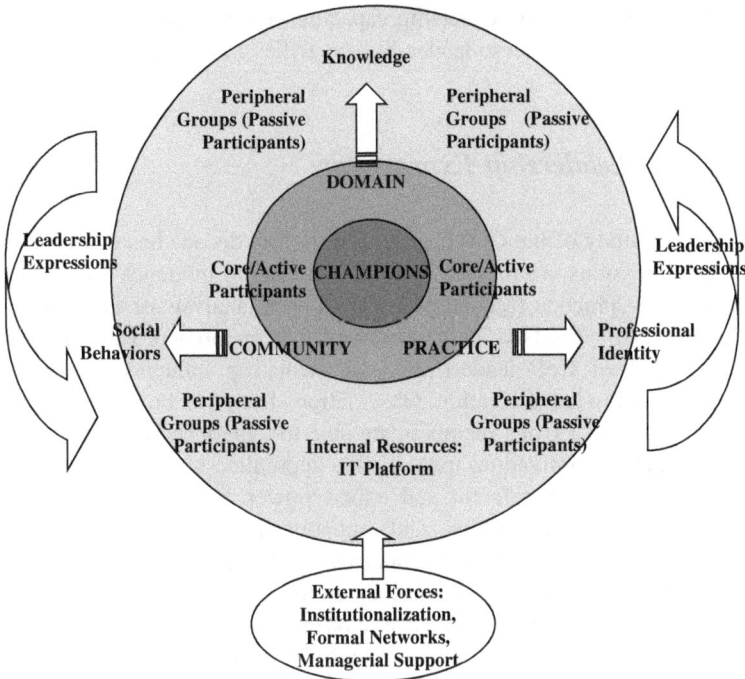

Fig. 13.3   Contemporary CoP model (Saldana 2012, 2014)

CoP members in key positions are fundamental to accomplish the goals of the community of practitioners. Not only do informal leaders serve as gatekeepers of knowledge, they communicate a vision, inspire by role modeling, and promote higher levels of trust (Bach and Carroll 2010).

A recent study (Saldana 2014) demonstrated that leadership is perceived as mediating factor in how CoPs produce knowledge and that this influence increases as the community becomes older. Members in mature CoPs are able to identify "quality leadership" role models and trust a process for which they feel compelled to share ideas and suggest new practice methods. The same study suggested that the transformational leadership paradigm seems to be leadership model best associated CoP activities, as it relates to knowledge creation and innovation (Wartburg and Teihert 2006). It might be suggested that CoP champions would be able to increase their capacities to lead innovation projects by integrating transformational behaviors to their repertoire of community skills. Furthermore, CoP memberships must integrate leadership support to advance common practice without becoming institutionalized to produce innovation (Zboralski et al. 2006). CoP members with transformational leadership capacities are able to influence how practitioners produce knowledge but organizations cannot force these conditions over innovation that happens spontaneously. Some studies (Saldana 2012; Saldana 2014) have attempted to identify which leadership capacities are present in the work of CoPs, and how much influence these leadership capacities have over group innovation.

13.3.2 CoP Leadership Expressions

The systematic study of the CoP literature of the last decade has demonstrated that leadership expressions are present both as a mediating influence and as outcomes from community practice (see Table 13.3). A meta-analysis of the CoP literature from 2000 to 2014 (Saldana 2014) observed that researchers from many nations have acknowledged CoP leadership as a mediating influence for both social interaction and knowledge creation. Observations from this body of literature have also demonstrated that CoPs members are able to experience and enact leadership expressions such as motivation, trust, visible apprenticeship, embedded leadership roles, shared leadership, referent and expert power, recognition, empowerment, self-efficacy, dyadic relationships, and empathy. The literature review analyzed research studies from more than 20 countries in 10 different industries.

Leadership is a mediating influence in the development of CoP memberships because power relationships influence closeness centrality, or the amount of interactions and engagement among members at the core of the community (Ranmuthugala et al. 2011). This mediating influence of leadership permeates the three dimensions of the CoP (i.e. community, domain, and practice). For example, in the community dimension, by mediating reflective collaboration, CoP leaders contribute to the careful and persistent consideration of practice and knowledge in

Table 13.3 Research observed leadership expressions from 2000 to 2014 (Saldana 2014)

Expressions	Frequency	Percentage (%)	Cumulative percentage (%)
Dyadic relationships	1	0.8	0.8
Empathy	2	1.6	2.4
Empowerment	5	4.1	6.5
Facilitation of activities	16	13.0	19.5
Leadership influenced socialization	20	16.3	35.8
Leadership influenced performance	23	18.7	54.5
Mentoring	8	6.5	61.0
Motivation	13	10.6	71.5
Power profiles	4	3.3	74.8
Rewarded expertise	7	5.7	80.5
Shared leadership	12	9.8	90.2
Trust	12	9.8	100.0
Total	123	100.0	

an area of expertise (Tal and Morag 2009). Embedded leadership behaviors facilitate knowledge transference and apprenticeship among music CoP memberships despite a vast diversity of levels of experience (Dabback 2010). It is at the community level that members of a CoP remove barriers to accept and legitimize knowledge. Individualized consideration is the transformational leadership behavior that empowers members of the community to enact socialized agency that generates mechanisms for innovation (Dionne et al. 2004).

The leadership literature also confirms that leadership can ignite sense of common purpose in the practice domain. Transformational leadership expressions, such as idealized influence and inspirational motivation not only explain the level of cohesiveness that a community of practitioners exhibit during critical moments, but also its subsequent vision to change systems and processes that are no longer effective, thus provoking paradigm shifts, new knowledge and changes in practice. For example, Fominaya (2010) emphasized that a sense of common purpose is necessary not only to reunite practitioners, but also to sustain innovation over time. Leadership factors that contribute to this sense of common purpose include shared direction, reciprocity, commitment, and solidarity (Fominaya 2010). More recently, Ready and Truelove (2011) reported that a sense of common of purpose also ensures the survival of communities during crises because members are able to sustain positivism during uncertain events. Although a sense of common purpose is identified as a sign of mature CoPs (evidence suggests that common purpose grows over time), Saldana's (2014) research suggested that common purposes could flourish among members during different stages of the community life cycles (i.e. inception, maturity, and stewardship). Nevertheless, it is accepted that homogeneous memberships with strong sense of common purpose are able to develop cohesive networking links through time.

Other leadership expressions, such as mutual (i.e. dyadic) relationships, unconditional trust, and motivation are evident at the practice and domain dimensions of a CoP and align with theories of prosocial contexts (Penner et al. 2005). Prosocial theory explains the tendency among members of a community to unify efforts (e.g. cooperative volunteering) when a crisis arises or when a new problem needs immediate attention. This phenomenon is observable during national emergencies or natural disasters (e.g. 9–11 terrorist attacks, Hurricane Katrina) when practitioners within a profession or domain manifest collaboration with more prominence than in usual circumstances, identifying creative solutions to the challenges at hand. Dane (2010) defined as *cognitive entrenchment* the ability of CoP members to develop new mental schemes that lead to creativity during critical moments.

In the domain dimension, leadership expressions also influence the motivation that members of a CoP exhibit to increase their expertise or their desire to solve industry problems. For example, intellectual stimulation is the transformational leadership behavior that encourages creativity, promotes constructive criticism to produce new solutions, and allows group members to develop their highest potential by empowering individual and distinctive skills. Therefore, leadership associates with innovation or the capacity to create roadmaps toward leading edge practices and processes. Anand et al. (2007) reported that CoP members are challenged to produce innovation, confronting obstacles such as capacity to attract expert members, access to communication platforms to share knowledge, and the creation of social processes and routines to promote innovation. However, reuniting members with high levels of expertise is not enough to promote innovation. Leadership expressions such as mentoring and coaching play a fundamental role in the development of CoP structures and knowledge sharing networks ability to solve industry problems creatively. Among professional communities, innovation is often the result of the imitation of champions who initiate effective actions, later replicated by followers as novel practice. Wenger et al. (2002) identified mentoring dynamics as capable of promoting sustainability and distributing workload burden among CoP memberships.

13.3.3 Emotional Intelligence as Leadership Expression

Emotional intelligence is an attribute of leadership vastly explored during the 1990s, when business organizations decided to implement emotional intelligence as a framework for work competencies which caused fast proliferation of emotional intelligence books, articles, and guidelines (Vaida and Opre 2014). Emotional intelligence has been associated with the ability of individuals to exhibit within occupational settings to collaborate. Furthermore, Mayer et al. (2001) proposed the emotional intelligence as the set of skills necessary to adapt successfully to uncertainty and change. According to this framework, emotional intelligence increases as individuals mature. Emotions happen most often in the context or relationships, and empirical research has demonstrated that relationships have universal character.

Goleman (1995) re-defined the framework of emotional intelligence competencies as empathy, motivation, self-awareness, self-regulation, and social adaptability. Brundrett et al. (2006) emphasized that common emotions among CoP members influence community behaviors and leadership identity, especially among members from different backgrounds. Emotional intelligence also equips CoP members with refined knowledge awareness. Mayer et al. (2001) emotional intelligence frame proposed that emotional competence resided in the individual ability to identify the significance of emotions, emotions within relationships, and use of emotions for decision-making. As emotions and intellect overlap in the learning experience, enhanced control of emotions will enhance, in turn, cognitive abilities.

Mayer et al. (2001) divided emotional intelligence into four main areas (also called 'branches': (a) perception of emotions, (b) utilization of emotions, (c) understanding of emotions, and (d) managing emotions. These four emotional intelligence areas interact to facilitate reasoning and managing of emotions, which simultaneously facilitate both social relationships and personal growth. Mentoring behaviors characteristic of emotional behavior include, for example, willingness to help others, understanding how helping others can help to develop self-esteem, understanding the fluctuations and escalation/de-escalation of emotions, remembering past emotions or emotional moments, and perceiving and identifying emotions in others. All of these have behaviors have been identified as the contributions of emotional intelligence theory to the practice of leadership.

13.3.4 Teamwork, Leadership from the Inside Out, and Theory U as CoP Leadership Expressions

The special nature of the CoP promotes environments in which relationships among members transcend the boundaries of contemporary teamwork. When groups of practitioners meet to solve industry issues in CoPs, their passion and reflective collaboration can progress them from a state of "not-yet-embodied" knowledge to a state of knowledge creation in which a deeper learning process emerges between participants (Wenger et al. 2002). Contemporary leadership paradigms, such as leadership from the inside out (Cashman 1998) and Theory U (Scharmer 2007) suggested that unconventional connections through intuition and awareness between individuals could increase cognition and critical thinking, or the "crystallizing" of a new mental states.

In analyzing innovations, Scharmer (2007) emphasized that the process of innovation is a discovery journey in which a professional community goes from familiar to unfamiliar knowledge. The Theory U of leadership analyzes a level of deep connection achievable by individuals, from which new values emerge. CoP structures facilitate this type of cognitive connection in which interconnected associations increase self-awareness that improves professional practice. Scharmer (2007) named *Landscape of Listening Model* to a seven-state inquiry process (see Fig. 13.4) that resembles the CoP process of knowledge creation.

Scharmer's Theory U (2007) presented a curvilinear form in U shape representing a deeper capacity of active listening through seven core capabilities (i.e. suspending, redirecting, letting go, letting come, crystallizing, prototyping, and institutionalizing). This leadership framework will follow a seven stage inquiry process using typical consumers as sample, as follows:

1. Receiving the story (i.e. suspending), in which community members stop their usual ways of perceiving and thinking to listen to the customers without biases.
2. Evaluating customer's relational experience (i.e. redirecting), in which team members direct their attention to the inner desires of customers.
3. Breaking mental models (i.e. letting go), in which team members are completely open to the customers' emerging desires and needs.
4. Receiving new mental models, in which team members reject their desire for controlling the situation and start a new experience with the customers.
5. Identifying the sources for change (i.e. crystallizing), in which team members should be able to crystallize their attention to the larger scenario, translating the customers' mental models in intuitions to guide strategic action.

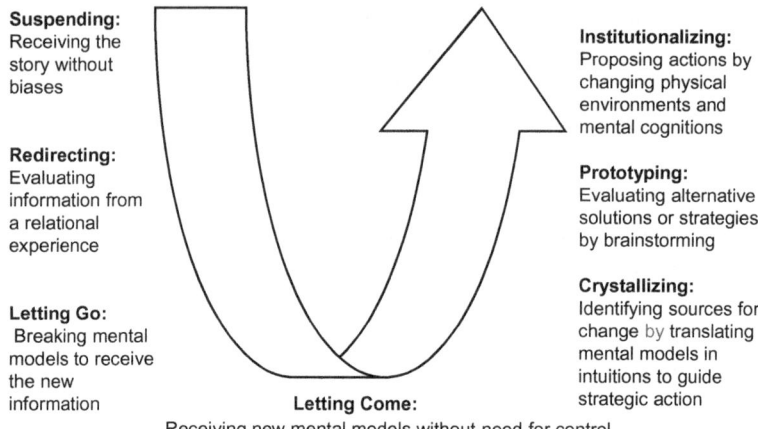

Suspending:
Receiving the story without biases

Redirecting:
Evaluating information from a relational experience

Letting Go:
Breaking mental models to receive the new information

Letting Come:
Receiving new mental models without need for control

Institutionalizing:
Proposing actions by changing physical environments and mental cognitions

Prototyping:
Evaluating alternative solutions or strategies by brainstorming

Crystallizing:
Identifying sources for change by translating mental models in intuitions to guide strategic action

Fig. 13.4 Landscape of Listening for Leadership (Based on Scharmer 2007; Printed with permission of the publisher from "Theory U: Leading from the future as it emerges", copyright©2007 by C. O. Scharmer, Berrett-Koehler Publishers, Inc., San Francisco, CA. All rights reserved. www.bkconnection.com

6. Evaluating alternative solutions or strategies (i.e. prototyping), in which team members assist customers to engage in brainstorming to generate improvements, ideas for new services, and a roadmap for excellent customer service.
7. Proposing actions (i.e. institutionalizing), in which team members make reality enduring changes associated to both customers' physical environments and mental cognitions.

Scharmer (2007) reported that most individuals can exercise a Theory U landscape of listening by a process of awakening. Furthermore, Theory U is a model based on the application of personal experience and self-awareness. As a paradigm to promote change, Theory U interjects with existing leadership theories about personality, emotions, idealized influence, inspirational motivation, intellectual stimulation, and individualized consideration (Antonakis and House 2008).

13.3.5   Significance of Leadership Expressions

Scholars agreed that new leadership models are necessary to find solutions to problems that evolve over time. Incipient leadership models suggest that optimal solutions emerge from the reflective collaboration of a group rather than single individuals. Organizations with supporting leadership structures could enable successful CoPs without interrupting their natural flow of knowledge sharing and creation. Mature CoPs create a repository of knowledge that helps harmonize global practices and identify best practices (Anand et al. 2007). Organizations and professional associations with parallel CoPs benefit from identifying leadership behaviors to ensure long-term sustainability (Saldana 2014).

Furthermore, diverse memberships sharing a common vocabulary of words, symbols, and emotions can feel isolation in the way they engage in leadership practices. Therefore, that exploring community behaviors and leadership challenges associated with innovation and professional identity will increase the advancement and growth of CoPs with memberships from different backgrounds (Brundrett et al. 2006). Organizations can use these leadership expressions to help CoPs to achieve innovation by promoting community behaviors related to knowledge awareness, adoption of knowledge management processes, and knowledge dissemination methods. CoPs can overcome environmental changes that alter the intensity and direction of knowledge creation by establishing strong leadership structures to promote active listening, conscious competence, and authenticity (Cashman 1998). Strong leadership structures reflect community behaviors such as reflective collaboration and spontaneous collaboration and networking.

CoPs produce leadership expressions conducive to innovation during day-to-day operations, and embed later these shared assumptions and knowledge to the organizational structure (Anand et al. 2007). Huang and Murray (2009) narrated how scholars examined the complex dynamics of production and accumulation of knowledge in firms, communities, and regions, finding that knowledge comes first through peer-to-peer socialization and later embeds in public and private spheres. The influenced of leadership over CoP increases that capacity of the community to produce knowledge, a concept clashes with the traditional concept of academia as only originator of fundamental knowledge. Professional CoP are proven structures that promote knowledge sharing, personal development, improved performance, innovation, and the application of best practices (Buckley and Du Toit 2009) without the direct intervention of academic forces.

The proliferation of global economies congregates individuals from different cultural and leadership backgrounds to discover together effective solutions to organizational problems. Global contemporary However, CoP members who operate within a shared leadership frame (West 2009) are able to be more effective during collective problem-solving. On the contrary, CoP memberships that perceive hierarchical differences can experience decreased participation and increased resistance to change (Bach and Carroll 2010). Community behaviors related to professional identity could support the development of working environments in which multiple voices find a common ground for shared leadership.

CoPs tend to develop better in conditions of flexibility, decentralization, and participative leadership. CoPs are shared leadership social structures as all members have the ability to expose different viewpoints, self-promote expertise, and build consensus about common industry vision. CoPs' egalitarian character enables flexibility, cross training, and job rotation within working environments. Cooperative social structures demonstrated direct influence over the development of commitment, common values, and loyalty (Hulpia et al. 2009). Effective programs for quality performance incorporate engaged leadership strategies. Schroeder (2010) reported the benefits of shared leadership in redefining changes of knowledge direction and intensity. Managers in charge of organizations sponsoring CoPs can learn to facilitate conditions for leadership networks capable to produce new industry solutions.

13.4 Managerial Implications

Organizations and professional associations around the world are promoting CoPs as strategy to induce innovation (Saldana 2014). Professional peers collaborating within collegial or community structures such as CoPs develop divergent thinking or the capability of breaking thinking patterns that originate novel solutions to existing problems (West 2009). Worldwide, organizations have been exploiting opportunities that come from communities of practitioners when they share a common body of knowledge and think creatively. Within these organizations, CoPs have shown to be useful in driving strategy, generating new businesses, generating problem-solving tools, disseminating best practices, and building expertise (Wenger et al. 2002).

Thompson (2005) summarized that CoPs adopt definable epistemological positions to achieve a "unique virtuous circle of increased participation, identification, learning, prominence within the group, and motivation" (p. 152). The shared passion of CoP members for topics that they can discuss empathetically facilitates shared knowledge, identity, and technical culture (Machles et al. 2010). Activities related to domain, community, and practice produce expressions of joint enterprise (including ways of doing things), shared repertoire (e.g. language and tools), collective cognition (Lindkvist 2005), collective innovation (Lee and Cole 2003), archival repositories, and community memory (Marshall et al. 1995). Managers who understand these conditions for industry socialization are able to facilitate leadership engagement that leads to the emergence or "championing" of new knowledge projects.

13.4.1 Recommendations for Organizational Managers to Facilitate CoPs

CoP managers are challenged continually with the issue of institutionalization. The risk of institutionalization increases when CoP managers attempt to intervene to enhance community outcomes and the emergence of champions (Wenger et al. 2002). However, organizations nurturing CoPs have found that these can propitiate opportunities to create and disseminate knowledge, and that innovation increases when memberships engage in collective collaboration. CoP managers must work strategically by ensuring championship of initiatives and technological resources without interrupting the way the CoP evolves. The distinctive voice of the community should be the main driver of ideas. Maintaining the balance between tight and loose-coupled processes is necessary to ensure the CoP domain advances in a way natural to the subject matter field. Loosely coupled structures give participants ample decision-making latitude to interpreting and implementing solutions while developing common sense (Abdullah et al. 2005; Holmström and Boudreau 2006). Simultaneously, tight-coupled processes can support structures for members to learn from their experiences and construct meaning by drawing from previous knowledge. Transformational leadership (i.e. inspirational motivation, idealized influence, intellectual stimulation, and individualized consideration) (Bass and Riggio 2010) seems to inspire and motivate CoP members to suggest new ideas. Nevertheless CoP managers cannot intervene in the way leadership evolves, neither controlling the personality traits of the membership. However, exposing champions to leadership theory could enhance the capacities of those in charge of igniting and sustaining knowledge projects (Saldana 2014).

The use of leadership expressions to motivate stewardship of knowledge is one of the gray areas of CoPs. Not all communities recognize stewardship as part of their activities, and those that cultivate stewardship see this activity to emerge in the maturity stage of CoP evolution (Wenger et al. 2002). CoP managers can help communities in facilitating leaders responsible to maintain repositories of knowledge from which members can draw information to make decisions. Producing knowledge as outcome of a CoP is not enough; CoP champions must be able to store and retrieve knowledge to sustain innovation (Price 2013). Knowledge management processes encompass integrating the totality of knowledge, and anticipating future needs to increase performance and innovation.

13.5 Recommendations for Future Research

The emergent CoP literature possesses a limited number of studies with leadership as the main research construct, despite evidence that effective leadership practices elevate the performance of practitioners in global communities (Lee and Cole 2003). Although, the contemporary theory of leadership (Bass and Riggio 2010) presents with numerous references on peer production, common good, communal values, and collaborative practice, leadership is not formally integrated the existing CoP theory (Wenger et al. 2002). More studies are necessary to understand the true role and influence of leadership over the works of these communities.

CoPs with visible participative leadership expressions are more effective in establishing actionable learning strategies, joint problem solving, multiple learning perspectives, organized activities for learning, and goal-oriented programs (Linehan 2010). Shared leadership enables communities of practitioners to improve motivation of peripheral subgroups and increases membership commitment to community values and loyalty (Hulpia et al. 2009). Moreover, emergent leadership paradigms such as Theory U (Scharmer 2007) relate intrinsically to the way members of a community connect by establishing a negotiation-and-dialogue mechanisms that often result in new institutional infrastructures. Leadership expressions allow professional CoPs to improve the motivation of existing members (Hulpia et al. 2009), learn negotiation-and-dialogue mechanisms (Scharmer 2007), and promote active listening, conscious competence, and authenticity (Cashman 1998). Other studies suggest that leadership is probably a strong influence in generating innovative solutions among professional CoPs.

Furthermore, documented challenges for CoPs to increase cohesiveness and efficiency represent a future area of leadership research. CoPs confront challenges related to multiple discourses (De Palma and Teague 2008), lack of technological support (Hew and Hara 2007), lack of motivation and participation (Linehan 2010), perceived hierarchical differences (Ferlie et al. 2005), cultural distance, and resistance to change (Vavasseur and MacGregor 2008). Contemporary CoPs confront challenges related to the existence of multiple epistemic discourses, or the implicit common language and practice philosophies that conforms the community of practitioners. The absence of a common discourse impairs the CoP's ability to sustain in-depth discussion and collaboration. In contrast, a cohesive discourse among members of a CoP demonstrated to increase collective engagement and created better integration of interrelated disciplines. Organizations promoting CoPs cannot underestimate the role of practice discourse in building an innovative and engaged community of practitioners. Eversole (2012) studied CoP challenges and concluded that additional efforts are needed with relation to, (a) challenging or contradicting assumptions about how to implement expertise, (b) recognizing the influence of individuals who serve as links between CoPs and peripheral communities and organizational forums, and (c) integrating CoPs with other organizations to accelerate progress and innovation. Further theory could be developed by studying these "hidden" CoP elements that act as impairment for the advancement of CoPs from different subject matter fields.

Another important topic to be explored in future research is the mediating influence of technology in supporting leadership efforts for the creation, stewardship, and dissemination of knowledge. Technology has previously been shown to facilitate increased capacity among CoP members to share knowledge within diverse subject matter fields, including education (Hew and Hara 2007), government (Venters and Wood 2007), technology (Lee and Cole 2003), and knowledge management (Griffith and Sawyer 2006). Web-based ideation platforms like GENEX have supported creativity among CoPs by facilitating cutting-edge technologies under four stages of (a) building knowledge upon previous knowledge, (b) facilitating powerful tools to ignite creativity, (c) refinement of social processes, and (d) dissemination of knowledge (Kipp et al. 2010). Nevertheless, Schlager and Fusco (2003) emphasized that building online technology exclusively as mechanism to create and disseminate knowledge is not sufficient to maximize the use of technologies among CoP members. In the meantime, case studies and research continues to prove the impact of technology in supporting both CoP collaboration and innovation (Dixon 2010). Since the origins of the existing CoPs' theory, technology has been an influential force for knowledge production among communities of practitioners, along with leadership, for which the influences of technologies is another CoP research area to explore.

13.6 Conclusions

Groups of practitioners, such as invisible colleges, and learning and epistemic communities are concepts that precede the theory of CoPs. These groups promote institutionalization of good practices and engage in activities to create and disseminate knowledge within industries and communities by sharing a field of expertise, mastering the same profession, and developing similar problem solving methods. Scholars have associated professional learning communities in general to the total quality management movement in Japan (e.g. Toyota), in which companies have been able to exploit the knowledge sharing capabilities of workers and transforming tacit to explicit knowledge. Communities of workers use their experiences, mutual understanding, and intuition to create and document working methods. Cashman (1998) and Scharmer (2007) emphasized how intuition is becoming key strategy in developing contemporary leaders able to innovate despite the challenges of these difficult times.

Wenger et al. (2002) used the concept of situated knowledge and learning exposed by Lave (1991) to guide their observations about groups of practitioners producing and stewarding knowledge. Similar to learning and epistemic communities, Wenger's concept presented how members of field can draw from their own experiences, intuition, and previous knowledge to innovate. They called this structure a CoP and soon other scholars (Brown and Duguid 1998; Orr 1996, as cited in Buderi 1998) elaborated research about how technical groups with similar cultural background, working contexts, and like-minded ideas develop cohesive collaboration methods that result in new working schemas. Members of learning communities often negotiate working methods that promote jargon, case stories, and professional artifacts. Semantics play a key role within the collaboration of like-minded professionals who need a common ground to germinate their ideas, which organizations can exploit to promote innovation (Wenger et al. 2002). Numerous scholars agree that knowledge relates to the epistemic self and proliferates within collaborative environments.

The distribution of groups with different degrees of participation is a distinctive characteristic of learning communities such as CoPs. Members with more passion for an enterprise often configure groups of people championing initiatives whereas members with interest but less passion remain as peripheral participants. It is usual that members with the most level of expertise initiate projects and become engaged for the longest time. However, CoP members in general seem to build sense of common purpose at all participatory levels. Saldana (2014) found that leadership is a mediating influence altering the landscape of contemporary CoPs. This mediating influence was achieved through the existence of dynamics such as embedded leadership roles, mentoring, and shared leadership which produced increased motivation, trust, expert and referent power, empowerment, self-efficacy, dyadic relationships, and empathy. In contrast, the existence of defective leadership dynamics contributed to the demoralization and decreased performance of CoP members.

One of the aims of this chapter has been to introduce leadership as mediating influence on how CoPs develop social interactions and consequent capacity to produce new knowledge and practice. Professional CoPs able to understand shared leadership during the identification of new practices can learn from these experiences, and add these lessons to the collection of processes and artifacts that community members use to perpetuate knowledge. Knowledge management scholars such as Nonaka et al. (2001) concluded that organizational structures often make poor use of workers' tacit knowledge, which they could accomplish through the creation of environments in which individuals might interact dynamically. The theory of knowledge management in an organization resembles the CoP theory in that it describes how individuals develop behavioral patterns in the way they identify, create, and disseminate knowledge.

The process of institutionalization continues to be a challenge for organizations promoting professional CoPs. As organizations try to create circumstances for spontaneous collaboration, the intervention of controlling agents, or the imposition of organizational policies are both factors working against the leaderless, fluid structure of learning communities (Wenger et al. 2002). Organizations learning the structural development of CoPs through research must study carefully how these lessons adapt to the distinctive culture and values of the community. When members from diverse communities develop shared vocabulary, artifacts, and symbols, they become more cohesive and productive (Brundrett et al. 2006). In contrast, when members of professional CoPs cannot find a common ground of shared expertise (Wenger and Snyder 2000), they build an environment conducive to poor performance and innovation. However, organizations continue promoting professional CoPs because stories of success in knowledge management (Yang and Wei 2010) and consulting firms (Anand et al. 2007) validate how groups of practitioners can achieve innovation when they engage in negotiated enterprise and collaboration. These case studies not only demonstrated how CoPs can generate improved performance, they also allow the replication of structural paths for the creation, compilation, and dissemination of knowledge. Several studies by Anand et al. (2007) demonstrated that CoPs build distinctive structural paths with communication and specialization as crucial indicators for building competences, learning, and sharing knowledge.

Leadership expressions manifest among CoP membership in many ways including increased motivation, cohesion, and power relationships. Scholars agree that these leadership expressions can also change through the life cycle stages of a community of practitioners. Leadership is present at the beginning of the CoP through the building of loose networks in which core members volunteer to lead during the growth stage through developing trust and increased dialogue among members; during the maturity stage through initiating projects, sharing vision and community focus; and during the stewardship state through developing openness toward new ideas and new members. Leadership seems to be a mediating influence throughout each of these different stages of collective knowledge creation.

Although CoPs operate better under flexible and decentralized structures, numerous authors concur that leadership expressions are visible as intervening factors or as outcomes of community socialization. Contemporary leadership paradigms such as Janusian leadership, transformational leadership, emotional intelligence, leadership from the inside out, and the Theory U have been identified as able to explain and predict the leadership behaviors of community members during knowledge creation activities. Systematic studies on CoP literature in more than 20 countries and more than 10 industry fields have also demonstrated that motivation, trust, visible apprenticeship, embedded leadership roles, recognition, empowerment, self-efficacy, and empathy are additional leadership expressions observed within communities of practitioners. Leadership also appears to influence CoP expressions of knowledge creation, such as reflective collaboration, sense of common purpose, dyadic relationships, prosocial behaviors, and motivation.

CoPs constitute a powerful forum for industry advancement and innovation, as proven by existing research among practitioners on different fields of expertise. This capacity to solve problems and create innovation is vastly documented in the existing CoP literature from the dimensions of community (e.g. social activity), practice (e.g. sense of common purpose), and domain (e.g. area of expertise). Although this existing literature seems to indicate that the presence of other mediating factors, such as leadership, is necessary to enhance problem-solving and innovation capacities, the existing CoP (Wenger et al. 2002) not only excludes leadership, but reports that leadership is an obstacle for creation and innovation as it can leads to legitimization. However, leadership is a mediating influence over the capacity that communities of practitioners have to socialize, develop sense of common purpose, and create solutions to everyday problems. All of these dynamics are necessary to emerge for CoPs to be able to capitalize on their ability to create, steward, and disseminate knowledge.

References

Abdullah, R., Sahibudin, S., Alias, R. A., & Selamat, M. H. (2005). Applying knowledge management system with agent technology to support decision making in collaborative learning environment. *Journal of American Academy of Business, 7*(1), 1–10.

Adkins, R., Bartczak, S. E., Griffin, K., & Downey, J. P. (2010). Improving military competitiveness by enabling successful communities of practice: Lessons learned over 10 years with Air Force knowledge now. *Competition Forum, 8*(1), 44–55.

Adler, E., & Haas, P. M. (1992). Conclusion: Epistemic communities, world order, and the creation of a reflective research program. *International Organization, 46*(1), 367–391.

Akkerman, S., Petter, C., & De Laat, M. (2008). Organizing communities-of-practice: Facilitating emergence. *Journal of Workplace Learning, 20*(6), 383–399.

Anand, N., Gardner, H. K., & Morris, T. (2007). Knowledge-based innovation: Emergence and embedding of new practice areas in management consulting firms. *Academy of Management Journal, 50*(2), 406–428.

Antonakis, J., Hourse, R. J. (2008). Instrumental leadership: Measurement and extension of transformational–transactional leadership theory. *The Leadership Quarterly, 25*(4), 746. doi:10.1016/j.leaqua.2014.04.005.

Ash, D., Brown, C., Kluger-Bell, B., & Hunter, L. (2009). Creating hybrid communities using inquiry as professional development for college science faculty. *Journal of College Science Teaching, 38*(6), 68–77.

Bach, P. M., & Carroll, J. M. (2010). December). Characterizing the dynamics of open user experience design: The cases of Firefox and OpenOffice.org. *Journal of the Association for Information Systems, 11*(12), 902–925.

Bass, B. M., & Riggio, R. E. (2010). The transformational model of leadership. In G. R. Hickman (Ed.), *Leading organizations: Perspectives for a New Era* (2nd ed., pp. 76–86). Thousand Oaks, CA: Sage.

Bishop, J., Bouchlaghem, D., Glass, J., & Matsumoto, I. (2008). Identifying and implementing management best practice for communities of practice. *Architectural Engineering and Design Management, 4*(3/4), 160–176.

Blanton, M. L., & Stylianou, D. A. (2009). Interpreting a community of practice perspective in discipline-specific professional development in higher education. *Innovative Higher Education, 34*(2), 79–92. doi:10.1007/s10755-008-9094-8.

Borzillo, S., Schmitt, A., & Antino, M. (2012). Communities of practice: Keeping the company agile. *The Journal of Business Strategy, 33*(6), 22–30.

Bowen, A. (2010). Factors that influence practitioners trained in Six Sigma principles in the development of a community of practice: A case study (Doctoral Dissertation, Capella University). *Dissertation Abstracts International, 71*(03)

Brown, J. S., & Duguid, P. (1998). Organizing knowledge. *California Management Review, 40*(3), 90–111.

Brundrett, M., Rhodes, C., & Gkolia, C. (2006). Planning for leadership succession: Creating a talent pool in primary schools. *Education, 34*(3), 259–268.

Buckley, S., & Du Toit, A. (2009). Sharing knowledge in universities: Communities of practice the answer? *Education, Knowledge & Economy, 3*(1), 35–44.

Burns, J., & Avolio, B. (2004). Transformational and Transactional Leadership. In G. Goethals, G. Sorenson, & J. Burns (Eds.), *Encyclopedia of leadership* (pp. 1559–1567). Thousand Oaks, CA: SAGE Publications Inc.

Buderi, R. (1998). Field work in the tribal office. *Technology Review, 101*(3), 42–50.

Carey, C., Smith, K., & Martin, L. M. (2009). Cross-university enterprise education collaboration as a community of practice. *Education & Training, 51*(8/9), 696–706. doi:10.1108/00400910911005244

Cashman, K. (1998). *Leadership from the inside out: Becoming a leader for life.* Provo, UT: Executive Excellence Publishing.

Cargill, B. J. (2006). Leadership in issues within a community of Practice. In E. Coakes & S. Clarke (Eds.), *Encyclopedia of communities of practice and knowledge management.* Hershey, PA: IGI Global.

Cheng, E. C. K., & Lee, J. C. K. (2014). Developing strategies for communities of practice. *International Journal of Educational Management, 28*(6), 751–764.

Clark, R. P. (2010, November). Developing our human capital: A mixed-method study of teacher use of online communities (Doctoral Dissertation, University of California). *Dissertation Abstracts International, 75*(05). (UMI Number: 3402053).

Contu, A., & Willmott, H. (2003). Re-embedding situatedness: The importance of power relations in learning theory. *Organization Science, 14*(3), 283–296.

Corso, M., Giacobbe, A., & Martini, A. (2009). Designing and managing business communities of practice. *Journal of Knowledge Management, 13*(3), 73–89.

Crane, D. (1969). Social structure in a group of scientists: A test of the invisible college hypothesis. *American Sociological Review, 34*(3), 335–352.

Crane, D. (1971). Transnational networks in basic science. *International Organization, 25*(3), 585–602.

Creech, A., Gaunt, H., Hallam, S., & Robertson, L. (2009). Conservatoire students' perceptions of master classes. *British Journal of Music Education, 26*(3), 315–331. doi:10.1017/S026505170999012X

Dabback, W. M. (2010). Exploring communities of music in Virginia's Shenandoah Valley. *International Journal of Community Music, 3*(2), 213–227.

Dane, E. (2010). Reconsidering the trade-off between expertise and flexibility: A cognitive entrenchment perspective. *Academy of Management Review, 35*(4), 579–603.

De Palma, R., & Teague, L. (2008). A democratic community of practice: Unpicking all those words. *Educational Action Research, 16*(4), 441–456.

Dionne, S. D., Yammarino, F. J., Atwater, L. E., & Spangler, W. D. (2004). Transformational leadership and team performance. *Journal of Organizational Change Management, 17*(2), 177–193.

Dixon, J. S. (2010). *Connecting creativity, technology, and communities of practice: Exploring the efficacy of technological tools in support of creative innovation. ProQuest Dissertations and Theses,* 275.

Eversole, R. (2012). Remaking participation: challenges for community development practice. *Community Development Journal, 47*(1), 29–41.

Ferlie, E., Fitzgerald, L., Wood, M., & Hawkins, C. (2005). The nonspread of innovations: The mediating role of professionals. *Academy of Management Journal, 48*(1), 117–134.

Fominaya, C. F. (2010). Creating cohesion from diversity: The challenge of collective identity formation in the global justice movement. *Sociological Inquiry, 80*(3), 377–404. doi:10.1111/j.1475-682X.2010.00339.x.

Griffith, T., & Sawyer, J. (2006). Supporting technologies and Organizational practices for the transfer of knowledge in virtual environments. *Group Decision and Negotiation, 15*(4), 407–423.

Goel, L., Johnson, N. A., Junglas, I., & Ives, B. (2011). From space to place: Predicting users' intentions to return to virtual worlds. *MIS Quarterly, 35*(3), 749–776.

Goldstein, B. E., & Butler, W. H. (2010). Expanding the scope and impact of collaborative planning: Combining multi-stakeholder collaboration and communities of practice in a learning network. *Journal of the American Planning Association, 76*(2).

Goleman, D. (1995). *Emotional intelligence.* New York, NY: Bantam Books Inc.

Guldberg, K., & Mackness, J. (2009). Foundations of communities of practice: Enablers and barriers to participation. *Journal of Computer Assisted learning, 25*(6), 528–553.

Hardy, M. (2010). Pareto's Law. *Mathematical Intelligencer, 32*(3), 38. doi:10.1007/s00283-010-9159-2.

Hawk, S., Zheng, W., & Zmud, R. (2009). Overcoming knowledge-transfer barriers in infrastructure management outsourcing: Lessons from a case study. *MIS Quarterly Executive, 8*(3), 123–139.

Hayes, K. J., & Fitzgerald, A. (2009). Managing occupational boundaries to improve innovation outcomes in industry-research organisations. *Journal of Management and Organization, 15*(4), 423–438.

Hew, K., & Hara, N. (2007). Empirical study of motivators and barriers of teacher online knowledge sharing. *Educational Technology Research and Development, 55*(6), 573–595.

Hodgkinson-Williams, C., Slay, H., & Siebörger, I. (2008). Developing communities of practice within and outside higher education institutions.

Holmström, J., & Boudreau, M. (2006). Communicating and coordinating: Occasions for information technology in loosely coupled organizations. *Information Resources Management Journal, 19*(4), 23–30.

Huang, K. G., & Murray, F. E. (2009). Does patent strategy shape the long-run supply of public knowledge? Evidence from Human Genetics. *Academy of Management Journal, 52*(6), 1193–1221.

Hulpia, H., Devos, G., & Van Keer, H. (2009). The Influence of distributed leadership on teachers' organizational commitment: A multilevel approach. *Journal of Educational Research, 103*(1), 40–52.

Kasper, H., Mühlbacher, J., & Müller, B. (2008). Intra-organizational knowledge sharing in MNCs depending on the degree of decentralization and communities of practice. *Journal of Global Business & Technology, 4*(1), 59–68.

Katja, Z. (2009). Antecedents of knowledge sharing in communities of practice. *Journal of Knowledge Management, 13*(3), 90–101.

Kipp, P., Wieck, E., Bretschneider, U., & Leimeiste, J. M. (2010). *12 Years of GENEX Framework: What did Practice Learn from Science in Terms of Web-Based Ideation?*. Kassel: Kassel University.

Kinsella, E. A., & Whiteford, G. E. (2009). Knowledge generation and utilization in occupational therapy: Towards epistemic reflexivity. *Australian Occupational Therapy Journal, 56*(4), 249–258.

Kopeikina, L. (2005). *The right decision every time.* Upper Saddle, NJ: Pearson.

Kouzes, J. M., & Posner, B. Z. (2000). The Janusian leader. *Executive Excellence, 17*(7), 3–4.

Lave, J. (1991) Situating learning in communities of practice. In L. B. Resnick, J. M. Levine, & S. D. Stephanie D. (Eds.), *Perspectives on Socially Shared Cognition* (pp. 63–82). Washington, DC, US: American Psychological Association.

Lave, J. & Wenger, E. (1991). *Situated Learning: Legitimate Peripheral Participation.* Cambridge: Cambridge University Press.

Lawless, A. (2008). Action learning as legitimate peripheral participation. *Action Learning: Research & Practice, 5*(2), 117–129.

Lee, S., Kim, Y. S., & Suh, E. (2014). Structural health assessment of communities of practice (CoPs). *Journal of Knowledge Management, 18*(6), 1198–1216.

Lesser, E. L., & Storck, J. (2001). Communities of practice and organizational performance. *IBM Systems Journal, 40*(4), 831–841. doi:10.1147/sj.404.0831.

Lee, G. K., & Cole, R. E. (2003). November/December. From a firm-based to a community-based model of knowledge creation: The case of the Linux Kernel development. *Organization Science, 14*(6), 633–649.

Li, L., Grimshaw, J. M., Nielsen, C., Judd, M., Coyote, P. C., & Graham, I. D. (2009). Use of communities of practice in business and health care sectors: A systematic review. *Implementation Science, 4,* 1–9.

Lindkvist, L. (2005). Knowledge communities and knowledge collectivities: A typology of knowledge work in groups. *Journal of Management Studies, 42*(6), 1189–1210.

Linehan, P. C. (2010). Communities of practice as a technical assistance strategy: A single-case study of state systems change (Doctoral Dissertation, The George Washington University). *Dissertation Abstracts International, 71*(04), AAT 3397351.

Mabery, M. J., Gibbs-Scharf, L., & Bara, D. (2013). Communities of practice foster collaboration across public health. *Journal of Knowledge Management, 17*(2), 226–236.

Machles, D., Bonkemeyer, E., & McMichael, J. (2010). Community of Practice. *Professional Safety, 55*(1), 46–52.

Marshall, C. C., Shipman, F. M., III, & McCall, R. J. (1995). Making large-scale information resources serve communities of practice. *Journal of Management Information Systems, 11*(4), 65–86.

Mayer, J. D., Salovey, P., Caruso, D. R., & Sitarenios, G. (2001). Emotional intelligence as a standard intelligence. *Emotion, 1*(3), 232–242.

Maistry, S. M. (2008). School-university CPD partnerships: Fertile ground for cultivating teacher communities of practice. *South African Journal of Higher Education, 22*(20), 363–374.

Moreno, A. (2001). Enhancing knowledge exchange through Communities of Practice at the Inter-American Development Bank. *Aslib Proceedings, 53*(8), 296–308.

Nonaka, I., Konno, N., & Toyama, R. (2001). Emergence of "Ba": A conceptual framework for the continuous and self-transcending process of knowledge creation. In I. Nonaka & T. Nishiguchi (Eds.), *Knowledge emergence: Social, technical, and evolutionary dimensions of knowledge creation* (pp. 13–29). Oxford: Oxford University Press.

Noriko, H. (2007). Information technology support for communities of practice: How public defenders learn about winning and losing in court. *Journal of the American Society for Information Science and Technology, 58*(1), 76–87.

O'Kane, M. P., Paine, M. S., & King, B. J. (2008). Context, participation and discourse: The role of the communities of practice concept in understanding farmer decision-making. *Journal of Agricultural Education & Extension, 14*(3), 187–201.

Orr, J. (1996). *Talking about machines: An ethnography of a modern job*. New York, NY: Cornell University.

Penner, L. A., Dovidio, J. F., Piliavin, Jane A., & Schroeder, D. A. (2005). Prosocial behavior: Multilevel perspectives. *Annual Review of Psychology, 56*(1), 365–392.

Price, M. (2005). Assessment standards: The role of communities of practice and the scholarship of assessment. *Assessment & Evaluation in Higher Education, 30*(3), 215–230.

Price, D. P. (2013). The relationship between innovation, knowledge, and performance in family and non-family firms. *Journal of Innovation and Entrepreneurship, 2*(1), 1–20.

Price, D. J., & Beaver, D. D. (1966). Collaboration in an invisible college. *The American Psychologist, 21*(11), 1011–1018.

Ranmuthugala, G., Cunningham, F. C., Plumb, J. J., Long, J., Georgiou, A., Westbrook, J., et al. (2011). A realist evaluation of the role of communities of practice in changing healthcare practice. *Implementation Science, 6*(1), 49–54.

Ready, D., & Truelove, E. S. (2011). Purpose and the power of collective ambition. *Business Strategy Review, 22*(3), 17–23. doi:10.1111/j.1467-8616.2011.00768.x.

Retna, K. S., & Ng, P. T. (2011). Communities of practice: Dynamics and success factors. *Leadership & Organization Development Journal, 32*(1), 41–59.

Rohlfing, K. J., Rehm, M., & Goecke, K. U. (2003). Situatedness: The interplay between context (s) and situation. *Journal of Cognition & Culture, 3*(2), 132–156.

Shin, J. H. (2011). Leveraging knowledge through communities of practice in a Korean company (Doctoral Dissertation, Columbia University). Dissertation *Abstracts International, 72*(02). (UMI Number: 3432899).

Sahin, N., Nijkamp, M., & Stough, R. (2009). Socio-cultural drivers of innovation. *The European Journal of Social Sciences, 22*(3), 247–249.

Saldana, J. B. (2014). *Comparison of community, practice, domain, and leadership expressions among professional communities of practice* (Order No. 3647745). ProQuest Dissertations & Theses Full Text. (1643246761).

Saldana, J. (2012). Community, practice, and domain behaviors, and the moderator influence of information technology among global communities of practice: A meta-analysis. *Hispanic Educational Technology Services Journal*, [Online Edition], 2, Fall Issue.

Scharmer, C. O. (2007). *Theory U: Leading from the future as it emerges*. San Francisco, CA: Berrett-Koehler.

Schlager, M. S., & Fusco, J. (2003). Teacher Professional Development, Technology, and Communities of Practice: Are We Putting the Cart Before the Horse? *Information Society, 19* (3), 203.

Schroeder, P. J. (2010). Changing team culture: The perspectives of ten successful head coaches. *Journal of Sport Behavior, 33*(1), 63–88.

Senge, P. M. (1993). Transforming the practice of management. *Human Resource Development Quarterly, 4*(1), 5–32.

Siebert, S., Mills, V., & Tuff, C. (2009). Pedagogy of work-based learning: the role of the learning group. *Journal of Workplace Learning, 21*(6), 443–454.

Smith, K. G., Mitchell, T. R., & Summer, C. E. (1985). Top level management priorities in different stages of the organizational life cycle. *Academy of Management Journal, 28*(4), 799–820.

Stuart, M. (1993). Themes from Thymos. *Journal of the American Planning Association, 59*(2), 147–151.

Tal, T., & Morag, O. (2009). Reflective practice as a means for preparing to teach outdoors in an ecological garden. *Journal of Science Teacher Education, 20*(3), 245–262.

Tapscott, D., & Williams, A. D. (2010). Wikinomics: The art and science of peer production. In G. R. Hickman (Ed.), *Leading organizations: Perspectives of a New Era* (2nd ed., pp. 48–62). Thousand Oaks, CA: Sage.

Thompson, M. (2005). Structural and Epistemic Parameters in Communities of Practice. *Organization Science, 16*(2), 151–164.

Tomcsik, R. (2010). Does gender matter? Collaborative learning in a virtual corporate community of practice (Doctoral Dissertation, Capella University). *Dissertation Abstracts International, 71* (05). (UMI 3402255). Retrieved from ProQuest Dissertations.

Vaida, S., & Opre, A. (2014). Emotional intelligence versus emotional competence. *Journal of Psychological and Educational Research, 22*(1), 26–33.

Vavasseur, C. B., & MacGregor, K. (2008). Extending content-focused professional development through online communities of practice. *Journal of Research on Technology in Education, 40* (4), 517–538.

Venters, W., & Wood, B. (2007). Degenerative structures that inhibit the emergence of communities of practice: A case study of knowledge management in the British Council. *Information Systems Journal, 17*(4), 349–368.

Wartburg, I., & Teihert, T. (2006). Leadership in issues in communities of practice. In E. Coakes & S. Clarke (Eds.), *Encyclopedia of communities of practice and knowledge management.* IGI Global: Hershey, PA.

Weaver, L., Pifer, M., & Colbeck, C. (2009). Janusian leadership: Two profiles of power in a community of practice. *Innovative Higher Education, 34*(5), 307–320.

Wenger, E. (2004). *Communities of practice: Learning, meaning, and identity* (7th ed.). Cambridge: Cambridge University Press.

Wenger, E., McDermott, R., & Snyder, W. M. (2002). *Cultivating communities of practice: A guide to managing knowledge.* Boston, MA: Harvard Business School Press.

Wenger, E. C., & Snyder, W. M. (2000). January/February). Communities of practice: The organizational frontier. *Harvard Business Review, 78*(1), 139–145.

Wenger-Trayner, E. & Wenger-Trayner B. (2015). Levels of Participation. http://wenger-trayner. com/project/levels-of-participation/. Accessed 22/12/2015.

West, R. (2009). What is shared? A framework for understanding shared innovation within communities. *Educational Technology Research and Development, 57*(3), 315–332.

Wright, N. (2007). Building literacy communities of practice across subject disciplines in secondary schools. *Language & Education: An International Journal, 21*(5), 420–433.

Yang, C. L., & Wei, S. T. (2010). Modelling the performance of CoP in knowledge management. *Total Quality Management & Business Excellence, 21*(10), 1033–1045.

Zboralski, K., Salom, S., & Gemuenden, H. G. (2006). Organizational benefits of communities of practice: A two-stage information processing model. *Cybernetics & Systems, 37*(6), 533–552.

Chapter 14
Revealing the Nexus Between Distributed Leadership and Communities of Practice

Sandra Jones and Marina Harvey

Abstract Distributed leadership is a leadership approach that aligns with, and supports, the creating and sustaining of Communities of Practice (CoP) in higher education. Agreeing with the editors' proposition that CoP need to be positioned within the broader social learning literature, the proposition is expanded to consider the relationship between CoP and distributed leadership (DL). This chapter argues that while the focus of DL is on building leadership capacity, its synergistic relationship with CoP results in it being indirectly linked to social learning. On the one hand, DL provides the context in which CoP are created and sustained, and, on the other hand CoP contribute to the enabling of distributed leadership. Together they support the social learning that occurs within the CoP. DL provides the 'best fit' for creating and sustaining a community of people within the CoPs and thus social learning (Green and Ruutz in Engaging communities, proceedings of the 31st HERDSA annual conference, Rotorua, pp. 163–172, 2008).

Keywords Distributed leadership · Community of practice · Collaboration · Relationships · Nexus · Reflection

14.1 Introduction

Communities of Practice (CoP) have been characterised by three factors—a domain of knowledge that creates common ground and a sense of common identity, a community of people who care about the domain and create the social fabric for

The original version of this chapter was revised: One of the author affiliation and the author name within the text have been updated. The erratum to this chapter is available at 10.1007/978-981-10-2879-3_29

S. Jones (✉)
RMIT University, Melbourne, VIC, Australia
e-mail: Sandra.jones@rmit.edu.au

M. Harvey
Queensland University of Technology, Brisbane, QLD, Australia

© Springer Nature Singapore Pte Ltd. 2017
J. McDonald and A. Cater-Steel (eds.), *Communities of Practice*,
DOI 10.1007/978-981-10-2879-3_14

learning, and a shared practice that the community creates to be effective in the domain (Wenger et al. 2002). The intersection of these three factors establishes the opportunity for learning through knowledge sharing between experts and new members (who move gradually from the periphery to the centre). Lave and Wenger (1991) initially proposed CoP as a conceptual means to enable learning as "an integral part of social practice in the lived world" (p. 35). In seeking to explain how learning occurs in a systematic way within CoP they describe "a process through which participants gain more knowledge as they move from the periphery to that of expert through Legitimate Peripheral Participation" (LPP), (p. 35).

This process accords with a social theory of learning that recognises learning as a cognitive process that takes place in a social context through observation (Bandura and Parke 1972). The link between CoP and social learning theory is recognised as learning moves from "the individual as learner to learning as participation in a social world" (Lave and Wenger 1991, p. 43). These changes go beyond the pragmatic to encompass social change in "the relational interdependency of agent and world, activity, meaning, cognition, learning and knowing" (Lave and Wenger 1991, p. 51). In other words, the design of more social learning models will inevitably lead to analysis of issues such as unequal relations of power. In a further advance of this early research, Wenger (2000) argued that CoP have the potential to combine organizational learning and strategic insights as the "latest wave in an ongoing evolution of organizational structure...*with*....the capacity to create and use organizational knowledge through informed learning and mutual engagement" (p. 4). Management and employment relations specialists proposed that CoP provide the potential foundation for new patterns of management-employee interactions based on value networks (rather than status, control and containment) resulting in greater employee satisfaction (Fontaine and Millen 2004). This can be seen as correlating with emerging theories of 'post heroic' (Fletcher and Kaeufer 2003), distributed and shared leadership. Such assumptions have led to identification of how to best train participants in specific roles to facilitate CoPs (Wenger et al. 2002; see also http://www.wenger-trayner.com). As a result empirically-based literature about CoP began to focus on how to create the internal conditions through which CoP have the capacity to be a "practical way to frame the task of managing knowledge" (Wenger et al. 2002, p. x).

It is not surprising that the potential of CoPs to improve knowledge sharing has been explored in the higher education sector. The open sharing of expertise is in accord with traditional notions of academic autonomy and collegiality that have characterised the sector (Coates et al. 2009). As a result, sectoral research has concentrated on how to improve the operation of CoPs, in particular how CoPs may be facilitated to network knowledge as a means of improving the quality of learning and teaching (McDonald et al. 2012; McDonald and Edwards 2014). Recognising the importance of this research, this chapter moves beyond this focus to locate CoPs within a broader context and culture. In so doing, the aim is to focus upon the question of whether a distributed leadership (DL) approach can provide the 'best fit' for creating and sustaining CoPs. Our conclusion affirms this question.

Reviewing the outcomes of empirical research undertaken in Australian into Distributed Leadership (DL) similarities are identified between the characteristics of DL and CoP.It emerges that DL can contribute to the process by which CoP contribute to social learning and indeed provides a 'best fit' context for CoP (Green and Ruutz 2008). An examination of these two variables may offer an explanation of how DL can contribute to the process by which CoPs are created and sustained.

In order to explain this it is first necessary to present the findings of research into the use of a distributed leadership approach to build leadership capacity in learning and teaching in the higher education sector.

14.2 Exploring Synergies Between DL and CoP

DL has been identified as offering a good fit for the complex nature of the higher education sector. Leadership in higher education, it is claimed, is "not a simple process… rather, it is a complex, multifaceted process that must focus on the development of individuals as well as the organisational contexts in which they are called to operate" (Marshall 2006, p. 5). There is a need, in higher education, for "clear leadership devolved from the top throughout the institution [with] management and leadership styles that are aligned with the specific nature of the university" (Coates et al., p. 31).

Building on the experience of DL in secondary schools in Australia and the USA (Gronn 2002; Spillane 2006; Spillane and Diamond 2007), research into DL spread to the post-secondary higher education sector in Australia and the UK (see for example Harris 2004, 2008, 2009; Bolden et al. 2008; Leithwood et al. 2009). In his initial Australian research Gronn (2000, 2002) described DL as a 'new architecture for leadership' based on 'concertive action' (Gronn 2002, p. 429). He differentiated concertive from numerical action by its holistic construct that he described as operating either through:

> collaborative models of engagement which arise spontaneously in the workplace…[OR]… intuitive understanding that develops as part of close working relations between colleagues…[OR]…a variety of structural relations and institutional arrangements which contribute attempts to regularise distributed action (Gronn 2002, p. 429).

From a study of the literature on DL in the UK in the early 20th century, Bennett et al. (2003) described DL as "the emergent property of a group or networks of interacting individuals… *[in contrast to]*… leadership as phenomena which arises from the individual" (p. 7). They arrive at a similar conclusion from their study into the variables that compose DL, explaining DL as being about groups of people working collectively rather than as individuals (Woods et al. 2004). Their key point is that in DL it is difficult to separate leaders from contributors, with the outcome being greater than the sum of the individual contribution. Next, they expanded Gronn's initial description of DL (as concertive action) to add two new characteristics— movable boundaries and a broader spread of expertise (Woods et al. 2004, p. 441).

In this way both the scope of DL was broadened as well as its emergent and flexible nature identified. In so doing, five components of DL were identified: a context of trust, a culture of respect for expertise, a process of change and development that involves many levels of engagement in collaborative activity and an agreed process to resolve conflict (Woods et al. 2004, p. 448).

From their empirical research into the use of DL approaches at the more fine grained level in Australian higher education institutional, Jones et al. (2011) provide a more detailed description of DL:

> a leadership approach in which individuals who trust and respect each other's contributions collaborate together to achieve identified goals. It occurs as a result of an open culture within and across an institution. It is an approach in which reflective practice is an integral part enabling action to be critiqued, challenged and developed through cycles of planning, action, reflection and assessment and re-planning. It happens most effectively when people at all levels engage in action, accepting leadership in their particular areas of expertise. It needs resources that support and enable collaborative environments together with a flexible approach to space, time and finance which occur as a result of diverse contextual settings in an institution (Jones et al. 2011, p. 21).

From this short overview of empirical research into DL it is clear that the focus of DL is on building leadership capacity rather than learning per se. However, synergies between DL and CoP can be identified whereby, on the one hand, DL provides the supportive context for, and action by which, CoP can be created and sustained. On the other hand, CoP contribute one of the means by which a DL approach is enabled. This synergistic relationship is explained further by a more detailed account of the empirical research into DL in Australia, before identifying that these synergies in fact identify a two-point nexus between DL and CoP.

14.3   Researching DL

Research in Australian higher education (2006–2013) extended beyond the theoretical conceptualisation and discourse on DL to reveal actions required to enable DL. This action-based research was funded by the national government agency established to improve the quality of learning and teaching across the higher education sector in Australia (initially the Carrick Institute which was later renamed the Australian Learning and Teaching Council and thence the Office for Learning and Teaching), to build capacity to lead change in learning and teaching. Research projects commenced within individual universities and developed through four key cycles over a period of 8 years. The factors that enable DL were first identified, followed by the design of an approach to evaluate effective implementation of these DL enabling factors and culminating in an inclusive conceptual model to explain DL.

A participative action research (PAR) (Kemmis et al. 2014) process was implemented that enabled change to be trialled and evaluated before a further action cycle was designed. The PAR methodology enables cycles of adaptive change, based on Plan, Act, Observe and Reflect and provided several beneficial outcomes. This was variously encouraged by appreciative inquiry (Barber et al. 2009), reflective practice (Fraser and Harvey 2008) and reflective journaling (Lefoe and Parris 2008).

While these research projects focused on DL as a means to build leadership capacity for learning and teaching, with no or little specific mention of CoP, an unplanned, but serendipitous, revelation arising from the research is the synergetic relationships between DL and CoP. Given the importance of the PAR process to the argument presented in this chapter concerning the nexus between DL and CoP, the four key action cycles that demonstrate this relationship are outlined before returning to the issue of the nexus between DL and CoP.

14.3.1 Cycle 1

In 2006, the Carrick Institute commenced a Leadership for Excellence in Learning and Teaching Program (Parker 2008). Two leadership approaches underpinned calls for projects designed to build leadership capacity for learning and teaching—one designed to use a traditional positional/structural leadership approach, the other to use a DL approach. Interestingly, while the positional/structural approach did identify the skills, traits and behaviours needed of individual leaders it also identified the important contribution of DL (Scott et al. 2008). It is the DL approach that is of chief significance to this chapter.

The DL projects consisted of four single university projects funded to overtly use a DL approach to different aspects of learning and teaching to: improve teaching quality (Barber et al. 2009, RMIT); develop online experts (Chesterton et al. 2008, Australian Catholic University [ACU]); improve assessment (Fraser and Harvey 2008, Macquarie University), and develop scholars as leaders (Lefoe and Parris 2008, University of Wollongong [UoW]). All projects engaged both formal/positional leaders and informal experts in a PAR process to trial and test change that resulted both in improved learning and teaching and increased leadership capacity in learning and teaching. Teams established as part of this PAR process were variously termed Action Research Teams (ART-RMIT), Action Research Enablers (ARE-ACU), Leaders in Affective Assessment Practice (LEAP-Macquarie University) and Faculty Scholar Networks (FSN, UoW).

14.3.2 Cycle 2

Following the successful outcomes of each of the individual university projects, a further multi-university project was funded (in 2009). The multi-university DL project (henceforth termed the DL 'synergies project') had as its aim to identify and synthesise the synergies between the experience of the four initial single-institutional projects. A PAR approach underpinned this synergies project that included: sharing and systematic documentation of the 'lessons learnt' reflections of the original project(s) leaders, team members and team participants. This data was collected through several cycles, each stage interrogated by research project team members, checked by the original project members and participants and validated by a cross section of university leaders of learning and teaching.

The outcome of this cycle was the acknowledgement that the operation of the original project teams was most aligned with the process of CoP in that they involved voluntary self selection, a sense of common identify and shared practice (Jones et al. 2011, pp. 38–41). The findings of the synergies project are: firstly, the identification of a mix of dimensions and criteria required for a DL approach to be activated. The dimensions of DL are: a *context* of trust rather than regulation; a *culture* of autonomy rather than control, recognition of the need for *change* from hierarchy to interdependent decision making, and the encouragement of *collaborative relationships* (Jones et al. 2011). The four criteria required to action a DL approach are: *involvement* of people, support of *processes*, provision of *professional development* and availability of *resources*. The relationship between each of these dimensions and criteria is outlined in Table 14.1.

Secondly, the researchers mapped these four dimensions and the four criteria for DL and cross-referenced them into a four-by-four matrix. Informed by the research data and literature, an evidenced-based action item was created for each cell of the matrix. This resulted in the identification of sixteen (16) actions required to enable DL that were designed into an Action Self Enabling Tool (ASET—Jones et al. 2011, see Table 14.2). In identifying 16 detailed enabling actions for a DL approach, this research added significant detail to the earlier UK conceptual research outcomes.

14.3.3   Cycle 3

Following the identification of the ASET, a further research project was funded to develop an evaluative process to assess the enabling actions. This research took the form of a national survey (in 2012) engaging 47 Australian higher education institutions that identified systems and frameworks employed to build leadership capacity in learning and teaching across Australian higher education institutions. Examination of the data by the project researchers confirmed that DL was linked to increased collaboration, and furthermore that there was a strong focus on the

Table 14.1 Dimensions of and criteria for, DL

Dimensions of DL	Criteria for DL
A context of trust rather than regulation	Involvement of people
A culture of autonomy rather than control	Support of processes
Recognition of the need for change from hierarchy to interdependent decision making	Provision of professional development
The encouragement of collaborative relationships	Availability of resources

Derived from Jones et al. (2011): see also www.distributedleadership.com.au

Table 14.2 Action self enabling tool (ASET)

Criterion	Dimensions and values			
	Context trust	Culture respect	Change recognition	Relationships collaboration
People are involved	Expertise of individuals is used to inform decisions	Individuals participate in decision-making	All levels and functions have input into policy development	Expertise of individuals contributes to collective decision-making
Processes are supportive	Distributed leadership is demonstrated	Decentralised groups engage in decision-making	All levels and functions have input into policy implementation	Communities of practice are modelled
Professional development is provided	Distributed leadership is a component of leadership training	Mentoring for distributed leadership is available.	Leaders at all levels proactively encourage distributed leadership	Collaboration is facilitated
Resources are available	Space, time and finance for collaboration are available	Leadership contribution is recognised and rewarded	Flexibility is built into infrastructure and systems	Opportunities for regular networking are supported

involvement of a broad range of people, the importance of support from formal, hierarchical leaders and the need to establish opportunities for collaboration (Jones et al. 2014). Of particular relevance was the contribution of CoP in developing collaborative relationships. Fifty-eight percent of survey respondents identified CoP as contributing to building collaboration (Jones et al. 2014).

The outcome of this cycle led to the design of an evaluative process using 'good practice benchmarks' identified from the national survey. This was based on the concept of best practice benchmarking (identified by Woodhouse (2000), cited in Stella and Woodhouse 2007). It offered the opportunity to create a framework through which institutions can self-evaluate current practices designed to enable distributed leadership against 'good practice' reference points. The benchmarking framework for DL consists of five domains—*engaging, enabling, enacting assessing and emergent*, each with an identified scope, elements and good practice descriptors. CoPs were identified as a good practice descriptor in the domain of *enacting*.

14.3.4 Cycle 4

Cycles one to three produced and confirmed the four dimensions, four criteria and 16 action items for a DL approach. Cycle four built on this established knowledge base and designed a 6E conceptual model of DL (Jones et al. 2014). The 6E

Fig. 14.1 Synergies between
DL and CoP

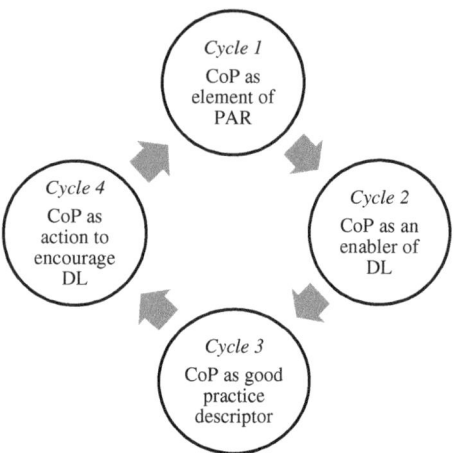

conceptual model identifies the six tenets upon which DL is based. These tenets are: *engaging* leaders and experts; *enabling* through trust, respect, change and the development of collaborative relationships; *enacting* through people, processes, support and systems; *encouraging* through actions; *evaluating* through bench-marking and *emergence* through cycles of change (Jones et al. 2014). CoP were identified as an action to encourage a DL approach.

In summary, as shown in Fig. 14.1, the empirical research into the design and implementation of a DL approach to build leadership in learning and teaching in Australian higher education identified synergies between DL and CoP in each of the four cycles of research.

In order to further analyse these findings the next section explores these synergies and suggests that they in fact create a nexus between DL and CoP at two touch-points, identified as a nexus of creating and a nexus of sustaining.

14.4 The Nexus of Creating

The first touch-point of the nexus between DL and CoP is formed by the conceptual synergy between DL and CoP. From the research findings presented above, DL is identified as creating the context for CoP. In turn CoP contribute to the enabling of DL. In the empirical research CoP were acknowledged as pivotal to the successful engagement of a broad range of experts in the learning and teaching domain under exploration at both institute-wide and specific faculty/department/school levels (see http://www.distributedleadership.com.au). The synergies form a nexus between DL and CoP:

1. Common domain of knowledge—each of the DL projects had a common focus of building leadership to enhance the quality of learning and teaching. While the specific learning and teaching topics varied (assessment practice; design for

Table 14.3 Conceptual synergies between CoPs and DL

DL practice	CoP characteristics
Build leadership capacity in enhancing the quality of learning and teaching	Common domain of knowledge
Self-selection based on experience and interest in learning and teaching	Community of people
Ability to lead developed over time	Shared practice

online teaching; improving student experience, and developing scholarly leadership) the dominant learning and teaching focus provided a common domain, as summarised in Table 14.3.

2. Community or people—each of the DL projects encouraged CoP with participation reliant on self-selected based on experience or interest in the domain. In some cases specific expertise or responsibility was encouraged by a line manager but participation in the CoP was voluntary rather than being a specific work requirement.

3. Shared practice—in each of the DL projects participants recognised and supported the expertise and strengths of each other, with decision making based on expertise rather than perceptions of leadership responsibility (Harvey 2014). Indeed, many of the participants stated that they did not initially perceive themselves as leaders, although by the end of each project most had accepted that, due to their expertise being recognised, they had become (informal) leaders. It is interesting that this social learning that occurs within CoP can be identified as extending beyond the specific domain to result in leadership capacity building.

The creating nexus is further evidenced through synergies identified between the tenets of DL and the characteristics of CoP. Table 14.4 demonstrates that the tenet of engaging aligns with the CoP sense of community identity; that of the tenet of enabling aligns with the CoP provision of a social fabric for learning, and that of the tenet of enacting and encouraging align with the CoP development of effective shared practice.

Table 14.4 Nexus between DL and CoP

Tenets of 6E model of DL	Characteristic of CoP
1. Engaging of leaders and experts	Community of people that creates a sense of common identify
2. Enabling through trust, respect, change and the development of collaborative relationships	Social fabric for learning
3. Enacting through people, processes, support and systems	Shared practice to be effective
4. Encouraging through actions	
5. Emergence through reflective cycles of change	Social learning through–Legitimate Peripheral Participation (see below)
6. Evaluating through benchmarking	To be further explored through research

Derived from: Jones et al. (2014) and Wenger et al. (2002)

Several participant reflections illustrate this nexus:

The most beneficial discussions I've had is with people involved in our group. FSN, University of Wollongong (Lefoe and Parrish 2008, p. 190).

Sharing progress, achievements and challenges often influenced how other scholar's (sic) responded to challenges and exercised leadership in the context of their own faculty-based projects. FSN, University of Wollongong (Lefoe and Parrish 2008, p. 190).

My experience was always one of being part of a collaborative effort. As such my experience throughout this project was quite different from the solitary experience I am used to when engaged in research. LEAP member, Macquarie University (Fraser and Harvey 2008, p. 31).

In summary, DL provides the context within which CoP can be created and thus supports the ability for CoP to support social learning that occurs. In turn CoP contribute to the enabling of a DL approach and, indeed, there is a suggestion that this learning may indeed extend to building leadership capacity and thus further support a DL approach.

14.5   The Nexus of Sustaining

The second touch point of the nexus between DL and CoP is evidenced by synergies in behaviours and activity that occur in both DL and CoP. The *behaviours* expected of participants in both DL approaches and CoP share a common characteristic of eschewing the centralisation of decision making in positional leaders and teacher-focused learning. One CoP member described the behavioural change needed for a DL approach as:

the 'need to overcome peoples' resistance to be scrutinised… at first it was hard to get people to share their experiences because it was so often personal…there was fear about sharing…once you had shared it was cathartic and led to further sharing ART RMIT University (Jones et al. 2011, Appendix 2, pp. 11)

This was otherwise identified as the need to:

work in collaboration with one another (Lecturer 2 LEAP, Macquarie University)

and

at different levels, with colleagues in our Department, across the University, Lecturer 1, LEAP, Macquarie University

becomes habitual (Program convenor, Macquarie University).

From the synergies project research into behaviours expected of participants in DL approaches, it was concluded that these behaviours have a closer alignment with a relational leadership paradigm (Fletcher and Kaeufer 2003) than traditional leader-centric leadership (Jones et al. 2011, pp. 12–14). These behaviours were classified into 4 characteristics: interdependence of participants (self-in-relation), creation of conditions for collective learning (social interaction), focus on learning

Table 14.5 Behavioural synergy DL and CoP

DL behavioural expectations	DL relational leadership	CoP relational interdependence
Adaptable Not ego centric Mentor Forthright but flexible Reflective	Self in relation (emphasis on interdependence)	Common domain
Proactive Resilient Peer sharing Beyond self-interest Critique not critical.	Social interaction (to create conditions for collective learning)	Shared practice
Represent issues not positions Accept free-ranging discussion Willing to listen Share goals	Dialogue (focusing on learning conversations)	Shared knowledge
Accept responsibility Work independently Work outside comfort zone Accept shared goals Not authoritarian Focus on growth Foster outcomes	Growth-in-connection (mutuality of self and others)	Legitimate Peripheral Participation

Derived from Jones et al. (2011) and Fletcher and Kaeufer (2003)

conversations (dialogue) and mutuality of self and others (growth-in-connection). These relational characteristics of DL can be viewed as analogous with the CoP conceptualisations of relational interdependence through which members move from the periphery to the core as they become expert (legitimate peripheral participation) as summarised in Table 14.5.

Activity associated with DL and CoPs are synergistic in their link to activity theory. In initially seeking to explain DL, Gronn (2000) turned to activity theory to explain the link between human behaviour in, and engagement with, the material (i.e. natural and social) world. (Vygotsky 1978; Leont'ev 1978), as flows that "comprise the constituent elemental stuff of human existence" (Leont'ev 1978, p. 66). Activity systems consist of actions and relationships that take place between subject and object, mediated by rules, community, division of labour and instruments (Gronn 2000, p. 327). Both the PAR process that underpins DL and LPP that informs CoP accord with activity theory. Both assume change and movement over time, described under PAR as cycles of change and by CoP as 'vicarious

Table 14.6 Action synergy

	CoP	DL
Behaviour	Relational interdependence	Relational leadership
Action	LPP	PAR

reinforcements'. The resultant flexible activity brings change with it. This is reflected in comments by DL project participants such as:

> …my observation was that the PAR model allowed for the required flexibility to respond to needs as they arise. LEAP member, Macquarie University (Fraser and Harvey 2008, p. 34).

> My experience was that the PAR approach is conducive to fostering a sense of ownership of the project by all participants. Indeed I think this approach serves to maximise the sense of ownership. LEAP member, Macquarie University (Fraser and Harvey 2008, p. 34).

> …the meetings are always a positive experience, it is always interesting to get in touch with others in other departments…I think the interaction is working well. Everybody is bringing something. Every time we have a meeting I think there are new ideas …good input from everybody. LEAP member, Macquarie University (Fraser and Harvey 2008, p. 41).

The behaviours required of participants in order to sustain DL through PAR is evidenced in statements such as

> an occasion to reflect on our own practice and a source of inspiration (Subject convenor, LEAP, Macquarie University).

> Reflection was important … we tended to reflect through discussion with one another rather than the team members reflecting individually (Head of Department, LEAP member, Macquarie University).

Individual reflection was practiced by

> Keeping a diary has been incredibly useful (Subject convenor) and it then

In summary a nexus between DL and CoP can be identified through synergies in the behaviours and actions that underpin both DL and CoP as summarised in Table 14.6.

14.6 Final Reflections

Drawing on Australian empirical research and primary data, this paper has identified that a synergistic relationship exists between DL and CoP in both the concepts and characteristics that underpin DL and CoPs. Further, these synergies create a nexus between DL and CoP at two touch points—creating and sustaining. These touch points identify a mutually supportive relationship that presents the opportunity to both enhance social learning and build leadership capacity. By extending both the conservative research discourse focus on the internal functioning of CoP and that of the leadership discussion on DL as a more relational form of leadership, it was nexus between DL and CoP does can impact social learning. The discussion of nexus at two-touch-point nexus between DL and CoP does suggests, as proposed at the beginning of this paper, that DL does provide a 'best fit' context in which CoP, and the social learning that occurs within them, can occur. In so concluding, however, the authors acknowledge that as the chapter relies exclusively on research directly related to DL, further research on this nexus from the perspective, or lens, of CoP is needed before a totally symbiotic relationship can be claimed. This research may explore possible synergies between how DL and CoP are evaluated using a similar benchmarking process for CoP as was developed for DL. With this caveat, for now the authors confidently conclude that DL provides a 'best fit' context for creating and sustaining communities of practice.

References

Bandura, A., & Parke, R. (Eds.). (1972). *Recent trends in social learning theory*. New York: Academic Press Inc.

Barber, J., Jones, S., & Novak, B. (2009). *Student feedback and leadership, final report to the Australian Learning and Teaching Council*. www.olt.gov.au/. Accessed 8 March 2015.

Bennett, N., Harvey, J., Wise, C., & Woods, P. (2003). *Distributed leadership: A desk study*, www.ncsl.org.uk/literature reviews. Leadership Foundation for Higher Education: UK. Accessed 8 March 2015.

Bolden, R., Petrov, G., & Gosling, J. (2008). *Developing collective leadership in higher education, final report, Research and Development Series*. Leadership Foundation for Higher Education: UK

Chesterton, P., Duignan, P., Felton, E., Flowers, K., Gibbons, P., & Horne, et al. (2008) *Development of distributed institutional leadership capacity in online learning and teaching project, Final Report Australian Learning and Teaching Council*. Strawberry Hills. www.olt.gov.au/. Accessed 8 March 2015.

Coates, H., Dobson, I., Edwards, D., Friedman, T., Goedegebuure, L., & Meek, V. (2009). *The attractiveness of the Australian academic profession: A comparative analysis, Research Briefing*, L.H Martin Institute, Education Policy Unit, ACER. http://research.acer.edu.au. Accessed 8 March 2015.

Fletcher, J. K., & Kaeufer, K. (2003). Shared leadership: Paradox and possibility. In C. Pearce & J. Conger (Eds.), *Shared leadership: Reframing the hows and whys of leadership* (pp. 21–47). Thousand Oaks, California: Sage Publications.

Fraser, D., & Harvey, M. (2008). *Leadership and assessment: Strengthening the nexus. Final report*. Strawberry Hills: Australian Learning and Teaching Council. www.olt.gov.au/. Accessed 8 March 2015.

Fontaine, M., & Millen, D. (2004). Understanding the benefits and impacts of communities of practice. In P. Hildreth & C. Kimble (Eds.), *Knowledge networks, innovation through communities of practice*. Hershey: Idea Group.

Green, W., & Ruutz, A. (2008). Fit for purpose: Designing a faculty-based community of (teaching) practice. In *Engaging communities, proceedings of the 31st HERDSA annual conference*, Rotorua, pp. 163–172.

Gronn, P. (2000). Distributed properties: A new architecture of leadership. *Educational Management Administration and Leadership, 28*(3), 317–338.

Gronn, P. (2002). Distributed leadership as a unit of analysis. *The Leadership Quarterly, 13*, 230–457.

Harris, A. (2004). Teacher leadership and distributed leadership: An exploration of the literature. *Leading and Managing, 10*(2), 1–9.

Harris, A. (2008). Distributed leadership: According to the evidence. *Journal of Educational Administration, 46*(2), 172–188.

Harris, A. (Ed.). (2009). *Distributed leadership—Different perspectives.* Dordrecht: Springer.

Harvey, M. (2014). Strengths-based approach. In D. Coghlan & M. Brydon-Miller (Eds.), *The SAGE encyclopaedia of action research* (Vol. 2, pp. 732–735). Thousand Oaks: Sage.

Jones, S., Applebee, A., Harvey, M., & Lefoe, G. (2010). *Scoping a distributed leadership matrix for higher education.* In M. Devlin, J. Nagy & A. Lichtenberg (Eds.), 33rd Higher Education Research and Development Society of Australasia (pp. 359–369). Milperra HERDSA.

Jones, S., Harvey, M., Lefoe, G., & Ryland, K. (2011). *Lessons learnt: Identifying synergies in distributed leadership projects, a report to the office for learning and teaching,* DEEWR, Sydney. www.olt.gov.au/. Accessed 8 March 2015.

Jones, S., Hadgraft, R., Harvey, M., Lefoe, G., & Ryland, K. (2014). *Evidence-based benchmarking framework for a distributed leadership approach to capacity building in learning and teaching, A Report to the Office for Learning and Teaching,* Department of Education, Sydney. www.olt.gov.au/. Accessed 8 March 2015.

Kemmis, S., McTaggart, R., & Nixon, R. (2014). *The action research planner. Doing critical participatory action research.* Singapore: Springer.

Lave, J., & Wenger, E. (1991). *Situated learning legitimate peripheral participation.* Cambridge: Cambridge University Press.

Leithwood, K., Mascall, B., & Strauss, T. (2009). *Distributed leadership according to the evidence.* London: Routledge.

Lefoe, G., & Parris, D. (2008). *The GREEN report: Growing, reflecting, enabling, engaging, networking, Final Report* Strawberry Hills. Australian Learning and Teaching Council. www.olt.gov.au/. Accessed 8 March 2015.

Lesser, E., Fontaine, M., & Slusher, J. (Eds.). *Knowledge and communities.* Boston, Massachusetts: Butterworth-Heinemann.

Leont'ev, A. (1978). *Activity, consciousness and personality* (M. J. Hall, Trans.). Englewood Cliffs, NJ: Prentice Hall.

McDonald J., Star, C., & Margetts, F. (2012). Identifying, building and sustaining leadership capacity for communities of practice in higher education. *Final Report to the Office for Learning and Teaching,* DEEWR, Sydney. www.olt.gov.au/. Accessed 8 March 2015.

McDonald, J., & Edwards, J. (2014). Community, domain, practice: Facilitator catch cry for revitalising learning and teaching through communities of practice. *Final report to the office for learning and teaching,* DEEWR, Sydney. Accessed 26th July 2015. www.olt.gov.au/. Accessed 8 March 2015.

Marshall, S. (2006). *Issues in the development of leadership for learning and teaching in higher education.* http://www.olt.edu.au/. Accessed 14 March 2015.

Parker, L. (2008). *Review of the Australian Learning and Teaching Council (ALTC) Program 2006–2008.* www.olt.edu.au/. Accessed 14 March 2015.

Scott, G., Coates, H., & Anderson, M. (2008). *Academic leadership capacities for Australian Higher Education. Final Report to ALTC.* www.olt.gov.au. Accessed 27 February 2015.

Spillane, J. (2006). *Distributed leadership.* San Francisco: Jossey-Bass.

Spillane, J., & Diamond, J. (Eds.). (2007). *Distributed leadership in practice.* New York: Teachers College Press.

Stella, A., & Woodhouse, D. (2007). *Benchmarking in Australian higher education: A thematic analysis of AUQA audit reports.* AUQA Occasional Publications Number 13. AUQA: Melbourne.

Vygotsky, L. (1978). *Mind in society: The development of higher education processes.* In M. Cole, V. Hohn-Steiner, S. Scribner & E. Souberman. (Eds.) Cambridge, MA: Harvard University Press

Wenger, E. (2000). Communities of practice: The key to knowledge strategy. In E. Lesser, M. Fontaine, & J. Slusher (Eds.), *Knowledge and communities* (pp. 3–20). Massachusetts: Butterworth-Heinemann.

Wenger, E., McDermott, R., & Snyder, W. (2002). *Cultivating communities of practice*. Massachusetts: Harvard Business School Press.

Woods, P., Bennett, N., Harvey, J., & Wise, C. (2004). Variables and dualities in distributed leadership. *Educational Management Administration and Leadership, 32*(4), 439–457.

Chapter 15
The Leadership Link: A Hybrid Professional Learning Network for Learning and Teaching Leaders

Trish McCluskey

Abstract Higher Education is awash with rich research outputs on the topic of Higher Education Leadership, however evidence of implementing recommendations emanating from such research is harder to find. This chapter will describe how a Professional Learning Network (PLN) was conceptualised and designed, utilising a range of collaborative spaces and digital technologies to extract Learning and Teaching Leaders from their operational 'silos' and engage them in collaborating and sharing their diverse experiences and wisdom about leadership in a contemporary university. The project aimed to shift Professional Development away from a traditional paradigm of 'workshop' delivered by an 'expert' and present it as a PLN where participants draw on the wisdom and experience of their peers, support each other to solve complex problems, and explore artefacts on Leadership in Learning and Teaching. The network model extended the concept of a Community of Practice and located it within a multiplatform digital space underpinned by the concept of 'connectivism'. The role of the author was that of Network Concierge rather than Leader or Facilitator which enabled a distributed leadership model to evolve.

Keywords Networks · Communities of practice, leadership · Professional development · Professional learning networks · Digital literacies · Higher education · Academic development

15.1 Introduction

Having never aspired to lead anyone anywhere, I consider myself an "accidental leader". Somehow, I found myself coerced into leadership positions that no one else wanted or have been left holding leadership positions by virtue of death or default. I now find myself with a wealth of experience in working and leading across the full

T. McCluskey (✉)
Faculty of Health, Deakin University, Burwood, Australia
e-mail: Trish.McCluskey@deakin.edu.au

© Springer Nature Singapore Pte Ltd. 2017
J. McDonald and A. Cater-Steel (eds.), *Communities of Practice*,
DOI 10.1007/978-981-10-2879-3_15

spectrum of tertiary education from course, program, and department leader to chair of Academic Board and University Council member.

My leadership experiences have engendered in me a healthy curiosity and passion for leadership development and an interest in how we build capability and nurture our emerging leaders to lead tertiary education into an unknown and precarious future.

Today's tertiary education leaders face a myriad of challenges and opportunities when choosing, or being chosen, to embark upon a leadership journey. The 'call' to leadership is often based on success in another realm such as teaching or research and the factors that contributed to success in a previous role don't always translate easily to the new context.

Contemporary leadership paradigms have evolved from accepting "received leadership wisdom" from a higher power to leveraging the wisdom of professional networks and building on this learning to create new symbiotic relationships which enable growth and progression.

So how do we ensure that our future leaders are supported to develop the capabilities and literacies required to warrant their success?

Across my career as a teacher, leader and manager I have had to endure many hours of lecture based "sit and git" professional development (PD) in my search for the magic potion that would authenticate me as anything but an imposter. I will never recover those many lost hours and the glossy ring binders which pay testament to them, continue to gather dust on my bookshelf.

So when I was recently invited to design an innovative leadership development program for learning and teaching leaders, I was confident about what I wasn't going to do—lectures and ring-binders!

This chapter will explore the design and development components of a Professional Learning Network (PLN) across a range of physical and virtual spaces using synchronous and asynchronous communication and digital technologies. I will outline the context in which the program was developed and the rationale for selection of a network model as an expansion of the concept of a community of practice. Wenger et al. (2002) seven key design principles for creating effective and self-sustaining communities of practice will be used to reflect on the effectiveness of the model.

15.2 Project Context

Universities are facing an unprecedented environment of change and uncertainty with increasing pressure to become more transparent, agile and responsive to the diverse needs of multiple stakeholders. To address these challenges many universities have instigated leadership development programs to build the capability of their staff to operate in complex environments.

I was engaged as a project manager to develop such a program for learning and teaching leaders at a large metropolitan university. The principle officer who commissioned the project envisaged that it would take the form of an elective module in the university's Graduate Certificate in Tertiary Teaching but was open to other ideas and suggestions.

Having managed and taught in an equivalent Graduate Certificate program at another university and participated on a number of reference groups for similar programs, I suspected that the uptake of such a module would not be high. Whilst I don't have a problem with this qualification per se, it tends to get bad press amongst academics and is often viewed as a burdensome compliance requirement imposed on the already burgeoning workload of academics. Many academics who move into learning and teaching leadership positions may already have a doctoral degree and some will have completed (or gained exemption from) the Graduate Certificate as most universities requires completion within the first three years of employment. So expecting busy leaders to enrol in an elective credit bearing module within a potentially inflexible course structure did not strike me as being very appealing to the target cohort.

I reflected deeply on what had worked and not worked for me in my formative leadership journey and consulted with colleagues on their experiences. I also consulted the literature on academic leadership development and the work of Scott et al. (2008) resonated with me. They surveyed 513 Australian university leaders and found that the learning preferences of university leaders are very similar to those of students. They suggest that university leadership programs need to be: "just-in-time, just-for-me; focused on learning through resolving real-world problems; peer supported and foster reflection on experience." To me this implied an authentic community based model of learning that allowed for reciprocal sharing of experience and collaborative exploration of issues.

Whilst the universities I had worked at had invested heavily in leadership development programs they were often 'off the shelf' products originating from the corporate business sector and consisted of numerous personality tests and poorly facilitated group activities with insufficient time for follow up debriefing. I recall having to travel to other campuses to attend professional development workshops, often at the most inconvenient times and usually clashing with other work priorities. Invariably there was the ubiquitous glossy, three ring binder with printouts of power-point slides and faded journal articles from business and management journals. This experience was echoed when I canvassed the opinions of a number of senior university leaders regarding what worked and hadn't worked for them in their leadership development.

The university where the project was undertaken was a complex organisation spread across a number of campuses. Learning and teaching quality and student engagement were both high on the institutional agenda and a concerted effort was being made to raise the profile and recognition of innovative practice in both these areas.

The pilot learning and teaching leadership program was to be promoted as an optional professional development activity for key staff across the university. However there was no effort to negotiate time release from other duties to engage with the program and discussions about workload points would need to wait until after the first pilot had been completed.

15.3 Needs Analysis

Being new to the university where the project was located I took a proactive approach and connected with a range of key stakeholders to get a sense of the 'culture' and identify the key issues impacting on this project and the role of Learning and Teaching Leaders. I met with a range of staff across a range of operational levels from schools, colleges, research centres, the library and central support units. Among those I spoke with were PVCs, Deans, Associate Deans, Heads of School, section managers and academics. I also used Google forms to survey 26 staff who occupied the target learning and teaching positions to ascertain their interest in such a program and explore their professional development preferences, needs and challenges. Some of the clear 'takeaways' from my conversations with stakeholders and from the survey were

- Talk with us not at us
- Don't make us do role-plays
- Make any professional development activity easily accessible and flexible
- Encourage conversations across organisational silos
- Don't use the university learning management system (LMS)
- Skip the consultants and use the expertise already in the university.
- Provide food if it's a lunchtime session
- Make it fun!

I concluded from this that that the model needed to be community focused and participant driven so the strengths, needs, fears and aspirations of the emerging leaders could be explored and addressed.

I was also influenced by a very positive experience as a participant in a Massive Open Online Course (MOOC). I had signed up for a 'connectivist' MOOC (well didn't we all?) called 'Personal Learning Environments, Networks and Knowledge' and it was here that I discovered first-hand the power and potential of social learning networks and how they can leverage rich discussion and idea sharing. The 'course' was transcended by the rich interactions between participants from all over the world, engaging and sharing their knowledge, ideas and resources through a network of social media platforms. It was fast-paced, chaotic, community-driven, but most importantly it was 'learningful' and I was overwhelmed by the very relevant and generous, resource and idea sharing that occurred. This was no fluke and I have subsequently undertaken numerous other MOOCs with similar enriching outcomes. I reflected that if I'd had access to such an "on tap" network of supportive peers in my early career I would perhaps have been spared much of the angst of 'not knowing' and encountered fewer struggles and mistakes along the way. Bates (2014) views connectivist MOOCs as being virtual communities of practice and an ideal way to bring together participants scattered around the world to focus on a common interest or domain.

So back to the project drawing board to consider how I might leverage the positive components of a connectivist MOOC design to address the stakeholder feedback and meet the requirements of the project brief.

The design questions I considered were:

- How can I engage learning and teaching leaders where they are at, both physically and developmentally, without disrupting their workflow?
- How can I model progressive 21st century learning and teaching practice and utilize the affordances of digital technology
- How can I engage this group in an open dialogue about leadership and draw on the experience and wisdom that already exists within the group?
- How can I construct a sustainable network using digital tools in a meaningful way to support learning.

I decided to frame the project as a Professional Learning Network (PLN) which is a rather recent construct, popularised through the exponential uptake of social media tools and on line learning via MOOCs. I envisioned that I would create a connected network of learning and teaching leaders who could engage with each other and the collective wisdom of the network using a range of social networking tools and Web 2.0 technology wherever they were and whenever they needed it. Mackey and Evans (2011) suggest that "networked interactions" provide opportunities for useful discourse and sharing of practice rather than positioning the participant as a passive recipient of expert knowledge.

I anticipated that the PLN would shift the focus of Professional Development away from a traditional event based paradigm of 'workshops', delivered by 'experts' and present it as a collaborative Professional Learning Network (PLN) where participants could connect to the wisdom and experience of their peers, support each other to solve common complex problems and feed forward learnings and artefacts on Learning and Teaching Leadership. The network would harness the flexibility, scope and connective power of the digital learning environment to enable and enrich conversations about leadership in learning and teaching.

The aims of the network were developed based on the project brief, survey responses from the target cohort and discussions with a range of other stakeholders.

Network Aims:

- establish a flexible, supportive and sustainable professional Learning Network for Leaders in Learning and Teaching
- enhance the digital literacy and confidence of network participants
- enable "just in time and just for me" professional learning about Leadership in Tertiary Education
- curate and share relevant, resources and artefacts
- create bridges across existing organisation silos.

15.4 So What's This All Got to Do with a Community of Practice (CoP)?

There are a multitude of interchangeable acronyms that capture network and community based learning: Communities of Practice (CoP), Communities of Inquiry (COI), Professional/Personal Learning Networks (PLN), Professional Learning Communities (PLC) to name but a few. I had initially considered a traditional Community of Practice model however stakeholder feedback indicated that Communities of Practice were a bit 'overdone' and in some cases very badly done at this particular organisation. Rightly or wrongly, they were perceived as a place you had to "go to" (usually during lunch hour and you had to bring your own lunch!) so essentially I needed a Community of Practice philosophy and approach but I needed to find a different and more appealing term to attract and engage those who were feeling a bit jaded by existing offerings.

According to Lave and Wenger (1991) "Communities of practice are groups of people who share a concern or a passion for something they do and learn how to do it better as they interact regularly". There are three essential elements required to be a community of practice (Wenger et al. 2002, pp. 27–29) and it is the interaction of these three that encourages the growth of the community. These are outlined in Table 15.1 in relation to the proposed Professional Learning Network.

Communities of Practice (CoP) are not called that in all organizations. "They are known under various names, such as learning networks, thematic groups, or tech clubs" (Wenger 2006) communities and networks can also be conceptualized as two components of social structures that involve learning:

- "The network aspect refers to the set of relationships, personal interactions, and connections among participants who have personal reasons to connect. It is viewed as a set of nodes and links with affordances for learning, such as information flows, helpful linkages, joint problem solving, and knowledge creation".
- "The community aspect refers to the development of a shared identity around a topic or set of challenges. It represents a collective intention—however tacit and distributed—to steward a domain of knowledge and to sustain learning about it" (Wenger et al. 2011).

Communities of Practice are important vehicles for engaging staff in continuing professional development because they:

- **Connect people** who might not otherwise have the opportunity to interact, either as frequently or at all.
- **Provide a shared context** for people to communicate and share information, stories, and personal experiences in a way that builds understanding and insight.
- **Enable dialogue** between people who come together to explore new possibilities, solve challenging problems, and create new, mutually beneficial opportunities.

Table 15.1   Alignment of professional learning network with community of practice fundamental elements

Essential elements	Network elements
A domain of knowledge creates common ground and a sense of common knowledge in the community. A well-defined domain legitimizes the community by affirming its purposes and value to members and other stakeholders. The domain inspires members to contribute and participate, guides their learning and gives meaning to their actions. Knowing the boundaries and the leading edge of the domain enables members to decide exactly what is worth sharing, how to present their ideas, and which activities to pursue	The knowledge domain applicable to the proposed network related to the concept of Leadership and its application to learning and teaching in a contemporary university Another domain was knowledge about digital spaces and the affordances of digital and social media tools
A community creates the social fabric of learning. A strong community fosters interactions and relationships based on mutual respect and trust. It encourages a willingness to share ideas, expose one's ignorance ask difficult questions and listen carefully. Community is an important element because learning is a matter of belonging as well as an intellectual process, involving the heart as well as the head	The community consisted of participants who held a specific job role in leading the learning and teaching functions within a school. There were many shared expectations and duties related to this role and the community would be built around authentic experiences and common challenges
The practice is a set of frameworks, ideas, tools, information, styles, language, stories and documents that community members share. Whereas the domain denotes the topic the community focuses on, the practice is the specific knowledge the community develops, shares and maintains. When a community has been established for some time, members expect each other to have mastered the basic knowledge of the community. This body of shared knowledge and resources enables the community to proceed efficiently in dealing with its domain	The practice relates to the many internal and external frameworks, tools, innovative practices and policies that govern and impact learning and teaching e.g. TEQSA, AQF, cloud based learning etc.

- **Stimulate learning** by serving as a vehicle for authentic communication, mentoring, coaching, and self-reflection.
- **Capture and diffuse existing knowledge** to help people improve their practice by providing a forum to identify solutions to common problems and a process to collect and evaluate best practices.
- **Introduce collaborative processes** to groups and organizations as well as between organizations to encourage the free flow of ideas and exchange of information.
- **Help people organize** around purposeful actions that deliver tangible results.

- **Generate new knowledge** to help people transform their practice to accommodate changes in needs and technologies (Cambridge et al. 2005)

All of the above components could equally be attributed to Professional Learning Networks.

The term Professional Learning Network (PLN) is more prevalent in web based learning spaces and communities. When someone joins an online learning community or subscribes to blogs, podcasts or social media they are essentially building a professional learning network and connecting with like-minded people. These 'nodes' provide real-time access to a wide array of experts, information and learning and are essentially transforming professional development. Wittel (2000) stresses that networks do not just consist of a set of people, but also reflect the set of connections or nodes between the people in the network. He believes that examination of the nodes, connections and flows (such as ideas and information) between nodes is what contributes to the success of the network.

For this project I felt that the term Professional Learning Network had a more contemporary feel and would be easier for me to promote to potential participants so I adopted it for the project. However my approach to the design was strongly influenced by the principles of the community of practice concept.

The PLN was premised on the principles of Connectivism which espouses the notion that "knowledge is distributed across a reciprocal network of connections, and that learning develops from the ability to construct and traverse those networks" (Siemens 2005; Downes 2012). Mackey and Evans (2011) claim that connectivism builds on the community of practice model and they investigated the complementary connections between communities of practice and how participants coordinate their engagement with others in the interests of professional development and socially networked learning. Downes (2006) describes connectivism as a theory that asserts knowledge is not located in one place and therefore not "transferred" but rather is distributed across a network of connections formed from experience and interactions with a "knowing community".

My goal was to establish a supportive and knowing community network that would leverage the wisdom and experience of its members in addition to the affordances of digital technology to connect participants where they were and whenever they needed it.

15.5   The Network Design

My initial brief was to develop the Leadership Module utilising the university learning management system (LMS) and incorporate it into the Graduate Certificate in Tertiary Teaching. However in light of the "collective groan" when I mentioned using the LMS and the limited interest in gaining credit towards a Graduate Certificate, I decided to utilise the more open, accessible and intuitive Google sites as a 'hub' for the network activity and a repository for the shared resources. I explored some other useful collaborative on-line options such as 'Wordpress' and 'Blogger' however Google was chosen as it was the existing enterprise system for the university and was used for all communications and scheduling. It was familiar and easily accessible to all participants without having to remember yet another password or learn a new navigation system. A number of the participants had limited digital literacy so keeping things familiar was desirable. Google also had the added potential to generate data analytics on participant activity and engagement.

The pilot Professional Learning Network was scheduled to run for six months and was designed as a blended mode of engagement.

It consisted of four key components which are listed below and will be further elaborated on later.

1. "The Leadership Link"

An interactive, on-line collaborative space hosted on a customised Google website and containing a range of multimedia resources: podcasts, videos, slide shows, readings, blog posts, infographics and scholarly works. The network was premised on six negotiated themes and these will be discussed later.

2. Meet-Ups

This term was used to capture an optional, monthly group catch-up, featuring guest speakers and network selected activities and topics. It was an effort to move away from the concept of meetings which are perceived as onerous and having a fixed agenda.

3. Webinars

A series of monthly webinars to discuss issues selected by the network and featuring invited guests.

4. Social Media

Engagement via Twitter, Facebook and Yammer and any other social media platform of choice on an as needs basis.

I felt it was important to locate the network activity across a range of spaces to afford participants choice and a variety of options for engagement in the network, as in reality most healthy groups and communities have many interactions and side conversations in various spaces and places. It's quite normal for some networking to remain low key and limited to a few nodes e.g. two participants engaging in a conversation on twitter. The most important thing is that the conversations get started and information gets shared, contemplated and fed forward.

15.5.1 The "Leadership Link" Google Site

This was essentially the hub of the network where members could "check in" and where key information was posted. The design was initially constructed as a loose scaffold underpinned by key leadership "big ideas" and strategic resources.

The content and process was negotiated with the group and co-constructed during the first face to face meet-up session. It was contextualised and categorised according to the needs and experience of the group.

Proposed engagement and activity within the network was premised upon a cyclical "action research" paradigm and was located across **three** separate activity spaces on the Leadership Link site. These were:

1. **Connect**: this space enabled participants to connect to:

   - other members of the network including contact details and bios;
   - leadership resources and artefacts;
   - ideas communicated in various modes;
   - leadership 'experts' connected to the site;
   - other sites for leadership development.

2. **Reflect**: this space was designed to encourage participants to blog about their learning and experience and provided participants with an opportunity to reflect

   - on own and others knowledge, skills, practice via postings and discussion;
   - on activities engaged in via the network;
   - on lived experiences relevant to the themes presented in the network.

3. **Create**: this space provided an opportunity to create

   - leadership action plans;
   - artefacts to feed forward to others in their organisational area.
   - innovative resources for learning and teaching design
   - future research plans.

This action reflection activity was communicated on the website and promoted through discussion based on the following visual model (Fig. 15.1).

The **Leadership Link** Site was designed to be flexible and easily navigated based on individual need. Participants could work through it sequentially, following the monthly themes or just dip into it randomly and target areas of interest or learning need. Everyone in the network had authoring access so they could comment, edit and upload artefacts as needed and time permitted (Fig. 15.2).

Leadership Themes Explored in the Network

I developed a draft list of themes to be explored based on identified needs of network participants and contemporary issues in the higher education sector. These were discussed and further developed at our launch and first meet-up. Below is an overview of what was explored over the course of each theme. This was generated through individual contributions and network conversations (Table 15.2).

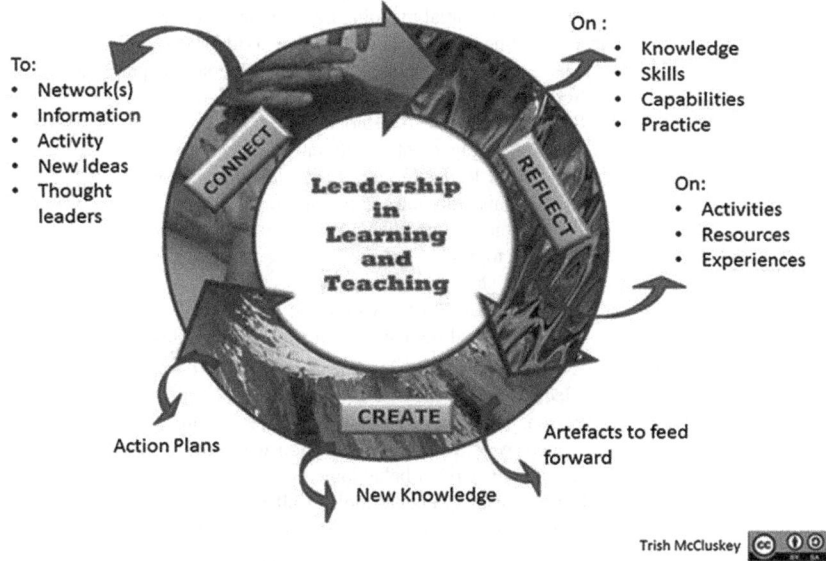

Fig. 15.1 Action research model

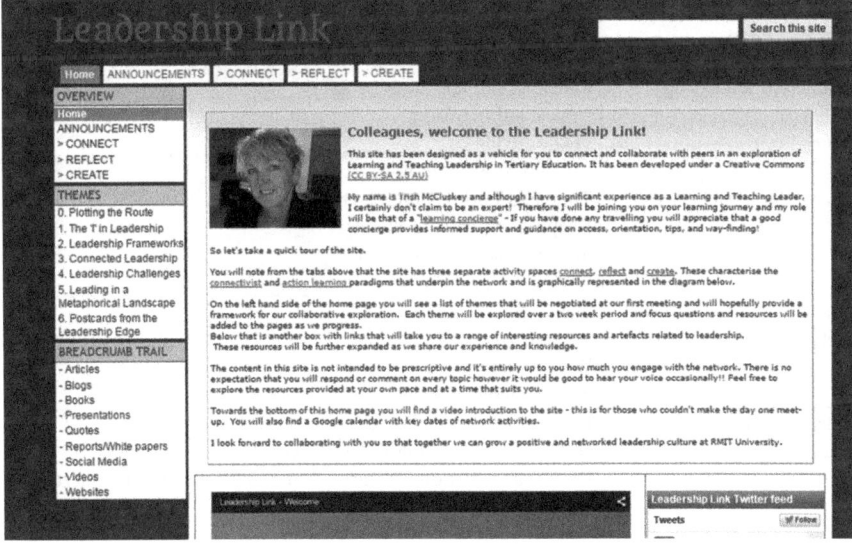

Fig. 15.2 Leadership Link screenshot (CC BY-SA 2.5 AU)

Table 15.2 Leadership themes explored in the professional learning network

Theme	Overview
Plotting the route	This was an initial mapping theme where we discussed in physical and on-line conversations how we conduct the network to best enable us to extend and enrich our leadership capabilities. Some of the issues considered were: Scenic routes and road blocks Rules of engagement—preferences, roles etc Drivers for leadership capability development at... Self-organisation and regulation Existing needs and challenges Webinar topics Tools for sharing and learning Leadership experience within the network Challenges and demands of our leadership roles
The 'I' in Leadership	Essential tools in the L&T leaders toolkit—the most valuable and effective tool is the awareness and use of self Personal characteristics, idiosyncrasies, strengths and limitations shaped by a lifetime of interaction with others Learned leadership behaviours Caring for the valuable tools—self care Discussion of shared resources to read, watch, listen to
Leadership Frameworks	Is leadership in learning and teaching distinctive from other leadership contexts and if so how? Who are the exemplary leaders currently showing the way in learning and teaching at ...... and what qualities and behaviours define their leadership performance? How does... acknowledge and reward good leadership? What Leadership paradigms are best suited to leading learning and teaching in Tertiary Education?
Connected leadership	Reaching out and 'leaning in' Nodes and networks Social Media Creating leadership identity
Leadership challenges	Time and information management Keeping the balls in the air Staying ahead of the curve Strategic management
Leading in a metaphorical landscape	Tsunamis, Avalanches Walled gardens Shifting landscapes
Postcards from the leadership edge	Looking back, moving forwards—learning reflections Notes to self—for future development HEA fellowship opportunity—Link with UK Higher Education Academy

15.5.2 Meet-Ups

The network met physically on a monthly basis. Although 22 leaders signed up to join the network not all of them participated and individuals had preferences for certain modes of engagement. Some people accessed and contributed to the collaborative Leadership Link site but never attended any of the meet-ups whilst others attended all the meet-ups but chose not to engage on line. Others didn't engage at all but sent feedback on how valuable they had found the resources on the site.

There were a number of very successful meet-ups with productive exchanges of intelligence and expertise. A very worthwhile session on distributed leadership hosted by a local expert and author in the field led to the Leadership Link network being featured at a National Summit on Distributed Leadership.

At the final meet-up we celebrated the publication of a book on leadership by one of the network participants. Although she was a published author on the topic and had a great depth of knowledge and experience she actively engaged in the network and shared her expertise willingly. This is the beauty of professional learning networks and communities of practice, it's not about individuals but about sharing and tapping into the collective wisdom.

15.5.3 Webinars

In an effort to encourage active engagement in real time on-line it was suggested by one of the participants that we make an effort to do what we expect our students to do and engage using Blackboard Collaborate video conferencing facilities. There had been a need identified to develop skills in the use of this tool. All I can say is "we tried". We tried very hard. In fact it was unintentionally very therapeutic as we spent one whole session laughing very hard at our inability to engage sound and vision without sounding like chipmunks. I can't say it was a success as a mode of engagement given that not many participants volunteered to host or even turned up for the session however we did learn about having a plan B when it comes to technology.

15.5.4 Social Media

We leveraged a range of social media tools to magnify and amplify the learning and network activity. Some stakeholders engaged daily online whilst others did so intermittently or chose to have stronger engagement at the physical meetings. Leadership Link, Facebook and twitter accounts were set up and used to connect participants and demonstrate the affordances of social media for network learning. The twitter page became quite popular and at one point had close to 100 followers. The account is still active and can be used for ongoing network engagement and promotion (Fig. 15.3).

Fig. 15.3 Leadership Link Twitter account screenshot

15.6 Reflections on Facilitating the Professional Learning Network

My role in hosting the PLN was a challenge to define and to navigate. From the outset I emphasised to the network participants that the PLN is intended to be "for you and by you". There is no 'top' in a network and I hoped that a distributed leadership model would emerge via the many connective nodes and these would vary with specific activities. I uploaded a short video introduction to the website and introduced myself as the "network concierge". I likened the role to that of a good hotel concierge—available to open doors, provide local tips, tricks, directions; listen to tales of travels; solve orientation issues. Wenger et al. (2009) in their book Digital Habitats outline how Technology has changed what it means for communities to "be together" and they provide guidance on the role of technology and the importance having a "technology steward" to support the community to achieve its goals. So the role of facilitator is multilayered and requires agility and responsiveness based on the varying needs and stage of development of the network. On reflection there was no dominant leadership that emerged from within the network, although some individuals contributed more than others which I attribute to a range of factors such as longer experience in the job and having significant tacit knowledge related to the role. Digital literacy and familiarity with the online environment was also a factor in this. I found myself initially having a more interventionist role as participants found their 'digital feet' and learned to engage and contribute more effectively to the Google site. In the face to face sessions most participants defaulted to typical student behaviour and waited for me to start the session.

The role of facilitator, concierge, steward, network weaver or whatever it should be described as is a challenging one that requires significant presence and responsiveness especially in the early phase of network formation and exploration.

15.7   Evaluation

Unfortunately the network was not set up formally as a research project and therefore no formal evaluation was completed. However, feedback from the participants to the project sponsor at the final meeting of the pilot phase, was unanimously positive and supported the continuation of the network.

As this chapter has mainly focused on the network design rather than outcomes and engagement of participants, I found it useful to reflect on Wenger et al. (2002) seven key design principles for creating effective and self-sustaining communities of practice (Table 15.3).

Table 15.3 Reflection on Design Effectiveness

Principle	Observation
Design for evolution: ensuring that the community can evolve and shift in focus to meet the interests of the participants without moving too far from the common domain of interest	I think involving the participants in populating the Leadership Link site enabled this to be achieved. The scaffold structure of the site and the focus on an action reflection cycle ensured sufficient props and prompts were in place to guide and shape activity
Open a dialogue between inside and outside perspectives: encourage the introduction and discussion of new perspectives that come or are brought in from outside the community of practice	Most of the multimedia content and resources uploaded to the Leadership Link site was sourced from the internet and was not limited to the education sector so provided a wide variety of perspectives and models. Inviting external speakers to attend and engage via social media was also a successful strategy and led to ongoing dialogue and collaboration
Encourage and accept different levels of participation The strength of participation varies from participant to participant. The 'core' (most active members) are those who participate regularly. There are others who follow the discussions or activities but do not take a leading role in making active contributions. Then there are those (likely the majority) who are on the periphery of the community but may become more active participants if the activities or discussions start to engage them more fully. All these levels of participation need to be accepted and encouraged within the community	Participation was a challenge for different participants in different spaces of engagement and at different times of the semester. Some needed take study or travel leave and were unable to connect however did express regret about 'missing out'. However all participants engaged at least in one space and most made an effort to develop their knowledge and skills by stretching themselves to engage in unfamiliar milieus such as social media. There was also significant contribution of expertise and resources back to the network

(continued)

Table 15.3 (continued)

Principle	Observation
Develop both public and private community spaces: communities of practice are strengthened if they encourage individual or group activities that are more personal or private as well as the more public general discussions; for instance, individuals may decide to blog about their activities, or in a larger online community of practice a small group that live or work close together may also decide to meet informally on a face-to-face basis	This was the key to the success of the network as participants could engage using a range of on-line tools to connect to the entire network or just reach out to individuals. Active participation was encouraged and sought however not everyone chose to connect or engage. This however is no different to many on line communities where 'lurking' can still result in learning
Focus on value. Attempts should be made explicitly to identify, through feedback and discussion, the contributions that the community most values, then focus the discussion and activities around these issues	As the network 'concierge' I made a concerted effort to link the nodes in the network to each other and to the many resources available. When areas of specific interest or need were identified every effort was made to address these through sourcing specific resources or key contacts
Combine familiarity and excitement, by focusing both on shared, common concerns and perspectives, but also by introducing radical or challenging perspectives for discussion or action	There were a number of organisational strategic issues that were of common interest and concern and we focused on action around resolving these however most of the resources shared were selected to be deliberately provocative and challenging
Create a rhythm for the community: there needs to be a regular schedule of activities or focal points that bring participants together on a regular basis, within the constraints of participants' time and interests	The schedule whilst negotiable was mapped across the six months and participants were aware of when the meet-ups and webinars were timetabled. However the nature of the network also encouraged regular and random engagement through the Leadership Link site and social media

15.8   Conclusion

One of the challenges facing contemporary tertiary education providers is how to prepare learners to engage and succeed in a complex hyper-connected world. Pedagogical practices in tertiary education continue to change and evolve and it's no longer enough for academics to only have mastery of their discipline knowledge and practice. Increasingly they are expected to engage students in digitally enhanced learning spaces and integrate an array of graduate capabilities into the curriculum. Leaders and managers of teaching teams must keep on top of these advances if they are to guide their colleagues in navigating the nuances of dynamic curriculum design and the inherent affordances of Web 2 technology. This will require creativity and responsiveness in the provision of leadership professional development programs.

The model of professional development presented in this chapter outlined how a Professional Learning Network (PLN) was initiated with a group of learning and teaching leaders to build their leadership capability and co-create support structures to enable them to succeed in this challenging environment. The rationale for the model was to create an alternative approach to professional development that engaged participants in any place and at any time that suited their needs rather than rolling out pre-packaged workshops within a predetermined schedule. A range of digital spaces, tools and strategies were utilized to facilitate connection and engagement anytime and anywhere. There was scope to contribute, share, co-create and repurpose resources to enhance leadership development in learning and teaching. Pathways through the program were self-determined and not necessarily linear, although they could be if required. Understanding the nature of the interactions among users in on-line networks and their interaction with the tools in these environments is one of the major challenges of researching socially mediated environments (Conole et al. 2011). Engaging with some of the tools and platforms proved challenging for some but it was acknowledged that it raised awareness of knowledge and practice deficits. Whilst it was useful to hear reflections from the network participants and track activity across this network using the analytics function of the Google platform, this information cannot be reported on at this time as ethical approval has not yet been obtained.

This pilot project was designed to test the interest and engagement of learning and teaching leaders in a new model of professional development and the outcome was certainly more positive than had initially been anticipated. Whilst it was expected that less than ten leaders would engage with the project there were 22 active participants. This could be an indicator that there is a need for flexible, ongoing support for leaders in such roles—or perhaps it was just curiosity about a novel way of engaging with colleagues in similar roles and finding support wherever they could. Although the program has concluded the infrastructure for the Professional Learning network remains in place and some activity continues on the google site that was developed.

The main recommendation emanating from this pilot project is that it be repeated and a formalized research and evaluation framework applied. The infrastructure developed for the PLN could easily be re-purposed and on reflection there is no reason to limit the network to one university as "a network is an open structure, able to expand almost without limits and highly dynamic" (Wittel 2000). The next step is to explore a collaborative research project on this issue with colleagues in other universities.

References

Bates, T. (2014). Online learning and distance education resources weblog. http://www.tonybates.ca/2014/08/14/special-edition-on-research-on-moocs-in-the-journal-distance-education/

Cambridge, D., Kaplan, S., & Suter, V. (2005). Community of practice design guide: A step-by step guide for designing & cultivating communities of practice in higher education. Louisville. http://net.educause.edu/ir/library/pdf/nli0531.pdf

Conole, G., Galley, R., & Culver, J., (2011) Frameworks for understanding the nature of interactions, networking, and community in a social networking site for academic practice. *International Review of Research in Open and Distance Learning*, 12(3). Open University, United Kingdom.

Downes, S. (2006). Learning networks and connective knowledge. *Instructional Technology Forum*. http://it.coe.uga.edu/itforum/paper92/paper92.html

Downes, S. (2012). Connectivism and connective knowledge: Essays on meaning and learning networks. National Research Council Canada. https://oerknowledgecloud.org/content/connectivism-and-connective-knowledge-essays-meaning-and-learning-networks

Lave, J., & Wenger, E. (1991). *Situated learning: Legitimate peripheral participation*. Cambridge: Cambridge University Press.

Mackey, J., & Evans, T. (2011). Interconnecting networks of practice for professional learning. *The International Review of Research in Open and Distributed Learning*. http://www.irrodl.org/index.php/irrodl/article/view/873/1682

Scott, G., Coates, H., & Anderson, M. (2008). Learning leaders in times of change: academic leadership capabilities for Australian higher education, Final report. Strawberry Hills, NSW: Australian Learning and Teaching Council. http://research.acer.edu.au/higher_education/3

Siemens, G. (2005) Connectivism: Learning as network-creation. http://www.elearnspace.org/Articles/networks.htm

Wenger, E. (2006) in Skalicky, J., & West, M., (Eds.) UTAS Community of Practice Initiative Readings and Resources Centre for the advancement of learning and teaching. University of Tasmania.

Wenger, E., McDermott, R., & Snyder, W. (2002). *Cultivating communities of practice*. Brighton: Harvard Business Press.

Wenger-Trayner, E., & Wenger-Trayner, B. (2011). Communities versus networks. http://wenger-trayner.com/resources/communities-versus-networks/

Wenger, E., Trayner, B., & de Laat, M. (2011). Promoting and assessing value creation in communities and networks: A conceptual framework. Ruud de Moor Centrum Open Universiteit. http://wenger-trayner.com/resources/communities-versus-networks/

Wenger, E., White, N., & Smith, J. D. (2009). *Digital habitats: Stewarding technology for communities*. Portland: CPsquare.

Wittel, A. (2000). Ethnography on the move: From field to net to internet. *Qualitative Social Research*. http://www.qualitative-research.net/index.php/fqs/article/view/1131/2517

Chapter 16
The Road Less Travelled: A Conversation Between Four Communities of Practice Facilitators About Their Experiences, Learning and Professional Outcomes from the Role

Kristin Warr Pedersen, Davina Boyd, Millie Rooney and Sarah Terkes

Abstract The facilitator role in a community of practice is widely recognised as a key position for ensuring the function, success and sustainability of a CoP. While a growing body literature and professional development resources have identified and aimed to enhance the skills and capacities of incumbents in this role, little research attention has been given to the in situ experience of facilitators as they undertake the role, nor to the professional outcomes and pathways afforded to CoP facilitators during and after their time in the role. This chapter begins to address this under-explored aspect of the CoP facilitator position through autoethnographic vignettes provided by four previous CoP facilitators from three different Universities who collaborated on the delivery of a multi-institutional CoP project over a 2-year period. The vignettes explore three themes, the extent to which the role provided the facilitators with opportunities to form new networks and friendships; the self-identified skills and capacities each facilitator developed through the role; and the professional pathways and outcomes for each facilitator following the conclusion of the role.

Keywords Community of practice · Facilitator role · Reflective vignette · Professional outcomes · Interdisciplinary teaching · Integrator

K.W. Pedersen (✉) · D. Boyd · M. Rooney · S. Terkes
Tasmanian Institute of Learning and Teaching, University of Tasmania, Private Bag 133, Hobart, TAS 7001, Australia
e-mail: Kristin.Warr@utas.edu.au

© Springer Nature Singapore Pte Ltd. 2017
J. McDonald and A. Cater-Steel (eds.), *Communities of Practice*,
DOI 10.1007/978-981-10-2879-3_16

347

16.1   Introduction

The facilitator of a community of practice (CoP) is often recognised as the lynchpin position for ensuring the function, success and sustainability of a CoP (Cox 2006; McDonald 2014; Ortquist-Ahrens and Torosyan 2009; Tarmizi and de Vreede, 2005). In particular, CoP facilitators are noted as critical to ensuring communication across a CoP; helping to establish and build trust between members; advocating for the group and its outcomes within an organisational context; and ensuring the ongoing and active participation of CoP members. While the existence of a facilitator within the structure of a CoP can seem counterproductive to the informal and organic nature proposed by this collaborative learning model, the positive impact of the facilitator role is recognised by decades of research and case study examples of CoPs in practice across the globe (Ardichvili et al. 2002; Barnett et al. 2012; Connected Educators nd; Garavan et al. 2007; Hildreth and Kimble 2004; Richardson and Cooper 2003).

A growing body of literature has explored the specific characteristics and skill sets required of a CoP facilitator (Cheng and Lee 2014; McDonald 2014; McFadzean 2002; Ortquist-Ahrens and Torosyan 2009; Sandell et al. 2004; Tarmizi and de Vreede 2005; Tarmizi et al. 2006). This work includes an identification of the responsibilities often assumed by this role and importantly, the benefits, and indeed the necessity, for supporting the existence and maintenance of this role in the establishment and management of CoPs. CoP facilitators are often responsible for managing the day-to-day administrative tasks of a CoP such as organising meetings, activities and information exchange between members. However, it is important to note that a CoP facilitator provides more than a basic administrative function (McDonald and Palani 2011; Ortquist-Ahrens and Torosyan 2009). As Prof Jacquie McDonald notes in her Australian Learning and Teaching Council fellowship that focused on the role of CoP facilitators, 'the facilitator plays an important role in creating and sustaining the organising structure and the culture that fosters community, collaborative learning and significant learning and teaching impacts' (2014, pp. 13).

The ability to create and sustain both the structure and culture of a dynamic group of practitioners requires CoP facilitators to possess a diverse and unique set of practical, intellectual and interpersonal skills. Importantly, facilitators also require the capacity to integrate these skills in an often complex environment, and in ways that build trust and motivate participation between CoP members (Ortquist-Ahrens and Torosyan 2009). Recent work has recognised the need for, and opportunities for professional development for CoP facilitators (Cox 2004; McDonald 2014; McDonald and Palani 2011; McDonald et al. 2012; Tarmizi et al. 2005). Particular areas of focus have included preliminary training resources for new CoP facilitators and in situ professional learning opportunities that aim to broaden understanding of the role of CoPs and enhance facilitation and group communication skills (Bellanet and TRG 2002; Cox 2004). A growing number of resources are also available to assist facilitators to carry out their role in the cultivation of a CoP (Kimball and Ladd 2004; McDermott 2004; McDonald 2014; Smith and McKeen 2004; Wenger et al. 2002). These resources are specifically aimed at supporting the achievement of such outcomes as establishing a CoP and enabling the learning and overall mission of that collaboration. Such resources are important because the 'first task [of a facilitator] is to serve the group and create the possibility for members to achieve their individual and their collaborative goals' (Ortquist-Ahrens and Torosyan 2009, pp. 32–33).

The CoP facilitator role is often recognised as a leadership position (McDonald and Palani 2011). Petrone and Ortquist-Ahrens (2004) have identified three specific leadership responsibilities assumed by the facilitator of a CoP—to be a champion, coordinator, and energizer of the CoP and its mission. They note however that 'the ultimate goal of a facilitator is not to maintain the leadership position but to help move the members of the [CoP] to the point where they gradually assume these three roles themselves' (pp. 64). By this model, a good CoP facilitator is one who can make themselves redundant as they build the capacity of the CoP to be self-sustainable, sharing the roles of champion, coordinator and energizer of on-going activities.

Despite growing interest in the facilitator role, little research attention has been given to the professional outcomes and pathways afforded to CoP facilitators, or how the role of the CoP facilitator might enhance or challenge the incumbent's professional opportunities following the role. There is great potential for in situ professional development and professional pathways to be forged through better understanding of the facilitator experience. The purpose of this chapter is to begin to address this underexplored aspect of the CoP facilitator position. Through a reflective conversation between four previous CoP facilitators from three different Universities in the Australian higher education sector, this chapter begins to examine the different professional motivations, positions, characteristics, pathways and outcomes afforded to staff in a defined CoP facilitator role. In doing so we highlight areas that warrant further investigation, particularly into ways to better support this role. The unique contribution of this chapter is in identifying pathways through which the leadership skills and opportunities afforded by the facilitator role might then be harnessed and promoted through the expansion of these skill sets into new contexts.

16.2   Background Context

The reflective accounts provided in this chapter come from four CoP facilitators who were simultaneously employed to support CoPs participating in a multi-institutional teaching grant funded by the Australian Learning and Teaching Council from 2009 to 2011 (Davison et al. 2012). The project focused on the establishment and support of interdisciplinary teaching CoPs in four Australian universities; the University of Tasmania, Murdoch University, the University of New South Wales Australia and the University of Wollongong. Due to the facilitator of the University of Wollongong CoP choosing to leave the higher education sector in the years following this project, this chapter will focus on the other three universities.

A shared CoP model, based on a successful pilot project run at the University of Tasmania in 2008, was used to guide CoP recruitment and reporting for this project. This CoP model aimed to bring together a collaborative teaching team from diverse disciplines around the shared concern of climate change to develop and deliver interdisciplinary, student-led learning activities across their individual classes and programs (Pharo et al. 2014). Student frustration levels at a lack of interdisciplinary undergraduate learning opportunities were noted in focus groups conducted at UTAS prior to the pilot project. Specific to climate change related studies, students stated that a lack of interdisciplinary opportunities often meant they received both repeated and conflicting information from lecturers in different disciplines. For example, students noted that in many of the physical science disciplines, they received the same greenhouse gas effect lecture content to explain global warming, sometimes in each of their four classes in a term. Other students noted that while some disciplines described climate change as a problem of science, others presented it as a problem of politics while others refused to recognise it as a problem at all. The premise of both the pilot and larger national projects was that students should be guided to make links between these disciplinary perspectives and helped to understand the tensions arising between them. This was perceived by the project team as particularly important for first year students who often trial three or more discipline areas across their first academic year. While divergent disciplinary perspectives on issues such as climate change are both realistic and useful for a well-rounded education (Hulme 2009), the lack of a formal space to discuss and learn from these disparate knowledges reflects a failure of the institution to provide students with the authentic and necessary learning opportunities that are so important for today's graduates.

The CoP model used in these projects centred on the existence of two key roles: that of the catalyst or 'activator' and that of the facilitator or 'integrator'.[1] This shared leadership model (described in Pharo et al. 2014) is distinct from other CoP models that outline the existence and roles of a single facilitator. The purpose for the division of roles in this project was two-fold. In the first instance, the model recognises the need for a dedicated facilitator to support the ongoing work of a CoP, hence the provision of the integrator role. However with a focus on leadership development, the model included an activator role at the start of the project to provide opportunities for junior level staff to collaborate with more senior members of staff in identifying and supporting the establishment of a CoP.

The 'activator' role for a CoP in this project was initially intended to be occupied by a mid-level academic staff member who committed to identify and recruit

---

[1]The term 'integrator' will be used to describe this role in the context descriptions and vignettes of the case studies provided in this chapter. This is to maintain the essence of the role in these cases. The term 'facilitator' will then be re-introduced to the Discussion section of this chapter to highlight how these cases can contribute to future research directions and scholarship in this space.

between 8 and 12 academic teaching staff from across a variety of disciplines. The motivation used to recruit individual members to the CoP was a commitment to collaboratively review and renew the interdisciplinary delivery of climate change curricula to ensure integration across disciplinary boundaries. The activator assumed a catalyst role; they were expected to inspire and motivate the start-up of the CoP. The ongoing support and motivation of the CoP following activation was delegated to the 'integrator' role.

The integrators in this project were responsible for facilitating the process of collaboration between members of each CoP. This included managing the practical needs of the project in terms of logistics, administration, data collection and reporting requirements of the larger national project. Additionally the integrator was responsible for facilitating communication between CoP members and motivating continued engagement of members in CoP activities. This was achieved by the integrator having responsibility for maintaining one-to-one contact with each CoP member to ensure ongoing engagement and attention to the needs of each individual in the group. The term 'integrator' was used to describe the expectation that this role would help to desegregate the bounded and often isolated disciplinary work of individual members of the CoP. With a birds-eye view of every CoP member's individual teaching practice, the integrator served as a focal point and repository of knowledge for the CoP itself. In many ways, the integrator role in this project delivered all of the identified roles of a CoP facilitator, however analysis of project outcomes revealed that each integrator also wound up fulfilling a variety of other roles based on the distinct, identified needs of particular CoPs at each institution. In essence the integrator role embodied the essence of the CoP; bringing together and sharing knowledge in a way that made the CoP greater than the sum of its parts. It is important to note that for the purposes of both the pilot and larger national project, the integrator was the only role in the CoP that received financial remuneration, giving them a workload commitment to the CoP that was not necessarily shared by other members.

Committing to participation in a CoP is often challenging for academic staff who work with an ever-present time-pressure of full workloads and often substantial teaching overloads (Davison et al. 2012). To ensure the integrators in this project were able to provide necessary and relevant support that would meet the needs of each institutional CoP and its members, the model flexibly allowed for a broad interpretation of the role. This was achieved through the active immersion of each integrator in the work of their CoP to help to determine the exact role they should take on and how this would contribute to CoP outcomes. As the following institutional context descriptions and accompanying vignettes will highlight, the role of the integrator in each context included a variety of positions based on CoP need. These included curriculum designer, co-teacher, recruiter, and publicity advocate, in addition to the core roles of facilitation and integration of CoP practice.

16.3   The Institutional Contexts

16.3.1   University of Tasmania

The University of Tasmania is a multi-campus institution with over 20,000 students. Until the recent introduction of interdisciplinary 'breadth units' in 2014, there have historically existed a number of structural and administrative barriers that challenge the delivery of truly interdisciplinary experiences for students in undergraduate programs. These challenges have included the siloed structure of course design and administration; the funding model for student enrolments; the lack of a general education or preparatory structure for incoming students; and the casualisation of the workforce (Davison et al. 2012).

The need to address the boundaries stifling interdisciplinary climate change education led to the internal funding (2008) and development of a University of Tasmania pilot CoP. This pilot CoP was made up of teachers interested in renewing their curriculum to enable more interdisciplinary delivery of climate change resources and learning activities. The larger multi-institutional project reported on in this paper, grew out of the pilot University of Tasmania CoP.

During this pilot, the CoP activator/integrator project model was created and successfully trialled in the University of Tasmania context. Following the funding of the multi-institutional grant, the University of Tasmania teaching CoP evolved through a cycle of replenishment and extension. The pilot CoP included eight teaching academics from five distinct faculties across the institution with an integrator who was hired after the CoP had been formed by the activators. This pilot CoP integrator was a professional staff member (author Warr Pedersen), who moved into an academic position towards the end of the pilot year. The second, consolidated CoP that ran during the nationally funded project (2009–2011) consisted of four new teaching academics from four additional disciplines and a new integrator who was a PhD student who did not have teaching responsibilities at the time of the role (author Rooney). Different to the other four institutions in this project, the University of Tasmania CoPs had two activators who worked together throughout the life of the project.

Both University of Tasmania CoPs focused on collaborating on the design and delivery of interdisciplinary student learning activities that could involve students from their combined disciplines. The pilot CoP collaborated on a number of team-taught teaching activities that were delivered throughout the year of the project. These included exploring the same climate change topic from different disciplinary perspectives and having students share their learning across classes; peer reviewing each other's lectures; and guest lecturing across classes. At the conclusion of the academic year, the pilot CoP then collaborated with students from across their discipline areas on the development of a new interdisciplinary climate change class that was then offered at the institution in 2010. The class was coordinated by the activators and integrator of the pilot CoP, with other CoP members contributing to lectures and learning activities based on disciplinary perspective.

Following this initial year, CoP activities stagnated substantially as first iteration members seemed satisfied with the outputs of the pilot collaboration and many retreated from participating in ongoing CoP activities. In the second iteration for the national project, new members were added and the CoP worked together to involve their students in an end of year, cross-disciplinary public forum on climate change. The CoP also continued to collaboratively deliver the new climate change class that remained under the central coordination of the activators and new integrator of the project. While the University of Tasmania CoP no longer exists today as a climate change specific CoP, the CoP model from this project has been used to inform the design of the whole of institution Communities of Practice Initiative (see Chap. 5). Many of the CoP members from this project now participate in this broader institutional initiative, with a large number of them being active participants in the award winning, Education for Sustainability CoP that stretches across the institution.

16.3.2 Murdoch University

Murdoch University (MU) has more than 22,000 students and 2000 staff in campuses onshore in Western Australia and offshore, predominantly in South East Asia. The University strives to be a leading international research-led institution with a focus on translational research, high quality teaching and learning and strong societal engagement. Course offerings at MU are student-centred and encourage interdisciplinary study, with students being required to take foundation courses in their first semester of study to develop an appreciation and understanding of different disciplines and the ways these address the complex societal problems that graduates face. Courses are structured flexibly, with the number of prescribed classes being kept to a minimum, in order to encourage students to take a broad range of courses from a range of discipline areas.

The University's commitment to interdisciplinary teaching and research made it a supportive environment for the MU CoP, at least in principle. However, the impediments to interdisciplinary teaching and research cited in the literature still remain. These impediments include the different languages and cultures of disciplines (Petts et al. 2008), that universities are compartmentalised (Lawrence and Després 2004; Petts et al. 2008), and that the publication culture, funding preferences, and reward mechanisms support disciplinarity as opposed to inter- or trans-disciplinarity (Kueffer et al. 2007; Petts et al. 2008; Evely et al. 2010). For many of the CoP members participating in the community was a way to overcome these impediments and collaborate around an area of shared interest… climate change.

The MU CoP included 14 members, ranging from early career to senior academics, and predominantly coming from the Faculties of Arts, Education and Creative Media, and Science and Engineering. In the first year of the project, two early career academics shared the roles of activator and integrator, working together to catalyse and support the collaboration. In the second year, one of the team moved away from the university and the remaining team member carried the combined role of activator/integrator as a sole position (author Boyd).

During the 2 years of operation the MU CoP enabled conversations, connections and curriculum changes. The CoP provided a space for individuals to share ideas and discuss teaching, climate change, climate change teaching and inter- and transdisciplinarity. The CoP also helped individuals better connect with colleagues from other disciplines and in particular researchers with teaching staff. This was seen to be particularly beneficial for supporting postgraduate students. Importantly, the CoP provided a source of motivation for individuals to rethink and improve their teaching and a number of members made curriculum changes during the project.

In addition, the CoP organised and/or contributed to three events focused on connecting academics, students and the wider public in conversations and action related to climate change. These included the (1) *Bike to Work Challenge* that encouraged people to participate in the annual 'bike to work' in spring challenge; (2) *Tackling Climate Change Student Creative Exhibition* that required students to create and exhibit an artwork that reflected their own personal and practical contribution to climate change and its resolutions; and, (3) *Climate Talk* a panel discussion that brought together practitioners, impassioned people, researchers, teachers and students to discuss burning questions and dilemmas relating to climate change that had been identified by students as important.

Since the end of the project the CoP has not been active, but the relationships and connections still remain for many of the members. There are members who have collaboratively published; bid for successful research grants; continue to teach into each other's classes; and others that are co-supervising higher degree students. The year 2 integrator/activator for this project has continued to benefit from these connections as highlighted in the below vignettes.

16.3.3 University of New South Wales Australia

University of New South Wales (UNSW) Australia has over 52,000 students and 7700 staff. A research intensive university established with a scientific, technological, engineering and medical disciplines focus, environmental research and teaching is undertaken in every one of the nine faculties across the institution. The UNSW Institute of Environmental Studies (IES) is a small unit located in the Faculty of Science, and is the hub for networking amongst staff with environmental research and teaching interests. The teaching collaboration for the project reported on in this paper was hosted by the IES, with the integrator for the CoP being simultaneously employed as the Research and Communications Coordinator for the IES (author Terkes). The activator in the UNSW CoP was a senior level Head of Discipline who was well connected with environmental groups on campus.

The network that existed prior to the formal CoP being established was a loose, informal affiliation of people with similar research and teaching interests. There were no formal meetings organised or specific network events, but people in the network were invited to regular seminars and public events and there were socialising opportunities throughout each year for people to connect. Key members of this existing network formed the basis of the CoP, which was built upon through a process of email call-outs sent by both the activator and the integrator to a university-wide list of students, academics and practitioners identified as having vested interests in improving teaching around climate change.

The UNSW CoP began in 2010 with 22 members including academic staff, students, PhD students and practitioners from across the nine faculties. The decision to include students and people from all levels (including practitioners) was due to the high profile of many student and practitioner activist groups—namely UNSW Sustainability, UNSWTV and the UNSW Enviro Collective—and their success in running campaigns and effecting change. The activator and integrator were also of the perspective that students would have valuable insights into teaching on campus, and they wanted to include their voices in the CoPs decision-making processes. As the profile of the CoP was raised and relative successes of CoP activities became known throughout 2010, more people became interested and expressed interest in joining. By 2011, this collaboration grew to include 45 participants. Additionally, an 'outer network' of mentors, including senior managers, consulted on various projects of the collaboration throughout the project.

Due to the large number of people in the UNSW CoP, the group was split into four teams focused on the following activities: Curriculum Development; Survey and Analysis; Communications and Filmmaking; and Public Events. In the Curriculum Development Group, members had their postgraduate students conduct climate change teaching research projects within their courses. In the Survey and Analysis Group, members had their students conduct institution wide student and staff surveys to scope and document key issues for climate change teaching and curriculum development. The Executive Director of UNSWTV led the Communications and Filmmaking Group to produce an entertaining but informative series of animated videos called 'Climate Change Simply Explained'. The Public Events Group led by a Research Fellow in the Faculty of Law developed models for a 'mock trial' and a 'climate adaptation game', as well as hosting a series of debates and conference presentations involving staff and students. While the teams worked on initiatives across a wide range of areas, the larger CoP was informed of the outcomes and lessons from each through the integrator and the communications she supported across the CoP. With IES as the 'home' for the UNSW CoP, this sharing of initiatives and broader networks between teachers and researchers in climate change still continues to be supported, even post funding and official function of the CoP.

16.4   Reflective Methodology

Reflective journaling (Janesick 1998; Jasper 2005) was used throughout the multi-institutional project to facilitate collaboration between the institutional CoPs and to enable the sharing of experiences and learning across the project team. Reflections were collected through individual written journals, interviews and focus groups between team members over the life of the project. This data contributed to the final reports of the funded project (Davison et al. 2012) and formed the basis for follow-up reflective work and collaborative publications by the whole project team (Pharo et al. 2014; Davison et al. 2014). One of the consistent messages highlighted in these project team reflections referred to the valuable contributions that the facilitator role provided to the success of each CoP. The trial of a shared CoP model in four different institutional contexts enabled a deeper exploration of the facilitator role, further enhanced by the existence of a variety of interpretations of that role in each context and the positions of the incumbent facilitators when they took on the role. It is important to note that all of the facilitators were junior staff members, only two of which had teaching responsibilities as academic staff. Another two were professional staff members in administration roles and the fifth, a PhD student.

The vignettes provided in this chapter draw on the reflective responses collected since the start of the project in 2010 and build on this information through further reflection from facilitators collected at time frames of 2 and 3 years following the conclusion of the project. These reflections were collected in collaborative focus groups in 2013 and through the collaborative publication of this paper in 2014/2015. The vignettes focus on the experience and professional outcomes of the facilitators to explore the impact of the CoP facilitator role on their learning and career trajectories in the higher education setting.

To guide the final reflective process, an interview schedule was drafted by authors Warr Pedersen and Boyd with the aim of further exploring themes identified in the multi-institutional project. These included: (1) the extent to which the position and identity of the facilitators influenced the direction and outcomes of the CoP; and (2) the extent to which the CoP initiated professional learning opportunities and career advancements for the facilitators. A series of four questions were used to guide a reflective focus group discussion between all four facilitators in 2013, the data from which was then used to instigate individual reflections by the authors in the form of the vignettes that are shared in this chapter. The focus of the reflections in this chapter explore the ways in which the personalities, motivations, existent job positions and skills of each individual facilitator helped, or challenged them to each find identity in the role, and how this ultimately influenced the function and outcomes of each CoP. The vignettes used in this chapter showcase our final stage of considered reflections on these themes through autoethnographic accounts of our individual and collective experiences as CoP facilitators (Ellis and Bochner 2000) marking the end of an evolving reflexive methodology that drove the multi-institutional project.

16.4.1 Vignette 1: Reflecting on New Networks and Friendships

A key outcome from the multi-institutional ALTC project on climate change CoPs was the establishment of new networks of interdisciplinary teaching staff at each institution. While the focus of this project was to catalyse collaborations that would improve interdisciplinary student learning opportunities, the enhancement of networks and friendships for the integrator was an additional positive outcome highlighted in many of the CoPs.

16.4.2 University of Tasmania: Integrator 1 (Kristin Warr Pedersen)

As a new staff member in an admin role, I really appreciated the CoP model as a method of building new networks and friendships that I would not have had the capacity to build myself at that stage in my career. I was able to walk into an already formed group of committed individuals and join the activities as an equal member who shared a mutual interest in climate change education. As a junior staff member with few contacts, the project was an amazing introduction to a variety of staff from across the institution. It is only now, 7 years later, that I can see how unique this start was. While most new staff are hired into one particular faculty or school to serve a discipline specific role, I was introduced to the institution in a truly interdisciplinary capacity. This lack of allegiance to any specific discipline or administrative area enabled me to imagine and propose linkages and courses of action for CoP activities that would never have been conceived of, or thought possible by other members of the CoP. This included co-developing curriculum and spruiking another's class in a 'competitive' discipline. The CoP found my perspective to approaching historical barriers to interdisciplinarity refreshing and they noted how they were more willing to innovate in their classrooms in non-traditional ways with my 'outsider' support.

Importantly, the objectives of my role were decided on by the whole group and all of the members were committed to my involvement. My connections with each of the members of the CoP centred around our collaboration on curriculum activities in each of their classrooms. This helped me to establish strong friendships with members of the CoP based on a growing trust and mutual respect for one another's ideas and ways of working. The best evidence of this was in my being invited to teach into four of the member's classes, which I would consider one of the deepest forms of respect and trust to show to another educator, especially one who at the time was not even a recognised 'teacher'. Following our first year, I continued to work with four of the educators in their classrooms, including working on the development and co-delivery of a new interdisciplinary climate change class that resulted from the CoP. In my current role as an academic developer, I have been able to draw on my networks and friendships from this initial year in a variety of capacities, and consider many of these colleagues some of my closest at the institution.

16.4.3   University of Tasmania: Integrator 2 (Millie Rooney)

Unlike all the other integrators in the project, I took on the role sometime after the CoP had already been established. This was both a positive and negative experience. In many ways it made my job easier; the CoP essentially ran itself and I was simply a conduit for any organisational questions. Less positive however was the fact that I did not develop particularly strong bonds with anyone in the CoP as we had not been through the shared process of creation. Indeed in a model that championed distributed leadership, I seemed to have been plonked into the CoP by the activators (based on previous work experiences with them), without any consultation of the group as a whole. This meant that the members were not given the opportunity to regroup and to consider what they wanted next from the CoP. In some ways this hindered my ability to develop networks personally as I added nothing particularly new to the group in terms of teaching opportunities (given at this stage I was not yet teaching into any classes).

While a part of my role was to recruit new members to the CoP, I struggled to do this effectively. This was because I was working within a CoP that already had a very clear idea of what an integrator was and their shared vision had been created without my involvement. Looking back over some of my project reflections at the time, I can see that I had underprepared in my recruitment role, failing to really engage properly with existing CoP members and getting a sense of what existed *before* attempting to recruit others. I think this was partially because many of the original members had gained what they needed from the CoP in the initial year and had lost the interest and the need for the CoP to continue (despite being very vocally supportive of its ongoing development). As a result, my ties with the broader CoP were relatively weak and my position unclear to many of the old and new members.

Despite the weakness of these ties, the very basic fact of having become acquainted with CoP members through the project has meant that I do feel more comfortable in contacting these people post project for various reasons. For example, I have recently contacted one of our CoP members to ask whether his marketing class could work with a volunteer project I am part of (he very readily agreed). Having entry points to different parts of the university is psychologically good for a new staff member, even if the ties are weak. As a PhD student, this was one of the few opportunities I was given that made me feel a part of the broader university community.

For me, the CoP was most effective in my developing stronger ties with the original integrator and the CoP activator, with whom I worked very closely throughout the project. These people were in the same department where I was undertaking my PhD. While being in the same department challenged my capacity to make unique contributions to our interdisciplinary CoP, there were also some benefits to this co-location. For example developing relationships with colleagues in my department that were not based on the power imbalances that often occur between staff and PhD students was invaluable. The establishment of these more equal relationships contributed not only to my professional development in the area, but also to my sense of belonging and wellbeing.

That said, I was working as the integrator and my PhD supervisor was one of the activators. Inherent here was a power imbalance that led to him being hesitant to ask me to do too much work that might distract from my PhD. As a result, I wasn't able to wholeheartedly throw myself into the role.

16.4.4 Murdoch University Integrator (Davina Boyd)

Murdoch University (MU) has a physical divide between the Natural Sciences and Social Sciences in the form of what is called Bush Court, this is a 100 m × 100 m of grass with iconic eucalypt trees scattered for shade. This space creates what urban planners call a severance, or barrier effect, which means many staff never cross it, except to visit the staff café, ATM or food outlets. I am perhaps unusual in that during my time as an academic staff member at MU I have spent 5 years on either side of this 'severance' and for 1 year I had office space on both sides. A consequence of this (as well as the extent of the activator's networks who as a lecturer in sustainability regularly involved other academics from different disciplines in his teaching) was that when the CoP was activated, I knew 11 of the 13 individuals who agreed to participate. This meant that for me new networks and friendships were not an outcome that I would attribute to my role as integrator. Today, out of the 13 other network members I am still regularly in contact with eight of them, but I would have called them colleagues, and many of them friends, before the CoP began. That said, it is possible that the CoP was another shared experience that contributed to that friendship making. Further, I recognise that the activator's relationship with some of the network members enabled me to develop stronger connections with others. I certainly enjoyed having the opportunity to spend more time working with them and the CoP afforded me that opportunity.

16.4.5 University of New South Wales Integrator (Sarah Terkes)

As a professional staff member with networking listed as a task on my job description, I relished the opportunity to take on this project and the role of integrator. This project gave me a license to approach all UNSW academics, practitioners and students who were passionate about climate change, and ask them to work with me on a problem I knew they were interested in. It seemed like a win–win situation.

I was already closely involved with a key group of environmentally-focused academics and PhD students that I knew I could count on to participate, so that left me to approach the people I wished would get involved. Needless to say, I enjoyed approaching people, introducing myself and the project, and asking them to join the network, subsequently acquiring many new useful contacts. This process benefited greatly from the CoP activator's database of contacts, thanks to his high-level position as Head of the School of Humanities and as a well-known and well-liked leader in the environmental humanities research group. I also really enjoyed investigating who the high-profile student activists were (the ones involved in environmental groups on campus). Approaching them and securing their involvement guaranteed a critical-mass of participants as well as publicity for our CoP.

Once we had established what we considered to be a large and diverse enough group of committed individuals, we started holding catered meetings. I mention the catering because I think it was crucial to securing attendance. Allowing people to indulge in delicious, free sandwiches while discussing topics they cared about, and encouraging them to brainstorm creative new ideas to potentially solve an issue they were already concerned about was invigorating for everyone. This helped create a comfortable and enjoyable atmosphere, and therefore helped everyone in the room form new, amicable relationships with the other CoP members.

In other words, it wasn't just me who benefited from the new networks and friendships—the other members of the CoP all met one another, realised they had common goals, and some of them even went on to co-author research papers and collaborate on projects together. As for me, my personal profile was raised at the university and since the project ended I have continued to collaborate and work amicably with CoP members such as the head of UNSWTV and the head of the UNSW Sustainability Office.

16.5   Vignette 2: Reflecting on New Skills and Capabilities

The skills and capacities required of CoP facilitators are well documented in the literature. The focus of the following vignettes are on the skills and capabilities that were developed as part of the integrator role in this project, and the impact these may have had on providing opportunities for future career pathways and professional opportunities in the higher education sector.

16.5.1   University of Tasmania: Integrator 1 (Kristin Warr Pedersen)

In many ways, my integrator role offered my first workplace learning opportunity, where I was able to apply and develop many of the skills I had explored and learned during my previous studies at university. All of those generic skills that we aim to develop in a university graduate, such as problem solving, critical thinking, communication and social responsibility are also key requirements of facilitating a CoP. Having just completed a research degree prior to taking on this role, I was also able to extend my developing skills in time management to a collaborative project focus, with deliverables that mattered to more than just me. The collaborative focus of the project also led to my developing understanding and skills in managing sometimes conflicting interests and perspectives across a group. I learned simple skills such as who preferred short emails and who preferred coffee and a chat when the project needed to be discussed. I also learned more complicated skills like how to present critique on curriculum and how to explain why some ideas or initiatives were not being supported by the group. These are all skills that I have found to be useful and transferable to other parts of my professional life, and honestly probably even my personal life!

Importantly, this role also gave me a broad, and first hand, understanding of many of the central university processes that often remain mysteries to junior academics. In our first year, we developed and successfully proposed a new class, pitched a new curriculum approach to the Associate Deans (Learning and Teaching); ran a student event; presented at three conferences; and established a team teaching approach not used before at UTAS. Through this role, I was given teaching opportunities that ultimately led to my securing an academic teaching position at the end of the pilot project. I also had the opportunity to participate as a member of a national consensus conference on climate change, a model which I then went on to use as a curriculum design strategy to guide the development of our interdisciplinary climate change class that involved students at every step. Our CoP often discussed how the informal education I received, as our CoP integrator, particularly in the role of co-curriculum designer, was exactly the interdisciplinary experience we were hoping our students could receive. If only that one-to-group attention could be delivered to each and every enrolled student.

16.5.2   *University of Tasmania: Integrator 2 (Millie Rooney)*

To be honest I'm not sure that the integrator role really gave me new skills and capabilities. I'd say that actually I wasn't proud of the job that I did in that role. I failed to acknowledge that I was stepping into an established CoP and the significance of this. Added to this was the fact that I had no other staff role at the university meant that I had no specific position from which to launch my integration role. I was unable to establish myself as a person at the University of Tasmania with whom others might get value out of connecting with. A part of this was also perhaps due to a flagging interest in re-energising the CoP by initial members, including the activators, and thus the job of gathering new members fell to me. This was a challenge due to my substantive role as a PhD student, where I found myself often working in isolation. This meant my own work, was less actively immersed in the CoP than the previous integrator and I often felt I had nothing concrete to contribute to the CoP.

Indirectly however, my role as integrator was an excuse for the activators in my department to employ me as a co-teacher into the interdisciplinary climate change class created by the pilot CoP. As I continued to be involved in this class I developed skills not only in classroom teaching but also in curriculum development and class planning, and I have continued in this role following my finishing the role of integrator for the CoP.

16.5.3 Murdoch University Integrator (Davina Boyd)

Reflecting on the new capabilities I developed from my experience as the MU integrator I would say that my experience impacted most on my capacity to collaborate. This collaboration was taking place on two levels: (1) as the integrator I was collaborating with the MU CoP; and, (2) as a researcher, I was collaborating with other researchers in the project.

My collaboration with the CoP was a constant source of reflection as I grappled and still grapple with whether a CoP requires an integrator or indeed an administrator to operate. Surely, if we just designed it appropriately and the University supported it (with a workload allocation) then participants could work together without someone doing the doing for them? I realise that it may be naïve to think that people can work across campuses without support or that academics will be given the time to commit to new things, but I like to think that with the right incentives/motivations then it is possible. More importantly at the time of the project I had a strong sense that without this commitment, the CoP would not be sustainable at the project end.

For the MU CoP, I don't think we tapped into the motivations of the group and it was difficult to discern what their motivations were when we had many individuals who were already collaborating across campus in climate change teaching. However, I do think I could have been more effective at supporting the CoP to function; at the very least I should have done a better of job of prioritising and defining some objectives/projects. I also now acknowledge that in the absence of workload points, my time should have better enabled the CoP members to do more with a smaller time investment, at least for the life of the CoP. I now realise that my fixation with creating a sustainable CoP meant that I lost sight of the fact that maybe it was about creating sustainable climate teaching outcomes, not a sustainable CoP. In my current role as project manager (and active researcher) of an international team of researchers I still struggle with how to motivate the team and be an enabler. I would say that my experiences as an integrator have contributed to my collaborative practice and my ability to continually reflect on and improve this practice.

In collaborating with the multi-institutional project team there were also new lessons to learn, particularly about how to navigate differences of opinions and ways of thinking. In collaborative activities that I have been involved in since, I take much more time to ensure there is clear communication between members and that differences of opinion are carefully navigated. In my research role this has become even more important because there are not only disciplinary differences, but differences in culture and language to navigate.

16.5.4   University of New South Wales Integrator (Sarah Terkes)

I came to the role with data analysis, project management and stakeholder management skills—what I didn't have were *qualitative analysis* skills. I approached the role with my usual action and results-driven mindset, hoping in the beginning that would be enough for the project to be a success. But it soon became apparent that I would need to *think*, and *reflect*, and *analyse* both my part in this project and the project as a whole. I was uncomfortable when I learned that our project reflections weren't supposed to focus on what we were doing and achieving—but what we were *learning* from this experience.

For me, deep and meaningful reflection (in relation to a research project) was a very new way of thinking. So, I would say that *learning to think reflectively* was a new skill I acquired along the way (which I am honestly still acquiring—I'm sure much to the chagrin of my very generous and kind co-authors). This role has also pushed me further into academic writing, as I had never co-authored an academic paper before, excluding written conference proceedings, presentations and technical reports.

16.6   Vignette 3: Reflecting on New Positions and Pathways

The following vignettes reflect on the ways in which the CoP facilitator role may lead to new positions and professional opportunities in the higher education sector. This theme came up as relevant to this cohort of integrators, as they were all junior level staff at the time of accepting the roles. Each of their roles have progressed in the higher education sector, with varying degrees of accountability being attributed to the integrator role and the skills developed in that role. It is worth noting, the fifth integrator in this project (whose experience has not been discussed in this chapter) also progressed in the higher education sector for a two year period following the conclusion of the project. After that point she chose to the leave the sector to pursue other interests.

16.6.1 University of Tasmania: Integrator 1 (Kristin Warr Pedersen)

I consider myself extremely lucky to have been offered the role of integrator in this project. I can say without a doubt that it was *the* door that opened for me at the University of Tasmania, which has led to the variety of roles and opportunities I have been offered in my almost eight year (now academic) career. My role in the project led to casual teaching opportunities in three schools, one of which I then continued on through a rolling contract for 4 years. I have had the opportunity to teach into both the undergraduate and postgraduate programs and I now coordinate a class in a staff professional degree. After the first pilot year of the project, the activators and I successfully won the federal grant funding for the national project discussed in this paper, giving me a significant run on the board for my research performance expectations as a new academic staff member. We also collaborated on the delivery of an interdisciplinary climate change class for which we won a teaching award in 2010.

Following a presentation on our work at our institution's central learning and teaching conference, I was approached by our central learning and teaching unit and asked to manage another multi-institutional federally funded, leadership grant. This role then led to my being offered a permanent academic development position in that central learning and teaching unit to assist project teams to develop grant ideas and proposals. I still work in this position today, with one my primary roles being the coordination of our institutions Communities of Practice Initiative (discussed in Chap. 5 of this book), which is based on the model of this project. I am also now an active member of the institution-wide Education for Sustainability CoP supported through this initiative. I work collaboratively with three other staff members to 'integrate' this large CoP, relying heavily on the skills and networks I developed as part of my original integrator role.

16.6.2 University of Tasmania: Integrator 2 (Millie Rooney)

For 2 years my work as integrator enabled me to continue developing my classroom teaching experience, which contributed to my being offered teaching positions at the University of Tasmania. I went from the occasional tutoring job, to being offered a temporary position as lecturer for a third year class (I turned this opportunity down due to a lack familiarity with the content of the class and the fact that it would have started the day I submitted my PhD). In 2014 I continued to teach (and assist coordination of) the interdisciplinary climate change class and was given significant responsibility in this work. While I would like to say that the integrator role has contributed to new positions and pathways, lack of funding for any non-permanent teaching staff has meant that teaching opportunities at the University of Tasmania have virtually disappeared, and this has significantly impacted on my ability to remain employed to teach this CoP founded class.

What the role did give me however was something concrete to put on a resume about my ability to network (something I consider to be a natural strength of mine) and the opportunity to show my ability and willingness to engage in paid work with staff within my own department. This has since indirectly led to the occasional short-term research assistant contract.

16.6.3   Murdoch University Integrator (Davina Boyd)

It would be difficult to directly attribute where I am now to my role and experiences as an integrator in this project, but I do believe it has contributed to my current position. This project ended in 2012 and later that year two colleagues from MU (including one that was part of the CoP) and I applied for a Category 1 Research Grant (this is a grant that is listed in the Australian Competitive Grants Register). We were successful, and as the Principal Investigator for this new project I have no doubt that being part of this multi-institutional research team, and having experience in working collaboratively on this CoP project (also funded by the Australian Government), helped demonstrate that I had a proven track record in being part of a successful research team. As mentioned previously, my capacity to work collaboratively also improved in my role as NA/NI and this has been asset in this new role.

16.6.4   University of New South Wales (Sarah Terkes)

The integrator role on this project served as a crucial stepping-stone to my current university position as a Digital Marketing Coordinator at UNSW Science. The diverse stakeholder management skills I was able to show evidence of, and the academic writing I was able to participate in were critical in helping me secure this role. These skills and evidence base also formed key aspects of my successful application to gain entry to a Masters degree here at UNSW. Incidentally, two CoP members served as referees on my job application, highlighting how the people I met and the friendships I formed during the project have continued to benefit me. In addition to this new position, the skills I gained as an integrator have also been critical in enabling me to continue studying, which will be a long term benefit for my professional outcomes directly, and indirectly, related to this role.

16.7   Discussion

The above vignettes demonstrate four case examples that have extended the facilitator role beyond one with specific, administrative responsibilities that support the growth of other members in a CoP. The vignettes highlight ways in which facilitators have a unique learning experience, and therefore set of outcomes, through the process of participation in a CoP. These included the establishment of relationships between the facilitators, as junior members of staff, with a broader range of colleagues across new networks and levels of experience; as well as the responsibility of undertaking leadership positions within the CoP that were not necessarily recognised across other aspects of the institution. The experiences discussed provide a starting point for exploring how the individual learning and professional outcomes of a CoP facilitator may be recognised as an additional indicator of the success of a CoP, and how the unique experience of a CoP facilitator as the integrator of a CoP's activities, may lead to opportunities for professional growth. Importantly, the above vignettes have highlighted how even when implementing a common CoP model across different contexts, the experience of the facilitator in a CoP is so unique and context dependent that it is hard to compare and contrast those experiences to the point of being able to make generalisations. What the vignettes do is provide a reflective account of four different experiences that begin to highlight the unique contributions that facilitators can make to CoPs, the higher education sector and scholarly inquiry into CoP literature.

The reflections of the facilitators in this project highlight differences in the ways the facilitator role was embodied in each context, which notably impacted on both the outcomes of individual CoPs and the facilitators' own professional pathways. For instance, the process of recruitment of participants in each CoP was distinctly different across the institutions, particularly the extent to which the facilitators themselves were involved in that process. The confidence of each facilitator to participate in recruitment was strongly based on the extent to which they had previous networks in the institution. The MU and UNSW facilitators had both worked at their institutions previously, and as such were able to draw on their own networks as well as the networks of the activators to engage participation in their CoPs. While the project gave them the credentials and purpose to approach new colleagues, the skill set and confidence in this task was already formed in some way. This level of confidence in participating in the recruitment process was significantly different to the experience of the University of Tasmania facilitators, who were both new staff members when they assumed the role. This was not such an issue for the first University of Tasmania facilitator, as when she came into the role the CoP had already been formed and she was given the opportunity to co-develop her own role in consultation with the full CoP. The second facilitator however found this lack of experience and personal clout at the University to significantly hinder her confidence in the role, and in effect, her ability to recruit new members or gain the trust of current members. The experiences of these four facilitators highlight the need for more effective initiation and confidence building in the early stages of the role, which using the first University of Tasmania facilitator's experience could simply come from suitable introductions at the start of the role.

The case of the second University of Tasmania facilitator provides a number of important lessons for CoP project leaders. In particular, when examined in relation to the experience of the first University of Tasmania facilitator, a number of questions arise regarding the success of transferring this critical role once a CoP has been established. While facilitator Rooney was allocated an identified leadership role in the CoP that had been previously recognised by the CoP members in relation to the first facilitator (Warr Pedersen), the lack of introduction to the role and the current members meant that her leadership capacity was significantly stunted from the outset. The result was a distinctly different experience for the two facilitators working with ultimately the same CoP. While the CoP model used was intended to provide for supportive development of the facilitator through a shared responsibility for recruitment between the integrator and the activator, in this instance, the activators did not provide the same level of initiation to the CoP for Rooney as they had for Warr Pedersen. This was in part due to the CoP already being formed and active for over a 2 years period. The result was a facilitator/CoP relationship that was not developed on shared experience and trust. This case highlights the need for consistent and ample initiation to the role for new facilitators, regardless of whether the CoP they will be facilitating has already been established. This case also highlights other areas for further investigation, including the perception of an on-going CoP regarding a change of facilitator, and the impact this might have on the continued sustainability and success of the CoP.

The initiation of the facilitator to the role deserves a great deal of consideration by CoP leaders, particularly considering the leadership responsibilities associated with the role (McDonald and Palani 2011). As the vignettes highlight, the leadership position of the facilitator within the CoP does not necessarily align with how leadership is conceived by the larger institution. The vignette of the second University of Tasmania integrator highlighted this challenge as a PhD student. Not only did she lack previous networks to draw on at the University, but she also had to contend with her parallel reality—being a PhD candidate and the power imbalances associated with working for her supervisor in a very different capacity. While the CoP facilitators in each case study assumed the leadership responsibilities of champion, coordinator, or energizer (Petrone and Ortquist-Ahrens 2004) at some point in the role, their achievements and abilities to excel at each of these varied in each institutional context and in relation to the individual positions of each facilitator. As junior level members of staff, championing the efforts and achievements of the CoP was limited to the professional contexts in which they each worked. As a professional staff member, the UNSW facilitator did not have extensive networks across the academic divisions of the institution, however through the CoP model her collaborative efforts with the activator in the project allowed for the development of a large, intra-institutional CoP. This is in contrast to the MU facilitator experience of taking on both the activator/integrator role and being limited to the networks of her own position. A comparison of these two cases highlights areas for further research into the potential benefits of a shared CoP leadership/facilitator model such as the one trialed in these cases. While the ALTC project these vignettes relate to did investigate the usefulness of this model in supporting the leadership development of the CoP members involved, these vignettes point out that further work is warranted to explore the leadership development opportunities provided to the facilitators themselves.

The vignettes also provide important prompts for a discussion about the opportunities provided by the facilitator role for the professional development of junior staff just starting out in the higher education setting. Such discussion is particularly pertinent considering the increased trend towards the provision of junior, casual positions across sector (Coates et al. 2009; Kogan et al. 1994; Ryan et al. 2013). All of the facilitators reflected in this chapter were junior level staff who undertook the role with the motivation to continue working in the higher education sector. The role was perceived as one that would open up networking opportunities to either extend teaching opportunities and/or broaden networking roles the incumbents were already working within. In the case of the University of Tasmania facilitators, the role opened up teaching opportunities for both incumbents and extended their professional networks well beyond their own discipline areas. The first University of Tasmania facilitator has even gone on to use the CoP model of the project to initiate a successful institution-wide CoP program. The second University of Tasmania facilitator has recognised the ways in which the role provided her with opportunities and in-roads to academic life at the institution that she felt sheltered from in her role as a PhD candidate. The MU facilitator recognises the impact of the role on providing opportunities for continued cultivation of already existent relationships, something that becomes increasingly difficult in a competitive, overloaded academic environment. Importantly, the MU facilitator has continued to cultivate these relationships and in fact recognises this collaborative skill she developed as a key part of her academic identity. As a professional staff member, the UNSW facilitator has commented on the ways the role has helped her start to extend her practical skill set to include new capabilities in reflection and academic writing, each of which have led her into new positions and new areas of study.

While the facilitator is often a recognised member of a CoP, the mission of a CoP is focused primarily on cultivating learning for members around their shared domain area and not on the professional learning outcomes of specific individuals in the group, arguably least of all the facilitator. In fact, as was previously noted, a good CoP facilitator is ultimately one that can bring a CoP to the point where they are no longer needed in the role, which has potentially led to the lack of research exploring what happens to facilitators after that point. However this project has highlighted that the unique experience had by facilitators can lead to them gaining a set of transferable skills that can be of great use to the higher education sector in a number of new contexts. The vignettes in this chapter warrant a call for more in-depth exploration of the facilitator experience in a CoP, which could uncover better ways to support the role, both during the time of facilitation and after when the incumbent proceeds down different professional pathways that may unfold as a result of the role. Of particular follow-up interest to the cases presented in this chapters, is the extent to which collaborative approaches to professional learning and engagement continue to be fostered, or sought out, by facilitators who find themselves on different professional journeys after their time in these roles.

The skill set required by the facilitators in each institutional setting reported on in this chapter has been recognised as capable of contributing to a number of institutional initiatives, including teaching, research and administrative collaborations. As such, it should be of interest to institutional managers to explore the ways in which the unique experiences of CoP facilitators can be designed to better develop these skill sets and provide professional opportunities to transfer the capacities of CoP facilitators into new initiatives. Through highlighting the different pathways and outcomes of the integrators in this project, this chapter has provided some points to consider when outlining the roles, responsibilities and futures of a facilitator of a CoP. Additionally, once formed, a CoP may want to consider ways in which the professional learning and outcomes of the facilitators themselves may be recognised as an additional success indicator of the CoP. In essence, this chapter argues for the potential for the CoP/facilitator relationship to be mutually beneficial, with the cultivation of learning and professional opportunities being a shared goal for each.

16.8 Conclusion

Communities of Practice as a field of inquiry provides a wide range of potential areas of exploration that include the theory behind CoPs through to the impact of this structure on the variety of domain areas on which CoPs may focus. Increased attention on the significant role of the facilitator in cultivating both learning and practice outcomes of CoPs has led to the provision of a number of justifications for the role as well as a suite of professional resources for incumbents to undertake the role. What has been underexplored and under resourced is an examination of the professional experiences of facilitators and how these may impact on the outcomes of the CoPs they support and on their own professional learning journeys in a higher education setting. The reflective vignettes of this chapter have provided insights into the unique experiences of four CoP facilitators, highlighting the distinctive skill sets, interpretations and executions of the role in different personal and professional contexts. While this work is not yet generalisable to the broader facilitator role across CoP studies, this chapter has provided a starting point and motivation to more strategically consider the role of the facilitator and the contributions this role can make to individual CoPs and the broader higher education sector.

Acknowledgments The authors would like to acknowledge all of the project team members of the ALTC Grant that funded this project, specifically Aidan Davison, Emma Pharo, Anna Wilson, Paul Brown, Peter Devereux and Helen McGregor. And a special acknowledgement to fellow integrator Pamela Aboudha, who we wish all the best in her new journey. We would also like to thank all of the CoP participants across each of our institutions, without whom our learning in this project would not have been possible.

References

Ardichvili, A., Page, V., & Wentling, T. (2002). Virtual knowledge-sharing Communities of Practice at Caterpillar: Success factors and barriers. *Performance Improvement Quarterly, 15*(3), 94–113.

Barnett, S., Jones, S. C., Bennett, S., Iverson, D., & Bonney, A. (2012). General practice training and virtual communities of practice: A review of the literature. *BMC Family Practice, 13*(1), 87.

Bellanet & TRG. (2002). *Facilitating a community of practice: Participant manual.* http://www.itrainonline.org/itrainonline/english/detail-eng.shtml?cmd%5B889%5D=x-889-5540504&cmd%5B996%5D=x-996-5540504. Accessed 15 March 2015.

Coates, H., Dobson, I. R., Goedegebuure, L., & Meek, L. (2009). Australia's casual approach to its academic teaching workforce. *People and Place, 17*(4), 47–54.

Connected Educators. (nd). *Online Communities of Practice in practice.* http://connectededucators.org/online-communities-in-practice/. Accessed 12 March 2015.

Cox, M. D. (2004). *The Faculty Learning Community program director's and facilitator's handbook.* Oxford, OH: Miami University.

Cox, M. D. (2006). Phases in the development of a change model: Communities of Practice as change agents in higher education. In A. Bromage, L. Hunt, & C. B. Tomkinson (Eds.), *The realities of educational change: Interventions to promote learning and teaching in higher education* (pp. 91–100). Oxford, UK: Routledge.

Cheng, E. C. K., & Lee, J. C. K. (2014). Developing strategies for communities of practice. *International Journal of Educational Management, 28*(6), 751–764.

Davison, A. G., Pharo, E. J., & Warr, K. (2012). *Demonstrating distributed leadership through cross-disciplinary peer networks: Responding to climate change complexity.* Sydney: Final Report to the Australian Learning and Teaching Council Ltd.

Ellis, C. S., & Bochner, A. (2000). Autoethnography, personal narrative, reflexivity: Researcher as subject. In N. Denzin & Y. Lincoln (Eds.), *The handbook of qualitative research* (pp. 733–768). London: Sage.

Evely, A. C., Fazey, I., Lambin, X., Lambert, E., Allen, S., & Pinard, M. (2010). Defining and evaluating the impact of cross-disciplinary conservation research. *Environmental Conservation, 37*(4), 442–450.

Garavan, T. N., Carbery, R., & Murphy, E. (2007). Managing intentionally created communities of practice for knowledge sourcing across organisational boundaries: Insights on the role of the CoP manager. *The Learning Organization, 14*(1), 34–49.

Hildreth, P., & Kimble, C. (2004). *Knowledge networks: Innovation through communities of practice.* London, United Kingdom: Idea Group Inc.

Hulme, M. (2009). *Why we disagree about climate change: Understanding controversy, inaction and opportunity.* Cambridge: Cambridge University Press.

Janesick, V. J. (1998). Journal writing as a qualitative research technique: History, issues and reflections. *Paper presented at the Annual Meeting of the American Educational Research Association,* San Diego, CA, United States, April 13–17, 1998.

Jasper, M. A. (2005). Using reflective writing within research. *Journal of Research in Nursing, 10* (3), 247–260.

Kimball, L., & Ladd, A. (2004). Facilitator toolkit for building and sustaining virtual communities of practice. In P. Hildreth & C. Kimble (Eds.), *Knowledge networks: Innovation through Communities of Practice* (pp. 202–215). London, United Kingdom: Idea Group Inc.

Kogan, M., Moses, I., & El-Khawas, E. (1994). *Staffing in higher education: Meeting new challenges.* London: Jessica Kingsley & Publishers.

Kueffer, C., Hadorn, G. H., Bammer, G., Van Kerkhoff, L., & Pohl, C. (2007). Towards a publication culture in transdisciplinary research. *GAIA, 16*(1), 22–26.

Lawrence, R. J., & Després, C. (2004). Futures of transdisciplinarity. *Futures, 36*(4), 397–405.

McDermott, R. (2004). How to avoid a mid-life crisis in your CoPs: Uncovering six keys to sustaining communities. *Knowledge Management Review, 4*(2), 10–13.

McDonald, J. (2014). *Community, domain, practice: Facilitator catch cry for revitalising learning and teaching through communities of practice*. Sydney: Project Report. Australian Learning and Teaching Council Ltd.

McDonald, J., Nagy, J., Star, C., Burch, T., Cox, M. D., & Margetts, F. (2012). Identifying and building the leadership capacity of community of practice facilitators. *Learning Communities Journal, 4*, 63–84.

McDonald, J. & Palani, A. (2011). Building leadership capacity for Community of Practice facilitators: Edgy professional development. In K. Krause, M. Buckridge, C. Grimmer & S. Purbrick-Illek (Eds.). *Research and development in higher education: Reshaping higher education, 34* (pp. 198–206). Gold Coast, Australia, July 4–7, 2011.

Ortquist-Ahrens, L., & Torosyan, R. (2009). The role of the facilitator in faculty learning communities: Paving the way for growth, productivity, and collegiality. *Learning Communities Journal, 1*(1), 1–34.

Petts, J., Owens, S., & Bulkeley, H. (2008). Crossing boundaries: Interdisciplinarity in the context of urban environments. *Geoforum, 39*(2), 593–601.

Petrone, M. C., & Ortquist-Ahrens, L. (2004). Facilitating faculty learning communities: A compact guide to creating change and inspiring community. *New Directions for Teaching and Learning, 2004*(97), 63–69.

Pharo, E., Davison, A., McGregor, H., Warr, K., & Brown, P. (2014). Using communities of practice to enhance interdisciplinary teaching: Lessons from four Australian institutions. *Higher Education Research and Development, 33*(2), 341–354.

Richardson, B., & Cooper, N. (2003). Developing a virtual interdisciplinary research community in higher education. *Journal of Interprofessional Care, 17*(2), 173–182.

Ryan, S., Burgess, J., Connell, J., & Groen, E. (2013). Casual academic staff in an Australian University: Marginalised and excluded. *Tertiary Education and Management, 19*(2), 161–175.

Sandell, K. L., Wigley, K., & Kovalchick, A. (2004). Developing facilitators for faculty learning communities. *New Directions for Teaching and Learning, 2004*(97), 51–62.

Smith, H. A., & McKeen, J. D. (2004). Creating and facilitating Communities of Practice. In C. W. Holsapple (Ed.), *Handbook on knowledge management 1: International handbooks on information systems* (Vol. 1, pp. 393–407). New York: Springer.

Tarmizi, H., & de Vreede, G. (2005). A facilitation task taxonomy for Communities of Practice. *AMCIS 2005 Proceedings Paper 485*. http://aisel.aisnet.org/amcis2005/485. Accessed 13 March 2015.

Tarmizi, H., de Vreede, G., & Zigurs, I. (2005). Leadership challenges in Communities of Practice: Supporting facilitators via design and technology. *International Journal of e-Collaboration, 3*(1), 18–39.

Tarmizi, H., de Vreede, G., & Zigurs, I. (2006). Identifying challenges for facilitation in communities of practice. In *HICSS '06. Proceedings of the 39th Annual Hawaii International Conference on System Sciences, 2006* (Vol. 1, pp. 26a-26a). IEEE.

Wenger, E., McDermott, R., & Snyder, W. M. (2002). *Cultivating communities of practice*. Boston: Harvard Business School Press.

Chapter 17
Facilitating a Community of Practice in Higher Education: Leadership Rewards and Challenges

Edward Rytas Pember

Abstract Facilitating a Community of Practice (CoP) has rewards and challenges. This chapter aims to highlight some of these in a practical way, employing a narrative style that chronologically describes the changing nature of the CoP environment. Although the chapter touches on some theory and research in order to elaborate some key ideas, it is not written from a theoretical perspective. The case study is purposely anecdotal and is written in a familiar tone. The main reason for this approach is twofold; firstly the experiences expressed are largely those of one individual. They are personal and inherently subjective thus, having an overly theoretical or scientific frame work seems somewhat paradoxical. Secondly, in the profusion of theoretical discussion on CoPs this piece aims to offer a lighter approach to the investigation of this field. As a final caveat to the reader I would like to express that this case study is about facilitation of a CoP. It is not designed to inform what one single CoP does but more to investigate the challenges and successes of leading such a community in a contemporary Higher Education environment. The chapter will firstly discuss how the author became interested in the CoP and their original motivation to join. As a CoP member in the early days of the CoP the activities and focus were somewhat 'free-form' and relaxed. This was ultimately the 'forming' and 'norming' stages of the group (Tuckman and Jensen in Group Facil Res Appl J 10:43–48, 2010). Once the inaugural facilitator (called a Champion) left the university, the author became one of the Co-Champions. The CoP then went through another 'norming stage' where upon the membership settled and the group's focus was somewhat open. At this stage of the narrative the CoP movement at the university went through a refocusing, largely due to directives from the Executive, who wanted a more outcome driven approach to all CoPs at the university. This increased the pressure of facilitation and meant that the CoP had to

The original version of this chapter was revised: Author affiliation has been updated. The erratum to this chapter is available at 10.1007/978-981-10-2879-3_29

E.R. Pember (✉)
Academic Learning Adviser, CQUniversity, Sydney,
400 Kent St, Sydney, NSW 2000, Australia
e-mail: e.pember@cqu.edu.au

© Springer Nature Singapore Pte Ltd. 2017
J. McDonald and A. Cater-Steel (eds.), *Communities of Practice*,
DOI 10.1007/978-981-10-2879-3_17

find more focus and achieve outcomes. The CoP adapted to the new paradigm and has again, to a degree, reached a 'performing' stage. Using examples of activities and projects accomplished, the case study highlights some of the difficulties of facilitating a diverse group of members, who may be less committed to achieving outcomes; while at the same time trying to maintain a degree of influence and traction within the institution. It discusses 'soft' and 'hard' benefits of CoP membership such as knowledge sharing and skills development. There are frustrations and rewards of leadership in this environment, but ultimately the case study shows that community and attitude is at the heart of CoP success.

Keywords Community of practice (CoP) · Cop facilitation · Cop champion · Soft and hard skills development · Cop challenges · Cop success(es)

17.1 Early Days: The Inception of the Internationalisation of the Curriculum CoP

In my first week of work at Central Queensland University (CQU) in 2011 my manager gave me time to peruse the university website and intranet to discover my new workplace. CQU is a multi-campus university with campuses all along the Eastern seaboard of Australia (from Cairns to Adelaide) so there is a lot to learn and lots going on. Being the inquisitive person I am, I soon came upon the concept of the Communities of Practice (CoPs) through the CoP Portal on the university intranet. At the time, these were advertised as informal meetings of like-minded people, where ideas and concepts could be freely discussed in an open and non-judgmental manner. It sounded great to me and, as I was mostly working with international students, the Internationalisation of the Curriculum CoP seemed a useful and fun group to join. Internationalisation of education is a concept that relates to the changes that have occurred in education (both globally and domestically) due to the growth of international students studying in foreign countries. The effects on the delivery, content and assessment of courses, as well as the impact on the student experience (both international and domestic) are some of the issues that this CoP aimed to discuss and address.

The CoP was in its early phases of development and the Champion (facilitator) worked on my campus. I approached her in person and was welcomed to the group not long after. Our meetings were (and still are) conducted through web based video links and are held every 6 weeks or so. Generally meetings begin by welcoming new comers and introducing members with a quick 'who am I, where do I work, why am I here'.

Initially, in the 'forming' stages of the group dynamic, meetings consisted of defining what we considered important in internationalisation. Culture was an obvious element of this and the group spent a good deal of time exploring concepts of culture, both formal definitions and personal insights. One of the memorable activities we engaged in was a workshop style exercise in which we wore plastic rubbish bags over our clothes in an attempt to understand how what we wear defines us and the culture (ethnic and corporate) that we subscribe to. The activities and meetings were fun and informal and yet we also had intentions to develop more practical best practice guides and information sharing forums.

Some of the practical work we achieved in the early days of the CoP included a 'Top Ten Tips' of Internationalisation, which was published on the CoP portal on the university intranet. This guide gave useful advice to academic and professional staff on how to internationalise the curriculum and better engage with international students. It must be said that although these Top Ten Tips are available on the Portal, the actual number of times they have been accessed is unknown, thus the impact of this work is impossible to gauge. The Portal is rarely accessed even by CoP members, it is on an intranet and thus requires secure login access. In a word, although this work is useful and available, we have no idea of its distribution to nor uptake by staff.

We also tried to establish a Chinese language class for staff and students. The class never eventuated but the idea was to engage a Chinese student, in a paid role, to teach basic functional Chinese. The aim of this activity was twofold—to broaden participants understanding of Chinese (thus helping to bridge any cultural divide with Chinese international students), as well as challenge participants to grasp the difficulties of understanding and learning a foreign language. The initiative ultimately failed due to funding constraints and a lack of interest from the group.

A year after the CoP's inception we had six meetings, of five or six regular members. We also had a working definition of culture and internationalisation, as well as a 'Top Ten Tips' for staff to help them to internationalise their courses. Additionally, the name of the CoP had been changed to 'Internationalisation of the Learning Experience Community of Practice' (IoLE CoP), to better align with our function—learning is not only about the curriculum and courses but also about extra-curricular activities and the institutional culture. The group was small but functional and had produced some useful work, although our impact on the university itself was minimal due to the level of exposure we had. We therefore vowed to increase membership and awareness of the CoP, as well as include more external speakers to present issues of interest in internationalisation. Overall it had been a modest but successful year.

17.2   Changing Times: Shifting Goal Posts

Change is the only constant in life and thus, with a down-turn in international student numbers, the university went through a restructure. This meant that the instigator and Champion of the CoP left the company and new leadership was needed. She approached me and another colleague to Co-Champion the CoP, something that appealed to me for a number of reasons. Firstly, I did not want the CoP to fail and a sense of duty encouraged me to agree. Secondly, the challenge of leading a group and the experiences that would bring inspired me. Lastly, I enjoyed being a member of the group, the relationship development and networking opportunities that were on offer are not always easily found in a multi-campus university. I therefore acquiesced to the position.

The CoP Champions have a group (called the METACoP) which meets every 4 or 6 weeks to discuss issues, share successes and mentor new Champions or CoP groups. Indeed, it was on the advice of the METACoP that the previous Champion opted for the Co-Champion model of leadership for the IoLE CoP. Other sound ideas for CoP leadership included asking members to honestly identify their motivations and interests, ideas for best times to hold meetings, how to 'manage up', help on connecting to Executive personnel in the university (CoP mentors) and general support for CoP facilitation.

One of the main attractions of the CoP movement when I first became involved was the informal, 'think tank' nature of participation. The CoPs were advertised as not being outcome driven, but more of a discussion forum, a place to discuss best practice and air shared frustrations. Through the sharing of such information, learning and collegiality would be fostered. However, with the restructure of the university the CoP agenda came under the spot light and CoP Champions were directed to 'refocus' and become more outcome orientated. Thus the goal posts shifted and we were required to take on projects that produced 'real' work.

Rising to the challenge, the IoLE CoP sought out activities that aligned with the CoP's focus and the universities values. One of these was to update a policy document that outlined the universities internationalisation activities. Although this was actually the remit of another directorate, the CoP discussed the document and re-wrote it, including adding some poignant activities that seemed essential to a policy document, such as it was. One of the activities we suggested was more training in the area of inter-cultural awareness. The updated draft was sent to the relevant area of the university and, as Co-Champion of the CoP, I politely requested that we be informed of the outcome of our work. As part of the policy update included more training, it seemed obvious that our next project should be to develop an intercultural awareness training module.

To this end, it was decided that we would create a pilot training video for student mentors. If, after feedback and evaluation, the pilot was successful we would make a similar video for staff and students. The CoP began the project and received a lot of interest from other non-CoP members. Indeed our membership had increased and this project helped to promote awareness of the CoP. After much consultation and a trial run of the presentation, it was recorded and given to the relevant department for release in the next term.

17.3   Challenges of CoP Facilitation

One of the biggest challenges of facilitating a CoP is finding traction in the institution, and actually getting positive work in use by the organisation. 'Managing up' is one way that this can be achieved but it is not always easily done. Managing up can be defined as developing mutually beneficial relationships with superiors that create mutual successes (Dobson and Dobson 2000). It is best achieved through understanding the vision of your superiors, as well as the pressures and issues they face, and then addressing these pre-emptively and autonomously (The Careers Group 2010). After waiting patiently, writing a few polite emails and making investigative phone calls to chase up the progress of our work, there was an astounding silence. The updated policy document had gone nowhere (indeed at the time of writing the old document was still on the university policy portal), while the training video was not used due to the fact that the staff involved had moved on because of the restructure. So while a lot of work was put into re-focussing the CoP and engaging in projects that produced real outcomes, none of our efforts saw the light of day, apart from within our group and to some key personnel. As a Co-Champion of the CoP I did my best to move our projects forward with the managers we were trying to support. I even engaged other departments and key personnel to try to get the work published or used, but to no avail. This was one of the most significant challenges of facilitating a CoP—a Champion leads a group of diverse and expert individuals but has little or no power to effect the changes or suggestions put forward by members. One is caught between a rock and hard place, with a small voice, whilst expected to 'produce' outcomes; it can be frustrating. Fellow CoP Champions talk of 'managing up' in this instance, and indeed it was for this purpose that each CoP was provided a 'mentor' at an executive level. This aligns with one of Probst and Borzillo (2008) ten key concepts for CoP success— having a sponsor who can communicate to, and promote the benefits of, the CoP to senior management. However, managing up is a tricky process and there is only so much of it that can be done before it becomes 'annoying the bosses'. Perhaps this is a skill that I didn't really manage well (pun intended).

Another challenge of being a CoP Champion is an apparent lack of interest, or investment from members. This may be a reality of life in a busy work place, but members may just not be as invested as the Champion, so it can sometimes seem like a lonely place. Indeed whilst on this matter, the METACoP advises that you need a core team while other members will come and go; and this is alright—it is the nature of a community group. Borzillo et al. (2011) highlight the movement of periphery members to core members; they also briefly discuss the difference between CoP leaders and facilitators. The authors outline that it is through a CoP leader's encouragement that members become more involved, and thus take on greater responsibility in the CoP. The difference between a leader (in our CoP— Champion) and facilitator (Co-Champion) is not very well defined. Indeed the concept of Co-Championing a CoP appears rather under researched, and may merit further research. The Co-Champion model adopted by CoPs at CQUniversity came about rather organically through METACoP discussions. The Co-Champion model for facilitation was something that I personally found very useful as you always have someone to talk to, someone who has an investment on par with yours and it makes the role much easier to manage.

Following on from the above, not being too emotionally invested is a common cry from CoP Champions at regular METACoP meetings. It is important to facilitate but remember that you are part of a group. The very nature of a Community of Practice is just that—a community. The Champions are only players in the field and each member has their own agenda and level of commitment. By placing too much onus on oneself for the CoP's succusses and failures Champions run the risk of burn out and depression.

17.4   Rewards of CoP Facilitation

There are many rewards to CoP facilitation and membership. One of them is the development of 'soft' and 'hard' skills. Andrews and Higson (2008) define soft skills as transferable skills, such as communication skills, analytical skills, interpersonal skills, professionalism, dealing with change and becoming more creative and confident in one's actions. Whereas hard skills are those that involve more technical skills, for example managing data, operating machinery or working with software (Culpin and Scott 2011). Andrews and Higson (2008, p. 414) define hard skills as knowledge of 'business specific issues'. The following paragraphs detail some of the soft and hard skills development gained from my CoP facilitation experience.

By far the most rewarding experience of Championing a CoP is the relationships that are built along the way, something that can be deemed a soft skill. Without a doubt I can honestly say that my career would not be the same had I not become involved, similarly my experience of the university would be poorer. I have come to know many people outside of my area of expertise, my campus, my department and directorate and indeed, my station. Other colleagues that have not become involved with the CoPs have taken a lot longer to get to know the different departments and understand 'who's who in the zoo'. Being a multi-campus, university, with locations all over Australia, we use video link much of the time for many meetings. This can be intimidating and somewhat strange; however my association with the CoPs has meant that in many video meetings I am already acquainted with other participants. This serves to bring us closer and arguably makes meetings more productive.

Another soft skill exercised was the experience of 'managing up'. Although at times difficult, is also a great privilege and benefit to interact with senior personnel on a somewhat equal footing. It is a very valuable to understand how the executive levels operate and what their guidelines and agendas are. Forming working relations with them and their executive assistants can have far reaching consequences (hopefully positive!). Here, it is really leadership skills and a better understanding of an organisation's components that facilitation provides, which is a great soft skill to gain.

Another soft skill gained from CoP membership is obviously shared knowledge. Not only can you learn more about your practice, but there are other useful titbits that you can gain. I got a much broader perspective on the industry in which I work and how policy and government impact upon it, amongst other things.

I most definitely exercised and developed my leadership and management skills through the CoP. I learnt a lot about time management and prioritising tasks (through titbits as mentioned above). I also had the pleasure of having an administrative assistant (not all to myself!), but nonetheless, someone who helped us to manage mailing lists, take minutes of meetings and such. The experience of managing people or interacting with those that help you is a great advantage, if you are not at that level in your 'real' job. Generally, the feeling that you are giving direction to a group is rewarding in itself. Including CoP facilitation and leadership skills on a CV is also very advantageous.

Obviously the 'hard' benefits are dependent on what a CoP achieves. As mentioned previously, the projects we engaged in did not always achieve their intended outcome. Nonetheless, the experience of producing a training video (learning to use new software) or writing a policy document (a business specific skill) is real and tangible and can thus be considered as hard skills development.

In conclusion, CoPs are what they are. Some of my colleagues shy from them as 'talk fests', but they are communities and are thus dynamic, at times challenging but also rewarding. Ultimately, as in all things in life, you get out what you put in. Being a member of a CoP has been beneficial in many ways, and although most soft skills development is unqualifiable, there are also real experiences and outcomes that can be measured. In terms of facilitating a CoP, for me at least, the benefits far outweigh the challenges. I have learnt many great things, about my industry, university and leadership, and that is just the beginning. I have made great friends and increased my professional networks. My CV has most definitely been improved by my work with the CoPs and because of all of this, my career as well. The challenges of a leading a diverse group are in some ways part of the benefits, as the old adage goes—what doesn't kill you makes you stronger. In terms of the difficulties and frustrations of being expected to produce outcomes, but then not having those outcomes aired and make a real impact, well, that's just work and life; you can't get too emotional about it all. So in the long run, I'd say that facilitating a CoP is a great thing to do but make sure you have a time frame on your tenure and always remind the CoP that it is a community affair.

References

Andrews, J., & Higson, H. (2008). Graduate employability, "soft skills" versus "hard" business knowledge: A European study. *Higher Education in Europe, 33*(4), 411–422.

Borzillo, S., Aznar, S., & Schmitt, A. (2011). A journey through communities of practice: How and why members move from the periphery to the core. *European Management Journal, 29*(1), 25–42.

Culpin, V., & Scott, H. (2011). The effectiveness of a live case study approach: Increasing knowledge and understanding of 'hard' versus 'soft' skills in executive education. *Management Learning, 43*(5), 565–577.

Dobson, M., & Dobson, D. (2000). *Managing up!: 59 ways to build a career-advancing relationship with your boss.* New York: AMACOM eBook Collection.

Probst, G., & Borzillo, S. (2008). Why communities of practice succeed and why they fail. *European Management Journal, 26*(5), 335–347.

The Careers Group. (2010). *Your academic career: Managing professional relationships*. London: University of London.

Tuckman, B. W., & Jensen, M. A. C. (2010). Stages of small-group development revisited. *Group Facilitation: A Research and Applications Journal, 10*, 43–48.

Chapter 18
The Role of Higher Education in Regional Economic Development Through Small Business CoPs

Sue Smith and Laurie Smith

Abstract The focus of this chapter is the learning experiences of a group of small business owner-managers on a leadership programme called LEAD. Small business leadership development is an ongoing aspiration of government to achieve regional economic development. LEAD was established to test this model and explores the need for governments to continue to support small businesses on this agenda through initiatives such as LEAD. LEAD was underpinned with Community of Practice design principles and the aim of the programme was to develop a learning community of small businesses with a focus to develop the leadership capabilities of the owner-managers. The chapter takes the point of view of the course designers and looks at the LEAD programme's development from the initial ideas which inspired it, through to the learning experiences as the programme Community of Practice developed. It explores how this learning influenced changes made to the programme which resulted in nearly 3000 SMEs participating in LEAD programmes based on this learning.

Keywords SMEs · Higher education · Communities of practice · Leadership

18.1 Introduction

This chapter looks at the purpose and impact of developing leadership in owner-managers of small and medium sized enterprises (SMEs) through a funded government initiative facilitated by a university. It explores how a pilot leadership programme was created drawing upon Community of Practice (CoP) design principles in order to create business growth and regional economic development.

S. Smith (✉)
Centre for SME Development, University of Central Lancashire,
Preston PR1 2HE, UK
e-mail: ssmith35@uclan.ac.uk

L. Smith
Lancaster University Management School,
Lancaster University, Lancaster LA1 4YW, UK

© Springer Nature Singapore Pte Ltd. 2017
J. McDonald and A. Cater-Steel (eds.), *Communities of Practice*,
DOI 10.1007/978-981-10-2879-3_18

Informed by two detailed evaluations, the chapter is written from the perspective of the course designers focusing on the learning experiences of the SMEs. The chapter looks at the LEAD programme's development from the initial ideas which inspired it, through to the learning experiences as the programme CoP developed. It examines the assumptions made from the point of view of the educators about how the participants would learn, what pedagogic methods would enable this, what the focus of the programme should be, and how the participants' previous experiences would prepare them for the LEAD programme. It explores how this learning influenced changes made to subsequent programme which resulted in nearly 3000 SMEs participating in future programmes based on this learning.

The chapter will be of interest to educators and facilitators in the fields of entrepreneurship and leadership development. The focus on the programme developers' point of view will be of interest to anyone involved in training provision for the SME sector.

18.2 SME Leadership Development

Small and medium sized enterprises (SMEs) are a significant part of most global economies. Small firms create a share of net new jobs that exceeds their static share of employment (Kirchhoff 1991; Kirchhoff and Phillips 1988). SMEs make up at least 95 % of enterprises in the European Community and within the UK, SMEs account for 99 % of all businesses (Carter and Jones-Evans 2006). By just about any measure the contribution small firms make to the economy of any country is increasing and their importance is fully recognised (Burns 2007).

A flourishing small business sector is central to the vision of economic growth in the UK. It has been highlighted that working with the owner-manager (or a decision maker) on their own development and the strategy of the business has a definite impact on the business's bottom line (see Wren and Jones 2006, 2012). In this sense the leadership of the owner manager is seen to have an impact on the performance of the business. A gap exists between the policy and research, which recognise that leadership development in SMEs is needed for SME survival and growth, and the reality of owner managers and senior teams in SMEs engaging with leadership development. Research shows that small business owners have little opportunity to learn leadership, especially in a social context, i.e. from other people (Kempster and Watts 2002; Kempster 2009). Kempster (2007) has shown that leadership can be learnt from notable people and that owner-managers lack the situations to learn leadership. Similarly, Smith and Peters (2006) note that working for themselves, at the head of their business, entrepreneurs find they have no management team or board of directors to bounce ideas off, share stress and worries with, and set levels of achievement to aspire to. A major weakness identified for the development of owner managers in understanding and enacting leadership is the restrictions on the richness of learning opportunities available—in striking contrast to large organisations (Kempster and Watts 2002). Owner managers also have limited opportunities to learn leadership and management techniques from others, or experience in-house training and appraisals and so on. Likewise, a small company is also usually constrained financially, meaning that courses and training take a back seat whereas training may be offered within a large company. Kempster and Watts (2002) argue that the significance and importance of leadership in large organisations is asymmetric to owner managers. In large organisations career success for a manager is judged against the degree to which they are seen to be a leader—the identity of leadership is most salient to them and as a consequence they absorb all observed and enacted learning opportunities in order to become this social identity. In contrast, owner managers have a very different career aspiration and do not identify themselves as a 'leader' and the social identity is of low salience (Kempster and Watts 2002; see also Smith 2011). Working for themselves, at the head of their business, owner-manager find they have no management team or board of directors to bounce ideas off, share stress and worries with, and set levels of achievement to aspire to. They also have limited opportunities to learn leadership and management techniques from others, or experience in-house training and appraisals and so on.

This chapter takes the view that leadership is a key component to the success and survival of SMEs and thus a contributory factor to the economy. This chapter argues that lack of leadership development of the owner manager can act as a barrier to growth, therefore, developing the leadership capabilities of the owner manager can give the business potential growth opportunities. It is argued that the Community of Practice model can, if managed and supported appropriately, enable this to take place.

18.3   Knowledge Exchange: Universities, SMEs and Government

In the UK universities are seen as one way of supporting and developing the small business sector through the knowledge exchange agenda to boost world class excellence and support regional economic development (see Lambert Review 2003; Benneworth 2007; Athey et al. 2007). Successive UK governments since the mid-1980s have argued that universities should be making a greater contribution to raising the global competitiveness of the UK economy (Cox and Taylor 2006, p. 117). This chapter uses the term knowledge exchange to indicate the dialogue between government, universities and SMEs. Lockett et al. 2009 identified an urgent need for relevant empirical research that examines how knowledge exchange policy is translated into practice, particularly in the area of small firms. This chapter responds to this call and explores the impact of CoPs of SMEs, funded by government and facilitated by a higher education institution Accordingly, it is less about technology transfer or research and development (other authors have addressed this is more depth, see Lendel 2010; Adams et al. 2001; Benneworth 2004) and more about the triple helix concept as summarised by Etzkowitz (2008, p. 294) as: "the interaction in university-industry-government." In the UK this is an increasing and dynamic role of universities and given the fairly recent change in the funding structure of (English) universities the exploration in this chapter of how to successfully work with the triple helix model is of importance. This chapter argues that the combination of government policy, business needs and university knowledge and expertise benefits from an approach which enables dialogue between all three stakeholders allowing for flexibility and innovative approaches to learning in order to meet the needs of all three stakeholders.

18.4 The Context of Knowledge Exchange: The LEAD Programme

The knowledge exchange activity under investigation is a leadership and management programme for owner-managers of SMEs designed, developed and delivered initially by a university in the North-west of England between 2004 and 2006. At the time, one of UK government's key aims as outlined in the Skills White Paper was to improve leadership and management capability: "Effective leadership and management are key to the development of competitive businesses" (DfES 2003, Chap. 2, 2.14). This university worked with the government to develop a leadership programme to respond to the lack of leadership provision for SMEs. This programme was initially funded by the government for 2 years (the total funding was £861,000), focusing on developing the leadership capacity of small businesses. It was called LEAD, standing for "Leading Enterprise and Development" and was piloted over 2 years engaging 67 owner-managers from micro SMEs which employ fewer than 20 people. The main objective of the programme was to raise regional productivity, competitiveness and skills by addressing issues of leadership within the context of the SME sector generally and in particular within the owner manager's business. LEAD was established using Community of Practice (CoP) principles, with the aim of creating a peer network of SME owner-managers (this will be discussed in more detail below).

The pilot programme was a resounding success demonstrating a positive growth impact and the role out of the programme, funded initially by the government. However, it was not all plain sailing; much learning was had along the way with trials and errors made about how to use a CoP model to develop the leadership capabilities of SMEs. Additionally, the engagement of SMEs has highlighted a challenge between continuing to support the economic development and business growth through funding (or part-funding) LEAD and engaging SMEs through such programmes at full economic cost. The aim of this chapter is to share the assumptions the course designers made on how LEAD was constructed as a CoP, the lessons learned and the resulting model of engagement. Accordingly, it is hoped this learning be useful to other educationists wanting to use the CoP approach for (regional) economic development and to contribute to debates of government funding for economic development through SME leadership development.

This chapter shares the learning over the past 10 years of developing the LEAD programme. The next section starts at the very beginning of designing a leadership intervention based on CoP principles in order to create peer networks where the SME owner managers could learn from one another and develop their leadership capabilities and grow their companies.

18.5   The LEAD Journey: Assumptions, CoP Principles and Design

In the development of CoP theory (Wenger 1998) presents three 'dimensions' that give coherence to a CoP: mutual engagement (the source of coherence for the community's participants); joint enterprise (organizing the community around a particular area of knowledge and activity); and shared repertoire (set of resources that allow for the engagement of the practice of the CoP). He argues that a CoP enters the experience of participants through their engagement with these three dimensions. Later debates draw on CoP theory as a tool to cultivate and manage CoPs. In their book *Cultivating Communities of Practice* (Wenger et al. 2002) move the theory to practice (i.e. to the organization) and as such they focus on the cultivation of CoPs as a potential managerial tool which organizations can use for competitive advantage. The three original dimensions of a CoP are replaced with domain, community and practice. Wenger et al. (2002, pp. 27–29) characterise these as follows:

- The *domain* creates the common ground (i.e. the minimal competence that differentiates members from non-members) and outlines the boundaries that enable members to decide what is worth sharing and how to present their ideas.
- The *community* creates the social structure that facilitates learning through interactions and relationships with others.
- The *practice* is a set of shared repertoires of resources that include documents, ideas, experiences, information, and ways of addressing recurring problems. In essence, the practice is the specific knowledge the community shares, develops, and maintains.

Based on the literature on how SME owner managers learn leadership and SME business growth generally, it was felt that LEAD could be designed drawing upon the CoP principles to provide leadership development to owner-managers of micro-SMEs. Creating a peer learning community was a key aim to alleviate the isolation of owner-managers and to provide a non-competitive environment for them to share knowledge and seek help. It was hoped then that the *domain* would be the membership of LEAD with owner managers committed to the *community* of like-minded people in similar situations, i.e. owner-managers wanting to grow their businesses. The *practice* would be that of leadership development through joint activities, largely through the social construction of knowledge and experiential learning.

The course designers made up the LEAD team consisting of academics, facilitators, a project manager and administrators. Along with colleagues within the university, the LEAD team already had much experience of developing the business growth of SMEs having worked with over 1500 SMEs on different projects and initiatives. These business support programmes were analysed and parts that were felt to benefit the CoP model of engagement were selected and refined.

A number of assumptions were made by the LEAD team about what learning methods the programme should entail, and what the desired outcomes of participation on the programme would be. Research showed that much entrepreneurial learning is an 'on the job' process—a vocational, practical form of learning (Cope 2003, 2005) and that entrepreneurs tend to learn best when the topic is directly relevant to their situation. The underlying factor behind the LEAD programme's chosen pedagogic methods was that entrepreneurs (in this case SME owner-managers) learn best when the learning is situational, meaning that they can relate the learning directly to a situation that is relevant to them (Cope 2003, 2005). With this in mind, the LEAD team made assumptions about what LEAD should consist of in order for the delegates to achieve maximum benefit by creating an environment that would help to ease the isolation they felt as owner-managers and enable them to learn from one another.

The pedagogy of LEAD supported a social view of learning that relied upon peer-to peer learning to make sense of the different elements of the programme as shown in Fig. 18.1. This pedagogy was based on constructionist views of knowledge which required the delegates to engage with the ideas that came from the different elements of LEAD and to develop skills and capabilities relevant to their own situations back in their businesses. It included learner-directed styles of learning and interactive approaches for the delegates to learn from each other and the knowledge they have about running small businesses. In CoP terms LEAD would enable them to address problems and share knowledge (Wenger 2004). It

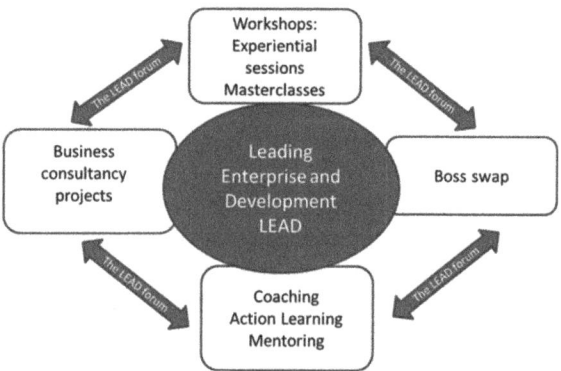

Fig. 18.1 LEAD learning interventions (initial CoP learning model)

was hoped that the circulation of knowledge within LEAD came largely from the delegates and their experiences of running small businesses. Accordingly, the approach focused on providing them the opportunities to learn leadership through social interactions from other SME owner-managers. Wenger (1998) notes that the primary focus of CoP theory is on learning as social participation and being active participants in the practice of social communities constructs identities in relation to them. This underpinned the development of LEAD whereby the aim of the different learning interventions was to bring together owner managers of SMEs to increase the salience of leadership and to take on the identity as both a member of the LEAD CoP and that of 'leader'.

The longer term goals of the programme were to help develop critical reflective thinking skills so that the delegates could solve current and future issues that they inevitably faced in their organizations. It was hoped that the reflective learning practices would be especially relevant in the SME environment where there is nobody for the owner-manager to turn to for advice, and limited access to training courses on offer to fill knowledge and skills gaps. LEAD then was designed so that participants (hereon in called delegates) could, in effect, teach themselves and then pass on this learning to their staff to encourage a culture of leadership and self-perpetuating development: double-loop learning (Deakins and Freel 1998; Cope 2003, 2005; Argyris 1976). Through engagement with the different learning interventions, it was hoped the delegates would, as one delegate later described: *"work on the business, not in the business"* (delegate, cohort 1).

Figure 18.1 gives an overview of the learning interventions involved in the pilot and is followed by a brief description of each element along with a rationale about why they were chosen.

The pilot programme consisted of four groups called cohorts with between 15 and 25 delegates on each cohort. In order to allow time for the circulation of knowledge and for the members of LEAD to develop a CoP, between 10 and 12 months were allowed for each cohort (depending on what time of year they started as there was a break allowed over the summer period to ensure that the delegates did not miss sessions due to holidays). The pilot cohorts were staggered over 2 years, each starting approximately 4 months apart. This was designed so that each cohort could be formatively evaluated as they experienced LEAD and make any necessary changes to the next cohort, if need be.

18.5.1 Recruitment and Selection

In order to create a peer learning community underpinned with CoP principles viewing learning as a social construction arising from participation in the community it was felt that each cohort needed to be made up of committed individuals who were willing to share their experiences and seek to develop new ways of thinking about themselves as leaders in order to help their businesses grow. Accordingly, it was felt that LEAD would not be suitable for every owner-manager and therefore a recruitment and selection process would be a way to engage with owner managers who would be willing to embrace this way of learning for up to a year whilst weeding out anyone wanting to use the network as potential customers (i.e. the focus of the CoP was to be about learning, not selling to one another which is often the focus of small business networking events). The recruitment process involved putting on taster events such as a breakfast, lunch or twilight masterclass on the benefits of leadership development to SMEs. Any owner managers who were interested in joining LEAD and taking advantage of the fully-funded place then needed to fill in an application form and attend a group interview, both of which focused on getting the owner manager to think about their own leadership style and what they wanted for the future of their company. The group interview was an interesting experiment which helped the LEAD team to see how willing potential delegates were to begin to share their thoughts and ideas. A total of 144 owner managers participated in the recruitment and selection process which resulted in 67 delegates participating in the LEAD pilot.

LEAD used a wide range of learning interventions which are now described. A cross-cutting feature of the entire programme was the ever-present element of peer-to-peer interaction between delegates, adding the opportunity for informal activity to occur around every session, however formal the delivery of that session. The aim of this was to increase the delegates' opportunities to share views and opinions, and learn from each other. Throughout LEAD, all delegates were prompted and encouraged to actively reflect on their experiences and learning from all parts of the programme, and from their deployment of that learning in their businesses.

18.5.2   Overnight Experiential (2 Full Days, Including Overnight)

Each cohort of LEAD began the programme by engaging with a 2 day, overnight experiential session. The aim of this was to lay the foundations of trust and confidentiality between the delegates through practical activities, discussion and reflection, and to ground the learning in the delegates' own businesses. It took place away from the university at a rural retreat. The delegates stayed overnight and there was an evening meal followed by optional socialising in the bar. During the 2 days a learning contract was developed which addressed what they wanted to learn from LEAD and from each other. Confidentiality was always emphasised during this process and the delegates unpicked what they meant by confidentiality for each other and for their cohort as well as how to deal with the information they shared between each other.

Masterclasses (50–60 h)
Over the 10–12 months, there were twelve half-day master classes: six on the theme of leadership, run by different leaders and inspirational speakers; and six on the

theme of business growth, run by the academic faculty. The masterclasses were designed to act as stimuli to generate discussion rather than content based teaching. Delegates were encouraged to find their own 'golden nuggets' of learning from each session and to share these on the LEAD forum (the virtual learning environment). Masterclasses took place in lecture theatres at the university and delegates were invited to bring appropriate guests from their companies if they felt they would benefit from the experience.

Coaching (7.5–8 h)

Each delegate was assigned a professional executive coach to provide a confidential forum to work through issues using a 'solutions focus' approach (see Jackson 2002). Each delegate was offered eight coaching sessions throughout the programme beginning with a one and a half hour face-to-face session and continuing with six one hour telephone coaching sessions. These sessions could be used flexibly as and when the delegate found them to be most appropriate. The coaches were all trained in, and adopted, a solutions-focused approach. The coaches were given ongoing training and supervision throughout the life of the programme. Normally, the first face-to-face coaching session took place in a meeting room at the university and then the coach and delegate decided where was appropriate to carry out the remaining sessions. The coaching was designed to give the delegates a space where they could explore the learning from the other elements of the programme which may in turn have raised issues they wanted to address about their own leadership development and/or business issues they wanted to work through.

Action learning (6 × ½ days)

Action learning sets (ALS) were designed to encourage peer learning and address real problems in the work place. They were made up of six to seven delegates with a facilitator, meeting six times over the 10–12 months. The ALS took place in a meeting room at the university and delegates sat in a circle on comfortable chairs to engender a relaxed and informal atmosphere. Ground rules were established by the members of each ALS. The facilitators followed the approach of Revans (1980, 1982) and matched the criteria set out by Pedler et al. (2005) whereby questioning was the main way to help delegates proceed with their problems, and learning was from reflection on actions taken (see Smith (2009) for a discussion on action learning and LEAD).

The LEAD team, in line with research (Kempster and Watts 2002), made an assumption that pedagogic methods such as ALS and coaching would be appropriate because of the isolated position held by SME owner managers, as described above. It was assumed these methods would enable delegates to learn effectively from themselves through the questioning processes of action learning and coaching, and then pass this learning and these techniques on to their staff. The LEAD team assumed that these methods, which require a high level of engagement on the part of the participant, would be more suitable for SME owner-managers than the formal pedagogic methods of traditional higher education.

Mentoring (at least 3 meetings)

Each delegate had the opportunity to be paired with a mentor from the business community. Mentors were given training by the university on how to use coaching and mentoring techniques. Fundamentally, the aim was for the mentor to share their experiences of running a successful business and for this learning to be shared with the delegate in order to help them grow their business.

Boss Swap (up to 3 days)

The boss swap was intended to be just that: a chance for a pair of delegates to run each other's business for a number of days. The intention was to allow participants to learn techniques from peers and to gain experience of working in a different environment to that of their own, to see what effect different leadership styles had on the working environment, the staff, and the overall running of a business. Again, the oft-reported isolation of SME owner-managers was the driver behind this. Having nobody else to compare themselves to meant that, in the eyes of the LEAD team at least, the participants would probably only have a limited and narrow understanding of leadership and how it impacts on a business. By immersing themselves in someone else's business, the participants were to gain important experience and knowledge that could not be provided through a normal teaching method such as a lecture or masterclass. Once again, following research into entrepreneurial learning (Cope 2005), the assumption was made that the participants would learn more by experience in a situation relevant to them (another small business) than by passive learning in a classroom.

The LEAD team was very aware that allowing someone else to run their business would take a huge leap of faith on the part of the participants. For this reason peer interaction, trust and social bonding were all very high on the list of priorities for the LEAD delegates. The boss swap was preceded with sessions on how to do this and was largely informed and designed by the delegates themselves. Trust was seen as absolutely essential for the participants to benefit fully from the course and for an exercise such as the boss swap it was fundamental.

Consultancy projects (up to 1 month)

The consultancy projects were designed to help the delegates work through a particular area or problem or opportunity they had identified throughout LEAD. A range of academics and students in the management school were available to carry out such a project (for example, accessing a new market, business planning, strategic planning).

18.5.3 The LEAD Forum

The term 'the LEAD forum' was used to refer to the virtual learning environment which predominantly focused on discussion through forums. It provided a confidential space for the delegates to ask questions, share learning points and to post and download resources. It was a closed space for the delegates and facilitators.

18.5.4   Evaluation and Methodology

As the design of the LEAD programme recognised the conjoined issues of leadership and business growth in the context of SMEs, the evaluation was designed to explore the objectives of the pilot project and assumptions of the LEAD team against project outcomes. Three main objectives driving the evaluation were:

1. Firstly, the evaluation was used formatively to address what worked in terms of the different types of learning mechanisms in order to adjust them as subsequent cohorts went through the programme.
2. Secondly, it was used summatively to assess both the economic impact the programme had on the businesses—an assessment which could also be scaled up to look at the regional impact—and also to look at the impact it had on the owner-managers coming through the programme.
3. Thirdly, it was used to evaluate which parts of the programme were creating the most success, with a view of taking this learning and rolling out similar programmes regionally and nationally.

With the pilot programme being funded, the LEAD team wanted to learn what worked and didn't, and to generate a sustainable model of leadership and regional economic development. Additionally, the funding body—the UK government—wanted to understand what return on investment looked like, i.e. would LEAD result in regional economic development?

Two evaluations were conducted to investigate the efficacy of the programme. The first was an extensive narrative evaluation conducted internally by the LEAD team; the second was a quantitative evaluation by an external body. The evaluation drew upon Pawson and Tilley's (1997) approach of realist evaluation which focused on the interplay between participants' perceptions of their needs, their perceptions of the 'usefulness' of the different parts of the programme, and the assumptions made by the LEAD team who were delivering the programme as to what sort of learning approaches would suit this group of professionals.

The LEAD team's evaluation consisted of many different methods, including interviews with each delegate before they started the programme, at the mid-point, and towards the end of the programme (totalling 150 transcribed interviews). The delegates were aware this was a pilot and were enthusiastic about being part of the co-construction. A number of formal feedback days were run with each cohort to help the LEAD team understand the experience of the delegates and to make improvements for future cohorts. There were also a number of questionnaires, comments through a comment box, conversations and emails, all of which contributed to the evaluation. This was supplemented with the LEAD team's own reflective accounts and specific sessions engaging deliverers such as the coaches and ALS facilitators to get their feedback and thoughts on what was working well and what might benefit from tweaking/changing.

The evaluation conducted by the external body was a quantitative assessment on the impact LEAD had on their businesses. This evaluation was carried out using a questionnaire at the end of the programme that focused on the business effects of LEAD, i.e. operations and outcomes, including sales turnover, employment, productivity and gross value added.

18.5.5   Reflections and Insights from the LEAD Pilot

Looking at the evaluation data revealed that the basic assumption—that the participants would learn best in a hands-on, practical, and situational way—was largely correct. The CoP model of engagement worked and delegates made significant changes to their businesses. Many LEAD delegates reported that the programme was so successful due to the fact that much of it they could easily and immediately relate back to their own businesses. The CoP principles largely worked, one of the biggest successes from this was the value and importance of a non-competitive environment that enabled peer interaction throughout the programme. The delegates felt that they improved their own skills and worked on their professional development through the peer interaction as well as building a community where they could ask any questions of their peers. The evaluation showed that LEAD built an excellent support network which has enabled many friendships to be formed as well business collaborations. In general the peer network allowed the participants to feel less isolated and provided them with affirmation on their own actions. However, the evaluation also provided insights into how the programme could be changed. This section looks at how the different elements of LEAD worked and the impact of programme. Each learning intervention is discussed in turn, supported with data from the delegates of the pilot programme evaluation.

Overnight Experiential

> I couldn't believe there were others who had the same issues as me, I really enjoyed the overnight experiential (Delegate, cohort 4)

> I found it daunting but enjoyed it. (Delegate, cohort 1)

All participants felt that the overnight experiential was a very useful way to begin to build trust between group members. Some delegates did not like the reflective aspects over the 2 days but also conceded that this was not their preferred way of learning. Many enjoyed the physical parts and the experiential aspects using simulated exercises to experience leadership in action. The evaluation highlighted that many felt there was too much packed into the 2 days and that some of the introductory aspects could have been done beforehand.

Masterclasses

> Masterclasses are a toolkit – I've taken something from each one. (Delegate, cohort 3)

The evaluation showed that in general the level of the masterclasses was suited to the needs of the participants. However, participants commented that they would have liked an additional session after the masterclass which focused more on their own businesses. The act of coming to the university and mixing with like-minded peers for the masterclass was seen to be beneficial, even though at first many had reservations about taking half a day away from the business. Once this benefit had been realised, many participants made the decision to stay on the campus for the entire day, making use of meeting rooms either to bring members of their own teams along to discuss the masterclass in relation to their own business, or to meet other members of their cohort for an improvised tutorial-style session.

Having masterclasses conducted by people who had direct experience of running an SME made the topics instantly relevant, and inspirational talks by well-known leaders provided food for thought about motivating oneself and one's team—vital tools in running a small business. Delegates spoke of 'lightbulb moments', when they realised how they could use knowledge learned in a masterclass. The delegates also fed back their wishes and skills gaps they felt they had which informed the choice of future masterclass topics and speakers.

Coaching

> The outcome from this part of the LEAD programme was by far the greatest influence on my business. (Delegate, cohort 2)

Due to the confidential nature of the coaching element it was difficult to understand the content of the coaching, though its impact could be seen through the changes the delegates were making and commenting on. The coaching element required a high level of self-reflection and input from the delegates which challenged some of them. In due course however, everyone valued the objectivity of their coach and felt that the solutions-focused approach was useful and made them step back to take a more objective view of their business. Many delegates worked on implementing the solutions focused coaching approach within their own organisations. Very few participants had a negative experience of coaching, though one person swapped their coach and one participant did not progress with the coaching. Some participants continued to work with their coaches after LEAD, funding this work privately. Some delegates struggled to fit all the sessions into the 10–12 months.

Action learning sets (ALS)

> I found the action learning sets to be a good forum to discuss things that I wouldn't be able to discuss with my colleagues. (Delegate, cohort 4)

Most delegates thought that the ALS were useful to discuss issues and share experiences with like-minded people. This helped them to see that their problems were not unique and that they could learn from others' real life experiences and knowledge. The delegates who were open to the action learning approach found it helpful and insightful and action learning helped these participants make important changes in their businesses.

Many delegates reported they were using the open questioning techniques of action learning and coaching with their staff, and that problems were solved much more easily or dealt with before they had a chance to develop. Also, the evaluation showed that where there was a lack of bonding between set members this was likely to result in a negative experience. This was mentioned by a few delegates. For the ALS to succeed, everyone in the group must attend each session and everyone must be fully committed.

Some delegates struggled with the concept of action learning and found it difficult to see the benefits of this approach. Some were expecting a more passive experience, rather than an active learning approach and therefore found it difficult to engage with the demanding level of self-reflection and examination required by action learning (and other parts of the programme which required this self-reflection). Generally these individuals preferred the more traditional learning approach offered by the masterclass lectures and were not open to engaging in what were, to them, new and unusual ways of learning.

Mentoring

> I enjoyed the mentoring part but I don't think I will continue with my mentor (Delegate, cohort 2)

> I took away some useful tips but I got more from the discussions with my LEAD peers (Delegate, cohort 3)

It was assumed that the delegates would benefit from having an experienced business leader on hand to offer advice and guidance as the programme reached its conclusion, and it was intended that this relationship would continue after LEAD, if so desired by the delegate and his or her mentor. The evaluation of the programme showed, however, that the mentoring aspect was not as successful as might have been assumed. The assumption was that the mentor would provide an on-going 'sounding board', similar to that provided by the coach or the peer group in an action learning set. Although the mentors received training, evidence seems to suggest that the mentoring element was out of step with the reflective elements of LEAD. Whereas coaching and action learning encourage the individual to question themselves and others to find solutions to issues, a mentor was more likely to give advice and offer opinions, drawing on their own experience. This is not meant to be a criticism of the mentors, who were all carefully chosen and were very experienced and well respected in their fields. It is more an observation that this element of LEAD was slightly out of synch with the rest of the programme. The assumption that participants would like a mentor who could offer advice and give opinions was, in the majority of cases, incorrect. Perhaps the mentoring did not fit with the self-reliant mentality of SME owner-managers.

Delegates perceived mentoring to be a good way to get advice from a more experienced business leader. The delivery model placed the mentoring towards the end of the programme and not everyone engaged with the process. This could be because the mentoring was not in line with the self-reliant needs of the LEAD CoP and reflective ethos of the pedagogy. Additionally, it could have been that mentoring did not fit in at this point of the course, as delegates effectively became one others' mentors by then.

Boss swap

> This was possibly the most difficult part of the course (Delegate, cohort 1)

Once the programme had begun, it became clear through feedback from the delegates that the idea of the boss swap in its initial form was off-putting, if not downright terrifying, to many of the delegates. It was clear to the deliverers that no amount of trust and bonding would be enough for a true boss swap to be feasible. The assumption that participants would be happy to let another person actually run their business was wrong: the LEAD team had underestimated the closeness of the link between owner-manager and their business. On the whole, the delegates resisted this element of LEAD; the thought of letting another owner-manager run their own business did not fit with the ethos of reflective and situational learning. Also, the thought of letting someone else look after or even run their 'baby' was not welcomed.

Consultancy Projects

> Although the consultancy idea is, in principle, a good idea, it wasn't beneficial to us at the time because I needed to lay some practical foundations for the business before I could consider which direction I wanted to take the research. (Delegate, cohort 2)

In general the consultancy element provided a trigger for the delegates, often enabling them to take certain aspects of the business forward or assisted in increasing their confidence as it often confirmed their own ideas. The evaluation showed that the business consultancy was highly valued by a few participants, but was not perceived this way by the majority. This may be because LEAD focused on situational learning and encouraged a reflective stance as opposed to providing information on the business or advising on strategy (i.e. the delegate would take the strategy forwards as opposed to an expert telling them how they should do it).

The LEAD forum

> The forum gave me the opportunity to discuss with members any issues they had in their businesses. And if other members had experienced similar problems, the members would then suggest ways to resolve the problems. (Delegate, Cohort 2)

> The forum hasn't caused any significant change at work but is good for communication. (Delegate, Cohort 3)

Not everyone embraced the online LEAD forum. In part this was due to the design and usability of the software which was changed and re-launched for cohorts three and four. In part it was due to lack of confidence using IT in this way. Time pressure also played a part in participants' reluctance or inability to use it.

18.6 Reflective Learning

Although not a learning intervention per se, reflective learning practices were built into all of the different elements. The evaluation revealed that although the reflective elements were the most taxing and required the most engagement and input, they were also the most rewarding to those delegates who immersed themselves fully. The chance to learn from 'themselves' was regarded as highly beneficial by some delegates and they expressed high levels of satisfaction with this side of LEAD, saying that it helped them feel less lonely and isolated, and able to explore issues at work in a more constructive manner. In this respect, with those who were prepared to open their minds to a new approach to learning, the assumptions about reflective learning were correct.

One possible oversight on the part of the LEAD team was that not all the delegates were receptive to this kind of learning, perhaps due to the levels of insight and introspection it required. The assumption was that all delegates would be eager to try out new ideas but the reality, in some cases, was that their previous experiences had not prepared them for a new learning method and they remained sceptical. Returning to a learning environment after a considerable length of time for some delegates would have required a period of adjustment, and some delegates reported they were not expecting to have to be as open with themselves and their peers as the reflective parts of the programme required. Of course, some individuals simply found that they did not enjoy the reflectivity on the programme, and that other learning methods were more beneficial to themselves.[1]

18.7 The Impact of the LEAD Pilot

The quantitative evaluation, as carried out by Wren and Jones (2006) showed that on average the SMEs increased their turnover by £200k per annum and 85–95 % of firms expected to increase the sales turnover, employment, productivity and profits after finishing the programme. A fifth of LEAD delegates created new businesses which were different to the existing one.

Whilst it is possible to measure the impact of LEAD in terms of growth in turnover, profitability and employee size, there are other areas of impact. Wren and Jones' (2006) work has also shown, amongst other things, that delegates felt more confident in taking risks, had a more motivated workforce, had better delegation

---

[1]At the mid-point one delegate reported he found a specific masterclass to be more useful than the whole of the LEAD programme. Four months after graduating, he attended a preview day for prospective participants and was able to explain how, in hindsight, he could see how the different elements of the programme interacted and the subsequent benefits to himself and his business.

skills and feel they had developed their leadership skills. The leadership development of owner managers has also shown to have an impact of the innovative capacity of the company. Delegates also reported relocation, expansion, diversification and acquisition activities. Increased confidence in, and awareness of, individuals' leadership roles was widely observed. This was often accompanied by elevated abilities to delegate effectively, leading in turn to staff empowerment and a commitment to work strategically on the business for further enterprise development.

Both evaluations showed that the pilot provided a successful framework for building cohesive and effective peer groups. These overcame many of the worst effects of the observed isolation that owner-managers experienced prior to LEAD. While important throughout the LEAD programme, many of these networks have endured after completion, for example, through the continuation of ALS and also follow on peer learning groups and subsequent initiatives such as the GOLD programme whereby delegates act as non-executive directors for one another.[2]

The pilot was effective in developing delegates' leadership skills and the CoP principles enabled effective engagement with, and support to, the micro business sector. The university continued to run LEAD drawing upon pockets of government funding available and between 2006 and 2008 the LEAD tam made changes to the model to increase the ability for LEAD to become a powerful learning community/CoP for the delegates. During this time ongoing discussions were being had with the government which led to a further collaboration between the government and the university which delivered the pilot. In 2008, the government supported a large scale roll out with £15m of public funding across 15 providers in the Northwest England and Wales, and subsequently a £1 m funded programme in the North East of England, and commercially (i.e. SMEs paying the full price) through a private training company in the Southwest of England. At the time of writing, nearly 3000 SMEs have participated in LEAD. The following sections highlights the changes made to the programme that the SMEs post the pilot programme have experienced.

18.8   Changes Made to LEAD

Figure 18.2 shows the resultant model that was rolled out and continues to be delivered in this way today. Many aspects of the original model are still in place but some important elements were changed as is now described.

---

[2]See   http://www.lancaster.ac.uk/lums/business/business-growth/programmes/gold/   and   http://www.quolux.co.uk/gold/.

Fig. 18.2 The resultant
LEAD CoP model

18.8.1 Inclusion of an Introduction Day

The CoP principles of knowledge construction through peer learning worked very well on the programme. LEAD did develop into a peer learning community and a CoP. The overnight experiential was recognised as a very precious time for the delegates to get to know one another so to begin this process prior to the 2 day overnight experiential, the LEAD team included an introduction day. This day focused partly on introducing the delegates to the university (or provider's institution) and partly on 'getting to know you' activities. Subsequent feedback from future cohorts highlighted how they enjoyed the introduction day, likening it to the first day at school and they felt nervous on arrival. This meant that when they arrived for the overnight experiential they had already met each other at least and knew something about one another.

18.8.2 Increase in Reflective Learning

Reflective learning methods were seen by the LEAD team as ideally suited to the needs of the LEAD participants. These methods encouraged the delegates to think more closely about issues and ask themselves questions which could help them resolve problems at work. Although some delegates struggled with the reflective elements of the programme, it was felt that this style of learning provided them with longer term 'lifelong learning' tools. The reflective practices and critical thinking activities the delegates engaged with (such as through the open questioning techniques in the action learning) had positive impacts for the delegates and their businesses. However, many delegates said they struggled to make the changes in their businesses at the pace they wanted to. This was a common theme, many delegates commented how they reflected after the programme had finished and only really began to make changes towards the end or after it had finished.

To allow delegates to absorb the learning, reflect on their own leadership, and importantly, how LEAD and learning from one another (i.e. the CoP) was working, specific 'learning and reflection days' were built into future programmes. These provide delegates a valuable opportunity to come together as the whole group (previously it was only the masterclasses that allowed for all of them to come together). Techniques such as reflective diaries and learning logs were used and the focus was on them sharing what they had learnt, what changes they were making, what they wanted to do and so on along with an action plan. Three learning and reflection days were built into subsequent programmes along with mini learning and reflection sessions during other parts of the programme (such as after master-classes). Subsequent feedback highlighted that this helped them compare their own experiences, reflect on their own situations, learn more effectively and have individual on-going action plans they could work to/from.

18.8.3 Boss Swap Changed to Shadowing and Exchanges

The principle of the learning method (i.e. looking at how another business is run and receiving feedback on the leadership styles and traits of the owner-manager) was acceptable but the execution had to be refined. The LEAD team were keen not to lose what they saw as an important way of giving the delegates a valuable, experiential learning opportunity, so changes were made to the element of the programme, and the boss swap became the 'business shadowing and exchanges'. This still involved the participants working in pairs, but replaced actually running each other's businesses with first, a shadowing activity whereby the pairs shadowed one another in their own organisation and gave each other feedback, followed by an exchange whereby they went into each other's business (a swap, at the same time). The exchanges involved the pairs carrying out pre-agreed micro-consultancy projects where they worked in each other's business for 2 or 3 days (examples included carrying out a cultural audit, doing a marketing analysis, getting feedback from staff on the owner manager, strategic analysis, and other projects that the pairs constructed between them). To prepare for this, they spent time 'shadowing' each other in their businesses to gain an insight into what working there might be like and to ease them into what could prove quite a challenging process. Subsequent feedback revealed that this was became one of the most rewarding aspects of the programme, for example: "This was possibly the most difficult part of the course and also the most rewarding for both parties. I learnt a great deal about myself and how I can appear to strangers but also gained experience on giving feedback" (LEAD delegate, cohort 5). Some providers of LEAD have evolved this model to include site visits to larger regional companies for delegates to observe different leadership styles in action across different sectors.

18.8.4   Mentoring and Consultancy Removed

The reflectivity that LEAD encouraged was at odds with the more one-way aspect of a mentor-mentee relationship and a directive consultancy project. Future programmes do not include the mentoring and consultancy elements. However, where LEAD is run by universities, the delegates are able to access the student body who work on live business issues as part of their course to help them on specific projects that come from the engagement with LEAD. In this way, the consultancy element may still be present for the delegates who wish to use the student body but it is not a constitutive element of the programme.

18.9   Summary and Conclusions

This chapter has shown that a group of small businesses brought together to construct a peer learning community using CoP principles can have a positive economic impact on the growth of those businesses and regional economic development. Kirchhoff and Phillips (1988) have argued that existing firms can grow by adding employees, or new firms can form and grow through increase in employees. They argue that investigation into the formation phenomenon has revealed that it is a significant component of and determinant of economic growth rates. LEAD has shown to both create opportunities for growth through increasing employee numbers and through the creation of new firms. Kirchhoff and Phillips (1988) argue that entrepreneurial entry is a necessary requirement for economic growth. The findings on the impact of LEAD show that developing the leadership capabilities of the owner manager can lead to skills for running businesses other than the one they were in/running when they commenced the programme. Additionally, LEAD provided a valuable forum for SMEs to come together in a non-competitive environment to learn, share knowledge, and seek help.

In terms of knowledge exchange and the relationship between government, universities and businesses, knowledge exchange itself is not prescriptive. Higher education institutions have been encouraged by successive governments to develop activities whereby the exchange of knowledge can benefit businesses and lead to regional development. There are no hard and fast rules of 'doing' knowledge exchange. Many activities are influenced by the funding bodies which support this type of activity. This chapter aimed to contribute to understanding better how higher education institutions can support SMEs through knowledge exchange using CoPs or programmes based on CoP principles. However, utilising support from universities in general and through knowledge exchange initiatives is an ongoing challenge for both universities and SMEs. SME owner-manager often do not know that business support is available or that programmes are being developed to meet their needs. Also, SMEs quite often do not engage with more traditional forms of education. The delegates enrolled on LEAD all had different levels of education.

Similarly, universities are still learning how to engage with SMEs effectively. The findings from this chapter suggest that CoP is an approach that can achieve effective business support to SMEs. Using a CoP approach focuses on connections between resources and people rather than delivery of taught programmes and gives a precedent for the positive impact of structured leadership development in that dominant sector of the economy.

Acknowledgments   The authors would like to thank all the delegates who participated in the pilot programme and the subsequent LEAD (and derivative) programmes. Acknowledgement is given to the Northwest Development Agency which provided the original funding and the team there who worked closely with the LEAD team to create the pilot. Thanks is also given to the wider team at the university and to the LEAD providers who participated in the roll out who have been open to the idea of an ongoing co-construction of a Community of Practice based approach for SME leadership development.

References

Adams, J. D., Chiang, E. P., & Starkey, K. (2001). Industry university cooperative research centers. *Journal of Technology Transfer, 26,* 73–86.

Argyris, C. (1976). Single-loop and double-loop models in research on decision making. *Administrative Science Quarterly, 21*(3), 363–375.

Athey, G., Glossop, C., Harrison, B., Nathan, M. & Webber, C. (2007). *Innovation and the city: how innovation has developed in five city-regions, NESTA.* http://www.centreforcities.org/assets/files/innovation_and_the_city_report_NESTA.pdf.

Benneworth, P. (2004). In what sense 'regional development?': Entrepreneurship, underdevelopment and strong tradition in the periphery. *Entrepreneurship and Regional Development, 16,* 439–458.

Benneworth, P. (2007). *Leading Innovation: Building effective coalitions for innovation, NESTA.* http://www.nesta.org.uk/publications/leading-innovation.

Burns, P. (2007). *Entrepreneurship and small business.* New York, NY: Palgrave Macmillan.

Carter, S., & Jones-Evans, R. (2006). *Enterprise and small business: Principles, practice and policy.* Harlow: Pearson Education Limited.

Cope, J. (2003). Entrepreneurial learning and critical reflection: Discontinuous events for 'higher level' learning. *Management Learning, 34*(4), 429–450.

Cope, J. (2005). Toward a dynamic learning perspective of entrepreneurship. *Entrepreneurship: Theory and Practice, 29*(4), 373–398.

Cox, S., & Taylor, J. (2006). The impact of a business school on regional economic development: A case study. *Local Economy, 21*(2), 117–135.

Deakins, D., & Freel, M. (1998). Entrepreneurial learning and the growth process in SMEs. *The Learning Organization, 5*(3), 144–155.

Dfes. (2003). *The government's white paper on the future of higher education.* http://www.dfes.gov.uk/highereducation/hestrategy/.

Etzkowitz, H. (2008). *The triple helix. University—industry—government, innovation in Action.* London: Routledge.

Kempster, S. J. (2007). Echoes from the past: An exploration of the impact of notable people on leadership learning. In *Academy of Management—Best Papers, 67.*

Kempster, S. J. (2009). *How managers have learnt to lead: Exploring the development of leadership practice.* Basingstoke: Palgrave Macmillan.

Kempster, S.J. & Watts, G. (2002). The Entrepreneur as Leader: An exploration of leadership development amongst small business owner-managers. *Paper presented at the 25th ISBA National Small Firms conference.*

Kirchhoff, B. A. (1991). Entrepreneurship's contribution to economics. *Entrepreneurship Theory and Practice, 16*(2), 93–112.

Kirchhoff, B. A., & Phillips, B. D. (1988). The effect of firm formation and growth on job creation in the United States. *Journal of Business Venturing, 3*(4), 261–272.

Lambert Review of Business-University Collaboration. (2003) *Final Report*, HM Treasury, London. http://www.hm-treasury.gov.uk.

Lendel, I. (2010). The Impact of research universities on regional economies: The concept of university products. *Economic Development Quarterly, 24*, 210–230.

Lockett, N., Cave, F., Kerr, R., & Robinson, S. (2009). The influence of co-location in higher education institutions on small firms' perspectives of knowledge transfer. *Entrepreneurship and Regional Development, 21*(3), 265–283.

Pawson, R., & Tilly, N. (1997). *Realistic evaluation.* London: Sage.

Pedler, M., Burgoyne, J., & Brook, C. (2005). What has action learning learned to become? *Action Learning: Research and Practice, 2*(1), 49–68.

Revans, R. W. (1980). *Action learning: New techniques for managers.* London: Blond and Briggs.

Revans, R. W. (1982). *The origins and growth of action learning.* Bromely: Chartwell-Brat.

Smith, L. (2009). Experiences of action learning in two SME business support programmes. *Action Learning: Research and Practice, 6*(3), 335–341.

Smith, S. M. (2011). How do small business owner-managers learn leadership through networked learning? In L. Dirckinck-Holmfeld, V. Hodgson, & D. McConnell (Eds.), *Exploring the theory, pedagogy and practice of networked learning.* New York, NY: Springer.

Smith, L. & Peters, S. (2006). Leading by design: the case of LEAD. *Paper presented at the British Academy of Management Conference.* Belfast.

Wenger, E. (1998). *Communities of practice: Learning, meaning, and identity.* Cambridge: Cambridge University Press.

Wenger, E. (2004). Knowledge management as a doughnut: Shaping your knowledge strategy through communities of practice, *Ivey Business Journal*, January/February, 1–8.

Wenger, E., McDermott, R., & Snyder, W. M. (2002). *Cultivating communities of practice.* Boston, MASS: Harvard Business School Press.

Wren, C. & Jones, J. (2006). *Ex-Post evaluation of the LEAD programme.* http://www.lums.ac.uk/leaddeval.

Wren, C. & Jones, J. (2012). *Quantitative evaluation of the LEAD Programme, 2004–2011.* http://www.ncl.ac.uk/nubs/research/publication/192709.

Chapter 19
Teacher Educators' Critical Reflection on Becoming and Belonging to a Community of Practice

Lenore Adie, Amanda Mergler, Jennifer Alford, Vinesh Chandra and Erika Hepple

Abstract Establishing communities of practice is a tenuous process fraught with a multiplicity of experiences and artefacts that come together and either strengthen or hinder the practice. In this chapter a diverse group of teacher educators reflect on their experience of being brought together to form a community of practice in the scholarship of teaching. Their task was to collaboratively consider and problem solve some of the key issues currently impacting on teacher education, and more broadly on higher education. How the group negotiated shared meaning and purpose is a focus of the chapter. There were many challenges and issues that the group needed to collaboratively and individually solve before progressing towards shared meaning. The experiences of the assigned leaders of this group are also considered, yet it is the evolving understanding of leadership through collaboration that is of greater importance. The interplay of the experiences of all group members along with the artefacts and practices that reify the group's purpose are considered. We explore how the group members began to understand how to work collaboratively across the boundaries of their disciplines, and how reflecting on their learning and participation in this group enabled them to work through issues that were constraining their progress.

Keywords Community of practice · Meaning making · Teacher educators · Negotiated practice · Scholarship of teaching · Higher education

L. Adie (✉)
Learning Sciences Institute Australia, Australian Catholic University,
Virginia, Australia
e-mail: Lenore.Adie@acu.edu.au

A. Mergler · J. Alford · V. Chandra · E. Hepple
Queensland University of Technology, Brisbane, Australia

© Springer Nature Singapore Pte Ltd. 2017
J. McDonald and A. Cater-Steel (eds.), *Communities of Practice*,
DOI 10.1007/978-981-10-2879-3_19

19.1   Introduction

This chapter presents a case study of a diverse group of teacher educators, in an Australian university, who were brought together to collaborate and research innovative ideas in improving the learning experience for preservice teachers. The purpose of the group was to draw from individual team projects and combine evidence to highlight and advance the key issues impacting on higher education and teacher education specifically. The chapter analyses the development of this group focusing on the social learning and collaborative problem solving that occurred in the initial stages of negotiating and establishing how the group would work together. These insights are explored via the reflections created by the academics involved in this community. Our learning from these reflections will be discussed in relation to the process of establishing a shared meaning and purpose within the group.

The value of 'public' thinking and shared problem solving has been highlighted as a means to create inspired and innovative practices (Timperley et al. 2007). Yet, public thinking or de-privatising thoughts is a fraught process complexified by the dynamics of the group and the assigned tasks. In this chapter, we describe the process that occurred as we, a diverse group of teacher educators, started to develop a sense of shared meaning and shared purpose in the initial stages of a developing community of practice. Lave and Wenger (1998) suggest that a community of practice is

> ...a set of relations among persons, activity, and the world, over time and in relation with other tangential and overlapping communities of practice... [and] an intrinsic condition for the existence of knowledge, not least because it provides the interpretive support necessary for making sense of its heritage. (p. 98)

Developing shared meaning and purpose is an initial stage of working together. In this self-reflective analysis, we draw on Wenger's belief (1998) that in all of the activities in which we engage, "it is the meanings that we produce that matter" (p. 51). However, the production of these shared meanings is a complex and dynamic activity, involving engagement with the task and a process of negotiation. The critical self-analysis of this group of academics is being used in this chapter to make visible how our learning was shaped through the social learning processes of negotiation and collaboration.

The theoretical position of this chapter is grounded in social practices, and specifically in learning as a part of these practices. Wenger (1998) defines practice as 'a process by which we can experience the world and our engagement in it as meaningful' (p. 51). Within this framework, knowledge is understood to be socially situated. In this chapter we explore how learning occurred for a group of teacher educators, as individuals moved towards understanding and taking responsibility for the group as collective action. This has been an iterative process of "discovering how to engage, what helps and what hinders; developing mutual relationships; defining identities, [and] establishing who is who..." (Wenger 1998, p. 95). Of interest is how the process of negotiation contributed to determining what the group as a collective considered to be worthwhile knowledge, and how participation in this practice changed over a period of 8 months during a series of meetings focused on clarifying our evolving community of practice. Three research questions guided us in exploring our practice:

1. What processes of negotiation defined this community of practice?
2. What were the challenges and issues in forming this community of practice?
3. How does reflective practice contribute to the ongoing formation of this community of practice?

19.2   Context

This chapter focuses on a community of practice composed of a diverse group of teacher educators in a Faculty of Education in an Australian university. The aim for this group was to promote a scholarship of teaching that involved critical enquiry into the theoretical, philosophical and conceptual knowledge of higher education teaching and learning practices. The rigorous interrogation of teaching in higher education, while linked to enhanced learning experiences for students, has been described as challenging (Bender and Gray 1999; Healey 2000). It has also been suggested that "there should be a much greater emphasis on collaboration amongst researchers" that results in an accumulation of evidence (Sleeter 2014, p. 152). Our goal was that this collaborative process of critical enquiry into teaching practice may respond to contemporary challenges of innovation and renewal in the changing landscape of higher education and teacher education.

The academics were brought together over the course of 8 months to collaborate on shared writing tasks. The larger group consisted of smaller project teams made up of one to five members each working on their own individual projects. Their task was to find the common themes in their projects that addressed overarching issues in teacher education, and collaboratively write about these issues, drawing on the findings from their individual projects to present a stronger body of evidence. These researchers did not normally work or write together.

The group consisted of teams of academics who had all applied for an internal faculty teaching and learning grant to improve some aspect of their teaching practice and two team leaders who held leadership positions within the university (referred to as Speaker 1 in the analysis) and the Faculty (referred to as Speaker 5 in the analysis). There were 12 academics in the group made up from five different teams with a range of one to five members in each team. Individually the teams were investigating aspects of practice such as enhancing preservice teachers' professional communication and relationships through visual media; developing intercultural learning and Asia literacy; developing digital storybooks as a collaboration between ICT and literacy subjects; developing an ICT preservice teacher special interest group; and enriching teaching and learning in mathematics.

The first interactions of the group aimed to develop a shared vision and collective responsibility for how the group would work as well as the anticipated outcomes of this work. This community of practice aimed to establish a space where thinking, talking, debating, negotiating and writing about teacher and higher education was an established practice. While university academics are experts in their own fields, 'higher education' and the 'scholarship of teaching' are other fields of practice.

Besides publishing about their own findings, the groups were asked to think more broadly about how together their projects were contributing to current debates in the preservice teacher education and higher education sectors. The process of working together required clear communication of their project, active listening to other's ideas and conceptualisations, clarification of individual projects, negotiation of ideas, and accommodation of differing perspectives. The reality of this process was complex and messy, requiring individuals to collaboratively navigate and construct the practice. This dialogic process was central to developing the community of practice, as Eckert and Wenger (2005, p. 583) have observed: "Legitimacy in any community of practice involves not just having access to knowledge necessary for 'getting it right', but being at the table at which 'what is right' is continually negotiated." It was an organic process where there was a problem of how to develop the practice and a desired outcome of collaborative writing. While the team leaders had a plan for meetings and topics for discussion, there were many barriers to the enactment of this linear plan.

In participatory pedagogies, such as communities of practice, there are no pre-established frameworks about the lifecycle of the community of practice and how much engagement or what type of engagement is necessary to maintain it (Davies 2005). It is the members who create their practice as a complex, jointly negotiated response to their perceived situation. These "amorphous community obligations" of educators in a community of practice provide the creative space to allow for the emergence of professional innovation, as the members give shape to their common enterprise (Lee and Shaari 2012, p. 459). It was envisaged that this community of practice, structured around thinking and publishing on the big issues affecting higher education, would gradually develop as a culture, a way of working within the faculty. The long-term goal was that the community of academics involved in these activities would be fluid, with members moving in and out as activities occurred, rather than a discrete group of members. In other words, this first coming together was to be the start of a culture of collaborative thinking and sharing of the broader issues affecting teacher education and more broadly higher education teaching and learning that would involve more academics than this initial group.

While a climate of collaborative activity was a goal of the group leaders, much discussion and negotiation was necessary to build trust amongst the group members, to establish the legitimacy of the group and to articulate the purpose of the group's formation. The leaders' aims for the group and the expected characteristics that would define the group broadly aligned with those that Stoll et al. (2006, pp. 226–227) describe in terms of a teacher professional learning community:

shared values and vision, collective responsibility, reflective professional inquiry, collaboration, and group, as well as individual learning. As one group leader explained:

> We were visionary leaders, but the team wasn't about being led. It was about everyone being leaders and coming together to make decisions. (Speaker 5)

The goal for this group was to collaboratively problem solve and learn together such that the collective knowledge of the group would result in authoritative comment in the field of teacher education and higher education teaching and learning.

In order to achieve shared values and vision the group engaged in a process of negotiating meanings. This negotiation of meaning is described as consisting of the dual processes of participation and reification. Participating in a practice involves a social, emotional and historical dynamic that separates participation from just the engagement or collaboration with others (Wenger 1998). The artefacts and experiences that are an aspect of the community also help to shape and define meaning within the community but are not directly involved in the negotiation process. In the negotiation of meaning, experiences are given form through the objects that are produced, and thus become a focus within the negotiation process. This projection of meaning is termed 'reification' (Wenger 1998). Meaning is reified in the naming of practices and groups, in the products that are created, and in the spaces that represent the group. Thus, reification can refer to both process and product.

Establishing a community of practice is not an easy task. By their nature such groups are informal and arise spontaneously at a grass-roots level through shared interests and concerns, rather than by being officially invited. Wenger and Snyder (2000) suggest that communities of practice cannot be mandated but they can be nurtured by taking action to "bring the right people together, provide an infrastructure in which communities can thrive, and measure the communities' value in non-traditional ways" (p. 140). By bringing these teacher educators together by invitation, tensions and uncertainties surfaced around the participants' understandings of the shared endeavour, which is at the heart of a community of practice. This highlights the importance of the relational aspect within communities, where "the critical dimension of community is a sense of belonging" (Healey et al. 2014, p. 28). Building this sense of belonging, so that members shared a feeling of personal relatedness, proved a lengthier process than originally anticipated.

The group met several times over monthly intervals, and areas of commonality in their research were discussed and brainstormed as 'big' ideas that connected to broad fields of investigation into higher education. However, the initial meetings of this group were not motivated by a collective desire to come together in the scholarship of teaching. The role of the group leaders and their associated institutional influence have great bearing on the problematic and iterative dynamic of coming to know and be in this group space. To understand this dynamic, it is necessary to outline the history of the group's formation. Figure 19.1 is an overview of meetings and communications that will provide a structure to the following description and discussion.

February	Submission of grant applications		
↓	↓		
March	Faculty leadership reframes applications and recommends alternate model	→	Email sent to grant teams re outcome of applications and invitation to be part of larger group
↓	↓		
May	1st group meeting outlining proposal for group	→	Email outlining meeting outcomes and attaching new proposal
↓	↓		
June	2nd group meeting – discussion of projects and mapping of broad issues that were being covered	→	Setting up of Google+ community with group documents including individual project proposals, new project proposals, mapping of ideas produced by group, timeline for group outcomes, associated reading
↓	↓		
July	3rd group meeting		
↓	↓		
August	4th group meeting		
↓	↓		
October	5th group meeting		
↓	↓		
January	Writing and reflection workshop		

Fig. 19.1 Overview of group meetings and communications

Individually each team had submitted a proposal for a Faculty grant applying for funding to work on their own teaching and learning project. The intended use of these funds included the payment of transcriptions of collected interview data, and/or the payment of a research assistant to help set up groups or to develop support materials including filming and video editing and developing web pages. However, institutionally there had been a shift in how these funds were to be used, and applications needed to demonstrate that the project results and findings could be applied across the university and scaled up to applications for national projects. The Faculty leadership team decided that these applications did not meet those criteria and a different approach to apportioning these funds was necessary. This meant that none of applications were successful but all teams were instead invited to participate in the larger scholarship of teaching project.

In the first meeting, the group leaders explained to the teams the purpose of the group. After this meeting, an email was sent by the group leaders with an overview of the meeting outcomes and providing the new proposal. The next meeting involved discussing how individual projects connected and could contribute to broader issues affecting teacher and higher education, and asked the group to envisage how they may set up processes to work together. At this meeting, groups discussed their individual projects then started to map the connections between them in terms of broad, overarching topics that would connect to larger issues affecting teacher education and teaching in higher education. An online community site was established so that groups could upload information about their individual projects, keep a record of their experiences and set up writing partnerships. Alongside these conversations each individual was asked to reflect on their own involvement in the group and the organic development that was an aspect of this group. The intent of the following meetings was to establish plans for collaborative writing and decide who may lead the writing on different papers. This goal has not yet been achieved as we reflect on the dynamic process of developing shared meaning and purpose.

19.3 Methodology

19.3.1 Research Approach

Qualitative methodology was used to explore the understandings and experiences of the participants within the specific context and within a time frame (Merriam 1998, 2002; Miles and Huberman 1994). A case study approach (Merriam 2002; Simons 2009) was taken with "the case" being the community of practice that was emerging as a result of broader institutional priorities.

The participants were ten teacher educators (seven females and three males) from three Schools within the Faculty of Education. They ranged in age and experience as teacher educators although all participants had been teaching in the Faculty for at least 3 years. One participant occupied a Professorial position and two held positions as course or program coordinators.

Data were collected in two phases. First, a 1-h face-to-face discussion amongst members of the group was video recorded. This prolonged discussion was captured as it came at a crucial point in the life of the community of practice. The group had been meeting for 8 months and the team leaders were keen for the group to start producing outputs. The discussion centred on the social and cognitive aspects of being a member of the evolving community of practice. Each member reflected on their trajectory from the commencement of the group up to this point. To aid the discussion, members were asked to use a Collaborative Problem Solving framework (Griffin et al. 2012) where they considered their developmental progression of working within the group. The collaborative problem solving framework focuses on dimensions of participation, perspective taking, social regulation, task regulation and knowledge building.

Self and public reflection has been used by academics to understand their work amid the complexity of changing sociopolitical contexts (Davies et al. 2005; Light et al. 2009). Public sharing is reported to support the development of identity within a practice (Jarvis et al. 2012). The power of peer group interaction to impact learning and personal development has been well-documented in a variety of educational contexts (Levine and Shapiro 2004; Visher et al. 2010). As teacher educators, we advocate reflective practice to our students and seek to enact this in our own daily professional practice. Such reflective practice is integral to establishing a 'collegial culture' within a community of practice, as noted by Lieberman and Miller (2008), who confirm the importance of mutually respectful discussion and sharing of ideas to achieve this.

The audio of this discussion was transcribed with the video aiding the transcriber to identify the participants' voices. Second, the de-identified transcription was distributed via email to all ten participants who were invited to engage in a respondent validation process (Simons 2009), clarifying and commenting on their own contributions via track changes. Whilst other studies have focused on analysing transcripts of participants' reflections (Cumming-Potvin 2009), it is not so common, outside of action research, that the analysis is conducted by the participants themselves. Yet we suggest that this is a powerful identity-shaping practice. In the case of this emerging community of practice, projection of meaning centred on the group's recorded discussion and the subsequent iterative process of participants analysing the transcript of that discussion. In identifying key elements in the transcript, participants were negotiating shared awareness of the community's emerging identity. This process of working with the transcripts then generated more refined data, for example, clarifications of content and meaning including providing referents for when pronouns were used (for example, you), as well as additional data in the form of new information as comments in the margins. Each revised transcript was then collated into a single transcript document containing all comments and changes.

19.3.2 Analytic Method

Four members of the group separately coded the transcript. Coding was used to "assign a summative, salient, essence-capturing attribute" (Saldaña 2009, p. 3) to portions of data in the margins on the transcript. These codes were then shared and discussed face-to-face by the four coders. Final codes were then agreed upon and these codes were grouped into overarching themes tracing the development of our community of practice over time and informed by the literature and the theoretical framework of making 'meaning' and 'reification' within communities of practice (Lave and Wenger 1991; Wenger 1998).

In the following section we present the findings and discussion of our emerging community of practice in relation to our research questions:

1. What processes of negotiation defined this community of practice?
2. What were the challenges and issues in forming this community of practice?
3. How does reflective practice contribute to the ongoing formation of this community of practice?

19.4   Findings and Discussion

19.4.1   Responding to a New, Overarching Agenda

The first meeting of this group was characterised by much tension as teams sought to understand why their applications for a grant were not successful and how the new vision of the leadership team applied to them. While there was no obligation to attend this first meeting, all teams that applied for grants did attend. However, while some were interested to hear of this new project, most also wanted to understand why the rules of the game (applying for a Teaching and Learning grant to enhance one's teaching) had changed. The broader, visionary, institutional agenda for the community of practice created a discombobulating shift for the individuals at the first meeting, and generated tension that needed to be resolved if these individuals were to work together. Each member of the community of practice came to the group as members of smaller collaborative groups who had applied for a small amount of funding through a Faculty Teaching and Learning grant. As such, individual members arrived connected to their smaller groups, and protective of the idea they had formulated for their teaching and learning project. For some they had invested a lot of their own time in their projects and they did not want their ideas to be "hijacked".

[People were] annoyed because the whole scenario seemed to have changed. (Speaker 5)

The collective writing that was the leader's aim for the group came to represent for some members a perversion of an institutional decision where they were the objects of the decision rather than part of the negotiations. Wenger (1998) points out that the reification of ideas and processes into artefacts can be double-edged. While symbolising the collective thinking of the group, the writing task also represented the lack of funding and the change in direction of grant giving to the group. By submitting their grant applications, team members were hoping for funds to complete their project; they did not sign up for this larger project. Rather than represent the collective thinking of group members, the writing came to represent an imposed purpose. The team leaders needed to have their vision become the group's vision and that required much conversation and debate.

In the initial meetings there was a discontinuity between the group leaders and the group members that was grounded in their differing perspectives. While team members were focussed on progressing their individual projects, and with projects at different stages of development, many were not in a space where they could commit to what appeared to be a different project. Many did not perceive that the projects could run in parallel, nor that this larger group thinking could contribute to their thinking about their individual project. Although group members acknowledged the common broad themes underpinning their projects, the differences between them, and the different stages of progression of individual projects was a barrier to progressing towards common meaning and purpose for the group. As a consequence there was a lot of confusion and resistance to the new model of collaboration.

> I think what we were saying was, "what are we supposed to be contributing?" Because of the confusion there was an element of resistance. (Speaker 4)

While the academics in this group were from the same faculty and knew each other, they were from different sub-groups within the faculty, they taught and researched into different disciplines, and they did not normally come together for these types and topics of discussion. Finding some commonality and synergy such that their engagement in the group was meaningful was challenging work. Participants felt they did not know what was expected of them, how their individual group projects connected to the wider project, and what it was that the group was trying to achieve. There was also a sense that these factors undermined the collaborative nature of the group, leading people to want to work on their small group projects.

> I am thinking of the very first meeting we ever had and I was just angry, frustrated, didn't want to be there. Didn't understand what we were trying to do. Couldn't make head nor tail of anything. "No one is getting any money! This is a waste of my time!" I was really cross. I felt really angry and frustrated about the whole process. (Speaker 2)

> I think when the task is unclear people become unfocussed. When the task became clearer I was more amenable to working with other people. Where the task was unclear I felt I was wasting my time and I would just go and do my own stuff. (Speaker 8)

Recognising similarities and differences between team members' individual projects was considered an important part of the negotiation of meaning. Conversations amongst group members sometimes clarified and extended our thinking, while at other times sent us off in different directions, or took us to what appeared to be dead ends. The conversations challenged team members to clearly articulate our intended meaning, and to clarify the terms we were using. For example, in the group were psychologists as well as sociologists who did not always share common understandings of terms. Negotiating a shared meaning also involved the social relationships among group members. Members needed to feel secure to question, challenge, and state their disagreement with others' opinions. This active process of negotiation required knowledge that was both based in the current events as they unfolded as well as historical knowledge of the broader social dynamic of academic professionalism which is the basis of this community.

Communities of practice and meaning develop as a result of other practices which have come before them, and inform group expectations which then contribute to the continued negotiations of the group. This was a group of academics who knew aspects of each other's practice but were not familiar with other member's individual ways of working. They were all familiar with a culture of academia, and the way of working within that context. There were commonalities of understanding, but there was much divergence in their perspectives. New meanings needed to be considered, and the group needed to find a convergence of their thinking if the group was to progress. Wenger (1998) acknowledges that this adoption of new meanings may be 'partial, tentative, ephemeral, and specific to a situation' (p. 53), such that the development of communities is a dynamic process that occurs gradually with much looping back and renegotiation of meaning. Davis et al. (2008) describe this development of meaning as a principle of knowing that is partial yet perceptively adequate.

> A knower's knowing is subject to constant modification; yet at the same time, one's sense of the world is curiously adequate. In spite of the partiality of knowing, *one* is typically unaware of the gaps in understanding and perception. That is, knowing has a certain sort of vibrant sufficiency (p. 16).

There were some underlying factors that led to the lack of clarity and progress for the group. While the group leaders had conveyed the purpose of the group in the first meeting and through email communications, many of the members could not understand how they could function as a group with a research focus.

> When we had our initial meeting, it was practical and made sense and then we were kind of moving back into our own individual projects and thinking, probably it doesn't make sense, maybe it doesn't make sense. (Speaker 4)

One tool the leaders of the group used to encourage engagement amongst group members was a closed group Google+ community site. It was anticipated that the development of the online community site would be a space where the group members would connect to share their projects and start to develop and negotiate their collective thinking and meaning. In our community of practice there was minimal uptake of this online community space until the last meeting of the group to date, where group members reflected on their experiences and started to commit to the goal of the larger group. At this time the online community site became a useful tool with group members contributing artefacts that could help build the knowledge of the group, and one they could refer to as a historic record of the group's collective thinking.

> So there was that whole misunderstanding, or maybe [the group leaders] were having things put up there [on the group's Google+ site] and we were thinking, well what does that have to do with me? And I was thinking, well that is not what we are on about (Speaker 4).

In a theory of situated learning, it is through participation in the community and building relationships and shared identities that meaning is developed (Handley et al. 2006). The initial meetings that included sharing information about each of their individual projects was for group members to start to see the intersections of their projects, such that these topics became the focus of discussion. Reifying the group's online space, the group's name and the artefacts that the group were being asked to produce into meaningful symbols that captured the work of this group was not a linear process of acceptance or evolution. Indeed, each time the group met, there was a toing and froing between discrete investigations and the common contributions to the bigger issues of teacher and higher education. A spiral of conversations more aptly illustrates the evolution of the practice and how shared meanings were being developed.

19.4.2 Negotiating a Way Forward

There were many challenges to progress the shared meaning for our group. These included the workload expectations of being an academic; the disconnect between individual team projects and the larger overarching project; and our different ways of working. Coming to understand the purpose of the group was uneven for group members. Members talked about moving backward and forward between understanding what they are trying to achieve in this collaborative group, and failing to understand this. While some understood the purpose of the larger group, others struggled to reconcile their individual projects to this larger vision. In this section we highlight the different responses of the group to the ambiguity of the project with which we were confronted.

The journey of creating the community of practice involved working in new ways with new people. Some members of the group highlighted the influence of other aspects in their lives, and how these considerations had fed into their capability to be involved in the community.

> I was meeting other academics [through being in this group] which, because I had maternity leave twice, I felt I was a bit disconnected, so I was coming back and I was meeting colleagues, so for me that was really exciting and because of where my life was at I was yes, let's get this going (our HERN group). (Speaker 2)

> I remember thinking I was being "hijacked". I think context is really important to be able to explain that because for me this [becoming a member of this community of practice] all came at the end of my PhD thesis. I was getting a huge six and a half year project finished and I was busy teaching, you know what it's like: "I don't think I can contribute to this. I don't know much about it. I am interested to learn more but I felt, how am I going to fit this into the rest of my life?" So that is where the resistance came in for me. I can comfortably say now…I feel much more open to learning more and to participate more. (Speaker 7)

Complicating this scenario was the busy lives of academics causing irregular attendance at group meetings for some, and lack of time to read email communications.

> If you are feeling overwhelmed at work, you just don't feel like this meeting, and you think I haven't done anything or read anything, I don't know what to talk about. Do I even want to go? I don't think I will go at all. So you need context in what is going on in your mind. (Speaker 4)

During reflections, 8 months after these events, the academics had different recollections of the events which may be attributed to their selective attendance and attention to details or a 'blinkered' perception of the events of which they were involved. Davis et al. (2008) discuss perception as 'more a matter of negotiating a relationship between current and past experiences' such that at times 'we don't see that we don't see it' (p. 22).

For those group members who attended every meeting, it appeared that little progress towards shared meaning was made as we constantly revisited previously covered ground. The lack of progress was causing problems. Nothing tangible was being achieved and for the members who were time poor this was a major issue.

> I think there was a point during the year where I came back to a second meeting and thought 'we just discussed that'. We don't seem to make a lot of progress because people come and go. (Speaker 8)

A challenge of coming together as a cohesive community of practice for our group was the fact that we had all started with separate small group projects. This meant that some people were very familiar with working together, while others had no previous exposure to each other. In addition, different groups were at different stages of their projects, and therefore finding a common place to start was challenging. Some groups had wanted funding to wrap up a project, while others had wanted funding to begin something new. This meant that some groups had a very clear formulation of what their individual project was, while other groups were quite unsure about what their smaller project would look like. This confusion then fed into wider confusion about what the community of practice was meant to achieve, and frustration at how to bring such diverse projects (in focus and stage of development) together.

> For our [small group] project, we have been going now for three years. It has a long history of [us] working together. It is still going. We are collecting our data and that has a big impact on how we see our role in this group. (Speaker 7)

> And I think the stage of the project is interesting, because ours is very much in the conceptual stage and we are still trying to look at what the project looks like, whereas yours is at the matured stage you know exactly what the direction is and where you want to go. So we are then trying to juggle these two completely different things [i.e., developing our project and integrating with the group] and this can be too much because of the group and so on, and then it is, "oh this is too much", and we are confused. (Speaker 3)

For one member of the community of practice, getting a fuller picture of the broader expectation of the group took a particularly long time. He remained firmly focused on his own small project, and he attended a number of meetings before he finally realised the purpose of the community.

> I know it is a group thing and I try to attend as many meetings as I can, but somehow the point I need to make [is that] I am doing numeracy. A part [of me feels like] I don't belong here, and people say "oh you too are in the group", and sometimes I feel a bit lonely. Nobody seems to understand my burning issue here. Unfortunately I don't belong here, maybe I should step out. (Speaker 9)

This community member is still focused very much on his individual project, and what it is he feels is necessary to achieve in his field of expertise. He has struggled to shift his focus toward the generation of a group outcome that, through his involvement, will be enriched by him, but he has continued to come to meet and discuss.

In response to the differential progress towards the anticipated outcomes for this group, one of the group leaders changed her leadership style over the course of the group's 8 months lifespan. She took on what she perceived to be a more directive and less collaborative approach.

> I tried to consider your perspectives from the first instance. When I came to it [the initial group meeting] I thought, I want to hear what you are going to say, and then I found [over time that] you were actually pulling apart in your own direction, and had we continued there, this wouldn't have been the goal I had, [which] was for collaboration. I thought we could come in with what you had and we could collaborate from there. But because there was a pulling apart then I had to shift back [to taking greater control]... you were looking for more direction, so I became more directive, through coming along to meetings with, "This is where we are at" and a bit more information up front at the beginning of each meeting. I think in some of the meetings I gave a thirty minute talk at the beginning. (Speaker 1)

There were those who needed more information and direction about the broader goals, while for others the ambiguity was an opportunity to do something different in terms of collaborating with colleagues. Even though the picture looked cloudy, the group was embarking on a challenge that was open ended—this initiative was creating a pathway for new opportunities.

> How do we actually make it happen? That was the challenge. I saw the opportunity that we could do different things.... (Speaker 6)

Despite the fact that the first meetings were characterised by confusion and anger, individuals chose to keep coming to meetings to discuss their projects and search for synergies between them. The shift from a focus on an individual small teaching project to a vision of high calibre research was hard work. But it was possibly this 'murkiness', the delving into the unknown and the challenge of moving into new territory and new thinking that compelled us to keep returning to progress our conversations. The project offered us a sense of freedom which allowed us to explore and deeply ponder aspects of interest both theoretically and conceptually. We see through these conversations the different ways in which people prefer to work, and while ambiguity is grasped by some as an opportunity, it is met with resistance by others. Following are a number of quotes from those who saw the open-endedness of the task as an opportunity.

> It was the second or third meeting that I finally realized that this is a situation where I am going to have freedom to do what I want to do, and once I got that I was excited about the possibilities. (Speaker 2)

> There needs to be something at faculty level because if we weren't in a group I wouldn't know what others are doing. There are wonderful pedagogies happening that all of us could be contributing to. (Speaker 4)

> I want to know more what are the possibilities here? This could be exciting. This could extend my thinking... That has been the beauty of this group and when you shared your projects, I have been inspired to do things better or differently... This came out of Speaker 6's [sharing of the work he does in his] unit and for me I took something immediately from his project, and [I thought] that is what I would like to do, and we took it back and worked from there. (Speaker 10)

> I think that everyone in the faculty should be a part of a collaborative network. They should all be interlinked and they shouldn't be in isolation, and that is what it is all about. (Speaker 8)

The emerging community of practice created new opportunities for participants which included: an awareness of what others are doing; stimulus to generate and apply ideas to their own teaching practice; opportunity to obtain additional value for the everyday teaching work of an academic; and a sense of connection to others who work in different parts of the Faculty. As the group is comprised of teacher educators, examining and reflecting on our practice with the purpose of continual improvement is fundamental to our daily teaching practice. The confusion in finding connections between projects eventually gave way to an eagerness to progress. The reactions of the group we consider are typical of any academics faced with open-ended projects such as was the nature of this one.

19.5 Conclusion and Implications

This chapter has provided an account of how one group of teacher educators traversed the emerging stages of a community of practice. The process of meaning making was more protracted than was initially expected by the group leaders, and was characterised by misunderstanding and confusion early on. This eventually led to greater openness to possibility. In investigating our own practice in establishing this community, we identified three key research questions:

1. What processes of negotiation defined this community of practice?
2. What were the challenges and issues in forming this community of practice?
3. How does reflective practice contribute to the ongoing formation of this community of practice?

The flexibility of a community of practice allowed the researchers to collaboratively create new foci and synergies beyond their smaller group domains, so that 'bigger' issues and new methodologies could be explored. In a heavily research and publications focussed milieu, communities of practice within teacher education, and higher education more broadly, can encompass a simultaneous dual focus on projects enhancing teaching and learning as well as expanding scholarly knowledge. Our self-reflective practice identified that the establishment of a community of practice is a complex and uneven process of negotiation and meaning making for group members. The dominant discourses of autonomy and competition within higher education often run counter to that which are required for a functioning community of practice that spans existing specialities within a Faculty. The challenges revolve around our individual identities and lives as academics, as well as our perception of ownership of the practice. Although working in uncharted terrain, the collaborative intent of the members has resulted in each individual's experience shaping the formation of this community and our responses to it.

The reflective practice that we participated in during our last gathering has contributed greatly to the meaning making and coming together of this diverse group. While this practice was a part of many of our meetings, and options were provided for group members to start this reflective practice, including suggested topics for reflection discussed at meetings and shared on our online community site, it took time to reach this point. It would be easy to recommend that this process occur earlier in the establishment of such communities of practice, but other factors such as time for deep thinking and trust need to be present. It takes time for all of these elements to connect, or for the "interplay of participation and reification" (Wenger 1998, p. 70) to balance.

The writing of this chapter documenting our process has proven to be a further step in forming a community identity. The production, distribution and review of the transcript of our most recent meeting in order to write this chapter has engaged various members of our community of practice in a process of reification (Wenger 1998). As Wenger noted, "Reification shapes... our experience of the world by focusing our attention in a particular way and enabling new kinds of understanding" (p. 64). Focusing attention and reflection on these transcripts as objects derived from collaborative problem solving, has enabled members to collectively question and refine their understandings of the shared enterprise, contributing to their developing sense of shared purpose. Including some formal focus on the process of becoming a community of practice, such as having reading workshops discussing key research in this area, could also be helpful in engaging group members in this process of reification.

In writing about our journey, new understandings of the potential and constraints that inhere in communities of practice have emerged. We did not come together thinking that we were developing a community of practice, but through our laughter and angst we wonder if we are on the cusp of developing such a community.

Acknowledgments The authors were a part of a team of academics who were involved in this community of practice and many of which contributed their reflections for analysis. We would like to thank our colleagues for their assistance in the conceptualisation of this chapter.

References

Bender, E., & Gray, D. (1999). *The Scholarship of Teaching. Research and Creative Activity, XXII* (1). http://www.indiana.edu/~rcapub/v22n1/p03.html

Cumming-Potvin, W. (2009). Social justice, pedagogy and multiliteracies: Developing communities of practice for teacher education. *Australian Journal of Teacher Education, 34*(3), 82–99.

Davies, B. (2005). Communities of practice: Legitimacy not choice. *Journal of Sociolinguistics, 9* (4), 557–581.

Davies, B., Browne, J., Gannon, S., Honan, E., & Somerville, M. (2005). Embodied women at work in neoliberal times and places. *Gender, Work and Organisation, 12*(4), 343–362.

Davis, B., Sumara, D., & Luce-Kapler, R. (2008). *Engaging minds: Changing teaching in complex times* (2nd ed.). New York: Routledge.

Eckert, P., & Wenger, E. (2005). Communities of practice in sociolinguistics. *Journal of Sociolinguistics, 9*, 582–589.

Griffin, P., Care, E., & McGaw, B. (2012). The changing role of education and schools. In P. Griffin, B. McGaw, & E. Care (Eds.), *Assessment and teaching of 21st century skills* (pp. 1–16). Dordrecht: Springer.

Handley, K., Sturdy, A., Fincham, R., & Clark, T. (2006). Within and beyond communities of practice: Making sense of learning through participation, identity and practice. *Journal of Management Studies, 43*(3), 641–653.

Healey, M. (2000). Developing the scholarship of teaching in higher education: A discipline-based approach. *Higher Education Research and Development, 19*(2), 169–189.

Healey, M., Flint, A., & Harrington, K. (2014). Engagement through partnership: Students as partners in learning and teaching in higher education. York, Higher Education Academy HEA (2014) Framework for partnership in learning and teaching. York, Higher Education Academy.

Jarvis, J., Dickerson, C., Chivers, L., Collins, C., Lee, L., & Solly, D. (2012). A personalised needs-led group approach to induction: Perceptions of early academics in a university School of Education. *Australian Journal of Teacher Education, 37*(11), 37–59.

Lave, J., & Wenger, E. (1991). *Situated learning: Legitimate peripheral participation*. Cambridge: Cambridge University Press.

Lee, D., & Shaari, I. (2012). Professional Identity or best practices?—An exploration of the synergies between professional learning communities and communities of practices. *Creative Education, 3*, 457–460.

Levine, J. L., & Shapiro, N. S. (2004). *Sustaining and improving learning communities*. San Francisco: Jossey-Bass.

Lieberman, A., & Miller, L. (2008). *Teachers in professional communities: Improving teaching and learning*. New York: Teachers College Press.

Light, G., Cox, R., & Calkins, S. (2009). *Learning and teaching in higher education: The reflective professional*. London: Sage.

Merriam, S. B. (1998). *Qualitative research and case study applications in education*. San Francisco, CA: Jossey-Bass.

Merriam, S. B. (2002). Introduction to qualitative research. In S. B. Merriam (Ed.), *Qualitative research in practice—Examples for discussion and analysis* (pp. 3–17). San Francisco, CA: Jossey-Bass.

Miles, M. B., & Huberman, A. M. (1994). *Qualitative data analysis—An expanded sourcebook* (2nd ed.). Thousand Oaks, CA: Sage.

Saldaña, J. (2009). *The coding manual for qualitative researchers*. Thousand Oaks, CA: Sage.

Simons, H. (2009). *Case study research in practice*. London, UK: Sage.

Sleeter, C. (2014). Toward teacher education research that informs policy. *Educational Researcher, 43*(3), 146–153.

Stoll, L., Bolam, R., McMahon, A., Wallace, M., & Thomas, S. (2006). Professional learning communities: A review of the literature. *Journal of Educational Change, 7*(4), 221–258.

Timperley, H., Wilson, A., Barrar, H., & Fung, I. (2007). *Teacher professional learning and development: Best evidence synthesis iteration*. Wellington: New Zealand Ministry of Education.

Visher, M., Schneider, E., Wathington, H., & Collado, H. (2010). *Scaling up learning communities: The experience of six community colleges*. New York: MDRC. http://www.mdrc.org/publications/550/overview.html.

Wenger, E. (1998). *Communities of practice: Learning, meaning, and identity*. Cambridge: Cambridge University Press.

Wenger, E., & Snyder, W. (2000). Communities of practice: The organizational frontier. *Harvard Business Review, 78*(1), 139–145.

Part IV
Communities of Practice Sustaining Professional Learning and Development

The chapters in this part explore the opportunities and challenges of applying CoP for professional learning and development.

Chapter 20 "Making an Impact: Utilising Faculty Learning Communities to Enhance Teaching and Learning" by Newman discusses use of topic-based Faculty Learning Community (FLC) in one institution to become a high-impact university.

Chapter 21 "The Faculty/Faculty Conundrum": Organizing Faculty Learning Communities to Support 'Singular' and 'Plural' Faculty Development" by Nelson and Cates outlines the use of a modified Faculty Learning Community (FLC) model for faculty development employed within a large academic department to create CoP.

Chapter 22 "Catalyst: Developing a Community of Practice for Supporting New Academics" by Kensington-Miller presents a CoP, which was introduced to support early-career academics.

Chapter 23 "Where's My Parking Permit? Bringing New Staff Together as a Learning Community" by Crawford and Saluja outlines the process taken to establish a CoP for new staff for a multi-campus university in Australia.

Chapter 24 "CoPs: Enhancing Quality Learning and Teaching With Sessional Staff" by Harvey and Fredericks examines the potential for CoP to support quality learning and teaching with sessional academic staff.

Chapter 25 "Communities of Practice and Negotiation of Meaning Among Pre-service Teachers" Martínez-Arbelaiz et al. presents an assessment of online asynchronous discussions provided by schools of teacher education and analyses the discourse generated in order to ascertain the degree of interactivity and identify instances of negotiation of meaning.

Chapter 26 "Forums, Fellowship and Wicked Problems in Teaching" by Beckmann reviews the characteristic CoP interactions that occur among participants in online discussion forums that augment face to face professional development and professional recognition workshops about teaching and learning at an Australian university.

Chapter 27 "From Project to Permanence: Growing Inter-institutional Collaborative Teams Into Long-term, Sustainable Communities of Practice" by Fraser et al. outlines learning from a research project in which the effectiveness of collaboration within funded projects and longer term outcomes—including staff engagement, enhanced networking opportunities and sustainable CoP was studied.

Chapter 28 "From Dream to Reality. Sustaining a Higher Education Community of Practice Beyond Initial Enthusiasm" by McCormack et al. describes the personal experience stories of community members who have taken their vision for a sustainable higher education CoP.

Chapter 20
Making an Impact: Utilising Faculty Learning Communities to Enhance Teaching and Learning

Tara Newman

Abstract This chapter discusses one institution's use of topic-based Faculty Learning Community in its journey to become a high-impact university. Through the program, a significant resource was created by and for academics to enrich teaching and learning in undergraduate curriculum through high-impact educational practices (Kuh in high-impact educational practices: what they are, who has access to them, and why they matter. American Association of Colleges and Universities, Washington, DC, 2008). A guiding emphasis of the program was to support successful, inter-disciplinary engagement in the Scholarship of Teaching and Learning to directly address gaps in undergraduate learning previously identified through institutional assessment measures. As participants, academics commit to a year-long journey in which they explore scholarly literature, attend a series of phased workshops, engage in collegial discussion, and ultimately redesign curriculum to enhance student learning. Preliminary data indicates positive impacts on students and academics, as well as an increased institutional focus on the value of teaching and learning.

Keywords Faculty learning communities · Quality enhancement · Academic development · Scholarship of teaching and learning

20.1 Introduction

It is commonly accepted in academe that university teaching can be an isolating profession. As academics traverse throughout the profession, they are met with many performance expectations they are told will have serious impacts on their future promotion and/or tenure at that institution. In addition, they are aware that their visible performance will have implications for their future career options in a

T. Newman (✉)
Learning and Teaching Services, University of Southern Queensland,
Toowoomba, Australia
e-mail: Tara.Newman@usq.edu.au

© Springer Nature Singapore Pte Ltd. 2017
J. McDonald and A. Cater-Steel (eds.), *Communities of Practice*,
DOI 10.1007/978-981-10-2879-3_20

way that is, perhaps, distinct from many other career paths. The quest to produce the "right" publications and presentations, serve on the "right" variety of committees, develop meaningful mentorships with students, and be an effective educator within the classroom walls (or virtual environment) doesn't always allow for significant professional reflection (Schön 1983). In fact, sometimes it seems the very environment designed to promote the teaching and learning of its students does the worst job promoting such opportunities for its educators.

Traditional professional development strategies tend to be "one shot" approaches. That is, educators attend a workshop or a conference over a brief period of time (perhaps a few hours for a workshop or a few days for a conference). At these sessions, educators frequently are excited about the concepts they are learning, feel motivation to try new things, and might even attempt to attempt changes to their practice upon their return to campus. Often, once they meet with opposition or struggle, there is generally no one to turn to for reinforcement or encouragement. This absence of support has a negative impact on the educators' self-efficacy to innovate his/her teaching (Postareff et al. 2007) and the anticipated pedagogical innovations fade away.

20.2 Supporting Academic Development

Fortunately, the literature is replete with insight on essential features for supporting academic development. While the scope of this topic extends beyond the parameters of this chapter, it is worth noting that successful developmental programs tend to include the use of experiential learning, relevant feedback, and collegial support, while adhering to principles of adult learning (Cox 2001; Lawless and Pellegrino 2007; Rienties and Hosein 2015; Roxå and Mårtensson 2009; Steinert et al. 2006). In addition, there is ample evidence that sustained developmental experiences result in more positive behavioural outcomes than isolated activities (Boylan 2002; Graziano and Kahn 2013; Lawless and Pelegrino 2007; Postareff et al. 2007; Steinert et al. 2006; Stes et al. 2010).

To incorporate the features described above, academic developers are turning to various forms of learning communities within and across institutions to provide opportunities for meaningful professional growth (Austin and Sorcinelli 2013; Furco and Moely 2012; Healy et al. 2013; Schwartz and Haynie 2013). While there is much written about the benefits of learning communities, the literature reveals that institutional support for such initiatives plays a key role in faculty buy-in and attributed value for such work (Furco and Moely 2012; Young et al. 2007). This chapter will discuss one institution's adaptation of the Faculty Learning Community model as described by Cox (2004) to simultaneously address identified gaps in student learning and contribute to a culture promoting the scholarship of teaching and learning.

20.3 Developing the Initiative

The development of the Make an Impact project was a collaborative institution-level initiative over the span of approximately 18 months. As a part of the reaccreditation process through the Southern Association of Colleges and Schools, institutions accept the requirement to develop a quality enhancement plan addressing an identifiable gap in student learning. While the plan is an externally-imposed expectation, its details are defined by each individual institution to address its particular needs. Admittedly, it is often challenging to introduce any institutional initiative associated with an accreditation review to faculty; however, the impending review date provided a sense of urgency and seriousness about identifying needs that might not have otherwise been present without that pressure (Shulman et al. 2004).

Seeking to identify areas that could be improved across the university, a steering committee was formed to conduct an institutional needs analysis. The committee solicited input from not only faculty and staff, but students, alumni, local business leaders, and other constituents as well. Internal data pertaining to standardized assessments, graduation rates, and student demographics were also compiled and analyzed. This process led to the identification of several areas of potential improvement which could contribute to greater faculty satisfaction and enhanced student outcomes, such as academic performance and engagement.

One area of concern that emerged pertained to students' achievement on assessments of their critical thinking skills. Students' scores were some of the lowest in this area when compared with peer institutions. When reviewing enrollment demographics, it was also noted that nearly 50 % students at the institution were the first in their family to attempt higher education. Combined with the high number of students leaving after their first year of study (35 %) and the low number of students achieving graduation within 6 years (42 %), it was determined that, overall, students had a lower probability for success at the institution than those at similar universities (Stephen F. Austin State University 2011). Simultaneously, the state of Texas was revising its funding structure to be based on student course completion rather than enrollment and modifying its educational core to include a greater focus on critical thinking. Since the institution relied heavily on state funding for its operational expenses, student course completion now had additional importance. At this point, it became clear that there was an established need to identify an innovative way to address multiple levels of concern rooted in student learning and achievement.

The work of the steering committee continued, and the group conducted several information sessions and focus groups, and later organized a design team to develop the details of the quality enhancement plan. The focus groups and design team were strategically comprised to promote dialogue amongst university constituents that might not otherwise have an opportunity to discuss an institution-wide educational initiative. The focus groups narrowed down the desired approach to addressing the academic needs with a revision of the current curricular approaches and recommended the inclusion of high-impact practices across the curriculum as a strategy. This information was presented to the design team, along with the possibility of using the Faculty Learning Community model to address the previously described concerns about student achievement, as well as the desires expressed by academics about the need for meaningful professional development.

20.3.1 The High-Impact Platforms

During the needs analysis process, focus group participants and other stakeholders overwhelmingly called for a strategic approach to incorporate specific active learning strategies. For example, service learning, required internships, small group-based activities (such as problem-based learning or team-based learning), and undergraduate research were all strategies proposed as ways to address the identified needs. The selection team identified a commonality across these approaches and proposed a strategy that would encompass the wide-range of learning activities under one framework. They suggested aligning an institutional teaching and learning approach with the educational practices promoted as high-impact.[1]

While there are a mix of curricular and co-curricular educational practices identified as high-impact (American Association of Colleges and Universities 2007; Kuh 2008), more significant than the individual practices are the six conditions that contribute to their effect. Therefore, the following elements of high-impact educational practices were adopted as essential components to curricular revisions at the institution. Any re-designed curriculum would ensure that students:

1. devote considerable amounts of time and effort to purposeful tasks;
2. interact with faculty and peers about substantive matters;
3. experience diversity through contact with people who are different than themselves;
4. receive frequent feedback about their performance;
5. discover how what they are learning works in different settings, on and off the campus; and
6. are prepared to connect to one another and the world through participation of these activities in the context of a coherent, academically challenging curriculum (National Survey of Student Engagement 2007).

These conditions describe the elements of programming associated with the boosts in academic performance sought by the institution. Kuh explained that to enhance student engagement and increase student success, institutions should,"… make it possible for every student to participate in *at least two high impact activities* during their undergraduate program, one in the first year, and one later related to

---

[1]A significant discussion of high-impact practices (or HIP) is beyond the scope of this chapter; however, for more information, refer to Kuh (2008).

their major field" (National Survey of Student Engagement 2007, p. 8). This statement led to a three-tiered, topical approach in the quality enhancement plan. It was determined that the institution would work directly with faculty to develop and implement a high-impact experience in the first-year seminar and also with third and fourth year students. Each of these transitions were deemed as important in the educational journey and served as a starting point for the institutional curricular re-design process.

To strengthen the initial contact students have with the institution, the target was set that all students enrolled in the first-year seminar would be engaged in some type of collaborative learning activity. To further these connections and solidify them into their chosen course of study, students in their final years of undergraduate study would be exposed to a research opportunity and/or a field-based learning experience, specifically related to their major.

The question of how to effectively facilitate the professional development necessary to undertake such a significant curricular overhaul was best answered by a model that not only provided the initial framework to educators, but the support to develop and implement curricular redesign. In addition, the project leaders were adamant that the initiative be one that resulted in a positive culture change and remained sustainable beyond the original plan. The design team overwhelmingly agreed that if implemented appropriately, incorporating Faculty Learning Communities would accomplish these goals.

20.3.2   Overview of the FLC Model

Strategically structuring professional development approaches to allow for adaptation and/or reuse over time is one way to demonstrate institutional support for—and foster sustainability in—teaching and learning initiatives (Brew and Cahir 2014; Furco and Moely 2012; Graziano and Kahn 2013). For example, an institution might decide to incorporate Communities of Practice (CoP) to connect faculty and contribute to shared resources. The CoP model unites those with a common concern or interest and, through regular interactions, encourages members to enhance and refine their skills in that area (Wenger et al. 2002).

One special type of CoP is a Faculty Learning Community, and two categories of Faculty Learning Communities (FLC) can be found in the literature: those that are cohort-based and those that are topic-based. Cohort-based FLCs address the needs of a specific group, such as early career academics, whereas topic-based FLCs are "designed to address a special campus teaching and learning need, issue, or opportunity" (Cox 2004, p. 8). Once the design team decided upon the plan's emphasis (high-impact practices across the curriculum), they needed to identify a way to engage faculty in the necessary professional development to bring the dream to a reality. It was determined that the using topic-based Faculty Learning Communities would be an ideal way to engage academics in a sustained professional development experience that would result in not only in the student learning outcomes desired, but in an important cultural shift for the institution as a learning community with a shared understanding of high-impact educational practices.

Miami University often receives recognition as the pioneer of Faculty Learning Communities in higher education. The initiative described in this chapter was rooted in the Miami FLC framework and definition to guide its efforts. Therefore, it is important to describe the definition applied to the FLC in this project to ensure that readers understand the premise upon which the work was founded and how the critical components were applied.

At its most fundamental level, an FLC can be described as a cross-disciplinary faculty and staff group of six to fifteen members that engage in "an active, collaborative, yearlong program with a curriculum about enhancing teaching and learning and with frequent seminars and activities that provide learning, development, the scholarship of teaching, and community building" (Cox 2004, p. 8). The FLCs are marketed as a "comprehensive and phased program combining study of scholarly literature, hands-on workshops, collegial discussion and support, and demonstration of objectives-based competencies" (Stephen F. Austin State University Center for Teaching and Learning 2015). Because the institution utilises topic-based FLCs, the sustained structure allows for individual and collective inquiry around targeted areas, contributing to a broader community of sub-communities focused on teaching and learning.

20.3.3   Institutional Support

Upon presentation of the comprehensive programming outlined in the plan, a commitment to delivering its significant added value to students' learning experiences further convinced participants that the work would transform the culture of the institution. The university community embraced the challenge and opportunity this project offered to improve student success.

Through the Faculty Learning Community (FLC) model, faculty and staff engaged in a year-long exploration of high-impact practices with the goal of designing or redesigning course methodology and delivery for a single course. Four initiatives were designed to facilitate this project:

- academic development;
- direct support;
- operational support; and
- sustainability.

A cultural shift toward the incorporation of high-impact practices across campus was fully endorsed through the institution's commitment to providing sufficient resources to sustain the various initiatives associated with the project. These efforts, which were critical to the project's success, are outlined in the remainder of the chapter.

20.4 Implementation

Because an important aim of the quality enhancement plan was to positively impact institutional culture, wide-spread influence of the initiative was desired. Successful implementation would require uniting diverse populations for a common goal, therefore the plan was developed to address the multiple objectives with a degree of flexibility that allowed for individual adaptation and personalized application within one's practice.

20.4.1 Academic Development

The FLC program was marketed as high-profile professional development activity across the institution. Participants were able to guide the direction of their activities based on their interest and experience, making the time investment meaningful to individuals. As one participant explained in the annual evaluation, "It was enriching to spend time with other faculty/staff sharing ideas and developing colleagial (sic) relationships".

In line with the Miami model, Faculty Learning Communities were comprised of cross-disciplinary staff groups of approximately 14 members. In order to encourage broad participation and target those who were working directly with students in the classroom, spaces were allocated for two members from each of the six academic colleges and two members representing student affairs. Deviations in this representation were due to unbalanced applications from specific areas. This variance was somewhat anticipated as the platforms explored in the FLC tended to lend themselves to disproportionate representation. For example, a high proportion of educators from student affairs teach in the first-year seminar, but few of them teach in the upper-level, discipline-specific courses. The configuration of teaching assignments contributed to a disproportionate number of student affairs personnel participating in the FLC targeting first-year students.

The FLC project was designed to enhance the pedagogical backgrounds of all those who work directly with students at the institution. Each participant committed to full involvement of the FLC for one year, divided into two distinct sections. The first half of the year was designated as the *Development Semester*. During this semester, faculty met biweekly to explore high-impact pedagogy and higher-order thinking and develop a plan to be implemented in a designated course the following semester. During the *Implementation Semester*, faculty incorporated their plans into the identified course and met with the FLC approximately every 3 weeks to engage in professional dialogue about their experience, sharing their successes and seeking feedback or guidance on implementation struggles. In anonymous post-program evaluation surveys, participants overwhelmingly expressed that the sustained support of the FLC enabled them to continue their newly developed practices in their work with students. Many of those completing one FLC applied to and participated in additional FLCs in a different topic area.

20.4.2 Direct Support

Certain direct support measures were implemented to accommodate the anticipated additional work. Participants were able to identify an enabler that they felt provided them with appropriate recognition and compensation for the significant amount of time associated with their involvement. Each participant was provided with the option of release from one of their course responsibilities, a graduate assistant, or additional compensation. These options allowed for each participant to determine his/her individual need for workload management and demonstrated institutional commitment to the initiative. Each participant could also apply for a small internal grant to implement their project, including money for travel to present at conferences.

20.4.3 Operational Support

Operational support was an important factor to promoting the value of the initiative. The FLC project was assigned a designated location on the first floor of the university library. This site provided a message of stability to the university community and ensured high visibility. A small staff was allocated to lead the project, including a full-time Director and administrative assistant and a part-time graduate assistant.

Reward and recognition were important aspects to FLC participation, with an annual appreciation social each December, and a conference to disseminate the work of FLC members each April. In addition, participants were presented to the Board of Regents upon the completion of the implementation semester for formal recognition. FLC members were also highlighted in the Alumni magazine.

20.4.4 Sustainability

To ensure that the program was sustained over time, a 5-year budgetary commitment was made and approved through the Board of Regents. A member of the steering committee was appointed as the director of the program and additional staffing allocations were made. The Director (High-Impact Practices) collaborated with the Director of Research, the Director of Instructional Technology, and the Teaching Excellence Center, whose programs were focused on related pedagogical matters. These collaborations established long-term partnerships that eventually resulted in the consolidation of similar services under one umbrella office, now called the Center for Teaching and Learning.

The value placed upon quality teaching and student learning at the institution is becoming firmly embedded into the culture. For example, academics receive recognition in their tenure and promotion applications for their efforts to enhance teaching and learning in their courses through high-impact practices. Many FLC participants have since been awarded teaching excellence nominations and/or moved into positions with increased responsibility. New staff members are introduced to the concept of high-impact practices at orientation and attend a compulsory Foundations of Teaching and Learning program.

As a result of the shared development and high degree of institutional support, the program had a successful start. In the first 2 years, 68 academics and professional staff completed Faculty Learning Communities focusing on the specific pedagogies targeted by the university. Representation spanned all academic colleges, student affairs, and university affairs personnel, contributing to a shared sense of community across areas that often report great divide.

20.5 Discussion and Conclusion

Some of the most significant challenges facing higher education at this time include declining resources and raised stakes for student success both for the student and for the institution. By incorporating a well-developed institutional FLC initiative, universities can efficiently address these challenges at the grass roots level. The structure of the FLC contributes to multi-disciplinary professional relationships that stimulate unity across the institution, as well as increases in student learning, retention, and engagement. As Shulman et al. (2004) explain,

> In confronting the challenges of constant change and the need for enhanced teaching and learning, there is no substitute for FLC collaboration—people choosing to come together for a common purpose and willing to support one another so that all can progress. (p. 45)

Throughout the process, both the system and the individual members function as learners (Baker 1999), resulting in a strong academic community focused on the scholarship of teaching and learning.

This chapter discussed the development and implementation of a comprehensive, outcomes-based Faculty Learning community model at one institution in the United States. Clearly, there are potential limitations for the applicability at other institutions, in cross-institutional implementations, and recreations in settings outside the United States system of higher education. However, the preliminary success of this initiative indicates that there is potential for inter-disciplinary academic-based learning communities to positively contribute to both individual professional growth and an enhanced institutional climate.

20.5.1 Institutional Impact

While many of the measureable outcomes related to students (i.e. the 6-year graduation rate and growth in critical thinking) are longitudinal in nature, outcomes of implementation appear to be correlated with a positive impact on preliminary data collected. For example, while overall freshmen retention (first-year students returning to the university to commence their second year) was reported at 35 %, nearly 70 % of first-year students who were enrolled in courses redesigned to have a high-impact focus were preregistered to return to study in the second year. While the figure can at this time only be presented as a projection, there are clear indicators of a positive impact on FLC participants and the institutional culture that are emerging.

In the post-participation program evaluation, 89 % participants reported that the FLC experience improved their effectiveness as a teacher. As one participant explained regarding the use of high-impact practices and higher-order thinking,

> The FLC gave me the vocabulary and the organization to better utilize those concepts in all my course planning work. It also helped me to better communicate with students *why* they do particular activities in class and how they connect to other ideas.

Another participant described how his involvement, "...gave [him] the motivation to develop both a new active learning teaching tool that led to a publication and a metric for critical thinking". These examples indicate that, at the individual level, participants found the experience to be beneficial to their professional practices related to the scholarship of teaching and learning.

The benefits seem to extend beyond the individual, however. For example, all participants completing the post-participation survey agreed or strongly agreed with the statement "I am a part of a cultural shift towards the incorporation of high-impact practices across the campus". This perspective was likely enhanced by the multiple efforts across the university designed to promote high-impact educational practices. The expectation of examples of high-impact practices (HIP) in promotion and tenure dossiers; recognition through departmental, college, and university teaching excellence awards; and career advancement opportunities around HIP resulted in a shared understanding about effective teaching and learning that continues to permeate the institutional culture.

20.5.2 Implications for Future Research

While initial examination of the cross-institutional impact is positive, permanent cultural changes can only be determined over an extended period of time. Future research is needed to identify the longitudinal outcomes of sustained professional development activities such as FLCs. Such longitudinal studies should include an exploration of behavioural outcomes, in addition to self-reports and academic perceptions.

The case study described in this chapter indicates a need for further investigation of the impact on students, as well. While Kuh (2008) identified a number of benefits to HIP on student achievement, determining the degree of relationship between FLCs and student outcomes is of critical importance. As with the shift in institutional culture, one might expect that student outcomes would improve over time as academics integrate and become more comfortable with their new skills over time. Research into how academics participation in FLCs influences student outcomes such as graduate attribute, course learning objectives, and degree completion could be of particular importance.

Furthermore, while academics report their teaching practices are improved, it is important to understand how students perceive their educational journey. It is this author's experience that students will initially complain when required to engage in learning approaches that are atypical and only later realise the true benefit of such activity. Therefore, following up with students post-graduation to reflect on the value of HIP could present a mature reflection on the educational experience from the learners' perspective.

Finally, while this chapter provides an overview of the core components of the FLC initiative, there is significant opportunity to explore the elements of leadership that contributed to the initial positive reception of the program. It will be important to consider the role that leadership plays not only in the introduction, but also the implementation and sustainment of institution-level initiatives to promote academic development. The program described is still in its infancy, yet appears to be strongly influencing the cultural value placed on teaching and learning. It will be noteworthy to revisit the long-term impact of such an initiative after inevitable changes in leadership, political climate, and/or economics occur.

20.6 Conclusion

Both student achievement and academic development are global concerns across the tertiary education sector. The possibility that institutions can address both of these targeted areas through the use of Faculty Learning Communities is one that warrants further attention. This chapter provides an overview of one institution's attempts to enhance student learning through a sustained academic development initiative using the FLC model. Preliminary data indicate the program model:

- has started strong;
- is projected to result in the long-term desired outcomes; and
- Supports previous work advocating sustained professional development for academics.

These initial outcomes provide an opportunity for institutions to consider the inclusion of adaptations of the FLC model that are appropriate for their individual context.

References

Association of American Colleges and Universities. (2007). *College learning for a new global century*. Washington, DC: Author.

Austin, A. E., & Sorcinelli, M. D. (2013). The future of faculty development: Where are we going? *New Directions for Teaching & Learning, 133*, 85–97. doi:10.1002/tl.20048

Baker, P. (1999). Creating learning communities: The unfinished agenda. In B. A. Pescosolido & R. Aminzade (Eds.), *The social worlds of higher education*. Thousand Oaks, CA: Pine Forge Press.

Boylan, H. R. (2002). *What works: Research-based best practices in developmental education*. Boone, NC: Continuous Quality Improvement Network with the National Center for Developmental Education.

Brew, A., & Cahir, J. (2014). Achieving sustainability in learning and teaching initiatives. *International Journal for Academic Development, 19*(4), 341–352. doi:10.1080/1360144X. 2013.848360

Carless, D. (2009). Trust, distrust and their impact on assessment reform. *Assessment & Evaluation in Higher Education, 34*(1), 79–89.

Cox, M. (2004). An introduction to faculty learning communities. *New Directions for Teaching and Learning, 97*, 5–23.

Furco, A., & Moely, B. E. (2012). Using learning communities to build faculty support for pedagogical innovation: A multi-campus study. *The Journal of Higher Education, 83*(1), 128–153.

Graziano, J., & Kahn, G. (2013). Sustained faculty development in learning communities. *Learning Communities Research and Practice, 1*(2), 1–15. http://washingtoncenter.evergreen. edu/lcrpjournal/vol1/iss2/5

Healy, M., Marquis, B., & Vajoczki, S. (2013). Exploring SoTL through international collaborative writing groups. *Teaching and Learning Inquiry, 1*(2), 3–8. doi:10.1353/iss. 2013.0021

Kuh, G. (2008). *High-impact educational practices: What they are, who has access to them, and why they matter*. Washington, DC: American Association of Colleges and Universities.

National Survey of Student Engagement. (2007). *Experiences that matter: Enhancing student learning and success*. Bloomington, IN: Indiana University Center for Postsecondary Research.

Newman, T. (2010). Engaging faculty in the assessment process: Recruiting missionaries and cheerleaders. *The Journal of Academic Administration in Higher Education, 6*(2), 9–14.

Pettrone, M. C., & Ortquist-Ahrens, L. (2004). Facilitating faculty learning communities: A compact guide to creating change and inspiring community. *New Directions for Teaching and Learning, 97*, 63–69.

Postareff, L., Lindblom-Ylänne, S., & Nevgi, A. (2007). The effect of pedagogical training on teaching in higher education. *Teaching and Teacher Education, 23*, 557–571. doi:10.1016/j. tate.2006.11.013

Rienties, B., & Hosein, A. (2015). Unpacking (in)formal learning in an academic development programme: A mixed-method social network perspective. *International Journal for Academic Development, 20*(2), 163–177. doi:10.1080/1360144X.2015.1029928

Roxå, T., & Mårtensson, K. (2009). Significant conversations and significant networks—Exploring the backstage of the teaching arena. *Studies in Higher Education, 34*(5), 547–559. doi:10.1080/03075070802597200

Schön, D. A. (1983). *The reflective practitioner: How professionals think in action*. USA: Basic Books.

Shulman, G. M., Cox, M. D., & Richlin, L. (2004). Institutional considerations in developing a Faculty Learning Community program. *New Directions for Teaching and Learning, 97*, 41–49.

Steinert, Y., Mann, K., Centeno, A., Dolmans, D., Spencer, J., Gelula, M., et al. (2006). A systematic review of faculty development initiatives designed to improve teaching effectiveness in medical education: BEME guide no. *Medical Teacher, 28*(8), 497–526.

Stephen F. Austin State University. (2011). *Make an Impact @SFA: Incorporating high-impact practices to enhance student learning*. Nacogdoches, TX: Author.

Stephen F. Austin State University Center for Teaching and Learning. (2015). *Faculty learning communities*. http://www.sfactl.info/#!faculty-learning-communities/cc04

Stes, A., Min-Leliveld, M., Gijebels, D., & Van Petegem, P. (2010). The impact of instructional development in higher education: The state-of-the-art of the research. *Educational Research Review, 5*(1), 25–49. doi:10.1016/j.edurev.2009.07.001

Wenger, E., McDermott, R., & Snyder, W. M. (2002). *A guide to managing knowledge: Cultivating communities of practice*. Boston: Harvard Business School Press.

Young, C. A., Shinnar, R. S., Ackerman, R. L., Carruthers, C. P., & Young, D. A. (2007). Implementing and sustaining service-learning at the institutional level. *New Directions for Teaching and Learning, 3*(29), 344–365.

Chapter 21
"The Faculty/Faculty Conundrum": Organizing Faculty Learning Communities to Support "Singular" and "Plural" Faculty Development

Thomas J. Nelson and Joseph W. Cates

Abstract This chapter outlines the use of a modified Faculty Learning Community (FLC) model for faculty development employed within a large academic department to create communities of practice. This model promotes faculty reflection and learning about pedagogy and also serves as a means for developing projects in different aspects of the scholarship of teaching and learning. Current intra-departmental discussion of this modified FLC model revolves around a question at the heart of faculty development—what exactly is being developed? There is a sense that faculty development should be about providing faculty members the opportunity for individual development (singular "faculty"), but this can be in tension with developing the collective strength of the faculty as a whole (in the plural sense) in fulfilling its mission to the University. We use an FLC model for faculty development in this multivalent sense, to address this dilemma that we have named "the faculty/faculty conundrum." FLCs are smaller circles within a larger community of practice intent on two goals: (1) developing individual projects in pedagogy and scholarship and (2) supporting the department mission by stimulating collaboration and creating knowledge. Our FLC model promotes faculty development in a multivalent (plural and singular) sense.

Keywords Communities of practice · Faculty development · Faculty learning communities · Organizational development · Teacher learning

T.J. Nelson (✉) · J.W. Cates
Department of Focused Inquiry, Virginia Commonwealth University,
Richmond, VA, USA
e-mail: tjnelson@vcu.edu

J.W. Cates
e-mail: jwcates@vcu.edu

© Springer Nature Singapore Pte Ltd. 2017
J. McDonald and A. Cater-Steel (eds.), *Communities of Practice*,
DOI 10.1007/978-981-10-2879-3_21

437

21.1 Introduction

The authors of the present chapter were friendly opponents in our department's most recent election for Faculty Development Coordinator, during which the discussion of "the Faculty/faculty conundrum" emerged. In his speech to the faculty in October of 2014, candidate (and co-author) Joe Cates argued for the need to support numerous faculty members' desire to publish in the field of the Scholarship of Teaching and Learning (SoTL). This issue had been weighing on the minds of many faculty members because it had recently emerged as an aid to promotion within our department and recognition without it. Following Joe's speech, Tom Nelson, the incumbent Faculty Development Coordinator (and co-author), described his continuing vision of faculty development, which depends on an understanding of faculty in what he called the "plural" sense—that is, to support a composite faculty's collective quest to fulfill the department's mission—as opposed to faculty in the "singular" sense which provides opportunities for individual faculty members to improve and advance. A few days later, the two authors of this chapter embarked a collaboration in which the overlap between these two fronts for faculty development could be explored. In this chapter we will seek to solve what we have come to call "the faculty/faculty conundrum." We agree that one means within our department that develops faculty in both singular and plural senses is our Faculty Learning Communities (FLC) program, a Communities of Practice (CoP) based model of faculty development and knowledge building which not only enhances the strength of the department as a whole but encourages individual development.

Our conundrum revolves around a question at the heart of faculty development: what exactly is being developed? There is a sense that "faculty development" should be about providing individual faculty members the opportunity for individual development and attendant career advancement (in the singular sense of "faculty"), but this can be in tension with developing the collective strength of the faculty as a whole (in the plural sense) in fulfilling its mission to the University. Our FLC model is designed to allow for individual development while working toward an end that benefits and strengthens our faculty as a whole. FLCs are smaller circles within a larger community of practice intent on two goals: (1) developing individual projects in pedagogy and scholarship and (2) supporting the department mission by stimulating collaboration and creating knowledge. Our FLC model promotes faculty development in a multivalent (plural and singular) sense.

In this chapter, we will examine how the FLC model promotes a vibrant community of practice within our large department. This model promotes faculty reflection and learning about pedagogy and also serves as a means for creating materials and knowledge that serve the departmental mission. These FLCs operate within the overlap between the traditionally separate domains of teaching, service, and scholarship. By producing scholarship, individually and collaboratively, faculty advance both singular and plural faculty development goals; scholarship related to teaching and learning serves the departmental goals of producing more effective learning outcomes for students while advancing the careers of faculty members.

21.2   Context: A Brief History of the Department

To appreciate this model, some background on the department will be necessary. The Department of Focused Inquiry at Virginia Commonwealth University is a large interdisciplinary department charged with providing key core education classes to first and second year university students and promoting student success in a learning-centered environment. Teaching these classes is, to say the least, a difficult and complex task for our large faculty (currently around 60 full-time faculty members). Small classes, capped at 22 or 25 students, engage with rotating themes and student interests. Focused Inquiry was from the beginning conceived of as providing a "student-centered, learning-centered, and learner-centered class-room" for VCU's first-year students (Marolla 2010, p. vii). The first courses offered by the department were Focused Inquiry I and II, a two-semester sequence designed to engage students in academic culture while cultivating the skills key to academic success, such as written and verbal communication, critical thinking, and information fluency. These classes are shaped by a shared curriculum: each key skill area has required learning outcomes, parameters for specific assignments are mandated (such as length and types of sources), and some common readings are shared across sections. Aside from this broad structure, instructors have a good deal of freedom in how they construct their classes. After a pilot year in 2006–2007, the program began full-scale operation with this two-course sequence in the 2007–2008 school year. In 2010, the department integrated another core education class, a required second-year writing class that had been housed in the English department. This course was soon to be retitled Inquiry and the Craft of Research and now operates as a continuation of the Focused Inquiry sequence, with its own shared curriculum. In this course, students conduct extended inquiries into topics of their own choosing as they research and craft arguments in multiple modes. By means of these three classes, intended to be taken during the first 2 years of a student's career, the Department accounts for a core of classes and basis for learning undertaken by students from all disciplines. In short, we seek to engender intrinsic motivation for students to think of themselves as emerging scholars in their chosen fields of study, along the lines that (Hase and Kenyon 2000) have described as "heutagogy." As we will develop below, this emphasis on self-directed learning has had a transformative effect not only of the culture of the student body over the last 8 years, but also on the approach we have taken to faculty development in both singular and plural senses.

Based from the outset on the learner-centered pedagogy as articulated by Barr and Tagg (1995) and Weimer (2002) (among many others), the new program was faced with the task of assembling a large faculty of skilled, learner-centered teachers. In the beginning, approximately half of the faculty were hired from the pool of adjunct instructors who had been teaching part time for the university, some for many years. The rest were hired as the result of a national search, drawing from new PhDs and experienced teachers looking for more stability. In the early years, department leadership made clear that the (collective) faculty was there to teach, and while individual scholarship was encouraged, it was understood to be additional, non-required work. The department's mission is articulated as follows:

> The purpose of this faculty and department will be to cultivate in all VCU students the skills, knowledge, and attitudes needed for collegiate and lifelong success through learning-centered experiences; to foster an environment of collaboration and fairness among its faculty; and to encourage excellence in the practice and scholarship of teaching and learning (https://focusedinquiry.vcu.edu/our-department/).

Note that while teaching is paramount, the department strives to support collaboration within its ranks and, perhaps as an outcome of that collegial environment, "encourage excellence in the… scholarship of teaching and learning."

The tension between departmental goals and individual career interests should be seen as useful in provoking genuine problems. A faculty working together can see these problems as opportunities to explore and develop better teaching practices, ones that make our lives as teachers more rewarding (if not easier). When we think about the impact this level of transparency has had on faculty feeling that their concerns are heard and addressed, we can easily make the connection that this is in part the reason why we have had such success in persuading a collateral faculty to take seriously their commitment to service and scholarship. Despite the lack of tenure lines within in our department, the faculty has remains remarkably stable from year to year.

The physical layout of the department can be seen as contributing to the level of interaction that takes place among faculty members. The entire faculty is housed on a single floor of a large building in the center of VCU's urban campus. Faculty offices form the outer ring with classrooms and meeting spaces located in the center. This arrangement helps facilitate informal conversations between classes, as does most faculty's open-door policy (when faculty are present their doors are almost always open.) This encourages not only students to come by and talk, but also drop-in consultations with colleagues. (While completing the final draft of this very document, "hall talk" between two faculty members who had presented on a panel at a service learning conference last year resulted in the decision to co-author a longer paper based on that research. These types of positive interactions occur frequently on our floor.)

If we imagine a bird's-eye view with the various networks of collaboration highlighted (such as leadership positions, department and university committees, service in professional communities of practice, cohorts associated with courses taught, cohorts associated by disciplinary background, and of course the FLCs), we would see a colorful sociograph depicting a highly integrated network of faculty. This horizontal organizational model values the input of all faculty members in shaping the actions we take to meet departmental goals, and serves as an example of a heutagogical approach to problem solving that mirrors the curriculum that we teach. Here there are many centers of gravity exerting their various pulls to shape the inquiries that faculty grapple with in an ongoing basis. We find most success when departmental goals align with collaborative groups' interests in seeking to better understand the questions associated with more effective teaching practices.

At present, the department has become an institutionalized part of the university's curriculum, but our identity and purpose continues to evolve. With the institution of a promotion policy in 2013, the traditional research component of academic life become a crucial determinant in advancing through the ranks. Nevertheless, it is essential that our commitment to new university students' education be maintained by cultivating a strong faculty. The remainder of this paper will explore the rationale for and execution of one aspect of this department's ongoing faculty development.

21.3 Theory: Underpinnings of Faculty Development Within the Department

Much writing on faculty development presupposes that it takes place within a center or program that supports teaching units across the university. However, the model under discussion here takes place within the confines of a single department. That fact notwithstanding, the university provides ample center-based support that many faculty members partake in. But the sheer size of the faculty and its complex shared curriculum creates certain unusual needs for the department that necessitate in-house faculty development (supplemented by other means sought out by individual faculty). Toward this end, the department's first faculty development coordinator was appointed in 2008.

Faculty development can be usefully defined as "an intentional set of educational activities designed to equip faculty to grow in their professionalism with the result of being partners in advancing all segments of the institution" (McKee and Tew 2013, p. 13). Even in this relatively straightforward definition, the simultaneous demands of singular and plural faculty are apparent. In this formulation, individual development results in a strengthened institution. Therefore, faculty development should function in a manner that simultaneously advances individual and collective needs. McKee and Tew (2013) and Lieberman and Guskin (2003) advocate for the necessity for faculty development to address transformations in higher education, including the growing role of technology in the classroom, changing conceptions of scholarship, and new understandings of learning, to name a few important issues.

Historically, faculty development has operated on three tracks. Schroeder (2010) describes a "three-pronged framework that include[s] individual, instructional, and organizational development" (p. 18). Individual support, or singular faculty development in our terms, is often manifested in time or money for individual faculty members to work on self-directed projects. Our department has been hard-pressed to provide course releases, but has maintained individual travel allotments even through trying budgetary times. We also provide opportunities for individual faculty members to present on their pedagogical or scholarly interests in symposia and more conversational settings within the department.

Instructional development can be understood as faculty development in the singular sense, but given our shared interest in learning-centered teaching, it is also properly understood in the plural sense. In higher education, many departments prioritize expertise in subject matter over teaching ability. Faculty development centers have often been called upon to respond to instructional needs, even deficiencies, through various means. As mentioned above, our faculty was hired based largely on the strength of their teaching records, but nevertheless the department is committed to continuing pedagogical development, organizing brown bag lunches, roundtables, and bi-annual institutes to continually examine and reinvigorate pedagogical practices. All faculty are encouraged to actively contribute presentations and workshops to these events that range in focus from practical aspects of classroom interaction and dealing with students in crisis, to subject and skill-oriented topics such as developing creative exercises to illuminate our shared texts, and adapting new technologies that enable more fluid communication in online environments. Our faculty also contribute presentations and panels at institution-wide conferences and institutes, such as ALTfest which focuses on learning innovation and technology and the Institute on Inclusive Teaching, which was founded by two of our faculty to disseminate best practices to the larger university faculty.

Perhaps the most complicated of the three "prongs" identified by Schroeder (2010) is "organizational" development, which can be understood as the planned, managed intervention in an institution's culture (p. 33 ff.). In this case, the department stands in as the representative of the institution as a whole, and the question behind organizational development becomes "what practices and structures can promote our mission?" Or put another way, "what are the conversations among faculty most worth having?" While this may sound like a sinister brand of social engineering, the amount of autonomy faculty members have in setting FLC agendas and work plans ensure a degree of egalitarianism:

> Learning communities, by their very nature, mandate collaborative work. They are an excellent vehicle for implementing the critical elements educators are endorsing as appropriate for higher-education... Learning communities change highly individualistic ways of working (my work) to collaboration and engagement (our work) and change the passive learning of unexamined assumptions to active learning and a culture of evidence. Learning communities facilitate democratic participation rather than elitism. (Evenbeck et al. 1999, p. 56).

FLCs, as outlined by Cox (2004), are interdisciplinary groups of faculty members "who engage in an active, collaborative, year-long program with a curriculum about enhancing teaching and learning...with frequent seminars and activities that provide learning, development, the scholarship of teaching, and community building" (p. 8). Wenger et al. (2002), Cox identifies an FLC as "a particular kind of community of practice" (p. 9). FLCs by nature are certainly "groups of people who share a concern, a set of problems, or a passion about a topic who deepen their knowledge and expertise in this area by interacting on an ongoing basis" (Wenger et al. 2002). As such, they are units of social learning, in which new members learn by the means of acculturation. This learning is situated in a social context:

the emerging picture of a CoP is of a community of individuals immersed in a domain of practice, who share their knowledge and experience of the domain in a variety of ways, very often informally. This sharing serves a variety of purposes: it enables good practice to be spread; it enables novices to become more knowledgeable and experienced; and it enables the community to develop new knowledge. (Klein and Connell 2008, p. 66)

As Cox (2001) argues, FLCs can transform institutions into "learning organizations" comprised of individuals willing and capable of continually learning to support the institution's goals. Therefore, in order for a "learning organization" to effectively learn it must look at faculty development as "both an unanticipated individual reward and a beneficial institutional outcome" (Evenbeck et al. 1999, p. 53). Klein and Connell (2008) posit that a CoP-based model "bridges the gap between organizational learning on the one hand, and individual learning on the other" (p. 67). In the following section, we argue that our FLC model does exactly this: it bridges the divide between singular and plural faculty development by encouraging individuals to learn and develop while simultaneously serving organizational needs.

21.4 The Model: Using FLCs for Departmental Faculty Development

Beginning in the 2008–2009 academic year, the Department of Focused Inquiry has utilized a modified Faculty Learning Community (FLC) model for ongoing faculty development. At the outset, FLC participation was considered a service obligation to the department, even though it provides a structure and support network for (individual) professional development. Despite the fact that the basic teaching load in the department is 4 classes a semester, numerous internal materials, faculty presentations, conference papers, and online resources have resulted from FLC work.

Cox (2004) identifies two types of FLCs: cohort-based and topic-based. Ours have tended to be the latter, which are convened to "address a special… teaching and learning need, issue, or opportunity" (p. 8). The former "address the teaching, learning, and developmental needs of an important group of faculty or staff" (Cox 2004, p. 8). Cohort-based CoP frameworks have been used as a means of teacher learning in elementary, secondary, and higher education. Work by Cuddapah and Clayton (2001) and Yildirim (2008) examines how novice teachers can use social learning in cohorts for the purpose of professional development. This type of model, which focuses on day-to-day teaching practice and classroom experience is without doubt valuable. However, our model differs in a few crucial ways. First, it is not predicated on educating and enculturating novices: in fact, there is currently no real distinction in the roles of new or experienced faculty members. (New faculty are supported through an in-department mentoring program.) As a result, there is no pressing call for FLCs to respond to the daily experiences and struggles of novice teachers. So for the most part, our FLCs are oriented toward creating knowledge on a pedagogical topic of shared interest. In 2 years of the department's history, we operated without FLCs as such, although we did sort the faculty into teams of 5–6 to discuss particular issues and problems with individual's teaching practice. Though not labeled as such, these faculty teams were essentially cohort-based FLCs. The 2 years that we employed these cohort-based FLCs were moments of transition in our history. In our first year, 2007–2008, much of our faculty was new —new to a full time position, new to the institution, or new to the unique course we were teaching, and all by definition new to the program. Seeded throughout the faculty teams were members with some relevant experience, such as teaching with the pilot program the previous year or at least teaching for another department of VCU. In the second year of cohort-based faculty teams, 2010–2011, the department was integrating new faculty members to teach the second-year course, Inquiry and the Craft of Writing, while a new theme was introduced to the existing first-year course sequence. Teams were therefore comprised of faculty members faced with similar teaching challenges.

As our faculty engages more and more with inquiry-based learning, the department organization has come to model what we teach in our own practices. Interestingly, the FLC-model based on groups formed around shared interests and loosely structured guidelines may be an example of how best practices have "trickled-up" from our courses to our departmental organization. For the most part, it is not merely the common enterprise of teaching that provides focus for the FLCs, but specific topics of interest within that larger domain. In this sense, these FLCs are smaller circles within the larger community of practice that is the faculty as a whole. Within our department, FLCs have been organized around shared interests such as the Scholarship of Teaching and Learning, Collaborative Teaching and Learning, Social Justice, Game-Based Learning, Visual Rhetoric and Multimodal Composition, and Online Teaching and Learning. We also maintain two cohort-based FLCs to provide support for faculty teaching Service Learning courses and for teaching with Undergraduate Teaching Assistants (These are based on both shared topical concerns and operational issues).

At the outset of each academic year, the Faculty Development Coordinator issues an open call for new FLC topics and also privately inquires after the health of existing FLCs. At the beginning of the year, faculty members decide whether to continue with the FLC they had been involved with or perhaps join a new one. While Cox (2004) defined FLCs as year-long endeavors, our department encourages them to continue as long as they are productive and self-sustaining. Some FLCs dissolve from lack of interest or by mutual agreement, but the common understanding is that they should continue for at least 1 year. Inevitably some FLCs will disband, but this has been fairly uncommon. In the past 3 years, only one has dissolved.

For organizational purposes, each FLC elects a facilitator as Cox (2004) suggests. New facilitators are advised not to operate as a chair of a committee tasked with certain jobs, but as a coordinator and cultivator of a group of peers with an open-ended set of goals. Ideally, common interests coalesce over time and the group collectively designs and implements a project that they work towards as a mutual goal. The faculty development coordinator occasionally meets with the facilitators (ideally once or twice a semester) to discuss progress and challenges in a sort of irregular cohort-based FLC.

Our FLCs have tended to be smaller than Cox suggests. While Cox suggests seven to fourteen members, we have operated with a minimum of five and no declared maximum (though the largest has been fourteen). On occasion, an FLC topic is deemed so important to the department's identity and mission that the chair and faculty development coordinator solicit additional membership or even suspend the minimum membership requirement. Our smaller size is also the result of the practical considerations of scheduling, and also to allow for a wider-range of individual choice in selecting the topics of the FLC. The largest FLC in the program's history, the Gaming FLC of 2013–2014, had too many members to find a regular meeting and had to break into two units.

FLC topics tend to be large and under-defined in order to allow for a multiplicity of interpretations and for individual interests and approaches to coalesce under a single banner. While Cox's original intent for Faculty Learning Communities was to support somewhat open-ended inquiries, we have asked that our FLCs pursue some specific end-goal (a "deliverable" in business terms) that is of value to either the department as a whole or to the professional development of individual members. Among these "deliverables" have been online resources, bibliographies of research, and conference presentations. These products have provided a sense of purpose for the FLCs and a focus for their practice.

The social learning fostered by the shared goal manifests itself in projects that strengthen the practices of the larger community. An example of the extent of social learning and collaboration might be supplied by the Gaming FLC, which originated from an informal conversation about how a shared text (Do Androids Dream of Electric Sheep? by Philip K. Dick) might be transposed into a role-playing game. This conversation led to one instructor implementing just such a game and another basing a course unit on a different cooperative game. These two instructors gave a symposium on their practice in the spring semester of 2013, which led to such interest in the general topic of gaming in the classroom that a large FLC on the topic was founded the following year. This FLC presented several gaming workshops for the faculty and seven members of the group presented at the CIDER CHEP conference in February 2015.

Though the FLC model is loose enough to allow natural situated learning to occur, the learning can be (and for a successful organization, should be) cultivated as well. Wenger et al. (2002) identify four strategic intents for CoPs which serve as the underpinning of this cultivation:

- Helping communities, which provide support for solving individual problems.
- Best-practice communities, which seek to identify best practices.
- Knowledge-stewarding communities, which develop and maintain knowledge.
- Innovation communities, which develop new knowledge.

At different times, any FLC might be operating with one or more of these intentions. The faculty teams were by nature helping communities, but the goal-oriented nature of the topic-based FLCs tend to move beyond solving individual problems to address collective concerns. Statements of best practices within a given domain are an acceptable FLC product, and most products represent knowledge-stewarding or innovation. As an example of knowledge-stewarding and best practices, the Visual Rhetoric and Multimodal Composition FLC compiled a bibliography of relevant scholarship in 2013–2014 which in Spring of 2015 was explored by the curriculum committee in developing best practices for multimodal composition. As an example of innovation, the Collaborative Teaching and Learning FLC has drafted a typology of student-student and teacher-teacher collaboration.

For most of the department's history, membership in one FLC was part of a faculty member's basic service obligation (along with service on one committee). From anecdotal discussion with FLC facilitators, participation in the FLCs has included all four types described by Goto et al. (2010): Networkers, Learners, Implementers, and Wait-and-seers. Networkers approach their FLCs as an opportunity to better know and understand the perspectives of their colleagues; Learners seek new knowledge to integrate into their practice; Implementers take advantage of the situation to integrate new practices; and Wait-and-Seers come with an open mind but no particular agenda. It is fair to add another category, the Resisters, who simply see the FLC as another meeting to attend, but over time this resentment seems to have died away (However, see Houghton et al. (2014) for resistance within faculty learning communities). As of the 2014–2015 academic year, FLC participation is no longer a required service obligation, though participation is not noticeably down: only 3 of 60 faculty members have elected not to participate. A practice that voluntarily enlists 95 % of the faculty (without the extrinsic reward of a stipend or course release) seems to indicate a healthy community of practice.

21.5   Future Directions

Recently, some FLCs have created web-based resources that promote knowledge and conversations about their topics of interest beyond our department to other interested parties. The Collaborative Teaching and Learning FLC has created a website cheekily entitled "The Collabalab" (for collaboration laboratory) which shares developing grey literature such as the above-mentioned typology of collaboration and various collaboration-based assignments faculty members have developed. The Gaming and Social Justice FLCs also maintain topic-defined portals that distribute their work and allow new knowledge to naturally grow in a network-mediated social setting. The online frontier allows for asynchronous creative partnerships in many ways, and learning how to make effective use of technology to facilitate these types of collaborative group work in the classes we teach allows for our faculty development model to mirror what we are learning about learning and how to apply it. The various means of open web communication is another way that the FLC model can value individual schedules, preferred methods of collaboration, and types of scholarship produced.

However, all of our FLCs meet formally and informally in various ways face to face as their primary means of interface. Again the physical layout of the department itself, coupled with online means of collaboration allows for an ongoing flow of discourse within the department. The corresponding online components are now being developed intentionally to reach a broader, connected learning network. This kind of networked blogging can result in conference panels and print publications, but we the department also value newer forms of scholarship because of the ease of dissemination of information, and also because "living documents" can grow and evolve as the department adopts new themes and reacts to new institutional goals.

With the evolution of the department into a knowledge-producing organization, some FLCs may be transforming into kinds of writing groups. In this model, a single collaborative deliverable is replaced with a variety of traditional and non-traditional scholarship (some of which will most likely will be jointly authored). In this transmutation, the FLC will still provide a structure of mutual support. Refaei et al. (2013) describe how writing groups at a 2-year community college serve to promote faculty development by providing structured writing time, peer support, and a pool of collective knowledge (p. 191). Refaei et al. begin their article with an almost idyllic image of this mutual support based FLC model:

> Consider this scenario: a college seminar room filled with faculty members from a variety of disciplines and career stages. Some sit at laptops; others write diligently with pen on paper. Over in the corner, two colleagues meet to talk about the assignment they're drafting for the class they're co-teaching. Occasionally, from the seminar table, someone breaks the silence to ask, "Did anybody see that article in the Chronicle," or "What's a better word for…?" (p. 190)

Aside from serving as an aspiration for faculty development, this description illustrates how these writing groups are still FLCs in spirit, even if they result more in individual products. While this represents a step away toward singular development, it will retain the essential duality of supporting the departmental mission and individual projects at the same time.

Both of these future directions still use the CoP-based organization development offered by the FLC model to promote individual and department-level concerns and thus solve the "faculty/faculty conundrum." All of our department's successful partnerships have arisen from faculty-directed inquiries that were given room and time to grow organically into meaningful collaboration. In writing this chapter, the authors have sought to model the process by which an inquiry of genuine interest to the department might result in a document that would be useful to our department and other similar organizations, while also providing an example of emergent faculty development in the form of an ad hoc FLC of two with a specific problem, loose structure, and shared goal.

References

Barr, R. B. & Tagg, J. (1995). From teaching to learning: A new paradigm for undergraduate education. *Change, 27*(6), 13–25.

Cox, M. D. (2001). Faculty learning communities: Change agents for transforming institutions into learning organizations. In D. Leiberman & C. Wehlburg (Eds.), *To improve the academy: Resources for faculty, instruction, and organizational development* (Vol. 19, pp. 69–96). Bolton, MA: Anker.

Cox, M. D. (2004). Introduction to faculty learning communities. *New Directions for Teaching and Learning,*. doi:10.1002/tl.129.

Cuddapah, J., & Clayton, C. D. (2001). Using Wenger's communities of practice to explore a new teacher cohort. *Journal of Teacher Education, 62*(1), 62–75. doi:10.1177/00224877110377507.

Evenbeck, S. E., Jackson, B., & McGrew, J. (1999). Faculty development in learning communities: The role of reflection and reframing. In J. H. Levine (Ed.), *Learning communities: New structures, new partnerships for learning* (pp. 51–58). Columbia, SC: University of South Carolina, National Resource Center for the First-Year Experience and Students in Transition.

Goto, S. T., Marshall, P., & Gaule, S. (2010). Assessment of faculty learning-communities: Considering social dimensions of participant choice. *Learning Communities Journal, 2*(1), 5–26.

Hase, S., & Kenyon, C. (2000). From andragogy to heutagogy. http://ultibase.rmit.edu.au/Articles/dec00/hase2.htm. Accessed June 20, 2015.

Houghton, L., Ruutz, A., Green, W., & Hibbins, R. (2014). I just do not have time for new ideas: resistance, resonance and micro-mobilisation in a teaching community of practice. *Higher Education Research and Development, 34*(3), 527–540. doi:10.1080/07294360.2014.973834.

Klein, J. H., & Connell, N. A. D. (2008). The identification and cultivation of appropriate communities of practice in higher education. In C. Kimble, P. Hildreth, & I. Bourdon (Eds.), *Communities of practice: Creating learning environments for educations* (Vol. 1, pp. 65–81). Charlotte, NC: Information Age Publishing.

Lieberman, D. A., & Guskin, A. E. (2003). The essential role of faculty development in new higher education models. In C.M. Wehlburg & S. Chadwick-Blossey (Eds.), *To improve the academy: Resources for faculty, instructional, and organizational development* (Vol. 21, pp. 257–272), Bolton, MA: Anker.

Marolla, J. (2010). A 21st-century education. In *A companion to focused inquiry* (pp. v–vii). Boston: Bedford/St. Matin's.

McKee, C. W., & Tew, W. M. (2013). Setting the stage for teaching and learning in American Higher Education: Making the case for faculty development. *New Directions for Teaching and Learning, 133*, 3–14. doi:10.1002/tl.20041

Refaei, B., Sipple, S., & Skutar, C. (2013). Writers groups: Composing a balanced faculty. In S. Sipple & R. Lightner (Eds.), *Developing faculty learning communities at two-year colleges: collaborative models to improve teaching and learning.* Sterling, VA: Stylus Publishing.

Schroeder, C. (2010). Faculty developers as institutional developers: The missing prong of organizational development. In C. Schroeder, P. Blumberg, & N. V. Chism (Eds.), *Coming in from the margins: Faculty development's emerging organizational development, note* (pp. 17–46). Sterling, VA: Stylus Publishing.

Wenger, E., McDermott, R. A., & Snyder, W. (2002). *Cultivating communities of practice: A guide to managing knowledge.* Boston: Harvard Business Press.

Weimer, M. (2002). *Learner-centered teaching.* San Francisco, CA: Jossey-Bass.

Yildirim, R. (2008). Adopting communities of practice as a framework for teacher development. In C. Kimble, P. Hildreth, & I. Bourdon (Eds.), *Communities of practice: Creating Learning environments for educations* (Vol. 1, pp. 233–251). Charlotte, NC: Information Age Publishing.

Chapter 22
Catalyst: Developing a Community of Practice for Supporting New Academics

Barbara Kensington-Miller

Abstract This chapter presents a community of practice, known as *Catalyst*, which was introduced to support new academics finding their feet within the university. *Catalyst* is a special type of community of practice; it is structured, multidisciplinary, one semester long, meets fortnightly and has no restriction on numbers. In addition, it includes peer mentoring, where the members of the community of practice meet in pairs or small groups between meetings to foster further support at a deeper, more personal level. These are structured in such a way that the members talk with each other about critical aspects of beginning an academic path and in the process learn more about each other, building strong professional friendships. *Catalyst* offers continuity throughout the first semester, but creates long-lasting networks. While the focus is always on building community, the aim is to introduce new academics to the expectations of the university enabling them to have a quicker and smoother transition into their respective departments. In the chapter, the lessons learned in setting up *Catalyst* for new academics, are discussed. The findings from a group of ten new academics from a range of disciplines, who were involved in *Catalyst* for one semester, are presented. In particular, provides space for the group away from their departments to work collaboratively while learning about institutional and departmental expectations, and to discuss difficult issues that often arise for them.

Keywords Community of practice · Peer mentoring · New academic · Early-career academic · Support

22.1 Introduction

> I feel quite isolated here … being newish to the university… what I need is someone I can actually bounce stuff off. I don't know where things are; I don't know anybody to ask. [pauses for a while] I don't know the rules, how things work in my department. (New academic)

B. Kensington-Miller (✉)
University of Auckland, Auckland, New Zealand
e-mail: b.kensington-miller@auckland.ac.nz

© Springer Nature Singapore Pte Ltd. 2017
J. McDonald and A. Cater-Steel (eds.), *Communities of Practice*,
DOI 10.1007/978-981-10-2879-3_22

Entering the academic world of universities can be both an exciting and daunting time. For new academics, however, excitement at getting the job is often dampened by the overwhelming prospect of being alone. It is not uncommon for new academics to feel isolated in an environment where colleagues look too busy to approach; as they need advice and yet hesitate to seek it, confidence drains and isolation intensifies. Although many institutions offer introductory programmes to induct new academics (Staniforth and Harland 2006), most are quite short and occur soon after arrival. Those who attend these programmes receive a broad overview on how the university operates, what is available, and a brief introduction to the fundamentals of teaching in one swift deluge of information. But, returning to their faculties, these new academics frequently report to the academic developers in our center that some departments are not providing enough, indeed any, support and many are unsure of what is expected of them in their new role when they return from induction to the reality of work within the faculty. Left unchecked, the excitement of the new position risks becoming rapidly lost to feelings of abandonment and loneliness, which leads to insecurities and doubts about the academic position they chose (Archer 2008; Gourlay 2011).

In this chapter I discuss the lessons learned in setting up a community of practice for supporting new academics, which came to be known as *Catalyst*. I describe how collective knowledge is generated through a shared practice and community is cultivated with members who are diverse in discipline and experience (Lave and Wenger 1991). Further to this, peer mentoring is introduced providing another dimension, where open, non-hierarchical conversations take place delivering another layer of support to strengthen the community of practice (e.g. Darwin and Palmer 2009; Nagy and Burch 2009). In this way, *Catalyst* is designed to support new academics while they are working in their departments through their first semester, where they all have heavy teaching and research responsibilities to fulfill.

The chapter follows a conventional structure beginning with some context and then background on why it is necessary to support new academics as they transition into academia. A section then follows on the literature that shaped the rationale for the development of *Catalyst*, favoring a community of practice approach incorporating peer mentoring. This includes a brief look at traditional mentoring, which although strongly recommended for new academics, with the advantages recognized, was not able to be implemented from a central position in our institution, prompting the conception of *Catalyst*. I present the findings from a group of ten new academics (seven women, three men) from a range of disciplines: Nursing, Education, Optometry, Mathematics, Sociology, Computer Science, Property, Psychology, Business, and Population Health, who were involved in the *Catalyst* community for one semester.

22.2   Context: Stories from Experience

Julie arrived in New Zealand with her partner a few weeks before starting her new position. She was English, her partner was American, and they had been working on post–docs in the United States when they met. They had both managed to get lecturing jobs at the University of Auckland and were keen to start a new life together in a new country. When I first met Julie she was still finding her way around the university and trying to cope with her teaching load whose content she had little experience with. Her PhD and post-doc had not prepared her for this. As well as attempting to establish her research Julie was also struggling to work through what she should be doing for her service component, 20 % of her job. In the short time they had been in New Zealand, she and her partner had moved house twice. Julie was desperately missing family and friends.

In the beginning months there is a lot of institutional knowledge for a new academic to be acquainted with, as well as establishing their teaching and research and finding a balance between these. Teaching involves many different aspects. For example, academics could be coordinating as well as lecturing on a course they may be unfamiliar with, or designing a new topic and including an assessment using an online tool. They may be working with new technology, or required to make their course blended or fully online. For many new academics, it will be their first time teaching in large lectures, or taking on supervision with postgraduate students. In many instances it is also the first time new academics have to face setting and marking assessments, a particularly daunting task if this is new to you—and especially meeting the 'standard' of the department or institution. There are numerous aspects of teaching that might be unknown and for new academics this is a time when they will have many questions.

At the same time, new academics are increasingly arriving from overseas and facing a new culture and the local way of life. Whatever the background, the adjustment or aspects of it can be harsh and unfamiliar. Trying to understand the requirements of the job, negotiate the balance between the demands of teaching and research when life outside of work is often more challenging, and doing this successfully requires support and reassurance.

Jack had joined a new department as his own discipline was small and would not be recruiting any time soon. He had been in the job three months and commented: "when I started I had these big ambitions for my research… I was told that this was all crucial for making any advancement… having this research… … but I have lost the energy for it. It has been all too hard in these beginning months getting started".

As academics, there is the expectation to be involved in productive research projects and along with this, to write papers for conferences or journals or books. New academics might be making the transition from writing a PhD, and subsequent post-doc, to their first journal or book publication. It may be there is an assumption from departments/employers that this transition is linear and unproblematic, but for many new academics becoming an active researcher in their own right can be a struggle. As well, balancing all the obligations of the new role can be physically exhausting and emotionally consuming, and thus constructing themselves as teacher and researcher simultaneously during the beginning months requires support.

> Nick had come to the university after working in industry for 10 years. He was accustomed to informal collaboration and collegiality in his workplace and was finding the new university environment artificial and closed. He had assumed that being a university, knowledge would be shared and open but this wasn't the case in his department and Nick felt that he was working in a silo. He commented: "I could very well be doing the same research as someone else across the hall and wouldn't know it".

Our academic development center was becoming increasingly aware of the urgency to provide more support for new academics in their beginning months. Mentoring was considered, as the literature is prolific on the merits, but we were mindful that "mentoring relationships are not always positive and sometimes manifest a dark and dysfunctional side" (Lunsford et al. 2013, p. 1). Mentoring, if it occurs, can sometimes be obscure or the relationship malfunctional, and "whether they succeed or fail often falls on the abilities of the people who volunteer or are chosen to fulfil the mentoring role" (Woodd 2001, p. 97). Although aware of the downside of mentoring, the positive features prevailed and we were keen to find a way, which would be relevant and sustainable for academics new to the university. At the time, our center was short-staffed and we did not have the resources to find and train mentors, so our aim was to find a strategy which could be easily set up and conceivably manageable by one person.

We were also aware of the volume of literature on communities of practice (e.g. Cox 2011; Gourlay 2011) and how academics become enmeshed in numerous communities of practices within their institutions. The challenge seemed to lie in how new academics make their transition into the new environment. The early stage of an academic career is inevitably characterized by competing pressures and yet making a quick and smooth transition into their respective departments is paramount to successfully finding one's 'feet' in the new job. How then do new academics inhabit communities of practice and become comfortable in them?

22.3   The Need to Support New Academics

Early-career academics usually enter the university with fresh ideas and enthusiasm, but, as with any job, there is often some initial trepidation and anxiety of what is required (Nir and Zilberstein-Levy 2006; Staniforth and Harland 2006; Trowler and Knight 2000). The reality of meeting expectations, and knowing that they must stack up when measured and evaluated for tenure, and later, promotions, can seem challenging for new academics as they try to orientate (Hemmings and Kay 2010; Nir and Zilberstein-Levy 2006). Archer (2008) argues that the path of becoming an academic is "not smooth, straightforward, linear or automatic, and can involve conflict and instances of inauthenticity, marginalization and exclusion" (p. 387).

There is an assumption that new academics 'learn the ropes' via the PhD process and then subsequently though informal communities of practice in their departments. However, Gourlay (2011, p. 68) argues that "the features of 'shared repertoire', 'mutual endeavor' and 'expert-novice interaction' (Lave and Wenger's key criteria for a community of practice) should not be assumed to pre-exist in academic departments. She claims that these commonly applied models of community of practice transition do not exist and need to be questioned. After examining the experiences of a small group of new lecturers, Gourlay found that the transition experience can result in confusion, inauthenticity and isolation for the new academic. Confusion arose around how to approach the new role in general, with the university and departments' expectations and requirements of them seeming opaque. Gourlay contends that many new academics lack confidence and a sense of legitimacy about their practice, and many experience physical as well as professional isolation. Furthermore, there is a lack of collegial team-work and instead a perceived ethos of academia being individualistic. This carries implications Gourlay argues regarding the applicability of the community of practice model being functional and implies a need for new dialogic spaces that are beneficial for new academics.

Learning how to negotiate the apparently democratic but actually hierarchical structure of academia can be challenging for new academics (Simmons 2011; Trowler and Knight 2000). It is hard for them to tell where the boundaries are, whereas for doctoral students these are more closely defined. Knowing how to talk to other academics when they have typically been a student is for many a difficult transition. The complex social system of academia does not commonly allow for support in helping new academics orientate themselves and get the knowledge they need.

For most, the role of the new academic will encompass a variety of tasks, some of which they may not have been exposed to while doing their doctorate. This might include conducting new research, fund-raising, publishing in books and professional journals, conferences, networking, teaching, and service within the university and community (Nir and Zilberstein-Levy 2006). These tasks all demand time, especially learning how to prioritize (Hemmings and Kay 2010) and the reality of the job can often be overwhelming, especially as academics "are increasingly required to objectively 'count' teaching hours ... as though higher numbers have impacts upon 'quality'" (Nagy and Burch 2009, p. 232).

Lack of support amongst early-career academics is a systemic problem (Nir and Zilberstein-Levy 2006; Staniforth and Harland 2006). A study by Sutherland and Petersen (2009) across two New Zealand tertiary institutions found many new academics were experiencing "a lack of mentoring from senior colleagues, an apathetic Head of Department, poor or non-existent advice about promotions and career planning, and induction processes that lacked specificity and timeliness" (p. 3). Such examples were preventing early-career academics from having "research success; collegiality or academic citizenship; and personal satisfaction and balance" (p. 6). In the United Kingdom, Staniforth and Harland (2006) found the role of heads of departments were pivotal in "protecting new staff from excessive workloads" (p. 194) and in Israel, Nir and Zilberstein-Levy (2006) found that prior to tenure, increasing stress about occupational uncertainty resulted in early-career academics making compromises at the expense of originality in order to increase productivity. These are the personal effects; there are also costs to departments and institutions when new academics take longer to settle in before being able to contribute to their full potential. What is needed, we were hearing in our university, was more 'backroom talk', the conversations and questions where new academics could talk freely about the complexity of juggling all the demands of the job.

22.4 The Development of *Catalyst*

22.4.1 *Communities of Practice*

Communities of practice have always existed in human societies. Wenger (1998) says they are so informal and pervasive that most do not have a name. There is now considerable literature describing communities of practice and what they offer. Essentially they are "groups of people who share a concern, a set of problems, or a passion about a topic, and who deepen their knowledge and expertise in this area by interacting on an ongoing basis" (Wenger et al. 2002, p. 4). Communities of practice have a set of meaningful connections among the people, the activity, and the world, over time and in relation with other peripheral and overlapping communities of practice (Lave and Wenger 1991).

Nagy and Burch (2009) discuss the changing university environment and how academics are encouraged to be autonomous and accountable, thereby diminishing both availability and willingness to engage in collegiality. They stress that universities should provide a contemporary context with opportunity to reconnect academics in communal engagement without coercion. However, Gourlay (2011) argues that when novice lecturers transition to new roles, the uncertainty and isolation can be so overwhelming that the suggestion by their departments they should feel part of a 'community' is a myth for them. Gourlay further argues that this "'community' should not be assumed to pre-exist in an academic department" and that there is "a need to develop ways of sharing these less observable practices more explicitly" (p. 76). Warhurst (2008) suggests that workgroups are better for anticipating newcomers' learning needs.

According to a number of scholars, by spending time together sharing information, pondering common issues and exploring ideas, knowledge accumulates, needs are met and in many cases a community of practice will form (e.g. Jawitz 2007, 2009; Nagy and Burch 2009). When this happens, Wenger (1998) maintains that individuals' social identities become forged and tied up with this community of practice, as they are built on a common purpose, with shared norms and practices, binding the group together. Driscoll et al. (2009) insist this takes time, as when academics from different disciplines meet together, physical, behavioral, cultural and professional differences are powerful and therefore time is needed for these changes to occur. They argue that only when collaboration and experiences are shared, a commonality of intellectual purpose, feeling, experience and resolve takes over and it is then that feelings of isolation and professional self-doubt diminish. In time, this provides incentives, which can be linked to career advancement, accelerated productivity, personal satisfaction and growth (see Darwin and Palmer 2009; Ehrich et al. 2004).

22.4.2 Introducing Peer Mentoring

The studies documenting mentoring for support are prolific (e.g. Allen et al. 1997; Chan 2008; Colvin and Ashman 2010; Darwin and Palmer 2009) with the merits well documented. There are, however, concerns as traditional mentoring is not always easy to access (Darwin and Palmer 2009); finding sufficient as well as suitable mentors can be a struggle; a lack of time to meet with a mentor is often problematic (Ehrich et al. 2004); poor planning and a lack of understanding of the mentoring process can arise; matching of mentors and protégés can be unsuccessful; there is often a lack of access to mentors from minority groups (Ewing et al. 2008), and more. The challenge of implementing a traditional mentoring programme and training both mentors and protégés, together with the expense of money and time, was going to be prohibitive for our relatively small center. Added to this, traditional mentoring can promote a hierarchical power relationship which can reinforce feelings of loneliness and professional self-doubt (Darwin 2000; Driscoll et al. 2009).

One adaptation of the traditional mentoring relationship is one-to-one peer mentoring, where the partners can be in comparable positions and levels. This seemed a promising compromise, which had potential to support our new academics. Searching through the literature produced further variations within peer mentoring that could be adopted to what was needed for our situation, for example: participants might be at the same level, but each partner comes with experience in a particular area providing skill and expertise (Colvin and Ashman 2010; Hargreaves and Dawe 1990); both participants could mentor each other and work on the same specific agenda (Diamond 2010; Jaworski and Watson 1994; Lick 1999); or both partners could help each other develop through a chosen method of reflection (Cooney and Krainer 1996; Farrell 2001; Saunders and Pettinger 1995). What was emerging was the opportunities that peer mentoring offered for open, non-hierarchical dialogue where partners could support, encourage and motivate each other. In this way, exchange of ideas on issues of survival would be more likely to occur than in a traditional mentoring relationship and anxieties that many have would also be more likely to be addressed (Harnish and Wild 1994; Webb et al. 2009).

Further variations included group peer mentoring or mentoring circles (Darwin and Palmer 2009), based on the notion from Kram (2004) that when participants collectively meet together on a regular basis to share and work, there are many benefits: closer and richer relationships grow, learning occurs, and support develops. Darwin and Palmer discuss the effects of a collaborative atmosphere which enables members "to discuss real issues relating to work, career and family with like-minded people … the greatest benefits coming from interacting with others and sharing experiences" (p. 134). The possibility therefore of creating simultaneously one-to-one or small groups of peer mentoring running alongside a community of practice started to take shape.

22.4.3 Catalyst

Creating *Catalyst*, a community of practice for our new academics, allowed us to focus on shared engagement in practice rather than individual actions. The practice (or practices) distinguishes the community of practice from other groups (Smith et al. 2013). Within *Catalyst* our new academics develop a sense of shared identity, along with individualized identities and roles. The members teach, learn, negotiate, and celebrate their corresponding practices and processes by engaging together on activities that are purposely enacted to benefit the whole community. From this, other activities may arise organically, which maximizes the opportunity to learn. For example, an invitation is extended to an experienced academic to share their knowledge of teaching large lectures, and the strategies she uses. The new academics then share within the community their experiences and practices they have seen or tried.

In addition, *Catalyst* includes peer mentoring as a learning mechanism and is contracted around a task. The new academics meet in pairs or sub-groups between the meetings to foster further support at a more personal level. These are structured in such a way that the members talk with each other about critical aspects of beginning an academic path and in the process learn more about each other, building strong professional friendships. By introducing peer mentoring within the community of practice, *Catalyst* recognizes that the members do not come as blank slates, without knowledge to share. *Catalyst* offers continuity throughout the first semester, and in the process provides the platform to create long-lasting networks. While the focus is always on building community, the aim is to introduce new academics to the expectations of the university enabling them to have a quicker and smoother transition into their respective departments.

The features of *Catalyst* are closely aligned to faculty learning communities (FLCs) found in the United States (Cox 2011, p. 18) which are described as:

> a special type of CoP in higher education that is structured, multidisciplinary, yearlong, voluntary, and of size 8–12, meeting tri-weekly with a focus on building community and developing a scholarly product, usually Scholarship of Teaching and Learning (SoTL).

Although *Catalyst* has many overlaps, in particular being structured and multidisciplinary, it also has distinctive features: it is one semester-long, meets fortnightly, has no restriction on numbers, and includes peer mentoring between the meetings. Cox discusses the problem of university academics being isolated from colleagues in different disciplines, and describes how they remain in their silos or 'tribes', do not cross 'borders' and are often defensive about their turf (Cox 2011,

p. 26). One of the aims of the FLCs is to counteract this by moving the institution towards becoming a learning organization, so that it connects its members closely to the mission, goals, and challenges of the organization. This is done through supporting groups rather than individuals, and promotes the sharing of informal learning that goes on in communities of practice. In a similar way, as the *Catalyst* community becomes involved in learning activities, meetings, and other practices they share together, their knowledge develops and they are supported as a group. However, with the added feature of the peer mentoring the individual can be supported as well.

22.5 The Structure of *Catalyst*

The participants in this study had just completed a 3-day introductory programme to the university and were part of a group of twenty-five new academics. Ten volunteered to take part (seven women, three men) in the *Catalyst* community to run for a 4-month period over the subsequent semester. They ranged in discipline: Nursing, Education, Optometry, Mathematics, Sociology, Computer Science, Property, Psychology, Business, and Population Health. The other fifteen participants chose not to participate for various reasons such as timetabling difficulties with the group meetings; located at other campuses and felt that travel would take up too much time; already being mentored; and, some were new academics to this university but not beginning academics and therefore felt they did not need the *Catalyst* community.

The ten participants attend six two-hour group meetings, every 2 weeks throughout the semester, at a central location with refreshments provided. At each fortnightly meeting the group is mentored by the author with the overall aim of learning about the different institutional expectations of academic life and finding ways of being more productive and strategic in their jobs, to become effective academics.

The six meetings are as follows:

Meeting 1: Balancing the roles
At this first meeting, the new academics receive teaching about what is involved with their research, teaching, and service and the importance of developing a nexus between these three. Discussion forms a major part of the meeting and this is interlaced into the teaching. The first discussion begins with what they understand their own teaching involves i.e. preparing course work, coordinating courses, team teaching, understanding the learning management system used by the university, and more; and then what they consider their service will involve and how much is expected i.e. institutional, faculty, departmental, and discipline. The focus then moves to the importance of integrating the three areas of research, teaching and service effectively into their academic practice; how this might be achieved; and, how they anticipate balancing these different roles. The group is introduced to the

concept of SMART (Specific, Measurable, Achievable, Realistic, Timely) goals and spend time identifying a goal from each of their research, teaching, and service that they can accomplish in the first semester. Each participant formulates a plan of how they will achieve these goals. Alongside their SMART goals the group also work individually on developing a personal work/life balance schedule for themselves (Boice 1991; Gray 2005).

Meeting 2: Academic performance reviews and continuation
The second meeting is concentrated around Academic Performance Reviews (APRs) and Continuation (similar to tenure) reports. An APR meeting is held annually with the academic's line manager and is an opportunity to discuss their career trajectory. The Continuation report is a document submitted in their fourth year and must show the development the academic has made over these initial years in order to be continued in the job. Failure to perform will result in a 2-year probationary period with strict deadlines to adhere to, and if not met can result in termination of the appointment. The two reports are discussed together as the APR should inform the Continuation report. A significant proportion of the time in this meeting is spent explaining what the APR and Continuation are and how to prepare for these processes/evaluations and the standard expected. The group spends time familiarizing themselves with the documents, matching them to the criteria for their own disciplines and outlining what is required for each year. The significance of developing a teaching portfolio follows and the need to start working on this document form the beginning so that they can easily track their development over the years to follow. Discussion within the group mainly involves what counts as evidence on their teaching and how to gather this for the portfolio. Interwoven into this discussion is an exchange on how to write strong applications.

Meeting 3: Promotion
The meeting on promotion draws attention to the different levels of the academic progression (lecturer, senior lecturer, associate professor, professor) and where there are bars requiring promotion to move over these points. Discussion commences again with why this is important to be gathering evidence from the beginning of the academic career, particularly with their teaching. This includes discussing the various ways of gathering evidence (formative and summative) and how to use this in the promotion document, particularly if it is not positive. The group spends time familiarizing themselves with the promotion document and each participant maps out when their first promotion might be with the steps required to get them there.

Meeting 4: Habits of highly effective academics
An invitation from a productive professor to talk about their career is the highlight of this meeting. The professor is given a brief to focus their talk about the three top tips they wish they had known when they were a new academic. The participants find this talk invaluable and have many questions for the professor.

The rest of the meeting is predominantly about research productivity and includes discussion about funding, what is available and how to access it, and what help is available to write grants; research teams, how to form these, and how to manage them; conferences, what ones to target, and how to fund them; and networking, why this is necessary. Finally, the discussion ends with the importance of integrating writing into everyday practice; how to keep the writing flowing easily; and, how to get past writers block if it occurs.

Meeting 5: Teaching in the lecture theatre
The fifth meeting also includes a guest; an expert in media production on voice projection, presentation, and more. Each participant presents a 3 min presentation in front of the group and receives feedback from the guest on what do they do well and how to improve it. The group is always anxious about this session but feedback indicates it is strongly recommended and everyone finds it extremely worthwhile.

In the second half of this meeting, discussion with the group covers three aspects of teaching: (1) effective ways for teaching small groups through to delivering large lectures, in both undergraduate and postgraduate; (2) different modes of delivery and what established colleagues are doing in their classes; and (3) teaching to diversity. The meeting ends with an introduction to student assessment and how to design peer-assessment and self-assessment.

Meeting 6: Where to from here
The final meeting involves an activity extensively mapping out the next 5 years for each participant's academic career. This includes how they can be strategic about their goals, such as when to set up new collaborations, what conferences are valuable for their career, when and how to plan for sabbaticals, attracting post-graduate students, and more.

This session concludes with a discussion about what professional development is available, what is useful and the value of attending if opportunities come along. The meeting ends with each participant briefly describing one thing that they found from the meetings the most useful for their career, and one thing that surprised them.

As well as working collectively as a group every 2 weeks over the semester, the group meet one-to-one or in small groups (of no more than four) for peer mentoring, at least once between the fortnightly meetings. The peer mentoring times are structured around tasks given out at the group meetings related to the topics that are covered each time.

In order to evaluate the programme ethics consent was obtained. Data was collected from post-programme interviews with each new academic and a focus group interview, together with journal notes the author made during reflections after each meeting. An independent researcher carried out the interviews, recording and transcribing these, rather than the author who facilitated the workshops, to avoid bias. Implicit in the interview process was the co-construction of meaning between the researcher and the new academic. In this way, semi-structured interviews allowed a point of interest to be explored in more detail (Hollway and Jefferson 2002), so that if there were factors that were overlooked they would surface.

The data collected from the interview transcripts and the journal notes from the author were analyzed using open coding (Corbin and Strauss 1990) to identify and classify recurring concepts. This involved an initial phase of familiarization with the data, which was achieved through multiple readings. This data was compared and revised with the independent researcher for consensus to ensure again that possible bias was avoided.

22.6 What We Learned

The new academics came together every 2 weeks and worked on the different topics for a 2-h session. Having a small group of ten participants meant there was time for everyone to have turns interacting as well as time for other activities. The group was often rowdy and animated as they shared together, enjoying the initial time when they met to 'unwind' and talk about their work and how they were coping.

> I feel I'm on the border so it is nice to have that contact with a bigger group. It makes you feel you're part of something and that you're all about the same. It's different from going somewhere else where you're the new person and everyone else has been there for yonks. I enjoyed it.

> It was good to see they had sort of the same concerns in different departments. It was helpful to know other people were in the same boat.

Overall, the meetings were a time to be mentored about the different aspects of the job and to gain more institutional knowledge, which would progress them more quickly than if they had been left on their own.

> There was a lot of useful stuff in those meetings, which we went up to the full two hours, how to manage your career but also do the teaching.

> I found the session on goal setting useful, especially when you have just started in your permanent position. Having to sit down and write a plan, to think about having short-term, mid-term and long-term goals was useful just to get that wake up call.

> I wish we'd had more of the teaching in the lecture theatre, I could go to three or four different versions of the same thing and pick up tips all the time. I find this the most scary part of the job.

> I'd seen reference to continuation in my contract but I hadn't really focused on it. It seems like it's very much left to the question of the individual departments, which if you're in one that isn't particularly useful or helpful to you then you're not left with much. As soon as you step in the door there should be something on continuation told to you.

The meetings were also an opportunity to be part of a bigger group to share stories and be encouraged by the others going through similar situations in their departments. Over the semester the group became very close and the comradeship that developed was evident.

> I was just trying to think about, reflect on my own department and yeah there's less informal collaboration and collegiality. When we were post docs we were all in the same boat and so you know you'd meet at coffee and you'd talk about things and therefore share information there. So this was actually great because we could share informally, especially as I'm in a small department.

> I was blown away by the experience and the diverse experiences and backgrounds of all the different people in the group. I found that intriguing and useful because I'm in a fairly small

department, and it's fairly mono, from the same background. Seeing the university in a better, wider context was fantastic.

The group was required to meet in pairs or in a smaller group at least once between the meetings to work on tasks together and mentor each other. Most chose to meet at a local café as they felt they could let their 'guards' down and not be worried about who might be listening if they were in offices or lunchrooms. Often, the conversations were what one participant described as 'backroom talk' meaning they would ask questions such as "What am I going to do about this?" or "Where do I find that?" They felt they should probably know the answers but might have forgotten or not really understood, and would be too embarrassed to ask senior colleagues to explain again or in some cases felt disapproval for being so needy.

> The peer mentoring was good. It's the informal side of the unsaid part of this course to be able to share information between different people.

At each peer mentoring meeting, the pairs or small groups would spend time recapping how their weeks were going, discussing what went well and what did not, and often touching on their personal lives as it usually affected their work-life balance. They would work on tasks given out at the group meetings, related to the particular topic of that week. These provided a focus and a structure, but more importantly a legitimate reason to meet as otherwise they felt they might not be so motivated, spending time away from their busy schedules talking with a colleague.

> They were helpful as a sort of icebreaking starting point. The task required people to get forced to talk about something.

> Having the task in front of you to talk about meant you automatically start talking about it, otherwise we'd be talking about the weather right?

> The task kept us honest. As we had to front up to the next meeting and say what you had or hadn't done and generally we went off topic but it was always useful stuff, it was still a good discussion.

Over these initial months, the value of having another new academic they could trust, to talk to about things that went well or not so well, the 'backroom talk', was noteworthy, and professional friendships grew remarkably strong. It was also easier to meet with one person at times and get to know them outside of the group.

> It was nice starting out just meeting up with one person and then when you went back to the bigger group it made it better. I think that was more useful than a bigger group all the time.

Peer mentors were encouraged to be from different departments or faculties, and as much as possible at similar academic levels. Meeting regularly one-to-one or in a small group gave an immediate feeling of belonging, which they said made them feel "part of the university structure, as we're all about the same, all newish to the university". One participant explained that having a colleague to meet with for coffee made her feel important, as she had no one else to do this simple activity with, and that:

In a strange sort of way we had similar roles and even though our titles and departments were quite different, there were lots of similarities when we started to dig down. We were able to encourage each other, exchange ideas and develop together.

Although the new academics enjoyed getting to know each other socially as a larger group and having new friends, it was the times in between when they met for peer mentoring that had a 'knock on' effect for the meetings. By meeting frequently and peer mentoring with someone from a different department meant trust developed faster which permitted them to be more open about issues:

If you're talking, you're probably talking about your job and someone nearby, you know, could hear what you're saying and so you would have to be careful about what you say and what is heard. You don't want to say the wrong thing.

If you have built up trust you can make contact and say, you know, I've got a problem, or can I run something past you, that kind of thing.

By the third meeting the camaraderie amongst the group was exceptionally strong and they were very open about what was or was not happening in their departments. Time and again the group had to be reminded of confidentiality as disheartening stories were shared. They valued the different perspectives and experiences each individual brought with them, and the alternative solutions to issues.

My knowledge was different being from a different discipline and so I felt I could offer other ideas about how to deal with things. I felt I could give a different perspective.

It gave me permission to ask things whereas normally I probably would have just carried on working, trying to figure it out myself. I didn't have to worry whether it was a silly question.

Working with nine other new academics from across the university gave the group a broader knowledge of how the university 'works' and a glimpse of how different departments worked and the type of work they did, compared to their own.

Some time spent on collaborative work was good because in my area we mostly work on our own, but we're being encouraged to work collaboratively. I can see now there are some interesting challenges that arise out of that so it was good to discuss this and get some ideas from the others how best to do it. There was a lot of variation between the faculties.

I learnt some amazing stuff. I learnt about contraception for opossums, which is not something if you're working in commercial law that you get exposed to. It gave me an appreciation of the different things they need to know.

Everyone seemed to be from a completely different background, even discipline and so the different things that came up were things that I hadn't necessarily considered because they weren't directly affecting me. So I could then sort of appreciate and fit into a broader context of where it could go or how it could apply to me at a later date.

The community of practice structure with peer mentoring added in was continually endorsed for the continuity provided.

It was quite good because of how the actual meetings were based to have this peer mentoring in between so you could just keep everything ticking over.

The meetings were once every two weeks so it's kind of like having at least something every week to keep the momentum going between the main meetings.

The findings suggest a number of benefits for establishing *Catalyst* and in the next section I delineate the details behind its success, while also noting its shortcomings.

22.7   Critiquing Catalyst: What Is Generalizable?

Catalyst provides space away from departments for new academics to work collaboratively while learning about institutional and departmental expectations, and to discuss difficult issues that often arise for them (Webb et al. 2009). This enables them to learn the ropes without having to pester colleagues when, as newcomers, they feel they are scrutinized. *Catalyst* also capitalizes on the individual knowledge, expertise and diversity of the members through sharing stories and celebrating successes, supporting Lave and Wenger's (1991) claim that shared practice generates collective knowledge. In this way, through participation and engagement with the group, new academics find they have a better sense of who they are professionally leading to more autonomy for them. The addition of peer mentoring with pairs or smaller groupings provides opportunity for job-related issues or concerns to be discussed on a more personal level, and without having to wait for the next meeting.

Some of the new lecturers purposefully selected who they wanted to interact with for peer mentoring, as they recognized their own learning needs and saw opportunities to develop their knowledge through engagement. During our first iterations of *Catalyst* pairing was done using the results of a simple questionnaire before the first meeting. New staff detailed their position and department, and established whether they were new to New Zealand, were parents, and what languages they spoke. The pairs were then matched according to personal similarities as much as possible. However, two of the pairs found the pairing problematic, which at one point caused much dilemma. Evaluations further confirmed that who they would be matched with added to the anxiety many felt. It was then decided to let them choose their own partner and this proved successful. I am still unsure as to whether preference around this is due to the serendipity of the individuals involved —if anyone felt that they were not chosen as a pair that might be a problem. Experimentation with small groups of three or four also had great success and I now encourage pairs to combine after the third week. This mitigates anxiety or dissatisfaction with pairing and means that they each get to share on a more personal and informal level with many more of the other new academics.

In early iterations, the group meetings, held once a fortnight, were too infrequent to sustain interest and energy on their own. Allocating more meetings was too difficult to timetable everyone attending. This was resolved with the addition of peer mentoring providing the continuity that was needed. Peer mentoring was scheduled at each meeting while participants were present and could compare their timetables. If necessary, these times could easily be changed later on but this was easier to manage than trying to organize peer mentoring once back in their disciplines. In pairs, contact could be maintained both digitally and informally, keeping issues alive. Partnerships gave the opportunity to work with a colleague(s) more closely; someone they could discuss job-related issues or concerns when they arose, rather than waiting until the next meeting. As a result, the group developed caring and strong friendships in a very short time, despite the enormous differences between them as individuals, their disciplines and their views. The peer mentoring gave participants agency in developing their careers. Talking together, they reflected on, and critiqued, their roles as academics and the expectations of their different faculties and the wider university. Building a commonality of purpose with academics from diverse backgrounds is not straightforward and Driscoll et al. (2009) emphasize that time is required for this, but having the two structures working simultaneously—community of practice group and peer mentoring—largely resolved time-expense.

The camaraderie that developed over the semester created a strong network of professional colleagues, which continues once the formal community of practice, *Catalyst*, has ended: "It was really good having colleagues outside the department that I could call on and that could actually help me, even when we had finished meeting together, that was special".

Being in similar positions made it easier for them to understand each other's challenges, which Gourlay (2011) says are inherent with faculty practices. The group was always quick to offer advice and encouragement to each other, which was then reinforced when they got together in the intervening weeks for peer mentoring. They worked through the different institutional and departmental expectations they were hearing about, voicing their concerns and discussing strategies, which resulted in a smoother transition to their jobs than had they been left alone.

> You're kind of being thrown in, you're teaching classes almost straight away and I think things we've learnt in this group have been really useful. To me the university is making a huge investment in its staff just in terms of salaries and overheads and all the rest of it and so it needs to put more emphasis on inducting them more effectively. It's a wee bit scary you know, for example I could be standing in front of 250 students within days of starting, with a lot of faith by the people that engaged me but no training so it was useful having this group to help me cope with it all.

Their level of connectedness and engagement in the university context increased, leading to better autonomy for each individual and a stronger sense of who they were professionally (Darwin and Palmer 2009; Kram 2004; Nagy and Burch 2009).

> Yeah it touches a nerve with me because I find having come out of practice where I have worked for 20 years there is less informal collaboration and collegiality here than the environments I'm used to working in. This is more of a silo kind of approach and yet a university is about sharing knowledge so there seems to be all these artificial, well not artificial but contrived situations and so this was useful for helping me understand what I am doing, yeah, who I was.

They also felt their choice of institution was good because induction was provided at a deeper level than with one rushed day: "At my last university there was a day of listening to people talk about what was expected on the job and so many things to take in. This is good here being able to talk about stuff as you do it in your job, you learn as you go".

The overriding benefit of being part of the *Catalyst* community was simply meeting colleagues from other disciplines and getting to know them on a deeper level; colleagues they could talk to confidentially about anything related to the job and receive advice and guidance in return. It is, however, recognized that the participants who are involved in *Catalyst* all volunteer to take part: they are all eager to be included and are cooperative, which impacts on the results. Making *Catalyst* compulsory for all new academics would be difficult because of the various reasons from those who did not take up the offer (described above). Voluntary participation brings with it intrinsic motivation, buy-in and accountability.

As new academics generate new knowledge, their learning is a process intrinsically tied up with their sense of identity (Lave and Wenger 1991). Access to participation and, thereby, to opportunities for learning are often restricted to what the power structures in the workplace are (Warhurst 2008). The first stage of the *Catalyst* community was about learning as experiencing and, in the beginning, disciplinary differences were apparent. Those in the sciences asserted that the nature of their subject determined its teaching and they had a strong preference for passive learning. This contrasted with the way they experienced learning within the group and opened the way for much discussion and debate about active engagement versus didactic teaching.

As the *Catalyst* community progressed through the semester, there was a notable sense of belonging which, according to Lave and Wenger (1991), is another stage of learning. Within their departments, new academics can often flounder as the more experienced academics may lack the interest to involve them, and may omit helping them make necessary interdisciplinary connections to build networks (see Trowler 2012). These networks are crucial to be able to cross the 'borders' of other disciplinary 'territories' and build institutional knowledge with potential collaborations. The degree to which departments felt like communities of practice was variable amongst the group, with some interacting with their colleagues about teaching more than others, but overall departmental community felt minimal to new arrivals. In general the group felt neglected by their workplaces and talked about feelings of isolation and lack of collegiality. This was particularly evident in smaller departments, where new academics are typically recruited specifically for their specialist contribution (see Warhurst 2008). The tendency in such departments was for very individualized working practices.

During the semester, the new academics were all involved in teaching in their respective departments; some were also given leadership responsibilities as undergraduate course conveners and some were teaching in very large lectures for the first time. Some had been allocated their teaching on the basis of a of colleagues' off-loading or resignation. For those new academics, there was no time spent on the periphery of their communities and invariably the courses had little or no documentation from previous years as scaffolding. For them, the *Catalyst* community was a space to share frustrations and to gain confidence.

By the end of the semester, the new academics were developing a stronger sense of their identity; who they were and where they were going. They knew that their research accomplishments were the things that 'counted' in their departments (see Warhurst 2008), but the *Catalyst* community enabled them to consider how their teacher identity could be strengthened. Whether these new academics retained this 'enlightened' sense of identity once *Catalyst* ends, is unknown. "Academic identity is found to largely be reinforced through the power and reward structures attributed to research" (Warhurst 2008, p. 464) so once academics have found their feet, they will be influenced by their surroundings.

When they settle into their departments, the pressure to conform is immense. For this reason, some scholars advocate building communities of practice within departments for early-career academics (Trowler and Knight 2000). However, advocates of interdisciplinarity believe that it allows knowledge production to be freed and transferred in ways more aligned with real need as expertise can be brought together, believing that disciplinarity can involve a partial, fragmented, understanding of the world (see Trowler 2012). The option of a peer-mentoring community of practice built across disciplines for early-career academics seems a strong benefit to those who take it up.

22.8   Final Words

The study presents tangible benefits and feasibility for a structure incorporating a community of practice with peer mentoring, to be offered to academics new to the university, following an initial induction programme. The aim is to speed up the transition into academia smoothly and quickly than if they were left alone. Academic jobs are structured as independent endeavors—publishing, teaching, getting promoted, etc. Faculty are burdened with tasks and responsibilities that are exhaustive and exhausting and creating departmental communities of practice to support new academics can seem counter-cultural to an individualistic culture (see Smith et al. 2013, p. 189).

If new academics are left in isolation without encouragement and support they will not be productive as quickly as those who receive this (Driscoll et al. 2009). The *Catalyst* structure provides support by fostering an inclusive, knowledge building community by capitalizing on individual knowledge, expertise and diversity of the members. The synergy between the community of practice and the peer mentoring provides continuity and offers frequent assistance, institutional knowledge, and guidance during the beginning months of the job. Although the benefits of *Catalyst* are not directly measurable in the short-term, it is arguable that new academics who are provided with support and guidance would not benefit.

The sense of belonging in a group is a powerful factor (Darwin and Palmer 2009) enabling new academics to grow in confidence and who they are professionally. While belonging is difficult to quantify, the awareness of group dynamics is unquestionably a factor worth considering for developing stronger groups. The significance of social learning as a purposeful process enables newcomers to the academy to learn expansively, and to establish themselves as productive academics more naturally. In practical terms, *Catalyst* is easily established, economical, and sustainable, with the potential to be generalizable to other fields. There is much scope for the model to evolve into other areas where groups require support.

References

Allen, T., Russell, J., & Maetzke, S. (1997). Formal peer mentoring: Factors related to proteges satisfaction and willingness to mentor others. *Group and Organization Management, 22*(4), 488.

Archer, L. (2008). Younger academics' constructions of 'authenticity', 'success' and professional identity. *Studies in Higher Education, 33*(4), 385–403.

Boice, R. (1991). Quick starters: New faculty who succeed. *New Directions for Teaching and Learning, 1991*(48), 111–121. doi:10.1002/tl.37219914810

Chan, A. W. (2008). Mentoring ethnic minority, pre-doctoral students: An analysis of key mentor practices. *Mentoring & Tutoring: Partnership in Learning, 16*(3), 263–277.

Colvin, J. W., & Ashman, M. (2010). Roles, risks, and benefits of peer mentoring relationships in higher education. *Mentoring & Tutoring: Partnership in Learning, 18*(2), 121–134.

Cooney, T. J., & Krainer, K. (1996). Inservice mathematics teacher education: The importance of listening. In A. J. Bishop (Ed.), *International handbook of mathematics education* (pp. 1155–1185).

Corbin, J. M., & Strauss, A. (1990). Grounded theory research: Procedures, canons, and evaluative criteria. *Qualitative Sociology, 13*(1), 3–21. doi:10.1007/bf00988593

Cox, M. D. (2011). The impact of communities of practice in support of early-career academics. *International Journal for Academic Development, 18*(1), 18–30. doi:10.1080/1360144X.2011.599600

Darwin, A. (2000). Critical reflections on mentoring in work settings. *Adult Education Quarterly, 50*(3), 197–211.

Darwin, A., & Palmer, E. (2009). Mentoring circles in higher education. *Higher Education Research & Development, 28*(2), 125–136.

Diamond, C. T. P. (2010). A memoir of co-mentoring: The "we" that is "me". *Mentoring & Tutoring: Partnership in Learning, 18*(2), 199–209.

Driscoll, L. G., Parkes, K. A., Tilley-Lubbs, G. A., Brill, J. M., & Pitts Bannister, V. R. (2009). Navigating the lonely sea: Peer mentoring and collaboration among aspiring women scholars. *Mentoring & Tutoring: Partnership in Learning, 17*(1), 5–21.

Ehrich, L., Tennent, L., & Hansford, B. (2004). Formal mentoring programs in education and other professions: A review of the literature. *Educational Administration Quarterly, 40*(4), 518–540.

Ewing, R., Freeman, M., Barrie, S., Bell, A., O'Connor, D., Waugh, F., et al. (2008). Building community in academic settings: The importance of flexibility in a structured mentoring program. *Mentoring & Tutoring: Partnership in Learning, 16*(3), 294–310.

Farrell, T. (2001). Critical friendships: Colleagues helping each other develop. *ELT Journal, 55*(4), 368–374.

Gourlay, L. (2011). New lecturers and the myth of 'communities of practice'. *Studies in Continuing Education, 33*(1), 67–77.

Gray, T. (Ed.). (2005). *Publish & flourish: Become a prolific scholar*. Las Cruces: Teaching Academy, New Mexico State University.

Hargreaves, A., & Dawe, R. (1990). Paths of professional development: Contrived collegiality, collaborative culture, and the case of peer coaching. *Teaching & Teacher Education, 6*(3), 227–241.

Harnish, D., & Wild, L. A. (1994). Mentoring strategies for faculty development. *Studies in Higher Education, 19*(2), 191–201.

Hemmings, B., & Kay, R. (2010). University lecturer publication output: Qualifications, time and confidence count. *Journal of Higher Education Policy and Management, 32*(2), 185–197.

Hollway, W., & Jefferson, T. (2002). *Doing qualitative research differently: Free association, narrative and the interview method* (1st ed.). London: Sage Publications.

Jawitz, J. (2007). New academics negotiating communities of practice: Learning to swim with the big fish. *Teaching in Higher Education, 12*(2), 185–197.

Jawitz, J. (2009). Learning in the academic workplace: The harmonization of the collective and the individual habitus. *Studies in Higher Education, 34*(6), 601.

Jaworski, B., & Watson, A. (1994). Mentoring, co-mentoring, and the inner mentor. In B. Jaworski & A. Watson (Eds.), *Mentoring in mathematics teaching* (pp. 124–138). London: The Falmer Press.

Kram, K. E. (2004). Forward: The making of a mentor. In D. Clutterbuck & G. Lane (Eds.), *The situated mentor*. Gower: Aldershot.

Lave, J., & Wenger, E. (1991). *Situated learning. Legitimate peripheral participation*. Cambridge: Cambridge University Press.

Lick, D. W. (1999). Proactive comentoring relationships: Enhancing effectiveness through synergy. In C. A. Mullen & D. W. Lick (Eds.), *New directions in mentoring: Creating a culture of synergy* (pp. 34–45). Lewes: Falmer Press.

Lunsford, L. G., Baker, V., Griffin, K. A., & Johnson, W. B. (2013). Mentoring: A typology of costs for higher education faculty. *Mentoring & Tutoring: Partnership in Learning, 22*(2), 1–24. doi:10.1080/13611267.2013.813725

Nagy, J., & Burch, T. (2009). Communities of Practice in Academe (CoP-iA): Understanding academic work practices to enable knowledge building capacities in corporate universities. *Oxford Review of Education, 35*(2), 227–247.

Nir, A. E., & Zilberstein-Levy, R. (2006). Planning for academic excellence: Tenure and professional considerations. *Studies in Higher Education, 31*(5), 537–554.

Saunders, S., & Pettinger, K. (1995). Prospective mentor's views on partnership in secondary teacher training. *British Educational Research Journal, 21*(2), 199–219.

Simmons, N. (2011). Caught with their constructs down? Teaching development in the pre-tenure years. *International Journal for Academic Development, 16*(3), 229–241. doi:10.1080/1360144x.2011.596706

Smith, E. R., Calderwood, P. E., Dohm, F. A., & Gill Lopez, P. (2013). Reconceptualizing faculty mentoring within a community of practice model. *Mentoring & Tutoring: Partnership in Learning, 21*(2), 175–194. doi:10.1080/13611267.2013.813731

Staniforth, D., & Harland, T. (2006). Contrasting views of induction: The experience of new academic staff and their heads of department. *Active Learning in Higher Education, 7*(2), 185–196.

Sutherland, K., & Petersen, L. (2009). *The success and impact of early career academics in two New Zealand tertiary institutions* (pp. 1–44). Ako Aotearoa Website: National Centre for Tertiary Teaching Excellence. https://akoaotearoa.ac.nz/download/ng/file/group-4/n3953-success-and-impact-of-early-career-academics-in-two-nz-tertiary-institutions—project-report.pdf. Accessed October 29, 2015.

Trowler, P. (2012). Disciplines and interdisciplinarity: Conceptual groundwork. In P. Trowler, M. Saunders, & V. Bamber (Eds.), *Tribes and territories in the 21st century: Rethinking the significance of disciplines in higher education* (pp. 5–29). London and New York: Routledge.

Trowler, P., & Knight, P. T. (2000). Coming to know in higher education: Theorising faculty entry to new work contexts. *Higher Education Research & Development, 19*(1), 27–42.

Warhurst, R. P. (2008). 'Cigars on the flight-deck': New lecturers' participatory learning within workplace communities of practice. *Studies in Higher Education, 33*(4), 453–467.

Webb, A. K., Wangmo, T., Ewen, H. H., Teaster, P. B., & Hatch, L. R. (2009). Peer and faculty mentoring for students pursuing a PhD in gerontology. *Educational Gerontology, 35*(12), 1089–1106.

Wenger, E. (1998). *Communities of practice: Learning, meaning, and identity.* Cambridge: Cambridge University Press.

Wenger, E., McDermott, R., & Snyder, W. (2002). *Cultivating communities of practice.* Boston, MA: Harvard Business School Press.

Woodd, M. (2001). Learning to leap from a peer: A research study on mentoring in a further and higher education institution. *Research in Post-Compulsory Education, 6*(1), 97–104. doi:10.1080/13596740100200095

Chapter 23
Where's My Parking Permit? Bringing New Staff Together as a Learning Community

Elise G.C. Crawford and Sonia Saluja

Abstract The process of adaption to a new work environment can be significantly accelerated through social learning opportunities. However, contemporary trends toward corporatisation of universities are seeing diminishing social encounters and this can have significant implications for new staff. This chapter offers that Communities of Practice (CoPs) can be a practical solution toward supplementing the diminishing levels of collegiality in modern universities. This chapter outlines the process taken to establish a CoP for new staff for a multi-campus university in Australia. Results from a 12 months review highlight the benefits of the three essential elements of CoPs, namely: 'feeling supported' (i.e. sense of *community*), 'increased total effectiveness as a staff member', and 'increased understanding and awareness of university systems and process' (i.e. building of *domain knowledge*). The most enjoyable aspects identified by survey respondents were 'the sharing of knowledge' and 'discussion's (i.e. *sharing practice*). Three core issues emerged from the review and advice is shared to increase awareness of their potential presence and to help CoP facilitators head off potential problems. Future directions for the CoP are provided and the chapter concludes with some guidance to readers who might be interested in establishing a similar CoP.

Keywords Community of Practice · Higher education · Grass-roots · Sensemaking · Multi-campus · Blended

A new staff member at a major university in Queensland approached his supervisor and asked where he could get his parking permit. Since no restrictions were placed on parking at the university, his supervisor was a little perplexed at this request, nevertheless he

E.G.C. Crawford (✉)
School of Human Health and Social Sciences, Central Queensland University, Rockhampton, Australia
e-mail: e.crawford@cqu.edu.au

S. Saluja
School of Medical and Applied Sciences, Central Queensland University, Rockhampton, Australia
e-mail: s.saluja@cqu.edu.au

© Springer Nature Singapore Pte Ltd. 2017
J. McDonald and A. Cater-Steel (eds.), *Communities of Practice*,
DOI 10.1007/978-981-10-2879-3_23

pursued further details. The new staff member explained that he sees many cars in the parking lots with permits displayed. He went on to add that these permits are colour coded. Some are red while others are green. It suddenly dawned on the supervisor the reason for his question, and with a smile, explained the laws regarding provisional licenses for new drivers in Australia. He clarified that provisional license holders must display P Plates to indicate their level of driving experience, and that the red P stands for less than two years' experience and green for less than three. New to Australia, the new staff member did not know this and left the room feeling a little silly for asking, 'where's my parking permit?'

23.1 Introduction

The commencement of a new job can be an exciting experience. However, it can also be daunting and disconcerting, as the cultural difference in the parking ticket scenario shared above has illustrated. The level and type of change experienced when adapting to a new environment differs amongst individuals and knowing the needs of new staff is not always apparent until one of those needs arises. New staff are often made welcome by attending some form of induction or orientation process and provided an information pack or directed to information associated with their new role. However, information alone is meaningless until it is related to one's own circumstances within a social context. In light of changes toward a more business-like approach in higher education, where opportunities for social learning are diminishing, this chapter presents a rationale for participating in Communities of Practice (CoPs). The process taken to develop a CoP for new university staff is outlined and results from a review after 12 months are discussed. Three core issues emerged from this review. The challenges these issues presented and how they were addressed is shared. Future directions for the CoP are shared and the chapter concludes with some guidance when establishing and sustaining similar CoPs in higher education settings.

23.2 Rationale for CoPs in Higher Education

23.2.1 Adaption and Sensemaking for New Staff

It is essential to adapt quickly to a new work environment and to learn to work within this environment effectively. In higher education, a large number of processes are likely to improve as a result of improved staff competence, including: governance, administration, student services, learning and teaching, industry and community partnership developments, and research outputs. For a new staff member, swift adaption can reduce stress associated with uncertainty and change. During the process of adaption and wayfinding, the employee creates new knowledge that provides meaningful insights on how their new environment relates to them. However, adapting to a new work environment can be challenging, as established assumptions about the world are tested when individuals are exposed to new experiences (Quinn 2012).

The example of the parking permit shared at the beginning of this chapter illustrates how individuals draw on past experiences to make sense of new environments. The process that enables people to create personal insights is known as sensemaking and involves synthesising information and experiences into meaningful insights that guide further actions. Sensemaking has been described as a cyclical process that continuously updates the mental model that guides further action (Seligman 2000, p. 361) from a series of bridging activities (White and Roth 2009). To fill gaps in knowledge, people think about new experiences and those of others to form insights of how this information relates to them individually. Therefore, sensemaking aligns with social learning theory, positing that individuals learn from their own experiences and from the experiences of others (Bandura 1977). However, sensemaking is easily taken for granted because it is ongoing, subtle, swift and social (Weick et al. 2005, p. 409). Therefore, to avoid inadvertently undermining or interfering with sensemaking activities, it can be useful to acknowledge and encourage its progress.

23.2.2   Learning from Social Exchange

Knowledge and the creation of new knowledge, which leads to greater personal insights, is not something that can be easily documented. Knowledge requires a social context and a social dialogue. McDermott (1999) draws a distinction between knowledge and information by identifying *knowing* as a human act and *knowledge* as the residue of thinking. In contrast, information is an artifact, something that can be documented and stored. Tricks of the trade, who to go to for help, and system shortcuts are acquired through experience and are difficult to articulate. Such learning is rarely documented and is instead contained in the form of ideas and insights known as 'tacit' knowledge (Polyani 1958).

To draw out knowledge rather than information requires an act of thinking with someone else and hence knowledge comes from a social exchange (McDermott 2000). Tacit knowledge needs to be discussed, thought about and shared to take on meaning. This form of knowledge may have never been documented or clearly articulated (McDermott 1999). Information provided at the start of a new job is of little relevance until it has personal meaning and this meaning is created during social exchanges. However, social interactions are increasingly diminishing in academic settings.

23.2.3   Modern Universities and Diminishing Social
Learning Opportunities

The changing nature of contemporary universities is creating a need for ways to create new knowledge under increasingly difficult circumstances. For the past 30 years, Western universities have been morphing away from a non-profit model to one more akin with private enterprise. Government pressure on universities to meet national objectives at reduced costs is changing the nature of higher education and redefining the role of the academic (Lingenfelter 2012). Modern universities need to become more financially self-sufficient and hence are looking to industry for solutions.

One notable change is the shift towards a managerial approach adopted from large corporations. Nagy and Burch (2009) refer to this trend as 'managerialism'. Other terms assigned include 'enterprise universities' (Quiggin 1996; Parker 2002), and 'corporate universities' (Churchman 2001; Blass 2005; Nagy and Burch 2009). The notion of a 'corporate university' began with the Walt Disney Corporation who established a university within the corporation to educate and build new knowledge amongst employees (Walton 1999). The new generation of universities focus on profit and loss and market competition (Walton and Martin 2004). These changes are having a significant effect on how new knowledge in universities can be created and transferred.

Government pressure to spend public funds responsibly is driving greater accountability from universities. In turn, universities demand greater accountability from their staff. As a result, universities are increasingly focused on measurable deliverables from their academic staff, such as: the number of teaching hours, articles published, grants awarded, awards received, scores attained in student evaluations, and the like. Often these measurable activities are linked to performance indicators and promotion processes. The effort concentrated on these activities reduces the time available and willingness to participate in collegial exchanges (Nagy and Burch 2009). Nagy and Burch (2009) predict that greater emphasis on quantitative rather than qualitative tasks is negatively impacting knowledge work practices. Therefore, the diminishing opportunities for social exchange in higher education have the potential to cause a profound impact on natural opportunities for learning and the creation of new knowledge for new and not so new staff.

Fewer face-to-face encounters reduce the chance for new staff to learn from others that can expedite the wayfinding process. As with organisations generally, tacit knowledge in universities is often created and transferred naturally in chance hallway meetings or lunch rooms (McDermott 1999). In universities, these spontaneous exchanges are known as intellectual collegiality, where problems are solved and innovative thinking and sharing take place in a collegiate manner (Tapper and Palfreyman 2000). In academia, collegiality can be a form of social support for new staff, where ideas and advice are shared in a socially informal manner as needs or ideas arise (Anderson et al. 2002). Fewer chance social encounters leave collegiality mute and untapped, creating a void of quality social learning opportunities for new staff.

Another trend in higher education is that universities are becoming more complex and diversified. One business solution is the consolidation of resources through mergers. A recent example is the merger of three higher education institutions to create the comprehensive University of Johannesburg (Burkley and Du Toit 2010). Mergers and the creation of 'super' or 'comprehensive' universities, such as the University of Johannesburg often result in restructured work arrangements and changes to roles and role descriptions. Changes to an organisation's strategic direction are also likely to be reflected in changes to the organisation's values and goals. In cases such as these, existing knowledge becomes redundant and is replaced with new tacit knowledge which develops in response to new demands.

In order to improve financial independence, universities try to attract more students through enhanced offerings and incentives, such as greater graduate employability and more flexible teaching delivery modes. These incentives give rise to new vocational degrees (Gourlay 2011) and distance delivery. Technical solutions to enable distance delivery require staff to become competent with a variety of technical skills (Roblyer and Doering 2013). Lecturers undertaking distance delivery are involved in connecting, running, and recording virtual collaboration sessions; developing storyboard animations; and preparing, editing and uploading pre-recorded messages, to name a few. The incorporation of teaching technologies is thought to make universities more useful and relevant (Davies and Petersen 2005).

The move towards more vocational degrees and distance modes of course delivery has significantly changed the nature of teaching and the nature of the teacher. To ensure programs of study reflect current industry practices, new staff are increasingly drawn from industry and, in many cases, with little research experience or familiarity with the organisational structure of universities.

One peculiarity in universities is the various roles within the organisation, particularly those associated with academia, such as: the Vice-Chancellor, Pro-Vice Chancellors, the Provost, Deans of Schools, Heads of Program, and a hierarchy of roles associated with teaching and research experience from Associate Lecturers through to Professors. Associated with the various roles are skills such as: course coordination, curriculum development, learning and teaching design, research, grant applications, and the use of teaching technology. Hence staff recruited from industry my need additional support as they adjust to a very different working paradigm.

An assumption is made that new lecturers will learn the ropes via the Ph.D. process (Barkhuizen 2002; Knight et al. 2006) which is developed through a discipline specific collegial process (Murray and Moore 2008). However, little is known about how Ph.D. graduates actually learn how to teach. Gourlay's (2011) raises the possibility that the academic role and scholarly practice relies on subtle processes involving tacit knowledge. Gourlay's (2011) study on novice academics transitioning into academia from industry found that participants experienced a great deal of confusion regarding how to adopt the academic role. Furthermore, participants noted that they could not find a system or a community that could support them in this process.

Experiences reported by industry-based staff include feelings of inauthenticity, a lack of legitimacy within the role as an academic (Archer 2008; Gourlay 2011), and feelings of isolation due to the perceived ethos of individualism regarding the nature of academia (Palmer 2002; Gourlay 2011). Gourlay (2011) suggests that the assumption of community in higher education today is erroneous and argues that a more explicit means of developing community in academia is necessary. Even if 'how to' guides exist, these alone would not help new staff develop a sense of community or to feel a valued member of the organisation (Baker-Eveleth et al. 2011). As episodes of natural collegiality decline, universities are beginning to proactively seek alternative strategies to encourage social learning opportunities. One way being explored is through Communities of Practice (CoPs).

23.3 Communities of Practice: The Theoretical Basis

Communities of Practice (CoPs) may offer a way to supplement the natural social learning processes of collegiality which appear to be in decline. CoPs provide a place for social learning opportunities by bringing together groups of people with a common interest to think together, to share knowledge and to create new knowledge (Wenger 1999). Lave and Wenger (1991) offer that sharing expertise and creation of new knowledge is a central tenet of a Community of Practice's (CoP's) existence. CoPs have recently been described as opportunities for 'voluntary situated learning and knowledge building activity where members negotiate identity, learning and purpose in collaboration' (Nagy and Burch 2009, p. 227). Although CoPs have been used in a variety of contexts, they share three common elements: a defined domain, shared practice, and a community (Wenger 1998).

CoPs are common-place in industry and are often organic in nature. That is, learning communities form spontaneously, because workers naturally look for help from others to solve problems, share insights and build knowledge on topics they care about (McDermott 1999). Businesses have learned to tap into this energy in order to achieve a competitive advantage including, building better products, reducing costs, increasing market share, etc. (Nagy and Burch 2009). To leverage existing learning communities of interest without 'killing' them, organisations formalise them by purposefully seeking out, nurturing and providing resource support (McDermott 1999). A variety of terms are used for CoPs in organisations, such as: learning communities (McDermott 2000), learning networks (Berkes 2009), and workgroups (Boud and Middleton 2003). Regardless of their name, the purpose of CoPs in industry is to provide an organisation sanctioned place for the sharing and creation of knowledge via social learning. Since CoPs have benefited industry, they have been thought to benefit universities.

23.3.1   Potential Benefits of CoPs for New Staff

The establishment of CoPs in higher educational settings is relatively new (McDonald and Star 2006). Increasingly, researchers are finding that CoPs have a positive influence on performance (Nistor et al. 2015). CoPs do more than create and share knowledge. For staff there are economic and social benefits, higher rates of tenure (Cox 1997, 2013), increased motivation to learn (Schmidt and Moust 2000), improved acquisition of knowledge that is otherwise unstated or implicit (Nonaka and Takeuchi 1995), faster skill development (Dochy et al. 2003), a greater sense of purpose (Lave and Wenger 1991), increased self-confidence (MacKenzie et al. 2010), a feeling of belonging and identity within the university, as well as an opportunity for meaningful engagement (Baker-Eveleth et al. 2011). The university benefits due to improved expertise in the teaching process (Cox 2002), increased research productivity (Hollingsworth and Fassinger 2002), improved research self-efficacy (Kozlowski et al. 2014), and greater interest in research (Bishop and Bieschke 1998).

23.3.2   Challengers for CoPs in Higher Education

While many benefits have been reported, Nagy and Burch (2009) argue that CoPs in higher education are more challenging to create and sustain. They offer that the reason CoPs have not been widely adopted is due to progressive corporatisation of universities. As universities trend towards private corporations, they begin to take on elements of institutions. For instance, Power (2007) notes that standards and guidelines are frequently introduced with the intention of improving governance. However, these more often simply facilitate the conducting of audits of various processes involving some form of risk without reviewing how effectively management is at overseeing these. The managerial changes can also have an impact on how well CoPs function within higher education. One obstacle to sustaining CoPs in higher education is that staff loyalties in universities tend to lie with individual academic units or disciplines, and not with the interests of the university as a whole and the corporate mission (Nagy and Burch 2009). Roberts (2006) adds that the context in which the CoP is embedded contributes significantly to the CoP's success and that issues of power and trust must be taken into consideration. McDermott (1999) warns that over formalisation by institutional leaders can 'kill' CoPs as participants lose interest and withdraw when they perceive they no longer have control. Nagy and Burch (2009) warn that too much organisational interference can undermine the effectiveness of CoPs in higher education. Therefore, it is important to be mindful that the tendency to control or to co-opt CoPs for institutional purposes may discourage staff participation.

Another challenge for CoP success in higher education is the tendency for CoPs to morph into simple committees (Ortquist-Ahrens and Torosyan 2009). It can be useful to draw the distinction between other forms of formalised groups common to higher education such as: committees, workgroups, and learning networks. There are similarities such as cross-disciplinary participation, the use of agendas, working toward goals and some form of record keeping (Ortquist-Ahrens and Torosyan 2009).

However, there are five distinguishing characteristics that set CoPs apart from committees: (1) their purpose is to manage, exchange and create knowledge that benefits both the group and the individual, within a particular *domain* of knowledge, (2) the personnel self-select into the *community* on the basis of expertise or passion, (3) the nature of the boundaries is less defined as participants vary their level of involvement within the community, (4) the cohesive factor is built around the nature of the expertise, and (5) their longevity is linked to continued relevance of the *practice* for individuals or the group and desire to continue learning together (Wenger et al. 2002, p. 42).

Furthermore, committees are often evaluated as: 'boring, waste of time, goes nowhere, busy work, time consuming, chair does the work, no need to do outside work' (Ortquist-Ahrens and Torosyan 2009, p. 33). By way of contrast, CoPs have been characterised as: enjoyable, have personal meaning, are non-threatening, are stimulating and offer a chance to grow and learn (Ortquist-Ahrens and Torosyan 2009). Additional components to CoP success include: safety and trust, respect, responsiveness, collaboration, relevance, challenge, enjoyment, esprit de corps and empowerment (Cox 2004, pp. 18–19).

Early writing on CoPs in higher education date back to the late 1970s in the United States (Austin 1990), and have taken on various forms under various titles. Some include: Learning Communities (Cox 2014), Facilitated Networking (Fasso 2010) and Faculty Learning Communities (FLCs) (Cox 2002, 2004). FLCs were established to cultivate positive collegial, interpersonal and collaborative relationships, through a spirit of appreciation for the collective, acceptance of others, support for all members' growth and willingness to engage in genuine collaboration (Ortquist-Ahrens and Torosyan 2009).

However, Zboralski (2009) suggests that an understanding of the factors influencing CoPs is limited and Baker-Eveleth et al. (2011) propose that little is known about the factors that contribute to the development of CoPs. This chapter shares a 12 month experience whereby a new CoP was established at Central Queensland University, Australia (CQU) for the purpose of supporting new staff. The chapter aims to shed more light on the factors that contribute to genesis and development of CoPs in higher education.

23.4 A CoP for New Staff at CQU

23.4.1 Context

Central Queensland University, Australia (CQU) is one of 40 public higher education institutions in Australia. In 2014, CQU achieved the largest university geographic footprint in Australia due to a strategic plan to increase the number of physical spaces available for students and staff and as a result of a merger with Central Queensland Institute of Technical and Further Education (CQ TAFE). To date, CQU has 24 delivery sites (campuses, distance study centres, and partner study hubs) in five Australian states, servicing around 38,000 students in local and distance arrangements (Pilbara Institute 2014). Under the current strategic plan, the Vice-Chancellor, Scott Bowman (Personal Communication 10 July 2015), plans to increase the number of delivery sites by 5–6 each year. The motivation behind this significant expansion was prompted by a need to increase productivity, to become a more attractive option for potential students and to improve community and industry partnership opportunities. Hence, CQU reflects many of the current global trends occurring in higher education institutions, such as: move to greater financial independence, taking on a corporate business-like approach, greater emphasis on measurable accountability from staff, introduction of more vocational degrees, employment of industry-based rather than research-based staff, and greater use of new technologies to enhance teaching flexibility and delivery.

Nagy and Burch (2009) identify two unique differences that explain the pronounced trend to corporatise higher education in Australia. Firstly, higher education in Australia is relatively young, with its first university established in 1850 (The University of Sydney 2015). Hence Australia does not have the history of patronage and heritage tradition apparent in North America and Western Europe. Secondly, Australian universities provide education to a relatively small yet geographically diverse population in the Asian-Pacific region.

In addition to these global differences, the multi-campus nature of CQU sets it apart from other universities within Australia. In this multi-campus working environment, professional and academic staff are likely to find themselves working with an array of technical and administrative systems which presents unique challenges to staff in general, let alone new staff who are just beginning their journey.

To give an example of the magnitude of changes experienced within CQU, within the first author's (EC) discipline area only, in 2011, five experienced academics were lecturing into the Bachelor of Occupational Health and Safety (BOHS). In 2015 the BOHS is taught by one experienced academic (20 years+) and 7 new staff members (with 1–4 years of experience at CQU) and 3 fractional appointments (each with less than 1 year experience at CQU). Most of the new staff are from industry rather than from academia. To further complicate matters, the 11 staff are spread across 7 different locations including one who resides in the United Kingdom. The significant growth and geographical spread is shared with many discipline areas at CQU, especially the newly added vocational degrees. It is easy to see the challenges new staff are likely to face, particularly in their first year as they make sense of their new role and learn how to work within existing university systems. The context of diminishing opportunities for collegial exchanges provides a strong rationale for introducing CoPs.

Communities of Practice have only recently been introduced into Australian universities. CQU established their first set of CoPs in 2009 and currently accommodate 15 individual CoPs as at the start of 2015. The driving force for introducing CoPs at CQU initially developed from a recognition that corporatisation in modern universities is increasingly alienating staff from participating in collegiality and collaborative pursuits in decision making and CoPs provided a means for reconnecting staff within their own terms of reference (Reaburn and McDonald 2015). Quiggin (2001) offers that university reforms towards private corporations is more pronounced in Australia. Peter Reaburn, the CoP founder and driver for CoPs at CQU states that the purpose of CoPs at CQU 'is a way of bringing together both academic and professional staff across disciplines, schools, faculties and divisions to share practice and learn from each other in a collegial and collaborative way' (Reaburn and McDonald 2015, p. xxx).

The creation of and participation in CoPs at CQU is encouraged by management and is financially supported. Each CoP has a personally chosen mentor and CoP advocate from the Vice Chancellor's Advisory Council who acts as a link to senior leadership in the university. Financial support is funded by the Learning and Teaching Directorate. However, CoPs can focus on any topic that supports the enhancement of university practice. Financial support provides for a dedicated CoP administration officer, catering costs, and costs associated with guest presenters or workshops. Each CoP is facilitated by a champion, a term given to denote CoP facilitators/conveners/leaders and to distinguish CoPs from other group types within the university.

23.4.2 New Staff CoP Initiation

CoPs at CQU represent both grass-roots (those created by the members) and strategic (those established to achieve a strategic purpose for the university) categories. The *New Staff CoP* is a grass-roots CoP that emerged from the common desire of a group of new staff to learn university systems and process. In line with Social Learning theory and the proven efficacy of CoPs, it is therefore anticipated that the benefits from this new CoP will improve university practice for both the individuals and collectively for the university in general.

The catalyst for establishing the New Staff CoP occurred during the CQU Foundation Day in June 2013. At this time many new staff were being employed just prior to (and in some cases after) the academic term had commenced. This possibly prompted a heightened awareness and need to quickly become familiar with university systems. After initial enquires from the group as to whether a CoP could be established for new staff, I (first author EC) volunteered to look into the possibility. Unbeknownst to me (EC), a cascade of activity commenced which catapulted me into a leadership role and creation of the CoP a few months later.

As a new staff member myself, the prospect of taking on additional responsibilities was quite daunting. However, the phone call from the overarching champion at CQU, was so warm and empowering, that my (EC) decision to take on the challenge as CoP champion came with the knowledge that I would be supported by a passionate leader. Around the same time the New Staff CoP was being considered, CQU was completing a major restructure and refocusing process. This resulted in the establishment of five core values, namely: engagement, leadership, a can-do approach, inclusiveness, and openness (Central Queensland University 2014). It was against this backdrop that the New Staff CoP was created.

23.4.3   Taking the First Steps

The first step towards the establishment of the New Staff CoP had already been taken, that is, the recognition that a need existed and that this need could be met through social learning. In this particular case, new staff identified the challenge of learning university systems and processes. Once sanctioned by the overarching CoP champion, the New Staff CoP was officially established at CQU.

The second step involved taking the initiative to start and facilitate (champion) the CoP. After an initial conversation with the leader of CoP champions, an email arrived containing seminal pieces of information: membership to the university's *MetaCoP*, the CoP for CoP champions; contact details for CoPs' administration support person, and a document, entitled: *Top Ten Tips: Creating and Facilitating Communities of Practice (CoPs)* (Reaburn et al. 2014). As the remaining steps were taken, the Top Ten Tips[TTT] for creating and facilitating CoPs was followed and these will be identified (i.e. [TTT1], [TTT2], [TTT3], etc.) as the rest of the journey unfolds. The *Top Ten Tips: Creating and Facilitating CoPs* are as follows:

- Select a domain name (title) for your CoP[TTT1]
- Make contact with the existing CoP network[TTT2]
- Make personal approaches to potential CoP participants[TTT3]
- Call your first meeting and create a relaxed atmosphere[TTT4]
- Lock in the calendar of meeting dates early[TTT5]
- Have a speaker for every meeting[TTT6]
- Engage every participant in every meeting[TTT7]
- Be patient and flexible and consider working with a fellow co-champion[TTT8]
- Have outcomes and share success[TTT9]
- Maintain regular contact[TTT10].

The third step was to select an appropriate domain name[TTT1], a title for the CoP that expressed the unique quality of the CoP. It was clear at the University Foundations Day that the common interest amongst the new staff was that they (both academic and professional) were in need of familiarization with their working environment. Therefore, it was decided to make the CoP available to both professional and academic staff. In the spirit of aligning with the universities values, it was felt that the blended membership would reflect an attitude of *inclusiveness* which it was thought would promote improved collaboration between the two staffing groups. Hence, the CoP title agreed upon would become the New Staff CoP.

The fourth step involved connecting with the existing CoP network[TTT2]. Participation at a *MetaCoP* session provided the first author (EC) with guidance on how a CoP session is run. Notable were the relaxed atmosphere, respect and inclusiveness of each participant, and flexible manner in which the session progressed[TTT4].

The fifth step was to make personal approaches to potential CoP participants[TTT3]. This was a little more difficult from the perspective of a new staff member with a limited network. However, all new staff who attended the University Foundations Day were contacted and informed that the New Staff CoP would be holding its first session before the end of the year. From this group, a professional staff member agreed to co-champion the CoP with the first author (EC). In addition to this, a list of new staff within 6 months of employment was generated to form a prospective membership list. This list was extensive, and comprised 380 individuals.

The sixth step involved planning for the first session and consideration of a guest speaker[TTT6]. A document entitled: *The Great Guide for CQUni Staff* was being developed and before its release staff developers were keen to have the document reviewed by those who would be using it. An introduction to this document was perceived to be an appropriate presentation and start for a group of new staff who could only benefit from this review exercise.

The seventh step came from a university directive to establish identifiable outcomes[TTT9] that aligned with CQU's (1) new strategic plan to become the most engaged university by 2020, and (2) initiative to transition from "Strong to Great" which would be reportable to the Vice Chancellor's Advisory Committee. Briefly, CQU's vision is to become one of Australia's great universities through partnerships with industry, students and the community. Engagement will enable these partnerships and be the driving force that directs all university activities.

Ordinarily, the CoP's goals and planned outcomes would be developed by the CoP members and usually during a CoP review or at the first meeting when establishing a new CoP (Parboosingh 2010). However, in this case and in light of expediency, the general aim for the New Staff CoP had been informally agreed upon by interested parties who attended the Foundations Day. While the aim of the CoP was clear, namely to provide a favourable environment whereby new staff could support each other while finding their way at CQU, the assignment of goals that had measureable outcomes was more difficult. Three proposed outcomes were set to align with the university's new strategic plan:

1. To encourage peer-support and mentoring (professional and academic).
2. To reduce university costs accrued from recruitment costs due to staff turnover and costs associated with mentoring new staff.
3. To contribute to the development of the *Great Guide for Staff at CQUniversity* through user experience.

Briefly, CQU's vision is to become one of Australia's great universities through partnerships with industry, students and the community. Engagement will enable these partnerships and be the driving force that directs all university activities. To transition from "Strong to Great" five values were established, namely: engagement, can-do approach, openness, leadership, and inclusiveness (Central Queensland University 2014).

In addition to ensuring CoP activities supported the new direction of the university, the Vice Chancellor's Advisory Committee also requested an outline of how each CoP might address issues related to attrition and retention. This request felt like an attempt to co-opt the new CoP to meet the needs of the university over those of the members. However, a statement was devised that reflected an outcome that supported the needs of the university after the needs of CoP participants were met. The below statement outlines the New Staff CoP's plans to address attrition and retention as noted in the first *New Staff Community of Practice (CoP) Refocusing Plan* for 2014 that was submitted to the committee for approval.

> Attrition and retention are addressed through improved new staff support. Improved system knowledge (e.g. administration, software for internal tasks as well as learning and teaching, academic policies and procedures) is likely to reflect on better services to students. As relationships develop within and external to the CoP, communication and activity between academic and professional staff is likely to be freer flowing and may help to improve university processes that occur between staff and between staff and students. Improved intrapersonal processes may increase time available for communication with students, and an ability to be able to respond more quickly to student needs thus expediting issue resolution. Additional time gained from greater efficiency, may increase the time required to monitor student progress which can help to identify those students at risk and to provide the necessary support in a timely manner. These actions are more likely to encourage students to stay and go on to complete their degrees.

The eighth step involved finding and appointing a CoP mentor. One further outcome from CQU's restructuring process was the need for all activities within CQU to be transparent, including those of CoPs. Therefore, each CoP was required to be overseen (and mentored) by a member of the Vice Chancellor's Advisory Committee. The mentor was to be a Dean of School that shared an interest in the CoP's aims. It is worth noting that while the Deans acted as overseers for the university, they were also important advocates who could act on behalf of their CoPs to ensure higher level decisions did not inadvertently, or intentionally, undermine CoP performance.

The ninth step, and most disconcerting at the time, was to call the first meeting and create a relaxed atmosphere[TTT4]. Official invitations were emailed to all new staff on the prospective membership list (i.e. 380 new staff, as developed in step five), and to the broader university community. The New Staff CoP held its first session on 12th November 2013.

The first meeting was a momentous occasion. Twenty-three staff members attended. The recommended number is 8–12 members (Cox 2004). The session was delivered from Rockhampton ($N = 12$) and connected to staff in Brisbane ($N = 4$), Bundaberg ($N = 2$), Mackay ($N = 1$), Noosa ($N = 2$) and Sydney ($N = 2$). Members attended in meeting rooms on campus as well as from their personal spaces via computers. This blended face-to-face and virtual meeting was achieved through videoconferencing Jabber technology. Recent research indicates that videoconferencing shows promise as an effective means of encouraging collaboration in learning and teaching settings (Groundwater-Smith 2010). The use of collaborative technology is not new to CQU and is well supported.

Most staff attending this first meeting were new to CQU. However, others were not but had taken on new roles within the university. Other attendees were simply curious to learn what this new CoP was all about. Introductions revealed some confusion regarding the purpose of the CoP. Some attendees thought that the CoP was compulsory for all new staff, something akin to an induction. A short discussion followed on the purpose of the CoP with specific mention of its informal, non-compulsory participatory nature and the opportunity for new staff to learn University systems in a non-threatening environment.

Facilitators of CoPs are advised to emulate the behaviour that they desire from members (Ortquist-Ahrens and Torosyan 2009). The arrival of 23 participants at the first session triggered some measure of stress and discomfort. However, this anxiety eased as the session got underway due to the presence of an experienced CoP Administration Officer who confidently made the necessary virtual connects, ensured lunch was available in Rockhampton, and calmly noted participant names as each introduced themselves to the group. At the end of the session, the CoP Admin Officer stated how relaxed she felt the participants were. As a new CoP champion I only felt more relaxed as time went on which I attribute to encouragement and practice. It was a comfort to discover that learning by practice is normal, with (Ortquist-Ahrens and Torosyan 2009) noting that the skills and knowledge associated with facilitating FLCs must be learned through practice.

The presentation on the *Great Guide for Staff* was received enthusiastically. Topics for future sessions were tabled and participants were encouraged to subscribe to the New Staff CoP webpage and continue discussions on topics of interest. Regular lunch time sessions were agreed upon by the members. During the meeting, a major goal was to engage every participant[TTT7]. To ensure all could participate, each member was asked if they had something to contribute to the discussion or wanted to express a concern or need.

The tenth and final step involved locking in the calendar meeting dates early[TTT5]. Outlook invitations served to help participants with time management (Reaburn et al. 2014). At the suggestion of the CoP mentor, it was decided to run monthly sessions to allow for a more frequent opportunity to support. The CoP Administration Officer made the necessary room bookings across the various campuses, which relieved the champions from this administrative duty.

23.5   New Staff CoP Review

To establish some form of baseline for future reference and to stimulate evidence-based progression into the future, the New Staff CoP was evaluated on its effectiveness over the past 12 months. The review process incorporated personal reflections of the first author (EC) and results from a small study that was conducted during December 2014 and January 2015.

23.5.1   Study Aim and Methodology

The aim of the New Staff CoP was to provide a favourable environment to help new staff find their way around systems and processes at CQU. To review whether this aim was met, questions to be answered were:

- Did the CoP provide a favourable environment for learning?
- Did the CoP enable increased understanding of university systems and processes at CQU?
- What lessons were learnt (to inform future offerings)?

An online survey tool was developed to explore perceptions of how well the New Staff CoP met the needs of participants. Aside from demographic questions, survey respondents were asked to rate their level of agreement to a list of 17 statements according to a 5-point Likert scale to identify aspects they enjoyed most from a list of possible choices. Open ended questions were included to provide an opportunity for participants to make additional comments.

23.5.2   Study Results and Discussion

Over the first 12 months since the New Staff CoP held its first session, a total of 78 individuals participated in at least one New Staff CoP session. This number represents: a CoP administrator, a CoP mentor, two CoP co-champions, and ten guest speakers. The remaining 64 members represented both professional and academic staff and two teaching staff from the vocational education and training (VET) sector. Members connected into the meetings from the following locations: Brisbane, Bundaberg, Cairns, Gladstone, Mackay, Melbourne, Noosa, Rockhampton, and Sydney. Most members were from Rockhampton, as is reflective of the higher proportion of staff numbers who work out of this campus.

Of the 68 individuals who were invited to participate in this study, 17 completed the survey, representing a 25 % response rate. This response rate only represents a quarter of the membership and therefore the results cannot be assumed to reflect the opinions of all CoPs participants. However, the results do provide the perceptions of a quarter of the members and serve as a useful base-line to suggest a direction for studies in the future.

Of those who responded, 53 % were academic staff and 47 % were professional staff. Within the academic cohort was representation from teaching, research and VET directorates. Respondents' mean length of employment at CQU was 11 months, ranged between 3 and 65 months and included staff who were contracted on continuing full-time, continuing part-time and yearly or sessional contracts.

In the study, participants were asked to rate their level of agreement, to 17 statements that indicate perceived benefits to members. Participants were asked to rate their opinions according to a 5-point Likert scale: 1 = highly agree, 2 = agree, 3 = neutral, 4 = disagree, and 5 = strongly disagree. Results showed that across all 17 statements, on average (Mean scores reported) academic respondents perceived greater benefits overall (M = 2.14, agree) than their professional counterparts who were less convinced (M = 2.71, almost neutral). These results could have resulted from the choice of topics presented and discussed which may have supported academic work more than that of professional staff. However, between two groups (academic and professional), the results indicate close consistency of opinion for all 17 statements. Note that, due to the small sample size, statistical significance is not sought.

The highest rated perceived benefit by respondents was that they felt supported. The next highest rated benefits were that respondents felt the CoP helped them increase total effectiveness as a staff member, increased their understanding and awareness of university systems and processes, achieved a heightened awareness and understanding of the various staff roles at CQU, and increased their general enthusiasm about their role (teaching or professional) at CQU. Table 23.1, shows the complete list of statements as rated by respondents with the associated average score across all survey respondents. The lowest rated statement 'Fast track work capability in general' received an average score of 2.88, indicating that the level of agreement by most respondents was slightly agreed with.

Comments provided by survey respondents support that participation in the CoP had a positive influence on member learning efficiency. Furthermore, comments made reflect the presence and effectiveness of the three essential elements of CoPs. Below are some of the comments made by participants to illustrate the aspects respondents felt helped them to transition into their new role:

Domain knowledge—Highlight key systems, contacts and information

- *By targeting some key and relevant university systems and* processes (Participant 1, academic)
- *I learnt more about who to contact for stuff* (Participant 10, academic)
- *It gave me a great feel for the high priority areas I needed to come to grips with* (Participant 11, professional)
- *Easier to find relevant information* (Participant 14, academic)

Table 23.1 Aspects of the New Staff CoP that helped members most to least

Rating	Statement	Mean
1	Felt supported	2.0
2	Increased total effectiveness as a staff member	2.06
3	Increased understanding and awareness of university systems and processes	2.12
3	Achieved a heightened awareness and understanding of the various staff roles at CQU	2.12
3	Increased my general enthusiasm about my role (teaching or professional) at CQU	2.12
4	Heightened awareness of who to contact for various purposes	2.18
5	Develop a sense of community with staff at CQU	2.29
6	Achieved heightened appreciation of professional practice	2.35
6	Increase comfort and confidence in my role as a staff member of CQU	2.35
6	Provide better quality of service to students	2.35
7	Increased reflection on and about my professional practice	2.41
8	Developed a community of colleagues who continue outside CoP meetings as an informal support system	2.65
9	Successfully complete work tasks	2.71
9	Contributed to activities designed to improve university services	2.71
10	Increase technical skills required for my job	2.82
10	Become more involved in university non-work related activities	2.82
11	Fast track work capability in general	2.88

Sharing of practice—Allowance for timely discussions

- *Interactive real time discussions* (Participant 2, professional)
- *Relevant and timely discussion with other new staff members* (Participant 6, professional)

Community—Provision of a 'safe' environment to learn

- *The ability to ask questions away from my particular school* (Participant 7, academic).

23.5.3 Did the CoP Provide a Favourable Environment for Learning?

In answering the first question regarding whether the CoP provided a favourable environment for learning, all the ratings from respondents were considered. Of those who participated in the study, most agreed with all 17 statements in the survey, indicating that they benefited from the CoP. When asked to indicate the most valuable aspect about the CoP, survey respondents rated the area of shared knowledge most highly. The overall responses are shown in Table 23.2.

Table 23.2 Aspects most liked about the New Staff CoP

No.	Reason	Respondents[a]
1	Sharing of knowledge	11
2	Discussions	10
3	The presentations	8
4	Opportunity to ask questions	7
5	Learning; supportive environment	6
6	Opportunity to network	4
7	Feeling of belonging; opportunity to review University documents and websites	3
8	Collaboration; lunch time meetings; common interest	2
9	Regularity of monthly meetings; meeting layout	1

[a]Multiple responses allowed from a total of 17 respondents

23.5.4 Did the CoP Enable Increased Understanding of University Systems and Processes at CQU?

Respondents overall indicated that the CoP did provide a vehicle for improving their understanding of university systems and processes. Below the top rated statement 'Felt supported' in Table 23.1, members rated statements relating to domain knowledge next highest: 'Increased total effectiveness as a staff member', 'Increased understanding and awareness of university systems and processes', 'Achieved a heightened awareness and understanding of the various staff roles at CQU'.

Results indicate that respondents were motivated to come together because of a common interest in a particular domain. The opportunity of being part of a community and the desire for sharing of practice were secondary motivations. However, the most enjoyed aspect of their participation was the opportunity to share practice.

23.5.5 Discussion of Lessons Learned

Upon reflection by the first author (EC), a number of further comments are shared in the following paragraphs regarding: member participation, meeting the needs of participants with different needs, and being new to CoP facilitation.

23.5.5.1 Member Participation

Study results showed that there was a core group of about five individuals who participated in at least half of the CoP sessions. However, 49 of the 68 members only attended one CoP session. This aspect of the CoP was difficult to manage as

Table 23.3 Types of membership roles as identified by members

Role	Leader	Peer supporter	Passive	Intermittent	Active	Receiver of knowledge	Giver of knowledge
Current	0	1	7	9	2	6	0
Future	0	2 (one maybe)	0	1	1 (maybe)	0	0

Participants could indicate more than one descriptor

each session required the learning of new member names and their particular needs. Also, thoughts on why staff did not continue their participation were worrying, and this led to feelings of failure as a facilitator from the first author (EC). However, encouragingly, for the facilitator (EC), all members who attended CoP sessions actively engaged in discussions post presentation.

Results from the study, regarding preferred engagement show that passive and intermittent engagement is preferred, as illustrated in Table 23.3 and by the comments made by participants regarding future involvement.

New staff may be reluctant to take on extra work, due to feeling overwhelmed with having to learn new systems and processes on top of their individual workloads. The following comments made in the survey support this view:

- *The volume of tasks included in my role increased on 14 Dec 2014. I do not expect to be able to participate in future* (Participant 12, academic).
- *Limited time so may not participate in the future* (Participant 9, academic).
- *Because I am new to everything* (Participant 8, professional).
- *I would like to be invited to a few additional future sessions* (Participant 14, academic).

The passive participation evident by New Staff CoP members could be reflecting a tendency to hold back until trust within the CoP is developed. Lave and Wenger (1991) suggest that peripheral participation is a legitimate way in which individuals learn, and a fuller participation relies on developing a sense of identity with the group.

The advice provided in the Top Ten Tips number 8 (Reaburn et al. 2014) is to 'use the collective wisdom of the CoP to decide the direction and activities the CoP want to engage in'. However, as indicated in the comments, new staff are time poor and this may be negatively influencing their willingness to participate. One of the driving forces for CoP participation is that members value their involvement and desire to be involved and have an interest in learning together (Wenger et al. 2002). Some ways to encourage future engagement are to ensure CoP activities are of value to the participants, and that the activities allow for genuine enquiry and deeper exploration (Ortquist-Ahrens and Torosyan 2009). Ortquist-Ahrens and Torosyan (2009), offer five essential elements that encourage collaboration for learning that are applicable to supporting new staff to find their way:

1. Take full advantage of different people's strengths;
2. Members are to be responsible and responsive to supporting one another's growth and development;
3. Each member is to be accountable for contributing to the team;
4. Members need to develop skills that help with small-group work; and
5. Periodically step back to consider and assess the work of the group in terms of outcomes and processes.

In taking this advice on board, New Staff CoP members could be given more responsibility for managing the topics presented, and for sourcing expert presenters. One of the benefits from this exercise is that it is likely to improve the individuals networking circle as internal experts are sought.

Another way to encourage member involvement is to share potential benefits that well-functioning mature CoPs might display and to ask participants to identify characteristics that exemplify maturity and success (Parboosingh 2010). Unfortunately, for members of the New Staff CoP, a sign of success is to reach the point that participation in the CoP is no longer relevant. How then can a CoP for new staff mature? Is the New Staff CoP by definition self-limiting? And if so, what can be learnt from these experiences in terms of supporting new staff? These issues are discussed later in the chapter.

23.5.5.2 Meeting the Needs of Participants with Different Needs

A challenge emerged half way through the year when newer participants began requesting topics that had already been covered earlier in the year, as expressed by Participant 7 in the survey:

- *I know you have covered great topics—however these were before I started—can you repeat some of these topics or record the sessions?* (Participant 7, academic).

This presents a dilemma for group cohesion and development of group maturity. The recommendation for sessions to be recorded is also difficult to address. While members may miss presentations that were delivered before they commenced at CQU, recorded sessions may discourage open discussion and may undermine the 'safe' and favourable learning environment that non-recorded sessions promote. One way to manage this was to direct members to session notes located on the CoP portal. An important lesson learned is to ensure new staff are provided information about the CoP portal, the documents available and instructions on how to subscribe to the discussion forum.

23.5.5.3 New to CoP Facilitation

At CQU the CoP facilitator is called a CoP champion. This is an apt title as it helps to distinguish a CoP from other types of groups at the university. Effective facilitation has been said to be at the heart of successful CoPs. Unlike the word's Latin root (facilis meaning 'easy'), facilitation is far from easy. Rather, the challenge to being an effective facilitator is to make the process easy for the members to work together to define and achieve shared goals (Ortquist-Ahrens and Torosyan 2009, p. 32). Experience as a CoP champion over the past 12 months has been challenging. Ortquist-Ahrens and Torosyan (2009) found that one of the pitfalls in facilitation is the tendency to take on a prescriptive role which can result in the work being charted out for the year leading to reduced flexibility, reduced meaningful activities for members and a lost sense of group ownership and commitment by members. The first author (EC) did fall into this trap.

Towards the middle of the year work commitments became overwhelming for the first author (EC). Around the same time, the co-champion left the university and the social support from this relationship left a void. Out of a desire to become more efficient, expert presentations were organised for the remainder of the year. While this improved efficiency, the action may have contributed to the high staff turnover and needs of current members may not have been met. It is encouraging to note that to be an effective CoP facilitator takes practice (Ortquist-Ahrens and Torosyan 2009). To support CoP champions at CQU, a CoP for CoP champions (i.e. MetaCoP) has been established and is facilitated by an experienced champion. This provides social learning opportunities for developing proficient CoP facilitators. This practice is highly recommended for any organisation when establishing new CoPs.

23.5.6 Conclusion

Results from this study indicate that CoP members who participated in the study found their participation in the New Staff CoP a beneficial experience and that their needs were mostly met. The most beneficial aspects of the New Staff CoP as indicated by respondents reflect the three essential elements of CoPs (i.e. *community*, *domain knowledge*, *sharing of practice*). Respondents agreed most highly that they felt supported (an element of *community*), and that they gained increased understanding and awareness of university systems and processes (an element of *domain knowledge*). Results also show that respondents enjoyed the element of *sharing practice* as the most enjoyable aspect of the participation experience, that is, the sharing of knowledge and discussions. Lessons learnt were shared for consideration for future offerings of the CoP. The following section provides a discussion of three core issues that emerged during the CoPs first 12 months of being.

23.5.7 Discussion on Three Core Issues

From this review, three core issues emerged, namely: (1) tension between meeting the needs of the members and being required to meet the needs of the university;

(2) issues with nurturing and sustaining a CoP where members were located at significant distances from each other in multiple locations; and (3) the potentially inherent issues with a CoP for new staff that is by definition self-limiting. Each of these issues is discussed and how these concerns were managed is shared.

23.5.7.1 Tension Between Needs of Grass-Roots CoPs and Institutions

As mentioned during the step taking process of establishing the New Staff CoP, the first meeting (step nine) had a rather confused group of individuals in attendance. Included in the group was a member of the university's People and Culture Directorate (e.g. similar to Human Relations Departments). This individual had extended great efforts to set up the Professional Development Training Program for the entire university and became quite animated due to the perception that the New Staff CoP was going to replace her well designed training plan. It was explained that the New Staff CoP was an informal forum for new staff to learn from each other and experts on selected topics and only intended to supplement, not replace, formal training. To help ensure the misunderstanding did not escalate, the New Staff CoP mentor (i.e. senior member of the university and CoP advocate) stepped into assure the staff member that CoPs were not in competition and to guard against potential future conflict.

Another factor contributing to tension is that CoPs can be co-opted to meet university needs rather than those of their members and, as explained earlier, staff are required to align with the university's new strategic direction. One of the key values is openness and transparency. The necessity to develop outcomes that demonstrate alignment with university goals is a form of management involvement that could begin to interfere with the core purpose of CoPs if greater demands are placed on the CoP in the guise of proving their worth. Parboosingh (2010) recommends handling management intervention with great care as this has been found to hamper or destroy CoPs. Parboosingh (2010) affirms the importance of reaching a delicate balance between member needs and organisational needs, and suggests that the primary value of participating in a CoP should be participant centred with a focus on their learning, meaning and identify, while value to the group and university leaders should be secondary. Parboosingh (2010) further asserts that CoPs are not part of an organisation's human relations program. Furthermore, McDermott (1999) offers that if CoPs become overly formal, they can turn into bureaucratic structures, that require documentation to keep a record of the CoPs 'official story'.

Therefore, CoP and institutional tensions can be resolved through mutual respect. From a CoP facilitator's point of view, it is important to recognise that CoPs need the support of the organisation to survive and therefore all CoP activities should not undermine the values of the university. Furthermore, alignment to the university's strategic direction is also important for organisational progress. However, the university's strategic direction should not drive the CoP's activities. Any attempts to co-opt CoPs into meeting needs other than their own, need to be addressed immediately to avoid escalation of the problem. The support of a powerful advocate who holds an influential position amongst senior decision makers can help to resolve problems such as these.

CoP Alignment with University Values as a Secondary Concern

It is important to illustrate how the New Staff CoP maintained alignment with CQU's values without allowing them to drive CoP decision making. Aspects of the CoP's significance were aligned to university values rather than fitting CoP actions around university values. The following alignment examples illustrate how the university values were maintained with the newly proposed CoP.

Leadership has been demonstrated by taking the initiative through the establishment a CoP that aims to support new staff as they find their way at CQU.

Engagement and inclusiveness has been demonstrated in that membership to the New Staff CoP provides an opportunity for staff of all types to engage internally. Furthermore, participation promotes the development of strong relationships that deliver mutually beneficial outcomes.

A can-do approach has been demonstrated through staff participation and by taking ownership of our own learning, through peer sharing and peer support. Inclusiveness has been exercised in that the CoP is open to all staff whether academic, professional, research or more recently from the VET sector. Furthermore, every staff member, whether full-time or sessional, with a desire to participate in CoP activities was welcomed.

Openness has been demonstrated by ensuring processes are transparent. Such actions include: posting session notes which are made available to all staff on the CoP portal; the provision of CoP annual reports to the Vice-Chancellor; by sharing CoP experiences with MetaCoP members; having a group mentor from the Vice-Chancellor's Advisory Committee overseeing individual CoP activities; and by sharing success stories with each other and with the university. Furthermore, one of the important aspects of the New Staff CoP was the provision of a non-threatening environment so that members could openly share experiences and concerns. This openness within a group can only occur in an environment of trust and respect, and thus has major emphasis in the CoP's support for social learning.

23.5.7.2   Nurturing and Sustaining CoPs at Distance

Establishing and sustaining a CoP across multiple locations, as is the case at CQU, can present challenges to overcoming issues of participation, power and decision making. Increased distance between staff is one of the issues associated with diminishing social exchange opportunities amongst staff in higher education. Furthermore, distance can significantly impact member participation, their power to make useful social exchanges and collective decision making for CoP activities and direction. One way to bring staff together in a fair manner is through virtual meetings. A further advantage is that internal expert presenters can also join these sessions which removes the barriers of time and travel.

However, technical problems, such as delayed access to the group, and intermittent connectivity can significantly undermine the effectiveness of discussions, dictate who can attend, who therefore benefits, and the ability to achieve collective decision making. To overcome the tyranny of distance that can be exacerbated by technical problems the following solutions used at CQU are shared.

To make it easy for members to participate, CQU supports CoPs with reliable technical support, in the form of virtual meeting spaces, software availability (e.g. Cisco Jabber) for personal and work computers, and help to trouble-shoot problems if and when they arise. Furthermore, the university assistance from a dedicated CoP administrator meant that room bookings and the scheduling of room connections were expertly accomplished. Furthermore, the collaboration with a co-facilitator can help to ensure decisions are member driven. New Staff CoP facilitators utilised an online survey (e.g. Survey Monkey) which allowed CoP facilitators to gather and collate member needs and preferences to ensure collective decision making could occur.

One further point to consider, is the suggestion by McDermott (1999) that before groups can effectively collaborate in virtual environments, they first need to build a relationship and these relationships are often best developed through face-to-face meetings. This did not seem to be the case for the New Staff CoP. However, the CoPs inception was born out of a group of new staff who were at the time located gathered together in one room during a staff Orientation day, and therefore, support to McDermott's view is unclear but worth consideration.

23.5.7.3   The Self-Limiting Nature of CoPs for New Staff Or Is It?

Reflection on the effectiveness of the New Staff CoP led the authors to contemplate whether a CoP for new staff could actually mature considering it had a 'revolving door' membership where new staff came and went throughout the year. This resulted in some already addressed needs resurfacing and the CoP champion had a sense of 'not getting anywhere'. Furthermore, although participants identified as 'new staff', their intention was not to stay 'new' and prolonged membership may have not been desired from the start. Therefore, the nature of a CoP for new staff is self-limiting as its domain name suggests and it may not reach a form of maturity.

In describing the phases that CoPs pass through, Reaburn and McDonald (2015) state that the 'maturing and sustaining phase' is reached when the CoP has an established identity and is demonstrating benefits to both CoP members and the university. Furthermore, the placing of the terms 'maturing' and 'sustaining' together, gives the notion that a CoP matures over time. In regards to this description, the New Staff CoP had matured, as participating members did align with the CoP's identity which was focused around the goal of improving knowledge and practice of university systems.

Table 23.4 Member stages of maturity

Stage	Actions
Awareness	The stage in which members recognise a need and that a CoP can meet personal needs and attend their first CoP session
Development	The stage in which members begin to learn what they do not know, or what they need to know. Participation is usually passive and learning often occurs from the periphery
Growth	The stage in which members learn new knowledge. Evidence of growth is realised when members begin to ask questions and actively seek new knowledge in discussions. Evidence may also be realised in improved practice
Focused adventure	The stage where members contribute to the creation of new knowledge by sharing practice and by applying their knowledge to another's situation
Maturing	The stage when members continue to participate in knowledge work (sharing and creating) and take on roles of greater leadership within the CoP (i.e. mentoring, facilitating, identifying needs within the group, etc.)
Celebration	The stage whereby members recognise progress and achievement. It is a time when members move on, signalling a time to celebrate and an end of their involvement

While staff joined the CoP with varying degrees of ability, most participated to learn what the expert presenter had to say. Therefore, sharing of practice was primarily led not by the members, but by the expert presenters. Topics for discussion were owned by the members, and some discussion and sharing of practice did occur amongst members, as staff began to make greater sense of what their role required them to know and do. However, it is our opinion that, without the expert presentations, it is unclear as to whether the CoP could be self-perpetuating, an attribute identified to be a strength of CoPs (Wenger and Snyder 2000).

Upon further reflection, the authors began to appreciate that members individually progress through stages of maturity (The Swiss Agency for Development and Cooperation 2011). So, while the CoP as an entity may mature as far as its facilitation, development of new knowledge, decision making and process goes, individual members also go through a maturing process. These stages of member maturity: awareness, development, growth, focused adventure, maturing and celebration, are outlined in Table 23.4.

Therefore, celebration occurs for individuals as each member no longer identifies with the group. The CoP for new staff is automatically self-perpetuating provided new staff continue to be employed. It is useful for CoP facilitators to appreciate this difference and to encourage maturing members to take on roles of leadership within the group, so that newer staff might benefit from the sharing of practice of less recently employed staff and hence expedite the creation of tacit knowledge as it relates to newer members.

23.6 Future Direction for the New Staff CoP

Based on the 12 month review, this section outlines some aspects that the New Staff CoP did well and will maintain for future offerings, as well as a list of changes to enhance CoP effectiveness in the future. Aspects to maintain and aspects that represent changes in the lists are provided below and are in no particular order.

23.6.1 Aspects to Maintain

- Maintain co-facilitation.
- For 2015, the New Staff CoP will be co-facilitated by three staff members to achieve both academic and professional representation.
- Continue membership for all staff types (i.e. professional, academic, from both university and vocational education and training sectors).
- Continue to encourage sharing and learning between members.
- Continue to align with the values and strategic direction of the university in an explicit way (i.e. engagement, leadership, can-do approach, inclusiveness and openness).
- Continue to invite expert presenters on topics of interest to members.
- Maintain a relaxed environment by avoiding strict committee-like processes.
- Continue to make attendance easy by organising lunch time sessions, reminder emails and calendar confirmations with sessions set at the same time each month to help members remember, i.e. every second Thursday at 12–1 p.m. each month.
- Continue to align with university values and strategic direction.
- Continue to draw on university support, both financial and technical.
- Contribute to the improvement of CoPs in higher education by reviewing the effectiveness of the CoP each year and publishing lessons learned so that others who are or wish to be involved in CoPs in higher education can benefit and make improvements.

23.6.2 Aspects that will Change

- Increase CoP awareness by sharing progress and achievements more openly with colleagues.
- Increase involvement and profile of core members, those that are active participants within the CoP and whose abilities are maturing.
- Review membership needs, CoP progress, and CoP facilitation more frequently (i.e. quarterly) to ensure member needs drive CoP actions.
- Share and encourage facilitation tasks across co-champions.

- Celebrate more frequently the small success stories, or accomplishments made within the group, to help build collective appreciation.
- Recognise the level of maturity that members may be at and aim to meet all needs (i.e. encourage more mature members to share practice).
- Connect more with members outside of CoP sessions to develop relationships further than CoP 'business' to build a greater sense of community.
- Alternate member needs to promote continued interest.
- When new staff join, send a follow up email with instructions on how to subscribe to the New Staff CoP discussion forum, and link them to pertinent documentation and help that has already been identified throughout the year.

23.7 Guidance for Creating Similar CoPs

Based on the lessons learned shared in this chapter, the following guidance is provided for anyone interested in creating a CoP similar to the one created for new staff at CQU. Advice is given on three areas deemed important to the success of CoPs by the authors. The areas addressed are: (1) establish the value of CoPs in higher education, (2) develop CoP facilitation skills, and (3) be flexible, patient and learn.

23.7.1 Establish the Value of CoPs in Higher Education

Organisations that understand the purpose for CoPs are more likely to value and therefore support and allow CoPs to function in a manner desirable to members. The New Staff CoP was supported by the university in a number of ways. Financial support was provided by the Office of Learning and Teaching. This support funded the assistance of a CoP administration officer who relieved the champion (facilitator) from a number of logistical chores, such as room bookings, lunch orders, maintenance of membership lists, taking notes, sending through session notices and organising and enabling virtual meeting connections.

Furthermore, funding was made available so that experts external to the university might visit and present pertinent topics to CoPs. Additionally, internal expert presenters were encouraged to take up invitations, and this activity could be used as evidence of internal engagement, one of CQU's performance indicators for staff members. Technical support was also provided that enabled members to participate as one group but from many locations. Virtual meeting spaces and requisite technology were provided, along with trouble shooting should connection problems occur.

To assist senior management to better understand the value and nature of CoPs the following recommendations are made: *Openly promote CoPs.* To build wider awareness of what CoPs are all about take every opportunity to spread the word about CoPs. Personally invite people you think may be interested to pertinent sessions. One of the Top Ten Tips for establishing and facilitating CoPs (document distributed at CQU) is to openly celebrate success. This is a good way to help members of the university understand the benefits of CoPs. This can be done in both formal and informal ways. Formally, achievements could be shared in school/department newsletters, in the university news, or by nominating for an award as the New Staff CoP had. Alternatively, awareness can be delivered via conversations in office corridors and email to colleagues. Another successful practice at CQU is the annual event, open to all staff, whereby CoP facilitators showcase their CoPs. Try to utilise every opportunity possible. The first author (EC) will soon be showcasing the New Staff CoP at the New Staff Orientation Day to build staff awareness of the CoP's existence and to extend a personal invitation to new staff.

23.7.2 Develop CoP Facilitation Skills

Be comforted to know that good facilitation takes practice: As defined by Reaburn and McDonald (2015), the role of CoPs is to provide a way to bring individuals together who would not otherwise meet, to share practice and to learn from each other in a collegial and collaborative way. Therefore, it is the role of the facilitator to uphold this ethos through genuine respect and acceptance of others and appreciation of the collective (Ortquist-Ahrens and Torosyan 2009). As Cox (2004) offered, the facilitator must help members feel safe and cultivate an environment of trust, responsiveness and genuine collaboration. Furthermore, the facilitator will need to ensure topics of discussion and activities are relevant, and that members become empowered from their participation. This can seem like a tall order and can be challenging. However, it is also comforting to know that good facilitation takes practice, that it is different from being a committee chair or project group manager, and that it is easy to slip into these more well-known roles. Therefore, it is recommended that new facilitators of CoPs be given support in three ways:

Provide clear and condensed guidance on how to facilitate. Ortquist-Ahrens and Torosyan (2009) point out that university staff are often too time poor to delve deeply into the literature. At CQU, a short one page guidance sheet is provided to new CoP champions in the form of Ten Top Tips. See the chapter from Reaburn and McDonald in this book for a copy of this guidance.

Establish a mentoring system. One very efficient way to help new CoP facilitators (called champions at CQU) is by establishing a CoP designed for CoP champions. At CQU a MetaCoP has been established for knowledge sharing and knowledge creation on CoP facilitation. Sessions are facilitated by CQU's CoP founder, an experienced CoP facilitator. This practice has been found very helpful by the authors and provides an opportunity for facilitation growth through discussion and through observation, actually seeing how someone more experienced approaches the role. It is also helpful to attend other CoPs to observe different styles that may suit you better.

Co-facilitate. There are advantages to sharing the task of facilitation, whether amongst members or with another facilitator/s. The authors have found co-facilitation very useful for a number of reasons. One is that the co-facilitator can help you take stock of your own practice, a form of audit and opportunity to improve. Additionally, a co-facilitator can be someone to bounce ideas off, to share decision making to ensure a focus is on the good of the collective membership. Another advantage of co-facilitation is the added support another person can give, particularly during times of doubt or frustration.

23.7.3 Be Flexible, Patient and Learn

Accept that CoPs have their ups and downs. One of the lessons learnt over the past 12 months is that facilitating CoPs is an emotional experience. At times, the CoP can be energising, as members actively participate and readily respond to each other's needs. At other times, the CoP can feel like it is going nowhere and its longevity or facilitation comes into question. An important lesson for CoP facilitators is to realise that CoPs naturally have a lifecycle. There will be times when growth occurs and times when this growth slows down. However, the CoP will eventually come to a natural end at which point the CoP or focus will be phased out, this stage being one of celebration or reorientation (Swiss Agency of Development and Cooperation 2011). The maturity of a CoP for new staff may be reflected more in its members than in the CoP's domain. This is one of those inherently self-limiting aspects of a CoP for new staff. As new staff begin to grasp the various systems and processes, their knowledge base matures, at which time they may make the decision to no longer participate. During the CoPs development, relationships are built and when members leave the group, there can be feelings of loss which can be emotionally trying for the facilitator. Ways to resolve potential concerns as a result of membership turnover, or feelings that the CoP is not maturing are as follows:

Remain flexible. Remember the CoP's direction is led by the members and you are there to be more like a 'director of traffic' and listener than a presenter or leader (Ortquist-Ahrens and Torosyan 2009). Regularly review whether the needs of current members are being met. Encourage regular members to take on leadership roles that give them added meaning and a recognised profile, such as: sharing the CoP facilitation, asking them for help to monitor and respond to queries on the discussion forum, or to source expert presenters.

Live and learn within the CoP. Remember you are also a member and the needs of the collective are the focus. So enjoy the experience, participate, share and help create new knowledge.

Do not take lack of attendance personally. As members leave and new ones replace them, treat this as a sign of success that the departing member has reached maturity. Regularly remind the group what has been learned and the topics that have been discussed, so that the progress of the members can be celebrated.

Take note of who is coming before you meet. One difficulty with a high membership turnover is the constant need to get to know the members. One tip is to gather a list of those who have acknowledged their attendance. At CQU the CoP administrator provides this. Before the CoP session, take a few moments to familiarise yourself with their names. New staff are not likely to have staff profiles set up, so facial familiarity may not be possible. Nevertheless, the experience of the first author (EC) is that familiarity with a person's name can help you remember who the person is when you meet.

23.8   Conclusion

Economic and government pressures are influencing changes in the operational nature of higher education institutions. For new university staff, tacit knowledge can have a significant influence on how they adapt to their new working environment. However, the creation of tacit knowledge developed between staff members is increasingly challenged by reduced social interactions due to greater distances between staff, less available time, and reduced willingness for staff to participate in collegial and collaborative activities.

As a result of diminishing social learning opportunities, researchers of higher education are finding that creativity and sharing is often inhibited and that the practice of collegiality needs to be supplemented, or in some cases revitalised with a more explicit way. Industry has adopted Communities of Practice (CoPs) as a viable strategy to nurture the sharing of knowledge and promote work efficiency. As higher education institutions become more aligned with a corporate model, CoPs are gradually being adopted with a number of reported benefits including socio-economic, socio-cognitive, and socio-emotional. The authors of this chapter support the notion that CoPs can provide a practical solution to the diminishing level of collegiality in modern universities, and in some cases revitalise social exchange that was once more active in past generations.

This chapter contributes to the understanding of CoPs in higher education, and shares the process taken to establish a grass-roots CoP for new staff in a modern Australian university (CQU). Results from a 12 month review revealed that the CoP was found beneficial to members. The top five benefits listed by respondents were that they: (1) felt supported, (2) gained increased understanding and awareness of university systems and processes, (3) gained increased total effectiveness as a staff member, (4) gained a heightened awareness of who to contact for various purposes, and (5) achieved a heightened awareness and understanding of the various staff roles at CQU.

In addition to the study, reflection on the past 12 months reveals three core issues in regards to CoPs in higher education, namely: (1) the tension between grass-roots CoPs and being co-opted into meeting institutional purposes, (2) the challenges associated with CoPs across multiple locations, and (3) the inherent issues associated with a CoP for new staff that is by definition self-limiting. In terms of supporting new staff, the following lessons learnt from managing these three issues are shared. These lessons can also help CoP facilitators be better prepared into the future by heading off potential problems before or when they occur. Firstly, CoP/institutional tensions can be resolved through mutual respect. Secondly, virtual meetings and video-conferencing technology with reliable IT support can reduce barriers from distance.

Finally, in relation to bringing the CoP to maturity, it is important to understand that maturity in a CoP for new staff is more readily realised from an individual rather than a collective perspective. In conclusion, the chapter shared some future directions for the New Staff CoP and offered some guidance to readers who might be interested in establishing a similar CoP.

If anyone is interested in learning more about the study conducted on the effectiveness of the New Staff CoP and its results, please contact Elise Crawford at e.crawford@cqu.edu.au.

References

Anderson, D., Johnson, R., & Saha, L. (2002). *Changes in academic work: Implications for universities of the changing age distribution and work roles of academic staff.* Canberra: Department of Education, Science and Training.

Archer, L. (2008). Younger academics' constructions of 'authenticity', 'success' and professional identity. *Studies in Higher Education, 33*(4), 385–403. doi:10.1080/03075070802211729

Austin, A. E. (1990). *To leave an indelible mark: Encouraging good teaching in research universities through faculty development: A study of the Lilly Endowment's teaching fellows program 1974–1988.* Nashville, TN: Vanderbilt University, Peabody College.

Baker-Eveleth, L., Chung, Y., Eveleth, D., & O'Neill, M. (2011). Developing a community of practice through learning climate, leader support, and leader interaction. *American Journal of Business Education, 4*(2), 33–40.

Bandura, A. (1977). *Social learning theory.* Englewood Cliffs, NJ: Prentice Hall.

Barkhuizen, G. (2002). Beginning to lecture at university: A complex of socialisation patterns. *Higher Education Research and Development, 21*(1), 93–109.

Berkes, F. (2009). Evolution of co-management: Role of knowledge generation, bridging organizations and social learning. *Journal of Environmental Management, 90*, 1692–1702.

Bishop, R. M., & Bieschke, K. J. (1998). Applying social cognitive theory to interest in research among counseling psychology doctoral students: A path analysis. *Journal of Counseling Psychology, 45*(2), 182–188. doi:10.1037/0022-0167.45.2.182.

Blass, E. (2005). The rise and rise of the corporate university. *Journal of European Industrial Training, 29*(1), 58–74.

Boud, D., & Middleton, H. (2003). Learning from others at work: Communities of practice and informal learning. *Journal of workplace Learning, 15*(5), 194–202.

Burkley, S., & Du Toit, A. (2010). Academics leave your ivory tower: Form communities of practice. *Educational Studies, 36*(5), 493–503. doi:10.1080/03055690903425532.

Central Queensland University. (2014). *CQUniversity Australia annual report 2014.* Rockhampton: Central Queensland University.

Churchman, D. (2001). Voices of the academy: Academics' responses to the corporatizing of academia. *Critical Perspectives on Accounting, 13*, 643–656.

Cox, M. D. (1997). Long-term patterns in a mentoring program for junior faculty: Recommendations for practice. *To Improve the Academy, 16*, 225–268.

Cox, M. D. (2002). The role of community in learning: Making connections for your classroom and campus, your students and colleagues. In G. S. Wheeler (Ed.), *Teaching & learning in college: A resource for educators* (pp. 1–38). Elyria, OH: Info-Tec.

Cox, M. D. (2004). Introduction to faculty learning communities. *New Directions for Teaching & Learning, 2004*(97), 5–23.

Cox, M. D. (2013). The impact of communities of practice in support of early-career academics. *International Journal for Academic Development, 18*(1), 18–30.

Cox, M. D. (2014). Learning communities as successful purveyors of evidence-based programs and scholarship: A message from the editor-in-chief. *Learning Communities Journal, 6*, 1–4.

Davies, B., & Petersen, E. B. (2005). Intellectual workers (un)doing neoliberal discourse. *Critical Psychology, 13*, 32–54.

Dochy, F., Segers, M., Van den Bossche, P., & Gijbels, D. (2003). Effects of problem-based learning: A meta-analysis. *Learning and Instruction, 13*(5), 533–568.

Fasso, W. (2010). Facilitated networking and group formation in an online community of practice. *Australian Educational Computing, 25*(1), 25–33.

Gourlay, L. (2011). New lecturers and the myth of 'communities of practice'. *Studies in Continuing Education, 33*(1), 67–77. doi:10.1080/0158037X.2010.515570.

Groundwater-Smith, S. (2010). *Connected Classrooms Program in Action*. Sydney: Connected Classrooms Program 2010.

Hollingsworth, M. A., & Fassinger, R. E. (2002). The role of faculty mentors in the research training of counselling psychology doctoral students. *Journal of Counselling Psychology, 49* (3), 324–330.

Knight, P., Tait, J., & Yorke, M. (2006). The professional learning of teachers in higher education. *Studies in Higher Education, 31*(3), 319–339.

Kozlowski, K. A., Holmes, C. M., & Hampton, D. D. (2014). The effectiveness of a college-wide research learning community in increasing the research self-efficacy of new faculty. *Learning Communities Journal, 6*, 55–74.

Lave, J., & Wenger, E. (1991). *Situated learning: Legitimate peripheral participation*. Cambridge, UK: Cambridge University Press.

Lingenfelter, P. E. (2012). Chapter 1: The knowledge economy: Challenges and opportunities for American higher education. http://www.educause.edu/library/resources/chapter-1-knowledge-economy-challenges-and-opportunities-american-higher-education

MacKenzie, J., Bell, S., Bohan, J., Brown, A., Burke, J., & Cogdell, B. (2010). From anxiety to empowerment: A learning community of university teachers. *Teaching in Higher Education, 15*(3), 273–284.

McDermott, R. (1999). Why information technology inspired but cannot deliver knowledge management. *California Management Review, 41*(4), 103–117.

McDermott, R. (2000). Knowing in the community: 10 critical success factors in building communities of practice. *IHRIM Journal*, March, 19–26.

McDonald, J., & Star, C. (2006). Designing the future of learning through a community of practice of teachers of first-year courses at an Australian University. In R. Philip, A. Voerman, & J. Dalziel (Eds.), *Designing the future of learning: Proceedings of the first international LAMS conference* (pp. 65–76). Sydney: The LAMS Foundation.

Murray, R., & Moore, S. (2008). *The handbook of academic writing: A fresh approach*. Cambridge: Open University Press.

Nagy, J., & Burch, T. (2009). Communities of Practice in Academe (CoP-iA): Understanding academic work practices to enable knowledge building capacities in corporate universities. *Oxford Review of Education, 35*(2), 227–247. doi:10.1080/03054980902792888.

Nistor, N., Daxecker, I., Stanciu, D., & Diekamp, O. (2015). Sense of community in academic communities of practice: Predictors and effects. *Higher Education, 69*, 257–273.

Nonaka, I., & Takeuchi, H. (1995). *The knowledge-creating company: How Japanese companies create the dynamics of innovation*. New York: Oxford University Press.

Ortquist-Ahrens, L., & Torosyan, R. (2009). The role of the facilitator in faculty learning communities: Paving the way for growth, productivity, and collegiality. *Learning Communities Journal, 1*(1), 29–61.

Palmer, P. (2002). Foreword. In W. M. McDonald & Associates (Eds.), *Creating campus community: In search of Earnest Boyer's legacy* (pp. ix–xv). San Francisco: Jossey-Bass.

Parboosingh, J. (2010). Tools for CoP facilitators: Materials for CoP workshop participants. University of Calgary, http://www.coffee-ab.ca/images/toolkit-2-pagers_v1jan2010.pdf

Parker, L. D. (2002). It's been a pleasure doing business with you: A strategic analysis and critique of university change management. *Critical Perspectives on Accounting, 13*, 603–619.

Pilbara Institute. (2014). CQUni to open study hub at Pilbara Institute. Retrieved 9 March 2015, http://www.pilbara.wa.edu.au/news/cqu-to-open-study-hub-at-pilbara-institute

Polyani, M. (1958). *Personal knowledge*. Chicago: The University of Chicago Press.

Power, M. (2007). *Organized uncertainty: Designing a world of risk management*. Oxford: Oxford University Press.

Quiggin, J. (1996). *Great expectations: Microeconomic reform and Australia*. Australia: Allen & Unwin.

Quiggin, J. (2001). Resolving the university crisis. Submission to the Senate Employment, Workplace Relations, Small Business and Education Committee into the capacity of public universities to meet Australia's higher education needs. Canberra.

Quinn, R. E. (2012). Deep change or incremental change? That depends on how easily you adapt. Retrieved 14 October 2014, http://leadingwithlift.com/2012/05/30/deep-change-or-incremental-change-that-depends-on-how-easily-you-adapt/

Reaburn, P., Khan, N., Kinnear, S., Owens, A., Cheney, K., Donovan, R., et al. (2014). *Top ten tips: Creating and facilitating communities of practice (CoPs)*. Rockhampton: Central Queensland University.

Reaburn, P., & McDonald, J. (2015). Creating and facilitating communities of practice in higher education: Theory to practice in a regional Australian university. In J. McDonald & A. Cater-Steel (Eds.), *Communities of practice—Facilitating social learning in higher education. Higher education dynamics series*. London: Springer.

Roberts, J. (2006). Limits to Communities of Practice. *Journal of Management Studies, 43*(3), 623–639. doi:10.1111/j.1467-6486.2006.00618.x.

Roblyer, M. D., & Doering, A. H. (2013). *Integrating educational technology into teaching*. Sydney: Pearson.

Schmidt, H., & Moust, J. (2000). Factors affecting small group tutorial learning: A review of research. In D. Evenson & C. Hemlo (Eds.), *Problem-based learning: A research perspective on learning interactions* (pp. 19–52). London: Lawrence Erlbaum.

Seligman, L. (2000). Adoption as sensemaking: Toward an adopter-centered process model of IT adoption. Paper presented at the international conference on information systems 2000. http://aisel.aisnet.org/cgi/viewcontent.cgi?article=1126&context=icis2000

Tapper, T., & Palfreyman, D. (2000). *Oxford and the decline of the collegiate tradition*. London: Woburn Press.

The Swiss Agency for Development and Cooperation. (2011). Steps involved with starting communities of practice. In S. Rodger (Ed.), *Title of fellowship: Building capacity among emerging occupational therapy academic leaders in curriculum renewal and evaluation of UQ and nationally*. Brisbane: The University of Queensland.

The University of Sydney. (2015). Origins and early years (1850–1900). http://sydney.edu.au/about/profile/history/origins.shtml

Walton, J. (1999). Human resource development and the corporate university. In J. Walton (Ed.), *Strategic human resource development* (pp. 412–437). Harlow, FT: Prentice Hall.

Walton, J. S, & Martin, M. C. (2004). Corporate universities v traditional universities: Comparison through published organisation documentation. http://files.eric.ed.gov/fulltext/ED491482.pdf. Accessed 1 July 2015.

Weick, K. E., Sutcliffe, K. M., & Obstfeld, D. (2005). Organizing and the process of sensemaking. *Organization Science, 16*(4), 409–421. doi:10.1287/orsc.1050.0133.

Wenger, E. (1998). *Communities of practice: Learning, meaning, and identity.* New York, NY, US: Cambridge University Press.

Wenger, E. (1999). *Communities of practice: Learning, meaning, and identity.* Cambridge, UK: Cambridge University Press.

Wenger, E., McDermott, R., & Snyder, W. M. (2002). *Cultivating communities of practice: A guide to managing knowledge.* Boston, MA, US: Harvard Business School Press.

Wenger, E. C., & Snyder, W. M. (2000). Communities of practice: The organizational frontier. *Harvard Business Review, 78*(1), 139–145.

White, R. W., & Roth, R. A. (2009). *Exploratory search: Beyond the query-response paradigm.* San Rafael, California: Morgan & Claypool.

Zboralski, K. (2009). Antecedents of knowledge sharing in communities of practice. *Journal of Knowledge Management, 13*(3), 90–101. doi:10.1108/13673270910962897.

Chapter 24
CoPs: Enhancing Quality Learning and Teaching with Sessional Staff

Marina Harvey and Vanessa Fredericks

Abstract The Australian higher education sector depends on sessional staff to undertake the majority of teaching. Despite the fact that sessional staff are central to the university, sessional staff report feeling isolated and invisible. There are few opportunities for sessional staff to participate in professional development or to engage in teaching teams and the wider academic community. Moreover, this reliance on sessional staff has been identified as a risk to quality learning in higher education. The Benchmarking Leadership and Advancement of Standards for Sessional Teaching (BLASST) framework has established national evidenced-based standards for systematising good practice for quality learning and teaching with sessional staff. Drawing on the BLASST framework, this chapter examines the potential for Communities of Practice (CoP) to support quality learning and teaching with sessional staff. Authentic examples are used to illustrate the ways in which CoPs can be used to improve quality learning and teaching, sustain good practice, and ultimately, to include sessional staff in academic communities. These CoPs can be implemented in a variety of ways—face-to-face, online or blended—and they may develop within traditional, structured university systems, or grow organically from a grassroots approach. Four factors for successful CoPs for sessional staff are identified: fit for purpose; a strengths-based approach; sharing of practice; and debriefing. The evidence suggests that learning and teaching CoPs for, and with, sessional staff are good practice.

Keywords Sessional staff · Casuals · Adjuncts · Communities of Practice · Learning · Teaching

The original version of this chapter was revised: Authors' affiliation have been updated. The erratum to this chapter is available at 10.1007/978-981-10-2879-3_29

M. Harvey (✉) · V. Fredericks
Queensland University of Technology, Brisbane, QLD, Australia
e-mail: dr.marina.harvey@gmail.com

© Springer Nature Singapore Pte Ltd. 2017
J. McDonald and A. Cater-Steel (eds.), *Communities of Practice*,
DOI 10.1007/978-981-10-2879-3_24

24.1   Introduction

Across the higher education sector, an emerging international trend is that of a reliance on sessional staff for teaching. In countries such as Australia, these staff now have a responsibility for the majority of teaching across the sector. This reliance raises issues for academic communities; professional and organisational development; quality assurance and enhancement of learning and teaching. These issues are identified and discussed.

One issue often cited by sessional staff is that they do not feel part of academic communities, with limited opportunities available to them to engage as members of Communities of Practice (CoP). Strategies to address this and other issues, including policy development, have had limited success. A national standards framework to support and enhance quality teaching with sessional staff is explored for its potential to lead and inform good practice strategies with sessional staff.

The focus of the chapter is the interplay between good practice strategies and the role of communities of practice. This interplay is illustrated through a series of authentic examples of communities of practice that have been created specifically for sessional staff. The range of examples shared have been selected to provide insights applications of how CoPs can support quality learning and teaching with sessional staff. It is hoped that these examples can act to educate and inspire the reader to consider the possibilities of how CoPs may be adapted and applied in their own higher educational context.

24.2   Role and Context of Sessional Staff in Higher Education

Sessional staff, also known as adjuncts, contingent, non-tenure track and casual staff amongst many other terms, are defined as "any teachers in higher education who are employed on a casual or contract or sessional basis. This may include lecturers, tutors, unit, program and subject convenors, demonstrators, and markers" (Harvey and Luzia 2013, p. 3). Beyond the classroom, the diverse cohort that make up sessional staff may also be responsible for a broad range of teaching-related tasks, for example marking or grading, curriculum design, laboratory or clinical practicals, and subject co-ordination roles (Harvey 2015a, b).

Australian universities rely on sessional staff to deliver the majority of their undergraduate teaching (May et al. 2013). This reliance on sessional staff is not restricted to the Australian higher education sector, but is part of an international trend of an increasing dependence on sessional staff (for example, across the United Kingdom, New Zealand, America and Canada, France and Germany) (Harvey 2015a). The reliance on sessional staff "reflects the unusual structure of universities" (Norton and Cherastidtham 2014, p. 35) and is predicted to be a constant feature of this workforce (Jaschik and Lederman 2015).

While sessional staff carry the majority of teaching responsibilities across the Australian higher education sector, systematic data is not collected or maintained on this significant workforce cohort. At best proxy measures, such as full-time equivalent numbers, are used to estimate sessional staff numbers. In addition, in countries such as Australia, non-university higher education providers do not report on their sessional staff data (TEQSA 2014).

Given this lack of data on sessional staff, they are located on the "tenuous periphery" (Kimber 2003, p. 41) of the academic community, often invisible (Leigh 2014; Ryan et al. 2013). These staff commonly experience a "powerful sense of marginalization" (Bryson 2013, p. 5) and isolation from the wider academic community. They are "frequently overlooked in discussion of policy and institutional strategy" (Coaldrake 1999, p. 4), and "participate only marginally in departmental and university activities" (Sutherland 2009, p. 149). These circumstances may impact negatively on quality as they can hinder quality enhancement due to the lack of "feedback from the 'coal-face' to educational policy, either within faculties or within the sector as a whole" (Brown et al. 2008, p. 26). Sessional staff have limited opportunities to network with colleagues compared with contracted staff (Hamilton 2008), and do not always have access to ongoing professional development opportunities (May et al. 2013, p. 20). Funding and opportunity is not always available for sessional staff members to attend meetings or participate in staff development programs, so sessional staff are "effectively cut off from legitimate participation in the cultural and organisational life of the faculty" (Green and Ruutz 2008, p. 166).

As a result and until recently, sessional staff and sessional staff issues have attracted limited attention across the higher education sector. They have not been recognised in institutional culture, nor systematically supported with professional development (Lefoe et al. 2013). Therefore, by default, they have not been the focus of Communities of Practice. They have not been included in organisational, strategic and operational plans (Harvey 2013a). Consequently there has been a general lack of any systematic approach to ensuring and enhancing quality learning and teaching with sessional staff.

The "significant reliance" on sessional staff, exacerbated by the negligible recognition of the role of sessional staff (Percy et al. 2008), has been identified as a "risk" to students (TEQSA 2012, p. 25). Action is needed to mitigate this risk. A few actions and strategies have been trialled, such as the development of organisational policies or projects, but these have been judged as neither successful nor sustainable (Bryson 2013). Given "that there are limited teaching focused development opportunities or resources available to sessional… teachers" (p. 8) and that sessional staff themselves "recognise a need for improved teaching-focused development" (Heath et al. 2014, p. 9) new approaches are needed to support quality learning and teaching with sessional staff.

24.3   The Need for a Systematic Approach to Ensure Standards for Quality Learning and Teaching with Sessional Staff

One "positive approach" (Brown 2015, p. 189) to ensure standards for quality learning and teaching with sessional staff that has been initiated in the Australia higher education sector is that of a national standards framework. The BLASST (Benchmarking Leadership and Advancement of Standards for Sessional Teaching) framework has established evidence-based criteria and standards for the multi-levels of a higher education organisation. Informed by seminal research in the field (e.g. Percy et al. 2008) and developed over a period of 10 years, a team of four universities then collaborated to successfully pilot the use of the framework in a range of higher education contexts (Harvey 2013a).

Referencing against the criteria and standards, individuals, departments, faculties or organisations can evaluate their current practices as either 'good practice', 'minimum practice' or 'unsustainable' practice. Criteria and their associated standards are categorised according to the three principles which underpin the framework: quality learning and teaching, sessional staff support, and sustainability (Luzia and Harvey 2013). The principles (detailed in Box 24.1), and their associated standards, were developed to be used not just to enable institutions to evaluate and benchmark but to perform an educative role in improving practice. The framework has been endorsed by the Tertiary Education Quality and Standards Agency (TEQSA) (Harvey 2015a).

Box 24.1 Three key principles underpinning the BLASST Sessional Staff Standards (Luzia and Harvey 2013, p. 6) (Used under Creative Commons Licence 3.0).

Principle One: Quality Learning and Teaching

This principle refers to those issues that affect the quality of teaching and learning with sessional staff. These issues include institutional and intra-institutional commitment to quality learning and teaching, to good practice learning and teaching approaches and values, principles and priorities, inclusivity and inclusion, and to professional development.

Principle Two: Support for sessional staff

This principle refers to the need for recruitment, employment, administration and academic systems that are consistent, appropriate and inclusive of sessional staff. It states the importance of support for sessional staff in the form of dedicated infrastructure and other resourcing in order for all staff to undertake their roles effectively and professionally.

Principle Three: Sustainability

This principle refers to the need for workforce planning that includes sessional staff, at all levels of the institution. The principle is associated with practices that enable retention of good sessional teachers, reduce turnover of sessional staff, and encourage sessional staff in the pursuit and development of quality teaching. It also acknowledges that this can be achieved by recognising and rewarding sessional staff for the contribution they make. This principle also recognises the need for appropriate resources to underpin processes, and the minimisation of the administrative load on all staff (including academic, administrative and human resources).

24.4 The Potential of CoPs for Systematising Quality Learning and Teaching with Sessional Staff

Communities of Practice (CoPs) are cited in higher education literature as a "successful way of building and sharing a scholarly approach to enhancing learning and teaching practice" (McDonald 2012, p. 11). There has been great emphasis on the "situated and social nature of learning" (Percy and Beaumont 2008, p. 8) that can occur through CoPs. CoPs can offer a unique form of professional development and community "founded on collegial, collaborative and personal contact" (McDonald 2012, p. 13). Supporting teachers with "professional formation" should be seen as "ecological", that is, "evoked by engagements with other colleagues and the 'lived' workplace environment" (Knight et al. 2007, p. 430). This is particularly the case for sessional staff, who should be included in teaching teams and departments (Knight et al. 2007). While formal professional development opportunities still have a place within universities, promoting peer learning opportunities in situated teaching communities (Boud 1999) has the potential to create a more meaningful professional learning experience for individual sessional staff members and lead to greater quality enhancement for the organisation (Percy and Beaumont 2008).

Drawing on the work of Wenger et al. (2002) we conceptualise CoPs as an amalgamation of three essential characteristics:

1. *Domain*—an area of knowledge, interest or expertise that provides the community with a shared sense of identity,
2. *Community*—which forges the "social fabric of learning" (Wenger et al. 2002, p. 29) by engaging in collegial and collaborative discussions and activities, and the exchange of information, and
3. *Practice*—a shared collection of ideas, tools and resources that the community develops and maintains (Wenger et al. 2002, pp. 27–29).

It is the fusion of these three characteristics which function to make communities of practice an ideal social structure that encourage the development and sharing of knowledge (Wenger et al. 2002, p. 29).

Engaging sessional staff in communities of practice is one way of including sessional staff in teaching teams, in learning, scholarly and higher education communities and thereby systematising quality learning and teaching practices. This strategy aligns with the BLASST Sessional Staff Standards framework. One criterion of the BLASST framework explicitly sets the standard that, "Sessional staff are included in academic communities of practice" (BLASST 2013a, p. 13), with good practice identified as sessional staff engaging in these CoPs. These national standards for quality learning and teaching with sessional staff, promote the role of CoPs in enhancing and in assuring quality learning.

Indirectly, several additional criteria that make up the standards framework may be interpreted as advocating the potential role and characteristics of CoPs. Examples of community and domain at the departmental level include, "Sessional and ongoing academic staff share good learning and teaching practice" (BLASST 2013a, p. 3) and that, "Sessional staff are involved in teaching teams" (BLASST 2013a, p. 4).

A CoP can be formed as a process and product of mentoring. The criterion of "Sessional staff receive professional academic supervision and mentoring" (BLASST 2013a, p. 4) could be achieved through a variety of both CoP and mentoring modes such as one-on-one; group; peer; online or compound mentoring (Cahir et al. 2010). Any level of peer review initiatives can also form CoPs whereby "Sessional staff teaching performance is monitored and evaluated" (BLASST 2013a, p. 5). Peer review CoPs for sessional staff can range from formal, integrated and aligned with professional development programs through to informal, collegial and reciprocated approaches (Harvey and Solomonides 2014).

The BLASST standards framework also establishes an expectation and responsibility of individual sessional staff to engage with professional learning opportunities. Relevant criteria at the individual level of responsibility include that sessional staff "… actively engage with ongoing professional development in learning and teaching" and "…maintain my professional role as a teacher and a disciplinary expert" (BLASST 2013a, p. 5). Learning and teaching, professional or disciplinary CoPs have the potential to provide these professional learning opportunities.

24.5   Identifying Examples of CoPs Supporting Session Staff: The Method

So, are there good practices amongst individuals, departments, faculties and organisations of using CoPs to enhance the quality of learning and teaching with sessional staff? The BLASST standards have been used as a stimulus for the awarding of National Good Practice Awards. A careful investigation of Australian good practice examples (BLASST 2013b), derived from award finalists, reveals an interesting and emergent pattern, that there *is* a role for Communities of Practice (CoPs) in supporting sessional staff.

Participatory Action Research (PAR) (Kemmis et al. 2014) was the approach used to investigate the emergence of CoPs in supporting sessional teachers. This approach offers a flexibility and adaptability of method through its cycles of Plan, Act, Observe and Reflect. It is an approach that is structured by a shared and collegial domain, or "sense of ownership" together with practices of "regular communication" including "communal reflection" and "involvement over time", (Harvey 2013b, p. 124), offering a philosophical and pragmatic alignment with the characteristics of CoPs themselves.

24.5.1 PAR Cycle 1

The secondary data drawn upon for this investigation were the original nomination documents submitted by national finalists and winners of BLASST good practice awards (for supporting quality learning and teaching with sessional staff). There were a total of 22 finalists (12 in 2013, and 10 in 2015) who had nominated against one of the key principles of the BLASST framework. These finalists had been determined by a national panel of four academic experts who judged against criteria that included: identification of factors for success as well as for improvement, outcomes of the practice, resourcing implications and evidence of impact. Although the finalists had not been judged by any criterion of creating and sustaining a CoP with sessional staff, review of these nominations revealed multiple examples of CoPs assuming a role in supporting sessional staff. Enacting the PAR cycle, we observed and then reflected on this data. Being intrigued by this observation, we applied "retroductive thinking" (Saldana 2015, p. 27) to plan a cycle of coding that would lead us from the idea (that COPs have a role to play in supporting quality learning and teaching with sessional staff) to the data pertaining to the idea (Richards and Morse 2007).

24.5.2 PAR Cycle 2

The original nomination submissions were reviewed for second level analysis. Reviewing text-based documents is an "excellent" method for retroductive thinking (Saldana 2015). In this cycle the plan was to code the documents originally categorised as "finalists" to either examples that incorporated CoPs, or not. The criteria for coding examples as CoPs were the three characteristics identified as crucial (Wenger et al. 2002), namely of the domain, community and practice. This "exploratory problem-solving technique" (Saldana 2013, p. 8) resulted in the identification of four examples (out of 22 finalists) that relied on CoPs to support sessional staff. In addition to this process, the literature that had been used to provide evidence of good practice and establish the research base for the development of the BLASST standards framework was used as a second set of data to be recoded using retroductive thinking. This resulted in identification of another five examples of CoPs for sessional staff.

In recognition of the diverse cohort that is sessional staff, possibly working across multiple and diverse locations, these CoPs are face-to-face, online and blended. CoPs to facilitate quality learning and teaching with sessional staff have been established at, and by, multiple institutional levels (departments, faculties, whole of institution and more recently by cohorts of sessional staff themselves). They are succeeding in not only enhancing quality learning and teaching, but in developing leadership capacity across their communities and enabling positive, developmental change in, and beyond, their institutions. The examples of CoPs supporting sessional staff are presented as short narratives and include a brief reference to how each aligns with the three crucial characteristics of CoPs.

24.6   Authentic Examples of Cops of Sessional Staff

A growing number of cases illustrate the contributions of CoPs in supporting sessional staff with quality learning and teaching. A range of such authentic examples are now presented. The examples have been chosen to illustrate their potential in achieving good standards as determined by the three guiding principles that underpin the BLASST Sessional Staff Standards Framework, which are to reiterate: quality learning and teaching, sessional staff support, and sustainability. In addition, the examples represent different modes and applications of CoPs used to support the diverse and varying needs of sessional staff.

24.6.1   Quality Learning and Teaching

The following examples demonstrate an acknowledgement of the role of sessional staff and their contribution to quality learning and teaching. They also illustrate the need to recognise and support sessional staff with professional development.

Sessional staff CoP example 1: Structured reflection communities

A reflective approach to CoPs has been implemented in one Engineering and Computing department. This has been structured as regular scheduled fortnightly meetings. As sessional staff gather for these meetings they are referred to as "reflective-practice groups" joining together as "teaching communities". This community shares good practice, learning and teaching strategies and pedagogical theories while acting as a supportive and collaborative community that also offers the opportunity to "debrief their practice". (Adapted from MacDonald and Edwards, cited in Percy et al. 2008, pp. 49–51).

This example demonstrates teachers in one disciplinary group, Computing and Engineering, as the domain for a CoP. They gather as a community through regular meetings where they share good practice and strategies as well as theorise about learning and teaching. The regular meetings provide the time for ongoing and sustained interactions.

Sessional staff CoP example 2: Online community

An online professional development and "community networking space" has been established for sessional staff. The Sessional Staff Hub has as its focus the sharing of good practice as a strategy for enhancing the quality of teaching. Sessional staff engage in this community of practice using an online forum. In addition, this online hub acts as a repository of a diverse suite of learning and teaching resources that sessional staff can engage with as needed. (Adapted from La Trobe University n.d.).

Teachers who identify as sessional staff is the domain of interest for this CoP. As a community, learning is made possible through online relationships where a focus of practice is the sharing of strategies and contribution of resources through the online repository.

Sessional staff CoP example 3: A university community

All new sessional staff are invited, and paid, to attend an annual conference and workshops which have been specifically designed and developed for the professional development of sessional staff. As this conference actively promotes and encourages networking across and beyond the sessional staff community, it acts as one key strategy for establishing a whole-of-university Community of Practice. Central to the conference's activities is the sessional staff sharing their good practices. The engagement of sessional staff is not a one-off occurrence as they are invited to continue their engagement with this community for as long as they are teaching at the university (adapted from UTS 2013).

Again, sessional staff who teach at the university is the domain of interest for this CoP. As an established annual event that lasts for several days, it sustains the community across the years while also growing the community by welcoming new members annually. The university's budget for such events is a demonstration of an organisational culture that supports the sharing of good practice and their sessional community.

24.6.2   Sessional Staff Support

The examples in this section illustrate how you can achieve positive outcomes for sessional staff through the resourcing of supportive communities of practice. The BLASST standards state a criterion of good practice as "The Institution has a funding model that allocates resources for sessional staff professional development" (BLASST 2013a, p. 6). Surprisingly, the resourcing of these supportive communities does not need to be onerous as demonstrated by the following examples. Indeed, investing in supportive CoPs can be efficient and provide effective outcomes.

Sessional staff CoP example 4: Professional learning communities

One structured program approach is that of funding sessional staff to engage with a whole-of-organisation professional learning community. Key elements of this program include: an orientation event, a focus on assessment and grading through workshops and student feedback sessions, and concluding with a community "debrief" session. "This strategy supports tutors and students to more fully engage with their faculty, tutor and learning community." (Adapted from Crimmins, Nash and Leibergreen 2012 as cited in BLASST 2013b).

The domain of interest for this CoP is that of a professional learning community, where the identity of members is that of being part of a broad learning and teaching community made up of sessional and permanent staff. Over time, members of this community engage in a series of workshops and professional learning sessions focusing on good learning and teaching practice.

Sessional staff CoP example 5: Tutor and subject co-ordinator community

An online "Tutors' Lounge" was established by a subject co-ordinator who managed a "geographically dispersed" cohort of sessional-staff. The aim was to assure quality through the sharing of good practice whilst building a collegial online community. This community of practice was "characterised by professional respect, reciprocity, and trust and professional development through dialogue with peers." (Adapted from Stirling as cited in Percy et al. 2008, pp. 45–48).

Online tutoring is the identity shared by this example of a sessional staff CoP. These tutors share a competence in online teaching. In spite of geographical separation, these CoP members are still able to share good learning and teaching practice through their online portal, or "Tutors' Lounge".

Sessional staff CoP example 6: Scholarly sessional community

One element of a nested and whole-of-institution approach is that of the STARS program (Sessional Teaching and Reflection Showcase). This program aims to provide support to sessional staff to develop scholarly teaching practice and then to showcase and share this practice, thereby achieving "scholarly and communication capacity building in a community of practice". Annually, it recognises and rewards the best of these practices at both the department and university level. Key features and activities of this program include academic mentoring, reflective practice, workshops, one-on-one meetings to support sessionals with the documentation of their good practice initiatives, presentations and official award ceremonies that engage multi-levels of the university: sessionals, tenured colleagues and executive.

Of special note, is that the STARS program was devised, initiated and led by a sessional staff academic. This was enabled due to the university's established Academic Development (AD) and Sessional Academic Success (SAS) programs

(adapted from Fox 2014 cited in BLASST 2015).

The identity of community members of the STARS initiative is that of sessional staff who wish to engage in scholarly enquiry into their teaching practice. This community supports such enquiry through a range of shared practices such as mentoring, workshops and consultations. Stories about good practice are then shared through faculty and institutional award ceremonies.

24.6.3 Sustainability

Given that the higher education sector is reliant on sessional staff for providing the majority of its teaching, the principle of sustainability is crucial. This principle pertains to the reduced attrition and turnover of good teachers, and includes new and experienced sessional staff in ongoing professional learning opportunities.

Sessional staff CoP example 7: Tutor professional development community

This university's professional development workshop for tutors draws on the "lived experience of each participant, thereby facilitating the creation of communities of practice". This university places the sessional staff as active community members and encourages them to "develop their own voice as educators". The sustainability of this community is evidenced by the fact that the tutor professional development has been offered for over a decade (adapted from Birbeck 2012 as cited in BLASST 2013a).

The domain illustrated by this example of that of tutors at one university. Practices such as workshops, for sharing information and discussing learning and teaching strategies, have as their focus the establishment of communities of practice for the tutor cohorts. Tutors are given a voice as they share their stories of good practice.

Sessional staff CoP example 8: Blended teaching communities

A strategy for building inclusive, engaged and "strong" sessional teaching teams has been the development of blended (online and face-to-face) teaching communities of practice at a faculty or discipline level. This strategy was developed in recognition of the perception by sessional staff of feeling "quite isolated". Team members in these communities undertake moderation, calibration, sharing of resources and debriefing activities. These communities of practice often thrive beyond a teaching session as "many tutors request to remain in the same teaching team in subsequent years" (Adapted from Chester 2012 as cited in BLASST 2013b).

Teaching teams of sessional tutors is the domain of this blended community. As a community they collaborate in good assessment practices of moderation and calibration as well as share resources. These interactions are sustained over time as tutors actively choose to remain in their communities. As a blended community, online interactions are pivotal to enabling collective learning. A more recent domain for sessional staff CoPs is that where the community engages in discussion, sharing of resources and collegial support in fully online communities of practice.

24.6.4 Emerging Sustainable CoPs: Cyber Communities of Practice

The previous examples of sessional staff CoPs are drawn from organisations that have some system in place for identifying their sessional staff. However, the lack of systematic data collection about sessional staff by many organisations (May et al.

2013) makes it challenging to identify these staff in order to be able to support their workplace and professional learning needs. Some sessional staff have responded to this challenge in innovative ways. The increasing sophistication and user-friendliness of web-based technologies are providing a new virtual or cyber medium for CoPs, whereby sessional staff can develop a sense of shared identity as their online communities collaborate to exchange stories, practices and advice (Murray-Johnson 2014). This has been most evident in the recent growth of the use of social media as a means of developing cyber communities of practice.

Cyber CoPs offer the advantage of connecting sessional staff across institutions, across a country and increasingly globally. They are easy to discover with names that clearly nominate their focus. Many of these cyber COPs originate in the United States, for example: #AdjunctChat; the Adjunct Project (adjunct.chronicle.com); AdjunctNation.com; adjunctaction.org; newfacultymajority.info, and precarious-facultyblog.com. The United Kingdom has UCUAntiCasualisation and Australia offers actualcasuals wordpress; hyperlinkacademia and UniCasual. These cyber CoPs have evolved through informal mechanisms and a grounded process (after Glaser and Strauss 1967), yet their development tend to follow good design principles (e.g. Cambridge et al. 2005).

A common form of social media employed is that of the web log or blog. Twitter was adopted early as a strategy for common collaboration of sessional staff in a cyber CoP. This is an example of a micro-blog, where practitioners are able to post 'tweets' of no more than 140 characters to their community members or followers. In turn, followers can either reply (publically or privately) or retweet the post.

Tweeters may accompany their micro-blogging with full blogs. These web blogs provide a broader scope to share issues and strategies through this form of online community. Commonly, CoPs can engage with, and respond to, these blogs through contributing and/or replying to online postings. An example of group blogging is that of CASA—Casual, Adjunct, Sessional staff and Allies in Australian Higher Education.

Sessional staff CoP example 9: Cyber communities—CASA

CASA brings sessional academics together as an "organised presence" in a "safe and neutral platform" where they can "share experiences and information on the academic career realities". Created by two academics who consider the casualisation of the academy as "a serious factor and we don't know enough about it", this CoP invites community engagement by supporting sessionals to "Speak candidly about their working lives and put forward ideas for change". As CASA grows, it is moving beyond national discussions to include the voices of colleagues in the US, the UK and Canada (adapted from Luzia and Bowles 2014, pp. 32–33).

The domain of this example is sessional teachers who are familiar and comfortable sharing in a fully online community. The predictable rhythm (Cambridge et al. 2005) of regular tweets and blog posts with the resultant discussion are key learning activities for this community.

24.7 Reflections: Key Success Factors and Future Directions

The research literature around quality learning and teaching with sessional staff in higher education is emergent. There is a limited research base that addresses the relationship between sessional staff and the role and benefits of Communities of Practice. This chapter has focused on sessional staff and communities of practice, reviewing the research for evidence to discover how communities of practice can enhance learning and teaching with sessional staff. The result is a contribution to knowledge about the potential of how Communities of Practice are created and enacted in relation to sessional staff.

24.7.1 Key Success Factors

Reviewing and synthesising each of the authentic case examples of the Communities of Practice that currently focus on sessional staff now enables a number of key success factors to be identified. The key factors that we have identified are: fit for purpose; a strengths–based approach; sharing of practice, and debriefing.

24.7.1.1 Fit for Purpose

Sessional staff are a diverse cohort, for example they may: be PhD candidates or retired industry professionals, present a 1 h lecture or facilitate 10 h of tutorials, teach face-to-face or online, teach at one or at multiple institutions and many other variations. Recognising this diversity, any CoP that is created will need to be fit for purpose (Green and Ruutz 2008). A good fit will ensure that the "domain of interest" (Wenger et al. 2002) is the main criterion on which the community is built. Depending on the needs of the targeted sessional staff group, the best fit may be offered by a face-to-face, online, blended, cyber, short or long-term CoP.

There is also a temporal feature to the fit for purpose factor. A successful CoP requires some temporal regularity. CoP activities are normally multiple in their iterations, as a community is not a "one off" event. Nevertheless these iterations may vary in frequency ranging from daily interactions through an online forum, to an annual major conference which can then lead to the development of an organisation-wide COP.

24.7.1.2 Strengths-Based Approach

Many sessional staff CoPs are inherently adopting a strengths-based approach. This approach recognises that each participant has knowledge and expertise that they can contribute to the CoP (Harvey 2014). This contribution may be consistent throughout the lifespan of the CoP, or may occur during various phases of the CoP. All the CoPs, featured as examples, rely on the contributions of many members to survive and to thrive. This success factor is especially analogous to the characteristic of "the community" (Wenger et al. 2002).

A strengths-based approach is also aligned with the concept of distributed leadership. Distributed leadership respects and works with traditional hierarchical leadership, but then in addition also distributes, or shares, leadership of a CoP between people and across and between the multi-levels and disciplines of an organisation (Jones et al. 2014).

The authentic examples illustrate a spectrum of leadership approaches to CoPS. Where some may initially start as formal and systematised with traditional, hierarchical leadership, at the universities "the organisational requirements of social learning systems often run counter to traditional management practices" (Wenger 2000, p. 243). When this is the case, the social learning systems that are these CoPs, move beyond traditional leadership models and organically develop towards a distributed form of leadership. Thus, the voice of sessionals is heard as they can share in leadership. In a more grounded approach, evident with many of the cyber communities, the sessionals assume and share the leadership of their CoP. Distributed leadership is also more likely to ensure the sustainability of a learning and teaching initiative such as a CoP (Jones et al. 2012).

24.7.1.3 Sharing of Practice

A key feature of the examples has been the sharing of practice between community members, one of the key characteristics of CoPs (Wenger et al. 2002). In addition, or synergistically, resources are also shared. This is one of the benefits offered by the CoP to the sessional staff members of that community. This feature also exemplifies good practice as assessed by the BLASST standards framework criterion of "Sessional and ongoing academic staff share good learning and teaching practice" (BLASST 2013a, p. 3).

The sharing of practice may take place in casual or formal settings, and in face-to-face or online environments. But, to enable this sharing of practice to be achieved through a CoP, resource investment is required. This resource investment is often small, with the cyber communities of practice illustrating impressive networks and outcomes for minimal or small financial investment, relying on the critical investment of human capital.

Sharing provides the potential for a range of positive outcomes for members of these scholarly learning and teaching communities, where the 'new' sessional staff can learn and become part of these practice communities and the 'old' sessional staff can continue to learn (Lave and Wenger 1991). As members contribute and share practices, these practices are then refined by the community and "sustained organisationally" (Wenger 1998), building the learning and teaching capacity of the community. Sharing of practice is also an effective strategy in countering the isolation often experienced by sessional staff. New academics who are part of a community of practice report feeling "part of something" (Warhurst 2006, p. 115).

24.7.1.4 Debriefing

Several sessional staff CoPs specifically attend to the need to include a debriefing session. The range of CoPs provided as examples each have different foci, aims and outcomes, but the majority have a focus on professional learning and development. Debriefing activities are valuable as they can extend and reconcile our learning (Billett 2011). These activities enable "the community to proceed efficiently in dealing with its domain" (Wenger et al. 2002, p. 29) and may be analogous with the characteristic of "the practice". In a CoP, participants may "reflect on action, identify performance gaps, discuss areas for improvement, and consolidate knowledge and skills so that the latter can be applied in real practice to improve ... outcomes" (Cheng et al. 2014, p. 658). This is another key feature that acts to develop the learning and teaching capacity of a sessional staff community.

24.7.2 Future Directions

Communities of Practice are evident throughout the higher education sector as illustrated by the examples throughout this book. They function to support a wide and diverse range of disciplines, cohorts and functions. When CoPs are created to support sessional staff they may result in a range of positive outcomes which then cascade into enhancing quality learning and teaching. These outcomes for both sessional staff and their learning communities are wide-scoping and include: an increased scholarly approach to learning and teaching which may also extend to contributions to scholarship; a stronger quality framework when sessional staff are able to contribute to curriculum design including providing feedback from the 'coal-face'; reduced attrition of good sessional staff as well as capacity development in leadership of learning and teaching. CoPs offer an effective strategy for moving the invisible sessional staff who are often located on the tenuous, but "legitimate" periphery "into full participation" (Lave and Wenger 1991, p. 37).

Readers are invited to broaden their practice to include sessional staff in their CoPs, and conversely, to consider establishing new, or contribute to existing, COPS as an effective strategy for enhancing, supporting and sustaining the "precariat class" (Standing 2014) of the academy, our sessional staff. These CoPs provide many benefits for both the organisation, and for the sessional staff members for whom they grant a new "associational freedom" (Standing 2014). The examples provide a starting point to imagine the possibilities of what type or mode of CoP may be created, with all of these initiatives offering transferability to other organisations and contexts. The emergence and growth of cyber CoPs increases the options available.

As universities continue to rely on sessional staff to provide teaching, CoPs offer an effective and flexible strategy for supporting these staff while also enhancing and assuring the quality of learning and teaching through the sharing of resources, practices and learning. Simply stated, it is good practice to enable sessional staff to engage in Communities of Practice. CoPs, however, are not a solitary panacea and we therefore recommended that they are realised in tandem with the suite of good practice strategies identified in the BLASST framework to enable the higher education sector to build its capacity for supporting sessional staff with quality learning and teaching.

Acknowledgments Support for this publication has been provided by the Australian Government Office for Learning and Teaching. The views in this publication do not necessarily reflect the views of the Australian Government Office for Learning and Teaching. We sincerely and gratefully acknowledge the BLASST team, reference group and the many members of the academy who have shared their good practice in establishing and using Communities of Practice with and for their sessional staff.

References

Billett, S. (2011). *Curriculum and pedagogic bases for effectively integrating practice-based experiences. Final Report ALTC Project.* http://www.acen.edu.au/resources/docs/Billett-S-Griffith-NTF-Final-report-2011.pdf

BLASST. (2013a). *The sessional staff standards framework.* http://blasst.edu.au/docs/BLASST_framework_WEB.pdf

BLASST. (2013b). *Benchmarking leadership and advancement of sessional staff standards, BLASST good practice awards.* http://blasst.edu.au/awards.html

BLASST. (2015). *BLASST good practice awards.* http://www.blasst.edu.au/awards.html

Boud, B. (1999). Situating academic development in professional work: Using peer learning. *International Journal for Academic Development, 4*(1), 3–10.

Brown, S. (Ed.). (2015). *Learning, teaching and assessment in higher education: Global perspectives.* London: Palgrave.

Brown, T., Goodman, J., & Yasukawa, K. (2008). Casualisation of academic work: Industrial justice and quality education. *Journal of the Academy of the Social Sciences in Australia, 27* (1), 17–29.

Bryson, C. (2013). Supporting sessional teaching staff in the UK—To what extent is there real progress? *Journal of University Teaching and Learning Practice, 10*(3). http://ro.uow.edu.au/jutlp/vol10/iss3/2

Cahir, J., Harvey, M., & Ambler, T. (2010). *Spectrum approach to mentoring. A guide for mentors and mentees.* North Ryde: Learning and Teaching Centre Macquarie University. http://staff.mq.edu.au/teaching/teaching_development/mentoring/mentor_spectrum/

Cambridge, D., Kaplan, S., & Suter, V. (2005). *Community of practice design guide: A step-by-step guide for designing & cultivating communities of practice in higher education.* EDUCAUSE Learning Initiative (ELI). https://net.educause.edu/ir/library/pdf/NLI0531.pdf

Cheng, A., Eppich, W., Grant, V., Sherbino, J., Zendejas, B., & Cook, D. A. (2014). Debriefing for technology-enhanced simulation: A systematic review and meta-analysis. *Medical Education, 48*, 657–666.

Coaldrake, P. (1999). *Rethinking university work*. Higher Education Research and Development Society of Australia (HERDSA) conference, Melbourne.

Glaser, B. G., & Strauss, A. L. (1967). *The discovery of grounded theory. Strategies for qualitative research*. New York: Aldine De Gruyter.

Green, W., & Ruutz, A. (2008). Fit for purpose: Designing a faculty-based community of (teaching) practice. In *Engaging Communities, Proceedings of the 31st HERDSA Annual Conference, Rotorua* (pp. 163–172), 1–4 July 2008.

Hamilton, J. (2008). *Teaching fellowship report. Unpublished report*. Brisbane: Queensland University of Technology.

Harvey, M. (2013a). Setting the standards for sessional staff: Quality learning and teaching. *Journal of University Teaching and Learning Practice, 10*(3). http://ro.uow.edu.au/jutlp/vol10/iss3/4

Harvey, M. (2013b). So you think you are doing action research? Indicators of enactment of participatory action research in higher education. *ALARj (Action Learning and Action Research Journal), 19*(1), 115–134.

Harvey, M. (2014). Strengths-based approach. In D. Coghlan & M. Brydon-Miller (Eds.), *The SAGE encyclopaedia of action research* (Vol. 2). Thousand Oaks: Sage.

Harvey, M. (2015a). Introduction. In M. Harvey & V. Fredericks (Eds.), *Quality learning and teaching with sessional staff*. Milperra: HERDSA.

Harvey, M. (2015b). *The role of the BLASST Framework for systematising and rewarding good practice*. Opening keynote, BLASST National summit, 10 April, 2015. http://www.blasst.edu.au/summit2015.html

Harvey, M., & Luzia, K. (2013). Editorial 10.3. *Journal of University Teaching & Learning Practice, 10*(3). http://ro.uow.edu.au/jutlp/vol10/iss3/1

Harvey, M., & Solomonides, I. (2014). Peer Review in a foundations in learning and teaching program. In J. Sachs & M. Parsell (Eds.), *Peer review of learning and teaching in higher education. International perspectives* (pp. 137–149). Heidelberg: Springer.

Heath, M., Hewitt, A., Israel, M., & Skead N. (2014). *Smart casual: Towards excellence in sessional teaching in law*. Sydney: Office for Learning and Teaching, Department of Education. http://www.olt.gov.au/project-smart-casual-towards-excellence-sessional-teaching-law-2013

Jaschik, S., & Lederman, D. (2015). *The 2015 inside higher Ed's survey of college & university chief academic officers*. Inside Higher Ed & Gallup. http://www.insidehighcred.com/download/form.php?width=500&height=550&iframe=true&title=Survey%20of%20College%20and%20University%20Chief%20Academic%20Officers&file=IHE_2015%20ProvostsSurvey(1).pdf

Jones, S., Harvey, M., Lefoe, G., & Ryland, K. (2014). Synthesising theory and practice: Distributed leadership in higher education. *Educational Management Administration and Leadership, 42*(5), 603–619.

Jones, S., Lefoe, G., Harvey, M., & Ryland, K. (2012). Distributed leadership: A collaborative framework for academics, executives and professionals in higher education. *Journal of Higher Education, Policy and Management, 34*(1), 67–78.

Kemmis, S., McTaggart, R., & Nixon, R. (2014). *The action research planner, doing critical participatory action research*. Singapore: Springer.

Kimber, M. (2003). The tenured 'core' and the tenuous 'periphery': The casualisation of academic work in Australian universities. *Journal of Higher Education Policy and Management, 25*(1), 41–50.

Knight, P., Baume, D., Tait, J., & Yorke, M. (2007). Enhancing part-time teaching in higher education: A challenge for institutional policy and practice. *Higher Education Quarterly, 61*, 420–438.

La Trobe University (n.d.) Sessional staff hub. Community and professional development site for sessional academic staff at La Trobe University. http://sessional-staff.blogs.latrobe.edu.au/

Lave, J., & Wenger, E. (1991). *Situated learning: Legitimate peripheral participation*. Cambridge, UK: Cambridge University Press.

Lefoe, G. E., Parrish, D. R., Keevers, L. M., Ryan, Y., McKenzie, J., & Malfroy, J. (2013). A CLASS Act: The teaching team approach to subject coordination. *Journal of University Teaching and Learning Practice, 10*(3). http://ro.uow.edu.au/jutlp/vol10/iss3/4

Leigh, J. (2014). "I still feel isolated and disposable": Perceptions of professional development for part-time teachers in HE. *Journal of Perspectives in Applied Academic Practice, North America,* 2, July. http://jpaap.napier.ac.uk/index.php/JPAAP/article/view/105

Luzia, K., & Bowles, K. (2014). CASA: the house that casualisation built. *NTEU Advocate, 21*(2), 32–33.

Luzia, K. & Harvey, M. (2013). *The BLASST guide. Benchmarking with the sessional staff standards framework*. http://blasst.edu.au/docs/A413_008_BLASST_Benchmark_Guide.pdf

McDonald, J. (2012). *Community, domain, practice: Facilitator catch cry for revitalising learning and teaching through communities of practice*. Project Report. Sydney: Australian Learning and Teaching Council. http://eprints.usq.edu.au/26128/1/McDonald%2C%20J%20USQ%20Fellowship%20report_FINAL%20April%202014.pdf

May, R., Strachan, G., & Peetz, D. (2013). Workforce development and renewal in Australian universities and the management of casual academic staff. *Journal of University Teaching and Learning Practice, 10* (3). http://ro.uow.edu.au/jutlp/vol10/iss3/4

Murray-Johnson, K. K. (2014). "Faculty professional development—A virtual reality?" A critical literature review of online communities of practice in post secondary settings. Paper presented at the 55th Annual AERC (Adult Education Research Conference) Conference June 4–7, Pennsylvania, USA, 2014. http://www.adulterc.org/Proceedings/2014/papers/Murray-Johnson.pdf

Norton, A., & Cherastidtham, I. (2014). *Mapping Australian higher education, 2014–15*. Carlton: Grattan Institute.

Percy, A., & Beaumont, R. (2008). The casualisation of teaching and the subject at risk. *Studies in Continuing Education, 30*(2), 145–157.

Percy, A., Scoufis, M., Parry, S., Goody, A., Hicks, M., Macdonald, I., et al. (2008). *The RED Report, Recognition–Enhancement–Development: The contribution of sessional teachers to higher education*. Strawberry Hills: Australian Learning and Teaching Council.

Richards, L., & Morse, J. M. (2007). *Readme first for a user's guide to qualitative methods* (2nd ed.). Thousand Oaks: Sage.

Ryan, S., Burgess, J., Connell, J., & Groen, E. (2013). Casual academic staff in an Australian university: marginalised and excluded. *Tertiary Education and Management, 19*(2), 161–175.

Saldana, J. (2013). *The coding manual for qualitative researchers* (2nd ed.). Thousand Oaks: Sage.

Saldana, J. (2015). *Thinking qualitatively. Methods of mind*. Thousand Oaks: Sage.

Standing, G. (2014). *A precariat charter. Form denizens to citizens*. London: Bloomsbury Academic.

Sutherland, K. A. (2009). Nurturing undergraduate tutors' role in the university teaching community. *Mentoring and Tutoring: Partnership in Learning, 17*(2), 147–164.

TEQSA. (2012). *Annual Report 2011–12*. Tertiary Education Quality and Standards Agency. http://teqsa.gov.au/sites/default/files/9206.4_TEQSAAnnualReport_Full%20Report_Web_06.5.pdf

TEQSA. (2014). *Statistics report on TEQSA registered higher education providers*. Tertiary Education Quality and Standards Agency. http://www.teqsa.gov.au/sites/default/files/publication-documents/StatsReportOnTEQSAregHEPs_0.pdf

UTS. (2013). *Casual academic staff*. http://www.iml.uts.edu.au/for/casuals.html

Warhurst, R. P. (2006). We really felt part of something: Participatory learning among peers within a university teaching-development community of practice. *International Journal for Academic Development, 11*(2), 111–122.

Wenger, E. (1998). *Communities of practice. Learning, meaning and identity.* Cambridge: Cambridge University Press.

Wenger, E. (2000). Communities of practice and social learning systems. *Organisation, 7*(2), 225–246.

Wenger, E., McDermott, R., & Snyder, W. (2002). *Cultivating communities of practice.* Boston, MA: Harvard Business School Press.

Chapter 25
Communities of Practice and Negotiation of Meaning Among Pre-service Teachers

Asunción Martínez-Arbelaiz, José Miguel Correa-Gorospe
and Estibaliz Aberasturi-Apraiz

Abstract Since more and more schools of teacher education all over the world are adding on-line asynchronous discussions to their pre-teaching education requirements, education practitioners need research to gauge their potential contribution to the development of future teachers' identity and, in particular, to the development of their shared repertoire. Ryan and Scott (Teach Teach Educ 24(6):1635–1644, 2008) already pointed out that these discussions offer opportunities for student teachers to link theory and practice, to identify discrepancies between the two, to set up problems, to uncover implicit assumptions in teaching and learning, etc. Nevertheless, we still felt the need for an assessment of these asynchronous discussions, given that they may easily become mere monologues where students uncritically repeat theories they have heard in their classes or just describe what they have seen in schools. In this chapter we analyse the discourse generated in order to ascertain the degree of interactivity and identify instances of negotiation of meaning. We propose that this particular type of interaction helps to develop a shared repertoire, one of the three characteristics of a community of practice.

Keywords Pre-school and primary school teachers · Teaching identity · Computer-mediated communication · Shared repertoire · Teacher education

25.1 Introduction and Purpose

Motivated both by growing accountability pressures in schools of education and critical voices that question the value of computer-mediated communication as a tool for professional growth among pre-service teachers (see Zydney et al. 2011 for

A. Martínez-Arbelaiz (✉)
University Studies Abroad Consortium, Donostia-San Sebastian, Spain
e-mail: asuncion@usac.unr.edu

J.M. Correa-Gorospe · E. Aberasturi-Apraiz
Universidad Del País Vasco-Euskal Herriko Unibertsitatea,
Donostia-San Sebastian, Spain

© Springer Nature Singapore Pte Ltd. 2017
J. McDonald and A. Cater-Steel (eds.), *Communities of Practice*,
DOI 10.1007/978-981-10-2879-3_25

a review), we decided to analyse the outcomes of the forum discussions among our student teachers. After several meetings and discussions about how to approach this data, we decided to analyse the logs that resulted from the asynchronous group discussion against social theories of situated learning and Communities of Practice (Lave and Wenger 1991; Wenger 1998).

In our preliminary analyses of the discussions, we realized that student teachers were juggling a double identity: (1) they positioned themselves (Harré and van Langenhove 1991, 1999) as students in the on-line discussion groups, and (2) they also self-positioned as beginning teachers in the periphery of the Community of Practice in the schools where their respective practicum was taking place. These two identities corresponded to their potential membership in at least two different communities: the emerging professional community of future teachers in the forum and the actual schools where they carried out their practicum.

The two types of belongings became clear in the analysis of our logs, but their natures were very different. First, it was not clear to us that the forum constituted a real or even an imagined Community of Practice (CoP). It is true that the discussion of their experiences and incidents during the practicum could be considered a joint enterprise—which they had to do through mutual engagement, and we questioned whether there was a shared repertoire being built. Although traces of the attributes of a CoP–joint enterprise, mutual engagement and shared repertoire—can be found in the interactions in the on-line forum, we need more research before we can confirm that the group of students in the practicum constituted a CoP. In this chapter, we focus on the third feature of the CoP, and analyse the on-line discussions in order to see whether there was some evidence that student teachers were developing a shared repertoire. If this is the case, we can say that one of the fundamental pillars of a CoP is formed. Moreover, we can prove the value of the discussions in forging a shared set of tools to collaboratively debate and discuss concepts relevant to education.

The present chapter, then, sits at a crossroads between assessing the value of the on-line discussions and their role in the building of a professional identity by pre-service teachers. Related to this professional identity, the background provided by the different CoPs that the student teachers belonged to helped us understand the meaning of the students' contributions.

25.2 Identity, Learning and Participation in Communities of Practice

The constructs of "subjectivity" (Weedon 1987, 1997) and "identity" (Bauman 2001) have made their way into practically all areas of the social sciences and are currently at the core of research that seeks to understand and account for any human behaviour. Postmodern views on identity have moved away from the traditional view of the self as a fixed or compartmentalized entity; rather it is conceptualized as being in constant evolution and going through multiple, and sometimes painful, contradictions, emphasizing its fragmentations and gaps. Thus, Weedon proposes "a subjectivity which is precarious, contradictory and in process, constantly reconstituted in discourse each time we think or speak" (Weedon 1997, p. 32).

This view of identity relies heavily on discourse, since as Bucholtz and Hall (2005) clearly formulate in their "Emergence principle", "identity is best viewed as the emergent product rather than the pre-existing source of linguistic and other semiotic practices and therefore as fundamentally a social and cultural phenomenon" (p. 588). In other words, it is through discourse, without discarding other semiotic practices that are beyond the goals of this study, that an identity is performed. But discourse and, consequently, identity enactment take place in the context of a community, since any identity has to be recognized by others. An individual has to create an intelligible self, so that others can recognize him or her. This process is what (Bucholtz 2003, p. 408) calls "authentication", that is, "the assertion of one's own or another identity as genuine or credible". Authentication occurs when the members of a given community accept the symbolic behaviour of an individual as appropriate and "real". Similarly, Gee (2001) calls this process "recognition work". Thus, a given identity has to be recognized though acts and discourse. This display that is necessary for identity recognition or authentication is roughly equivalent to what Wenger calls the shared repertoire, which usually consists of "routines, words, tools, ways of doing things, stories, gestures, symbols, genres, actions, or concepts that the community has produced or adopted in the course of its existence, and which have become part of its practice." (Wenger 1998, p. 83).

From this perspective, learning entails acquiring the shared repertoire and displaying it through participation in social activities. This participation shapes not only what we do but also who we are and how we interpret what we do. In this sense, learning shapes our identity (Wenger 1998, p. 227). Through a process called "legitimate peripheral participation" (Lave and Wenger 1991), newcomers, those who are learning, interact with old timers within the community and gradually become more experienced in the practices that characterize the community. Lave and Wenger help us pay attention to the practices of a community, recognizing that some groupings can either limit or facilitate movement towards full participation.

CoPs correspond to the different subject positions (Harré and van Langenhove 1991, 1999), performances or enactments that individuals adopt on a moment-to-moment and day-to-day basis, and indeed throughout their lifetimes. Individuals gain entry by means of the abovementioned "legitimate peripheral participation". This peripheral participation is achieved via exposure to "mutual engagement with other members, to their actions and their negotiation of the enterprise, and to their repertoire in use" (Wenger 1998, p. 100).

While identity is conditioned by social interaction and social structure, at the same time, it conditions social interaction and social structure. Thus, interaction is crucial since it is constitutive of and constituted by the social environment. This is the two-way action commonly described in the work of sociologists such as Bourdieu (1985) and Giddens (1995).

Summarizing, Lave and Wenger claim that the identity of the novice or the beginner is built through performing tasks and the subsequent reflection and automatization of the new concepts and activities. According to Wenger (1998), the sources of coherence in a CoP are mutual engagement, joint enterprise and shared repertoire. The meaning of belonging to a community is negotiated in practice through participation in a dynamic that is characterized by social interaction among participants through the contribution of their competencies and personal experiences. This negotiation is a fundamental feature of identity since it involves both the creation and adoption of meaning.

25.3   CoP Theory and Teaching Identity

The theory of CoP has been mainly developed through an anthropological perspective, with an examination of practices such as Yucatan midwives, native tailors, navy quartermasters, meat cutters (Lave and Wenger 1991), as well as insurance claims processors (Wenger 1998). Nevertheless, there are growing attempts to extend this framework to education in general (Barab and Duffy 2000; DePalma 2009; Gee 2005; Warriner 2010) and teacher education research in particular (Bathmaker and Avis 2005; Clarke 2009; Correa, Martínez-Arbelaiz and Gutierrez 2014; Kwan and Lopez-Real 2010; Niesz 2010; Sim 2006; Yandell and Turvey 2007; Woodgate-Jones 2012). In this body of research the situation of student teachers is discussed with analytical lenses provided by the CoP Theory and it shows that in these schools, student teachers are entitled to legitimate peripheral participation, learning in an apprenticeship fashion. Thus, they are gradually given some responsibilities in the schools, although they are not fully responsible for the students, they do not attend meetings and they follow the lesson plan the practicum instructor designs. They usually follow a trajectory from peripheral to hopefully full participation once they reach graduation.

In addition to being members of the CoP of their practicum school, student teachers are also members of their classes in the School of Education, where they interact with other student teachers and their practicum supervisor. Interactions are often face-to-face through regular discussion format, but they also happen via mandatory on-line asynchronous discussions. Although some researchers (see Haneda 2006) have argued that classes can become CoPs, others, such as Hanson-Smith (2006), cast doubt on the notion by noting that classroom communities are usually too short lived and homogeneous to allow a genuine CoP to develop. Our own view is that we do not assume that simply participating in a forum discussion with other pre-service teachers leads to membership in a CoP. We believe, following Wenger, that "[m]embership is not just a matter of social category, declaring allegiance, belonging to an organization, having a title, or having personal relations with some people" (p. 74). Thus, we do not have enough evidence to assert that a CoP has formed through these interactions, but at the same time we cannot deny the idea that the existence of a CoP is possible. In this chapter we analise the on-line discussions of student teachers in order to gauge their value in building a teaching identity. As we will discuss further, the student teachers that were doing the practicum were engaged in the teaching practices but to the eyes of the CoP of the school, they were still considered students.

25.4 Liminality and the Practicum

This double membership reflects the liminality involved in being a student teacher. Although the concept of liminality has been applied to novice teachers (Pierce 2007) since they are caught in between two stages and they are in transition, we believe that this notion can also characterize the situations lived by student teachers. During their practicum they no longer act as students, but they have to start forging a new professional identity, in this case a teaching identity, for the first time (Beauchamp and Thomas 2009). The transition is gradual and as was pointed out above, they are allowed legitimate peripheral participation in the schools that act as CoPs. As opposed to novice teachers, student teachers do not have what Gee (2001) calls I-identity, since a given school of education has not yet granted them a degree, although this is obviously not enough to be considered a teacher. Applying Bucholtz's (2003) construct to education, newly-qualified teachers still need the authentication of the CoP, in this case, the school where they start their careers. We have proposed elsewhere that the role of colleagues in student teachers' (Correa et al. 2014) and newly qualified teachers' (Correa et al. 2015) first encounters with the profession are crucial. Nevertheless, when we discuss the trajectory of student teachers, the roles of both the instructor in the schools (the practicum instructor) and the university professor that supervises the student teachers (the practicum supervisor) should not be underestimated.

The university professor in charge of the practicum and also one of the authors of this study asked student teachers to post 600 words about an experience that was considered to be a critical incident, and the rest of the group members were required to reply to the initial posting. This pedagogical intervention is reminiscent of case-based pedagogy, which has been advocated by some teacher educators (Harrington et al. 1996; Hsu 2004). The main difference between the case-based approach and the one described here is that in both Harrington et al. and Hsu, the case studies came from a textbook or were presented by the professor. In contrast, in our project, the student teachers had to narrate an experience related to their teaching in the schools. Thus, the cases and discussion were not only relevant to the members of the group, but also highly realistic.

Student teachers were given a definition of critical incidents (Flanagan 1954), in which critical incidents are those events in our professional practice that cause perplexity, doubts, surprise or that have bothered or worried us because they lack coherence or they are unexpected. Critical incidents are events from daily life that impact us or surprise us and thus trigger reflection. In the case of teachers, for

Kelchtermans (1994) a narrated event is a critical incident because that is how the teacher perceives it.

Pre-service teachers' participation in asynchronous on-line discussions has been a crucial and mandatory part of the teaching practicum in the School of Teacher Education in Donostia-San Sebastián (University of the Basque Country, Spain) since 2004. From the onset of this experience, the benefits and possibilities of these on-line discussions became apparent (Martínez-Arbelaiz et al. 2008), particularly in providing opportunities for pre-service teachers to link theory and practice, to identify discrepancies between the two, to raise problems for discussion, to uncover implicit assumptions in teaching and learning and in schools in general (Tyack and Tobin 1994), etc. Nevertheless, some critical voices (Aviv et al. 2003; Pawan et al. 2003; Ryan and Scott 2008; Zydney et al. 2011) claim that the discourse in asynchronous forums can easily turn into mere monologues, without real interaction, particularly if the instructions and tasks are not carefully designed. In those cases, students uncritically repeat theories they heard in their classes or just describe what happens in schools. Even worse, since students may feel they are in a panopticon (using Foucault's metaphor) and observed by the teacher, they may tend to avoid certain topics or repeat the "official curriculum". This is why we decided to look critically at the discourse student teachers produced in the forums. By analyzing the discourse we can see if there is evidence of the emergence of a shared repertoire, one of the three characteristics of a CoP.

25.5 The Problem of Meaning: Negotiation of Meaning and the Development of a Shared Repertoire

According to Gee (2004), situated meanings do not simply reside in individual minds. Instead, they are negotiated between people through communicative social interaction. In the logs of the discussions among the student teachers, we want to see if there are instances of what has been called "negotiation of meaning" (Varonis and Gass 1985). In our research those would be cases where student teachers crucially co-constructed meaning regarding issues pertaining to education. These instances of negotiation of meaning were identified and codified using a fixed scheme developed by Garrison et al. (2001) and modified by Lee (2011). This schema consist of Triggering (the utterances that cause the interactive episode to develop), Exploration (where doubts, concerns or inconsistencies are expressed), Integration (when the student who uttered or wrote the critical incident discusses, expands, explains or tries to clarify or solve the misunderstanding) and Resolution (where there is an acknowledgment by any student that the episode can be considered closed). In applying this simple and intuitive coding schema to the discourse generated by student teachers, we were able to see whether there were instances of negotiation of meaning with regard to their practices in the schools.

The negotiation of meaning is not only a sign that there is interaction among the forum participants, but it also indicates that they are engaging in the development of a shared repertoire or a conceptual toolbox whose meaning they are negotiating together. This shared repertoire is the one that can facilitate further discussion and critical thinking about issues in education. Thus, the research question we want to address in this chapter is whether the discourse generated in the forums contains any evidence of the negotiation of a shared repertoire. If this were the case, we could claim that the pedagogical intervention fostered the development of thinking tools for student teachers' participation in future professional CoPs.

25.6 Methodology

In order to ascertain whether the discourse was produced collaboratively and whether it showed episodes of negotiation of meaning, we analysed the logs of three random groups in the School of Teacher Education: (1) a group of 6 students in 2007–2008, (2) a group of 5 in 2008–2009 and (3) a group of 4 in 2009–2010. The ideal number of students that should interact through a computer is hotly debated in the literature on education, and the literature usually points to the benefits of small sized groups (Hewitt and Brett 2007; Schellens and Valcke 2006), like the ones analysed here.

In addition, one or two practicum supervisors participated in the discussions, although they did not act as discussion leaders. In fact, there were some discussions where they did not participate at all. The first group held its discussion in Spanish while the last two did so in Basque. The language choice was determined beforehand as part of the course description of the practicum students opted to register for. In our logs there were no language switches and the students and supervisors adhered to the language listed in the course description.

All the postings of the student teachers and the instructors were collected in the form of logs, which told us the date and the name of the student who was in control of the discussion. Each week a student teacher explained a critical incident and opened the discussion, and the other student teachers were required to participate. In order to codify the discourse, we applied (Lee's 2011) adaptation of Garrison et al.'s (2001) model. If there were doubts among the three researchers, these were discussed until we reached agreement about what constituted an instance of negotiation of meaning and what could not be considered one.

25.7 Results: Instances of Negotiation of Meaning in Student Teachers' On-Line Discussions

In what follows we reproduce verbatim the discourse that was used by the student teachers to co-construct the meaning of relevant constructs in education. We have coded the postings according to the role they have in the development of the negotiation of meaning. In terms of their frequency, they are rather serendipitous and there were many forums in which we could not find any. However, when student teachers engaged in one of these negotiated interactions, we could actually observe the steps in the collaborative construction of the shared repertoire.

We have selected four instances of negotiation of meaning which illustrate different approaches to this co-construction of meaning: in the first one, two students discuss the meaning of a commonly repeated phrase, "learning for life", which they adopted from the lectures of a previous professor. In the second case, the initial posting triggers a cascade of questions, which the student teacher responded to and integrated one by one; not surprisingly this critical incident describes a complex situation of a child with a hearing impairment. The third case crucially discusses the behaviour of the practicum instructor, who seems to have a wonderful rapport with the children and she never forces them to do anything. Finally, the fourth case deviates a little from the previous three, since what the students negotiate is their feelings about the practicum and the anxiety that posting in this forum entails.

The four cases illustrate the possibilities of the forum as a site for critical thinking and sharing emotions during this liminal stage that is a hallmark of being a student teacher.

Case 1: "Aprendizaje para la vida" or learning for life

A student teacher (Luisa) writes about a critical incident where a young girl receives physical abuse from a young boy on the playground. After describing the events in chronological order and sharing with the other student teachers her contradictory feelings about how to react, the student teacher remembers and brings to the forum a sentence heard from a university professor in one of their previous classes. This quote is the triggering of an instance of negotiation of meaning, since another student teacher (Amaia) interprets the university professor's quote differently. This second student's posting is the Exploration, where there is evidence that there has been some misunderstanding or the former message has to be negotiated so the students come to an agreement. After Amaia says that she understands "education for life" to mean something else, Luisa has to explain her understanding of the quote further. We call this phase Integration, where the source of the misunderstanding is revised by the first student, former assumptions are challenged and eventually, there is agreement. In this interaction, there is a resolution, since the student who initiated the routine also closes it by saying that the meaning of the sentence is now clear.

> Triggering: Luisa: Esto me dio mucho que pensar y me vino a la cabeza una frase que nos ha dicho varias veces un profesor de Universidad: "La educación obligatoria sirve para lograr aprendizaje para la vida".

> This made me think a lot and a sentence repeated several times by a university professor came to mind: "Compulsory education helps lead to learning for life".

> Exploration: Amaia: La escuela para aprender a manejarte en la vida, como comentabas, ¿qué significa? Que esa niña tiene que comerse ese malrato (sic) e irse acostumbrando a que la vida es así? Pues no sé, no sé si somos los maestros las personas adecuadas para dar un

abrazo, o simplemente ofrecer afecto mediante una conversación amable, hablando del tema y ofreciendo herramientas para estas situaciones.

School is for learning how to handle things in daily situations, as you commented, what does it mean? That the child has to come to terms with the bad treatment and get used to the idea that life is like that? Well, I do not know if we teachers are the appropriate people to hug her or simply offer affection through a nice conversation, talking about the issue and offering tools for these situations.

Integration: Luisa: Hola a tod@s!

He leído los comentarios sobre lo que escribí y, al leer el comentario de Amaia me han entrado dudas sobre si había quedado claro lo que yo quería expresar. Cuando escribí que en la educación obligatoria se aprende aquello que nos va a servir para la vida, me refería a que durante esta etapa escolar se aprender a leer, a escribir, a realizar funciones matemáticas y conocimientos de cultura general, es decir, aprendizajes funcionales que luego nos servirán para la vida. No me refería para nada a que se deban permitir todo tipo de situaciones (abusos, agresiones…) en la escuela porque también nos lo vamos a encontrar en la vida. (…)

Hello, everybody! I have read the comments about what I wrote and when reading Amaia's comments I had doubts about whether what I wanted to convey was clear or not. When I wrote that in compulsory education we learn those things that are needed for life, I meant that during schooling we learn to read, to write, to do math and general cultural knowledge, that is, functional learning that is good for life. I did not mean that all types of situations (abuse, aggression…) could be allowed in the school because we are going to find them in real life (…)

Resolution: Amaia: Hola Luisa, creo que has explicado perfectamente tu planteamiento…

Hello, Luisa, I think you have explained your proposal clearly.

This long interaction between the two members of the group shows how a coined phrase that has been repeated and taken from a former university professor without much thinking needs to be further explained in the context of the practicum. Where do we place the violence that is occurring in our schools? How should the ideal teacher react to it? Should student teachers get used to it? These are relevant questions that student teachers posit in this discussion, and in the negotiation of the meaning of the phrase "learning for life" they decide to leave aspects related to abuse or aggressions out of the definition.

Case 2: The Roma child with a hearing impairment

Not all negotiation of meaning occurs in a dyadic fashion. In the following case, after the first student teacher describes the critical incident, there is more than one student who needs further explanation, reformulation or clarification. The on-line nature of these discussions facilitates different negotiations of meaning at the same time. This is something that could not take place in face-to-face interaction, where floor-sharing conventions rule (Sacks et al. 1974).

In this discussion, the student posted a case of a Roma child who has a serious hearing impairment and has not acquired a sign language. In addition to this, he seems to have some behaviour problems. This first posting triggers four additional messages that explore the intended meaning of the original posting. Two of those messages come from the university professor who supervises the practicum.

Triggering: Susana:

El no tener lenguaje más que el labial también provoca un conflicto de intereses en el colegio ya que se le tiene muy sobrepotegido sobre todo en el aula. Aunque también provoca muchos conflictos en el comedor porque el chaval se siente agredido por ejemplo en el comedor y se pelea con todo el mundo ya sean compañeros o personal del comedor.

Not having any language other than lip reading also causes a conflict of interest in the school because he is overprotected, particularly in the classroom. Although he also creates many conflicts in the lunchroom because the kid feels attacked, for example in the lunchroom and he fights with everybody, be they schoolmates or lunchroom personnel.

Exploration 1: Itziar:

¿cómo se relaciona con el resto de niños de la clase? ¿han aprendido a hablarle de manera que él pueda llerles (sic) los labios? Y, ¿con otros niños sordos, que supongo que no mueven los labios como el resto? ¿Cómo comunica él sus necesidades?

How does he relate to the other children in the class? have they learned to talk so he can read their lips? And, with other deaf children, who I suppose do not move their lips like the others? How does he communicate his needs?

Exploration 2: Begoña (practicum supervisor):

¿Cómo se comunica la P(edagoga) T(erapeuta) con él? ¿Y la tutora? ¿Y el resto del profesorado? ¿Qué esfuerzo real de acercamiento y de implicación en crear un vínculo afectivo se lleva a cabo? ¿Qué sentido tienen las horas fuera de la clase ordinaria? ¿Y encima con contenidos alejados de su momento cognitivo?

How does the E(ducational) T(herapist) communicate with him? And the tutor? And the rest of the teachers? What kind of real effort is being made to get closer and involve themselves and create an affective link? What meaning do the hours outside the regular classes have? On top of content that is far away from his cognitive situation?

Exploration 3: Miren: Lo que no entiendo muy bien es que conozca tan pocos signos estando escolarizado en una escuela bilingüe, donde la lengua de signos se supone que está tan presente como la lengua oral.

What I do not understand is how he knows so few signs being in a bilingual school, where sign language is supposed to be as present as oral language.

Exploration 4: Miren: Y en cuanto al desarrollo cognitivo y emocional, creo que en este caso lo necesario sería darle al niño una vía de comunicación por la que pudiese expresarse y recibir la información de su entorno, favoreciendo tanto el desarrollo cognitivo como el emocional. (…) Pero lo que no tengo muy claro es cuánta repercusión tiene sobre el desarrollo cognitivo, ya no tanto la sordera como la no disposición de una lengua o sistema que posibilite la comunicación con el entorno, perdiéndose la mayor parte de lo que pasa.

Regarding cognitive and emotional development, I think that it is necessary to provide this child with some communication tool so that he can express himself and receive information from his environment, thus favoring his emotional and cognitive development. But I have doubts about the impact of not only deafness but the lack of a language or communication system on his cognitive development, because he is missing the most of what is going on.

At this point the student in charge of the critical incident opts to respond to each one of the explorations one after the other:

Incorporation: Susana to Practicum upervisor 2 (Begoña): En cuanto al uso o no de la lengua de signos, que no lenguaje, Begoña preguntas con quién va a poder comunicarse en el tiempo que pase alejado del entorno escolar usando la lengua de signos, pues con el resto de personas sordas con las que tarde o temprano va a terminar juntándose. Todos necesitamos relacionarnos con los demás, y por mi experiencia, te puedo decir, que las personas sordas, buscan la compañía de personas sordas, estando entre ellos, o con personas oyentes ussarías (sic) de lengua de signos, es cuando se sienten plenamente integrados, donde acceden a la información y participan realmente en una conversación, sienten que pertenecen al grupo.

Regarding the use of sign language, not sign language capacity, Begoña you ask who he can communicate with during the time he is away from the school environment using sign language, well, with all the rest of the deaf people he will sooner or later meet with. We all need to engage with others and according to my experience, I can tell you that deaf people look for deaf people's company, being among them or with hearing people who use sign language; that is when they feel totally integrated, where they can access information and really participate in conversations; they feel they belong.

Incorporation Susana answers to Miren: En cuanto a la escuela, tiene que facilitar el acceso a la información y a la comunicación de las personas sordas, ¿cómo? En mi opinión (sic), contando con profesionales sordos y oyentes, técnicos/as de lengua de signos, asesores sordos e intérpretes de lengua de signos. No debemos olvidar que las nuevas tecnologías podrían ayudar mucho en el contexto escolar. La información y la formación sobre las necesidades del alumnado sordo van a ser imprescindibles para su desarrollo y autonomía.

Regarding the school, it has to facilitate deaf students' access to information and communication, but how? In my opinion, with the help of deaf and hearing professionals, experts in sign language, deaf counselors, sign language interpreters. We should not forget that new technologies can help a lot in the school context. Information and training about deaf students' needs are going to be indispensible for their development and autonomy.

Incorporation: Susana to Miren: En cuanto al desarrollo cognitivo se refiere, debemos tener en cuenta todas las cosas, todos los estímulos que nosotros recibimos por el oído, todas las cosas que aprendemos simplemente porque las oímos ellos no tienen esa posibilidad, por lo que hay que aprovechar cualquier situación cotidiana para explicar cosas, hacer que les llegue la información a través de vivencias, imágenes, explicaciones, etc. (...)

Regarding cognitive development, we have to take everything into account, all the stimuli that we receive through the ear, all the things we learn just because we hear them, they do not have this possibility, that is why we should take advantage of every single daily situation to explain things, so that they get the information through experiences, images, explanations, etc. (...)

Incorporation: Susana to Itziar

Itziar preguntaba que como mostraba el (sic) sus necesidades, pues de una manera oral con la poca comunicación que tiene y por diferentes gestos que los han ido creando en la escuela.

Itziar was asking how he shows his needs, he does it orally with the little communication he has and through different gestures that they have been developing in the school.

Incorporation: Susana to Miren and also to Practicum Supervisor 2:

Además en la escuela como ya dije estan dando lengua de signos pero con el vocabulario del día a día, y los niños oyentes tambien (sic) están aprendiendo diferentes palabras. La P (edagoga) T(erapeuta) y el resto del profesorado se comunica con el (sic) a partir de la lectura labial y con la lengua de signos.

In addition, as I told you, they are studying sign language in the school, but with everyday vocabulary and the hearing children are also learning different words. The E(ducational) T (herapist) and the rest of the teachers communicate with him through lip reading and sign language.

Estoy de acuerdo con Miren que la lengua de signos es necesaria para que llegen (sic) a comprender en su totalidad el mensaje, y que lo que al fin y al cabo se quiere llegar a conseguir es que Ibon sepa desenvolverse de una manera normal en la sociedad.

I agree with Miren that sign language is necessary so that they completely understand the message and, when all is said and done what we want is for Ibon to learn how to function normally in society.

In this particularly lengthy discussion of a critical incident, the student teachers do not give closure to the multiple explorations afforded by the initial posting. In other words, we do not find a resolution. However, after the forum was closed (each one lasted a week), the student teacher continues giving detailed explorations of the case:

Resolution: Susana:

Hola ya se (sic) que el foro está cerrado pero es que ayer anduve liada y no saqué tiempo para contestar. Volveros a dar las gracias y contestar a Miren, los niños oyentes si saben las pautas que deben seguir con los niños sordos, se les ha ido enseñando, por otra parte dos veces al mes mas (sic) o menos recineb (sic) una clase de lengua de signos, donde los niños sordos son los principales protagonistas.

Hello I know that the forum is closed but I was busy yesterday and I did not have time to answer. I want to say thanks again and answer Miren, hearing children know the guidelines they have to use with deaf children, they have been taught to, on the other hand, twice a month more or less, they receive a class in sign language, where the deaf children play the starring role.

The discourse helped student teachers to face disabilities that they had never encountered before. Very often, hearing problems affect speaking abilities and in this case, since the child did not receive any early intervention, his sign language development seems very low. The situation triggers a great deal of curiosity and student teachers negotiate their understanding of children with special needs. Although we as readers of this discussion are left with a very superficial understanding of what it means to have a child with disabilities in a class, this is not surprising since no expert of inclusive education was part of it. In their research with high school teachers, Vermeulen et al. (2012) found that there could be negative beliefs and emotions among teachers in response to the inclusion of deaf and hard of hearing students. In particular, they "recommend teacher educators and school principals to create opportunities for teachers to gain positive experiences with inclusive education" (p. 181).

Case 3: What does the teacher do if children do not collaborate?

In the third case, the student teacher responsible for posting the critical incident writes about the rapport the practicum instructor has with the children. The student teacher describes the behaviour of this teacher in great detail and with admiration.

She observes that the practicum instructor does not have to force the children to do anything, but she convinces them that it is the best thing to do. This ideal situation where no coercion or threats are used triggers a negotiation of meaning, since another student teacher is not sure if she has properly understood the situation. In fact, this second student teacher, Sofia, casts some doubts on the techniques this ideal practicum instructor (Izaskun) uses to motivate her students.

Triggering: Sara:

Izaskunek ez die ezer egitera behartzen. Normalean haurrek egin beharrekoa ondo hartzen dute eta hobeto edo okerrago egin egiten, badakitelako "hala" egin behar dela. Kasua ematen bada batek ez duela lan konkretu bat egiten (gutxitan, baina gertatu da). Instructoreak zera esaten dio: "Bueno, zuk ikusi, bi aukera dituzu: bat kareta bukatu eta arratsaldean jarrita eraman etxera, edo bestea, ez egin eta arratsaldean karetarik gabe joango zara, beste laguntxo guztiak ez bezala. Zuk ikusi". Hau da, aukerak aurkeztu, ondorioak ere, eta berak erabaki dezala.

Izaskun does not force them to do anything. Normally, the kids have a good attitude and they do their tasks better or worse because they know they have to do them. In the case that someone does not want to do something (seldom, but it has happened), the instructor says: "OK, you will see, you have two options: finish the mask and take it home with you in the afternoon, or don't do it and go home without the mask, unlike your little friends. You can choose". That is, she presents options, consequences, and he chooses.

Exploration: Sofia: Baina nire duda zera da, haur batek fitxa bat egin nahi ez duenean Izaskunek ze nolako aukerak eskaintzen dizkio? Hau da, egin edo ez egin? Edo bihar egingo duzu gaur egin ez duzuna? Edo nola?

But my question is the following, if a child does not want to finish his or her assignment, what kind of options does Izaskun give? That is, do it or not do it? Or you can finish tomorrow what you have not finished today? And how?

Incorporation: Sara: Haur batek fitxa egin nahi ez duenean Izaskunek zer eskaintzen dion galdetzen duzu, edo zer egiten duen. Normalean haur guztiek egiten dituzte fitxak, gustora batzuk, ez hainbeste besteek. Inoiz ez zen gertatu tematu eta fitxa egiten hasi nahi ez izatea. Gerta liteke bat asko moteltzea edo gogorik ez izatea. Orduan Izaskun motibatzen saiatzen da, edo pizten pixka bat, esanez "orain ez baduzu bukatzen hurrengo txokoan bukatu beharko duzu", edo "zuk ikusi, gero karpeta polit-polita eta lan guztiekin txukun-txukun etxera eramaten dituztenean ez da bertan zure lana egongo eta pena izango da", edo horrelako zerbait. (…)

You are asking what Izaskun asks or does if a child does not want to do his or her assignment. Usually all the kids do their assignments, some with pleasure, others not so much. It has never happened that a child becomes stubborn and does not want to finish the task. It might happen that they are slow or they do not feel like it. Then Izaskun tries to motivate them or give them energy by saying "if you don't finish now, you will finish it in the next room" or "you'll see it, but when you bring home your beautiful portfolio with your neat assignments, this one won't be there".

Resolution: Sara: Espero dut zure zalantzak argitu izana.

I hope I have clarified your doubts.

In this particular negotiation, the student teachers go in depth into what to do when children do not participate and the modeling of the practicum instructor becomes the main source for learning teaching techniques. In this discourse, we see the power of observing and reflecting on the practices of the experienced teachers, which are shared and discussed collaboratively. In this fashion, a particular feature of the shared repertoire of the CoP of the school where Sara is doing her practicum, namely, how to treat uncooperative children, is shared with the group of the student teachers in the forum. We can thus see how by delving deeper into the questions that student teachers posit, the shared repertoire gets refined and its meaning is being built.

Case 4: Negotiation of emotions

The last case we selected and discuss shows the emotions, particularly tension and dissatisfaction that emerge from the liminal situation of the student teachers. The discussion of the critical case is abandoned, and the student teachers and the practicum supervisor discuss the strong emotions that the teaching situation generates. As we have argued elsewhere (Correa et al. 2014), the delicate and liminal position that student teachers occupy makes them very vulnerable, and in some cases, this feeling of being on the periphery in the CoP of the school makes them pay an emotional toll. Usually, their ideas and proposals are not taken seriously, as Woodgate-Jones (2012) already observed. This is why in this context it is particularly valuable that student teachers can talk to each other and share the emotional rollercoaster they experience. In the forum exchange we reproduce below, besides using some metaphors to express these emotions, such as standing before the sea, the other student teachers recognize that they all have similar feelings and they can relate to the feelings being described. We reproduce the discussion between Aintzane, Ana, who had posted a previous message, and Alicia.

Aintzane: Esperientzia hau bestelakoa da: itsasoaren aurean egotea bezalakoa. Sakona, misteriotsua, erakargarria, errespetua sortzen duena, nondik joko duen ez dakizu eta horrexegatik kontzentrazio maila izugarria da. Bere pozak izugarrizko poza sortzen dizu.

"Berritzaile hauek ez dute ikasgelako errealitatea ezagutzen". "Egunerokoak, eginbeharrak definitzen ditu". Aditutako komentario bat.

Aintzane: This experience has been different, like standing before the sea. Deep, mysterious, attractive, one that brings respect, one that makes you feel lost and because of this, it requires concentration. Their satisfaction creates an incredible feeling of satisfaction inside of you.

"These innovators do not know the reality of the classroom" "The daily routine and work that has to be done define it" Comments that I have heard...

Aintzane to Ana: Zure animoak eta interesak hunkitu naute. Mila esker ezer baino lehen. Foroaren asunto honek antsietate apurtxo bat sorzen dit eta gaia atsegin duzula jakiteak aurrera jarraitzeko indarra eman dit.

Aintzane to Ana: Your interest and support have moved me. First of all, thank you. This forum thing is making me anxious and to hear that you liked the topic has given me strength to move on.

Alicia: Zuk sentitutako amorru eta ezintasun berdina sentitu dudala uste dut.

I think I have felt the same anger and the anxiety that you have felt.

Aintzane: Mila esker nire kontutxoak jasotzeko eta ideak gakoak identifikatzen laguntzeko. Uste dut magisteritza hasi nintzenetik ez naizela hain "taldekide" sentitu. Entzuna izana, feed-back konstruktiboa jasotzea edo zure ideia osatuta edo buelta emanda ikustea esperientzia potentea da, oso.

Thank you very much for telling me these little stories and for helping me to identify the key ideas. I think that this is the first time that I have felt "part of a group" since I started studying teacher education. Being heard, receiving constructive feedback or seeing your idea completed or changed is a very moving experience.

In this last case, the value of these interactions is not to enhance the toolbox or shared repertoire that will make them gain authentication as teachers, as the first three cases showed, but their value comes from sharing emotions that, as Aintzane said, tied the group together. Her actual words cannot be more revealing: "I think that this is the first time that I have felt 'part of a group' since I started studying teacher education". This shows that it is not only the sharing and co-construction of concepts, ideas or techniques regarding education that can make us part of a CoP, but also the sharing of feelings and emotions. As was mentioned earlier, these emotions are particularly salient in the confrontation with the experienced teachers or the practicum instructor in the schools, as the comments Aintzane heard at her school show.

25.8 Discussion

We started this chapter by casting doubt on the value of on-line discussions in the overall professional identity-building of the teacher of the future. Besides reducing their sense of isolation while they complete their practicum, we wondered whether this discourse was helpful in terms of developing a CoP of professionals, where the shared repertoire was negotiated. By applying the model of negotiation of meaning, we have been able to document that student teachers discussed and problematized important concepts in education. Specifically, we observed how student teachers discussed among themselves what is meant by "school learning is learning for life", what it means to have students with special needs in our classroom, how to motivate students and how to cope with the emotions that being a student teacher and not a regular teacher entails. Thus, to clarify our initial doubts, the analysis of the on-line discourse reported here has proved to be very interactive and we have observed that there are some instances of negotiation of meaning in the discussions. In addition, the presence of two practicum supervisors did not seem to induce variation in the amount of breakdowns in communication. We can conclude that this particular form of interactions is rich in terms of presenting explorations and incorporations from different members of the group at the same time, as was seen in Case 2.

The practicum supervisors did not always act as an expert. In fact, in Case 2 the student teacher corrects the supervisor's expression "lenguaje de signos" for the one commonly used in Spanish, "lengua de signos". Through this discourse move, the student self-positions herself as the expert. Recent studies in the field of language acquisition, such as Reichert and Liebscher (2012), contend that the division between experts and novice is "an unrealistic model for students working cooperatively to carry out activities. The display and acceptance of expertise is strongly situated in interaction." (p. 607)

In our data, the practicum supervisors not acting as experts reduced the opportunities for negotiations of meaning. However, there could be an additional explanation for the absence of negotiations initiated by the practicum supervisors. It may very well be that student teachers do not want to give an image of incompetency. Adopting Goffman's (1959) understanding of how individuals project a self-image, it is clear that pre-service teachers will do everything they can to hide gaps in their knowledge of pedagogical theories or constructs. They are in this liminal stage where they want to be perceived as competent, and indicating that something needs to be further reformulated can be a face-threatening discourse move. The forum is clearly a public space, which means that everybody is reading what everybody says and drawing conclusions about the teaching identity of the others. Thus, misunderstandings, which could interfere with the authentication process (Bucholtz 2003), should be kept to a minimum, unless someone clearly points to the source of confusion and asks for further elaboration. In the discourse analysis presented here some explorations were made explicit, and these were usually resolved. This happened at a comfortable rate that let the interactions flow at an adequate speed.

Summarizing, the interactions described and analysed here are evidence that collaborative thinking is at work. They also give evidence of the negotiation work required to construct what (Wenger 1998) named the shared repertoire, which can act as a thinking tool to reflect on their experiences in the schools. By shaping this shared repertoire, one of the ingredients of the CoP is built among the student teachers discussing in the forums. We do not want to conclude that this is enough to state that a CoP has been built, but minimally there is evidence that the student teachers are on their way to forging a professional CoP.

Finally, we believe it is crucial for teacher education programs to address the feelings of frustration among the future teachers, which are reflected in the forum discourse in Case 4. We should not forget that teaching, also in teacher education, involves not only enhancing critical thinking and giving the student teachers the theoretical tools they need, but also caring for and forming relationships with them. Although the value of forums in teacher education has been convincingly shown through the analysis of the discourse with the documentation of instances of negotiation of meaning, we should acknowledge the role of the forums as a valuable venue for expressing the feelings of frustration and vulnerability that being in the periphery entails. This is an area that has been marginally addressed in this chapter, but it will undoubtedly have to be further discussed by those in charge of preparing teachers for the schools of the future, including the authors of these lines.

25.9 Concluding Thoughts

Drawing on a wide range of notions coming from CoP theory, we have examined data from the on-line discussions of three groups of students while doing their teaching practicum. Following previous research (Correa et al. 2014; Yandell and Turvey 2007; Woodgate-Jones 2012), we assumed that these student teachers were in the periphery of the CoP represented by each of the schools where each student did the practicum. In addition, we questioned whether a CoP of future teachers was being forged among them with the participation of the practicum supervisor through the computer-mediated discussions. We understood that the discursive moves which are part of the negotiation of meaning are indicators that student teachers were building a shared repertoire.

The model of negotiation of meaning was a useful model against which the generated discourse could be analysed. It proved to be a simple tool that allowed us to identify the development of a shared repertoire of a number of concepts regarding the field of education, such as learning for life, children with special needs, motivation, as well as how to cope with the emotions that arise during the practicum. Schools of education and professors in particular should think critically when implementing technology-based innovations, but a close analysis of the outcomes, like the one exemplified here, can give them some understanding of their role in the building of students' professional identity.

Acknowledgments The authors are members of the Elkarrikertuz Research Group (IT 563 13) and REUNI+D, The University Network for Educational Research and Innovation (http://en. reunid.eu/). This chapter is part of the research project entitled "Building the identity of pre-school and primary education teachers during initial training and the first years of work" (EDU2010-20852-C02-02, 2010–2013), funded by the Ministry of Economy and Competitiveness of Spain. We thank Wendy Baldwin for her editing help and particularly for making sure that the English translations of the student teachers' words maintained the same register and tone.

References

Aviv, R., Erlich, Z., Ravid, G., & Geva, A. (2003). Network analysis of knowledge construction in asynchronous learning networks. *Journal of Asynchronous Learning Networks, 7*(3), 1–23.
Barab, S. A., & Duffy, T. (2000). From practice fields to communities of practice. In D. Jonassen & S. M. Land (Eds.), *Theoretical foundations of learning environments* (pp. 25–56). Mahwah, NJ: Lawrence Erlbaum Associates.
Bathmaker, A. M., & Avis, J. (2005). Becoming a lecturer in further education in England: The construction of professional identity and the role of communities of practice. *Journal of Education for Teaching, 31*(1), 47–62.
Bauman, Z. (2001). Identity in the globalizing world. *Social anthropology, 9*(2), 121–129.
Beauchamp, C., & Thomas, L. (2009). Understanding teacher identity: An overview of issues in the literature and implications for teacher education. *Cambridge Journal of Education, 39*(2), 175–189.
Bourdieu, P. (1985). *¿Qué significa hablar? Economía de los intercambios lingüísticos.* Madrid: Akal, DL.

Bucholtz, M. (2003). Sociolinguistic nostalgia and authentication of identity. *Journal of Sociolinguistics, 7*(3), 398–416.

Bucholtz, M., & Hall, K. (2005). Identity and interaction: A sociocultural linguistic approach. *Discourse Studies, 7*(4–5), 585–614.

Clarke, L. (2009). The POD model: Using communities of practice theory to conceptualise student teachers' professional learning online. *Computers and Education, 52*(3), 521–529.

Correa, J. M., Martínez-Arbelaiz, A., & Aberasturi-Apraiz, E. (2015). Post-modern reality shock: Beginning teachers as sojourners in communities of practice. *Teaching and Teacher Education, 48*, 66–74.

Correa, J. M., Martínez-Arbelaiz, A., & Gutierrez, L. P. (2014). Between the real school and the ideal school: Another step in building a teaching identity. *Educational Review, 66*(4), 447–464.

DePalma, R. (2009). Leaving Alinsu: Towards a transformative community of practice. *Mind, Culture, and Activity, 16*(4), 353–370.

Flanagan, J. C. (1954). The critical incident technique. *Psychological Bulletin, 51*(4), 327–358.

Garrison, D. R., Anderson, T., & Archer, W. (2001). Critical thinking, cognitive presence and computer conferencing in distance education. *American Journal of Distance Education, 15*(1), 7–23.

Gee, J. P. (2001). Identity as an analytic lens for research in education. In W. G. Secada (Ed.), *Review of research in education, 25* (pp. 99–125). Washington, DC: American Educational Research Association.

Gee, J. P. (2004). Learning languages as a matter of learning social languages within discourses. In M. R. Howkins (Ed.), *Language learning and teacher education: A sociocultural approach* (pp. 13–31). Clevedon: Multilingual Matters.

Gee, J. P. (2005). Semiotic social spaces and affinity spaces. In D. Barton & K. Tusting (Eds.), *Beyond communities of practice. Language, power and social context* (pp. 214–232). Cambridge: Cambridge University Press.

Giddens, A. (1995). *Modernidad e identidad del yo: el yo y la sociedad en la época contemporánea*. Barcelona: Península.

Goffman, E. (1959). *The presentation of self in everyday life*. New York: Doubleday Anchor Books.

Haneda, M. (2006). Classrooms as communities of practice: A reevaluation. *TESOL Quarterly, 40* (4), 807–826.

Hanson-Smith, E. (2006). Communities of practice for pre- and in-service teacher education. In P. Hubbard & M. Levy (Eds.), *Teacher education in CALL* (pp. 301–315). Amsterdam: John Benjamins.

Harré, R., & van Langenhove, L. (1991). Varieties of positioning. *Journal for the Theory of Social Behavior, 21*(4), 393–407.

Harré, R., & van Langenhove, L. (1999). *Positioning theory*. Oxford: Blackwell.

Harrington, H. L., Quinn-Leering, K., & Hodson, L. (1996). Written case analysis and critical reflection. *Teaching and Teacher Education, 12*(1), 25–37.

Hewitt, J., & Brett, C. (2007). The relationship between class size and online activity patterns in asynchronous computer conferencing environments. *Computers and Education, 49*(4), 1258–1271.

Hsu, S. (2004). Using case discussion on the web to develop student teacher problem solving skills. *Teaching and Teacher Education, 20*(7), 681–692.

Kelchtermans, G. (1994). Biographical methods in the study of teachers' professional development. In I. Carlgren, G. Handal, & S. Vaage (Eds.), *Teachers' minds and actions: Research on teachers' thinking and practice* (pp. 93–108). London: The Falmer Press.

Kwan, T., & Lopez-Real, F. (2010). Identity formation of teacher–mentors: An analysis of contrasting experiences using a Wengerian matrix framework. *Teaching and Teacher Education, 26*(3), 722–731.

Lave, J., & Wenger, E. (1991). *Situated learning: Legitimate peripheral participation*. Cambridge: Cambridge University Press.

Lee, L. (2011). Blogging: Promoting learner autonomy and intercultural competence through study abroad. *Language Learning and Technology, 15*(3), 87–109.

Martínez-Arbelaiz, A., Gutierrez Cuenca, L. P., Jimenez de Aberasturi, E., Correa Gorospe, J. M., & Ibañez Etxeberria, A. (2008). ICT in teacher education: Designing a practicum for reflection and inquiry. In K. McFerrin, R. Weber, R. Carlsen, & D. A. Willis (Eds.), *Proceedings of the society for information technology and teacher education international conference 2008* (pp. 3341–3346). Chesapeake, VA: AACE.

Niesz, T. (2010). Chasms and bridges: Generativity in the space between educators. *Teaching and Teacher Education, 26*(1), 37–44.

Pawan, F., Paulus, T. M., Yalcin, S., & Chang, C.-F. (2003). Online learning: Patterns of engagement and interaction amongst in-service teachers. *Language Learning and Technology, 7*(3), 119–140.

Pierce, K. A. (2007). Betwixt and between: Liminality in beginning teaching. *The New Educator, 3*(1), 31–49.

Reichert, T., & Liebscher, G. (2012). Positioning the expert: Word searches, expertise, and learning opportunities. *The Modern Language Journal, 96*(4), 599–609.

Ryan, J., & Scott, A. (2008). Integrating technology into teacher education: How online discussion can be used to develop informed and critical literacy teachers. *Teaching and Teacher Education, 24*(6), 1635–1644.

Sacks, H., Schegloff, E. A., & Jefferson, G. (1974). A simplest systematics for the organization of turn-taking for conversation. *Language, 50*(4), 696–735.

Schellens, T., & Valcke, M. (2006). Fostering knowledge construction in university students through asynchronous discussion groups. *Computers and Education, 46*(4), 349–370.

Sim, C. (2006). Preparing for professional experiences—Incorporating pre-service teachers as 'communities of practice'. *Teaching and Teacher Education, 22*(1), 77–83.

Tyack, D., & Tobin, W. (1994). The "grammar" of schooling: Why has it been so hard to change? *American Educational Research Journal, 31*(3), 453–479.

Varonis, E. M., & Gass, S. (1985). Non-native/non-native conversations: A model for negotiation of meaning. *Applied Linguistics, 6*(1), 71–90.

Vermeulen, J. A., Denessen, E., & Knoors, H. (2012). Mainstream teachers about including deaf or hard of hearing students. *Teaching and Teacher Education, 28*(2), 174–181.

Warriner, D. S. (2010). Competent performances of situated identities: Adult learners of English accessing engaged participation. *Teaching and Teacher Education, 26*(1), 22–30.

Weedon, C. (1987). *Feminist practice and poststructuralist theory*. Oxford: Blackwell.

Weedon, C. (1997). Teaching post-structuralist feminist theory in education: Student resistances. *Gender and Education, 9*(3), 261–269.

Wenger, E. (1998). *Communities of practice: Learning, meaning, and identity*. New York: Cambridge University Press.

Woodgate-Jones, A. (2012). The student teacher and the school community of practice: An exploration of the contribution of the legitimate peripheral participant. *Educational Review, 64*(2), 145–160.

Yandell, J., & Turvey, A. (2007). Standards or communities of practice? Competing models of workplace learning and development. *British Educational Research Journal, 33*(4), 533–550.

Zydney, J. M., de Noyelles, A., & Seo, K. J. (2011). Creating a community of inquiry in online environments: An exploratory study on the effect of a protocol on interactions within asynchronous discussions. *Computers and Education, 58*(1), 77–87.

Chapter 26
Forums, Fellowship and Wicked Problems in Teaching

Elizabeth A. Beckmann

Abstract Many of the concerns of university teachers constitute 'wicked' problems—wicked not in the sense that they are evil, but rather in the way that they resist definition and analysis, are presented differently by different stakeholders, and at best are 'resolved' rather than 'solved'. This could explain why there are no globally-, nationally- or even institutionally-accepted 'right' ways to teach in any discipline, and why communities of practice have become important mechanisms for pooling and sharing the knowledge, experiences and skills of university professionals who are focused on teaching and learning in a given context. Can the encouragement of shared reflective thinking as a tool of inquiry in a fairly transient community of practice (CoP) provide these university teachers some respite from the constant search for 'the' right answer by helping them understand the realities of finding 'an' answer? This chapter reviews the characteristic CoP interactions that occur among participants in online discussion forums that augment face to face professional development and professional recognition workshops about teaching and learning at an Australian university. Even though these online interactions are relatively fleeting, cross-disciplinary, and constituted by diverse groups of participants, empirical analysis suggests they provide adequate evidence of the nine thematic signals of effective communities of practice described by Wenger (Communities of practice: A brief introduction, 2012), and illustrate the kinds of wicked problems with which university educators grapple on a daily basis.

Keywords Community of practice · Online discussion · Professional development · Professional recognition · Reflective practice · Teaching self-efficacy · Wicked problems · University teaching

E.A. Beckmann (✉)
Centre for Higher Education, Learning and Teaching, Australian National University,
Canberra, Australia
e-mail: elizabeth.beckmann@anu.edu.au

© Springer Nature Singapore Pte Ltd. 2017
J. McDonald and A. Cater-Steel (eds.), *Communities of Practice*,
DOI 10.1007/978-981-10-2879-3_26

26.1   Introduction: Wicked Problems and the World of University Teaching

If we acknowledge that problems are 'discrepancies between the state of affairs as it is and the state as it ought to be' (Rittel and Webber 1973, p. 165), it is clear that many—if not most—university teachers have problems. These teachers design courses, plan learning activities, create assessment tasks, spend time marking and giving feedback, and yet are often puzzled—even disappointed—in how, or how much, or when, or even why, their students learn. The desire to succeed is nevertheless strong in these teachers, as they all seek the magic bullet of teaching. This leads the innovators to try something completely new, the followers to try the latest innovation craze—peer learning, groupwork, flipped classrooms, massive open online courses—and the researchers to study them (alas, often without a guiding theoretical framework; Bulfin et al. 2013). Yet, whatever the teachers try, as their career lengthens they note that the problems persist: some students are committed but nonetheless fail, some students don't come to classes but still pass, some students learn from boring activities, and some find it hard to learn no matter how exciting or engaging the teacher tries to be. One lesson is always found to be true, however: 'you can't please all the students all the time'.

Could it be that the concerns that plague university teachers fall into the category of 'wicked' problems? These are problems that resist definition; that require you to think of all the possible solutions before you can even understand the problem properly; that are presented differently by different stakeholders, and shift shape even as you try to find out about them; that are not accessible to trial-and-error testing, because every tried solution generally involves a significant, potentially irreversible, change to the problem; and that, at best, are 'resolved' rather than 'solved' (Conklin 2003; Knight 2007; Rittel and Webber 1973). Certainly, despite every university in the world teaching very similar discipline areas, and the very same knowledge in many cases (especially in the 'hard' sciences), we have not discovered the 'right' way to teach simply by trying many different approaches, averaging the outcome data, and achieving consensus. Schön (1983, p. 43) explained that this inaccessibility to relatively simple technical solutions occurs in education because the important problems lie not in the 'high, hard ground' of research-based knowledge but rather in the 'swampy lowland'. Hence, while we imagine that teaching 'problems' would be soluble *if only* we could apply sufficient evidence, reason and resources, in reality we find solutions that are only partially satisfying (Borko et al. 2009). Moreover, even those partial solutions may well be providing evidence not so much about teaching and learning but more about how universities exercise the power of assessment and accreditation—students may well 'learn', but only because they want a degree, not because we have created an environment where learning is easy.

Henderson (2008) demonstrated that teachers' professional learning is intimately connected with their professional identities, which develop over time and are not easily changed simply by providing technical training in new skills. Nevertheless, most universities expect professional development to help their academic staff become 'better' teachers (Dearn et al. 2002; Gibbs and Coffey 2004; Hicks et al. 2010). The notion of what exactly constitutes 'better' in this context is obviously contested, but a general consensus—at least in Western-style higher education—is first, that teachers become more student-centred, in that they become more concerned with students learning (Biggs 1999) and secondly, that they increase their own self-efficacy (Bandura 2000), that is, their "confidence in their ability to promote students' learning" (Hoy 2000).

As someone facilitating a teaching professional development program, I found myself wondering how I could help both early career and more experienced academics engage with an understanding of teaching as an archetypal wicked problem —that there may be no one 'right' way to approach any teaching task (although there may be some greater clarity around 'wrong' ways). Brown (2010) argues that, if we are even to begin to engage with the complexities posed by wicked problems, cross-disciplinary Communities of Practice (CoPs) are a key strategy. Certainly CoPs—whether named as such or not—are increasingly becoming a preferred way of engaging with thinking about university teaching and learning. For example, McDonald et al. (2008, p. 222) reported on a CoP comprising a group of Australian academics who taught first year courses, and reported a range of benefits: 'real communication and ongoing dialogue across institutional barriers; a sense of trust required to open up a safe place to share common challenges and enable social learning; support and professional development; and a model of strategic thinking and strategic action'. But how structured does a CoP have to be to ensure its success? Several successful Australian peer engagement projects—such as the Peer Assisted Teaching Scheme (Carbone 2014) and the Science and Mathematics Network of University Educators (Sharma et al. 2014)—have had diverse structures but underlying philosophies that reveal CoP principles (Wenger et al. 2002; Wenger 2012). First, they comprise "groups of people who share a concern or a passion for something they do and learn how to do it better as they interact regularly" (Wenger 2012). Secondly, over "time and sustained interaction", these practitioners come to develop a "shared practice" (Wenger 2012) and become a "knowledge-based social structure" (Wenger et al. 2002, p. 5). The time element is important, and requires thinking beyond casual encounters: "a good conversation with a stranger on an airplane may give you all sorts of interesting insights, but it does not in itself make for a community of practice" (Wenger 2012).

With the notion of time as potentially a key limiting factor for today's academics becoming involved in a CoP, several driving questions became paramount. Was it possible for the potentially powerful influences of a CoP to be at play even when time-frames are short? Could the impacts of CoP learning still occur even when exchanges between members of the CoP are short-term rather than sustained, but nonetheless occur within a structured framework? Could one find evidence of CoP characteristics even within the fairly broad context of groups of diversely-experienced participants attending professional development workshops blended with online forums for reflection on each workshop? In particular, were such online discussion forums acting to 'stretch' the interactive time among CoP members, and thus adding an extra dimension to the benefits of face to face sharing and peer learning? Importantly, would the questions raised by academics in these online discussion forums be essentially trivial, or would they stretch into the realm of wicked problems?

In this chapter, I discuss these questions—with a focus on the last two—based on evidence from a case study of university teachers engaged in blended (face to face and online) communities engaged in professional development and professional recognition at an Australian tertiary institution. First, I consider some of the special issues related to the online aspect of this professional learning environment. Then I describe the analytical methodology used to examine online discussions to characterise them in terms of the nine representative 'exchange of practice' categories that (Wenger 2012) has identified as characteristic of CoPs, showing that even relatively transient engagements can have serious impacts in terms of exchanges of practice. Moreover, many of these transient CoP-type experiences were centred on the wicked problems of teaching that participants encounter in their working lives. Finally, I leave readers with a vision of the future where professional learning and recognition pathways provide university educators with CoPs that are relatively rapidly formed and re-formed.

26.1.1 Special Aspects of the Online Environment

Establishing the CoP framework in a blended learning context has required thoughtful use of technology (as advocated by Wenger et al. 2009). For example, the creation of an online private dialogue option as well as the group forum proved vital for those participants who (Wenger et al. 2009, p. 208) call 'readers' (those who read others' postings but never or rarely post themselves, often because of lack of confidence or active discomfort in the online space; Beckmann 2011):

> I liked the option of private feedback as I'm not from the share everything generation. (Anonymous participant feedback 2014).

Participants who do not wish to post in the public forum but do want a certificate of their engagement in the program, will post in the private space:

> I think it's a great idea that you give participants the option of submitting their reflections privately and publicly. A fine example of flexible learning in action. (Anonymous participant feedback 2014).

Here, the facilitator can respond not only in terms of the content but also by pointing out that at least part of the participant's private post describes ideas or experiences that would be valuably shared with the broader group. Some participants, emboldened by positive encouragement from the 'expert', will then progress to sharing on the open forum, which creates the opportunity for members of the broader CoP to respond. In keeping with the experiential and reflective learning tone of the workshops, some participants applied personal learning from this approach to their own teaching practice:

> I like having both options—I personally prefer to have a private conversation, but in this course, I pushed myself to put some posts in the general forum. This actually made me think that I will also put both the general forum and the private dialogue in my [online course site] for this coming semester. (Anonymous participant feedback 2014)

Undeniably, all the discursive characteristics of a CoP are evident in each face to face module of the professional development program, with its many small- and large-group discussion during the twenty hours of contact. However, by introducing the requirements for online discussion elements into the course, the facilitator was deliberately maximising the opportunities for participants to engage in productive reflective practice in writing as well as through individually cognitive or pair/group conversational exchanges. This level of facilitation 'expertise' comes from the facilator's avowed belief that every participant is not simply an attendee seeking to learn from the facilitator as 'expert', but is actually already an informed practitioner within an emergent CoP. The facilitator's leadership, in this sense, is most closely aligned with the concepts of 'quiet leadership' (Badaracco 2002).

The idea of a 'virtual CoP' in the continuing professional development of teaching academics pre-dates today's Internet of social networks and instant communication by almost two decades:

> … faculty need new ways of working together to prepare for and shape their professional future. Community … combined with computer mediated communication technology can help redefine teaching, learning, research, service, and professional development in higher education (Di Petta 1998, p. 54).

Not surprisingly, Houghton et al. (2014) report that virtual, or partially virtual, CoPs are quite common today, including among university academics, with peer to peer communication mediated partly, largely or entirely through technology. However, Dubé et al. (2006, p. 70) raised concerns that, while such approaches may conquer the tyrannies of space and time, they may also make CoP activities more difficult: "building mutual knowledge, trust among members, and a sense of belonging … may be more difficult through computer-mediated interactions". These authors' empirical research suggested that academics tend to have difficulty with the (then available) technology as an effective communication tool—they lacked trust in the online environment, and they were likely to show more "time jealousy" online than in face to face gatherings (Dubé et al. 2006). When Houghton et al. (2014) tried to test whether a virtual CoP was effective at advocating and spreading professional practice, they found that—even when their CoP members had a strong commitment to sharing practice and supporting others in face to face meetings—the same individuals tended to approach online activities with a view to 'direct, personal benefit' rather than group outcomes.

26.2   Case Study Context and Background

The case study describes an informal CoP that has been nurtured for several years within an Australian university's short course of professional development and recognition of university teaching, open to all engaged in teaching or supporting learners (academic staff, professional staff involved in student support services, and doctoral students already tutoring or anticipating an academic career). Facilitated by the author through 20 iterations since 2009, with 25–35 participants in each cohort, the *Foundations of University Teaching and Learning* course involves up to 25 h of face to face and, increasingly over time, online engagement. Participants' satisfaction ratings have been outstanding (averaging 95 %), with many participants reporting that the program was 'transformative'.

A key feature of the program has been its emphasis on multiple layers of reflective practice. Participants are encouraged, in the terms of Schön (1987), to reflect both 'on action' (thinking about what happened after an event) and 'in action' ('where thinking and doing coincide in a moment-to-moment adaptation'; Bleakley 1999, p. 322), and also to practice reflection 'as action' (reflexivity), seeking both to apply theory-in-practice and practice-as-theory in challenging personal and societal assumptions about teaching and learning (Bleakley 1999).

This emphasis on reflectivity and reflexivity is accomplished in three ways. First, reflection 'in action' and 'on action' (Schön 1983) are modelled during face to face sessions. Reflection is integrated interactively into all the learning activities, such that the participants learn to value one another both as peer learners (of the professional development concepts being presented) and as (more, or less, experienced) practitioners of the art of university teaching. At moments throughout the face to face learning activities, for example, participants are asked to 'stop the clock' and think about why an activity was structured in a particular way, or to question their assumptions leading into that activity. Do they actually believe what they are being told? If so, is this because they are constantly testing (reflecting on) the ideas against their own experience, or simply because they trust the facilitator? If the former, what happens when what they hear from others—the facilitator or their peers—doesn't match their own experiences: who do they believe? If the latter, what happens if the facilitator is wrong? Reflexivity is brought into play as the participants then reflect on what this would mean for their students.

Second, reflective practice (especially mediated through the written form) is presented theoretically and practically as an activity that is strongly advocated for teachers (e.g. Brookfield 1995; Schön 1983, 1987) because of its powerful capacity to lead to improvements in the quality of teaching and the satisfaction of teachers. Emphasis is especially placed on the importance of critical incidents (Brookfield 1995) in teaching as key stimuli for deep reflection.

Finally, reflection is presented as a course certification requirement. This is done in a blended learning context, requiring participants to post online a series of short but 'substantive' reflections on individual sessions or topics, either in a general forum that can be read, and responded to, by all participants or in a private dialogue with just the facilitator. As many of the participants have never before written on their thoughts on teaching, nor shared these with others, the process is considered another learning opportunity: participants are led through a face to face activity that scaffolds reflective writing before they make their first online postings and it is understood (and explained) that some may be further along the path of written reflective practice than others.

While the peer learning opportunities that occur face to face have been self-evident in students' responses and feedback, a question I have returned to again and again is to what extent this kind of short-term professional development—and especially the online reflections—can engender, and facilitate, a genuine CoP, rather than simply supporting a gathering of individuals with a shared focus on finding out more about the teaching work they do. Wenger (2012, p. 2) is very clear that simply 'having the same job or the same title does not make for a community of practice unless members interact and learn together'. Participants' shared domain of interest in this case is teaching and learning in a university context, to which the participants are committed, have an existing level of competence, and demonstrate (by their participation, which is not compulsory) a desire to extend that competence. However, while it is the participants' choice to "pursue their interest in this domain", it is the facilitator's (the author's) role to ensure that participants begin to "engage in joint activities and discussions, help each other, and share information … [and] build relationships that enable them to learn from each other." The third constituent element of a CoP is, of course, the shared practice: the members are practitioners (in this case, university teachers) who "develop a shared of resources: experiences, stories, tools, ways of addressing recurring problems" (Wenger 2006, p. 2). All these elements are just as valid in the case of developing technology-mediated CoPs online, but greater care must be taken in the mediation processes (Wenger et al. 2009).

26.3 Analytical Methodology

Noting that communities develop their practice through a variety of activities, Wenger (2012) gave nine focal examples of distinct outcomes that might be sought by communities in sharing their practice, and illustrated these with the typical kinds of questions that characterise those outcomes (Box 26.1).

Box 26.1 Nine characteristic outcomes sought by members of a Community of Practice, and questions that typify these outcomes (Wenger 2012)

Problem-solving   "Can we work on this design and brainstorm some ideas; I'm stuck."

Requests for information	"Where can I find the code to connect to the server?"
Seeking experience	"Has anyone dealt with a customer in this situation?"
Reusing assets	"I have a proposal for a local area network I wrote for a client last year. I can send it to you and you can easily tweak it for this new client."
Coordination and synergy	"Can we combine our purchases of solvent to achieve bulk discounts?"
Discussing developments	"What do you think of the new CAD system? Does it really help?"
Documentation projects	"We have faced this problem five times now. Let us write it down once and for all."
Visits	"Can we come and see your after-school program? We need to establish one in our city."
Mapping knowledge and identifying gaps	"Who knows what, and what are we missing? What other groups should we connect with?"

To establish empirically whether the online engagements among the workshop participants could be characterised as those of a CoP, these nine categories were used as thematic codifications with which to review and analyse the professional development participants' online forum postings and responses. The 15-month period from January 2014 to March 2015 was used as the sampling time, as this covered a large group of about 200 participants who had been involved over that time-frame, with a fairly consistent approach to the way the six iterations of ten professional development workshops had been run. As participants have no time limit as to when they post after the face to face workshop, this also maximized the likelihood that online conversations were 'complete' before analysis. This approach allowed for purposive sampling of 1500 posts from 134 participants from January to December 2014, and 500 posts from 65 participants from January to March 2015.

As the aim of the analysis was to look at online interactions between participants, postings from workshop forums were included in the study sample only if they had at least one response from another participant (excluding the facilitator). A suite of responses to an initial posting was treated as a single element for analysis. Importantly, because the online forums existed in the context of ten face to face workshops, many reflective postings on the forums that did not elicit written responses, and so were excluded from this analysis, were nonetheless probably read by other participants (being delivered to their email address as a daily digest), and were also often known to have stimulated a peer response in the subsequent face to face gatherings.

Two analysts (the author and a research assistant) then independently reviewed the study sample. The first task was to identify the more generic evidence—usually a response of gratitude to the original poster—that a participant had been stimulated by a posting into a practice-based interaction. The second task was to review the kinds of questions and comments in each discussion in the study sample to see if they matched the context of the characteristic questions of the nine categories of CoP outcomes (Wenger 2012) until the analysis had been exhausted. This led to a collection of example exchanges in each category. For the purposes of this chapter, one sample was then chosen from each category, with effort made to ensure that the breadth of examples selected represented the diversity of participants, including both men and women, both first-language English and English-as-an-additional-language speakers, and a range of relevant teaching experience.

This methodology has thus provided a set of examples of ways in which the online forums provide evidence of a CoP in action. All examples have been de-identified in terms of name, gender and discipline (in line with the university's Human Research Ethics protocol). However, to aid in interpretation, the quoted participants are identified as less experienced teaching academics (LETAs; in their first 2/3 years of teaching), more experienced teaching academics (METAs; with four 4–7 years teaching experience), or highly experienced teaching academics (HETAs; with more than 7 years teaching experience), with numbers denoting individuals. In addition, for the sake of brevity and focus, the examples reported here are generally excerpted to focus on the key aspect of the posting and response with relation to the CoP characteristic. By considering these examples in some depth, one by one, it becomes possible to see how the defining elements of a CoP are evidenced in the workshop participants' online interactions, and how this binds the participants of these professional development workshops together as they share their experiences, thoughts, concerns, and learning.

Notably, after this research was completed, Wenger-Trayner and Wenger-Trayner (2015) published an update to this categorisation of outcomes, adding two more: Building an Argument (How do people in other countries do this? Armed with this information it will be easier to convince my Ministry to make some changes.") and Growing Confidence ("Before I do it, I'll run it through my community first to see what they think.") Although these are not included in the analysis below, readers are encouraged to keep these in mind as they read the participants' exchanges.

26.4   Empirical Evidence of CoP Characteristics in the Case-Study

Before delving into the detail of the exemplar online interactions, two key points about the case study data must be made. First, many—if not most—of the participant interactions in this professional development course take place in the twenty face to face workshop hours, and there is little doubt that these interactions have

CoP-like characteristics and impact, as many participants report in their evaluation feedback:

> the group discussion facilitated in each of the modules was for me, the most important aspect (anonymous participant evaluation feedback 2014).

As face to face interactions lay outside the scope of this case study, however, they remain completely unreported here. The online forum examples discussed here thus constitute just a tiny sliver of the totality of interactions.

A successful technology-mediated CoP will show evidence of interactions between participants. In the online forums, there were multiple examples of participants responding directly to ideas, concerns, practices and reflections posted by others, as illustrated by just a few given here (Box 26.2). It is notable that these examples express gratitude for the sharing of practice, and then often move into a questioning mode as the participant seeks to further the discussion.

Box 26.2 Example of forum exchanges that demonstrate CoP-style interactions stimulated by individual postings

Hi [name], Thank you for sharing your experience and insightful thoughts. I begin with your last sentence where you …

Thanks for your reflection, [name]. You have inspired me to take a closer look at [named university's] framework that was introduced to us in this session.

Thanks for sharing this, [name]. You've inspired me to revise my teaching…

[Name 1] and [name 2]—thanks again for your insights [in the face to face session today]. Your thoughts … [provided] an inspired idea. I especially like that ….

Hi [name], thanks for that reflection. I am so impressed that you were able to apply [your idea] so quickly and that you had immediate results. … Can you give me an example of how you … ?

I also agree with what [name 1] said, that the most important thing is we teachers are able to reflect on our own teaching. … [name 1] mentioned …. [name 2] said that …. What do you think?

Beyond the simple stimulation to engage with other members, Wenger (2012) identifies nine distinct ways in which CoP participants develop their shared practice (Box 26.1)—problem-solving; requests for information; seeking experience; reusing assets; co-ordination and synergy; visits, discussing developments; mapping knowledge and identifying gaps; and project documentation. In the following sections, exemplar extracts derived from the analysis of the online discussions illustrate each of these nine activities.

26.4.1 Problem-Solving

Wenger (2012) gives the exemplar question that suggests a CoP is attempting problem-solving as 'Can we work on this design and brainstorm some ideas; I'm stuck". This is illustrated by a series of online postings by four participants. The thread is started by a less experienced academic, new to teaching, who is concerned about perceptions by peers when dealing with students who make factually incorrect statements in class:

> How to be hard but fair in feedback – I have been criticized by peers for being too soft on students when they make factually inaccurate statements. (LETA1)

After some further explanation and situational analysis, the academic ends with a description of practice, and a question:

> I tend to correct them once they are finished, and gently too. How can I ensure that observers do not confuse this with going easy on them? (LETA1)

Another LETA gives support and a tentative answer to the question, but then identifies his personal challenge in the same situation, which is potentially causing students who make errors to lose face in front of their peers by correcting them:

> … Perhaps you would try explaining to your colleagues that you need to understand the student's thinking to best explain the correct answer? … My own biggest challenge in this area has been when students are giving presentations or facilitating tutorials for their peers and they get it wrong. … (LETA2).

Going on to explain what her own response in this situation has been, LETA2 notes that she would like to improve on this 'compromise' approach, and again ends on a question: "Any ideas?" At this point, a highly experienced academic enters the discussion:

> I think it is important to nod and say 'yes' to indicate to students 'I am listening to you, and I am interesting in what you are saying'. I don't think that is being 'soft'. …. But I don't think 'correction' needs to equal 'embarrassment'. Maybe you can create some kind of culture within your class with a message: someone's mistake is a learning opportunity for the others? … You are already doing it by saying things like "that's a tricky concept, let's revise it again" – I think I will try that myself next time. (HETA1)

In this response, the highly experienced academic has acknowledged the situation as being an important one, has fine-tuned the understanding of the context, and has added more suggestions for possible action by the teacher. The post notably ends not with a question but with an endorsement of one of the approaches already described by the LETAs: "I think I will try that myself next time." A fourth participant, still early in his career but more experienced, now contributes:

> I think this is a real issue for those newly graduated. … while still doing my PhD I felt a strong need to 'correct' the students. … from my own experience [in peer review of my research] I am now a bit more sensitive about both the level and style of criticism. As you say, there is a need to ensure that you are actually giving the student useful feedback.

What I try to do is phrase any criticism by reference to what they could do better in the future. (META1)

Here, META1 first acknowledges the problem as one that is a particular risk for new academics, but then describes how personal experiences (notably, as a researcher, not as a teacher) has increased sensitivity to the value of feedback being couched constructively, and suggested a practical way of doing this.

In this example, therefore, four academics—from different disciplines, different educational contexts, different cultures and different stages of career—have engaged online in a problem-solving exercise around something that they have all experienced and are concerned about, in a way that shares and acknowledges both the problem and their current practices, and suggests some possible new approaches to the problem (while reinforcing acceptance of their existing approaches). In addition, although the discussion ends still with a focus on students, it has broadened out to include research aspects of the participants' academic practice.

26.4.2 Requests for Information

Evidence that a CoP is providing space for members to seek and exchange information can be found in a simple question such as "Where can I find the code to connect to the server?" (Wenger 2012). Such interactions online may be brief, a straightforward answer often being all that is needed. However, one might expect that peers relating in a CoP-like manner might also supply more substantive responses, as in example:

I don't know much about the different approaches to internal assessment [in honours degrees]. In your field is it simply by one supervisor, two faculty or a panel? I have a very different experience in [another country] which relies on internal assessment at all levels of research education. (LETA3)

Response: To assess honours theses, our department … uses an internal panel of three academics (at least one of which is not a specialist in the thesis topic), and the supervisor has nothing to do with assessment. [Continues with more detailed information] (LETA4)

In this exemplar exchange, which occurred within a broader discussion on university policies around teaching and learning, a newcomer to the university identified a lack of knowledge around the supervision of honours students, and was quickly given an informed answer, notably by another relative newcomer.

26.4.3 Reusing Assets

Effective sharing of knowledge in a CoP can be evidenced not only by straightforward questions and answers, but also by the open sharing of specific tools or activities in response to an idea. Wenger (2012) exemplifies this as "I have a

proposal for a local area network I wrote for a client last year. I can send it to you
...". In the case-study, a good example of this was shown when two less experienced academics became aware of a shared interest:

> ... I also found the introduction about analytics helpful – I didn't know that I could find out
> how the students were progressing via the statistics and reports in [the Learning
> Management System]. I think that will be very useful for analysing the content and its
> appeal/usefulness. (LETA5)

> Response: I am also interested in learning analytics ... I have found this [named] software
> tool really interesting and would like to share it to you just in case you want to find out
> at-risk students in your course. .... I guess it's worth a try if you're interested. (LETA6)

Here we see not only a sharing of potential future practice as these academics
start a joint journey into the new world of learning analytics, but also the identification of a potentially wicked problem (understanding what kind of online content
might appeal to students, and how they preferentially use that content in online
environments).

26.4.4 Discussing Developments

The need to balance research and teaching has been a crucial issue for academia for
decades (e.g. Kalivoda 1995; Pan et al. 2014), and almost certainly constitutes one
of the wicked problems of higher education. Managing the research-teaching nexus
is a key topic in the workshop face to face discussions, and often spills into the
online reflections. The multi-opinion aspect of this topic seems to mesh with the
'discussing developments' activity of CoPs, where the exemplar question is "What
do you think of the new CAD system? Does it really help?" (Wenger 2012). This
more open-ended form of discussion is exemplified by an online exchange in which
LETA7 initially notes satisfaction that teaching is accorded equivalence with
research, but then voices some doubts about rhetoric versus reality, which a more
experienced academic acknowledges:

> The 'value' of teaching in universities – It is great that [the University's strategic plan] is
> one of excellent teaching on par with excellent research. It is brilliant that it is written down,
> but is it really believed by leaders and decision makers?... Is there a true sense of parity
> between teaching and research? ... (LETA7)

> Response—I am new to [the University] so I had not heard of [the strategic plan] until
> today ... You've raised some interesting points about government and changed programs,
> and the impact that those changes have had upon [the University]. ... (META2)

Noting the concerns raised by these two participants, a third academic feels
comfortable in raising additional puzzlement:

> What I worry about (in line with the two previous posts) is that this positive message about
> teaching and its value to both the individual and the schools is not uniform across [the
> University]... [provides detailed examples] (LETA8)

This online interaction thus involved three participants identifying challenges to the idealistic concept of research-teaching balance, testing the concept against their experienced realities, and openly identifying and sharing their concerns. The language used by the participants ('It was somewhat alarming …'; 'What I worry about…'; 'But is this possible?') demonstrated a genuine sharing of affective responses, and echoed the face to face discussions on this topic.

26.4.5 Visits

A very clear-cut example of shared practice in teaching comes when members of a CoP invite other members to visit their classes or other learning environments, actions indicative of the 'Visits' category of CoP activity, exemplified by the direct question and rationale "Can we come and see your after-school program? We need to establish one in our city" (Wenger 2012). In the case-study, direct invitations could be expected to occur more often in the face to face environment. However, the analysis identified examples of indirect invitations in this mode. For example, LETA9 starts what appears almost a stream of consciousness reflection, concisely and thoughtfully articulating ideas about 'reflection in action', and conveying a level of reflexivity as to the assumptions behind what constitutes reflection in an online environment and what is mere commentary in a social space. Moving from reflecting on teaching to reflecting on learning, LETA9 queries whether students are being encouraged to become reflective learners, and whether they actually need teaching how to do this:

> Great to understand that the thought processes (reflections – self criticisms) that naturally go on when you teach is normal AND in fact you can harness that evil and put them into a good planning and professional development cycle. Are forums on [the Learning Management System] an effective teaching tool? Perhaps 'reflection in action'. …. I wonder though … who is telling the students about reflective practice in learning/teaching? Is it a fine line between a reflective thought and a [social network] comment in teaching space? Do these need to be outlined/taught just like reviewing a paper? (LETA9)

Another academic responds:

> We do a little bit of this [teaching students about reflecting'] in one of the courses I teach …
> if you want to chat about it sometime. (LETA10)

This could be interpreted as an invitation to 'visit' the learning environment that LETA10 has created, and is augmented by another reflection:

> I have been thinking today about how we might be able to strengthen it, perhaps by introducing more of the scaffolding [the facilitator] demonstrated to us [in the face to face session]. (LETA10)

This latter comment suggests that the facilitator's practice is equally being shared, and that the facilitator is thus accepted as a member of the CoP.

26.4.6 Seeking Experience

A crucial feature of CoPs is that they allow members to seek knowledge from, and vicariously share in, others' experiences. Wenger (2012) identifies this with the exemplar question "Has anyone dealt with a customer in this situation?" In the online forums, an example of this followed discussions about student-feedback evaluations of teaching:

> … many participants have mentioned that they haven't had much experience teaching at university – so it may be instructive. … I'm attaching my [student] evaluation from last semester – to illustrate some of the points I made [in a previous posting]. (META3)

Such open sharing with the group—of both the physical layout and examples of authentic feedback—was immediately met with gratitude:

> Thanks for this alternative perspective on [student evaluations], and thanks very much for attaching an example of the feedback you received – it struck me that there were some really disparate comments there. … I too am concerned about the use of [these evaluations] for performance management … (LETA11)

How teaching should be evaluated, and the role that student feedback does, and should, play in this evaluation is definitely another wicked problem in teaching (Darwin 2014), and it is exciting to see the sharing of experiences moving so clearly into the virtual space.

26.4.7 Mapping Knowledge and Identifying Gaps

In any CoP, the sum of knowledge across all its members is generally greater than the knowledge of any one member, so there is generally great value in mapping the group's knowledge and identifying any gaps—"Who knows what, and what are we missing? What other groups should we connect with?" (Wenger 2012). In the case study, the final module includes a small-group structured activity focused on critical reflection on teaching materials brought in by one of the group. This leads to an intensity of focus on listening to, and sharing, insights on practice. In the post-module online discussion, the participants from one group reflected on the activity, and found a focus on discipline-specific terminology. First one of the group members posted a commentary entitled 'Designing a syllabus with students in mind':

> I found it instructive to look over a syllabus designed by [someone in another discipline] today because it illuminated an issue that all academic disciplines have in communicating to students. When we spend a lot of our time as graduate students and lecturers with other people from our discipline, read journals from our discipline and socialise with other people from our discipline, it can be difficult to remember how much vocabulary and how many words we take for granted are hard for outsiders to understand … a good solution to this is to have someone from a very different discipline look at your communication with students

560   E.A. Beckmann

… and see what they don't understand and what needs to be explained to them. If they don't get it, chances are the students won't either. (LETA12)

Another group member responded:

That was one of my thoughts from today, too. … your comments illuminated aspects of the course (technical language, assumptions that we made about prior knowledge and skills development) that we might otherwise have entirely missed. (HETA2)

A third group member then contributed:

I have also found learning from teachers in other disciplines a very valuable component of this … course. (LETA13).

Finally, the fourth group member—the leader of the activity—concluded the discussion:

Thanks [named group members] for your comments on my course. I found it very useful in getting me to think more carefully about … the use of specific terms that may make perfect sense to [a specialist in my field], but are unclear to students not familiar with my discipline. I also found it helpful to test some ideas about assessments with the group … Based on [your] comments … I think more work needs to be done …. (LETA14).

In this exchange, the four participants demonstrate not only reflective practice (thinking about what they experienced during the activity, and the knowledge shared), but also reflexive practice (understanding that they needed to challenge their own assumptions, and doing so). They come to a joint realisation of the importance of involving those outside their discipline to help review and think through teaching plans and materials, and identify the gap that exists when their usual CoP is solely discipline-based. They are thus, almost unknowingly, confirming their need for, and the importance of, their membership of a CoP that is based around their domain interest of teaching, as well as one based around their discipline interest.

26.4.8 Documentation Projects, and Co-ordination and Synergy

The two final characteristic activities that (Wenger 2012) identifies as indicative of CoPs are documentation projects—"We have faced this problem five times now; let's write it down once and for all"—and co-ordination and synergy—"Can we combine our purchases of solvent to achieve bulk discounts?" While examples solely of the former were the most difficult to find among the online forum postings (because the diverse professional development participants were less likely to have common procedures to document), there was evidence of these activities in combination. For example, a less experienced academic made a posting, entitled 'Reflecting more deliberately', noting the commonality between teachers and students, and the need to document practice:

Both of the courses I currently tutor ask students to reflect upon their practice of learning, so it seems only fitting that I should also be continually reflecting upon my teaching practice.... I also need to consciously record examples of the details of what does and does not work well in classes, and analyse why. (LETA15)

The posting continues positively about peer sharing practices, and ends with a personal intentional statement:

I am lucky to have colleagues who are also passionate about teaching, and have participated in shared, informal reflections with them. Reflecting is more enjoyable over coffee. I do think though, that I am missing some of the opportunities to maximise learning from my own experience, particularly 'critical incidents'. To counter this, I would like to start writing a teaching journal, and be more deliberate in setting aside a few minutes to analyse what works and what does not. (LETA15)

A more experienced academic responds:

... I agree with you about consciously recording what seemed to work in the class and what didn't. ... more importantly, by writing the reflections down, it will likely force me to order my thoughts a bit more, and to actually practice what I was thinking about. ... (META4)

The following set of four postings, after the final workshop, demonstrated the intensity of collegial engagement, co-ordination of ideas and activities, and responses stimulated not by a desire to answer questions posed, but rather by a genuine synergy of cognitive and emotional reactions to shared events and activities:

I had a great opportunity to share my course design with a panel of [my peers] today ... Thanks again to [the facilitator] and other colleagues who have shared with me their thoughts, ups and downs in teaching. I appreciate your support a great deal. (LETA16)

Response—Thanks for your reflection. I agree the final module was a wonderful opportunity to discuss aspects of my course design with knowledgeable and creative people. ... I particularly appreciated the opportunity ... to discuss ideas with knowledgeable teachers who are not a part of my immediate teaching team. The clarity and fresh thinking they brought to the table was so valuable for me because they saw things in different ways... (META5)

Response: [This] was my first experience of designing a course and thanks to my peers, a fruitful one. ... (LETA17)

Response: This was also my first opportunity to design a course... Going through the process itself ... was powerful, but the opportunity to discuss it in my group was where the real magic happened. It was fantastic to have the opportunity to talk through the course and its logic with supportive peers. (LETA18)

Response: I completely agree with all of you...This was an excellent opportunity to use all skills and knowledge acquired during all [previous workshops]. ... all participants were happy for this interesting opportunity. I would like to do similar activities when ... I go back to the academic position I have in my country. (LETA19)

This final example shows how far these participants have come in their journey together, and the depth of reflective thought that they share online. One can feel that, while participants may now be more aware of just how wicked the problems are that beset university teachers, a genuine CoP relationship has arisen among the participants as a result of their shared learning, and especially as a result of understanding how they share the same practices, concerns, and joys.

26.4.9 Validating the Analysis

Two possible limitations of the interpretations above concern first the methodological validity of the thematic analyses of the postings, and second the role of the facilitator (the author) in the process of CoP development.

The analysis of forum postings can be validated by considering to what extent participants' evaluation of the professional development workshops and forums refer directly to the reflective and peer-based aspects of the course as an interactive 'CoP-like' endeavour. In this context, confirmation of the CoP nature of the online forums is indicated by the many feedback comments similar to the following on what had been 'most worthwhile':

... to be able to meet new people and to share ideas;

... to share experiences across different disciplines;

[My] reflective practice posts, reading other peoples' posts;

... to share thoughts and ideas with people outside my own course. They opened my eyes to things I had not seen before.

This evidence strongly supports a perception of the course having succeeded in engaging participants not just in a cognitive journey with regards to university teaching and learning, but also on a shared journey with fellow practitioners.

The second potential limitation is not so much on the methodology but on the role played by the facilitator (author), who in this case plays the de facto role of the CoP's initiator and leader. Having facilitated these workshops over 18 iterations since 2009, the author has seen significant evolution of CoP thinking in both the facilitation role and the emphasis on reflective practice, which has worked towards emphasising an environment that engenders a CoP state of mind among participants of the program (rather than one of attendance simply to gain information or practice 'tips and tricks'). It has to be acknowledged, therefore, that the outcomes reported here may be generalisable to similar professional development situations only in the context of similar facilitation styles.

26.5 The Future: From *Foundations* to Fellowship

Active participation and engagement with others pursuing a similar path can be transformative, but they are dependent on the social and cultural relationships among the participants (Carlen and Jobring 2007; Henderson 2008). Wenger (1998, p. 5) has argued that learning within a CoP depends both on an act of 'doing' and an act of 'becoming'. In leading a CoP that is linked so directly to a professional development course (*Foundations*) of limited duration, there is a real concern about the potential impact of 'short-termism', leaving reflective practitioners adrift without a CoP when they complete the program. On the other hand, having a cohort of several hundred participants who have been through professional development workshops in the past 6 years means that an understanding of reflective practice is slowly spreading among the university's teaching academics.

The University has recently augmented its professional development program with a professional recognition scheme, involving four experience-differentiated categories of internationally-accredited fellowship. In its first two years, the scheme attracted more than 200 applicants, including more than 50 from other universities, who had successfully proclaimed their experience of, and commitment to, a range of practices, knowledge and values around university teaching and learning. The application/recognition process involves a reflective narrative mapped against a set of standards. Many of the highly experienced academics who have applied are already familiar with the notion of communities of practice, albeit informally structured:

> Some of my best learning experiences—and many ideas about improving my teaching practice—have come from informal conversations with colleagues around the morning-tea table, or over a coffee. ... Even colleagues from vastly different disciplines and backgrounds can share common problems ... (Known respondent A, pers. comm., 2014)

For this reason, a key design feature of this recognition scheme is a CoP model, underpinned not only by collaborative mentoring, peer review and peer assessment elements, but also by the frequent bringing together in Fellowship Forums of those already recognised as 'fellows'. Regardless of category of fellowship, the Fellowship Forums provide opportunities for a genuine CoP of shared ideals and shared practice, as participant feedback is already showing:

> I especially like how Fellowship Forums are non-hierarchical. As a [relatively inexperienced academic], this has helped me mix with more of the very experienced teachers and listen and learn from their stories and experiences. So far I have felt respected, included, and part of the community of practice. (Known respondent B, pers. comm., 2014)

> I [left the Fellowship Forum] ... optimistic that a room full of such engaged, experienced and diverse individuals were meeting and wanting to seek change. (Known respondent C, pers. comm., 2014)

The future looks bright, with the continuing induction of less experienced academics—well-primed by their introduction as reflective practitioners in the professional development program—into the fellowship scheme as fully-fledged members of an institution-wide CoP:

> ... I [now] have many colleagues in almost every department on campus whom, if I need help ... will be there as mentors. (Known respondent D, personal communication 2014)

This chapter has demonstrated how characteristics of an effective CoP can be clearly recognised even in a time-limited, cross-disciplinary context, such as within the postings and responses of university teaching professional development participants in online forums that support face to face modules. The engagement of reflective practice as a tool of inquiry, and effective modeling and mediation of communication, can foster the development of an authentic, though somewhat fragmented, community of practice. The strengths of the latter lie in its capacity to allow participants to recognise for themselves the nature of the 'wicked' problems with which university educators must grapple, and allows some respite from the need to discover 'the' answer to an understanding of the realities of finding 'an' answer.

References

Badaracco, J. L. (2002). *Leading quietly: An unorthodox guide to doing the right thing*. Boston: Harvard BP.

Bandura, A. (2000). *Self-efficacy: The exercise of control*. New York: W.H. Freeman.

Beckmann, E. A. (2011). A community of opinion and debate: Postgraduate students' reactions to compulsory online discussions. In K. Moyle & G. Wijngaards (Eds.), *Student reactions to learning with technologies: Perceptions and outcomes*. Hershey, PA: IGI Global.

Biggs, J. (1999). What the student does: Teaching for enhanced learning. *Higher Education Research & Development, 18*(1), 57–75.

Bleakley, A. (1999). From reflective practice to holistic reflexivity. *Studies in Higher Education, 24*(3), 315–330.

Borko, H., Whitcomb, J., & Liston, D. (2009). Wicked problems and other thoughts on issues of technology and teacher learning. *Journal of Teacher Education, 60*, 3.

Brookfield, S. (1995). *Becoming a critically reflective teacher*. San-Francisco: Jossey-Bass.

Bulfin, S., Henderson, M., & Johnson, N. (2013). Examining the use of theory within educational technology and media research. *Learning, Media and Technology, 38*(3), 337–344.

Brown, V. (2010). Can there be a community of practice of practice? In V. A. Brown, J. A. Harris, & J. Y. Russe (Eds.), *Tackling wicked problems through the transdisciplinary imagination* (pp. 285–296). London: Earthscan.

Carbone, A. (2014). A peer-assisted teaching scheme to improve units with critically low student satisfaction: Opportunities and challenges. *Higher Education Research and Development, 33* (3), 425–439.

Carlen, U., & Jobring, O. (2007). Perspectives on the sustainability of activities within online learning communities. *International Journal of Web Based Communities, 3*(1), 100–113.

Conklin, J. (2003). Dialog mapping: Reflections on an industrial strength case study. In P. Kirschner, S. J. B. Shum, & C. S. Carr (Eds.), *Visualizing argumentation—Tools for collaborative and educational sense-making*. London: Springer-Verlag.

Darwin, S. (2014). Ensuring improvement or improving assurance: Student feedback-based evaluation in Australian higher education. PhD thesis, Australian National University.

Dearn, J., Fraser, K., & Ryan, Y. (2002). Investigation into the provision of professional development for university teaching in Australia: A discussion paper. A DEST commissioned project funded through the HEIP program. http://nla.gov.au/nla.arc-50804

Di Petta, R. (1998). Community of practice online: New professional environments for higher education. In K. Gillespie (Ed.), *The impact of technology on faculty development, life, and work. New directions for teaching and learning* (Vol. 76, pp. 53–66). San Francisco: Jossey-Bass.

Dubé, L., Bourhis, A., & Jacob, R. (2006). Towards a typology of virtual communities of practice. *Interdisciplinary Journal of Information, Knowledge, and Management, 1*, 69–92.

Gibbs, G., & Coffey, M. (2004). The impact of training of university teachers on their teaching skills, their approach to teaching and the approach to learning of their students. *Active Learning in Higher Education, 5*(1), 87–100.

Henderson, M. (2008). Relationships are more important than content: designing effective professional development within a community of practice approach. In K. McFerrin, et al. (Eds.), *Proceedings of society for information technology and teacher education international conference 2008* (pp. 1432–1439). Chesapeake, VA: AACE.

Hicks, M., Smigiel, H., Wilson, G., & Luzeckyj, A. (2010). *Preparing academics to teach in higher education (PATHE)*. Report to Australian Learning & teaching Council. http://www.flinders.edu.au/pathe/ALTC_report_final.pdf

Houghton, L., Ruutz, A., Green, W., & Hibbins, R. (2014). I just do not have time for new ideas: Resistance, resonance and micro-mobilisation in a teaching community of practice of practice. *Higher Education Research & Development,*. doi:10.1080/07294360.2014.973834.

Hoy, A. W. (2000). Changes in teacher efficacy during the early years of teaching. In *Paper presented at the annual meeting of the American educational research association*, New Orleans.

Kalivoda, P. (1995). Exemplary senior faculty at research universities: Their guiding principles for balancing teaching and research. *Innovative Higher Education, 29*(2), 95–116.

Knight, P. (2007) *Fostering and assessing wicked competencies*. http://www.open.ac.uk/opencetl/resources/pbpl-resources/knight-2007-fostering-and-assessing-wicked-competencies

McDonald, J., Collins, P., Hingst, R., Kimmins, L., Lynch, B. & Star, C. (2008). Community of practice learning: Members' stories about their academic community of practice of practice. In *Engaging communities, proceedings of the 31st HERDSA annual conference, Rotorua*, 1–4 July 2008 (pp. 221–229).

Pan, W., Cotton, D., & Murray, P. (2014). Linking research and teaching: Context, conflict and complementarity. *Innovations in Education and Teaching International, 51*(1), 3–14.

Rittel, H. W. J., & Webber, M. W. (1973). Dilemmas in a general theory of planning. *Policy Sciences, 4*(1973), 155–169.

Schön, D. (1983). *The reflective practitioner. How professionals think in action*. London: Temple Smith.

Schön, D. (1987). *Educating the reflective practitioner*. San Francisco: Jossey-Bass.

Sharma, M., Rifkin, W., Jones, S., Yates, B., Beames, S., Zadnik, M., et al. (2014). *Fostering institutional and cultural change through the Australian network of university science educators: 'SaMnet'*. Final report to Office for Learning and Teaching. http://www.olt.gov.au/system/files/resources/LE11_1967_Sharma_Report_2014.pdf

Wenger, E. (1998). *Communities of practice: Learning, meaning, and identity*. Cambridge: Cambridge University Press.

Wenger, E. (2006). *Communities of practice, a brief introduction*. http://wenger-trayner.com/wp-content/uploads/2012/01/06-Brief-introduction-to-communities-of-practice.pdf

Wenger, E., McDermott, R., & Snyder, W. (2002). *Cultivating communities of practice*. Boston: Harvard Business School Press.

Wenger, E. (2012). *Communities of practice: A brief introduction*. http://wenger-trayner.com/wp-content/uploads/2012/01/06-Brief-introduction-to-communities-of-practice.pdf.   Accessed February 23, 2016.

Wenger, E., White, N., & Smith, J. D. (2009). *Digital habitats: Stewarding technology for communities*. Portland: CPsquare.

Wenger-Trayner, E., & Wenger-Trayner, B. (2015). *Communities of practice: A brief introduction*. http://wenger-trayner.com/wp-content/uploads/2015/04/07-Brief-introduction-to-communities-of-practice.pdf. Accessed February 23, 2016.

Chapter 27
From Project to Permanence: Growing Inter-institutional Collaborative Teams into Long-Term, Sustainable Communities of Practice

Cath Fraser, Judith Honeyfield, Fiona Breen, Mervyn Protheroe and Victor Fester

Abstract The opportunity for academics to draw on concepts, methods and insights from colleagues in disciplines and organisations other than their own is well recognised as an effective strategy to promote the interconnectivity of knowledge, and pursue new learning and understanding. In the right circumstances, with the right nurturing, one-off project collaborations can become long-term communities of practice, ensuring social and professional learning well past the original project's expiry date. This chapter outlines learning from a recently completed research project in which the five authors, representing three New Zealand Institutes of Technology and Polytechnics (ITPs), conducted a first-of-its-kind national survey, together with follow-up interviews, of the effectiveness of collaboration within funded projects and longer term outcomes—including staff engagement, enhanced networking opportunities and sustainable communities of practice. We begin with a brief description of the New Zealand higher education

---

The original version of this chapter was revised: Authors' affiliation have been updated. The erratum to this chapter is available at 10.1007/978-981-10-2879-3_29

C. Fraser (✉) · J. Honeyfield
Toi-Ohomai Institute of Technology, Tauranga, New Zealand
e-mail: fraser.cath@gmail.com

J. Honeyfield
e-mail: Judith.Honeyfield@toiohomai.ac.nz

F. Breen · M. Protheroe
Weltec, Wellington, New Zealand
e-mail: Fiona.Breen@weltec.ac.nz

M. Protheroe
e-mail: Mervyn.Protheroe@weltec.ac.nz

V. Fester
Unitec Institute of Technology, Auckland, New Zealand
e-mail: vfester@unitec.ac.nz

environment and the role of Ako Aotearoa, together with a commentary on the authors' own community of practice, followed by an outline of the recently completed research project entitled *A national evaluation of inter-institutional collaborations*. Next, a survey of the literature is summarised in which the concept of communities of practice and the nature of collaborative communities are interrogated. Following this, the findings of the study are shared—these include: factors that affected collaborative communities, accounts of the development of relationships that progressed from initial collaboration through to more well-developed communities of practice, and evidence of benefits to multiple stakeholders. Finally, details of the good practice guide we produced to assist future collaborative project teams in the higher education sector are shared, together with an identification of several related areas that warrant further study.

Keywords Inter-institutional · Across discipline · Collaborative advantage · Collaborative communities · Sustainability

27.1 Introduction

One thing that most teachers would probably agree on: they have come to the profession because they like working with others, because it is a good match with their persona, and because, likely, they pride themselves on their communication, team work and relationship building skills. A logical assumption would be, therefore, that collaborative endeavours are a natural fit, and that collegial partnerships will automatically run smoothly and produce strong outputs and enhanced workplace satisfaction. Unfortunately, this aint necessarily so!

This chapter outlines learning from a study of collaborations in higher education which suggest that while most succeed, it is often due to sheer grit and determination, rather than a streamlined and transparent process. Arising frustrations and stress, whether passing or entrenched, stymie the potential of collaborative teams to move beyond the project at hand into a longer term community of practice. This means that the individuals involved, their students and their organisations, forfeit the rich rewards that come with membership of a sustained and supportive professional community. How can any such mismatch between expectation and experience be addressed? Perhaps with timely and mindful strategic planning, using available tools and resources, and following established good practice.

The first section of this chapter offers a brief introduction to the research environment in higher education in Aotearoa New Zealand, and the national framework which supported a study of efficacy within inter-institutional collaborations. We outline our research objectives and data collection instruments, and describe our own community of practice and the deliberate way in which we fostered some of the core principles of good practice in our purpose and processes. The next section introduces some of the literature we found particularly helpful in understanding the "collaborative advantage" as we analysed our findings, enabling us to then move into a discussion of what makes some inter-institutional collaborations more successful than others, and how this can be measured. One of our key measures is an extended shelf-life for the collaborative team as they leverage established relationships to pursue new opportunities and grow personal and group capability. We flesh out some of the benefits—for practitioners, learners and institutes—documented from our study, before summarising the factors which we now consider as essential for developing communities of practice.

The chapter concludes with a description of a new resource to support inter-institutional collaborations and communities, which we hope will assist colleagues to develop their own teaching and learning partnerships and find a similar measure of professional satisfaction and growth.

27.2 Setting the Scene

27.2.1 New Zealand's Higher Education Research Environment

In New Zealand, higher education has many faces. Our eight universities, the youngest of which was established as recently as 2000, account for 33 % of our post-secondary students. The remaining two thirds are dispersed between 18 institutes of technology and polytechnics (ITPs), two colleges of education, three wānanga (a publicly owned tertiary institution that provides education in a Māori cultural context) and an ever-changing array of private training establishments (PTEs), with 604 registered as members of the New Zealand Association of Private Education Providers at the time of writing. Clearly there will be a correspondingly wide range of subjects, levels, quality and research interests among the teachers and other academic staff.

Improving the quality of teaching has become a high priority, both on an institutional and a national level. In 2007, New Zealand's Ministry of Education established Ako Aotearoa, The National Centre for Tertiary Teaching Excellence as a specialist body to fund research related to teaching and learning. A Creative Commons publishing platform and a national register of educational research facilitates the sharing of ideas and learnings across the breadth of the sector (Ako Aotearoa n.d.). An apt name indeed: "Aotearoa" is the Māori word for New Zealand: literally "land of the long white cloud", and the concept of "ako" means both to teach and to learn, with an emphasis on reciprocity and shared learning experiences.

The three types of projects which account for the majority of Ako Aotearoa's investment in New Zealand's tertiary sector are research, resource development and teaching and learning initiatives. There are three pots of money: one for a few large national projects which often run over a number of years; one for small e-book chapters about good practice; and the third and most sizeable group for regionally sponsored projects, most often with an applied research focus. Contestable funding requirements emphasise demonstrable, tangible evidence that the outcomes will benefit the target population and produce measurable improvements in performance. In addition to "quality", a central tenet of Ako Aotearoa's vision is collaboration (Ako Aotearoa n.d.).

Approximately a third of the projects funded through Ako Aotearoa's three Regional Hubs (Northern, Central and Southern) involve team members from two or more organisations. The rationale is that inter-institutional collaboration in tertiary education has far-reaching potential as a means to share good practice and investigate new directions across the sector. Yet as Wolff (2002) notes, "those who work closely with collaborations on a regular basis know that the effectiveness in operations and outcomes … varies widely" (p. 1). The design or implementation of the collaboration process is an intangible factor often overlooked in reporting or evaluation, yet it is one which has the potential to either derail or enhance a project. Prior to the study which we describe shortly, no formal inquiry into this aspect of the national funding agency's work had been undertaken.

27.2.2 Our Own Community of Practice

Over the past 8 years since Ako Aotearoa's inception, the authors of this chapter have participated in several funded inter-institutional research collaborations, separately and together. We have experienced different roles as contributors, partners and leaders, and have worked with colleagues from a range of organisations, including universities, ITPs, PTEs and wānanga. Through this earlier work we feel that we have built an extensive community of practice, and been able to draw on our colleagues for assistance with other projects—further research, but also peer-review and quality assurance, specialist expertise and oversight, as workshop facilitators and guest speakers and as a source of literature and institutional benchmarking in our fields. Others often comment on the strengths and rigour of our professional networks, and we realised that for many, the relationships established during a project do not automatically extend beyond its completion. These observations and considerations led us to propose a first-of-its-kind national study of inter-institutional collaborations which was approved and attracted support from all three Regional Hubs.

Given our focus on collaborative process and our objective of creating a good practice guide (described at the end of this chapter) to assist others develop their own partnerships and communities, it was vitally important to us as a group of researchers that we managed our own inquiry process in an exemplary fashion. First, we tried to make sure that a high level of trust and respect was established from the beginning. We made sure that all proposal discussions, budget items, timelines and responsibilities were copied to all partners, and input was invited from each. Second, we felt that face-to-face meetings were important to build our personal and professional relationship. To maintain a sense of balance, we planned and allocated resources for all members to be able to travel to each other's organisation for these meetings, so that all had hosting duties as well. All meetings included provision for us to discuss our own collaboration and how we were feeling, and what our own challenges and issues were at any particular point. A third consideration in our process was recognising one another's strengths when allocating roles, tasks and responsibilities, following an ethos of distributed leadership (Gronn 2000) throughout the different stages of the project: big picture planning and management, online tool development, statistical analysis, grounded theory coding techniques, writing and reporting. We also made sure that discussion and dissemination activities showcased different strengths, and that all members shared lead presenter/author status across the various outputs we planned.

A great deal of our work together has relied on a platform of technology, allowing us to become "time and place independent" (Hoadley 2012, p. 295). In particular, we use a suite of services provided by Microsoft OneDrive, a cloud based storage system, for sharing and editing documents as well as file management. We also used OneDrive to create the on-line survey described below; a useful feature is that respondent data automatically uploads into a Microsoft Excel document in OneDrive, thus making the analysis more efficient.

27.2.3   The Study: A National Evaluation of Inter-institutional Collaborations

The five authors and researchers, representing three institutions, suggested that while Ako Aotearoa monitor quality and outcomes of each project, there had been little reporting of the work behind the scenes, and the processes by which the work took place. We posited that it was highly likely that the sustainability of the newly forged professional community, and the ongoing value to members, was largely due to the intangible factors: the relationships and interactions within the collaboration itself.

Accordingly, we developed a series of specific research questions:

- What makes inter-institutional collaborations successful and how is success best measured?
- How many Regional Hub projects have led to successful and on-going professional communities, and how desirable do participants see this as an outcome?
- What are the uses and benefits to members of successful collaborations/ communities, and to their organisations?
- What factors account for the sustainability of inter-institutional collaborations, and how can these be built into projects and fostered?
- How does successful collaboration in research projects lead to improvements in teaching and learning, and directly contribute to learner benefit?

Our methodology drew on the case study approach, where the "real-life context" (Yin 1989, p. 23) of institutions was an important element. Other theoretical elements were the embedded researcher-participant interface (Denzin 2009) and ethnographic fieldwork (Willis and Trondman 2000), both perspectives of which supported the prominence of self-reporting participant narrative and voice. This methodology and the research design are discussed more fully in Breen et al. (2015a, b).

There were four phases to the project, beginning with a literature review to inform the research, to guide our own collaborative practice as we carried out the evaluation, to examine work and commentary around the use of the selected survey tool and ensure any identified flaws or features were addressed in our own application. Second was a document analysis of 122 completed Regional Hub projects to determine those which included inter-institutional collaborations, arriving at a final tally of 44. The third phase was an anonymous online survey of team members from these eligible projects based on the Wilders Collaboration Factors Inventory (Mattessich et al. 2001a). This widely used inventory provides 20 indices by which to gauge participants' engagement in the collaboration and allows calculation of the mean rating for each factor, creating a sound measure by which to compare projects. The developers of the tool have made it freely available to any organisation or collective wishing to evaluate the strengths and shortcomings of their collaboration and teamwork, with customization allowed to suit the context (http://wilderresearch.org/tools/cfi/index.php). As we wished to examine the longer-term effects and sustainability of the collaboration beyond the end-point of the research study itself, we developed an additional 10 questions over four new domains: Post-research benefits; Learner benefits; Retention/workplace satisfaction; and Personal value (see "Appendix: Revised Wilder Collaboration Factors Inventory"). We developed a database of potential survey participants (past inter-institutional collaboration team members) still working in higher education; 121 contacts prompted 41 survey responses (34 %), with 22 projects (50 %) represented. The fourth and final phase of the research was a series of semi-structured interviews with a representative sample of 18 participants from different projects across all three regional Hubs.

Survey data analysis was largely quantitative, taking the ranking provided by participants and assigning each ranking value a numerical score, to aggregate and quantify the scores by project, and by factor. So we allocated "Strongly Disagree" responses -2; "Disagree" -1; "Neutral" 0; "Agree" $+1$; and "Strongly Agree" $+2$. The majority of factors contained multiple questions, which were then averaged. We then used the project scores to identify high, medium and low scoring projects which would suggest useful interview candidates. In contrast, the interview analysis used a grounded theory approach in which we aimed to construct our ideas about what constitutes good practice in inter-institutional collaborations through analysis of the data—looking for repeated ideas and concepts, and tagging these with codes to identify the emerging themes (Breen et al. 2015a, b).

27.3 The Collaborative Advantage in Principle

A review of the literature reveals a wealth of studies and discussion about education-based collaborations and communities of practice of all shapes and sizes: internal and external, pan-institutional and interdisciplinary, some informal and serendipitous, others highly structured with formal contracts or memorandums of understanding. Some disappear once the finish line is crossed, others cover a stipulated time period, and some are "multi-generational" with team members passing the collaboration role onto their replacement so that the organisation's place at the table is assured.

27.3.1 In the Beginning…

A common starting point for discussions is the work of theorists Jean Lave and Etienne Wenger, who in 1991, wrote about the social learning that occurs when practitioners with a common interest or domain meet and collaborate regularly to share ideas, resources, solutions and support (Smith 2009). In 2000, Wenger further defined his vision of a 'Community of Practice' as being bounded by joint enterprise, mutual engagement and a shared repertoire of communal resources. One of the most significant implications of his concept was that learning is not just something individuals do, with a measurable beginning and end, but rather, it comes from participation and interaction with like-minded others, providing opportunities to learn how to do things better through shared enterprise (Learning Theories Knowledge base 2009). As the concept of communities of practice began to be applied across a spectrum of activity by governments and business, agencies and associations, in public and private enterprise, Wenger (2006) has continued to refine and define his vision. He and his closest followers focus on describing the purposes of communities of practice (such as creating, sharing and managing knowledge, and linking learning and performance) and characteristics (including autonomy, practitioner-orientation, and informality and crossing boundaries).

27.3.2 Community of Practice Theory

As Cumming (2008) notes, the focus of such work is on the collaborative and meaningful activities undertaken in socio-cultural-historical contexts, for example, in higher education. Yet there is a parallel development in recent literature, which some are terming Community of Practice Theory (Cox 2005; Jakovljevic et al. 2013). Hoadley (2012) for example, summarises discussions about how learning and knowledge-building occur. He distinguishes between "feature-based" and "process-based" definitions (p. 287), with a focus in the former area on the nature of knowledge transfer and practice, and in the latter, on systems and participants' enculturation through movement from tangential positions to those of centrality.

There is also debate around terminology, and as Kimble (2006) says, the very utility and popularity of the term "Community of Practice" has led to it being used in a variety of different, and potentially conflicting, ways by academics, consultants and practitioners, who also debate what such communities are supposed to achieve. Hoadley and Kilner (2005) note several alternatives: "knowledge building communities"; "communities of learners"; "communities of interest" and "knowledge networks" (p. 293). Andriessen (2005) prefers the term "knowledge communities" and offers a taxonomy based on two dimensions of variability: connectivity (about people) and institutionalisation (about organisation, structure and deliverables). Wolff (2002) writes about "professional communities" including "coalitions, collaborations and partnerships" (p. 1), while Hogue (1993) offers five levels of engagement: "networking, cooperation, coordination, coalitions, or collaboration", according to the purpose, structure, and process involved.

In another emerging trend, Cox (2005) notes a rise in discussions whereby communities are "necessarily virtual" (p. 10), driven by both the impact of globalisation in higher education with the advent of phenomena like MOOCs (massive open online courses) (Lyon et al. 2015), as well as the needs of large, multinational organisations to tie together disparate individuals across their enterprises. Hoadley also notes the growing importance of technology in shaping modern, online communities of practice, contributing a useful "C4P" model (Hoadley and Kilner 2005) which maps the links between the five elements of "content, conversation, connections (information) context and purpose" (p. 33). Terms such as "social networks" and "social capital" are further indications of new areas of exploration (Tyler et al. 2003).

Another concern which exercises many authors is the debate round what (Wenger 2006) called "intentionality" (p. 1). In the original iteration of the concept, communities of practice were self-organising and voluntary, with "aliveness" based on "natural, spontaneous and self-directed" organic growth (Jakovljevic et al. 2013, p. 1110). Yet as organisations seek to harness the potential of these groups, the movement has been first, to "cultivation" (Cambridge et al. 2005), and onward to designing, developing and harnessing the work of these groups, arguing that "management needs to play an active role in the development of

CoPs if CoPs are to be successful" (Buckley and Giannakopoulos 2012, as cited in Jakovljevic et al. 2013, p. 1111). The issue of even "light handed management" in coordinating communities for organisational agenda, has therefore become one of "control and [or] empowerment" (Cox 2005, p. 11) for some commentators. Meaning, as Hoadley (2012) puts it, "we must be careful to distinguish between a community of practice as a phenomenon (naturally occurring or otherwise), versus an intended or designed learning environment" (p. 296).

These strands traversed in the current literature—the role of members and organisations, the variation between communities and resulting definitional ambiguity, the role of technology and the issue of where creation of the community should reside—were all apparent to some degree in the data generated from our study.

27.3.3   The Nature of Collaborative Communities

Turning from theoretical views of what collaborative communities of practice *are*, there is an arguably even larger field of scholarship about what they *do*. Mattessich et al. (2001a) describe collaboration, as "a mutually beneficial and well defined relationship entered into by two or more organizations to achieve common goals" (p. 39). Or, as Wood and Gray (1991) put it "[collaboration] occurs when a group of autonomous stakeholders of a problem domain engage in an interactive process, using shared rules, norms, and structures, to act or decide on issues related to that domain" (cited in Czajkowski 2007, p. 3).The best type of collaborative process, conducted with deliberation and forethought, creates "genuine partnerships, characterized by respectful and critical dialogue" (Gewirtz et al. 2009, p. 567) to make outcomes meaningful and productive for all participants. This creates what (Huxham 1996) calls the "collaborative advantage", achieved when something unusually creative is produced - perhaps an objective is met - that no single organization could have produced.

There is, in general, fairly widespread consensus on the characteristics of successful collaborative communities: a degree of formality in time, resourcing and budgets, strong leadership, high level trust and productivity with ideas and decisions equally shared through well-developed communication systems (Wolff 2002) with shared authority and responsibility for planning, implementation, and evaluation of a joint effort (Moxley 2005).

A key aspect of collaboration is that all participants must feel the personal value and have a belief that they have skills to offer the project. The collaborative approach also puts all participants on an equal footing, with each member being able to offer their specialised knowledge for the benefit of the entire project (Kristoff 2005; Lucas 2005). Studies on collaboration success factors seem to indicate that there is no single factor responsible for ensuring successful outcomes; rather that institutions need to align several factors to suit the context (Mattessich et al. 2001b). In 2006, Czajkowski conducted studies of 52 American tertiary institutions, including community colleges and universities, which were at that time involved in collaborative communities and partnerships. The outcome from her research was the delineation of six widely applied key collaboration success factors: trust and partner compatibility; common and unique purpose; shared governance and joint decision making; clear understanding of roles and responsibilities; open and frequent communication; and adequate financial and human resources. Moxley (2005) adds one further element, observing that an "alliance" culture must be egalitarian and participatory. While such collaboration must accommodate difference, generally "alike" institutions (size, sector and relatively equal power and/or prestige) find collaboration easiest and members of communities of practice find more in common with colleagues from same-status workplace environments.

Again, many of these factors and features discussed in the literature were apparent in the findings from our study; particularly notable was the strong emphasis placed on distributed leadership, personal relationships, immediate and longer-term benefits and transformative learning—as discussed in the following sections of this chapter.

27.4　Collaborations in Practice

27.4.1　Most and Least Important Factors in Collaborative Communities

Our first and overarching research question about what makes some inter-institutional collaborative communities especially successful was addressed by participants' responses to the revised Wilder Collaboration Factors Inventory survey tool (see "Appendix"). The study population was 121 participants (past inter-institutional collaboration team members) still working in higher education; emailed invitations to participate, along with information sheets and the survey link yielded 41 responses (34 %), with 22 projects (50 % of those eligible) represented. All participants therefore had first-hand experience and knowledge of inter-institutional project work, and were well qualified to offer inferences about the communities of practice which arose from these endeavours. Using the scoring system outlined earlier, we were able to determine the descending order of factors which participants identified as having been present in their inter-institutional collaboration experience. The top five factors are shown in Table 27.1.

The factor ranked the highest, 'Skilled leadership' related to just one question which asked whether leaders in the project possessed good skills for working with people and organisations. There were twenty-five responses which strongly agreed with this comment and thirteen which agreed, with only response disagreeing. The role of leadership is discussed in greater detail below. The 'Personal Value' factor was not an original factor present in the Wilders Collaboration Factors Inventory; this was added later by the project team. As part of the research it seemed fitting to identify whether involvement in the collaborative project was a rewarding experience and that this contributed to a successful collaborations. There were twenty-nine responses which strongly agreed with the statement and seven which agreed, with two where there was strong disagreement. 'Mutual respect, trust and understanding' is a factor that according to the literature is prevalent within collaborations, coming in just behind the second highest factor by half a point. Over

Table 27.1 Top ranked factors

Ranked	#	Factor	Strongly agree	Agree	Disagree	Strongly disagree	Total
1	20	Skilled leadership	50	13.0	−1.0	0.0	62.0
2	24	Personal value	58	7.0	0.0	−4.0	61.0
3	4	Mutual respect, understanding and trust	50	12.5	−2.0	0.0	60.5
4	15	Establish informal relationships and communication links	44	16.5	−0.5	0.0	60.0
5	16	Concrete, attainable goals and objectives	44	16.0	−0.7	−2.0	57.3

thirty-seven of the forty one respondents had a positive response for this factor. The difference between the first and fourth placed ranking factor was minimal. The findings illustrate that there were far fewer 'Strongly Agree' responses, but an increased number of 'Agree'. This identifies that establishing informal relationships and communication links was not as prevalent as other indices. The fifth place high scoring 'Attainable Goals and Objectives' appears to indicate that this is a focussing point for most, if not all collaborations.

What, then, were the factors participants found to be less important when evaluating the overall value of participating in an inter-institutional community of practice? The factor that scored the lowest was 'Multiple layers of participation'. This result indicated that participants did not feel that they could represent their whole organization and in some instances they felt that they did not have enough time to confer with colleagues outside of the project group to inform their decision. 'History of collaboration or cooperation in the tertiary sector' was also scored low, as project participants felt that collaboration in their area of practice was not common and had not been done to a great extent in the past. Also seen as relatively less important to the experience were: 'Collaborative group seen as a legitimate leader in the tertiary sector,' indicating that project members did not feel that others in the industry would necessarily see them as either the right organization to complete the project or indeed would not expect that they would achieve a final result; and 'Sufficient funds, staff, materials, and time,' illustrating that some aspect of funding, staffing, materials and or time did not meet the needs of the project.

Overall, the survey responses indicate that factors such as flexibility, ability to compromise and communication were not as prevalent as the literature would suggest. The authors speculated that this may have been because while the projects were still successful, they may not have resulted in a sustained community of practice with participants continuing with collaborative endeavours. Many of the interviewees made comments which shed light on the ranking of the inventory's factors.

For readers who are interested in using this tool, we would like to briefly acknowledge two limitations: first, the Wilder Collaboration Factors Inventory is a quantitative tool designed to provide numerical results for statistical analysis—it is concerned with respondents' ranking of elements of their experience, but not with any explanatory details. We hoped that the follow-up interviews would allow us to address this gap, but we are aware that some of the survey participants would have liked the option of comment boxes to augment their entries. Second, as with any large online survey, it took a considerable effort to prompt the level of responses received, with follow up emails in which we attempted to personalise the request to the email recipient's own project. This was time consuming, and also, we had no way of knowing who had already responded (since the OneDrive survey tool uses an anonymous submission). We were reluctant to pester people to increase the response rate, at 34 % a respectable return for a survey, but still below what we had hoped for, given the target population had all received funding and support for their involvement and might be presumed to have an interest in the project and its outcomes. It is perhaps useful to note that a number of potential respondents had moved to different institutions or had retired since completion of their collaborative projects and so did not respond to the survey, further lowering the response rate. We hope that foresight might enable others to find alternative approaches, if considered relevant, in their own implementations.

27.4.2 Collecting and Analysing Individual Experiences

Reflection on the survey responses suggested to the team that it would be useful to focus on a range of collaboration examples to extend understanding about individuals' experiences of inter-institutional communities of practice, both positive and negative, as well as associated strategies, longevity, and outcomes. The 18 semi-structured interview candidates were selected to represent a sample of projects with high and low collaborative rankings, as well as those from the mid-range. An equally important consideration was to include projects which included participants from a range of organisations: universities, ITPs, PTEs and ITOs, and which covered projects with a Māori and Pasifika focus, eLearning, staff development as well as classroom initiatives, and industry partnerships. At the end of this selection process, ten of our interviewees came from the Northern hub, three from Central and five from the Southern hub.

Interviews were generally face-to-face, with one conducted by email, and three by telephone when this suited the informants better. The interviews, averaging 45 min, were recorded and transcribed, then sent to the interviewee for verification. The 18 collaborative experiences described by interviewees were gathered as individual case studies, prior to collation and analysis which sought recurrent themes and transferable success strategies. Participants were keen to share their ideas of what worked, what didn't and their recommendations for how others might approach a similar collaborative endeavour in the future. This interest in research about collaborations and a resource to facilitate them supports (Doz's 1996) call for a focus on the process dynamics of the project, rather than just what it achieved.

In keeping with the semi-structured interview approach, often commentary ranged across the topics as interviewees told their story and shared anecdotes and examples. No attempt was made to pigeonhole contributions to match separate survey factors, so that this fairly fluid and flexible data collection method provided a good complement for the more bounded survey framework. Participant comments were recorded anonymously, and are identified here with the code A–R.

The sheer volume of data collected from the interviews meant that while we had used a case study approach to inquire about participants' contextualised experience of what worked well, and what didn't, we needed to combine these narratives for analysis, and to synthesise the learning from multiple projects and extract key principles and examples.

A grounded theory approach was used to construct a framework for ideas about what constitutes good practice in inter-institutional collaborations through analysis of the data—meaning the team read and re-read the data collected, identifying repeated ideas and concepts, and finally tagging these with codes for emerging themes. This general research method was a good fit for this project, the team felt, as it is not associated with any one field or discipline, and in fact has been advocated by others as ideal for studying interdisciplinary teams (McCallin 2007).

Transcript responses were separated out under each of the ten interview questions, so that each question document had 18 sections of comments, pasted into a table. Three additional columns were added, allowing us to refine the comments through "Initial coding" to "Intermediate coding" to arrive at a "Theme". Finally, themes were collated and a selection of representative quotes to support each theme were assembled to allow us to include participant voice to cement their status as partners in the research process, to add authenticity, and to provide interest to reporting in various fora. Additional rigour was provided through supervision by the research department head in the lead institution and the team's own use of a critical reflection review cycle.

27.4.3 Collaboration Enablers

The question "What aspects of the collaboration worked well?" drew the largest response of any in the 18 interviews conducted for our study. Most of the identified themes reflected findings from various studies of collaborative communities discussed in the literature review, albeit with details and examples distinct to the Ako Aotearoa context and the Regional Hub funding platform. Social connectivity and institutional drivers (Andriessen 2005) were both important imperatives for involvement in inter-institutional communities of practice, as these representative comments show:

> Research is lonely and isolating, so the social aspect plays a big part and enables me to be more productive. (Participant L)

> [We] are convinced that working in collaboration with someone else results in a far better product. Both X and I are capable of doing projects on our own but we know that that result would not be nearly as good as when we work together and can bounce ideas off each other, stimulate each other's thinking, and give each other honest feedback. (Participant N)

> Because I think once you understand there's a problem, you have some responsibility to find out more, at least. (Participant P)

For some, therefore, "purpose is paramount" (Cambridge et al. 2005, p. 2) and the collaboration was completely goal-driven, but this was not always the case, and Participant A told us about one community she was invited to join: *"Initially they didn't really know what they wanted to do—they just wanted to do a research project"*.

Mutual trust, respect and understanding were important to all interviewees, directly echoing (Czajkowski's 2007) first factor for success:

Everyone felt valued and empowered in what they were doing. (Participant H)

When you are working as part of a team you've got to make sure that you are on track and do your share. (Participant O)

Importantly, it was not just personal relationships which were valued, but the combination of skill sets, experience and expertise. In the most highly performing collaborative groups (based on members' rankings in the online survey) there was an appreciation of what each group or individual brings into a project or piece of work, and recognition of the need to make sure that everyone has equal input or the opportunity to make input on decisions. Participant I's story offers one example:

We each complemented one another well – X had a good contribution about how we publish and what's needed – and for a workbook that's really important – if I'd tried to do this on my own, it may not have had the same quality. I think I added clarity around the purpose and process; another colleague added visual clarity.

Structure and strategic planning were also seen by many in our study as key enablers for strong working relationships and achievement of group goals. Participants named "*clear guidelines and objectives*"; "*clear direction*"; "*task focussed*"; and "*clear milestones*" as important, not only in underpinning the community's work, but also as part of what members did together—a clear demonstration of the overlap between the "feature-based" and "process-based" interpretations of communities of practice (Hoadley 2012) outlines, suggesting that these boundaries may not be so distinct in practice as they are in theory. An example here is a story from one interviewee who told us she had responded to an invitation on a practitioner website asking if anyone wanted to do some collaborative research. The collegial endeavour which followed from this began with a group of individuals unknown to one another negotiating possible topics, identifying separate needs and suitable collective goals, agreeing roles, tasks and responsibilities, and developing personal and professional relationships—all more or less concurrently.

An essential enabler for several of the communities we studied, including the one above, was technology. Yet for most groups, even those which were bonded by a common interest in e-learning and online practice, technology was a means to progress the community's work and members still valued opportunities to meet in person:

Skype worked well. [But] The best bits were when we were actually together…we decided to use the funding to travel to join each other's campus and…gathering the data together. Putting the publication together, this was necessary…We used our times when we visited centres to plan meetings too, which worked well. (Participant L)

27.4.4   The Role of Leadership

Leadership which is shared among team members respects individual strengths and expertise and allows collegial synergies and camaraderie by sharing the "load" (Ramsden 1998), as members in inter-institutional collaborations manage competing responsibilities within and outside the project. In most evaluation tools for assessing the strength of collaboration within a multi-organisational project, issues around leadership roles and delegation processes are high on the list of critical features. In the Wilder Collaboration Factors Inventory used by our study, 'Skilled Leadership' is one of 20 factors participants use to rank their experience of a collaborative project; it was also the one which received the highest overall score.

Where much of the literature viewed as a background to this account focussed on how organisations can create and direct communities of practice (for example, Cambridge et al. 2005; Jakovljevic et al. 2013), implying at least initially, external and management leadership, this was not the case with most of the collaborative communities we investigated. A closer match was (Gronn's 2000) model of "distributed leadership", which he describes as vested in groups of people, not individuals. It has aspects of facilitation and turn-taking, and is synonymous with the concept of leading from the front, from the side, and from behind. Several participants' experience of collaborative, multiple and complementary activity by teams of people sharing responsibility for a successful outcome, directly mirrored this perspective:

> I took the lead at the beginning and coordinated, and she gave me lots of advice – *what lines to pursue, the shape of the field and where and what research was happening. She knew the literature. She was definitely the senior person – I wrote the application and she gave me feedback.* (Participant C)

> X had been quite close to the research initially and she was fairly hands-*off until the end of the collaboration where she came in and helped to structure the research outputs.* (Participant P)

We did also hear stories of communities of practice where a particular collaboration had not been as successful, and a lack of overt and/or committed leadership had played a large part in a loss of focus. Leaders who had "owned" a project, managing budgets, external liaison and reporting responsibilities, and who then left their organisation, meant that projects with little succession planning faltered in their absence. There was also an account of a community which comprised members from different types of organisations, in which many members saw themselves as novices and peripheral participants (Hoadley 2012) and expected that the member from a university would take responsibility for the work:

> From the very first meeting…I guess in their mind it was decided that I was going to lead it. I didn't realize that at the time until a bit further down the track. (Participant A)

Participants spoke about personal enrichment and a renewed satisfaction with their work role and environment (Cumming 2008), sometimes taking up leadership roles where they would have felt unprepared in the past (Ramsden 1998).

Distributed leadership, then, is a powerful model for academic autonomy in collaborative communities (Woods et al. 2004), and provides an effective process for multiple people contributing across a broad arena of activity—but only when members know about it, talk about it, and agree to abide by it!

27.5 From Collaboration to Community of Practice

27.5.1 Sticking Together

> Our evaluation of collaborations in funded higher education projects asked the representatives of 18 inter-institutional groups whether they had continued to work with members of the group, after the initial project which got them together. This relates to our second research question about the formation of long term, sustainable "professional communities" (Gerritson 2007). Five participants said "No"; two said "Partly" (meaning with some members of the group but not others), and 11 (61 %) said "Yes". Of the five participants who had not continued to work with the collaborative team past the completion of the original goal, three told us that they would have been happy to continue the relationship, but hadn't pursued further shared opportunities with these external partners due to *"being busy"*, *"time and resource constraints"* and *"logistically, it's easier to work in-house"*.

Those whose original collaborative project had strengthened into a true community of practice, as measured by the components nominated by Wenger (2006): a shared domain of interest, reciprocal learning relationships and a shared practice with a repertoire of resources, relished the opportunity:

> We have. The number of projects we have done since that first project, we just continued. What shall we do this year? We make plans…we were both elected to become the new convenors of an international…organisation, for worldwide networking… Also we're going to plan for the symposium at the next congress at Rio in 2017. That would never have happened if we weren't working so well together. (Participant K)

> We do a lot of article writing, book chapters and reviewing. (Participant L)

> You learn so much about the issues and then you go and tell other people about it and then, because we were on the radar, we were able to connect with the Office of Ethnic Affairs, I… ended up on their Intercultural Awareness and Communication workshops and developing a diversity management strategy and becoming known as an expert, different ITO [Industry Training organisations] people would ring me up and ask me about stuff – *it [the research project] mostly started that journey.* (Participant Q)

Others told of visiting one another's institutes, speaking invitations, shared problem-solving, resource sharing, sourcing information, and mapping knowledge and identifying gaps for future research inquiries. Many of these benefits align with what (Wenger 2000) says are typical activities of communities of practice.

One thing that none of our participants mentioned, and yet which generates some concern and warnings in the literature, was competition. A number of writers argue that the current higher education climate actually works against long-lasting inter-institutional collaborations. A recent article published on the New Zealand Ministry of Education website "Education Counts" by Smart et al. (2013) states "Concerns have been raised that the Performance-Based Research Fund [New Zealand's mechanism for disseminating funding based on institutional ranking according to quality of research produced] Quality Evaluation has had a negative impact on research collaboration between researchers in New Zealand universities" (p. 1). These authors speculate that issues of academic competition may be undermining some collaborations which don't perform well.

Although this issue was not apparent in our findings, it may not mean that participants were unaware of the potential tension, but could instead indicate that they found ways to work past it. Moxley (2005) notes that the realities of collaboration among higher education providers include that often, the partners in the collaboration will remain competitors. This, she says, can be accommodated if the people in the collaboration also remain friends, and if their behaviours toward each other and on behalf of the alliance demonstrate generosity and good will. She counsels that "alliance participants cannot skip the hard parts of alliance building— the disagreements, the divergent policies, the engagement of other functional entities at the partner institutions, who may perceive the alliance to be a burden rather than an asset" (p. 9). A representative comment bears this out:

> I think it was because we very rapidly got to a stage where we could be really honest with each other... You've got to be able to disagree because how are you going to progress if you can't disagree. (Participant N)

27.5.2   Trying Again

We also asked interviewees whether being part of this first collaborative group would encourage them to participate in other inter-institutional/interdisciplinary collaborative communities. The overwhelming response from 17 of the 18 practitioners interviewed was "*Yes, absolutely!*" Respondents felt that they had a better understanding of both the collaborative process and purpose, as well as a growth in professional skills and capability, and personal satisfaction. The following comments are representative of the range of gains mentioned:

> I think that's given me a skill to work sort of with others. To cooperate with other people... to listen to each other...That has actually helped me a lot with the other two groups as well. I feel I've become more, I care, but I'm not (what is it called?), egocentric. (Participant K)

> I think the perspectives from different sectors of the community and of education are enriching and motivating. It was always fascinating to see different areas of 'life'...As well, each made different contributions and sought different recognitions, in that our values and what we viewed as important were often very different. (Participant M)

My attitude towards the inter-institutional collaboration has definitely changed because of the experience. I think it's critical for the success of research that these endeavours do take place because of the expertise that lies outside of your own institution that you need to be able to tap into, so that you can produce better outputs and you can just give back to society in a more rapid fashion. (Participant R)

27.5.3 Workplace Satisfaction

The issue of workplace satisfaction as a result of collaboration is not one which appears to be widely discussed in the literature from higher education, and may suggest a gap for future research. However, it is an area which engages authors in the field of business and knowledge management, where a reluctance to recognise what Sveiby and (Simons 2002) call "a collaborative climate" (p. 425) not only stymies organisational growth, but fails to address staff turnover. A critical issue today, staff turnover is almost triple what it was only 15 years ago, they say, and "every time somebody walks out the door they are taking an amount of expertise with them" (p. 425). Hence, by helping to retain that expertise, or promoting opportunities to share information knowledge, organisations will have more motivated, fulfilled and productive employees.

Two of the 18 respondents in our study felt that being a part of their particular inter-institutional collaboration had been negative and stressful; both attributed this to the frustration of working with partners who were less committed than themselves to the project's success and completion. However, the remaining 16 interviewees offered a rich testimony to their satisfaction as practitioners, with the learning which resulted. A sample of comments offered about workplace satisfaction include:

If I think very specifically about how good I feel coming to work every day, having projects that are going on that take me out meeting people and doing things where I feel there's a benefit – not just to me but to other people - that gives me satisfaction. If I wasn't able to do research, and projects, I think I'd leave. It's that important to me...Keeps you going through the tough times. (Participant A)

Satisfying. I enjoy researching. More rewarding when you are working with others too. When you can see others gaining from the project. (Participant O)

My directors are really proud and so are the staff in what we have done. (Participant G)

It probably has given me opportunities that I wouldn't have found at the polytechnic...it also affirmed that I can take a leadership role in collaborations...knowing strengths and when to call on others. (Participant P)

Overall, the results from this study indicate that the opportunities created through this type of funded, inter-institutional research projects are enriching and reinvigorating the working lives of educators who may otherwise be limited by the confines of their job description, and that everyone is benefitting: the individuals themselves, the organisation, and especially the learners.

27.6 Who Benefits, and How?

Two of our research questions specifically addressed the benefits to practitioners, organisations and learners which arose from educators' involvement in inter-institutional collaborations, and thence, in communities of practice.

27.6.1 Practitioner Benefit

As referred to in some of the sections above, when the 18 interviewees reflected on the benefits they had experienced or observed from being part of an inter-institutional collaboration, there was a wealth of positive testimony. Only one person felt that they had not gained from the experience; all others were positive about the benefits, regardless of how well they thought the collaboration had gone. The strongest category of responses here was the personal gain: building capability, learning and confidence, and a strong sense of satisfaction, with "*lots of positive feedback both nationally and internationally*" (Participant L).

Individuals also told us they gained professionally: they had developed practical and fit-for-purpose resources for their own workplace use, had achieved professional outputs (conference presentations and invitations, publications and subsequent funding grants), and had developed or extended valuable professional networks and communities of practice:

It's been a useful resource for my job – I use it and share it with staff. I've run workshops …here and at other organisations. (Participant B)

Developed a research whānau [extended family] with the people we were working with. (Participant P)

27.6.2 Organisational Benefits

Tangible gains for practitioners' organisations were also evident, and included learning from both the project itself, and from working alongside other institutions:

One [participating institution] in particular I remember having their EER [external evaluation review] right in the middle of the project, so they took their summary of the focus group, showed it to the evaluators. (Participant A)

If you've been exposed to other different types of processes, then we can perhaps become more efficient within our own organizations. (Participant R)

Other organisational benefits included: showcasing the organisation ("gave us some credibility …adds to the portfolio of projects we've been successful with" (Participant A) and "the organization came to be seen as a regional leader" (Participant D)); building longer term inter-institutional relationships ("Some of the people that we met were amazing, doing incredible work in institutions that were almost next door... several people in Wellington doing amazing work that didn't know each other.... Some people in Auckland that didn't know each other" (Participant P)); and generating income ("The organisation does very well out of it, 'cos we've produced lots. We've got publications, we were both ranked with PBRF [performance based research fund]. We're both C rankings, so we're bringing money into the organization" (Participant N)).

27.6.3 Benefits to Learners

The issue of linking teachers' professional development to student outcomes is one which has long taxed higher education teaching and learning specialists, and is notoriously difficult to "prove". A number of studies in the New Zealand context have attempted to do so, such as case study accounts of learning adviser interventions and outcomes (Manalo et al. 2009) and a meta-analysis of literature about effective practice and outcomes (Prebble et al. 2004). Prebble et al.'s two principal conclusions are that "good teaching has positive impacts on student outcomes, and teachers can be assisted to improve the quality of their teaching through a variety of academic interventions" (p. 91).

While learner benefit as a result of teachers engaging in communities of practice is hardly discussed in the literature, it was very important to our own study, as positive impact on students is a key criterion for Ako Aotearoa's Regional Hub funding. Our interviewees therefore understood this line of questioning, and almost all felt strongly and were able to articulate a variety of ways that students had benefitted—either directly or through the "trickle-down effect"—which participant D explained as *"If the tutors are gaining experience, surely it will impact back on the learners."*

A first theme which was frequently referenced was reflection as part of the learning cycle for organisational improvement in supporting students:

> Just participating... required people to think about – How do we support our learners? What are the things we do? How do we know what works? ... They really wanted to know, not just the things they were doing well that their learners were telling them, but what were the things their learners were saying they needed to improve? (Participant A)

> Providing people with a rigorous process of exploring their teaching and learning ... people can see the need for major improvements in their practice as a result of having to think and write about it. So students get the gains of this reflection. (Participant B)

Another benefit to students was that many of the collaborative research projects included them as partners in the research; allowing their voice to be heard and using their comments to inform reporting and decision-making:

> Students taken seriously...acknowledged and validated in the way the [researchers] did in research collection is really important in itself. (Participant J)

> Being singled out and identified as someone who was contributing more and differently was really personally significant to many of those learners. (Participant M)

Participants also talked about improved teaching and learning pedagogy, and consistency and equitability of student experience:

[Did your students gain?] Yes. Definitely. Because I became more knowledgeable in what I was doing. It was a complete eye opener to me just how the strategies and techniques that you can use, and how you use them, and how you deal with the problem. (Participant N)

Happy teachers make happy students ... We saw stressed tutors who felt unprepared and how this caused student dissatisfaction ... tutors all get the same experience now - *step by step more consistence, not such big difference from experienced and new tutors.* (Participant F)

[We developed] some practices and tools and strategies that could help broaden design educators to better understand how to work with Māori students, and ... I have implemented these. We now have a 100 % *Māori retention and success and increasing numbers of Māori students joining the Bachelor...programme.* (Participant P)

Other learner benefits mentioned included: changes to organisational systems and curriculum leading to improved employability for learners and better work-readiness; growing community relationships and networks; concrete opportunities for learners; strengthened cultural identity; and changes to learner support/service provision, and new materials and resources. Some, like Participant I, noted that larger communities of practice offered significant advantages in this area, as in general, the broader the project, the broader the potential impact on learners. In his collaborative e-learning community, he suggested that members use group-generated activities with over 1000 learners each year: *"learners benefit from better quality resources and educators from having greater confidence to use new activities."*

27.6.4 Transformative Learning Through Communities of Practice

Ako Aotearoa are committed to supporting projects and initiatives which bring about change, and the research team were aware that (just as with Ako's other core focus, learner benefit) establishing tangible and demonstrable evidence of shifts in practice can be extremely nebulous. We deliberately included our question about shifts in personal and organisational practice as the last topic in the interviews. The intention was that the interviewee had had ample time to reflect on and remember various elements within their inter-institutional collaborative experience; while the interviewer had gained some insight into the project and was likely to be as well-informed about the project as possible by this point, in order to prompt useful insights and examples.

Several of the themes here echoed earlier points (building and consolidating networks with other providers; collaboration as a natural fit for teachers; critical reflection; enhanced learning and capability; a focus on student feedback; and tactics, strategies and resources for success). Participants also talked about the value of professional development for teaching through involvement and practical modelling:

> It's not just the resources but the experience of producing them which is a rich professional development experience…One way of extending the shelf life of research projects is by making people think about them. (Participant B)

> My teaching changed completely, as a result of the research I was doing… when there's group work that isn't working we point our fingers at the students, and we say – oh they're cheating – they're not pulling their weight – they're giving it to one person in the group to do – but it all comes back on the tutor. That if you know as a tutor how to design assignments properly, if you know how to assess properly, if you know prepare students for groups, if you know just elementary things like the appropriate size for groups. If you know all that sort of stuff, then your group work's successful. (Participant N)

In addition to comments like those above, which referred to enacting findings and sharing ideas, and implementing evidence based change, it was exciting to see an emerging theme of "transferability" as interviewees shared examples of taking learning across settings, both from one institute to another, and also internally, across disciplines:

> As an organization, we recently used the same framework to develop a set of activities around social justice – *so the value of the project to us has lived on, being able to develop the existing model in another context.* (Participant I)

27.7 Fostering Sustainability

27.7.1 *Community of Practice Design Models*

One of our guiding research questions was to investigate the factors which account for the sustainability of inter-institutional communities of practice in higher education, and mechanisms to build these into future collaborative projects sponsored by Ako Aotearoa. Our search of the literature found ample discussion around the features and purposes of communities of practice, and considerable debate in community of practice theory about different aspects of operationalization, as alluded to earlier in this chapter. There were, however, not a great many examples of guides and models available to assist novices establish their own collaborative communities. Jakovljevic et al. (2013) introduce their own work in this area, stating: "The current problem is that there is no specific guidance to form communities of practice in higher education institutions to guide learners' practical and theoretical knowledge and learning experiences" (p. 1107).

Jakovljevic et al. (2013) started from a similar position to ourselves, examining the literature for ready-made solutions. Their article cites two examples: that of Buckley and Giannakopoulos (2012) which addresses the topic via the management challenge, the academic challenge and the technological challenge; and that of Hanna and Robinson (1994) who looked at community empowerment and

Table 27.2 Criteria for communities of practice (CoP)

No.	Criteria for CoP
C1	CoP should support agile methods and strategies
C2	CoP should develop a learner's practical skills, attitudes and values through experiential and guided participatory learning
C3	CoP should develop a learner's reflective experiences
C4	CoP should shape a learner's behaviour through sequencing of instruction
C5	CoP should engage a learner in emotional reflection
C6	CoP should empower consciousness and meaning through joint, collective activity and feedback contro
C7	CoP should utilise the dynamics of the activity system: artefacts, rules and division of effort
C8	CoP should emphasise an activity which leads to an innovative outcome
C9	CoP should pay attention to the 'individual style of activity
C10	CoP should acknowledge individual features of personality
C11	CoP should support joint enterprise between management, academics and technology
C12	CoP should engage attention, memory, motivation and retention
C13	CoP should encourage multidisciplinary tacit knowledge-sharing between learners, supervisors in academia and entrepreneurs
C14	CoP should acknowledge that learning is a function of the activity, context and culture
C15	CoP should support learning through cognitive and practical apprenticeship

contrasting models of social change. However, they concluded that neither model covered their requirements. Instead, they propose a predetermined framework of 15 criteria for communities of practice, summarised in Table 27.2.

We reproduce the table here as we wish to acknowledge the closest summary to our own findings that we have discovered to date, and have ensured that we have captured all these points in our own version. However, this set of criteria is more a check-box guide for those external facilitators choreographing a group's activities, than our own vision of a "how-to" resource for users to work out their own moves, for themselves.

Cambridge et al.'s (2005) *Community of Practice Design Guide* is another example which partly addresses what we want to provide for our own context. The lifecycle approach to communities is useful, with six stages recognised: Inquire; Design; Prototype; Launch; Grow; Sustain—each stage with key questions to explore and supporting activities for each (pp. 4–7). Across this is a four step planning activity: Knowledge building; Learn and develop the practice; Take action as a community; and Create knowledge in the domain (p. 3). Finally there are four "Core technical features" to consider: Relationships, learning, Action and Knowledge (p. 8). This time, there is almost too much specificity—at least for our intended readership of busy practitioners. We are looking for less of a text-heavy manual, and more of a user-friendly "kit".

27.7.2   Development of the Good Practice Guide

A primary objective of our evaluation of collaborative practice across the 44 represented projects was to use the findings to develop a new resource to guide future project teams. Based on our analysis of existing models in the literature, including the two outlined above, we felt there was still a need for a concise and practicable good practice guide. The research team discussed the audience, purpose, contents and structure—while all the time referring to existing Ako publications and resources, freely available through their Creative Commons publishing platform (https://akoaotearoa.ac.nz/resource-centre).

We determined that the material we presented needed to be guided by a similar ethos: simple, accessible language; content restricted to just-in-time practical suggestions; and a focus on relatable and transferable strategies which could be adapted to a range of contexts and projects. By combining our learnings from the survey's ranked factors of effectiveness within the collaborations, along with the narratives offered by our interviewees, we created a resource based on a "before-during-after" format. This document offers suggestions about discussions which are useful to have at various points in the life-cycle of the original collaboration, and suggests way markers and pause points to reflect on the meta-process which can all too often become lost in the task-focused practice of the group. The resource also contains mini case study examples to address specific points we wished to highlight—these are included as shaded sections designed to stand alone, and to add some personalisation without overwhelming the text.

The result of these decisions is the resource: *Getting on: A Guide to Good Practice in Inter-Institutional Collaborative Projects,* is now published, downloadable from www.akoaotearoa.ac.nz.

27.8   Conclusion

The discussion of collaborative learning and the work of inter-institutional communities of practice covered in this chapter has drawn significantly on a recently completed study which evaluated the collaborative element in a range of externally funded, higher education research projects in Aotearoa New Zealand. Our research was designed to meet the requirements of Ako Aotearoa, our funding body, and also to ensure that we were addressing gaps in both organisational knowledge and the literature about inter-institutional collaborations and what makes them reach, exceed, or fail their potential to deliver long term value and benefits to participants. This is research which from its inception, was intended to be both applied and practicable in its outcomes, with a high relevance to our practitioner community.

The mixed method data collection (survey and interviews) generated a great deal of data, both quantitative and qualitative. Participants' narratives testified to experiences which traversed the spectrum of collaborative practice and project undertakings—from personal challenges to career highlights. Establishing agreement about the factors which are most important in collaborative endeavours, and identifying what enables effective communities to function, including the contribution made by distributed leadership, has directly contributed to the new good practice guide, described in the section immediately above.

We were particularly pleased to collect and present strong confirmation of individual, organisational and learner benefit and changes to practice which result from inter-institutional collaborative communities. Above all it is heartening that our colleagues' experiences in the real world bear out the claims made in the literature of the potential of this simple way of working together to improve personal performance and professional satisfaction in the world of academia.

27.8.1 Future Directions

A number of ideas raised in this discussion would merit further investigation. First, the literature appears to lack significant discussion of the benefits to the larger network of stakeholders when higher education practitioners are involved in shared activities in a thriving community of practice. The particular group discussed in this chapter is learners, but another interesting area to investigate could also include industry connections, given that employability is a growing focus for higher education in most western countries today.

Workplace satisfaction is another topic which seems not to be much discussed in connection with participation in external collaborative ventures. This would appear ripe for further research, given that there are plenty of business models which quantify the cost to an organisation when employees leave a professional role, and a similar database of studies about reasons for workplace disengagement, in which social connectivity, a sense of being valued and adding value, and opportunities to learn feature highly—there seems a logical convergence here!

Finally, just as there are few models to guide new collaborative community endeavours, so there are even fewer accounts of how these models work in a real world trial. As one of our participants noted, any resource or tool needs to be reviewed and refined, and reflected upon. As a community of practice ourselves, a future assessment of how well our own good practice guide works for others will be high on the list of future work for the research team, aka the authors. The work of communities of practice is rich with potential, and one in which we hope to be involved in exciting and stimulating learning adventures for some time to come!

Appendix: Revised Wilder Collaboration Factors Inventory (amendments to original statements and ten new statements added)

Factor	Original statement	Our revised statement
History of collaboration or cooperation in the community tertiary sector	1. Agencies in our community have a history of working together. 2. Trying to solve problems through collaboration has been common in this community. It's been done a lot before.	1. Colleagues in the tertiary sector have a history of working together. 2. Trying to solve problems through collaboration has been common in the tertiary sector. It's been done a lot before.
Collaborative group seen as a legitimate leader in the community tertiary sector	3. Leaders in this community who are not part of our collaborative group seem hopeful about what we can accomplish. 4. Others (in this community) who are not part of this collaboration would generally agree that the organizations involved in this collaborative project are the "right" organizations to make this work.	3. Leaders in the tertiary sector who are not part of our collaborative group seem hopeful about what we can accomplish. 4. Others (in the tertiary sector) who are not part of this collaboration would generally agree that the organizations involved in this collaborative project are the "right" organizations to make this work.
Favorable political and social climate	5. The political and social climate seems to be "right" for starting a collaborative project like this one. 6. The time is right for this collaborative project.	5. The political and social climate seemed to be "right" for starting a collaborative project like ours. 6. The time was right for our collaborative project.
Mutual respect, understanding, and trust	7. People involved in our collaboration always trust one another. 8. I have a lot of respect for the other people involved in this collaboration.	7. People involved in our collaboration always trusted one another. 8. I have a lot of respect for the other people involved in our collaboration.
Appropriate cross section of members	9. The people involved in our collaboration represent a cross section of those who have a stake in what we are trying to accomplish. 10. All the organizations that we need to be members of this collaborative group have become members of the group.	9. The people involved in our collaboration represent a cross section of those who have a stake in what we were trying to accomplish. 10. All the organizations that we needed to be members of this collaborative group have become members of the group.

(continued)

(continued)

Factor	Original statement	Our revised statement
Members see collaboration as in their self-interest	11. My organization will benefit from being involved in this collaboration.	11. My organization has benefitted from being involved in this collaboration.
Ability to compromise	12. People involved in our collaboration are willing to compromise on important aspects of our project.	12. People involved in our collaboration were willing to compromise on important aspects of our project.
Members share a stake in both process and outcome	13. The organizations that belong to our collaborative group invest the right amount of time in our collaborative efforts. 14. Everyone who is a member of our collaborative group wants this project to succeed. 15. The level of commitment among the collaboration partners is high.	13. The organizations that belonged to our collaborative group invested the right amount of time in our collaborative efforts. 14. Everyone who is a member of our collaborative group wanted this project to succeed. 15. The level of commitment among the collaboration partners was high.
Multiple layers of participation	16. When the collaborative group makes major decisions, there is always enough time for members to take information back to their organizations to confer with colleagues about what the decision should be. 17. Each of the people who participate in decisions in this collaborative group can speak for the entire organization they represent, not just a part.	16. When the collaborative group made major decisions, there was always enough time for members to take information back to their organizations to confer with colleagues about what the decision should be. 17. Each of the people who participated in decisions in this collaborative group could speak for the entire organization they represented, not just a part.
Flexibility	18. There is a lot of flexibility when decisions are made; people are open to discussing different options. 19. People in this collaborative group are open to different approaches to how we can do our work. They are willing to consider different ways of working.	18. There was a lot of flexibility when decisions were made; people are open to discussing different options. 19. People in this collaborative group were open to different approaches to how we could do our work. They were willing to consider different ways of working.
Development of clear roles and policy guidelines	20. People in this collaborative group have a clear sense of their roles and responsibilities.	20. People in this collaborative group had a clear sense of their roles and responsibilities.

(continued)

(continued)

Factor	Original statement	Our revised statement
	21. There is a clear process for making decisions among the partners in this collaboration.	21. There was a clear process for making decisions among the partners in this collaboration.
Adaptability	22. This collaboration is able to adapt to changing conditions, such as fewer funds than expected, changing political climate, or change in leadership. 23. This group has the ability to survive even if it had to make major changes in its plans or add some new members in order to reach its goals.	22. This collaboration was able to adapt to changing conditions, such as fewer funds than expected, changing political climate, or change in leadership. 23. This group had the ability to survive even if it had to make major changes in its plans or add some new members in order to reach its goals.
Appropriate pace and development	24. This collaborative group has tried to take on the right amount of work at the right pace. 25. We are currently able to keep up with the work necessary to coordinate all the people, organizations, and activities related to this collaborative project.	24. This collaborative group tried to take on the right amount of work at the right pace. 25. We were able to keep up with the work necessary to coordinate all the people, organizations, and activities related to our collaborative project.
Open and frequent communication	26. People in this collaboration communicate openly with one another. 27. I am informed as often as I should be about what goes on in the collaboration. 28. The people who lead this collaborative group communicate well with the members.	26. People in this collaboration communicated openly with one another. 27. I was informed as often as I would be about what went on in the collaboration. 28. The people who led this collaborative group communicated well with the members.
Establish informal relationships and communication links	29. Communication among the people in this collaborative group happens both at formal meetings and in informal ways. 30. I personally have informal conversations about the project with others who are involved in this collaborative group.	29. Communication among the people in our collaborative group happened both at formal meetings and in informal ways. 30. I personally had informal conversations about the project with others who were involved in this collaborative group.

(continued)

(continued)

Factor	Original statement	Our revised statement
Concrete, attainable goals and objectives	31. I have a clear understanding of what our collaboration is trying to accomplish. 32. People in our collaborative group know and understand our goals. 33. People in our collaborative group have established reasonable goals.	31. I had a clear understanding of what our collaboration was trying to accomplish. 32. People in our collaborative group knew and understood our goals. 33. People in our collaborative group had established reasonable goals.
Shared vision	34. The people in this collaborative group are dedicated to the idea that we can make this project work. 35. My ideas about what we want to accomplish with this collaboration seem to be the same as the ideas of others.	34. The people in our collaborative group were dedicated to the idea that we could make this project work. 35. My ideas about what we wanted to accomplish with this collaboration seem to be the same as the ideas of others.
Unique purpose	36. What we are trying to accomplish with our collaborative project would be difficult for any single organization to accomplish by itself. 37. No other organization in the community is trying to do exactly what we are trying to do.	36. What we were trying to accomplish with our collaborative project would be difficult for any single organization to accomplish by itself. 37. No other organization in the community was trying to do exactly what we were trying to do.
Sufficient funds, staff, materials, and time	38. Our collaborative group had adequate funds to do what it wants to accomplish. 39. Our collaborative group has adequate "people power" to do what it wants to accomplish.	38. Our collaborative group had adequate funds to do what it wanted to accomplish. 39. Our collaborative group had adequate "people power" to do what it wanted to accomplish.
Skilled leadership	40. The people in the leadership positions for this collaboration have good skills for working with other people and organizations.	40. The people in the leadership positions for this collaboration had good skills for working with other people and organizations.
New Questions		
Post-research benefits		41. I have continued to work with members of the original collaborative group in new areas/activities. 42. Involvement in our collaborative project has led to

(continued)

(continued)

Factor	Original statement	Our revised statement
		other personal or professional opportunities. 43. Participation in the original collaborative project has encouraged me to join other collaborative groups.
Learner benefits		44. My students have benefitted from my involvement in our collaborative project. 45. Students in my organization have benefitted from the outcomes of our collaborative project. 46. My teaching/professional practice has been enhanced through my involvement in our collaborative project.
Retention/workplace satisfaction		47. My involvement in our collaborative project has contributed towards my workplace satisfaction. 48. My organization has valued my participation in our collaborative project. 49. My involvement in this collaborative project has contributed to my desire to remain with my current organization.
Personal value		50. Involvement in our collaborative project was a rewarding experience.

References

Ako Aotearoa. (n.d.). https://akoaotearoa.ac.nz/ako-aotearoa. Accessed 6 November 2015.

Andriessen, J. H. E. (2005). Archetypes of knowledge communities. In P. van den Besselaar, G. De Michelis, J. Preece, & C. Simone (Eds.), *Communities and technologies* (pp. 191–213). Milan: Springer.

Breen, F., Protheroe, M., Fraser, C., Honeyfield, J., & Fester, V. (2015a). A national evaluation of funded inter-institutional research collaborations: A work in progress. In *Southland institute of Technology journal of Applied Research (Special Edition: 2014 NTLT conference proceedings)*. https://www.sit.ac.nz/SITJAR

Breen, F., Protheroe, M., Fraser, C., Honeyfield, J., & Fester, V. (2015b). Research collaborations: What are the benefits for Learning Advisors? In *ATLAANZ Refereed Conference Proceedings 2014*. www.atlaanz.org

Buckley, S., & Giannakopoulos, A. (2012). Knowledge sharing through communities of practice. Proceedings of the 3rd European Conference on Intellectual Capital. April18–19, 2011, Nicosia, Cyprus. pp.103–112. Reading: Academic Publishing International Limited.

Cambridge, D., Kaplan, S., & Suter, V. (2005). *Community of practice design guide: A step-by-step guide for designing and cultivating communities of practice in higher education.* http://net.educause.edu/ir/library/pdf/nli0531.pdf

Cox, A. (2005). What are communities of practice? A comparative review of four seminal works. *Journal of Information Science, 31*(6), 527–540.

Cumming, J. (2008). Acknowledging conflict in communities of practice: A case study from doctoral education. In *Engaging communities, proceedings of the 31st HERDSA annual conference*, Rotorua, NZ. 1–4 July 2008 (pp. 117–125).

Czajkowski, J. M. (2007). *Leading successful inter-institutional collaboration using the collaboration success measurement model.* http://www.mc.maricopa.edu/community/chair/conference/2007/papers/leading_successful_interinstitutional_collaborations.pdf

Denzin, N. K. (2009). The elephant in the living room: Or extending the conversation about the politics of evidence. *Qualitative Research, 9*(2), 139–160.

Gerritson, J. (2007). Trust and collegiality at heart of quality teaching. *New Zealand Education Review, 12*(36), 2–3.

Gewirtz, S., Shapiro, J., Maguire, M., Mahony, P., & Cribb, A. (2009). Doing teacher research: A qualitative analysis of purposes, processes and experiences. *Educational Action Research, 17* (4), 567–583. doi:10.1080/09650790903309433

Gronn, P. (2000). Distributed properties. *Educational Management Administration and Leadership, 28*(3), 317–338.

Hanna, M., & Robinson, B. (1994). Strategies for community empowerment. Lewiston, NY: Edwin Mellen Press.

Hoadley, C. (2012). What is a community of practice and how can we support it? In D. Jonassen & S. Land (Eds.), *Theoretical foundations of learning environments* (2nd ed., pp. 286–300). Mahwah, NJ: Lawrence Erlbaum Associates.

Hoadley, C., & Kilner, P. G. (2005). Using technology to transform communities of practice into knowledge-building communities. *SIGGROUP Bulletin, 25*(1), 31–40.

Hogue, J. (1993). *Community based collaboration: Community wellness multiplied.* http://www.uvm.edu/crs/nnco/collab/wellness.html

Huxham, C. (1996). Collaboration and collaborative advantage. In Huxham (Ed.), *Creating collaborative advantage*. Thousand Oaks, CA: Sage.

Jakovljevic, M., Buckley, S. & Bushney, M. (2013). Forming communities of practice in higher education: A theoretical perspective. In *Proceedings of MakeLearn conference*, 19–21 June 2013, Zadar, Croatia. ToKnow Press, Bangkok.

Kimble, C. (2006). Communities of practice: Never knowingly undersold. In E. Tomadaki & P. Scott (Eds.), *Innovative approaches for learning and knowledge sharing*, EC-TEL 2006 Workshop Proceedings. https://pdfs.semanticscholar.org/c0a3/680fe2a1d1789ccade7875c68ccafbbeebff.pdf#page=229

Kristoff, Y. (2005). Collaboration: Why and how. *The Medium, 45*(1), 25.

Learning Theories Knowledgebase. (2009). *Communities of practice (Lave and Wenger)* at Learning-Theories.com. https://www.learning-theories.com/communities-of-practice-lave-and-wenger.html

Lucas, A. O. (2005). International collaboration in health research. *Bulletin of the World Health Organisation, 83*(7), 482.

Lyon, D., Steele, L., & Fraser, C. (2015). Smaller by design: How good practice features from MOOCS can be adapted to enhance core curricula delivery. In M. Childs, C. Karp, M. Keppell, & S. Reushle (Eds.), *Open learning and formal credentialing in higher education: Curriculum models and institutional policies. Open learning and formal credentialing in higher education.* Hershey: IGI Global Publishers.

Manalo, E., Marshall, J., & Fraser, C. (Eds.) (2009). *Student learning support programmers that demonstrate tangible impact on student retention, pass rates and/or completion.* Auckland: ATLAANZ. Retrieved from http://www.atlaanz.org/research-and-publications

Mattessich, P., Murray-Close, M., & Monsey, B. (2001a). *Collaboration: What makes it work: A review of research literature on factors influencing successful collaboration* (Vol. 2). Saint Paul, MN: Wilder Research Center.

Mattessich, P., Murray-Close, M., & Monsey, B. (2001b). *Collaboration factors inventory: Assessing your collaboration's strengths.* Saint Paul, MN: Fieldstone Alliance.

McCallin, A. M. (2007). Pluralistic dialoguing: A theory of interdisciplinary teamworking. In B. G. Glaser & J. Horton (Eds.), *The grounded theory seminar reader.* Mill Valley, CA: Sociology Press.

Moxley, V. (2005). *Inter-institutional academic alliances—when, why, who and how.* Paper presented at the Academic Chairpersons Conference, Orlando, Florida. Retrieved from http://www.k-state.edu/iaa/Resources/Alliances.doc

Prebble, T., Hargraves, H., Leach, L., Naidoo, K., Suddaby, G., & Zepke, N. (2004). *Impact of student support services and academic development programmes on student outcomes in undergraduate tertiary study: A synthesis of the research.* Report to the Ministry of Education, Ministry of Education: Wellington.

Ramsden, P. (1998). *Learning to lead in higher education.* London: Routledge.

Smart, W., Smyth, R., & Hendy, S. (2013). *An analysis of collaborative journal article authorship at New Zealand universities.* http://www.educationcounts.govt.nz/publications/tertiary_education/130421

Smith, M. K. (2009). Communities of practice. *The encyclopedia of informal education.* www.infed.org/biblio/communities_of_practice.htm

Sveiby, K.-E., & Simons, R. (2002). Collaborative climate and effectiveness of knowledge work—An empirical study. *Journal of Knowledge Management, 6*(5), 420–433.

Tyler, J., Wilkinson, D. M., & Huberman, B. A. (2003): Email as spectroscopy: Automated discovery of community structure within organizations. In *Proceedings of the First International Conference on Communities and Technologies;* C&T 2003, Amsterdam.

Wenger, E. (2006). *Communities of practice: A brief introduction.* http://www.ewenger.com/theory/index.htm

Wenger, E. (2000). Communities of practice and social learning systems. *Organization, 7*(2), 226.

Wood, D. J., & Gray, B. (1991). Toward a comprehensive theory of collaboration. *The Journal of Applied Behavioral Science,* 27, 139–162. doi:10.1177/0021886391272001

Woods, P., Bennett, N., Harvey, J., & Wise, C. (2004). Variables and dualities in distributed leadership. *Educational Management Administration and Leadership, 32*(4), 439–457.

Willis, P., & Trondman, M. (2000). Manifesto for Ethnography. *Ethnography, 1*(1), 5–16.

Wolff, T. (2002). A practical approach to evaluating coalitions. In T. Backer (Ed.), *Evaluating community collaborations* (pp. 57–112). New York: Springer Publishing.

Yin, R. (1989). *Case study research: Design and methods.* Beverly Hills, California: Sage Publications.

Chapter 28
From Dream to Reality: Sustaining a Higher Education Community of Practice Beyond Initial Enthusiasm

Coralie McCormack, Robert Kennelly, John Gilchrist, Eleanor Hancock, Jesmin Islam, Maria Northcote and Kate Thomson

Abstract This chapter is set within the complex context of academia where challenges facing sustainability of learning communities are yet to be explored in detail. It presents a narrative of one such exploration with a focus on the personal experience stories of community members who have taken their vision for a sustainable higher education community of practice called Talking about Teaching and Learning (TATAL) from dream to reality. The focus of this chapter, the 2009 and 2011 TATALs, are two of seven on-going TATAL communities. Their journey suggests that to maintain long-term sustainability, learning communities need to be both individually sustaining places and collectively sustainable spaces. These places and spaces are characterised by connection through professional and social relationships, engagement through purposeful collaborative reflective inquiry, ownership through shared commitment to each other, safety based on multiple trusts and permissions, and holistic facilitation as weaving. Knowing more about

C. McCormack (✉) · R. Kennelly · J. Islam
University of Canberra, Canberra, Australia
e-mail: Coralie.McCormack@gmail.com

R. Kennelly
e-mail: Robert.Kennelly@canberra.edu.au

J. Islam
e-mail: Jesmin.Islam@canberra.edu.au

J. Gilchrist
Australian Catholic University, Banyo, Australia
e-mail: John.Gilchrist@acu.edu.au

E. Hancock
University of NSW Canberra, Canberra, Australia
e-mail: e.hancock@adfa.edu.au

M. Northcote
Avondale College of Higher Education, Cooranbong, Australia
e-mail: maria.northcote@avondale.edu.au

K. Thomson
University of Sydney, Sydney, Australia
e-mail: kate.thomson@sydney.edu.au

© Springer Nature Singapore Pte Ltd. 2017
J. McDonald and A. Cater-Steel (eds.), *Communities of Practice*,
DOI 10.1007/978-981-10-2879-3_28

individual and collective sustainability enhances individual, community, and institutional understanding of the value of informal learning for teachers. This knowledge better positions individuals to negotiate the challenges of the shifting higher education landscapes.

Keywords Community of practice · Collaborative reflective practice · Narrative, story writing · Teaching philosophy

28.1 A Complex and Challenging Context

Internationally, university teachers live and work in continually "shifting land-scapes" (Clandinin et al. 2009) where much has changed and where change will continue (Clandinin et al. 2009). In such landscapes, "there are significant chal-lenges" (McDonald and Star 2008) in relation to implementation and sustainability of communities of practice (CoP). Sector-wide drivers of higher education insti-tutional accountability, and their links to institutional funding, now focus univer-sities' attention on institutional and individual research and publications and on teaching and teacher quality assurance through quantitative measures of student learning. To a significantly lesser extent, attention has focused on the profession-alisation of teachers through formal and informal professional learning opportuni-ties. The current higher education landscape has become one in which teachers experience high workloads and focus on extrinsic motivation, and these are likely to compromise teacher health, productivity and work satisfaction (Baron and Corbin 2014). This complex and challenging environment is "not conducive to reflection, critique and dialogue" (Baron and Corbin 2014), the practices which form the heart of communities of practice.

The focus of the narrative that follows is the personal experience of members of a community of practice who have taken their vision for a sustainable higher education community called Talking about Teaching and Learning (TATAL) from dream to reality. The narrative 'From dream to reality' is composed of four stories:

- TATAL began as a dream.
- From dream to reality.
- Sustaining the dream.
- Time to dream again.

28.2 TATAL Began as a Dream

The idea for TATAL emerged from a series of conversations between two of the authors (Kennelly and McCormack); the kind of conversations "that bring people closer to the heart of a shared concern, give them new eyes to see both problems and possibilities, and set the stage for creative action" (Palmer et al. 2010). The passing of time had seen us in our roles as academic developers initiating conversations about teaching and learning with groups of colleagues. "Participants in such conversations agreed that they were valuable, yet, inevitably, the conversations petered out" (McCormack and Kennelly 2011). We were intrigued. Why did these carefully planned and sensitively facilitated conversations with colleagues peter out while our conversations continued to flourish through both pleasurable times and times of perturbation? Our investigation of the higher education literature revealed that others too were concerned about the increasing difficulty academics were experiencing in finding space and time to undertake sustained inquiry into their teaching and students' learning (for example, Palmer 1993, 2007; Lyons 1998; Warhurst 2006). Harper's (1996) conversation with a colleague sums up the experience of many academics.

> My conversations as I hurry around campus end up being staccato fragments of talk … 'I'm going to teach the qualitative research class in spring. I would like to hear your ideas about it. Yes. We *must* get together and *really* talk' I hear myself saying to a colleague as we both continue to stride in different directions. (pp. 251–252)

It was time to move from dream to reality, that is, from informal conversations with each other in which we dreamt about collaborative reflective conversations in communities of practice, to reality, a community where collaborative reflective inquiry into learning and teaching was the norm. The Australian Learning and Teaching Council Promoting Excellence Initiative funding and in-kind support from the University of Canberra and the Higher Education Research and Development Society of Australasia (HERDSA) provided the opportunity to stop dreaming. In 2008, the first TATAL community formed.

28.3   From Dream to Reality

TATAL is a community that seeks to:

- Provide a safe collaborative cross-discipline and cross-institutional environment where participants can investigate both the successes and challenges of learning and teaching.
- Enable its members to develop skills and confidence in sharing teaching and learning experiences and writing about them.
- Provide collegial support for TATAL members who are preparing teaching awards and fellowships.

TATALs begin as 'nurtured' communities guided by external co-facilitators. In its own time, each TATAL community moves beyond the 'group establishment' phase to travel at its own pace through 'group maintenance'. This phase introduces community members to the practice of facilitation (one external facilitator co-facilitates with a group member). As time passes, the community moves into 'self-organisation'. In this phase, facilitation rotates around the group with each person taking a turn to facilitate a meeting. At this point, the external facilitators choose whether to remain as members of the community and move from facilitator to participant roles or to leave the group.

TATAL members and facilitators are volunteers. TATALs are a cross-institutional higher education community whose members are geographically dispersed across Australia, Hong Kong, The People's Republic of China, and New Zealand. Community members come from a variety of disciplines including allied health, academic development, accounting, building and construction management, business, education, geography, history, law and theology. Their teaching experience ranges from early career to retiree. TATAL conversations may be face-to-face, via audio conferencing (for example, using Skype), or a combination where some community members are face-to-face and others are participating via Skype. Communities of 6–8 members meet for 2 h every 4–6 weeks. The authors of this chapter are both members in, and facilitators of, a TATAL community.

- TATAL conversations draw together the literatures around:
- Experiential learning (Kolb 1984; Boud et al. 1985).
- Social models of reflection (Brookfield 1995; Boud et al. 1985; Mezirow 2000a, b; Schön 1983).
- Transformation through action research (Carr and Kemmis 1986; Mezirow 2000a, b; Shulman 1993).
- Teaching philosophy statements and teaching portfolios (Lyons 1998; Chism 1998; Schonwetter et al. 2002).
- Writing stories as reflective inquiry (Brookfield 1995; Richardson 2000).

TATAL conversations connect community members through the stories they tell of their teaching and their collaborative reflection on these stories. Writing and telling stories of learning and teaching experiences helps academics "to see into themselves, to see what they may not have seen previously, or to see the familiar through different eyes" (McCormack 2009). Collaborative reflection is more than a congenial conversation (Kennelly and McCormack 2014). Rather, it involves robust discussion that supports individuals to "move beyond a purely emotional response to their experiences to a position where they have the confidence to acknowledge and then make sense of their emotions", to "develop their capacity to view things through another's perspective", and to "wrestle with complex, difficult questions that do not yield an easy answer" (Kennelly and McCormack 2014).

TATAL conversations move through cycles of collaborative reflective inquiry with a shared purpose and the support of facilitators.

Three portfolio-based activities (Fig. 28.1) form a common framework within which each TATAL shapes its cycles of collaborative reflective inquiry. As the community shapes the portfolio-based framework to meet their needs, the facilitators provide targeted and specific support. For example, during the development of a teaching philosophy statement, the facilitators use guided discussion to introduce frameworks for writing a teaching philosophy (for example, Chism 1998;

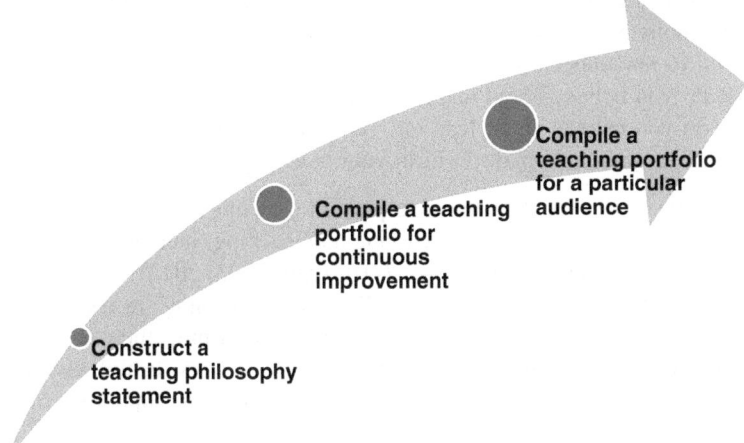

Fig. 28.1 TATAL portfolio-based framework

Schonwetter et al. 2002). In the structured dialogues, members consider which framework they would and wouldn't feel comfortable using for their teaching philosophy statement. The dialogue is structured around the following questions: What makes a framework comfortable? What would help you start writing? and What might hinder you getting started writing?

During a community meeting, each member undertakes a cycle of collaborative reflective inquiry (Fig. 28.2). The cycle begins with each member critically questioning their personal beliefs and values about learning and teaching and how these inform their teaching practice using **guided story writing** as a mode of inquiry; "a way of finding out about yourself and your topic' through "discovery and analysis" (Richardson 2000). The following questions guide members as they write the stories that construct their teaching philosophy statement.

Fig. 28.2 Collaborative reflective inquiry cycle underlying TATAL interactions

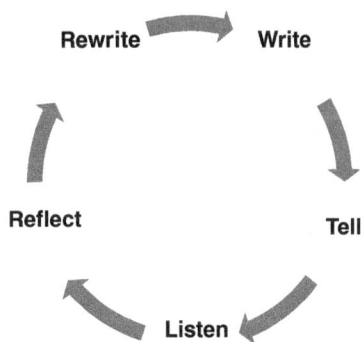

- Why is being a teacher important to you? What personal experience(s) inform/motivate your teaching today? Why is this experience important enough for you to remember it today?
- What do you believe about teaching? Why do you hold these beliefs?
- What do you believe about learning? Why do you hold these beliefs?
- How are these beliefs played out in your teaching context?

To compile stories for their teaching portfolio, members are asked to recall and record in writing, stories of critical learning and teaching 'incidents' (Harper 1996; Brookfield 1995; Hughes and Moore 2007; Tripp 1993, 2012). Critical incidents can be times when they felt students 'really learnt something' (a narrative of success) or times when they felt 'nothing was working to inspire students' learning' (a personally confronting narrative). A critical incident story is not just a factual description. The following guided story writing process supports community members as they re-construct a critical incident.

- *Story writing*: Return to the experience and describe when and where it happened and what happened.
- *Story analysis*: Attend to feelings associated with the experience: What were you thinking and feeling at the time and just afterwards? How were the students feeling?
- *Story evaluation*: Interrogate the story: Why did this incident stand out? What did you learn from the incident?

Telling a story to others sets the scene for a collaborative conversation during which the storyteller **listens and responds to others** as they ask questions of clarification, share with the storyteller words, phrases, or metaphors frequently used or suggested to them by the story; and identify points of tension or opportunity in the story. This conversation concludes with community members reflecting back to the storyteller the key point they have learnt from the story. The purpose of this conversation is to enable deeper reflection and understanding which will provoke a rewriting of the story and another cycle of collaborative inquiry. Collaborative reflective inquiry can do this because it gives the individual 'permission' to "stand back from their taken-for-granted assumptions about teaching and enter into a shared inquiry into the meaning and significance of the event at hand" (Harper 1996).

Each storyteller concludes their inquiry cycle by **reflecting** on what they have learnt and sharing their response to the question: What will I do next? Between meetings, a community member **rewrites** their story to reflect their new learning. Another cycle of story writing, storytelling, and collaborative reflection occurs at the next meeting. Most stories proceed through several cycles of collaborative reflective inquiry.

When members move to compiling a portfolio for a particular audience, specific requirements of that portfolio guide the process of story writing. For example, the requirements of a HERDSA Fellowship portfolio can be viewed at http://www.herdsa.org.au/?page_id=5. As the life of the community extends beyond the

portfolio-based activities illustrated in Fig. 28.1, each community identifies personally meaningful scholarly inquiries to investigate using cycles of collaborative
reflection (Fig. 28.2). These inquiries may result in individual or collaborative
authorship of a scholarly publication. For example, members of the 2008 TATAL
community published a HERDSA Guide titled "Using stories in teaching" (Miley
et al. 2012). Ongoing inquiry has led the 2009/2011 combined TATAL to develop a
collaborative reflective inquiry process to explore the role of facilitation in TATAL
communities from their perspectives as both community members and facilitators.
Community members often take up the opportunity to extend their leadership
capacity and capabilities beyond their 'home' TATAL community by joining with
members from different TATAL communities to facilitate new communities formed
through a series of workshops at the annual HERDSA conference, while continuing
their membership of their 'home' TATAL community. Kennelly et al. (2013)
describe the TATAL workshops at the 2013 HERDSA conference in Auckland
facilitated by members from four different TATAL communities.

Before commencing the inquiry reported in the following chapter sections, the
authors negotiated an ethical code based on the TATAL community's ground rules
which members felt had served them well (over the 4 years of meeting by the 2011
TATAL and the 6 years of meeting by the 2009 TATAL). As academics, a large
part of our work involves interaction with other human beings, as this research did.
It is therefore important that our inquiry abides by ethical standards. Participation in
the inquiry was voluntary and participants were able to cease their participation and
withdraw their stories (if they wished) at any time. In this chapter, quotes have been
anonymised and pseudonyms adopted for the purpose of confidentiality. The main
purpose of this negotiated ethical framework was to promote respect, concern and
care for the physical, social and emotional dimensions of participating TATALers.

28.4   Sustaining the Dream

Early evaluation of TATAL communities reported that while members used positive terms to describe their overall experience, such as "wonderful", "encouraging"
and "refreshing", their comments about reflection and interaction in the groups
revealed that something else was also happening which sustained their involvement.
TATAL members became engaged and dedicated to their TATAL communities and
expressed a willingness to spend time participating in the group despite other time
pressures such as "working around 70 h per week" (2008 participant, email 27
February 2009). TATAL meetings felt like the "only time in the week I can reflect
on what I'm doing; a refuge" (TATAL session 7 conversation, 2009 participant). In
this "refuge" there was time to talk, listen, reflect and engage in continuous
self-improvement:

> I learned that though I have been teaching for a very long time, I have been teaching without having ever asked myself why I am doing this as a profession. (2008 participant, mid-program survey)

> My involvement in this group is scaffolding my preparation for a HERDSA fellowship in a way that is measured and systematic. The group provides a clear direction, purpose and helped me to clarify my own thinking behind the application. (2011 HERDSA TATAL participant)

Discussions that occurred in the communities were typically diverse and far-ranging. Nevertheless, this diversity did not seem to reduce the quality of scholarly conversation that happens in "border crossing" (McAlpine 2005) groups such as TATALs. In fact, this very diversity often sparked recognition of the value of having members from different disciplines, with different teaching experience, involved in the same TATAL community.

> One of the community's strengths is the mix of disciplines in the group because we each come from a different perspective. I think it helps to have different levels of teaching experience in the group too. For instance, some of [name of participant] comments have really made me think about things I have been doing without much thought for years. (2008 participant, email 23 October 2009)

Perhaps it was the community's open approach to talking about identity that fostered sustained engagement as the informal, yet guided group process offered a place where teachers could reflect on their practice as well as their own journey as practitioners.

> I explored my inner self and discovered a gap between the inner 'self' and the teaching 'self'; you need to be true to yourself. (2009 participant, TATAL session 7 conversations)

While the reasons behind the sustainability of a TATAL community may be difficult to define, there is more than one factor that contributes to the longevity of a community. Instead, there appear to be multiple and multi-layered reasons why TATAL community members remain in the group across sustained periods of time, often years, even though participation is voluntary. There are no extrinsic rewards, no marks or grades, no performance indicators to recompense each person. Yet, more often than not, members extend their engagement in TATAL communities well beyond the establishment period. Evaluation of the 2008 and 2009 TATAL communities by the first two authors (see McCormack and Kennelly 2011) suggested that 'glue' was needed to bring individuals together and to sustain the group as a community (Allard et al. 2007; Mitchell and Sackney 2001).

The story 'Sustaining the dream' begins with an exploration of three factors: connection, engagement and safety. These were the factors identified by the early TATAL communities as key in sustaining communities in the short-term. More recent reflections by members of the 2009 and 2011 TATAL communities, shared in the second part of this story, have revealed a more nuanced understanding of these factors and also, the particular role of ownership and facilitation in the longer-term sustainability of TATAL communities.

28.4.1 Sustainability: An Initial Exploration

An initial exploration undertaken by the first two authors (McCormack and Kennelly 2011) identified the constituents of the 'glue' that sustained TATALs through continuous cycles of collaborative reflective inquiry were connection, engagement, and safety. When moulded together as glue, connection, engagement and safety provoke 'knowing why' conversations. Such conversations are exploratory and delve "deep[ly] into the experience of each participant" (Belenky et al. 1986) to open opportunities to construct and reconstruct teaching identity.

Part of what makes a TATAL community sustainable is the **connections** it fosters, between individuals, between individuals and facilitators, and within the entire community. These connections are largely based on the combination of shared interests and different backgrounds. Community members represented various disciplines, a range of academic appointments and roles, teaching and learning experiences, and they have come together for a shared purpose. This purpose is to TATAL—talk about teaching and learning, with a view to developing a teaching portfolio. The variety within the community served to validate individuals as teachers, when members realised that what they were experiencing in their teaching was not unique to them. For example, they discovered that "[t]eachers have common concerns/issues/ideas regardless of discipline" (2009 participant, TATAL session 1). Differences in context encouraged community members to understand and learn from the perspectives of their community colleagues, and to introduce their own perspective to the group, and this worked to foster collaborative learning about teaching.

> TATAL provides a place where we can discuss our ideas with colleagues and get their feedback. (2008 participant email, 25 March 2010)

> Exchange of ideas with other academics, especially from other universities helped me learn. (2009 participant, mid-program survey)

TATAL communities represent the type of learning about teaching from colleagues that Brookfield argued for—"[t]alking to colleagues about problems we have in common and gaining their perspectives on these increases our chances of stumbling across an interpretation that fits what is happening in a particular situation" (Brookfield 1995). Connections were formed as TATAL members talked about and shared their experiences. These connections formed the basis for further engagement.

TATAL communities **engage** members by encouraging them to think deeply and learn about their teaching through an ongoing process of conversations, writing, and reflection. Community members are engaged as teachers, and as learners; they reflect on their beliefs about teaching and how these relate to their beliefs about, and experiences of, learning. These processes are individual and collaborative, and support members, validating existing practice at the same time as developing their teaching repertoire and generating new ideas. Some members described community meetings as the time to "think fundamentally about my beliefs and philosophy"

(2010 participant, mid-program survey) and for "learning beyond teaching" (2010 participant, mid-program survey). This deeper engagement with their own practice, and ability to articulate this in a teaching philosophy, changed the teaching practice of some TATAL members.

> TATAL is an important opportunity to strengthen my reflective practice in a way that has directly influenced and enhanced my learning and teaching … [It] provides me with a regular opportunity to gain and share stories about learning and teaching and has provided me with new knowledge about the role of the teaching philosophy statement, teaching portfolio, and the application for formal recognition of learning and teaching practice. (Excerpt from a successful teaching award application)

In the contexts of research-intensive universities and the performativity agenda of higher education, investing time in teaching can be seen as less than worthwhile and, consequently, is difficult to achieve. Furthermore, in a competitive environment, acknowledging that you face challenges in your teaching is seen as a problem that should be fixed, and is not necessarily something that you would be eager to share with colleagues (Bass 1999). The TATAL communities are distinct in that they are characterised by mutual trust and respect, and this led to a sense of **safety** in a broad sense—community members were physically comfortable, and professionally secure, and therefore able to be honest with one another about their experiences without concerns for their well-being or employment. Members felt that the group was "… all there to help each other, which is a strength of TATAL—so no one has to go it alone" (2008 participant, email 12 July 2009). Community members felt they could be "open about their apparent failures and weaknesses as teachers" (Gilchrist et al. 2013) and, accordingly, not just share their experiences, but inquire meaningfully into their teaching philosophies and practices.

28.4.2 Sustainability: A Further Exploration

As time passed, and more TATAL communities formed and more existing communities continued, the authors sought to learn more about sustainability of TATAL communities. In particular, we wondered about the long-term sustainability of the initial TATAL communities. TATALs begun in 2009 and in 2011 were continuing well beyond initial enthusiasm. Had the components of the 'glue' sustaining TATALs during their early years remained the same, changed or …?

TATAL stories written in 2014 by 2009 and 2011 community members revealed the continuing importance of connection, engagement and safety as ingredients of the 'glue' that sustains TATALs. In addition to the similarities, the stories revealed a more nuanced understanding of the role of connection and safety. The 2014 stories unpacked the role of ownership, a 'glue' element acknowledged in the initial sustainability framework (McCormack and Kennelly 2011) as growing from the interaction of connection, engagement and safety, with little further explanation. More explicit too was the role of facilitator as an ingredient of the sustainability glue; an ingredient assumed but not explored in the construction of the earlier framework.

Over time the value of **connecting** teachers across disciplines and institutions continued to be valued by TATAL members as Therese describes.

> Learning about the challenges and successes of other like-minded academics enabled me to learn from their experiences and provided me with plenty of chances to share stories of my own success and challenges…Because we work in a range of different institutions in the higher education sector, it is very useful to hear about how we all face these issues on a day-to-day basis.

For Fatima, TATAL connected her with other colleagues, also passionate about student learning; a connection missing from her discipline environment.

> I find it hard to talk with colleagues of my own discipline about teaching and learning. Their focus is more on teaching technical aspects and getting that right, rather than the more sensitive issues of teaching and learning in my discipline. So when I received an invitation under my office door to participate in TATAL I agreed. Others regard this as a strange thing to do. I am passionate about my students' learning and I don't find such passion in my colleagues in the same discipline. TATAL has given me an opportunity to connect with similar minded colleagues from other disciplines and institutions.

Not only did connection with other like-minded colleagues enhance individuals' self-confidence but also, the collective belief in the individual held by the TATAL community further strengthened individuals' self-belief. For Fatima, her TATAL community's belief "that I can do it" gave her the confidence to continue writing her stories for her HERDSA Fellowship application. Aisha also noticed the importance of the community's belief that an individual could complete a Fellowship application "when this writing process seemed daunting".

As expected from the experiences of the early TATAL communities, a **safe environment** for learning and teaching conversations contributed to the sustainability of the 2009 and 2011 TATALs. In addition, our recent stories revealed that the safe environment of TATAL was also characterised by a sense of **equality** and **freedom** that has sustained both Fatima and Therese's participation.

> I come from a different cultural/religious background. I am a first generation migrant from an Asian country. There are very few academics like me in the Australian universities – an Asian country Muslim lady with hijab (scarf on head)…What sustained my continued participation in the group was participants' ready acceptance of my different cultural/religious background and continued respect and support of my participation in the group. I think this has also helped me survive in my job because I can not only discuss about my teaching and learning issues, but I have also found a safe haven for discussing job related issues without the fear of adverse consequences. So in that sense another factor for me which helps in sustaining the dream of TATAL is…being able to talk safely about my career related issues. (Fatima)

> ..a place where I am free to talk about teaching and to consider, with like-minded colleagues, how teaching can be applied to research and how research can be applied to teaching…a TATAL group seems to create a place where…it's acceptable and even honourable to discuss the value of teaching in university contexts. (Therese)

It was not unexpected that trust, understood as a willingness to place oneself in a position of vulnerability, would be evident in the more recent stories about safety in TATAL communities. What was unexpectedly revealed was that trust is both complex and dynamic. It forms through multi-dimensional social and professional relationships. Trust has both time-based dimensions described as initial trust and longitudinal trust by Swift and Hwang (2013) and affective and cognitive dimensions identified by Chowdhury (2005).

Affective trust is based on emotional connections with others that create a feeling of openness without vulnerability (Chowdhury 2005). Cognitive trust arises from connections based on professional credentials and pedagogic theory and practice knowledge which "improve professional relationships and enhance professional collaborations" (Chowdhury 2005). Initial trust develops through social and professional interactions during group formation (that is, during the period of initial enthusiasm). It is built on expectations created by facilitators. Longitudinal trust is based on actual experiences within the community over time. Longitudinal trust that sustains TATALs beyond initial enthusiasm builds on initial trust through on-going strengthening of affective and cognitive trust (see Fig. 28.3).

Suzanne and Lyn's stories ("Appendices 1, 2") illustrate the strength of affective and cognitive trust grown over time to become longitudinal trust. The strength of such trust increases community members' (in this case Suzanne) and facilitators' (in this case Lyn) willingness to take risks beyond those taken in the early days of the community. Suzanne shared her story titled 'How to deal with hurtful student comments' ("Appendix 1") based on cognitive trust, her belief that other TATAL members, whatever their discipline or career experience, would have a professional understanding of the context described in the story. The affective trust already established within Suzanne's community also contributed to her willingness to take the risk of sharing the hurtful student comments. In her story about facilitating the meeting in which Suzanne told her story ("Appendix 2"), Lyn recalled that affective and cognitive trust built over time gave her permission to step back from the role of facilitator to become a group member. In her reflections on her story Lyn concluded:

> …It's the particular way trust and safety works in TATAL groups that enable more than the textbook expected creation of a safe environment. Trust and safety in TATAL give group members the permissions necessary to share their inner teaching selves and contradictions between their inner teaching self and their everyday teaching self (the self that is visible to colleagues, heads of school, etc.). The inner teaching self is a 'raw' self, unshareable (except in TATALs), in contrast to the functional self of everyday academic life. Events which touch the inner teaching self are events that touch the spirit. The risk of sharing/making visible one's teaching spirit is a big one to take.

Affective and cognitive trust, built from initial trust into longitudinal trust, provided the safety needed by Suzanne and Lyn to take this 'big risk'. These 'multiple trusts' give individuals permission to relax and be themselves and to invest in time to talk about and investigate their teaching away from their faculty. As noted by Phillip, TATALs provide "respite and renewal and a feeling of rebooted enthusiasm for engagement as a teacher and learner".

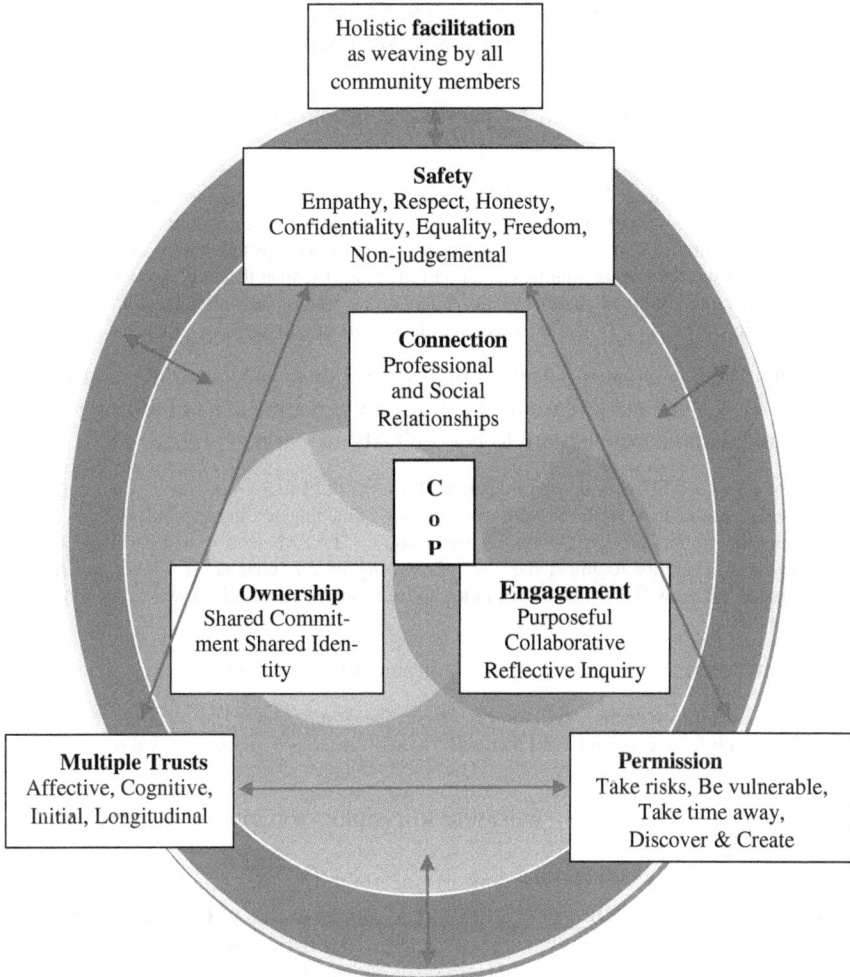

Fig. 28.3 The elements of the 'glue' that promote long-term sustainability of a TATAL community and their inter-relationships

That a sense of **ownership** has been created is evident in the language community members use in their stories to talk about TATAL. Words such as 'our', 'we', 'us TATAL members' or 'TATALers', were repeated across each individual's stories and across story writers. The use of capitals by Therese and her metaphor of an Irish hedge school (scoil chois clai, Adams 1999) illustrates the strong sense of ownership felt by TATAL members.

> During my time in Ireland last year I learned a lot about the plight of oppression suffered by most of the Irish population in days gone by. One thing that struck me about their oppressed years was that the things that mattered to them mostly lived on because of their clandestine activities that took place despite the presence of their oppressors...In a way, the existence

of TATAL reminds me of the defiance of an Irish hedge school - we WILL still care about teaching, we WILL still talk about teaching, we WILL still research our teaching, we WILL still express our concern about student learning.

Ownership is strengthened by personal connections fostered within a TATAL community as told in Tatem's story.

We had one wedding themed TATAL meeting (or it felt that way to me). There was a poem/song and a virtual toast in the lead up to my wedding…there were references to Irish sports and comments in Gaelic when Therese was away. The gestures seem simple enough, but at the time, they were significant. Upon reflecting, I realise that this was a way to help us to stay connected to each other, with content and a process beyond what would typically happen in a workshop or similar academic development activity.

Working together creates a feeling of responsibility, accountability and commitment to each other and a sense of shared identity. Fatima talks of a strong sense of commitment and accountability to her TATAL members.

I have no forced obligation to participate in TATAL, but I feel a sense of accountability… At the moment, I am quite busy/concerned about finishing writing my unit outline…But despite having that pressure I have decided to do the TATAL writing first because I feel a shared responsibility to finish the TATAL writing of this chapter. If I can't finish my writing in time I will feel like I have failed to fulfill my responsibility towards my TATAL colleagues.

Tatem describes this sense of commitment to each other as:

… you prioritise listening, and contributing to the group, you try to meet the deadlines, because you feel supported. And then when you do meet as a group, you feel re-energised and reconnected.

Ownership provides the motivation to continue to connect, engage, and work safely together.

The more nuanced understanding of sustainability that emerged from TATAL stories suggests a **holistic understanding of the practice of facilitation** where the role of the facilitator is that of a weaver. Holistic facilitation goes beyond observable actions (such as conducting icebreakers, scaffolding individuals' learning through feedback) to include aspects of facilitation less frequently recognised and articulated by facilitators or group participants. That is, the ways of being and doing that form the "inner practice of group facilitation" (Thorpe 2011). The role of the facilitator is to weave together the observable and the inner practices of facilitation to nurture the whole person and the community as a whole as Tatem recognised.

I had a sense that TATAL was about me (and each one of us) growing and developing as a whole person. The TATAL, as individuals, and as a group, were whatever we needed at the time, and there was always patience and mutual respect. This meant that the support was tailored, connected to me as a person, as a learner, as a PhD student, as a developing academic, and an academic developer, as a teacher, (even as a bride to be). It's pretty amazing really that facilitators can achieve this.

In TATAL effective weaving seamlessly fuses personal, spiritual and intellectual ways of being, knowing and working. For Phillip, this involves:

> …the fusion in TATAL of the academic/intellectual and the personal, emotional, social and professional. It is a chemistry (or alchemy) which academics do not experience overall, in what is generally expressed as an objectivised evidence-based world.

For Tatem, this alchemy results in a seemingly magical transformation in which the role of the facilitator is invisible.

> It also seemed like we did things because we chose to do them, brilliant facilitation (manipulation?) [even though] we did still achieve the agenda for each meeting, it somehow felt like that happened organically… Facilitation happens but you don't see it happen, you feel it changing the way you think about learning and teaching.

She suggests that this 'invisibility' enables the storyteller to "go deeper into the 'puzzle' of their story, providing a climate where the TATAL members feel free, indeed motivated, to explore their own story almost as though no one was in the room".

28.4.3   Learning from Our Explorations

For long-term sustainability, communities of practice need to be both **individually sustaining places** and **collectively sustainable spaces** in which facilitation as weaving is distributed amongst community members who see themselves as both facilitators and community members. The 'glue' that enables and promotes **long-term sustainability** is constructed by the interactions of the following five ingredients, as illustrated in Fig. 28.3.

- Connection through professional and social relationships.
- Engagement through commitment to purposeful collaborative reflective inquiry.
- Safety based on 'multiple trusts' and permissions.
- Ownership through shared commitment to each other.
- A holistic practice of facilitation as weaving.

Each TATAL group develops a personal and collective understanding of these factors. In this way the dream of long-term sustainability beyond initial enthusiasm is realised. It's now time to dream beyond individual community sustainability to consider a role for TATAL in responding to the widely expressed concern that teaching, in comparison to research, is not sufficiently rewarded and recognised in universities (for example, Chalmers 2011; Debowski and Blake 2004; Ramsden 2009).

28.5 Time to Dream Again

The prevailing university culture is characterised by an approach to getting things done described by Robbins et al. (2003) as "the degree to which people are pragmatic, maintain emotional distance and believe that the ends justify the means". Universities constantly spin the importance of teaching and learning as though they were serious about all the implications of doing so. The knowledge that teaching is under-valued (Ginns et al. 2010; Devlin et al. 2012; Chalmers 2011; Ramsden 2009) contributes to increasing alienation among academic staff. Full-time academics work far beyond an 8 h day, often into their evenings and weekends (Coates et al. 2009; Baron and Corbin 2014). In fact, in comparison with their international peers, Australian academics work among the longest hours per week (Coates et al. 2009). 'Flexible learning' can lead to more frequently scheduled classes, often at weekends or at night. Students' queries are received day and night, regardless of the mode of delivery.

In addition, financial pressures suggest that universities to some extent have lost their mission to foster students' learning and prepare them for a career. Many universities are businesses with the normal motivation of earning income and profits to enable them to survive at a time when government funding is a declining proportion of total university income. Teaching and learning then becomes a commodity to be sold in competition with other universities. Consequently, many universities devote their limited resources towards technical innovations which are promoted at the expense of professional growth. Teaching-active academics are quickly becoming de-personalised.

This final story dreams of a higher education landscape that equally values teaching and learning and research. Our dreaming suggested three strategies.

- Use formal teaching and learning programs already supported by university managers as springboards.
- Develop a network of TATAL-based strategies aligned with the dimensions of an institution's 'cultural web'.
- Adopt an alternative approach to learning and teaching leadership based on values and processes aligned with those underpinning TATAL communities.

28.5.1 Vision 1

In this vision formal teaching and learning programs already supported by university managers become springboards that increase the number of advocates for teaching and learning within an institution. For example, embedding TATAL-based processes and practices into induction and mentoring programs for new academics provides an opportunity to have a TATAL 'lite' experience. Ideally, these opportunities would be cross-disciplinary experiences in a safe context as suggested by

TATAL experiences. Taking advantage of current technology, TATAL 'lite' opportunities could be cross-institutional.

TATAL 'lite' opportunities, described by Clancy (2013) as "possibility portals" (p. 82), have been created by her in the Graduate Diploma in University Teaching and Learning offered at the University College, Dublin. 'Possibility portals' in this context were defined as:

> …a developmental space; a protected space; a portal free from the criticism and bias of students and colleagues where academics began to discover themselves in a new, exciting but often troublesome way. In addition, and perhaps more significantly, this portal had a joint mission in that it also encouraged academics to embark on a journey of self discovery through its collaborative nature (Clancy 2013).

This 'possibility portal' enabled diploma participants to grow and develop as teachers and had the potential to move academics to contribute to the scholarship of learning and teaching and to academic leadership in their department. Participants indicated that "they would become advocates of teaching and learning" (Clancy 2013).

In a similar context (the Graduate Certificate in Tertiary Education at the University of Canberra), a TATAL group was formed at the beginning of semester 1 2010 and continued to meet outside formal 'class' time over the semester. At the end of the semester participants agreed that they had learnt to "learn beyond teaching" and that this increased their understanding of their beliefs about teaching and student learning (2010 TATAL participants, end of semester survey). They recognised that "students are not empty vessels" and "teaching isn't about a text-book" (2010 participants, TATAL session 7 discussions). Seen through the prism of 2015, this TATAL community was successful for the semester life of the Graduate Certificate. All participants composed a teaching philosophy statement and were introduced to the concept of a teaching portfolio. A current university program was used and a dozen new academics were exposed to the TATAL process.

28.5.2 Vision 2

To extend institutional participation in collaborative reflective practice beyond TATALs, and other 'pockets of resistance' such as those suggested in the first vision, strategies aligned with Johnson's (2000) three dimensions of an institution's cultural web (symbolic, structural and political dimensions) are needed (Kennelly and McCormack 2015). Such strategies for the symbolic dimension could include regular formal social and developmental activities constructed around rituals and symbols. Strategies aligned with the structural dimension of organisational culture could integrate TATAL perspectives into the ways the organisation works by strategically positioning individual TATAL community members in discipline and faculty conversations as members of formal committees, reference groups or working parties. Strategies aligned with the political dimensions of the organisational culture could include briefing sessions for groups of learning and teaching leaders (e.g., Associate Deans, Teaching and Learning) to familiarise them with the language of TATALs to increase the exposure of this language and its legitimacy within the institution.

However, as was noted with vision 1 strategies, the vision 2 strategies above are still creating 'pockets of resistance', though the pockets would be somewhat larger and have greater institutional breadth and legitimacy. Developing a 'package' of interacting strategies with each strategy aligned with one or more of the dimensions of the institution's 'cultural web' and then 'rippling out' this package across a faculty would have the potential to increase the 'elbow room' for collaborative reflective practice and the extent of institutional advocacy for learning and teaching.

28.5.3   Vision 3

Our third vision advocates for a shared learning and teaching leadership framework to replace the more common hierarchical leadership model and in so doing, create more 'elbow room' for collaborative reflective practice in universities. One possibility is the TATAL-inspired interactional approach to leadership with the acronym of HILOTALM (Heads of Schools, Interactional, Leadership of Teaching and Learning, and Metaphors) (Kennelly and McCormack 2015). This approach seeks to promote learning and teaching leaders at the 'meso' level of an institution who have learning and teaching competency and passion and an ability to use metaphors and political acuity to sell this leadership model to managers and executives. Distributive leadership in a collaborative framework proposed by Jones, Lefoe, Harvey and Ryland (2012, 2013) has many similarities to the HILOTALM approach.

Both frameworks have the potential to create more 'elbow room' when implemented in conjunction with TATALs as 'possibility portals' because the underpinning values and processes of these models exhibit a strong degree of alignment. Both value a context of trust, a culture of respect, recognition of change, and collaborative relationships. Both involve people in facilitated collaborative processes which include some professional development, supported and resourced to encourage space and time for collaborative reflective practice. Both engage a broad range of participants, are sustained through cycles of participative action inquiry and are evaluated by gathering evidence of increased collaboration and growth of leadership capacity.

To extend their vision into practice Jones et al. (2013) have developed good practice benchmarks for distributed leadership to enable institutions to identify and evaluate their own learning and teaching leadership practice. Applying this benchmarking process provides a systematic and significant step towards increasing advocacy for learning and teaching in universities.

28.5.4 Learning from Our Visions

Dreaming again can also mean dreaming differently. In dreaming again, differently, we must be awake to the possibilities that the following question may trigger: What do active, former, and future TATAL community members need to support institutional strategies to make more 'elbow room' for collaborative reflective practice? Currently we are calling on TATAL members to act as pioneers and missionaries, to sustain the dream themselves, and bring its benefits to others. The challenge is now not just to write down and explain our dreams but to actually commit and continue to commit to doing something more to advocate for learning and teaching.

28.6 Coda

Academics have and will continue to have competing commitments, and may not have the time, interest, or support, to participate long-term in a TATAL community. This means that TATAL communities will change over time; as members are unable to prioritise a focus on their teaching, or they discover that the style of a TATAL community doesn't suit them. This doesn't reflect negatively on those individuals or on that TATAL community, but it does make those TATAL communities that are sustained long-term, significant.

Optimistically, the TATAL experience reminds us that a community of practice can achieve long-term sustainability. TATAL communities formed in 2009, 2011, 2012, 2013, 2014 and 2015 continue to meet. A new TATAL community will form in July 2016 at the HERDSA annual conference.

Acknowledgments The authors wish to acknowledge support for the TATAL communities from the Higher Education Research and Development Society of Australasia (http://www.herdsa.org.au/). We also wish to thank the members of the 2008, 2009, 2010, 2011, 2012, 2013, 2014 and 2015 TATAL communities for their enthusiasm and willingness to take the risk of talking to others about their teaching.

Appendix 1: An Example of a TATAL Member's Story Titled: 'How to Deal with Hurtful Students' Comments'

Just a day or so before our last TATAL meeting I received the USS data for the units I taught in semester 1. I teach (post) graduate students in the TESOL (Teaching English to Speakers of Other Languages)/FLT (Foreign Language Teaching) programme. More than half of my students are international students from various backgrounds; the other half is Australians. In addition to the diversity in students' ethnic and cultural background, students' age also varies considerably, i.e. from early 20s to 60s or above.

Looking at the figures first, I was very pleased with the overall results. However, when I looked at the 'open questions' comments', I read the following two comments:

> The course convenor should be sent back to china because she does not like or respect other students from other countries only chinese she likes and gives more office time to them.

> The change of the teacher of the course will be the best solution to the unit.

I found these two comments very disturbing. I also felt that especially the first one was not justified. One of my principles is to treat each and everybody fairly. In addition, my office hours are actually very quiet most of the time; so there is plenty of time to chat with students if they came to see me. What I found and still find so upsetting about these two comments is that they are so disrespectful. They are personal attacks, insults; I find this hurtful.

The first one is particularly disturbing since the student is reproaching me of being biased towards one group (the Chinese students) in my class. I don't think I am. Indeed, because of the very diverse backgrounds of my students (e.g. Chinese, Indonesian, Korean, Japanese, Saudi, Australian) I always make sure that all students 'mix and mingle' in my classes so that they experience a firsthand cultural and linguistic exchange.

I also regret that this student has not talked with me about his/her concerns and drawn my attention to his/her feelings of being disadvantaged at an earlier stage; I always encourage students to talk with me if there is a problem. The mid-semester evaluations that I conduct in all my units had not alerted me to this issue, either.

Finally, another reason why I felt so upset when I read these comments was that they brought back a negative incident that I had when I started teaching in New Zealand and encountered such student satisfaction evaluations for the first time in my academic career (they were not standard at the universities of my birth country at that time). In my first semester at the New Zealand University, one of my students ticked the weakest mark for each question and wrote "You suck" in big letters on the back of his/her questionnaire. I remember that at the time, I was even more upset than I was a few weeks ago. I sought advice from the Higher Education Centre and shared my experience. I felt a little bit better after having shared this incident with the colleague who was very kind and supportive. I found it comforting when he said that I was particularly "vulnerable", given the fact that I had just arrived at the university in a new country, that I was teaching new units, in a new context etc. etc. He made sure that this particular questionnaire was not counted, which did not make much of a difference in the overall score, but felt 'just'.

I wish I would be 'cooler' when reading such hurtful comments, especially since they are the exception, but somehow they do upset and hurt me. I keep on thinking about them at least for a few days, which annoys me even more, since I think that I should not give that much attention to such disrespectful comments. I wonder what I could do to avoid such comments, regardless of how rare they are, and what to do when they happen.

Appendix 2: An Excerpt from a TATAL Member's Story Titled: 'Trust Enables Risk Taking'

This event happened at a scheduled TATAL meeting during the phase where the group was being co-facilitated by the two external facilitators…On this afternoon Suzanne shared a story about student comments she had received in response to open-ended questions on her student feedback survey (mandatory surveys, all units have the same questions). Soon after she began telling her story I could see and feel the risk she was taking. At this point I wasn't sure what my role as co-facilitator would be. As the story unfolded my concern for Suzanne and for the group members increased. While as part of my role as an academic developer I had seen many negative student comments and worked with staff to make sense of these comments, most of the derogatory comments were about a teacher's clothes, appearance or mannerisms. Suzanne's student comments were different. They were hurtful, mean and offensive. As she told the story I could hear in her voice the feelings these comments had provoked: surprise, fear, anger and self-questioning; a sense of loss of her teaching self. This story was touching my heart as it was the hearts of all group members…As co-facilitators we had worked over time to create both social and professional relations of trust and an environment in which trust was not a theoretical or superficial concept but a living concept that became a 'natural' part of the TATAL process and conversations. Trust is like a complex system. It's not something that facilitators 'set up' but rather it's the interconnections that are created between people and process. It is the interweaving of multiple 'trusts' that facilitates learning and growth in a complex system. Trust is like the interconnections that form the global climate system rather than the single events that we describe as everyday weather. I made the decision to trust in our safe place and space…With these relations in place Suzanne shared a story she had told no one else…At the end of the meeting Suzanne felt that talking about her experience, and how she felt about receiving belittling comments, could be a fruitful way of dealing with hurtful student comments. Later, Suzanne contributed to an article in her professional association newsletter that offered ways for teachers 'to deal' with hurtful student comments.

References

Adams, J. R. R. (1999). The hedge schools and popular education in Ireland. In J. S. Donnelly & K. L. Miller (Eds.), *Irish popular culture, 1650–1850*. Dublin: Irish Academic Press.

Allard, C. C., Goldblatt, P. F., Kemball, J. I., Kendrick, S. A., Millen, K. J., & Smith, D. M. (2007). Becoming a reflective community of practice. *Reflective Practice: International and Multidisciplinary Perspectives, 8*(3), 299–314.

Baron, P., & Corbin, L. (2014). The academic role: Service, compliance, freedom. In A. Kwan, E. Wong, T. Kwong, P. Lau, & A. Goody (Eds.), *Research and development in higher education:*

Higher Education in a globalised world. Refereed papers from the 37th HERDSA Annual International Conference (Vol. 37, pp. 10–19). Hong Kong SAR, People's Republic of China.

Bass, R. (1999). The scholarship of teaching: What's the problem? *Inventio: Creative thinking about learning and teaching. 1*(1), 1–28.

Belenky, M. F., Clinchy, B. M., Goldberger, N. R., & Narule, J. M. (1986). *Women's ways of knowing: The development of self voice and mind.* New York: Basic Books.

Boud, D., Keogh, R., & Walker, D. (1985). Promoting reflection in learning: A model. In D. Boud, R. Keogh, & D. Walker (Eds.), *Reflection: Turning experience into learning* (pp. 18–40). London: Kogan Page.

Brookfield, S. D. (1995). *Becoming a critically reflective teacher.* San Francisco: Jossey-Bass.

Carr, W., & Kemmis, S. (1986). *Becoming critical. Education, knowledge and action research.* Lewes: Falmer.

Chalmers, D. (2011). Progress and challenges to the recognition and reward of the Scholarship of Teaching in higher education. *Higher Education Research and Development, 30*(1), 25–38.

Chism, N. V. N. (1998). Developing a philosophy of teaching statement. Essays on teaching excellence. *Professional and Organizational Development Network in Higher Education, 9*(3), 1–2.

Chowdhury, S. (2005). The role of affect- and cognition-based trust in complex knowledge sharing. *Journal of Managerial Issues, 17*(3), 310–326.

Clancy, A. (2013). Possibility portals: Building sustainability amongst academics in challenging times. In C. O'Farrell & A. Farrell (Eds.), *Emerging issues in higher education III. From capacity to building sustainability* (pp. 82–94). Athlone: Educational Developers in Ireland Network.

Clandinin, D. J., Downey, C. A., & Huber, J. (2009). Attending to changing landscapes: Shaping the interwoven identities of teachers and teacher educators. *Asia-Pacific Journal of Teacher Education, 37*(2), 141–154.

Coates, H., Dobson, I., Edwards, D., Friedman, T., Goedegeburre, L., & Meek, L. (2009). The attractiveness of the Australian academic profession: A comparative analysis. In *Research briefing. Changing academic profession* (pp. 1–34). Melbourne: LH Martin Institute, University of Melbourne & Australian Council for Educational Research & Educational Policy Institute.

Debowski, S., & Blake, V. (2004). The developmental needs of higher education academic leaders in encouraging effective teaching and learning. In *Seeking educational excellence, Proceedings of the teaching and learning forum 2004* (pp. 1–7). Perth, WA: Murdoch University.

Devlin, M., Smeal, G., Cummings, R., & Mazzolini, M. (2012). *Seven insights for leading sustainable change in teaching and learning in Australian universities* (pp. 1–8). Sydney: Office for Learning and Teaching.

Gilchrist, J., Hancock, E., Islam, J., McCormack, C., & Northcote, M. (2013). Collaborative mentoring: Reflection on the role of TATAL in the aftershock of a HERDSA fellowship application. *HERDSA News, 35*(3), 16–18.

Ginns, P., Kitay, J., & Prosser, M. (2010). Transfer of academic staff learning in a research-intensive university. *Teaching in Higher Education, 15*(3), 235–246.

Harper, V. (1996). Establishing a community of conversation: Creating a context for self-reflection among teacher scholars. In L. Richlin (Ed.), *To improve the academy* (Vol. 15, pp. 251–266). Stillwater, OK: New Forms Press and the Professional and Organizational Development Network in Higher Education.

Hughes, J., & Moore, I. (2007). Reflective portfolios for professional development. In C. O'Farrell (Ed.), *Teaching portfolio practice in Ireland: A handbook* (pp. 11–23). Dublin: Centre for Academic Practice and Student Learning (CAPSL), Trinity College Dublin and All Ireland Society for Higher Education (AISHE).

Johnson, G. (2000). Strategy through a cultural lens. Learning from managers' experiences. *Management Learning, 31*(4), 403–426.

Jones, S., Lefoe, G., Harvey, M., & Ryland, K. (2012). Distributed leadership: A collaborative framework for academics, executives and professionals in higher education. *Higher Education Policy and Management, 34*(1), 67–78.

Jones, S., Lefoe, G., Harvey, M., & Ryland, K. (2013). *A user guide for benchmarking distributed leadership*. Sydney, Australia: Office of Learning and Teaching

Kennelly, R., Gilchrist, J., McCormack, C., Partridge, L., Ruge, G., Schonnell, S., et al. (2013). Why make time at the HERDSA Conference in Auckland to TATAL? *HERDSA News, 35*(1), 13–16.

Kennelly, R., & McCormack, C. (2015). Creating more 'elbow room' for collaborative reflective practice in the competitive, performative culture of today's university". *Higher Education Research and Development, 34*(5), 942–956.

Kolb, D. A. (1984). *Experiential learning: Experience as the source of learning and development*. Englewood Cliffs: Prentice-Hall.

Lyons, N. (Ed.). (1998). *With portfolio in hand. Validating the new teacher professionalism*. New York: Teachers College Press.

McAlpine, L. (2005). Conversations: Negotiating professional learning and power. *Journal for Academic Development, 10*(1), 1–2.

McCormack, C. (2009). Stories return personal narrative ways of knowing to the professional development of doctoral supervisors. *Studies in Continuing Education, 31*(2), 139–154.

McCormack, C., & Kennelly, R. (2011). 'We must get together and really talk…'. Connection, engagement and safety sustain learning and teaching conversation communities. *Reflective Practice: International and Multidisciplinary Perspectives, 12*(4), 515–531.

McDonald, J., & Star, C. (2008). The challenges of building an academic community of practice: An Australian case study. In *Engaging communities: Proceedings of the 31st HERDSA annual conference* (pp. 230–240). Rotorua, New Zealand.

Mezirow, J. (Ed.). (2000a). *Learning as transformation: Critical perspectives on a theory in progress*. San Francisco: Jossey-Bass.

Mezirow, J. (2000b). *Learning as transformation: Critical perspectives on a theory in progress*. San Francisco: Jossey-Bass.

Miley, F., Griffin, A., Cram, B., Kennelly, R., McCormack, C., & Read, A. (2012). *Using stories in teaching. HERDSA Guide*. Milperra, NSW: Higher Education Research Development Society of Australasia.

Mitchell, C., & Sackney, L. (2001). Building capacity for a learning community. *Canadian Journal of Educational Administration and Policy, 19*(24 February).

Palmer, P. J. (1993). Good talk about good teaching. *Change, 25*(6), 8–13.

Palmer, P. J. (2007). *The courage to teach. Exploring the inner landscape of a teacher's life (10 anniversary ed.)*. San Francisco: Jossey-Bass.

Palmer, P. J., Zajonc, A., & Scribner, M. (2010). *The heart of higher education: A call to renewal. Transforming the academy through collegial conversations*. San Francisco: Jossey-Bass.

Ramsden, P. (2009). *Reward and recognition in higher education. Institutional policies and their implementation*. University of Leicester: The Higher Education Academy and the Genetics Education Networking for Innovation and Excellence (GENIE) CETL.

Richardson, L. (2000). Writing: A method of inquiry. In N. K. Denzin & Y. S. Lindoln (Eds.), *Handbook of qualitative research* (2nd ed., pp. 923–948). Thousand Oaks: Sage Publications.

Robbins, S. P., Bergman, R., Stagg, I., & Coulter, M. (2003). *Foundations of management* (3rd ed.). Frenchs Forest, NSW: Prentice Hall.

Schön, D. (1983). *The reflective practitioner: How professionals think in action*. New York: Basic Books.

Schonwetter, D. J., Sokal, L., Friesen, M., & Taylor, K. L. (2002). Teaching philosophies reconsidered: A conceptual model for the development and evaluation of teaching philosophy statements. *The International Journal for Academic Development, 7*(1), 83–97.

Shulman, L. S. (1993). Teaching as community property: Putting an end to pedagogical solitude. *Change, 25*(6), 6–7.

Swift, P. E., & Hwang, A. (2013). The impact of affective and cognitive trust on knowledge sharing and organizational learning. *The Learning Organization, 20*(1), 20–37.

Thorpe, S. (2011). Editorial. The inner practice. *Group Facilitation: A Research and Applications Journal, 11*, 3.

Tripp, D. (1993, 2012). *Critical incidents in teaching: Developing professional judgment*. New York: Routledge.

Warhurst, R. P. (2006). 'We really felt part of something': Participatory learning among peers within a university teaching development community of practice. *International Journal for Academic Development, 11*(2), 111–122.

Erratum to: Communities of Practice

Jacquie McDonald and Aileen Cater-Steel

Erratum to:
J. McDonald and A. Cater-Steel (eds.),
Communities of Practice, **DOI 10.1007/978-981-10-2879-3**

The book was inadvertently published with incorrect information in FM, Chaps. 2, 4, 14, 17, 24, and 27 which have been corrected now as below:

In P. xxix, Jeanne Keay's; P. xxxi, Helen May's; P. ii, Marina Harvey's; and P. xxix, Sarah John's biographies have been corrected.
In Chap. 2, P. 30, Line 2 in Para 1: Remove "," after was. It should read "It was embedded". In P. 31, Last line: Add " ' " after Knowles, i.e., "Knowles' work…".
In Chap. 4, P. 73, affiliation of J. Keay was corrected.
In Chap. 14, P. 313, affiliation of M. Harvey was corrected; P. 322, Lefoe and Parris 2008, p. 190 was replaced with Lefoe and Parrish 2008, p. 190.
In Chap. 17, P. 373, affiliation of E.R. Pember was corrected.
In Chap. 24, P. 505, affiliation of M. Harvey and V. Fredericks was corrected.
In Chap. 27, P. 567, affiliation of C. Fraser, J. Honeyfield, and V. Fester was corrected.

The updated original online version for this book can be found at 10.1007/978-981-10-2879-3

J. McDonald (✉)
University of Southern Queensland, Toowoomba, QLD, Australia

A. Cater-Steel
University of Southern Queensland, Toowoomba, QLD, Australia

© Springer Nature Singapore Pte Ltd. 2017   E1
J. McDonald and A. Cater-Steel (eds.), *Communities of Practice*,
DOI 10.1007/978-981-10-2879-3_29

CPI Antony Rowe

Chippenham, UK

2017-02-09 22:48